The
New International
Lesson Annual

2014–2015

September–August

Abingdon Press
Nashville

PREFACE

Welcome! You hold in your hands a resource used by the global community of Bible students and teachers who study resources based on the work of the Committee on the Uniform Series, known by many as the International Lesson Series. *The New International Lesson Annual* is designed for teachers who seek a solid biblical basis for each session and a step-by-step teaching plan that will help them lead their classes. *The New International Lesson Annual* can be used with any student curriculum based on the International Lesson Series. In many classes, both the students and teacher rely on *The New International Lesson Annual* as their companion to the Bible.

The four themes that support our study during the 2014–2015 Sunday school year are *hope, worship, God: The Holy Spirit,* and *justice.* The thirteen lessons for the fall quarter, "Sustaining Hope," explore portions of Jeremiah, Habakkuk, Job, Ezekiel, and Isaiah. As we turn to "Acts of Worship" in the winter quarter, we will study twelve lessons rooted in Hebrews, Psalm 95, Luke, Matthew, John, James, Daniel, and Ephesians. We will trace God's work through the Holy Spirit in the fourteen lessons of the spring quarter, "The Spirit Comes," by investigating selections from John, Mark, 1 Corinthians, 1 John, 2 John, 3 John, and Acts. Over the course of the thirteen lessons of the summer quarter, we will learn how "God's Prophets Demand Justice" by studying the work of seven prophets: Amos, Micah, Isaiah, Jeremiah, Ezekiel, Zechariah, and Malachi.

As you examine *The New International Lesson Annual,* notice the following features that are especially valuable for busy teachers who want to provide in-depth Bible study experiences for their students. Each lesson includes the following sections:

Previewing the Lesson highlights the background and lesson Scriptures, focus of the lesson, three goals for the learners, a pronunciation guide in lessons where you may find unfamiliar words or names, and supplies you will need to teach.

Reading the Scripture includes the Scripture lesson printed in both the *New Revised Standard Version* and the *Common English Version.* By printing these two translations in parallel columns, you can easily compare them for in-depth study. If your own Bible is another version, you will then have three translations to explore as you prepare each lesson.

Understanding the Scripture closely analyzes the background Scripture by looking at each verse. Here you will find help in understanding concepts, ideas, places, and people pertinent to each week's lesson. You may also find explanations of Greek or Hebrew words that are essential for understanding the text.

Interpreting the Scripture looks at the lesson Scripture, delves into its meaning, and relates it to contemporary life.

Sharing the Scripture provides you with a detailed teaching plan. Written by your editor, who is a very experienced educator, this section is divided into two major sections: *Preparing to Teach* and *Leading the Class.*

In the *Preparing to Teach* section you will find a devotional reading for your own spiritual enrichment, as well as ideas to help you prepare for the session.

The *Leading the Class* portion begins with "Gather to Learn" activities designed to welcome the students and draw them into the lesson. Here, the students' stories and experiences or other contemporary stories are highlighted as preparation for the Bible story. The next three headings under *Leading the Class* are the three "Goals for the Learners." The first goal always focuses on the Bible story itself. The second goal relates the Bible story to the lives of the learners. The third goal encourages the students to take action on what they have learned. You will find diverse activities to appeal to a wide variety of learning styles. These activities suggest listening, reading, writing, speaking, singing, drawing, conducting research, interacting with others, and meditating. The lesson ends with "Continue the Journey," where you will find closing activities, preparation for the following week, and ideas for students to commit themselves to action during the week.

In addition to these weekly features, each quarter begins with the following helps:

- **Introduction to the Quarter** offers you a quick survey of each lesson to be studied during the quarter. You will find the title, Scripture, date, and a brief summary of each week's basic thrust. This feature is on the first page of each quarter.
- **Meet Our Writer**, which follows the quarterly introduction, provides biographical information about each writer, including education, pastoral and/or academic teaching experience, previous publications, and family information.
- **The Big Picture**, written by the same writer who authored the quarter's lessons, is designed to give you a broader scope of the materials to be covered than is possible in each weekly lesson. You will find this background article immediately following the writer's biography.
- **Close-up** furnishes additional information, such as a time line, chart, overview, short article, map, or list that you may choose to use for a specific week or anytime during the quarter, perhaps even repeatedly.
- **Faith in Action** describes ideas related to the broad sweep of the quarter that the students can use individually or as a class to act on what they have been studying. These ideas are usually intended for use beyond the classroom.

Finally, two annual features are included:

- **List of Background Scriptures** is offered especially for those of you who keep back copies of *The New International Lesson Annual*. This feature, found immediately after the "Contents," will enable you to locate Bible background passages used during the current year.
- **Teacher enrichment article**, which follows the "List of Background Scriptures," is intended to be useful throughout the year. We hope you will read it immediately and refer to it often. "Getting to Know the Bible:

Prophecy, Gospels, and Letters" explores these three types of literature that you will encounter in this year's sessions.

We are always open to your suggestions! We want *The New International Lesson Annual* to be the first resource you consult when planning your lesson. Please send your questions, comments, and suggestions to me. I invite you to include your e-mail address and/or phone number. I will respond as soon as your message reaches my home office in Maryland.

> Dr. Nan Duerling
> Abingdon Press
> P.O. Box 801
> Nashville, TN 37202

All who use *The New International Lesson Annual* are blessed by the collective community of readers. We pray that you and your study partners will be guided by the Word of God and the power of the Holy Spirit so as to be transformed and conformed to the image of our Lord and Savior Jesus Christ.

> Nan Duerling, Ph.D.
> Editor, *The New International Lesson Annual*

CONTENTS

First Quarter: Sustaining Hope
September 7, 2014–November 30, 2014

UNIT 1: THE DAYS ARE SURELY COMING
(September 7–September 28)

UNIT 2: DARK NIGHTS OF THE SOUL
(October 5–October 26)

UNIT 3: VISIONS OF GRANDEUR
(November 2–November 30)

Second Quarter: Acts of Worship
December 7, 2014–February 22, 2015

UNIT 1: IN AWE OF GOD
(December 7–December 28)

UNIT 2: LEARNING TO PRAY
(January 4–January 25)

Third Quarter: The Spirit Comes
March 1, 2015–May 31, 2015

UNIT 1: THE PLEDGE OF GOD'S PRESENCE
(March 1–March 29)

UNIT 2: THE COMMUNITY OF BELOVED DISCIPLES
(April 5–May 3)

UNIT 3: ONE IN THE BOND OF LOVE
(May 10–May 31)

Fourth Quarter: God's Prophets Demand Justice
June 7, 2015–August 30, 2015

UNIT 1: AMOS RAILS AGAINST INJUSTICE
(June 7–June 28)

UNIT 2: MICAH CALLS FOR JUSTICE AMONG UNJUST PEOPLE
(July 5–July 26)

UNIT 3: ADVOCATES OF JUSTICE FOR ALL
(August 2–August 30)

LIST OF BACKGROUND SCRIPTURES, 2014–2015

Old Testament

Ezra 7:1, 6, 21-28	August 9	Jeremiah 32	September 21
Job 1	October 5	Jeremiah 33	September 28
Job 5	October 19	Ezekiel 18	August 16
Job 19	October 12	Ezekiel 40:1–43:12	November 2
Job 24	October 19	Ezekiel 43:10–46:24	November 9
Job 42	October 26	Ezekiel 47:1, 3-12	November 16
Psalm 33	November 30	Ezekiel 47:13-23	November 23
Psalm 55:12-23	October 19	Daniel 1:5, 8-17	February 1
Psalm 56	October 5	Amos 2:4-16	June 7
Psalm 57	October 12	Amos 5	June 14
Psalm 86	October 26	Amos 6	June 21
Psalm 89:11-18	August 2	Amos 8	June 28
Psalm 95:1-7a	December 14	Micah 2	July 5
Proverbs 21:2-15	August 16	Micah 3	July 12
Isaiah 30:18-26	August 23	Micah 6	July 19
Isaiah 52:1-2, 7-12	November 30	Micah 7:11-20	July 26
Isaiah 59	August 2	Habakkuk 1–3	October 5
Jeremiah 7:1-15	August 9	Zechariah 7:8-14	August 23
Jeremiah 30	September 7	Malachi 3:1-12	August 30
Jeremiah 31	September 14		

New Testament

Matthew 6:16-18	February 1	Acts 2:1-21	May 24
Matthew 7:12	August 30	Acts 2:37-47	November 23
Matthew 9:9-17	February 1	1 Corinthians 12:1-11	May 10
Matthew 14:22-36	December 28	1 Corinthians 12:12-31	May 17
Matthew 25:31-46	February 15	1 Corinthians 13	May 31
Mark 11:1-11	March 29	1 Corinthians 14:1-25	May 24
Luke 2:1-20	December 21	1 Corinthians 15:1-22	April 5
Luke 10:25-37	February 8	Ephesians 6:10-20	February 22
Luke 11:1-13	January 4	Hebrews 1:1-9	December 7
John 1:29-34	March 1	Hebrews 4:14–5:10	January 18
John 14:15-26	March 8	James 5	January 25
John 16:4b-15	March 15	1 John 3:11-24	April 12
John 17:1-26	January 11	1 John 4–5	April 19
John 20:19-23	March 22	1 John 5:6-12, 18-20	April 26
Acts 1:4-8	March 22	2 John	April 26
Acts 2:1-4	March 22	3 John	May 3

TEACHER ENRICHMENT ARTICLE:
GETTING TO KNOW THE BIBLE: PROPHECY, GOSPELS, AND LETTERS

Do you like to read a newspaper? If so, you probably have a favorite section or two that you turn to immediately. Perhaps you're a big fan of the comics, or you want to be the first one in the house to read the sports pages, or can hardly wait to get your hands on the section with the book reviews and listings of movie, art, and musical events. Whatever your taste, you are surely aware that each section of the publication only makes sense if it is viewed through the appropriate "lens." Who, for example, would make the mistake of reading the obituary notices as if they were comics? Would anyone think that letters to the editor or an op-ed page carry the same in-depth investigative reporting as the news pages?

Just as we know how to read different portions of a newspaper with different expectations, so too we approach the various parts of the Bible with different expectations and distinct ways of reading the material we encounter. In this article, we will explore three different types of writings found in the Bible—prophecy, Gospels, and letters—to discern their purposes, characteristics, and structure. With this knowledge we will be better able to comprehend and appreciate the Bible passages found in this year's lessons of *The New International Lesson Annual*.

Prophecy

In the Old Testament we find a number of figures referred to as prophets. Some are unnamed (for example in 2 Kings 17:13, 23); sometimes they work together in a group, such as the four hundred prophets mentioned in 1 Kings 22:6 or the "company of prophets" called by Elisha in 2 Kings 9:1. Others are named, including Nathan (2 Samuel 7; 12), Elijah (1 Kings 17–2 Kings 2), Elisha (1 Kings 19–2 Kings 13), and the prophetess Huldah (2 Kings 22:14). Fifteen prophets have entire books associated with their names. Three of those—Isaiah, Jeremiah, and Ezekiel—are referred to as Major Prophets because of the length of the scrolls attributed to them. The twelve Minor Prophets, whose works are much shorter, are found in the books from Hosea through Malachi. What ties all of these prophets together is an openness of heart to God that allows them to hear divine messages and thus serve as intermediaries between God and the people. This was not a one-way street, though, for the prophets interacted with the people and communicated their concerns and the prophet's own concerns to God. Despite hearing a word from the Lord, the people were free to reject prophetic messages—and they often did so. During 2014–2015 we will study texts from Isaiah, Jeremiah, Ezekiel, Amos, Micah, Habakkuk, Zechariah, and Malachi.

The Old Testament prophetic books generally contain collections of the prophets' speeches, written in poetry and prose, and often, though not always, arranged in some meaningful order. Works of prophecy may also include descriptions of incidents from the prophets' lives.

Writing in Volume 6 of *The New Interpreter's Bible*, scholar David L. Petersen identifies seven types of prose accounts found in Israel's prophetic literature. Prophetic actions that convey a message are described in a *symbolic action report*. The action itself, not any words the prophet may proclaim, is important. For example, Isaiah 20:3 records that the prophet "has walked naked and barefoot for three years as a sign and a portent against Egypt and Ethiopia." A *commissioning report* records the prophet's call to ministry as seen in Isaiah 6; Jeremiah 1:4-10; and Ezekiel 1–3. Usually these calls are presented in six parts: God confronts the one who is being called, God pronounces an introductory word, the commission is announced, the one being called objects, God provides reassurance, and a sign is given. A *vision report* refers to something that the prophet witnessed with his eyes. Sometimes the prophet can interpret the significance of what he has seen, but at other times he asks for an explanation. *Legend* may state something about a holy person, such as the tale of two boys who taunted Elisha and then died after he cursed them (2 Kings 2:23-24), or tell a story about some miraculous event, such as Elisha providing large quantities of oil for a widow (2 Kings 4:1-7). *Prophetic historiography* is seen when events that appear in the Bible's history books also appear in a prophetic book. Such overlaps attest to the important role the prophet played with respect to Israel's political and military affairs. *Biography* looks at both the prophet's life and the larger context of his times. *Divinatory chronicles* report on help the prophet provides from beyond the world of normal human knowledge, such as when the prophet is the intermediary between those seeking information and God (Zechariah 7–8).

Poetic speech is the most prevalent form of prophetic literature. In the case of *divine oracles*, the prophet serves as a mouthpiece for God. In contrast, *prophetic speeches* are given when the prophet speaks from God's perspective but does not purport to utter God's exact words. Some speeches are introduced with the words "thus says the Lord," and then followed by an indictment and the pronouncement of judgment, such as would have been used in a court of law. Another type of poetic speech is the *oracle of woe*, which often begins with "ah" (Isaiah 5:8), "alas" (Amos 5:18), "ha" (Isaiah 29:15), "oh" (Isaiah 30:1), or "woe" (Isaiah 45:9). An example of a *lament* is found in Jeremiah 8:18–9:3. Another type of prophetic speech, *the hymn*, begins with a plural verb that calls people to "sing" or "praise" and then gives testimony to the character of the God who is worthy to be worshiped.

In sum, prophecy is not an exercise in fortune-telling, but a means by which a person who has been called and equipped by God may communicate the divine word with God's people.

Gospels

When Paul refers to "gospel" in his writings, he is not referring to a specific kind of book, but rather to the entire message of the good news, especially Jesus' death and resurrection as related to God's plan of salvation. Some early literary texts, such as the Gospel of Mary and the Gospel of Thomas, also bore the name "Gospel," but their structure is different from the four books that were eventually deemed authoritative and included among the sacred Scriptures. Since the second half of the second century four books that now appear in our Bible, and which we will study this year, have been designated Gospels: Matthew, Mark, Luke, and John.

The careful reader will notice that Matthew, Mark, and Luke—known collectively as the Synoptic Gospels—share common stories and sequences, but they are not identical. Scholars generally agree that Mark's Gospel was written first. By studying Matthew and Luke alongside Mark, one can discern what the two later Gospels borrowed from Mark. We also know that Matthew and Luke each had sources that Mark apparently did not use. The Gospel of John, believed to have been written last, is based on altogether different sources and, therefore, tells the story of Jesus from another perspective. Scholars debate the relationship among the four and the sources upon which each relied, but those issues need not concern us here.

What, then, ties these four books together so that we may think of them as being closely related? All four spotlight the appearance of John the Baptist at the beginning of the story. They then go on to tell the story of Jesus' life, teachings, and actions, though few of the stories are found in all four Gospels. All include information about the final week of Jesus' life, his trial, and the empty tomb being discovered on Easter morning, though there are some variations in the details.

Until early in the twentieth century, readers understood these books to be essentially biographies. Although they are not biographies according to our modern understanding of this genre that would probe his personality and reveal details about his entire life, they do tell episodes from the story of Jesus' life. Yet they are not simply biographies. Nor were they intended to be objective reports about Jesus. Each of the four writers strongly supported Jesus and believed that he had been crucified and resurrected. Each author was purposefully writing to a specific community of faith. Matthew wrote so that his community could recognize that Jesus fulfilled Old Testament prophecies (for example, Matthew 1:22); Mark's persecuted community needed to hear "the good news of Jesus Christ, the Son of God" (Mark 1:1); Luke did careful research to write an "orderly account" to help readers "know the truth" (Luke 1:3, 4); John wrote so that readers "may come to believe that Jesus is the Messiah, the Son of God" (John 20:31). Each author captured the story of Jesus in ways that would continue to guide the church now that he was no longer physically present. Jesus was not only a historical figure but also the living Lord of the church. Thus, the writers told Jesus' story so as to be relevant to the faith community for which each Gospel was written, which helps to explain why the four Gospels do not agree on all points.

As we read the Gospels, we find different kinds of stories within them. Some of these stories are to be read and understood as what we would call nonfiction. For example, when we find stories of healings and exorcisms, we understand that real people with needs encountered Jesus, who met their needs. Similarly, stories of controversies, such as when religious leaders object to Jesus "working" on the sabbath by healing people, are understood as actual encounters between Jesus and living people. Some stories that involve real people also include a miracle, such as Jesus' feeding of the five thousand or altering the forces of nature to rescue someone, such as the disciples being tossed about in a storm. Matthew, Mark, and Luke record parables. Jesus usually told these stories as examples or comparisons, generally using objects and characters that would be familiar to people who worked the land. The stories themselves are fictional, but the point, which was often used to help listeners understand life under the reign of God, revealed an important truth.

Letters

The twenty-one letters that are part of the sacred Scriptures for Christians were written in a particular time and place to address theological concerns and specific issues within the early Christian communities. The letters that we have are divided into two collections, the Pauline Collection and the non-Pauline Collection. Although these collections are from different points of view, as a group they present beliefs and ethical understandings that shape the lives and communities of Christians.

The Pauline Letters are further divided in several ways. One division is based on whether scholars believe that Paul actually wrote the letter bearing his name. The issue at stake is whether the theology in the letter is that of Paul himself or someone who knew him well and was interpreting his teachings. Scholars believe the authentic letters are Romans, 1 Corinthians, 2 Corinthians, Galatians, Philippians, 1 Thessalonians, and Philemon. The disputed letters include Ephesians, Colossians, 2 Thessalonians, 1 Timothy, 2 Timothy, and Titus. Another way to categorize the letters attributed to Paul is to refer to one group—Ephesians, Philippians, Colossians, 2 Timothy, and Philemon—as "prison letters," though there is disagreement as to where and when Paul may have been imprisoned when each letter was written. A third way to classify these letters is to think of Romans, 1 Corinthians, 2 Corinthians, and Galatians as "major" because of their length. The letters from Ephesians through Philemon, which are shorter, are considered by some to be less influential in shaping the early church's theology. Although the early church also included Hebrews in its list of Paul's letters, his authorship was questioned as early as the third century and modern scholars agree that he was not the writer.

Eight letters—Hebrews, James, 1 Peter, 2 Peter, 1 John, 2 John, 3 John, and Jude—are diverse and written by persons other than Paul. This collection is loosely related by the hostile environments in which the readers of these letters live. The poverty, alienation, persecution, marginalization due to one's faith, and values being in conflict with the larger world lead to suffering. Whereas Paul's letters helped people focus on their beliefs, the non-Pauline letters often helped powerless believers shape their behaviors as they strived to live in an age and world that was antagonistic toward their faith.

Our study for the 2014–2015 Sunday school year will include letters from both the Pauline and non-Pauline collections, namely, 1 Corinthians, 1 John, 2 John, 3 John, Ephesians, Hebrews, and James. As we consider the literary context of these letters, remember that these letters were meant to be read aloud. They followed accepted rhetorical conventions in order to persuade listeners to make desired responses. They therefore reflected what the writer would have said had he been present among the congregation. In some cases the letters were intended as substitutes for personal visits (see Romans 1:9-12). In other letters the writer is responding to questions or crises that have arisen and need immediate attention. As we read them centuries later, we are both eavesdropping on mail written to our spiritual ancestors and finding teachings that empower us to live as Christian believers.

FIRST QUARTER
Sustaining Hope

SEPTEMBER 7, 2014–NOVEMBER 30, 2014

The thirteen lessons for the fall quarter focus on the theme of hope. Unit 1 concentrates on the hope for restoration that exiled Israel will experience as seen through the eyes of the prophet Jeremiah. The lessons of the second unit feature Bible readings from Habakkuk, Job, and the psalmist, all of whom seek hope from God in times of trouble. The final unit is a five-lesson study of God's glory as Ezekiel and Isaiah envisioned it.

Unit 1, "The Days Are Surely Coming," begins on September 7 with "A Vision of the Future," which reviews God's promise as recorded in Jeremiah 30 to restore the people to their land. We move ahead to Jeremiah 31 on September 14 to explore God's new covenant that not only ensures forgiveness but also promises a renewed relationship between God and Israel. On September 21 we consider "A New Future" as we turn to Jeremiah 32 to hear about the prophet's hopefulness as he buys a field while awaiting an invasion by the Babylonians. "Improbable Possibilities," the lesson for September 28, examines God's promise that forgiveness and restoration will follow punishment.

"Dark Nights of the Soul," a four-session unit that begins on October 5, opens with "Rejoice Anyway," which looks at background Scripture from Job 1, Psalm 56, and Habakkuk 1–3 to discern God's message of patience and assurance that God will act on behalf of justice. On October 12 we will study "Even So, My Redeemer Lives," based on Job 19 and Psalm 57, to understand that Job had an unwavering belief in God's redemption. "Hope Complains," the session for October 19, delves into Job 5, 24, and Psalm 55:12-23 to hear Job's complaint that God appears to do nothing to call wicked people to account for their actions. On October 26 we turn to Job 42 and Psalm 86 to hear the conclusion of the conversation between God and Job and become aware that "Hope Satisfies."

The third unit, "Visions of Grandeur," begins on November 2 with "God's Divine Glory Returns," which glimpses the vision of God's holy and merciful glory in the Temple as seen in Ezekiel 40:1–43:12. We review the instructions that the prophet was given to build a new altar and make offerings as told in Ezekiel 43:10–46:24 in the lesson for November 9, "The Altar, A Sign of Hope." On November 16 we catch a glimpse of Ezekiel's vision of life-giving water, as recorded in Ezekiel 47:1, 3-12, in a session titled "A Transforming Stream." "Transformation Continued," the lesson for November 23 from Ezekiel 47:13-23 and Acts 2:37-47, helps us to hear God's Word about sharing our inheritance with those who live among us. Unit 3 concludes on November 30 with "Let Zion Rejoice," where we hear the prophet's words of hope, good news, and rejoicing from Isaiah 52:1-2, 7-12 and Psalm 33. These words seem especially appropriate on this first Sunday of Advent.

MEET OUR WRITER

REV. JOHN INDERMARK

John Indermark lives in the town of Naselle, located in the southwest corner of Washington state. His wife, Judy, recently retired from her work as an E-911 dispatcher for Pacific County, Washington. Their son Jeff works on the Quality Assurance team that oversees the counseling programs in the Juvenile Rehabilitation Administration facilities in the state of Washington.

John grew up in St. Louis, graduating from Northwest High School, St. Louis University, and Eden Theological Seminary. Ordained in the United Church of Christ, John served as a parish pastor for sixteen years before shifting to a ministry of the written word. He has also served in a variety of interim and extended pulpit supply positions for Presbyterian, Methodist, and Lutheran congregations in southwest Washington and northwest Oregon. In the spring of 2013, he served a three-month associate pastor term at Church of the Holy Cross (U.C.C.) in Hilo, Hawaii.

John's ministry of writing focuses on spiritual formation books and Christian education curricula. Among his most recent books are *Way Words: A Daily Itinerary for Lent* and *Gospeled Lives*. John and coauthor Sharon Harding have a new book, *Advent: A to Z: Prayerful and Playful Preparations for Families*. The curricula projects he currently writes for include *The Present Word*, as well as *The New International Lesson Annual*. He wrote the New Testament materials for youth and leaders in *Crossings: God's Journey with Us*, a confirmation resource published by Logos Productions, Inc., and also did a revision of that resource for use with adults.

In their spare time, John and Judy enjoy walking their region's trails and logging roads and traveling the Southwest, Hawaii, and British Columbia.

THE BIG PICTURE: KEEPING HOPE ALIVE

What Do You Hope For?

Your answers to that question will rely, to some degree, upon your age. What a young adult, who seemingly has all of life ahead, hopes for will likely differ from the hopes of an elder who has journeyed through many years and experiences. Indeed, those accumulating years of experiences may nurture or suffocate hopes once held. That final point underscores the significance of attaching the modifier of "sustaining" to "hope" in the title of this quarter's sessions. At any isolated moment in life, hope might seem reasonable or even self-evident. But what happens when the passage of days, or years, results in no fulfillment of that hope? *Having* hope then depends on the more difficult discipline of *sustaining* hope.

This matter of sustaining hope greatly concerned the writers (and audiences) of the passages explored in this quarter. In the wake of exile, in the aftermath of extraordinary personal and national tragedy, in the face of others who want to blame victims (or messengers) for their suffering, the prophets and psalmists and sages of Israel sought to frame a way for hope to be sustained when hope's possibilities seemed most under siege and out of sight. Sustaining hope is a task and discipline taken up in the New Testament as well. There is, for example, Paul's perspective in Romans 8:24-25, as well as the hope given witness in the prayer Jesus taught to disciples of all times: "your kingdom come." The church and individual Christians have been offering that prayerful hope for two millennia. So after almost two thousand years of waiting, what enables our hope in God's reign to be sustained—and more practically, what enables us to translate that hope so long-delayed into the conduct of our lives as individuals and communities?

Biblically speaking, the question raised at the opening this article ("What do you hope for?") is grounded in an even more fundamental question: "*In whom* do you hope?" Biblical hope is grounded in the character and trustworthiness of God. The passages that we will consider this quarter largely have to do with God's promises. Whether those promises themselves generate hope—and hopeful living—depends upon the prior determination of whether we trust God to bring the promises to fruition.

So as you lead those who will engage these sessions and texts with you, seek ways to keep hope's horse before its cart. That is, keep before you the primacy of trust in the One who makes such promises (and the purpose of God in their offering). This focus will be especially critical when you reach the third unit of the quarter, where hope's sustaining is linked to some extraordinarily detailed promises related by Ezekiel regarding the vision of a new temple.

The remainder of this article will consider overviews of the quarter's three units. These overviews will not only provide biblical backgrounds for the wider context of the book(s) from which each unit's passages are drawn but also thematic entry points into each unit's emphases. Taken together, these units and their passages witness to vital components for what makes possible the *sustaining* of hope.

The Days Are Surely Coming

Psychiatrist and Holocaust survivor Viktor Frankl observed in his book *Man's Search for Meaning*: "The prisoner who had lost faith in the future—his future—was doomed." Frankl went on to expand that thought, gained from his experience in the concentration camps, to its application to life beyond the camps. Having and sustaining hope are not optional appendages to life. Without hope, despair sets in. Without the promise of better days, the oppressiveness of difficult times can close us off to life, figuratively and sometimes literally.

The first unit in this quarter explores four passages from the prophet Jeremiah. On the one hand, Jeremiah might seem an odd choice to begin a study on hope. Most of the material in the first twenty-five chapters of his book is largely devoid of hope. In those sections, "the days are surely coming" tends to be imaged primarily in texts of national judgment and personal despair. But the Book of Jeremiah, like the Book of Isaiah, has a pivot point. After exile has ended the despair over the immediate future of judgment shifts to the long-range hope of new days marked by God's promises. Understanding the nature of these pivot points in the Prophets is key to making sense of their words—not simply in their original setting, but in applying them to contemporary matters both inside and outside of the church. Simply comparing the first half of Jeremiah to the second half might make it seem as if the prophet has had a sudden change in mind—or worse yet, that the prophet is not consistent in saying contradictory things. *Which is it? Judgment or hope, threat or promise?* we might ask.

But as Jeremiah and Isaiah perceived, the message hinges on the situation. In an era of prosperity and ease, when justice ignored did not seem to matter, complacency is the enemy. Hope has little or no appeal, because folks are fat and happy, so to speak. In those times, Jeremiah and others sounded calls to repentance, and urgings to turn aside lest judgment fall. When those calls went unheeded, when justice and mercy went ignored by those in power, and when people did not want to be disturbed by such troubling summons to renewal, judgment sounded.

Yet once exile came, and despair set in among a people separated from land and home and a now-destroyed Temple (Psalm 137:1) it was no longer the time to pronounce judgment. It was the time to bring forth hope in the form of God's promises of a new day (Isaiah 40:1-2). As taken up in the passages covered in this unit, God's promises to which Jeremiah witnesses relate to the coming of days marked by restoration and new covenant, by homecoming and healing. What enables Jeremiah and those whom he addresses the ability to trust these promises and the One who makes them? The character of God revealed in commitment to relationship (Jeremiah 30:22), in covenant grounded in forgiveness (31:31-34), and in God's "steadfast love," a word that speaks of God's loyalty to those with whom God covenants.

The church has much to learn from the prophets, particularly when it comes to speaking the truth most needed in our times. Sometimes, both in the church and in the wider culture, we get the order mixed up. In times of prosperity and ease, when budgets are bulging and pews are filling, we presume those are the days to not rock the boat, to speak only of good things that make our comfort even more comfortable. In times of crisis, when conflict arises or threats appear, we take as times to scold and blame (usually others, not ourselves). Yet the prophets remind us of God's call to be contrarian. They announced judgment when all seemed well. They spoke hope when all seemed lost. The likes of Jeremiah understood that the proclamation of "the days are surely coming" needs to be framed in ways, and with a message, that reminds us our trust is not in ourselves or our accomplishments or our power (or the lack thereof): Our trust is in God. The promises of God keep us from confusing good times with the reign of God—and from letting bad times defer our hopes for and labors toward that same reign.

Dark Nights of the Soul

Dark Night of the Soul was originally a poem written by the sixteenth-century Spanish mystic known as St. John of the Cross. The poem lyrically describes a spiritual journey that leads into encounter with the Divine. Saint John later wrote a lengthy prose exposition on the poem and more on the spiritual journey described therein. In literature and popular culture, the phrase "dark night of the soul" has come to represent any moment of crisis or deep questioning, spiritual or otherwise, from which we struggle to emerge.

The four sessions in this unit pair a psalm in the background readings with print passages from the prophet Habakkuk (one session) and the Book of Job (three sessions—actually four, as the first session also has Job 1 for one of the background readings).

Habakkuk is one of the shorter prophetic books in the Old Testament. Unlike books such as Jeremiah and Isaiah, where some historical context is provided to "locate" the prophet's work, no such information is given in Habakkuk. While there is an approximate range of one hundred years within which Habakkuk might have been written, most scholars set its composition at the verge of Babylon's initial deportation of Jews in 597 B.C., yet before Jerusalem's destruction in 587 B.C.

Habakkuk's "dark night of the soul" is clearly and powerfully stated in the prophet's complaint to God recorded in the second verse of the book: "O LORD, how long shall I cry for help, and you will not listen? Or cry to you, 'Violence!' and you will not save?" Where other prophets open with indictments of Israel's wrongdoing, Habakkuk takes God to task for the ruin he sees overtaking the people in the form of the Chaldeans (another name for Babylonians, see 1:6). Habakkuk does not merely call out to God in the darkness he experiences; the prophet wonders whether God's seeming absence will continue, thus deepening that darkness.

Joining Habakkuk in the focus passages for this unit is the Book of Job. Job may well be a book with which most are familiar, but few have deeply explored.

Part of the reason for maintaining a safe distance may be in the difficult questions the book raises. In the first chapter, the background reading for the first session, the flood of tragedies that fall upon Job are said to result from God's willingness to let Satan's question "does Job fear God for nothing?" (Job 1:9) into an allowance for severe suffering to fall upon Job. Indeed, Habakkuk 1:2 could easily serve as a viable response to what befalls Job. He suffers through no fault of his own. That, however, does not stop his friends from presuming Job's suffering is because of his guilt. The second and third sessions are parts of dialogues between Job and those who presume to know the mind of God on such matters. The fourth session is Job's response to the voice of God who speaks to him through the whirlwind in chapters 38–41.

Paired with each session's primary texts are psalms; in particular, they are psalms of lament. The lament (or complaint) psalms have been woefully ignored at times by the church, particularly in liturgical use. Psalms of praise (Psalm 8) or thanksgiving (Psalm 104) are more frequent accompaniments as calls to worship. Good Friday may be the one exception to our flight from lament, when we read Psalm 22:1, "My God, my God, why have you forsaken me," in remembrance of Jesus' own cry from the cross. Even then, we are quick to move to the second half of that psalm, where praise returns. But our avoidance of lament misses a key element of faith, namely, God is to be called upon in all our times, good and bad, including the dark nights of our souls. The enemy of faith is not lament, but silence in the face of what weighs down upon us. Indeed, as the very structure of lament songs teaches us, trust arises out of, not in spite of, lament. For when we bear the whole of our selves and our lives to God, we avail ourselves of the gift of Holy Presence. Faith in those dark nights, as Job and Habakkuk well knew, comes not by denial of the darkness, but in holding on to God come what may.

Visions of Grandeur

"Where there is no vision, the people perish" (Proverbs 29:18 KJV). The wisdom of this counsel in Proverbs neatly ties together the flow of this quarter's units. "The days are surely coming" relies intrinsically on a vision, an insight, into what those days will bring. Enduring the "dark nights of the soul" requires a vision that draws one forward and upward and lightward. Indeed, the overall theme of "Sustaining Hope" depends on an overarching purpose that gives hope its energy and promises their durability when conflicting or contradictory experiences arise.

And so it is fitting that the final five sessions take up "visions" of those coming days meant to sustain hope that come to us, four from the prophet Ezekiel and one from Isaiah.

While Ezekiel may primarily be associated with his vision of "a wheel within a wheel" (1:16) that opens the book or the later vision of a valley of dry bones brought to life by God's Spirit (37:1-14), the visions of days to come explored in this unit are grounded in God's promises of a restored temple. The Temple stood at the core of Israel's religious practices and identity—but exile stripped it away, first in distance and later in destruction. Ironically, the time of exile produced an institution that much later would provide Judaism with the resiliency to survive after the Roman destruction of Jerusalem after the time of Jesus: the synagogue. But for Ezekiel, the hope of homecoming and restoration was envisioned by an idealized temple clearly defined not only by the rites and rituals within but also by the construction of its precincts and beyond that to the borders of the land that would safely enclose it.

The final session, which focuses on an oracle of Isaiah, is a clarion call to be on the move—for exiles from Babylon, for persons of faith in every generation. "Your God reigns" (Isaiah 52:7) is the core proclamation of this vision—and in that gospel declaration are also our marching and missional orders. For when all is said and done, our hope as persons and communities of faith is sustained by God's reign. We are hopeful not because of who we are, but because of who God is: the One who reigns over all, the One whose character is grounded in steadfast love and justice.

The promises can be trusted, because God can be trusted.

So we hope, and so we live.

Thanks be to God!

CLOSE-UP:
Time Line of the Babylonian Exile and Return to Judah
(All Dates B.C.)

- 612 Babylonians and Medes conquer Assyria; Assyrian capital Nineveh falls.
- 609 Jehoahaz (Shallum) succeeds his father, Josiah, but rules only three months before Pharaoh Necho sent him to Egypt as a prisoner, where he dies.
- 609 Judah becomes a tribute state of Egypt.
- 609 Jehoiakim (Eliakim) becomes king of Judah after his brother Jehoahaz is removed; he reigns until 598.
- 609 Jeremiah gives Temple sermon (Jeremiah 26).
- 609–605 Egyptians control Judah.
- 605 Babylonians defeat Egyptians and Assyrians at Carchemish.
- 605 Judah becomes a tribute state of Babylon.
- 605 Nebuchadnezzar succeeds his father, Nabopolassar, and becomes king of Babylon.
- 601 Babylonians battle Egypt; both sides suffer losses.
- 601 Jehoiakim of Judah decides to realign Judah with Egypt while the Babylonians are regrouping after battle with Egypt.
- 598 Jehoiachin (Jeconiah) becomes king of Judah and reigns until 587.
- 597 Babylonians invade and capture Jerusalem as punishment for siding with Egypt.
- 597 Babylonian Exile begins with the first deportation to Babylon from Judah (see Jeremiah 52:28-30). Most deportees are prominent or skilled citizens.
- 597 Ezekiel taken captive to Babylon.
- 597 Zedekiah (Mattaniah) becomes king of Judah and reigns until 586.
- 593 Ezekiel begins to prophesy.
- 586 Babylonians invade and destroy Jerusalem and Solomon's Temple.
- 586 Second deportation to Babylon from Judah (see Jeremiah 52:28-30).
- 582 Third deportation to Babylon from Judah (see Jeremiah 52:28-30).
- 539 Babylon falls to the Persian ruler Cyrus II.
- 538 Cyrus II issues a decree allowing the Jews to return home (see Ezra 1:1-4; 6:3-5).
- 520 Haggai prophesies.
- 520–518 Zechariah prophesies.
- 520–515 Zerubbabel, the governor of the Persian province Yehud (central Judah) leads the Jews in rebuilding the Temple, despite local opposition.
- 515 The Second Temple in Jerusalem is completed and dedicated (see Ezra 6:13-18).

FAITH IN ACTION: FINDING HOPE

"Sustaining Hope," the title of the fall quarter's course, explores hope from different perspectives. The second unit, "Dark Nights of the Soul," finds hope amid even life's most crushing blows. As Unit 1 reminds us, "The Days Are Surely Coming" when we will experience a future that perhaps at this moment seems impossible.

Psalm 130 is a penitential psalm. The psalmist cries out for help, hoping and trusting in the Lord, who forgives. As this individual waits in hope, he encourages the community of faith to "hope in the LORD" (130:7).

Read this psalm aloud to the class as expressively as possible. If class members have copies of *The New International Lesson Annual*, encourage them to underline phrases that speak to them. Alternatively, distribute paper and pencils and invite students to jot down these phrases. Provide time for meditation, suggesting that the adults focus on their special phrases and consider how this psalm speaks to their own needs for hope.

Psalm 130
¹Out of the depths I cry to you, O LORD.
² Lord, hear my voice!
Let your ears be attentive
   to the voice of my supplications!
³If you, O LORD, should mark iniquities,
   Lord, who could stand?
⁴But there is forgiveness with you,
   so that you may be revered.
⁵I wait for the LORD, my soul waits,
   and in his word I hope;
⁶my soul waits for the Lord
   more than those who watch for the morning,
   more than those who watch for the morning.
⁷O Israel, hope in the LORD!
   For with the LORD there is steadfast love,
   and with him is great power to redeem.
⁸It is he who will redeem Israel
   from all its iniquities.

Recommend that the adults follow up at home by completing at least one of the following activities, which you will list on newsprint prior to the session:

- Memorize this psalm and recite it when you need to hear a word of hope.

- Call to mind times when you have felt dejected and were buoyed up by hope in God. Give thanks for the way God has moved—or will move—to help you resolve challenging situations.
- Share a story of hope from your own experience with those who long to know that the God of love can redeem and sustain them.
- Use this psalm as a prayer for those who are in difficult circumstances and see no light at the end of the tunnel.
- Offer tangible support to someone in need of hope.
- Page through the Psalms to find other poems that touch your heart with hope.

UNIT 1: THE DAYS ARE SURELY COMING
A VISION OF THE FUTURE

PREVIEWING THE LESSON

Lesson Scripture: Jeremiah 30:1-3, 18-22
Background Scripture: Jeremiah 30
Key Verse: Jeremiah 30:3

Focus of the Lesson:
People often find themselves in situations where they feel lost and alone. How do they regain a sense of belonging? Jeremiah tells of God's promise to restore the fortunes of the people, Israel and Judah, and to reestablish the covenant with them.

Goals for the Learners:
(1) to review God's written promise to restore the people and the land of Israel and Judah as of old.
(2) to imagine and express the feelings of safety in a community that has great promise for the future.
(3) to plan a way to invite persons who are not a part of the covenant community to become members of the church and Sunday school.

Pronunciation Guide:
Torah (toh´ ruh)
yasha (yaw shah´)

Supplies:
Bibles, newsprint and marker, paper and pencils, hymnals

READING THE SCRIPTURE

NRSV

Lesson Scripture: Jeremiah 30:1-3, 18-22

¹The word that came to Jeremiah from the LORD: ²Thus says the LORD, the God of Israel: Write in a book all the words that I have spoken to you. ³**For the days are surely coming, says**

CEB

Lesson Scripture: Jeremiah 30:1-3, 18-22

¹Jeremiah received the LORD's word: ²The LORD, the God of Israel, proclaims: Write down in a scroll all the words I have spoken to you. ³**The time is coming, declares the LORD,**

the LORD, when I will restore the fortunes of my people, Israel and Judah, says the LORD, and I will bring them back to the land that I gave to their ancestors and they shall take possession of it.

18 Thus says the LORD:
I am going to restore the fortunes of
   the tents of Jacob,
  and have compassion on his
    dwellings;
the city shall be rebuilt upon its
   mound,
  and the citadel set on its rightful
    site.
19 Out of them shall come
   thanksgiving,
  and the sound of merrymakers.
I will make them many, and they
   shall not be few;
  I will make them honored, and
    they shall not be disdained.
20 Their children shall be as of old,
   their congregation shall be estab-
    lished before me;
  and I will punish all who oppress
    them.
21 Their prince shall be one of their
   own,
  their ruler shall come from their
    midst;
I will bring him near, and he shall
   approach me,
  for who would otherwise dare to
    approach me?
               says the LORD.
22 And you shall be my people,
  and I will be your God.

when I will bring back my people Israel and Judah from captivity, says the LORD. I will bring them home to the land that I gave to their ancestors, and they will possess it.

18 The LORD proclaims:
I will restore Jacob's tents
  and have pity on their birthplace.
Their city will be rebuilt on its ruins
  and the palace in its rightful place.
19 There will be laughter
  and songs of thanks.
I will add to their numbers
  so they don't dwindle away.
I will honor them
  so they aren't humiliated.
20 Their children will thrive as they
   did long ago,
  and their community will be established before me.
  I will punish their oppressors.
21 They will have their own leader;
  their ruler will come from among
   them.
I will let him approach me,
  and he will draw near.
Who would dare approach me
  unless I let them come,
   declares the LORD.
22 You will be my people,
  and I will be your God.

UNDERSTANDING THE SCRIPTURE

Introduction. With some exceptions, the first twenty-nine chapters of Jeremiah are laden with oracles of judgment and warning against Judah. Exile was inevitable. As those chapters draw to a close, the prophet had instructed the captives now in Babylon to prepare for an extended time away that would involve multiple generations (29:4-7). But in verse

10 the undisclosed time in exile is "capped" at seventy years. Even more significantly, God's intent to levy judgment against Judah (7:16-20) reverses course. God's plans now involve "a future with hope" (29:11). The unfolding of this new vision for the future takes places in Jeremiah 30–33, sometimes called the "Book of Consolation" or "Book of Comfort." Its first two chapters are primarily poetry, while the second two chapters are almost exclusively prose. Today's passage, Jeremiah 30, bears its witness not simply within the particular situation of Israel in exile, but more broadly to the character of God evidenced in gracious and powerful fidelity to promises of restoration, compassion, and covenanted community.

Jeremiah 30:1-4. "The days are surely coming" is a hallmark phrase in Jeremiah, occurring here as well as in ten other places in his work (7:32; 9:25; 16:14, 33:14, and so on). The effect of the expression is to assure that what is written is not speculation, but certainty, about the future. What evokes such certainty is the threefold affirmation with which Jeremiah begins: What he has to say is not his own but what he has received from God ("The word that came to Jeremiah from the LORD. Thus says the LORD. . . . all the words that I [God] have spoken to you" —30:1, 2). The command in verse 2 to "Write in a book" is congruent with this work's interest in underscoring the written record left by this prophet (see especially chapter 36). The coming days, in contrast to days of judgment whose announcement dominates the first twenty-nine chapters of Jeremiah, are revealed in verse 3 to be days of restoration and return to the land of promise. The notation

of "Israel and Judah" suggests that Jeremiah perceives not only an end of Judah's exile in Babylon but also a restoration of the once united but eventually divided northern (Israel) and southern (Judah) kingdoms.

Jeremiah 30:5-11. The panic and terror that open these verses reflect the situation of hopelessness and despair into which these words were cast. The imagery of men acting as if they are in labor may symbolize the impossibility of human action alone to generate new possibilities in the face of verse 5's distress. This crisis finds sudden reversal when the prophet declares that Jacob (Jewish exiles) shall be "rescued" from it. "Rescue" translates the Hebrew *yasha*, which is also the root for "Joshua," the one who first led the Hebrew tribes into the Promised Land. God's salvation interrupts the cycle of despair of the previous verses, and opens into the promises of verses 8-11. The initial promises in verses 8-9 take on a decidedly political-national edge by pointing not only to a removal of foreign yokes but also more pointedly to the raising up of "David." David was Israel's idealized king, who reigned over a united kingdom. The promise of God's "saving" is repeated in verse 11. Interestingly, this verse asserts not only the judgment against those who scattered Israel but also affirms, "I will by no means leave you unpunished." Covenant takes seriously those who breach it, and God holds the guilty accountable, even in the midst of their deliverance.

Jeremiah 30:12-17. This section opens, as did 30:5-11, with the portrayal of dire circumstances that reflect both the cause and consequence of exile. Only here, the imagery shifts from the earlier one of childbirth to that of incurable illness and grave wounds. Verses 12-15 speak of the consequences of Israel's breaking covenant in terms as severe as any other in Jeremiah's earlier chapters in judgment. But similar to the abrupt reversal announced at the end of verse 7, so verses 16-17 overturn these severe consequences. The reversal comes initially in a turn of fortunes for those who took advantage of Israel—the captive-takers will now themselves become the captives. More significantly, verse 17 declares in a dramatic about-face that the incurable illness and wounds for which there was no medicine or healing (30:13) will find restoration to wholeness and healing.

Jeremiah 30:18-22. An interesting progression of restoration is reflected in the rehabilitated places identified in verse 18: tents, to dwellings, to city, to citadel. The movement flows from the most simple of habitations (tents) to citadels, guarantors of power and thus symbols of security for cities and nations. The imagery employed in verses 19-21 is liturgical, ranging from the resumption of thanksgiving to leaders whom God will "bring near" and who will "approach" God.

These are priestly acts, and this passage thus weds the roles of priestly functions (drawing near to God on behalf of the people) with governance (rule exercised on behalf of the people). Verse 22 closes this section by decisively identifying the tie between God and the exiles: "You shall be my people, and I will be your God." The expression echoes earlier affirmations of covenantal relationship in the Torah (Exodus 6:7; Leviticus 26:12).

Jeremiah 30:23-24. The changes God is about to bring about are depicted in the ominous metaphor of "storm." Exile cannot be ended until Babylon's power is broken—and such power does not yield without disruption. That disruption will come is revealed in evocative language: wrath, whirling tempest, fierce anger. There is no specificity in these terms of how or by what means the storm will be unleashed. That much remains mystery, to be understood in hindsight rather than foresight (30:24). What is clear, however, is that God's purposes for saving and restoring will not be deterred—not even by powers that have enforced captivity upon Israel. That is Jeremiah's vision of, and hope for, the future.

INTERPRETING THE SCRIPTURE

Write It Down

Don't commit anything to writing that you would not want to be held accountable for—even, perhaps especially, in this digital age of ours. Undocumented conversations can be denied ("I don't recall") or slanted ("that's not what I said") for one's own protection. But put something in writing, whether on paper or in

e-mail, and there is a trail left that can be traced. The commission God gives to Jeremiah in the opening of today's passage summons the prophet to take such a risk: "Write in a book" (30:2).

There is defiance in that command. Like the urging to Habakkuk to "Write the vision: make it plain on tablets, so that a runner may read it" (Habakkuk 2:2), God is directing Jeremiah to lay down a marker for which both God and the prophet can be held account-able. After all, what happens if these words do not come to fruition? The safe way would have been to limit words of restoration and hope to oral communication alone. That way appeals to "I don't recall" or "that's not what I said" could always be summoned—or to use contemporary political discourse, a "spin" could be put that would ensure ultimate deni-ability. But neither God nor prophet seeks deniability. They seek hope.

The other defiance in this com-mand to "write it" aims not at the people whose hopes God and the prophet are seeking to stir, but rather those who have held down those hopes for so long. Put something into writing, and authorities can build a case against you. Keeping things secret from oppressors requires stealth in communication. Either never commit it to writing—or if you do, as with the Book of Revelation, encode it in such hyperbole as to defy attempts to charge the author(s) with treason. But God's interest with Jere-miah is not in stealth, but in clear and open communication. It is, if you will, drawing a line in the sand so that the captives may see hope, and so that their captors may see their grasp on power drawing to an end.

"Write it in a book" asserts that restoration of community and return to land is not a secretive dream held in the dark, but public promises brought into the light for all to see. As for Israel of old, the question for us is this: Do we trust such promises? Are we willing to "write" our hopes so as to be accountable to them, in *defiance* of words and ways that still hold peo-ple captive to powers whose time is running out?

Safety and Promise

What measures do we use to assess the "safety" or "security" of a com-munity? Gates that control access to who's allowed in, and, more import-ant, who's kept out? Dusk-to-dawn lights and home-security systems? Well-stocked gun cabinets? Or do the more accurate measures of safety and security of communities reside in intangibles, unable to be purchased? For example, the cultivation of rela-tionships between neighbors? Or, more ominously, the homogeneity of those who live there, whether deter-mined on the basis of skin color or national origin or economic status?

There is nothing wrong with seek-ing safety and security in one's life, for one's community, whether under-stood as neighborhood or nation. The crunch comes in what we strive—or settle—for to achieve safety and secu-rity. In the promises God brings to the exiles through Jeremiah, the desire for safety and security are strong undercurrents. People who have been stripped of homeland and freedom do live at risk, and would likely be keenly interested in promised actions of rescue (30:7) and saving (30:11).

Except, daring to open oneself to a promised future can jeopardize the present's status quo. Even if exile was not ideal, it was what the exiles knew. The walls of Babylon, not to men-tion its armies and imperial power, did provide a measure of safety not unlike some of the things mentioned in the opening paragraph above. To trust the promises of God required no small risk: the risk of stepping out in faith, holding on to what the future promised more than what the present assured.

That tension is always with us: in

our lives within neighborhood and nation, in our lives within the faith community. We are a people who are the caretakers of great promises infused with lofty ideals. In the case of the nation: liberty and justice for all. In the case of faith community: the justice, mercy, and compassion of God's coming realm. But those visions constantly face "on the ground" realities that tempt us to live solely in the moment and not for the sake of the future. Like Esau, we sometimes even sell the birthright of promise for the "pottage" of immediate gratification, which frequently takes the form of shortcuts to security and safety.

The community to which God bid the exiles was one of trust in promises and Promise-maker, trust that empowered the risk of living in their light and hope rather than settling for the "safe" and familiar environs of exile. God still bids the community of faith to do the same. If we ask how or why we should take such a risk, the answer today is the same promissory answer God gave through Jeremiah to the exiles: "You shall be my people, and I will be your God" (30:22).

Sharing the Vision

"You shall be my people, and I will be your God." It is possible to twist that promise of God's gracious inclusion into an assertion of exclusionary self-righteousness. That is, the "you" and "your" in that declaration can be defined narrowly to a limited number of folk—not surprisingly, those who think like me or believe like me, or who share the same color of skin or

nation of origin or view of Scripture as me. Once such limits begin to be applied as to who gets included in "you are my people," then it becomes increasingly easy to slip into judgments as to who is *not* one of God's people.

Such devolutions of God's gracious vision can impact the church and its understanding of mission. In severe ways, some traditions see actual numerical limitations placed on who constitutes "my people"—for example, casting the symbolism of the 144,000 in Revelation 7:4 into predestined limits on those God saves. But one need not go to those extremes to impact the faith community. Sometimes, we grow so comfortable in our congregational circles that it seems as long as we have one another's company, there is no urgency to expanding "my people" in that local context. Outreach and evangelism become, if anything, relegated to pastors we hire to do this for us or outgoing church members who have the gift of gab.

But remember where this interpretive commentary began: with God's call to "write it down," which is to make it public. Our calling in the faith community is not to hold the promises of God close to our vest so that no one can steal them from us. It is up to us broadcast those promises and invite folks to experience what it means to live not simply *with* a future of hope, but more to the point to live *toward* the future *with* hope. To do so on the basis of the promises, and the Promise-maker, we encounter in Jeremiah's writing—and ultimately, the promises kept in Jesus Christ.

SHARING THE SCRIPTURE

PREPARING TO TEACH

Preparing Our Hearts

Meditate on this week's devotional reading from Jeremiah 29:10-14. What plans for a bright future do you hope that God has for you? How might you discern these plans? What steps will you take to act on them?

Pray that you and the students will seek God and trust the promises God has made for your benefit.

Preparing Our Minds

Study the background Scripture from Jeremiah 30 and the lesson Scripture from Jeremiah 30:1-3, 18-22.

Consider this question as you prepare the lesson: *When we find ourselves in situations where we feel lost and alone, how do we regain a sense of belonging?*

Write on newsprint:

❏ information for next week's lesson, found under "Continue the Journey."

❏ activities for further spiritual growth in "Continue the Journey."

Review the "Introduction," "The Big Picture," "Close-up," and "Faith in Action," which all precede this first lesson of this quarter. Consider how you might use any of this material in today's lesson.

LEADING THE CLASS

(1) Gather to Learn

❖ Greet the class members and introduce guests.

❖ Pray that those who have come today will feel a sense of belonging in this group.

❖ Read these two quotations from famous authors and invite the students to comment on what gives them a sense of belonging.

- **"He was part of a whole, a people scattered over the earth and yet eternally one and indivisible. Wherever a Jew lived, in whatever safety and isolation, he still belonged to his people."** (Pearl S. Buck, *Peony*)

- **"That is part of the beauty of all literature. You discover that your longings are universal longings, that you're not lonely and isolated from anyone. You belong."** (F. Scott Fitzgerald)

❖ Read aloud today's focus statement: **People often find themselves in situations where they feel lost and alone. How do they regain a sense of belonging? Jeremiah tells of God's promise to restore the fortunes of the people, Israel and Judah, and to reestablish the covenant with them.**

(2) Goal 1: Review God's Written Promise to Restore the People and the Land of Israel and Judah as of Old

❖ **Option:** Read or retell "The Big Picture: Keeping Hope Alive" in order to give the adults a sense of direction for this quarter. You may want to emphasize the first unit and return to this overview later in the quarter to look more closely at the second and third units.

❖ Set the stage for today's lesson by reading "Introduction" in Understanding the Scripture.

❖ Select a volunteer to read Jeremiah 30:1-3, 18-22.

❖ Discuss these questions:

1. **Why do you think Jeremiah was instructed to write God's words in a book?** (See "Write It Down" in Interpreting the Scripture.)

2. **What promises do you hear in verses 18-22?**

3. **How will people respond when God restores them?**

4. **What places does God promise to restore—and why might these be important?** (See "Jeremiah 30:18-22" in Understanding the Scripture.)

5. **Read again Jeremiah 30:22. Also read 1 Peter 2:10. What does it mean to you to know that you are one of God's people?**

❖ Provide quiet time for the learners to consider this question: **What does God need to restore to make your life whole again and give you a sense of fully belonging to God?**

(3) Goal 2: Imagine and Express the Feelings of Safety in a Community that Has Great Promise for the Future

❖ Read or retell "Safety and Promise" in Interpreting the Scripture and ask:

1. **How do you measure the safety and security of the community in which you live or work?**

2. **How do you measure the safety and security of your faith community?**

3. **How do you experience God as the provider of safety and security for you and your loved ones?**

❖ Distribute paper and pencils. Encourage the students to create their own vision for a community where all people will feel safe and secure. Consider what the community will be able to offer each person and the opportunities that each person will have to contribute the best that he or she has to offer. Also imagine the kinds of relationships people will have so that they can work together in harmony for the common good. Think about the role that material goods will play in such a community, as well as the attitudes community members will have toward nonessential possessions.

❖ Suggest that the adults work with a partner or threesome to describe their ideas to one another.

❖ Bring everyone together and give each person an opportunity to answer this question in a few words or sentence: **How would you feel if you were able to live in such a community?**

(4) Goal 3: Plan a Way to Invite Persons Who Are Not a Part of the Covenant Community to Become Members of the Church and Sunday School

❖ Read or retell "Sharing the Vision" in Interpreting the Scripture.

❖ Form small groups and distribute newsprint and a marker to each. Reread this sentence: **It is up to us to broadcast those promises and invite folks to experience what it means to live not simply *with* a future of hope, but more to the point to live *toward* the future *with* hope.** Encourage each group to brainstorm ways in which your class (and the congregation) can broadcast promises of hope to those who are not currently part of a faith community.

❖ Reconvene and ask each group to report its ideas.

❖ **Option:** Encourage one or more of the groups to roleplay one of their ideas in order to show how they would go about broadcasting God's promises of hope.

❖ Challenge the class members to invite at least one person to attend Sunday school and/or worship with them next week. Suggest that they use ideas they have gleaned from today's lesson as part of their invitations.

(5) Continue the Journey

❖ Pray that as the learners depart they will be open to God's leading as to whom they are to share God's promises with and invite to attend next Sunday.

❖ Post information for next week's session on newsprint for the students to copy:
- ■ Title: Restoration
- ■ Background Scripture: Jeremiah 31
- ■ Lesson Scripture: Jeremiah 31:31-37
- ■ Focus of the Lesson: Sometimes agreements and relationships must be revised and renewed. How can the faithful make sure all aspects of their lives encourage wholeness and spiritual growth in present circumstances? Jeremiah assures the people that God will make **a new covenant with God's people that will nurture and equip them for the present and future.**

❖ Challenge the adults to grow spiritually by completing one or more of these activities related to this week's session, which you have posted on newsprint for the students to copy.

(1) **Pray about the person(s) you feel God is leading you to invite to class. Think about how you might approach this person in a winsome, appealing way.**

(2) **Research the prophet Jeremiah. What do you learn about the man, his times, and his message? How do you think you might have responded to him?**

(3) **Identify some groups for whom the present seems hopeless. What might you be able to do to help these people—perhaps the hungry, homeless, lonely, ill— feel that they are cared about and belong?**

❖ Sing or read aloud "Great Is Thy Faithfulness."

❖ Conclude today's session by leading the class in this hope-filled benediction from Psalm 55:16, which is the key verse for October 19: **I call upon God, and the LORD will save me.**

UNIT 1: THE DAYS ARE SURELY COMING
RESTORATION

PREVIEWING THE LESSON

Lesson Scripture: Jeremiah 31:31-37
Background Scripture: Jeremiah 31
Key Verse: Jeremiah 31:31

Focus of the Lesson:
Sometimes agreements and relationships must be revised and renewed. How can the faithful make sure all aspects of their lives encourage wholeness and spiritual growth in present circumstances? Jeremiah assures us that God will make a new covenant with God's people that will nurture and equip them for the present and future.

Goals for the Learners:
(1) to know God's new covenant to reveal God's self to all the people, forgive their sins, and hold them accountable.
(2) to sense the relief and joy that come from starting over in agreement with someone.
(3) to make plans for renewing their personal covenant with God.

Pronunciation Guide:
Decalogue (dek´ uh log)
Ephraim (ee´ fray im)

Supplies:
Bibles, newsprint and marker, paper and pencils, hymnals

READING THE SCRIPTURE

NRSV
Lesson Scripture: Jeremiah 31:31-37

31The days are surely coming, says the LORD, when I will make a new covenant with the house of Israel and the house of Judah. 32It will not be like the covenant that I made with their ancestors when I took them by

CEB
Lesson Scripture: Jeremiah 31:31-37

31The time is coming, declares the LORD, when I will make a new covenant with the people of Israel and Judah. 32It won't be like the covenant I made with their ancestors when I took them by the hand to lead them the hand to bring them out of the land of Egypt—a covenant that they broke, though I was their husband, says the LORD. ³³But this is the covenant that I will make with the house of Israel after those days, says the LORD: I will put my law within them, and I will write it on their hearts; and I will be their God, and they shall be my people. ³⁴No longer shall they teach one another, or say to each other, "Know the LORD," for they shall all know me, from the least of them to the greatest, says the LORD; for I will forgive their iniquity, and remember their sin no more.

³⁵Thus says the LORD,
who gives the sun for light by day
　and the fixed order of the moon
　　and the stars for light by night,
who stirs up the sea so that its waves
　　roar—
　the LORD of hosts is his name:
³⁶If this fixed order were ever to cease
　from my presence, says the LORD,
then also the offspring of Israel
　would cease
to be a nation before me forever.
³⁷Thus says the LORD:
If the heavens above can be
　measured,
　and the foundations of the earth
　　below can be explored,
then I will reject all the offspring of
　Israel
　because of all they have done,
　　　　　　　　　says the LORD.

out of the land of Egypt. They broke that covenant with me even though I was their husband, declares the LORD. ³³No, this is the covenant that I will make with the people of Israel after that time, declares the LORD. I will put my Instructions within them and engrave them on their hearts. I will be their God, and they will be my people. ³⁴They will no longer need to teach each other to say, "Know the LORD!" because they will all know me, from the least of them to the greatest, declares the LORD; for I will forgive their wrongdoing and never again remember their sins.

³⁵The LORD proclaims:
The one who established the sun to light up the day
　and ordered the moon and stars to light up the night,
　　who stirs up the sea into crashing waves,
　　whose name is the LORD of heavenly forces:
　³⁶If the created order should vanish
　　from my sight,
　　declares the LORD,
　only then would Israel's descendants ever stop being a nation
　　before me.
³⁷The LORD proclaims:
If the heavens above could be
　measured
and the foundation of the earth
　below could be fathomed,
　only then would I reject Israel's
　　descendants
　for what they have done,
　declares the LORD.

UNDERSTANDING THE SCRIPTURE

Jeremiah 31:1-14. "Samaria" and "Ephraim" were names associated with the Northern Kingdom of Israel. It comprised the territories of the so-called "lost ten tribes of Israel" who disappeared after the Assyrian conquest of the Northern Kingdom in 722 B.C. "Remnant" (31:7) carries forward earlier prophetic traditions. The theology of the remnant declared the disobedience that resulted in the judgment of exile would result in far fewer "returnees" than those taken away (Amos 3:12; see also 5:15). That same theology could also be framed far more positively: God would bring life out of what seemed like an unmitigated catastrophe, as here in Jeremiah 31:7 and Isaiah 11:11. Remarkably, those who are restored and gathered for return are not the ones most capable on their own strength for making such a journey, but rather those whose frailties assert that such restoration relies upon God. While God's rule in the judgment of exile is clear (31:10), God's new purpose to restore the scattered ones promises to transform sorrow into joy (31:13).

Jeremiah 31:15-20. This poignant poem reflects a mother's grief for her lost children. It is invoked in Matthew 2:17-18 to express the grief arising from Herod's slaughter of Bethlehem's children. Rachel was the wife of Jacob, the mother of Joseph and Benjamin, and the grandmother of Ephraim. The mother whose death was grieved by her own children now, in Jeremiah's metaphor, is the one who grieves the death of her children. Into this metaphor of a mother's grief, Jeremiah injects

the promise of return and "hope for your future" (31:17). The poem closes in verse 20 with an intriguing and powerful word. God hears Ephraim repenting—and God confesses that, having spoken against him (in judgment), "I still remember him." Such remembrance, as in Exodus 2:24, brings life.

Jeremiah 31:21-26. Verses 21-22 use another set of feminine images to speak of restoration and return in which Israel now is portrayed as a "daughter" and a "woman." The final sentence of verse 22 has long baffled interpreters in terms of what "encompasses" means. The previous reference to "virgin" Israel might suggest this final clause aims at affirming the fruitfulness of life being restored in the land and among the people who will return. Verse 26 closes this section in a curious way: "I awoke and looked . . ." Does this mean the oracle of hope in verses 23-25—or perhaps the entire chapter or more—has been a dream or vision granted to the prophet? Dreams are closely related to imagination. To break the "reality" of the present circumstances of the exiles, dreams and imagination may be precisely what is needed to see beyond what is immediate (and oppressive) to what is possible and liberating by the workings of God.

Jeremiah 31:27-30. The reunion of the "houses" of Israel and Judah stands at the fore of the promised restoration, along with fruitfulness in the land. The reversal of God's purposes from judgment to restoration uses language that almost exactly parallels what God had commissioned

Jeremiah to speak in 1:9-10. Verses 29-30 contain what was apparently the "conventional wisdom" among exiles, perhaps especially for those who had been born in Babylon. They had not committed the disobedience that brought down the judgment of exile, yet they lived in exile. So it must be that children (and grandchildren) must suffer for their parents' mistakes, and exile must continue. Verse 30 declares no! While phrased negatively ("all shall die for their own sins"), the declaration opens the door to the possibility of restoration. No longer will exiles be consigned to suffer the consequences of a previous generation. Each generation chooses its own path.

Jeremiah 31:31-34. "Covenant" is at the heart of prophetic theology. The breaking of covenant had brought on the disaster of exile. But now, what might have seemed as irreparable is given new life—the promise of a new covenant. The invocation of the memory of God leading the people out of Egypt clearly has in mind the Sinai covenant that ensued. And just as that covenant had been symbolized by words written on stone, so this covenant will be written "on their hearts" (Jeremiah 31:33). How the knowledge of this covenant is disseminated is imagined to take place not by the standard of people in the "know" instructing those in the dark. All will hold this knowledge (31:34). And the nature of such knowledge is revealed by Jeremiah to be grounded in the experience of God's forgiveness.

Jeremiah 31:35-37. The tone of Jeremiah's work takes a different direction in these verses. While the emphasis remains on the restoration of Israel, the portrayal of this assurance shifts to the realm of creation. Before, hope in Jeremiah's work had largely been expressed in God's turn from judgment to renewal. In these verses, the prophet uses the steady purposes of God revealed in the constancy of creation as a metaphor for the unshakable hope extended to Israel. God has fixed the order of the skies, mastered the chaotic waters (see Genesis 1:1-2), and set in place the foundations of the earth. Just so, the continuity of the natural order is linked to the continuity of God's covenanting with Israel. That is, to conceive of God's voiding covenant relationship with Israel would be akin to conceive of creation ceasing to be. As for the latter possibility, see the promise of Genesis 8:22—the prelude for covenant with Noah.

Jeremiah 31:38-40. Yet another shift occurs in these closing verses of the chapter. They are prose rather than poetry, and they are also somewhat prosaic in nature. That is, Jeremiah moves from dreams and words engraved on heart and the entirety of creation to measuring sticks. Similar to what Ezekiel does in far more detail, Jeremiah imagines what the restored Jerusalem will look like and where it will be. The specificity reminds every generation that God's promises are not finally about transporting us out of our circumstances, but rather setting our feet on sacred ground and living here in light of God's promises and covenant.

INTERPRETING THE SCRIPTURE

Old, New, and the Tie that Binds

"I will make a new covenant." Have you ever been in a relationship where a new beginning was decided upon? It takes a lot of energy and investment of self to set aside what may have led to an argument or a dead end. Some of what is "old" does indeed need to be cast off in order for room to be made for the new.

Even in those new starts, the relationship does not start from scratch. Indeed, the very reason for seeking renewal may be deeply grounded in remembrances of the good that has been in that relationship. Keep in mind that today's theme is restoration. And restoration presumes there is some fundamental continuity in all of the "housecleaning" that must take place. Restoration seeks to reestablish that which has somehow been lost.

Jeremiah's "new covenant" is such an act of restoration. That which has been lost can be summed up in the word "exile." Home. Land. Freedom. That which needed to be set aside has already been summed up by Jeremiah and others: injustice, disobedience.

But the promise and hope of restoration, of "starting over" that comes from Jeremiah is not, as noted before, a starting from scratch. The covenant partners remain the same: God and Israel. It is the means and core of the covenant that Jeremiah describes as new, as will be explored in more detail in the next section.

Now the church, precisely at this point, needs to take a deep breath and understand that Jeremiah is directly addressing the people of Israel in exile with the promise of new covenant. "Old" and "new" covenants are not shorthand for Judaism and Christianity. It is not as if Jeremiah's words and promise do not apply until Jesus enters the scene some 500-plus years later. To be sure, the church has interpreted Jeremiah's promise of new covenant through the lens of Jesus' life and ministry—and for good reason when it comes to the nature of the new covenant that Jeremiah announces (more on this shortly). But the truth of the matter is that the promise of Jeremiah's new covenant belongs first to Israel, and through that grounding secondly to the Christian faith that sprouted from its Hebrew roots. The synagogue and the church are not simply claimants of the same promise—they, we, are *claimed by* the same promise.

The Heart of Covenant

A covenant is basically an agreement between two parties. In the ancient Near East, covenants often took the form of political treaties whereby the parties involved made promises regarding conduct toward one another, and also delineated sanctions when those promises were not met. The most expansive example of covenant in the Old Testament is that which God enacted with Israel at Sinai after deliverance from Egypt. The books of Exodus and Deuteronomy contain long sections devoted to the obligations of Israel (traditionally summed up in the Decalogue or Ten Commandments, though also including numerous ethical and ritual commands) along with both the blessings

God promises for obedience and the curses looming for disobedience (see Deuteronomy 28).

The chief symbol of the Sinai covenant were the tablets with the Decalogue engraved on them, which were kept in the ark of the covenant (yes, of Indiana Jones fame—and a continuing mystery as to its whereabouts today). Thus, it was a covenant associated with what had been written on stone.

Jeremiah's "new" covenant plays on that written nature. Newness arises where God, speaking through the prophet, "locates" the new writing: on the hearts of the people. In many respects, old and new covenant have the same purpose: to shape the conduct of the people not only in relationship to God but also in relationship to one another.

Part of the distinction Jeremiah draws between old and new comes in the "exteriority" of the old and the "interiority" of the new. As you listen to verses 33-34, the old relied upon outside experts to rightly interpret the covenant's meaning. As the earlier prophetic critique of Israel and Judah's leaders revealed prior to exile, it was precisely the failure of those "outside experts," be they kings or priests, who led to covenants breaking (see, for example, Jeremiah 5:31 and Ezekiel 34:1-10).

Part of the distinction Jeremiah draws between old and new comes in the basis of how God is known. In the Decalogue, the God of covenant is known as the One who brought the people out of the land of Egypt (Exodus 20:2). In Jeremiah's new covenant, the God of covenant is known as the One who forgives (Jeremiah 31:34). A covenant of the heart reveals forgiveness at the heart of covenant.

Such a covenant is powerful—and not simply because individuals are forgiven. What is at stake here in Jeremiah, and what these promises of Israel's restoration hinge on, is God's commitment and power to enact a fresh start, a new covenant, for the whole people of God. Forgiveness creates that; forgiveness unbinds communities, and not individuals alone, from pasts and exiles who might not otherwise be escaped.

Creation, Hope, and Trust

I watched a political commentator I greatly respect critique a senator for appealing to Genesis 8:22 in comments that were seemingly intended to soft-pedal the issue of global warming and climate change. I understand totally the reason for such a critique. The senator apparently used that verse to argue that God's promise to maintain the rhythms of seasons and temperatures meant that human beings could not really do any significant damage to the planet without God's intervening. Really? The same argument could be made that since God covenanted with Israel, then we really didn't need to worry what Hitler was doing since God would not let significant damage happen there either.

Human folly and sin have very few limits, it would seem from the most casual reading of history, and I side with my political commentator friend in taking issue with that verse being used to excuse degradation of the planet.

Scripture can be twisted—just ask Jesus in the wilderness.

But I also have to admit: Jeremiah makes some rather extraordinary claims about creation and covenant in the closing verses of today's passage. Pay attention to verses 35-37, particularly 36 and 37. What the prophet is saying to the exiles is a radical word of assurance. The idea of God backing off from covenant with Israel would be akin to God backing off from creation itself. To me, this doesn't mean a carte blanche to those so covenanted with—and since I take Jeremiah's promise of new covenant to apply to the church and the synagogue, I include us in this caveat. The purpose of such assurance is not to give free rein to an "anything goes" attitude *since God avowed never to reject us*. That is, after all, the attitude that led to the breaking of covenant that set in motion exile in the first place. No, to me the purpose is to assert the utter fidelity of God to covenant and to those with whom God has covenanted. It is to say that as surely as the sun rises in the morning, so is God's faithfulness to God's people.

SHARING THE SCRIPTURE

PREPARING TO TEACH

Preparing Our Hearts

Meditate on this week's devotional reading from Hebrews 8:1-7, 13. How do you perceive Jesus to be the mediator of God's covenant? Although the writer of Hebrews claims in verse 13 that the first covenant is "obsolete," many contemporary Christians would disagree that God has canceled or reneged on that covenant with the Jews. Where do you stand—and why?

Pray that you and the students will open your hearts to know the covenanting God more fully.

Preparing Our Minds

Study the background Scripture from Jeremiah 31 and the lesson Scripture from Jeremiah 31:31-37.

Consider this question as you prepare the lesson: *How can the faithful make sure all aspects of their lives encourage wholeness and spiritual growth in present circumstances?*

Write on newsprint:

❏ information for next week's lesson, found under "Continue the Journey."

❏ activities for further spiritual growth in "Continue the Journey."

Review the "Introduction," "The Big Picture," "Close-up," and "Faith in Action," which all precede the first lesson of this quarter. Consider how you might use any of this material in today's lesson.

Familiarize yourself with "The Heart of Covenant" in Interpreting the Scripture. Decide whether you will create a lecture from this material or use it to help answer discussion questions under "Know God's New Covenant to Reveal God's Self to All the People, Forgive Their Sins, and Hold Them Accountable."

LEADING THE CLASS

(1) Gather to Learn

❖ Greet the class members and introduce guests.

❖ Pray that those who have come

today will seek ways to grow spiritually in all circumstances.

❖ Read the first two paragraphs of "Old, New, and the Tie that Binds" in Interpreting the Scripture.

❖ Encourage partners or threesomes to talk about situations in which they have tried to make a fresh start. They need not focus on the reasons for the rupture in the relationship, but they can explore the challenges they faced in deciding that the relationship was worth saving and in trying to make a fresh start that did not allow the past to create stumbling blocks for the present.

❖ Call everyone together and invite participants to comment on ideas they heard for making a successful new start.

❖ Read aloud today's focus statement: **Sometimes agreements and relationships must be revised and renewed. How can the faithful make sure all aspects of their lives encourage wholeness and spiritual growth in present circumstances? Jeremiah assures the people that God will make a new covenant with God's people that will nurture and equip them for the present and future.**

(2) Goal 1: Know God's New Covenant to Reveal God's Self to All the People, Forgive Their Sins, and Hold Them Accountable

❖ Read or retell the information in Understanding the Scripture though the portion labeled "Jeremiah 31:27-30" to prepare the adults for today's lesson.

❖ Select a volunteer to read Jeremiah 31:31-37.

❖ Use information from "The Heart of Covenant" in Interpreting the Scripture to address these questions, either in a lecture or as part of a discussion.

1. **How would you define "covenant"?**
2. **What role does writing play in covenant making?**
3. **Where does Jeremiah "locate" the new covenant?**
4. **What difference does this location make when compared with the first covenant?**
5. **What is the basis for restoration under the new covenant?**
6. **What role might forgiveness play in your own covenant keeping?**

(3) Goal 2: Sense the Relief and Joy that Come from Starting Over in Agreement with Someone

❖ Lead the class in this guided imagery activity.

• **Imagine yourself sitting in a comfortable space in your home as you look through a photograph album. Continue paging through until you come to a picture of someone with whom you were once estranged. Focus on this person and recall what led to the break in your relationship.** (Pause)
• **Try to recall how you felt when the two of you were able to patch up your differences, forgive each other, and start anew. What words or actions led to your recommitment to each other? What did you both say? What emotions swept over you?** (Pause)
• **Think about the new covenant that enables you to be in a relationship with God where you can experience**

unconditional divine forgiveness. Ask God to allow you to experience this divine forgiveness right now as you recall reasons why you may feel estranged from God. (Pause)

❖ Bring the group together and ask: **How is the experience of forgiveness from God similar to the experience of restoring a relationship with a person from whom you have been estranged?**

(4) Goal 3: Make Plans for the Learners to Renew Their Personal Covenant with God

❖ Distribute paper, pencils, and hymnals. Turn to "Take My Life, and Let It Be." (This Frances Havergal hymn, which is no longer protected by copyright, may also be found at www.cyberhymnal.org/htm/t/m /tmlalib.htm if it is not included in the hymnal you use.) Invite the group to join you in *reading* this hymn in unison so as to focus on the words.

❖ Suggest that the learners read this hymn again silently. Tell them to be open to any ideas this song suggests as to how they can renew their personal commitment to God. Once they have an idea, they are to write their commitment on the paper. For example, perhaps their "lips" (verse 2) have not been "filled with messages from [God]" but rather with gossip or other words that hurt. The students could commit themselves to asking forgiveness not only from God but also from the persons they have hurt. They could also pledge to think about how their words will be heard before they speak and promise not to knowingly offend or belittle anyone.

(5) Continue the Journey

❖ Break the silence by praying that as the learners depart they will feel assured of God's covenantal commitment with them.

❖ Post information for next week's session on newsprint for the students to copy:
- **Title: A New Future**
- **Background Scripture: Jeremiah 32**
- **Lesson Scripture: Jeremiah 32:2-9, 14-15**
- **Focus of the Lesson: Even in dire circumstances, some people take hopeful actions. What gives them the confidence to do so? While Jerusalem was under siege, God instructed the prophet Jeremiah to purchase property as a sign that there was a future for the people and their land beyond defeat and exile.**

❖ Challenge the adults to grow spiritually by completing one or more of these activities, which you have posted on newsprint for the students to copy.

(1) **Identify a relationship in your life that you value so much that you will work to restore it. Pray about how God wants you to proceed and then act on those insights.**

(2) **Use a Bible dictionary or other reference to research the biblical theme of "covenant." Also look at Isaiah 55:3; 61:8; Ezekiel 16:60; 34:25; and 37:26 to read about an eternal covenant that cannot be broken. How do you see yourself as being**

in a covenant relationship with God?

(3) Encourage someone who feels that he or she needs to make a fresh start with God or a person. Let this person know that forgiveness and a new sense of wholeness are gifts that God will give to those who seek restoration.

❖ Sing or read aloud "Dear Lord and Father of Mankind."

❖ Conclude today's session by leading the class in this hope-filled benediction from Psalm 55:16, which is the key verse for October 19: **I call upon God, and the LORD will save me.**

UNIT 1: THE DAYS ARE SURELY COMING
A New Future

PREVIEWING THE LESSON

Lesson Scripture: Jeremiah 32:2-9, 14-15
Background Scripture: Jeremiah 32
Key Verse: Jeremiah 32:15

Focus of the Lesson:

Even in dire circumstances, some people take hopeful actions. What gives them the confidence to do so? While Jerusalem was under siege, God instructed the prophet Jeremiah to purchase property as a sign that there was a future for the people and their land beyond defeat and exile.

Goals for the Learners:

(1) to recapture the hopefulness of Jeremiah's purchase of a field while he awaits the siege of Israel.
(2) to appreciate hope and hopeful actions in the face of deep hardship.
(3) to review their personal times of hardship in the past that held, and hold, hope for the future.

Pronunciation Guide:

Anathoth (an´ uh thoth)   Nebuchadrezzar (neb uh kuh drez´ uhr)
Chaldean (kal dee´ uhn)   Shallum (shal´ uhm)
Hanamel (han´ uh mel)   Zedekiah (zed uh ki´ uh)
Molech (moh´ lek)

Supplies:

Bibles, newsprint and marker, paper and pencils, hymnals

READING THE SCRIPTURE

NRSV

Lesson Scripture: Jeremiah 32:2-9, 14-15

²At that time the army of the king of Babylon was besieging Jerusalem, and the prophet Jeremiah was

CEB

Lesson Scripture: Jeremiah 32:2-9, 14-15

²At that time, the army of the Babylonian king had surrounded Jerusalem, and the prophet Jeremiah was

confined in the court of the guard that was in the palace of the king of Judah, [3]where King Zedekiah of Judah had confined him. Zedekiah had said, "Why do you prophesy and say: Thus says the LORD: I am going to give this city into the hand of the king of Babylon, and he shall take it; [4]King Zedekiah of Judah shall not escape out of the hands of the Chaldeans, but shall surely be given into the hands of the king of Babylon, and shall speak with him face to face and see him eye to eye; [5]and he shall take Zedekiah to Babylon, and there he shall remain until I attend to him, says the LORD; though you fight against the Chaldeans, you shall not succeed?"

[6]Jeremiah said, The word of the LORD came to me: [7]Hanamel son of your uncle Shallum is going to come to you and say, "Buy my field that is at Anathoth, for the right of redemption by purchase is yours." [8]Then my cousin Hanamel came to me in the court of the guard, in accordance with the word of the LORD, and said to me, "Buy my field that is at Anathoth in the land of Benjamin, for the right of possession and redemption is yours; buy it for yourself." Then I knew that this was the word of the LORD.

[9]And I bought the field at Anathoth from my cousin Hanamel, and weighed out the money to him, seventeen shekels of silver. . . . [14]Thus says the LORD of hosts, the God of Israel: Take these deeds, both this sealed deed of purchase and this open deed, and put them in an earthenware jar, in order that they may last for a long time. [15]For thus says the LORD of hosts, the God of Israel: Houses and fields and vineyards shall again be bought in this land.

confined to the prison quarters in the palace of Judah's king. [3]Judah's King Zedekiah had Jeremiah sent there after questioning him: "Why do you prophesy, 'This is what the LORD says: I'm handing this city over to the king of Babylon, and he will occupy it; [4]and Judah's King Zedekiah will be captured and handed over to the king of Babylon; he will speak to the king of Babylon personally and see him with his very own eyes. [5]And Zedekiah will be carried off to Babylon to live out his days until I punish him, declares the LORD. If you make war against the Babylonians, you will fail.'"

[6]Jeremiah said, The LORD's word came to me: [7]Your cousin Hanamel, Shallum's son, is on his way to see you; and when he arrives, he will tell you: "Buy my field in Anathoth, for by law you are next in line to purchase it." [8]And just as the LORD had said, my cousin Hanamel showed up at the prison quarters and told me, "Buy my field in Anathoth in the land of Benjamin, for you are next in line and have a family obligation to purchase it." Then I was sure this was the LORD's doing.

[9]So I bought the field in Anathoth from my cousin Hanamel, and weighed out for him seventeen shekels of silver. . . . [14]"The LORD of heavenly forces, the God of Israel, proclaims: Take these documents—this sealed deed of purchase along with the unsealed one—and put them into a clay container so they will last a long time. [15]The LORD of heavenly forces, the God of Israel, proclaims: Houses, fields, and vineyards will again be bought in this land. "

UNDERSTANDING THE SCRIPTURE

Jeremiah 32:1-5. Verse 1's references to the particular years of reign for Zedekiah and Nebuchadnezzar set this passage in 588 B.C. In less than a year, Jerusalem will be destroyed and the vast majority of its inhabitants carried off into exile or dispersed across the eastern Mediterranean region. King Zedekiah had been installed as a "puppet" king of Judah by Nebuchadnezzar in 597 B.C., when the Babylonians first conquered the land and exiled some of its citizens. Over the years, Zedekiah came under the influence of Judean nobles and "prophets" who urged rebellion against Babylon and alliance with Egypt. Jeremiah vehemently opposed those efforts, and was rewarded with imprisonment (32:2-3). The words in verses 4-5, which Zedekiah mimics back to Jeremiah, reflect Jeremiah's prophecy of the inevitability of exile—particularly now that rebellion had resulted in Babylon's armies laying siege to Jerusalem. "Chaldeans" is a synonym for Babylonians. The repeated "[thus] says the LORD" reveals that exile—and Zedekiah's fate—arises not out of random historical factors, but out of the purpose of God.

Jeremiah 32:6-8. Anathoth was the hometown of Jeremiah (1:1), situated several miles northeast of Jerusalem. The earlier notation in 32:2 that the armies of Babylon were laying siege to Jerusalem would indicate that the family field in Anathoth was likely already "lost" to the invaders. "Right of redemption" in verse 7 relates to the Jubilee traditions in Leviticus 25:25-31 (see also Ruth 4:1-6). The repeated "the word of the LORD," coupled with the fulfillment of what

God said Jeremiah's cousin would do, underscores that this exchange is no mere financial transaction. As with earlier purchases made by Jeremiah of a linen loincloth (13:1-11) and an earthenware jug (19:1-13), this purchase of land will become a symbol of what the future holds. In contrast to the other two purchases, however, which both became symbols of judgment and destruction, verse 15 will make clear that purchasing land in enemy territory stands as a radical act of hope in the future.

Jeremiah 32:9-13. This section carefully records the methodical details of Jeremiah's purchasing of this family plot of land. Money is weighed and exchanged. A deed is signed and sealed in the presence of witnesses. The sealed deed and the "open copy" are entrusted to Baruch, later identified as the scribe who will write down Jeremiah's prophecies (36:4). *The Interpreter's Bible* offers an explanation for the "two" deeds identified in this passage. It suggests that the deed would have been written twice on a single sheet of papyrus, which was then cut in the space between the two copies. Once signed, the first deed would have been rolled and then sealed for official documentation, while the second deed would have been left unrolled, so that verification of its details could be made without breaking the seal.

Jeremiah 32:14-15. Earthenware jars provided secure storage for documents. Most of the Dead Sea Scrolls survived almost two thousand years by being stored in such vessels. Verse 15 makes clear why the storage of Jeremiah's deeds so that they may "last" (the Hebrew verb literally means "to stand") is not simply a legal attestation. This plot of land becomes a witness to the hope of return from exile. The basis of the "right of redemption," that forms the appeal of Hanamel to Jeremiah, is not simply a right to retain family lands. More fundamentally, it is founded on the Jubilee assertion that the land belongs to God (Leviticus 25:23). "Houses and fields and vineyards" is an inclusive term by which Jeremiah proclaims that the whole of life, familial and social and vocational, shall be restored.

Jeremiah 32:16-25. These verses form a prayer that Jeremiah raises to God. The immediate context of the prayer is his purchase of the land, which he alludes to in both its opening (32:16) and its closing (32:25). In between, Jeremiah moves from praise of God as Creator to remembrance of God's saving acts in the past—and now, to the disaster of exile God is about to bring for the breaking of covenant. The prayer's more general sense of God's repaying the guilty (32:18) takes on the specificity of calling upon God to see the equipment set in place to lay siege to Jerusalem (32:24). In the midst of such threat that God had said would come to pass (often through the words of Jeremiah himself), Jeremiah concludes the prayer in verse 25 with a kind of marveling at all that has come to pass—and all that is yet promised to be: "Yet you . . . said to me, 'Buy the field.'"

Jeremiah 32:26-35. God's reply to Jeremiah's prayer comes in two segments, the first in these verses and the second in 36-44. This first segment confirms that judgment and exile will fall. Babylon and Nebuchadnezzar are viewed as the instruments of God—an assertion that could easily be heard as traitorous by the political and religious leaders who still held forth in Jerusalem. The details and causes of Jerusalem's destruction are cast in severe terms (32:29-30). The very city itself is indicted in verse 31, again an assertion that would have cut against the grain of Jerusalem's commonly accepted position of privilege. According to verse 32, no group is exempt from the guilt that brings down exile. The denunciation reaches a climax in verse 35 with the sacrilege of child sacrifice to Molech (see Leviticus 20:2-3).

Jeremiah 32:36-44. The utter condemnation in the first half of God's reply to Jeremiah's prayer pivots on verse 36's "Now therefore." As bleak as the previous segment had been, this second half asserts God's saving purposes for the people. In the face of broken covenant, God unilaterally declares the establishment of an "everlasting" covenant. An allusion to Jeremiah's purchase comes in verses 43-44, which underscores the promise in 32:15. Note the assertion that begins and ends this segment (and appears as well in the reversal promised in verse 42): "[thus] says the LORD." Hope is not Jeremiah's wishful thinking. Hope is grounded in the promissory—and trustworthy— word of God.

INTERPRETING THE SCRIPTURE

Who Holds the Future?

The values—and hopes—that faith instills can sometimes force hard decisions to be made. Such decisions reveal our priorities, and our "bottom lines" of what and who wields power over our future, more than any creedal statement. A German Christian in the 1930s had to decide whether to risk opposing the increasing rhetoric of hatred and militarism gaining a stranglehold on the nation—or to keep silent for fear of retribution. For an American Christian in the 1950s and early 1960s, particularly those who lived in communities where the dividing lines between races were strictly (and unevenly) enforced, the hard choice would have been whether to take a public stand against segregation, knowing it could cost friends and business and worse. For a Christian today, one of the hard choices may be—you fill in the blank. What word or act, grounded in your understanding of discipleship, could land you in hot water with your community, or your church? And what would your resulting decision reveal about what, or who, you ultimately believe to hold the future?

Consider Jeremiah. No prophet is as grieved at times for the message of judgment he is commissioned to proclaim (8:18-22). The decision to heed that commission had been hard, as can often be seen in his laments to God scattered through this book. As today's passage opens, two factors weigh on Jeremiah's decision and what it reveals of his view of who holds the future. Most immediately, Jeremiah is in prison on the order of King Zedekiah (32:3). Jeremiah's offensive prophecy (32:3-5) suggests why the king would do such a thing. It would appear that King Zedekiah holds the final word over Jeremiah and his destiny. But second, there is also the detail that the Babylonian armies are laying siege to Jerusalem. So as much as Zedekiah might seem to hold the upper hand over Jeremiah's future, even that control appears

short-lived. For Nebuchadrezzar seems to hold overarching control over the futures of king and prophet and nation. Right?

Wrong. At least, not in Jeremiah's assessment as to who holds the future. Zedekiah does not, even though he can imprison. His day will all too soon draw to a close. Even Nebuchadrezzar does not, even though he can conquer. His empire is on the rise, but it will be eclipsed in just slightly more than one generation by another whom God will raise up (Isaiah 45:1).

The future is not held by those who exercise injustice or command by brute force. The future is held by God. The challenge is this: Do our lives, and choices, and priorities reflect that hope when it becomes costly for us to do so?

Putting Your Money
Where Your Hope Is

I once came across a story of an experienced tightrope artist, known as Charles Blondin, who walked blindfolded across a rope strung over Niagara Falls—and did so pushing a wheelbarrow. The crowd cheered wildly when he made it across. When the cheering died down, he asked: "Do you believe I can carry a person across in this wheelbarrow?" Affirming that Blondin was the greatest tightrope walker in the world in the mid-1800s, the crowd roared a resounding yes. To which he replied: "Okay, get in the wheelbarrow!" But no one did.

This story provides us with a clear example of how it is one thing to make some assertion that involves no risk of self. It is quite another, however, to have one's words or confession require an investment of one's own self.

It is one thing for Jeremiah to prophesy that God will restore the people of Israel to their homeland. Words can be cheap. It is quite another thing for Jeremiah to buy a plot of ground currently under Babylonian control, at the very moment when the siege weapons of their armies surrounded the city walls, and would soon destroy the city in which king and people and prophet took refuge. Unless there was a miracle, the land was in the process of being forcibly taken, and exile was imminent.

In point of fact, there was no miraculous deliverance. Jerusalem fell. Those who were not killed in the assault were either taken as captives to Babylon, or scattered to Egypt or other environs. The land was lost.

Except for this plot of land Jeremiah had sunk his own money into at the height—or should I say, depth—of the crisis. Except for the deed to the land that Jeremiah had arranged to be stored in a safe place "for a long time" (32:14).

To buy land in a place to which you will never return is an act of supreme folly. But to buy land as an act of defiant hope? That is investing oneself in the future. There is risk, but it is risk grounded in where—and in whom—one places trust. Parallel to the Understanding the Scripture comments regarding 32:14-15, what Jeremiah does is place a "down payment" on the Jubilee hope that all the land ultimately belongs to God. In buying this plot, Jeremiah puts his money where his hope is.

Do we?

What Stands for You?

Imagine that you could drop in on a gathering of your descendants fifty years from now. What might you hope they point to as the legacy you left for them? What of your life will "stand" long after you have departed?

In Jeremiah 32:14, Jeremiah instructs Baruch to store the deeds "in order that they may *last* for a long time" (emphasis added). As noted earlier, that Hebrew verb literally means "to stand." "To stand" can be taken at least two ways in that verse and in our lives. One way is suggested in the opening paragraph's imagined visit to your future family. To "stand" for something can mean to symbolize, or to remind one of something or someone else. The act of Jeremiah's instructions for preservation can be heard as the prophet's desire to have this purchase stand as a symbol of hope in a despairing situation.

But to "stand" can also mean to endure. Something that stands the test of time is something that holds its value or meaning through changing circumstances. That, too, is part of Jeremiah's meaning here. The storage of the deed becomes a means to ensure that what has been done this day, as foolish as it seems now, will "stand." That land and its ownership by Jeremiah—and by implication of the Jubilee "right of redemption" referenced earlier, its ownership by God—will stand.

It is like how Paul closes 1 Corinthians 13. He notes the enduring values of faith and hope and love, but the greatest of these, the most enduring, that which gives the others meaning and significance is love.

Far more than a simple financial transaction that purchases a small plot of ground, Jeremiah's action is asserting that God's promised restoration and the eventual return of exiles will "stand." In spite of Zedekiah's ineffective alliance building, in spite of Nebuchadrezzar's forcible leading off of the captives to Babylon, God's word of return and hope will stand. It will endure.

It has been said that those who don't stand for something will fall for anything. What do we see enduring in life, in faith, come what may? In other words, what stands as "magnetic north" for us, by which we then direct our lives and hopes and efforts?

SHARING THE SCRIPTURE

PREPARING TO TEACH

Preparing Our Hearts

Meditate on this week's devotional reading from Isaiah 12, which takes the form of a psalm of thanksgiving. What does the prophet say about God? What does the prophet reveal about his own relationship with God? For what will you give God thanks and praise this day?

Pray that you and the students will appreciate the greatness of God and share that good news with others.

Preparing Our Minds

Study the background Scripture from Jeremiah 32 and the lesson Scripture from Jeremiah 32:2-9, 14-15.

Consider this question as you prepare the lesson: *What gives people the confidence to take hopeful actions even in dire circumstances?*

Write on newsprint:

❏ information for next week's lesson, found under "Continue the Journey."

❏ activities for further spiritual growth in "Continue the Journey."

Review the "Introduction," "The Big Picture," "Close-up," and "Faith in Action," which all precede the first lesson of this quarter. Consider how you might use any of this material in today's lesson.

Prepare a lecture using information from Understanding the Scripture for "Jeremiah 32:6-8" through "Jeremiah 32:14-15" to be used under "Recapture the Hopefulness of Jeremiah's Purchase of a Field While He Awaits the Siege of Israel."

LEADING THE CLASS

(1) Gather to Learn

❖ Greet the class members and introduce guests.

❖ Pray that those who have come today will find the confidence to take hope-filled actions even in the midst of difficult situations.

❖ Read: **In his book for young readers, A Child's Garden: A Story of Hope, Michael Foreman tells the story of a boy living in a war-torn land strewn with rubble and bordered with a barbed-wire fence. The boy noticed a tiny green plant, began to care for it, and soon had a beautiful grapevine that not only hid the wire but also provided a gathering place for birds, butterflies, and friends. The boy was heartbroken when soldiers ripped out the vine. In that process, some seeds fell** on the other side of the fence, which a girl tended. Green plants sprouted not only on her side but also again on the boy's side of the fence. Eventually the plants on both sides intertwined, completely hiding the fence. The boy dared to dream that one day the fence would be gone.

❖ Ask: **What gives you hope to take bold action?**

❖ Read aloud today's focus statement: **Even in dire circumstances, some people take hopeful actions. What gives them the confidence to do so? While Jerusalem was under siege, God instructed the prophet Jeremiah to purchase property as a sign that there was a future for the people and their land beyond defeat and exile.**

(2) Goal 1: Recapture the Hopefulness of Jeremiah's Purchase of a Field While He Awaits the Siege of Israel

❖ Select a volunteer to read Jeremiah 32:2-9, 14-15.

❖ Discuss these questions:
1. **Why would Hanamel turn to Jeremiah to sell his plot of land?** (Include Leviticus 25:47-48, which concerns the right of redemption.)
2. **What is the process by which one made such a purchase?** (After hearing comments from the students, present the lecture you have prepared to clarify this process.)
3. **From a business perspective, Jeremiah's purchase is foolhardy. What role does his purchase serve?**

❖ **Option:** Use "Close-up: Time Line of the Babylonian Exile and Return to Judah" at the beginning of this quarter to provide some dates for the

students to get a sense of what is happening and when.

(3) Goal 2: Appreciate Hope and Hopeful Actions in the Face of Deep Hardship

❖ Read or retell the first paragraph of "Putting Your Money Where Your Hope Is" in Interpreting the Scripture and ask these questions:
1. **How is Charles Blondin's story similar to that of Jeremiah?** (Information from the rest of "Putting Your Money Where Your Hope Is" will be helpful here.)
2. **What other examples can you think of where people have courageously acted with hope even in a dire situation?** (Here are some possibilities: *band on board the* Titanic *playing to calm passengers, though they lost their own lives; members of the armed forces who risk—and sacrifice—their lives to save their compatriots; teachers at school in Newtown, Connecticut, who shielded children from danger during a gunman's attack; emergency personnel who rescue victims of disasters.*)

❖ Brainstorm answers to this question: **How can we show appreciation to people who have acted in hope in the face of hardship?** List ideas on newsprint. Discuss what the class might do to recognize at least one such person.

(4) Goal 3: Review the Learners' Personal Times of Hardship in the Past that Held, and Hold, Hope for the Future

❖ Distribute paper and pencils and invite the students to jot down answers to these questions.

1. Recall a situation when you experienced a time of personal hardship. What was going on? (Pause)
2. How did you find hope in this situation? (Pause)
3. What role did your faith play in helping you to get through this tough time? (Pause)
4. As you look back on this difficult time, what lessons did you learn that you can carry forward to meet the challenges of another hard time? (Pause)

❖ Call time and ask the class to form several small groups. Encourage the students to talk about their answers to questions 3 and 4. They need not explain the nature of the hardship, but rather, will comment on how God helped them and how the fact that they got through that hardship gives them hope that they can successfully face another challenge with God's help.

❖ **Option:** If time permits, allow each group to report to the class one or two lessons they learned.

(5) Continue the Journey

❖ Pray that as the learners depart they will hold hope in their hearts.

❖ Post information for next week's session on newsprint for the students to copy:

- Title: Improbable Possibilities
- Background Scripture: Jeremiah 33
- Lesson Scripture: Jeremiah 33:2-11
- Focus of the Lesson: So many times when they have done wrong things, people reach a point where they stop and

wonder which way to turn. How can people seek renewal and accept help to turn their lives around? Jeremiah says God is willing to forgive and bring recovery, healing, and restoration.

❖ Challenge the adults to grow spiritually by completing one or more of these activities related to this week's session, which you have posted on newsprint for the students to copy.

(1) Procure a copy of *A Child's Garden* by Michael Foreman. Share this story with a child to demonstrate how signs of hope can arise in the most hopeless-looking situations. Note how the nearly colorless pictures of rubble turn to brightly colored pictures of life.

(2) Take whatever action you can to help a family or community that is facing hardship and needs to find hope in the midst of a crisis.

(3) Locate several Bible stories in which a person demonstrated faith and hope in a time of crisis. Consider, for example, the widow of Zarephath offering her last bit of meal and oil to Elijah (1 Kings 17:1-16) or the woman with the issue of blood touching Jesus' garment (Mark 5:21-43).

❖ Sing or read aloud "This Is a Day of New Beginnings."

❖ Conclude today's session by leading the class in this hope-filled benediction from Psalm 55:16, which is the key verse for October 19: **I call upon God, and the LORD will save me.**

UNIT 1: THE DAYS ARE SURELY COMING
IMPROBABLE POSSIBILITIES

PREVIEWING THE LESSON

Lesson Scripture: Jeremiah 33:2-11
Background Scripture: Jeremiah 33
Key Verse: Jeremiah 33:11

Focus of the Lesson:
So many times when they have done wrong things, people reach a point where they stop and wonder which way to turn. How can people seek renewal and accept help to turn their lives around? Jeremiah says God is willing to forgive and bring recovery, healing, and restoration.

Goals for the Learners:
(1) to realize God's promise to follow punishment with forgiveness and restoration is still a valid promise.
(2) to affirm that with God, punishment, forgiveness, and healing come as a package.
(3) to design a "thank offering" for hope, healing, and forgiveness they receive from God.

Pronunciation Guide:
Chaldean (kal dee´ uhn)   shalom (shah lohm´)
emeth (eh´ meth)   Zedekiah (zed uh ki´ uh)
hesed (hee´ sid)

Supplies:
Bibles, newsprint and marker, paper and pencils, hymnals

READING THE SCRIPTURE

NRSV
Lesson Scripture: Jeremiah 33:2-11
   ²Thus says the LORD who made the earth, the LORD who formed it to establish it—the LORD is his name:

CEB
Lesson Scripture: Jeremiah 33:2-11
   ²The LORD proclaims, the LORD who made the earth, who formed and established it, whose name is the

³Call to me and I will answer you, and will tell you great and hidden things that you have not known. ⁴For thus says the LORD, the God of Israel, concerning the houses of this city and the houses of the kings of Judah that were torn down to make a defense against the siege ramps and before the sword: ⁵The Chaldeans are coming in to fight and to fill them with the dead bodies of those whom I shall strike down in my anger and my wrath, for I have hidden my face from this city because of all their wickedness. ⁶I am going to bring it recovery and healing; I will heal them and reveal to them abundance of prosperity and security. ⁷I will restore the fortunes of Judah and the fortunes of Israel, and rebuild them as they were at first. ⁸I will cleanse them from all the guilt of their sin against me, and I will forgive all the guilt of their sin and rebellion against me. ⁹And this city shall be to me a name of joy, a praise and a glory before all the nations of the earth who shall hear of all the good that I do for them; they shall fear and tremble because of all the good and all the prosperity I provide for it.

¹⁰Thus says the LORD: In this place of which you say, "It is a waste without human beings or animals," in the towns of Judah and the streets of Jerusalem that are desolate, without inhabitants, human or animal, there shall once more be heard ¹¹the voice of mirth and the voice of gladness, the voice of the bridegroom and the voice of the bride, the voices of those who sing, as they bring thank offerings to the house of the LORD:

"Give thanks to the LORD of hosts,
 for the LORD is good,
 for his steadfast love endures
 forever!"

For **I will restore the fortunes of the land as at first, says the LORD.**

LORD; ³call to me and I will answer and reveal to you wondrous secrets that you haven't known.

⁴This is what the LORD, the God of Israel, proclaims about the houses of this city and the palaces of the kings of Judah that were torn down to defend against the siege ramps and weapons ⁵of the invading Babylonians. They will be filled with the corpses of those slain in my fierce anger. I hid my face from the people of this city because of all their evil deeds, ⁶but now I will heal and mend them. I will make them whole and bless them with an abundance of peace and security. ⁷I will bring back the captives of Judah and Israel, and I will rebuild them as they were at first. ⁸I will cleanse them of all the wrongdoing they committed against me, and I will forgive them for all of their guilt and rebellion. ⁹Then this city will bring me great joy, praise, and renown before all nations on earth, when they hear of all the good I provide for them. They will be in total awe at all the good and prosperity I provide for them.

¹⁰The LORD proclaims: You have said about this place, "It is a wasteland, without humans or animals." Yet in the ravaged and uninhabited towns of Judah and the streets of Jerusalem, ¹¹the sounds of joy and laughter and the voices of the bride and the bridegroom will again be heard. So will the voices of those who say, as thank offerings are brought to the LORD's temple, "Give thanks to the LORD of heavenly forces, for the LORD is good and his kindness lasts forever." **I will bring back the captives of this land as they were before, says the LORD.**

UNDERSTANDING THE SCRIPTURE

Jeremiah 33:1-3. The notation that this is the "second time" that the word of God came to Jeremiah hearkens back to the previous time (32:1). Jerusalem is under siege. Then, Jeremiah bought from his cousin a plot of family land, now in enemy territory, as a sign of God's promise of the (soon-to-be) exiles' eventual return to the land—an action taken while Jeremiah was already in prison for prophecies that disturbed King Zedekiah (32:2-3). Chapter 33 opens with Jeremiah still in prison. Verse 2 asserts the power and authority of God in perhaps not so subtle defiance of Zedekiah and, eventually, the Babylonian (Chaldean) empire now laying siege to Jerusalem. Jeremiah grounds that power and authority in God as Creator of all. The importance of the "name" of God summons remembrance of the name of God given to Moses at the burning bush (Exodus 3:13-15) so that he might tell the Israelites who the One is who will save them. That saving purpose echoes here in Jeremiah 33:2-3, where the assertion of God's name is immediately followed by the invitation to call upon God with the assurance of divine answer.

Jeremiah 33:4-5. These verses reveal the setting of this portion of the oracle to be in the midst of the siege. "Chaldeans" is an ancient name for the people who inhabited the region of which Babylon was capital. An interesting irony is that Genesis 11:27-31 reveals that "Ur of the Chaldeans" was the original home of Abram—and now, the people of Abram/Abraham are to be taken into captivity into that land from which he came. The desperation of Jerusalem's inhabitants is portrayed in the severe measures taken to defend themselves. They demolish their own homes to shore up the walls, but to no avail. The failure is not simply the military superiority of the Chaldeans, but the underlying prophetic cause for judgment and exile: the "hiding" of God's face. Similar to other prophets, Jeremiah grounds the cause for God's withdrawal in the wickedness that prevailed in the land and from its rulers (Ezekiel 34:1-10; Amos 8:4-8).

Jeremiah 33:6-9. The passage pivots back to the themes of hope and restoration. Verses 6-8 are punctuated with a series of first-person declarations of what God is about to do ("I am going to . . . I will . . ."). Bring recovery. Heal. Reveal. Restore. Rebuild. Cleanse. Forgive. The God whom Jeremiah has just said is hidden will be disclosed in such saving interventions. Of particular importance are two other words Jeremiah uses in verse 6. The first word, translated as "prosperity," is the Hebrew *shalom*. Often translated as "peace," shalom references a broad and inclusive meaning of well-being: material, political, spiritual, relational. Shalom will come from God's saving intervention. The second word is *emeth*, translated here as "security." This word strongly connotes the sense of faithfulness or reliability. Affirmed here is the fidelity of God as the basis for trusting in such promises, and in the hope of God's shalom. The significance of that comes in remembering this oracle is not set in the time when exile is about to end, but rather, when it is about to begin. These ensuing words and promises make no sense unless God's fidelity is trusted.

Jeremiah 33:10-11. As noted by Walter Brueggemann in *A Commentary on Jeremiah*, verse 10 in Hebrew begins with the phrase that the NRSV and other English translations place at the end: "There shall once more be heard." Keeping that original order places hope at the very beginning of what becomes a despairing view of a land desolate of life. Those descriptions reflect what the people perceive to be collapsing around them in the siege. The dominant image in verse 11 is that of "voices": voices of mirth and gladness, voices of bridegroom and bride, voices of singers giving thanks by lifting up the affirmation of Psalm 136:1. This image is made even more restorative by recalling that, in several earlier passages, Jeremiah anticipated the coming of God's judgment with the silencing of such voices (7:34; 16:9; 25:10). The sung refrain of Psalm 136:1 in verse 11 merits deeper consideration. The second half of every verse of Psalm 136:4-25 affirms, as here in Jeremiah, the enduring nature of God's steadfast love. But it is to be noted that the first half of those same verses in the psalm confess the unfolding narrative of God's power revealed in creation and then in deliverance from Egypt. Today's lesson Scripture thus begins and ends with affirmations of God's power, where recollection of God's past actions summon anticipation of God's promised deliverance.

Jeremiah 33:12-18. The two "oracles" or declarations of hope in these verses invoke several images of nation and rulers. "Shepherds" is a common symbol for kings in the prophetic literature—and the providing of pasture for shepherds to graze their sheep subtly weaves the theme of creation and kingdom renewed. Verse 13 lists regions associated with the boundaries of Judah (see also 32:44). Verses 14-18 comprise a specific promise regarding the promise not only of reinstated Davidic rule but also the association of this coming reign with "justice and righteousness in the land" (33:15)—the absence of which had been cause for God's judgment in the first place.

Jeremiah 33:19-26. This concluding portion of the chapter makes a case for viewing the covenant God has made and will keep with Israel through the prism of the broadest of all biblical covenants, wherein God promises fidelity to the whole of creation (Genesis 8:22; 9:8-17). Jeremiah 33:19-22 applies that perspective to the promise of Davidic leadership. Jeremiah 33:23-26 expands that perspective to God's covenant with the peoples of Israel and Judah. The passage concludes with an affirmation of God's "mercy" (*hesed*), which is the same word appearing in the song of verse 11, translated there as "steadfast love." Thus, the "final word" for the improbable possibility of restoration is *hesed*: the covenant-keeping loyalty of God to those with whom God covenants.

INTERPRETING THE SCRIPTURE

Judgment to Hope: In the Mean Time

"In the meantime" is a phrase that can simply refer to what takes in some sort of interval, between one event and another. "Mean," after all, has for one of its meanings "middle." But "mean" can also have a harsher meaning of something lacking in goodwill or kindness, something (or someone) malicious. In that sense, today's passage from Jeremiah can clearly be anchored in "mean" times for both prophet and people.

For the prophet, the time is mean because he suffers imprisonment—not for doing anything wrong, but for speaking the truth to power. For the people, the time is mean because judgment falls upon them in the siege that would soon eventuate in Jerusalem's destruction, and their death or exile.

In the midst of imprisonment, in the face of national and spiritual catastrophe (the Temple will be destroyed, and the question of "where is God" is certainly up for discussion): In this "mean time," Jeremiah pivots. Judgment is not denied; how could it be? The armies of Babylon are massed outside the walls, and Zedekiah's gamble to trust in secret alliances to rebel against Babylon is about to come crashing down. Yet in the face of judgment, in the midst of "mean" times, Jeremiah sees cause for hope. Hope whose movement comes not in turning the clock back, but rather in moving forward toward the promised time of God.

It is a movement that we sometimes get confused over today. Perhaps like the contemporaries of Jeremiah, we see the "mean times" in our lives as obliterations of the promises of God. We come to think and believe, thanks to purveyors of various forms of the prosperity gospel, that if we only had deeper faith or gave more God would bless us with good times or, at the least, help us avoid the mean times. In truth, the promises of God find their greatest power and hope precisely in such times.

Religious progressives and conservatives alike stumble on the matter of judgment, and the path that leads to hope. Some progressives consider God's intervention in judgment an old-fashioned idea whose time has passed. Hope arises from the vision of what we can make of life if only we all work together. Some conservatives consider God's intervention in judgment typically falling on those who offend God on one of several hot-button social issues for which they, invariably, are on the right side. Hope arises from the vision of maintaining a moral and political uprightness that causes no offense to God. Both extremes end up providing little if any consolation when mean times fall. The improbable possibility Jeremiah provides comes in holding together both judgment and hope as interlaced means by which God seeks renewal of individuals and institutions, of church and society. For only then can promissory words speak genuine hope and offer the means of transformation when mean times fall.

A Grammar of God's Salvation

Grammar. The name may evoke memories of grade school textbooks that hammered away at the differences between nouns and verbs, and why prepositions ought not be left dangling. Or of times spent at blackboards (or are they all now marker boards, and soon to be wide-screen versions of iPads?) diagramming sentences, and remembering what kind of diagonal lines are used for adverbs, or subjunctive clauses, or all manner of things grammatical. All of those exercises, which likely seemed tedious at the time, really did have a solid purpose: to help us communicate. To give us a basis to relate and connect ideas. To differentiate between who (subject) does (verb) what (object) to whom or for whom (indirect object).

In that light, consider Jeremiah 33:6-8 as a "grammar" of sorts: a grammar of God's salvation. The first task of grammar, to discern the subject, is a piece of cake here. There is only one: "I." And that "I" is not the prophet speaking, rather Jeremiah relating the "thus says the LORD, the God of Israel" of verse 4. God is the subject of every sentence and clause in verses 6-8. The second task of grammar, to discern the verb, is equally clear-cut though certainly diverse: bring, heal, reveal, restore, rebuild, cleanse, forgive. According to Jeremiah, the grammar of God's salvation involves a lot of action on God's part. This is not to say that human beings, then or now, have no part to play. But to take the word of Jeremiah seriously, God is at the very least the initiator of all these actions.

And for whom? In the case of this passage, the grammar in terms of the objects of these actions involves a bit more exploring. "It" in verse 6a references back to the "city" in verse 5. The actions of God are not limited to the sphere of the human heart or spirit. The welfare of the city—the place(s) where people live and worship and engage in social relationship—is the object of God's "recovering and healing" action. In verse 6, "Judah and Israel" become the objects of God's restorative activity. Those whose sin and rebellion prompted the response of God's judgment will now be the recipients of God's forgiving and cleansing (33:8).

Why bother with the grammar of an ancient text? The grammar of salvation in many ways remains the same in our time as Jeremiah's. As much as we would like to claim we pull ourselves up by the bootstraps, whether by actions of social justice or rigidly adhering to orthodox (in our view, anyway) doctrine, the truth of the matter is that God's salvation still comes at and depends on God's initiative. The actions God takes in extending salvation continue, as Jeremiah reported, in ways that are restorative and reconstructive and forgiving. All of which gives us a clue, by the way, as to how we might then conduct our own lives and reform our own institutions: to engage in acts of restoration; to reconstruct lives and relationships and institutions in ways that mirror the love and grace and justice of God; and to extend forgiveness to others as well as to accept it for ourselves.

Celebrating and Sharing God's Shalom

Twice in this passage, Jeremiah speaks of the promise of God's providing shalom to God's people. As noted in the comments on verses 6-9 in Understanding the Scripture, *shalom* is a word that encompasses far more than temporary cessations of fighting. God's shalom envisions the provision of all that is needed for life. Not just the absence of war, shalom is the fullness of life wherein no one goes lacking for life's necessities, by way of food or justice. The enactment of shalom is the realization of life as God intended in our creation.

Such a promise is not something to be held tight to the vest, disclosed only to those who are "in the know." Verse 11 closes today's print passage with a cacophony of voices. Voices of joy and gladness, celebrating the goodness of God's creation and the promise of God's hope. Voices of bridegroom and bride, celebrating the richness of human relationship. Voices that sing as they bring offerings to God, thus translating words of praise into actions of sharing. All of these voices flow in response to God's promised shalom.

And all of these voices bid us to join with them: to bring our experiences of God's steadfast love to their songs of that same persistent grace, to add our offerings to theirs in joyful response to God. For with them, God's promises beckon us to the improbable possibility of living by hope even now.

SHARING THE SCRIPTURE

PREPARING TO TEACH

Preparing Our Hearts

Meditate on this week's devotional reading from Jeremiah 9:17-24. How do you mourn your losses? Why would you boast? What reasons do you have for boasting in God?

Pray that you and the students will support those who are mourning and recognize that change will come and laughter will return.

Preparing Our Minds

Study the background Scripture from Jeremiah 33 and the lesson Scripture from Jeremiah 33:2-11.

Consider this question as you prepare the lesson: *How can people who do not know which way to turn seek renewal and accept help to turn their lives around?*

Write on newsprint:

❏ words from Jeremiah 33:11: "Give thanks to the LORD of hosts, for the LORD is good, for his steadfast love endures forever" for "Design a 'Thank Offering' for Hope, Healing, and Forgiveness We Receive from God."

❏ information for next week's lesson, found under "Continue the Journey."

❏ activities for further spiritual growth in "Continue the Journey."

Review the "Introduction," "The Big Picture," "Close-up," and "Faith in Action," which all precede the first lesson of this quarter. Consider how you might use any of this material in today's lesson.

Be prepared to present information as recommended under "Realize God's Promise to Follow Punishment with Forgiveness and Restoration Is Still a Valid Promise."

Practice reading Isaiah 43 for "Affirm that with God, Punishment, Forgiveness, and Healing Come as a Package." If you prefer, contact a reader early in the week and ask him or her to read the entire chapter.

LEADING THE CLASS

(1) Gather to Learn

❖ Greet the class members and introduce guests.

❖ Pray that those who have come today will be open to seeking renewal when they need help turning their lives around.

❖ Read: **Known as both a "brilliant political strategist" and a "dirty tricks artist," Charles W. Colson once bragged that he would "walk over my own grandmother" to get Richard Nixon reelected. Colson had compiled of list of Nixon's enemies and been involved in the Watergate scandal. But it was his illegal scheming to discredit Pentagon official Daniel Ellsberg, who was suspected of leaking a "top secret" history of the Vietnam War, which led to Colson's imprisonment on an obstruction of justice conviction. Colson described his guilty plea as part of "a price I had to pay to complete the shedding of my old life and to be free to live the new." After serving seven months in prison, Colson was released in January 1975. He became an advocate for prison reform and a leader in the evangelical movement. His autobiography, _Born Again,_ has been read by millions.**

❖ Ask: **What motivates and enables people who have done wrong to turn their lives around?**

❖ Read aloud today's focus statement: **So many times when they have done wrong things, people reach a point where they stop and wonder which way to turn. How can people seek renewal and accept help to turn their lives around? Jeremiah says God is willing to forgive and bring recovery, healing, and restoration.**

(2) Goal 1: Realize God's Promise to Follow Punishment with Forgiveness and Restoration Is Still a Valid Promise

❖ Select a volunteer to read Jeremiah 33:2-11.

❖ Help the adults understand this passage by reading or retelling "Jeremiah 33:1-3" through "Jeremiah 33:10-11" in Understanding the Scripture.

❖ Form small groups to study Jeremiah 33:6-8, which reveals God's intentions and promises for the people. Ask the groups to focus on the action words (verbs) that show what God intends to do. Invite each group to be prepared to present their findings to the class in some creative way. They might, for example, create a pantomime, or construct a word search or crossword puzzle, or write a poem. Have paper and pencils and newsprint and markers available as groups request them.

❖ Encourage each group to present its interpretation of verses 6-8. Compliment their efforts. Wrap up by repeating again God's actions as found in these verses: bring, heal, reveal, restore, rebuild, cleanse, and forgive.

❖ **Option:** Read or retell "A Grammar of God's Salvation" in Interpreting the Scripture. This option would be especially helpful if you are unable to do the suggested group work.

(3) Goal 2: Affirm that with God, Punishment, Forgiveness, and Healing Come as a Package

❖ Read Isaiah 43 in which God promises to restore, protect, and forgive the people, who as Isaiah writes are captives in Babylon. Suggest that the students try to hear these words as if God is speaking to them.

❖ Encourage the students to call out any words or phrases that grabbed their attention. Ask why these words seemed so meaningful. (They may wish to look at their Bibles.)

❖ Close this activity by asking:

1. **Where in this chapter do you see evidence that God's punishment, forgiveness, and healing come as a package?**

2. In what ways do you hear the same message in Jeremiah 33:2-11?

(4) Goal 3: Design a "Thank Offering" for Hope, Healing, and Forgiveness the Learners Receive from God

❖ Read "Celebrating and Sharing God's Shalom" from Interpreting the Scripture.

❖ Note that the words of thanks in verse 11 are taken from a refrain in Psalm 136. Ask the adults to read this psalm silently, taking note of why the people are giving thanks.

❖ Post newsprint on which you have written the words of Psalm 136 quoted in Jeremiah 33:11. Encourage participants to call out reasons why they have to be thankful, particularly for the gifts of hope, healing, and forgiveness. Write their responses underneath the quotation.

❖ Combine the students' ideas with the quotation to create a closing litany. Ask half of the class to read the first of the suggested reasons for thanks. All then join in reciting the quotation. The other half of the class will read the second suggestion, followed by the refrain, and so on.

(5) Continue the Journey

❖ Pray that as the learners depart they will trust God to do all that God promises to bring them hope, healing, and forgiveness.

❖ Post information for next week's session on newsprint for the students to copy:

- **Title: Rejoice Anyway**
- **Background Scripture: Job 1; Psalm 56; Habakkuk 1–3**
- **Lesson Scripture: Habakkuk 2:1-5; 3:17-19**

■ Focus of the Lesson: Some people experience so many difficulties in life that they lose all hope for the future. Where can they turn for direction when things get really bad? Job, the psalmist, and Habakkuk all affirm that no matter what calamities might come their way, they will trust God, rejoice in God's presence in their lives, and praise God for strength to carry on.

❖ Challenge the adults to grow spiritually by completing one or more of these activities related to this week's session, which you have posted on newsprint for the students to copy.

(1) **Read Charles Colson's autobiography,** *Born Again.* **Ponder how God enables people who have done wrong and been punished to receive forgiveness and begin anew.**

(2) **Use a Bible concordance, dictionary, or other references to investigate the image of God's face. What can you learn about God's face shining on Israel and remaining hidden from Israel?**

(3) **Make it a practice to identify and give thanks for God's forgiveness at the end of each day. Give thanks with a prayer, hymn, psalm, movement, art work, or by whatever means you can best express yourself.**

❖ Sing or read aloud "Amazing Grace."

❖ Conclude today's session by leading the class in this hope-filled benediction from Psalm 55:16, which is the key verse for October 19: **I call upon God, and the Lord will save me.**

UNIT 2: DARK NIGHTS OF THE SOUL
REJOICE ANYWAY

PREVIEWING THE LESSON

Lesson Scripture: Habakkuk 2:1-5; 3:17-19
Background Scripture: Job 1; Psalm 56; Habakkuk 1–3
Key Verses: Habakkuk 3:18

Focus of the Lesson:
Some people experience so many difficulties in life that they lose all hope for the future. Where can they turn for direction when things get really bad? Job, the psalmist, and Habakkuk all affirm that no matter what calamities might come their way, they will trust God, rejoice in God's presence in their lives, and praise God for strength to carry on.

Goals for the Learners:
(1) to hear God's message of patience for the people and assurance that God will act for justice.
(2) to experience the feeling of joy when they have patiently awaited God's promises.
(3) to practice responding to difficulties by trusting in God's presence and by praising God for strength to endure.

Pronunciation Guide:
Achish (ay kish´)   Sheol (shee´ ohl)
Chaldean (kal dee´ uhn)   theodicy (thee od´ uh see)
emuna (em oo naw´)   *yad* (yawd)

Supplies:
Bibles, newsprint and marker, paper and pencils, hymnals

READING THE SCRIPTURE

NRSV
Lesson Scripture: Habakkuk 2:1-5
¹I will stand at my watchpost,
    and station myself on the rampart;
I will keep watch to see what he will
    say to me,

CEB
Lesson Scripture: Habakkuk 2:1-5
¹I will take my post;
    I will position myself on the
      fortress.
I will keep watch to see what the

and what he will answer concerning my complaint.
²Then the LORD answered me and
said:
Write the vision;
make it plain on tablets,
so that a runner may read it.
³For there is still a vision for the
appointed time;
it speaks of the end, and does not
lie.
If it seems to tarry, wait for it;
it will surely come, it will not delay.
⁴Look at the proud!
Their spirit is not right in them,
but the righteous live by their
faith.
⁵Moreover, wealth is treacherous;
the arrogant do not endure.
They open their throats wide as
Sheol;
like Death they never have
enough.
They gather all nations for
themselves,
and collect all peoples as their
own.

Habakkuk 3:17-19
¹⁷Though the fig tree does not
blossom,
and no fruit is on the vines;
though the produce of the olive fails,
and the fields yield no food;
though the flock is cut off from the
fold,
and there is no herd in the stalls,
¹⁸**yet I will rejoice in the LORD;**
I will exult in the God of my
salvation.
¹⁹GOD, the Lord, is my strength;
he makes my feet like the feet of a
deer,
and makes me tread upon the
heights.
To the leader: with stringed
instruments.

Lord says to me
and how he will respond to my
complaint.
²Then the LORD answered me and
said,
Write a vision, and make it plain
upon a tablet
so that a runner can read it.
³There is still a vision for the
appointed time;
it testifies to the end;
it does not deceive.
If it delays, wait for it; for it is
surely coming; it will not be
late.
⁴Some people's desires are truly
audacious;
they don't do the right thing.
But the righteous person will live
honestly.
⁵Moreover, wine betrays an arrogant
man.
He doesn't rest.
He opens his jaws like the grave;
like death, he is never satisfied.
He gathers all nations to himself
and collects all peoples for himself.

Habakkuk 3:17-19
¹⁷Though the fig tree doesn't bloom,
and there's no produce on the
vine;
though the olive crop withers, and
the fields don't provide food;
though the sheep is cut off from
the pen, and there is no cattle in
the stalls;
¹⁸**I will rejoice in the LORD.**
I will rejoice in the God of my
deliverance.
¹⁹The LORD God is my strength.
He will set my feet like the deer.
He will let me walk upon the
heights.
To the director, with stringed
instruments

UNDERSTANDING THE SCRIPTURE

Introduction. Today's session and the three that follow engage passages that explore this unit's theme, "Dark Nights of the Soul." Each session includes in the background Scripture a psalm of lament or complaint, recording the psalmist's plea for deliverance from some treacherous situation. Each session also includes a passage from the Book of Job, a work that powerfully explores the theme of "theodicy"—literally, "God-justice"—in a world where evil and suffering fall on the just and unjust alike. The remaining three sessions after today use narratives from Job as the print passage. Today, however, the print passage is from the prophet Habakkuk. The connection between Habakkuk and this unit's overall theme is made clear in the prophet's core question to God posed in 1:13b: "Why do you look on the treacherous, and are silent when the wicked swallow those more righteous than they?"

Job 1. The first two chapters of Job, along with its final eleven verses (42:7-17), are written in prose. Otherwise, the entire book is poetry. Scholars view the prose portion as an earlier folktale about someone who suffered greatly but refused to curse God, and the poetic section as a later exploration (perhaps during or after the Babylonian exile) of the question of God's justice and presence in the experience of suffering. Chapter 1 begins by detailing the wealth and family of Job, then a dialogue (1:8-12) between God and the "Accuser" (Satan); a similar dialogue occurs in 2:1-6). Faced with the Accuser's charge that Job is faithful only because of his prosperity and protection from God, God puts into Satan's power everything that is Job's. It is fascinating to note that "hand" and "power" translate the same Hebrew word *yad* that occurs four times in verses 10-12. To be in another's hands is to be in their power.

Psalm 56. The superscription to this psalm connects it to an incident in David's life (1 Samuel 21:10-15). Fleeing for his life from Saul, David so fears what his host, King Achish of Gath, might do to him that he pretends to be mad. The psalm twice asserts the writer's trust in God that banishes fear (56:4, 11). Does the repetition owe to the writer's certainty of that refrain's confession, or does it serve more as a mantra meant to convince the psalmist of its truth by repeating it again? The verbs used of the enemies in the psalm make clear that the situation is severe: trample, oppress, fight, injure. Thank offerings are offered for God's deliverance of the psalmist from death (56:12).

Habakkuk 1. Habakkuk provides no introductory verses that pinpoint the historical setting. Most scholars place this work shortly before the fall of the Southern Kingdom and Jerusalem to the Babylonians. The opening four verses of this chapter lift the prophet's complaint about the disintegration of order and justice in society. Earlier prophets charged Israel and then Judah with the breaking of covenant in the midst of prosperous times. The tone of Habakkuk, however, suggests a collapsing of societal order. The cry of verse 2, "O Lord, how long" not only reflects laments in the Psalms but also provides a first taste of this prophet's willingness to speak directly and bluntly to God. God's initial reply to Habakkuk comes in 1:5-11. God's role in the coming upheaval is affirmed (1:6), though God does not portray the Chaldean invaders as holding any moral edge to the Judeans against whom judgment falls. The prophet's second complaint begins at verse 12 and runs through the remainder of the chapter. The prophet challenges God's reply, as he wonders aloud how the One confessed to be unable to look on evil can now bear to look at the treachery being unleashed against the "righteous" (1:13). The chapter closes on the note of the absence of "mercy," one of the core characteristics attributed to God.

Habakkuk 2:1-5. Habakkuk now watches/listens for God's answer to his complaint (2:1), referring to chapter 1's addressing and questioning of God. Habakkuk 2:2 begins that answer. Called by the prophet to give an accounting, God instead replies with a command: "write the vision." The imagery of making it readable to one who runs can be taken several ways. One interpretation draws on the imagery of destruction in chapter 1, suggesting that the vision be made plain so that even those fleeing from the disaster about to overtake them can still see and read—and as a result, still have hope. Another interpretation is that the prophet and other messengers of the vision are to set out running with the news of the vision, acting as its heralds. The second half of verse 4 becomes a key verse in Pauline theology, quoted in both Romans 1:17 and Galatians 3:11 to assert Paul's primacy of faith. The word translated as "faith" in Habakkuk, *emuna*, carries the connotation of "firmness" or "fidelity." It is not a doctrinal or propositional word so much as it is a relational word.

Habakkuk 2:6–3:16. This "interlude" between today's two segments of the print passage begins with a set of five "alas" statements in 2:6-20 that offer prophetic warnings against self-aggrandizing or idolatrous behavior (see Isaiah 5:8-23 for a parallel series). The first sixteen verses of Habakkuk 3 take the form of a prayer by the prophet who pleads for God to act in saving ways "in our own time" (3:2).

Habakkuk 3:17-19. The "tarrying" of that saving action, hinted at in 2:3, need not lead to despair. The final three verses of chapter 3 hold together in remarkable and dynamic tension circumstances of despair and hope that remains resolute. Each of the "though" statements in verse 17 represents disastrous cycles in society and economy, perhaps in anticipation of the fall of exile. "Yet"—the word that begins verse 18—even in the face of such circumstances, trust in God's salvation is possible. Indeed, such trust is what makes these intervening circumstances bearable. The assertion of 2:4 that "the righteous live by their faith" is no mere figure of speech. When all around seems to be collapsing, as verse 17 suggests, life is still possible. God may still be trusted, for the basis of faith is not the ability to suspend doubt or deny reality, but to trust God's fidelity.

INTERPRETING THE SCRIPTURE

Making Things Plain

"Plain speaking" has come to connote a form of communication that does not mince words or "beat around the bush." Meanings are clear. There is no deception. All the cards are on the table.

The prophet's announcement in verse 1 of today's passage in chapter 2 of taking his stand and keeping watch comes in the wake of his own "plain speaking" to God in chapter 1. Looking back at what was said there, the prophet does not mince words with God. The situation is bad (most likely, the approach of the Babylonian army to lay siege to Jerusalem)—and in the short run is liable to get worse. The former teachings of a God too pure to look upon evil or always inclined to hear cries for help seem, for the moment, to be suspended. Cries of "violence" result in no saving—God seems silent in the face of evil. That is what Habakkuk plainly says to God in chapter 1. He models faith that is willing to bare the soul and spirit to God, holding nothing back.

In return, God speaks plainly to the prophet. God calls upon the prophet to "write the vision; make it plain" (2:2). God does not seek followers who would dissemble the truth, to speak it in ways that leave meanings unclear or purposes up in the air. The prophet has already rightly seen, and plainly spoken, the approach of judgment. But now, to a people whose world and even faith is collapsing before their eyes God calls on the prophet to make it plain that things are not always what they seem, nor is judgment the final word.

God will act, even if our timetables are not met (thus, "if it seems to tarry, wait for it," 2:3). These are not easy words to speak, nor is this an easy vision to see and hold on to, when the evidence of societal breakdown (1:3b-4) and vicious enemies (1:15-17) questions even the possibility of mercy. But that is precisely why plain speaking is called for in Habakkuk's time. And that is why plain speaking is called for whenever the people of God endure times of upheaval. In the face of persistent injustice, God's people need the assurance of God's good purposes—not simply to settle troubled spirits, but to engage faithful and courageous witness. If those who speak for God do not speak plainly in such times, who will?

Trusting God's Fidelity

At the center of today's lesson Scripture is the assertion that Paul later brought front and center to his theology: "the righteous live by their faith" (2:4; see Romans 1:17 and Galatians 3:11). Paul, and later Luther, will emphasize the centrality of faith over works. But note here that the contrast in Habakkuk is *not* faith versus works, but rather faith versus arrogant pride or treacherous wealth (2:4-5). The distinction is an important one, not only in Habakkuk's time but also in our own.

Faith invests oneself in another—in the case of religious faith, in God. Faith understands that life without that other is less than whole. The arrogance of pride and the treachery of wealth undermine that understanding. They suggest we can stand on our own, isolated, apart from God or others, so long as we maintain the illusion that we are the final arbiters of right and wrong, either by the arrogance of self-importance or the power of wealth or influence. The issue here is not faith versus works; the issue is faith *expressed* in works grounded in covenant, or *denied* in works that are grounded in arrogant self-centeredness.

The righteous, Habakkuk declares, live by faith. That is, we live by entrusting ourselves to God, whose fidelity to covenant is the very basis of our own fidelity. In its deepest meaning, faith is not a set of propositions to be accepted or explained. Faith is relational. Faith is an active engagement with the God whom we confess to be faithful.

The contrast Habakkuk draws is clear. The proud do not need faith, for they have their own self-proclaimed assertion that they are in the right. As for whether the treachery is wealth (NRSV) or wine (CEB)—the Hebrew text in verse 5 is unclear on this point— the basic point is the same. Altered states of mind leave us just as deceived as overabundance of wealth, for both can suggest the final word in life to be self-gratification. Or as Habakkuk puts it: "they never have enough" (2:5).

In contrast, faith trusts that we always have enough. Covenant provides relationship with God, community with one another, and hope in God's promises. Is that enough for you?

Subversive Joy

"How Can I Keep From Singing?" is a nineteenth-century song created in and for the American Sunday school movement. Its original verses asked "how can I keep from singing" in spite of the inevitable sorrows that come in life. In the 1950s, in the wake of the Senator Joseph McCarthy hearings, a woman named Doris Plenn wrote another verse. It, too, asked the same question, even when friends are imprisoned and oppressors still inflict hardships: "how can I keep from singing?"

It is not simply that added verse to this old hymn that speaks of joy as a subversive act when the times are troubled. Verse 17 of today's passage invokes a litany of dire events that may be seen as a harbinger of exile's judgment: crops fail, flocks and herds dwindle, food disappears. But instead of funeral dirges and mournful cries, the very next verse begins: *yet*. Yet I will rejoice. Yet I will exult in God.

Habakkuk is not at all interested in Pollyanna versions of faith that deny or minimize the reality of what the current days bring. Habakkuk speaks plainly. But Habakkuk also speaks faithfully. Even when all else seems in retreat, the prophet will not be deterred from joy.

There is subversiveness to such joy. It celebrates, in the face of hardship and a very unpromising future, the very future of God. In the time of Habakkuk, such joy confesses that the might and destructiveness of Babylon cannot do away with hope. In our time, such joy confesses that we are not finally victims of the circumstances that may fall upon us. We are, rather, heirs of God's future—a future that cannot be taken from us.

In the letter to the Philippian church, Paul counsels: "rejoice in the Lord always" (4:4). Like Habakkuk, the context of that epistle makes clear that joy is not self-congratulation, but subversive trust in God. For when Paul writes this, he is in prison. Roman prisons were not enjoyable places. There are even some scholars who suggest that Philippians may be Paul's final letter, written shortly before his execution. Yet— and there is that same word that Habakkuk uses in 3:18—yet, in spite of imprisonment, Paul invites his community to rejoice. Such joy is not celebration that Paul is a prisoner, or that they themselves face difficulties. Rather, the invitation to rejoice arises from God's trustworthiness to God's promises. Joy cannot be helped, for God cannot be deterred.

So how can we keep from singing?

SHARING THE SCRIPTURE

PREPARING TO TEACH

Preparing Our Hearts

Meditate on this week's devotional reading from Psalm 56:8-13, the prayer of one who is persecuted, which is part of our background Scripture. What assurance do you have that God is "for" you? How do you demonstrate your trust in God? What words of praise will you offer to God right now?

Pray that you and the students will praise the God who cares for you in all of life's circumstances.

Preparing Our Minds

Study the background Scripture from Job 1; Psalm 56; and Habakkuk 1–3.

The lesson Scripture is from Habakkuk 2:1-5; 3:17-19.

Consider this question as you prepare the lesson: *Where can people who have lost hope for the future turn for direction when things get really bad?*

Write on newsprint:
❏ information for next week's lesson, found under "Continue the Journey."

❏ activities for further spiritual growth in "Continue the Journey."
Review the "Introduction," "The Big Picture," "Close-up," and "Faith in Action," which all precede the first lesson of this quarter. Consider how you might use any of this material in today's lesson.

LEADING THE CLASS

(1) Gather to Learn

❖ Greet the class members and introduce guests.

❖ Pray that those who have come today will turn to God, especially when they have lost all hope and do not know which way to go.

❖ Brainstorm answers to this question and write them on newsprint: **What kinds of situations may create such desperation that people will lose all hope for the future?**

❖ Review the list and invite the students to comment on what people who are faced with such situations might do to find hope and new directions. Note that in some cases the final outcome will not likely be changed, but people can find a more hopeful way of coping with the situation.

❖ Read aloud today's focus statement: **Some people experience so many difficulties in life that they lose all hope for the future. Where can they turn for direction when things get really bad? Job, the psalmist, and Habakkuk all affirm that no matter what calamities might come their way, they will trust God, rejoice in God's presence in their lives, and praise God for strength to carry on.**

(2) Goal 1: Hear God's Message of Patience for the People and Assurance that God Will Act for Justice

❖ Set the stage by reading "Habakkuk 1" from Understanding the Scripture.

❖ Choose a reader for Habakkuk 2:1-5 and then discuss these questions. Use information from "Habakkuk 2:1-5" in Understanding the Scripture and "Trusting God's Fidelity" in Interpreting the Scripture as appropriate.

1. **Habakkuk had complained to God (chapter 1), but now stands watch to hear God's reply. How does God answer him?**
2. **What does God say to the prophet concerning those who are proud?**
3. **How are the righteous ones different from the proud?**
4. **How does verse 4 support Paul's understanding of justification by faith as expressed in Romans 1:17 and Galatians 3:11?**

(3) Goal 2: Experience the Feeling of Joy When the Learners Have Patiently Awaited God's Promises

❖ Select a volunteer to read Habakkuk 3:17-19.

❖ Explain this information by reading "Habakkuk 3:17-19" from Understanding the Scripture.

❖ Read again these words: **"The assertion of 2:4 that 'the righteous live by their faith' is no mere figure of speech. When all around seems to be collapsing, as verse 17 suggests, life is still possible."** Read aloud this question and invite the students to discuss it with a partner or small group: **What examples can you give from your own life to demonstrate that even when you faced serious difficulties, you were able to affirm life and live by your faith?**

❖ Bring the groups together and direct attention to a sheet of newsprint on which you write the words "When God fulfills promises, the joy I feel is like . . ." Encourage students to call out answers and write them on the sheet. Some adults may want to comment about how they felt concerning a fulfilled promise.

❖ Conclude this portion of the lesson by reading together these words from verses 17-18: **Though the fig tree does not blossom, and no fruit is on the vines; . . . yet I will rejoice in the LORD; I will exult in the God of my salvation.**

(4) Goal 3: Practice Responding to Difficulties by Trusting in God's Presence and by Praising God for Strength to Endure

❖ Form several groups. Tell them that you will read a scenario and then in their groups they will roleplay the situation, perhaps trying out different ways to respond to the difficulty you will describe: **The Jensens had just completed their dream home—a modern log cabin set within a community amid hundreds of acres of** forest. After much planning and hard work, all their possessions were neatly arranged and ready to be enjoyed. Two weeks after the Jensens had unpacked their last box, disaster struck in the form of a raging wildfire. The family was all safe, but their home was among eleven that was burned to the ground. You have been dispatched to the area to bring spiritual comfort and support to these residents. What might you say to these people who have lost everything, including their dreams?

❖ Bring the groups together and ask:

1. What words or ideas seemed most helpful in supporting these devastated people?
2. What challenges would you have faced in trusting in God's presence in such a situation?
3. Where do people find the strength to praise God and resilience to endure in such crushing circumstances?

(5) Continue the Journey

❖ Pray that as the learners depart they will rejoice in God even in the midst of troubles.

❖ Post information for next week's session on newsprint for the students to copy:

■ Title: Even So, My Redeemer Lives
■ Background Scripture: Job 19; Psalm 57
■ Lesson Scripture: Job 19:1-7, 23-29
■ Focus of the Lesson: Even when people admit their shortcomings, they are often ostracized by others and

receive no justice. Where can they get strength and reassurance? Job and the psalmist proclaim that—no matter what happens—God, the Redeemer, lives and constantly sends forth steadfast love to all people.

❖ Challenge the adults to grow spiritually by completing one or more of these activities related to this week's session, which you have posted on newsprint for the students to copy.

(1) Learn more about God's passion for justice by studying the parable of the widow and the unjust judge in Luke 18:1-8. How does this parable give you hope that God will act with justice as you encounter unjust situations in your life and in the community?

(2) Express your feelings of joy as you recall a promise that God has recently fulfilled for you by singing a hymn, drawing a picture, or writing a poem.

(3) Tell someone about how you experience God with you in the midst of a difficult situation. Step out in faith by declaring to your listener that you believe God will give you the strength to endure.

❖ Sing or read aloud "My Life Flows On (How Can I Keep from Singing)" found in *The Faith We Sing*.

❖ Conclude today's session by leading the class in this hope-filled benediction from Psalm 55:16, which is the key verse for October 19: I call upon God, and the LORD will save me.

UNIT 2: DARK NIGHTS OF THE SOUL
EVEN SO,
MY REDEEMER LIVES

PREVIEWING THE LESSON

Lesson Scripture: Job 19:1-7, 23-29
Background Scripture: Job 19; Psalm 57
Key Verse: Job 19:25

Focus of the Lesson:
Even when people admit their shortcomings, they are often ostracized by others and receive no justice. Where can they get strength and reassurance? Job and the psalmist proclaim that—no matter what happens—God, the Redeemer, lives and constantly sends forth steadfast love to all people.

Goals for the Learners:
(1) to understand that Job had unwavering belief in God's redemption even as he was made to suffer.
(2) to affirm that, though they suffer much, God loves them and offers them redemption.
(3) to acknowledge ways they are loved and blessed during times of trouble.

Pronunciation Guide:
avath (aw vath´)   Eliphaz (el´ i faz)
Bildad (bil´ dad)   Zophar (zoh´ fahr)

Supplies:
Bibles, newsprint and marker, paper and pencils, hymnals, pictures of people who are suffering

---

READING THE SCRIPTURE

NRSV	CEB
Lesson Scripture: Job 19:1-7, 23-29	Lesson Scripture: Job 19:1-7, 23-29
[1]Then Job answered:	[1]Then Job responded:
[2]"How long will you torment me,	[2]How long will you harass me

and break me in pieces with
words?
³These ten times you have cast
reproach upon me;
are you not ashamed to wrong me?
⁴And even if it is true that I have
erred,
my error remains with me.
⁵If indeed you magnify yourselves
against me,
and make my humiliation an argument against me,
⁶know then that God has put me in
the wrong,
and closed his net around me.
⁷Even when I cry out, 'Violence!' I am
not answered;
I call aloud, but there is no justice.
²³"O that my words were written
down!
O that they were inscribed in a
book!
²⁴O that with an iron pen and with
lead
they were engraved on a rock
forever!
²⁵For **I know that my Redeemer
lives,**
**and that at the last he will stand
upon the earth;**
²⁶and after my skin has been thus
destroyed,
then in my flesh I shall see God,
²⁷whom I shall see on my side,
and my eyes shall behold, and not
another.
My heart faints within me!
²⁸If you say, 'How we will persecute
him!'
and, 'The root of the matter is
found in him';
²⁹be afraid of the sword,
for wrath brings the punishment of
the sword,
so that you may know there is a
judgment."

and crush me with words?
³These ten times you've humiliated
me;
shamelessly you insult me.
⁴Have I really gone astray?
If so, my error remains hidden
inside me.
⁵If you look down on me and use my
disgrace to criticize me,
⁶know then that God has wronged
me and enclosed his net over
me.
⁷If I cry "Violence!" I'm not
answered;
I shout—but there is no justice.
²³Oh, that my words were written
down, inscribed on a scroll
²⁴with an iron instrument and lead,
forever engraved on stone.
²⁵But **I know that my redeemer is
alive and afterward he'll rise
upon the dust.**
²⁶After my skin has been torn apart
this way—
then from my flesh I'll see God,
²⁷whom I'll see myself—my
eyes see, and not a stranger's.
I am utterly dejected.
²⁸You say, "How will we pursue him
so that the root of the matter can
be found in him?"
²⁹You ought to fear the sword
yourselves,
for wrath brings punishment by
the sword.
You should know that there is
judgment.

UNDERSTANDING THE SCRIPTURE

Introduction to Job. Although technically outside the confines of this day's passage from Job, the presence and rhetoric of Job's three friends (Eliphaz, Bildad, and Zophar) are critical to the understanding of the book in general and today's passage in particular. Chapters 3–27 comprise three cycles of speeches that, until the third cycle, follow the pattern of Eliphaz/Job, Bildad/Job, and Zophar/Job. A careful reading reveals that both the friends and Job do not so much talk to each other as past each other. The arguments of the friends essentially boil down to a settled view of the universe where faithfulness is rewarded and evil punished. Thus, by the time of the third cycle, the friends assert Job's punishment is due to his guilt, rather than the extraordinary scene set in Job 1 that they know nothing about. Ironically, Job's defense oftentimes comes down to the same understanding of the world—and his later demands to be shown his guilt with protestations of his innocence (chapter 31).

Job 19:1-7. The statement that Job "answered" in verse 1 refers to the reply Job now makes to the friend named Bildad in the second cycle of speeches. The "torment" that Job assigns to his friends may be underscored by the final declaration of Bildad in 18:21: "Such is the place of those who do not know God." The charge has now come down not simply to Job's guilt, but his godlessness. The "ten times" in verse 3 is figurative rather than literal: Bildad's most recent attack was the fifth speech made by Job's three friends. Verse 4 is unclear. Is Job saying that

it is not the friends' place to assign error to him—or that his error is his business alone (an idea that does not reflect understandings current in that day)? In verse 5, Job describes his friends' efforts as "magnify[ing] yourselves against me," that is, placing themselves morally above and apart from him. The folly of such an attitude comes in the startling assertion of verse 6: "God has put me in the wrong." "Put me in the wrong" translates the Hebrew *avath*, whose meaning suggests "to overthrow" or "to subvert." The consequence of such action is spelled out in verse 7: Job's cry of "violence" is not heard, and in the silence there is no justice.

Job 19:8-22. This bold assertion in verses 6-7 is now given extended treatment. Each of the verses (8-13) begins with "He" or "His"—and each verse brings an indictment of what God has done to Job. The verbs that describe God's actions are bold to the point of violence: "walled up . . . set darkness . . . stripped . . . taken . . . breaks me down . . . uprooted . . . kindled . . . put family far from me." Like Habakkuk 2:1, where the prophet spoke of taking his stand and watching to see how God would answer his complaint, so now does Job in these verses speak bluntly in search of an answer.

Job then describes how his relatives and friends have abandoned him. Even servants otherwise bound to obedience and little children defy him. These verses depict the collapse of familial and social orders that would otherwise provide support. These verses are bracketed at beginning and end with Job's assessment that God is responsible for family turning against him (19:13) and friends "pursuing" him like God, "never satisfied" (19:22).

Job 19:23-27. In the midst of such defiance Job expresses confidence in his "Redeemer." Job longs for his words to be "inscribed in a book," written on a lead tablet with an iron pen, or "engraved on a rock" (19:23). The three "media" can be seen as a "progression" of enduring material, rock being the most long-lasting ("forever"). In Judaism, a "redeemer" was a male kinsman who took responsibility for defending a family member in a situation of vulnerability. Sometimes it involved repurchasing property that had been lost (the levitical traditions of Jubilee in Leviticus 25, and the story of Boaz serving as the redeemer of Ruth in Ruth 4:4-6). Scholars debate who Job has in mind when he refers to "my Redeemer." While God is portrayed as redeemer in some passages, the first half of this chapter can be interpreted to suggest Job's redeemer would need to advocate for him in the face of God who has put him in the wrong and alienated family from him (19:6, 13). Christian tradition has interpreted Job's "Redeemer" and its accompanying imagery of Job's "seeing" God as an expression in life after death. Difficulties in translation and multiple ways of interpreting verses 25-27 preclude any singular view of its meaning but

Job's words in these verses reflect his hope for exoneration.

Job 19:28-29. The final two verses seem directed at the three friends whose accusations he has endured. These verses speak of the possibility of reversal: that those who speak judgment risk judgment themselves; that those who say the "root of the matter (guilt) is found in him" neglect to take into account the guilt they themselves bear.

Psalm 57. The psalmist weaves together lament and trust, so that one cannot be separated from the other. The cry for God's mercy (57:1) comes in the midst of a desperate and even violent situation. The core of the complaint occurs in verses 4-6, where enemies are portrayed first as predatory animals and then as scheming enemies. Verse 5 "interrupts" that flow by confessing God above all, a powerful affirmation given the circumstances that preface and follow it. In verse 7, the psalmist confesses that his own heart is steadfast—an expression that may be heard to assert both innocence as well as perseverance. The earlier cry for mercy now moves to the psalmist's confession of the greatness of God's love and faithfulness. Lament and complaint do not contradict such confession. Rather, they assert that God can be and is to be trusted in the midst of crisis and threat.

INTERPRETING THE SCRIPTURE

With Friends Like These . . .

You have likely heard the saying that begins with the words of this section's title, and ends with "who

needs enemies?" The familiarity of the adage is likely not simply with its words, but with its experience: times when a friend has let us down, or actively worked against us. Why such things happen often remain unclear. Did we do something that sowed the seeds of betrayal? Was the friendship a ruse all along?

The great part of the entire Book of Job is taken up with a series of speeches that alternate between Job and his "friends." The degree of Job's anguish at their turning upon and against him becomes clear in portions of today's text: "How long will you torment me . . . are you not ashamed to wrong me?" (19:1, 2). It is said that strangers cannot hurt us as deeply as friends, those upon whom we have trusted and leaned upon for support. We hear that in Job's words.

But there is an even darker turn of relationship to which Job lifts up his voice in anguished protest: "Know then that God has put me in the wrong and closed his net around me" (19:6). Job in his suffering alludes to the possibility that even God has become distant if not, in fact, adversarial. The intervening verses of 8-13, in this chapter though not technically part of today's passage, very much belong to this cry Job lifts up that questions God's fidelity to him. For in those verses, God is the source of what has befallen him. Indeed, in verse 13, God is the one who has alienated Job from his family.

"With friends like these" takes on an even more ominous cast in Job's protest. For the God of Israel, celebrated as the One who hears those who call upon him, instead is depicted by Job in these words: "Even when I cry out, 'Violence!' I am not answered; I call aloud, but there is no justice" (19:7).

Such words might spark righteous indignation against Job—how dare he speak of God in such a way! But notice: Job still speaks of God, and to

God. To disengage from a relationship with God results in silence. Job is not silent. Job remains engaged with God: in the midst of his suffering; even in the face of the seeming silence of God. Given the scenario in chapters 1 and 2 where God gives Satan ability to disrupt Job's life so severely, that perceived silence is close to the narrator's understanding of exactly what has happened here.

Even in his torment, even in the desertion of his friends, Job will not let God go. It is a lesson about faith that persists for us all. Would we persevere, would we cry out, as does Job—or would we fall into silence, unwilling to engage with God?

Redeeming Hope

In ancient Jewish life, a redeemer was an advocate. Typically, it was a family member who takes action to deliver an otherwise vulnerable family member (or property) from debt or slavery or dishonor. In Judaism, this familiar term became expanded to describe the work of God in the deliverance of Israel: first from Egypt (Exodus 6:6), and later from Babylon (Isaiah 44:22-24). Given that national experience of God as redeemer, it became natural for that understanding to come into play with regard to the lives of individuals ("Draw near to me, redeem me, set me free from my enemies," Psalm 69:18).

These streams of meaning all flow into Job's assertion in 19:25: "I know that my Redeemer lives."

The question is this: Who does Job have in mind as his redeemer?

Traditionally, in Israel's national and devotional use of the term "redeemer" it refers to God: God is Job's redeemer. That understanding is clearly behind the aria in Handel's *Messiah*, "I Know That My Redeemer Liveth," which asserts that Christ is the Redeemer. Some interpreters, however, draw another conclusion. Based upon the previous assertions by Job as to God's silence, they interpret the redeemer Job has in mind as one who will serve as Job's advocate before God. Job does not identify who such an advocate might be. The other curious element here is that the work of this redeemer Job has in mind seems to be depicted as occurring after his (Job's) death.

But whether one lands on the side of traditional interpretation of God as redeemer, or redeemer as one who will advocate on behalf of Job before God, Job links the work of redemption with hope. Even though death might come, as his circumstances might suggest sooner than later, Job lives with hope that he will see God. And clearly, that sight in these verses is not one of dread but one of anticipation by such redeeming.

In addition to the meanings of "redeem" that come from Judaism, consider also the suggestion of that word in English. Re-deem. To deem something (or someone) is to give it value. To re-deem it is to restore value. Consider that possibility in the life of Job—and your own life. In the midst of suffering and loss, Job experienced devaluing that was only multiplied by the inept intervention of his friends. But the hope of redemption brings with it the anticipation of finding oneself again valued by others, and by God. Keep that before you in those times and circumstances where you find yourself devalued, either by the judgment of others or the sometimes harsher judgment of self. As Genesis 1 asserts, in our creation God deemed us good. And now, in the love and grace of God as revealed in Jesus Christ, God re-deems that goodness in our salvation.

God's Love: Confession and Caution

While "love" does not occur per se in Job 19, the hope that we are given of One who will redeem us assures of such love and blessing in our lives. But there is a caution Job adds at the end precisely out of that confession. The caution is aimed at Job's friends, who have made Job too easy a target for their righteous indignation. Their "how will we persecute him" and the "root of the matter is found in him" (19:28) point the accusatory fingers at the distressed (and seemingly un-deemed) Job. But their attitude, and the caution it evokes here, calls to mind a similar warning by Jesus: "Do not judge, so that you may not be judged. For with the judgment you make you will be judged, and the measure you give will be the measure you get" (Matthew 7:1-2).

When the love of God is at stake, a cavalier attitude as to who is worthy and who is not can get one into trouble—and not simply with the one who is being reproached, but with the God whose love is being impinged upon by human judgment. Neither Job nor his friends is aware of the narrative of chapters 1–2, which make clear Job is not the cause for all his woes. Likewise, you and I do not possess the God's-eye perspective to determine how others are held in the sight of God when things go bad, or perhaps more seductively, when things go well. God's love is meant to be a blessing that affirms us and others, not a weapon by which we measure who measures up to us.

SHARING THE SCRIPTURE

PREPARING TO TEACH

Preparing Our Hearts

Meditate on this week's devotional reading from 1 Chronicles 16:28-34, which is part of David's thanksgiving to God when the ark of the covenant was returned to Jerusalem and restored to its place in the tent (16:1). What reasons do you have to worship God joyfully today? How have you experienced God's goodness and steadfast love this week?

Pray that you and the students will rejoice in God in all situations.

Preparing Our Minds

Study the background Scripture from Job 19 and Psalm 57. The lesson Scripture is from Job 19:1-7, 23-29.

Consider this question as you prepare the lesson: *Where can people who admit their shortcomings get strength and reassurance?*

Write on newsprint:

❑ information for next week's lesson, found under "Continue the Journey."

❑ activities for further spiritual growth in "Continue the Journey."

Review the "Introduction," "The Big Picture," "Close-up," and "Faith in Action," which all precede the first lesson of this quarter. Consider how you might use any of this material in today's lesson.

Collect pictures depicting people suffering for a variety of reasons such as illness, loss of loved ones, loss of jobs, destruction of homes, victimization by criminals, or accidents.

LEADING THE CLASS

(1) Gather to Learn

❖ Greet the class members and introduce guests.

❖ Pray that those who have come today will recognize that strength comes from God our Redeemer.

❖ Distribute hymnals and invite the students to turn to "O God, Our Help in Ages Past." Either sing this hymn or assign different groups to read verses 1, 2, and 6.

❖ Ask: **Assuming that you knew nothing about God except what you have just read, how would you describe God—and why would you want to know this God?**

❖ Read aloud today's focus statement: **Even when people admit their shortcomings, they are often ostracized by others and receive no justice. Where can they get strength and reassurance? Job and the psalmist proclaim that no matter what happens, God, the Redeemer, lives and constantly sends forth steadfast love to all people.**

(2) Goal 1: Understand that Job Had Unwavering Belief in God's Redemption Even as He Was Made to Suffer

❖ Encourage students to say what they know about the story of Job. Add information from the "Introduction to Job" in Understanding the Scripture as appropriate.

❖ Choose a volunteer to read Job 19:1-7. Remind participants that this reading is part of Job's response to Bildad (Job 18). Discuss these questions adding information from "With

Friends Like These . . ." in Interpreting the Scripture:

1. **How would you characterize Job's response to Bildad, his supposed "friend"?**
2. **What do you learn about Job's relationship with God in this passage?**

❖ Prepare to study the second passage by first reading "Redeeming Hope" in Interpreting the Scripture.

❖ Select another volunteer to read Job 19:23-29 and then discuss these questions:

1. **What would Job have expected from a redeemer?** (See "Job 19:23-27" in Understanding the Scripture.)
2. **Notice that the "R" in "Redeemer" is capitalized in verse 25 in some translations, including the NRSV and NIV, though not in the KJV or CEB. Which way would best represent Job's understanding of the word?** (Job likely would have used a lowercase *r*, for he was talking about an unnamed heavenly individual who would redeem him. He was probably not talking about God—who would be indicated by the use of and uppercase R in Redeemer—since in Job's view he needed to be redeemed or defended from God. The uppercase Redeemer, associated with God and especially with Christ, reflects a Christian understanding.)
3. **What is Job saying to his friends? Why should we remember his words when trouble comes to our friends?** (See "Job 19:28-29" in Understanding the Scripture.)

(3) Goal 2: Affirm that, Though the Learners Suffer Much, God Loves Them and Offers Them Redemption

❖ Do a comparative Bible study by reading Psalm 57, which is part of today's background Scripture. Invite two volunteers to read this psalm responsively from the same Bible translation. Form small groups and ask each group to discuss (1) how the psalmist seems to be similar to Job in terms of his relationship with and expectations of God, and (2) how the psalmist seems to be different from Job.

❖ Bring the groups together and distribute paper and pencils. Invite the learners to reflect on these ideas, which you will read aloud: **Both Job and the psalmist had suffered, but both could affirm God's faithfulness and redemption. What trials are you encountering? What do you believe about God's desires for your life? How do you experience God's love and redemption in your life?**

❖ Call on volunteers who are willing to relate their experiences of God's love and redemption.

(4) Goal 3: Acknowledge Ways the Learners Are Loved and Blessed During Times of Trouble

❖ Show the pictures you have collected of persons who are in the midst of trouble. Invite the students to create a brief story about each picture. Talk about the way those who are suffering may be experiencing God's love and blessings even as they suffer. For example, a good Samaritan may have stopped to render assistance, a friend may be hugging the sufferer and even crying with him, the community may be erecting a makeshift memorial with candles and stuffed toys. List ideas on newsprint.

❖ Invite the learners to recall silently a time when they experienced trouble. Encourage them to review the list and acknowledge any of the ways shown there that they received love, and then add other ways that they experienced.

❖ Conclude by inviting the adults to affirm God's love by saying in unison today's key verse, Job 19:25.

(5) Continue the Journey

❖ Pray that as the learners depart they will hold fast to the God who loves and redeems them, even in times of trouble.

❖ Post information for next week's session on newsprint for the students to copy:

- **Title: Hope Complains**
- **Background Scripture: Job 5; 24; Psalm 55:12-23**
- **Lesson Scripture: Job 24:1, 9-12, 19-25**
- **Focus of the Lesson: Sometimes it seems as though the wicked people in the world get all the breaks and cannot be stopped from doing terrible things. How can this picture be changed? Job 24 complains that God supports the evil ones, but only for a while; however, Job 5 and the psalmist affirm that, even so, God saves the needy and**

gives the poor hope in the battles they are waging.

❖ Challenge the adults to grow spiritually by completing one or more of these activities, which you have posted on newsprint for the students to copy.

(1) **Remember that even in the midst of his suffering Job did not turn away from God, but instead kept trying to engage God. Has someone you know felt like turning away from God because things were not going well? Talk tenderly with this person about continuing to seek God, just as Job did.**

(2) **Recall "dark nights" of your own soul when you wondered if God was on your side. Recite today's key verse, Job 19:25, to remind yourself that God is the One who will vindicate you.**

(3) **Make a list before you go to bed of all the ways God has blessed you this day. Meditate on how these blessings affirm God's desires for your life.**

❖ Sing or read aloud "Precious Lord, Take My Hand."

❖ Conclude today's session by leading the class in this hope-filled benediction from Psalm 55:16, which is the key verse for October 19: **I call upon God, and the LORD will save me.**

UNIT 2: DARK NIGHTS OF THE SOUL
HOPE COMPLAINS

PREVIEWING THE LESSON

Lesson Scripture: Job 24:1, 9-12, 19-25
Background Scripture: Job 5; 24; Psalm 55:12-23
Key Verse: Psalm 55:16

Focus of the Lesson:
Sometimes it seems as though the wicked people in the world get all the breaks and cannot be stopped from doing terrible things. How can this picture be changed? Job 24 complains that God supports the evil ones, but only for a while; however, Job 5 and the psalmist affirm that, even so, God saves the needy and gives the poor hope in the battles they are waging.

Goals for the Learners:
(1) to explore Job's complaint about the appearance that God does nothing to call wicked people to account.
(2) to appreciate that although the timing of God's justice is often mysterious to us it is certain.
(3) to determine ways to help God bring justice to the poor and weak.

Pronunciation Guide:
Eliphaz (el´ i faz)   Sheol (shee´ ohl)

Supplies:
Bibles, newsprint and marker, paper and pencils, hymnals

READING THE SCRIPTURE

NRSV	CEB
Lesson Scripture: Job 24:1, 9-12, 19-25	Lesson Scripture: Job 24:1, 9-12, 19-25
[1]"Why are times not kept by the Almighty, and why do those who know him never see his days?	[24]Why doesn't the Almighty establish times for punishment? Why can't those who know him see his days?
[9]"There are those who snatch the orphan child from the breast,	[9]The orphan is stolen from the breast; the infant of the poor is taken as

and take as a pledge the infant of
the poor.
[10]They go about naked, without
clothing;
though hungry, they carry the
sheaves;
[11]between their terraces they press
out oil;
they tread the wine presses, but
suffer thirst.
[12]From the city the dying groan,
and the throat of the wounded
cries for help;
yet God pays no attention to their
prayer.
[19]Drought and heat snatch away the
snow waters;
so does Sheol those who have
sinned.
[20]The womb forgets them;
the worm finds them sweet;
they are no longer remembered;
so wickedness is broken like a tree.
[21]"They harm the childless woman,
and do no good to the widow.
[22]Yet God prolongs the life of the
mighty by his power;
they rise up when they despair of
life.
[23]He gives them security, and they
are supported;
his eyes are upon their ways.
[24]They are exalted a little while, and
then are gone;
they wither and fade like the
mallow;
they are cut off like the heads of
grain.
[25]If it is not so, who will prove me a
liar,
and show that there is nothing in
what I say?"

Key Verse: Psalm 55:16
[16]But **I call upon God,**
and the LORD will save me.

collateral.
[10]The poor go around naked, without
clothes,
carry bundles of grain while
hungry,
[11]crush olives between millstones,
tread winepresses, but remain
thirsty.
[12]From the city, the dying cry out;
the throat of the mortally wounded
screams, but God assigns no
blame.
[19]Drought and heat steal melted
snow,
just as the underworld steals
sinners.
[20]The womb forgets them;
the worm consumes them; they
aren't remembered, and so
wickedness is shattered like a
tree.
[21]They prey on the barren, the
childless,
do nothing good for the widow.
[22]They drag away the strong by force;
they may get up but without guarantee of survival.
[23]They make themselves secure; they
are at ease.
His eyes are on their ways.
[24]They are exalted for a short time,
but no longer.
They are humbled then gathered
in like everyone else; cut off like
heads of grain.
[25]If this isn't so, who can prove me a
liar
and make my words disappear?

Key Verse: Psalm 55:16
[16]But **I call out to God,**
and the LORD will rescue me.

UNDERSTANDING THE SCRIPTURE

Job 5:1-16. Job 5 forms the second half of the initial speech by Job's friend Eliphaz, the first of the three friends to speak. The opening seven verses provide a challenge for interpreters, stemming both from inconsistencies in logic as well as textual difficulties in verse 5. Eliphaz uses the image of the "fools" (5:3) in rebuttal of Job's opening protest in chapter 3. In Wisdom Literature and the psalms in particular, the "fool" is one who does not know or acknowledge God (Psalm 14:1). Beginning at verse 8, Eliphaz makes a confessional (or is it self-congratulatory?) statement as to why he would commit his cause to God—with the implied assumption that Job has not done so. The universe Eliphaz describes in verses 9-16 is an orderly one, with praise of God's providence and justice. What goes unspoken in the creed of Eliphaz is the present suffering of the one he lectures.

Job 5:17-27. The closing argument of Eliphaz is uttered from the safety of his own well-being: Those whom God punishes and disciplines should be happy. Eliphaz depicts God, perhaps unintentionally, in callous terms that rival any of Job's protests: "He wounds . . . he strikes . . ." (5:18). To be sure, Eliphaz affirms God as one who heals and binds up—but only after he has identified God as the source of the violence done to Job.

Verses 21-26 offer a series of promissory "you shalls" to Job in terms of what God will do for him. There is nothing in this list that departs from the promissory nature of Israel's (and later, the church's) faith regarding God's deliverance. What is painfully silent, however, and thus undermining the very promises of what Job shall experience, is any acknowledgment of the suffering and loss Job has experienced. In the closing verse, Eliphaz cavalierly declares: "We have searched this out; it is true." He claims to speak not only for the community but also in one sense for God. And therein lies the weakness of the argument of Eliphaz. Only God knows the truth of the origin of Job's sufferings that unfolded in chapters 1 and 2. Eliphaz speaks of a faith, grand though it is, that is separated from the experience of Job and the mystery of God.

Job 24:1-12. A large jump in narrative has been made. From the first speech of the first friend to speak, chapter 24 takes up with the second half of Job's reply to the *third* speech of Eliphaz in chapter 22. The core of Eliphaz's final words to Job is twofold: "Is not your wickedness great" (22:5) and "Agree with God, and be at peace" (22:21). In other words, you are bad to the core, so shut up and take it. Job wonders in chapter 23 where he could possibly find God (23:8-9 offer a reversal of sorts of Psalm 139:7-9's affirmation of God's omnipresence). Job 24 becomes, in one sense, an explication of what Job finds instead of God and God's justice upon the earth. Verse 1 opens with a frustrated cry about the hiddenness of God's time. Jewish faith, especially in its prophetic writings, avowed that God had set a time for the judgment of the wicked. Beginning at verse 2, Job spells out the absence of that "time" in present actions of injustice. Breakdowns in societal boundaries and obligations form one set of witnesses to justice delayed (24:2-4). In verses 5-7 Job compares the poor with wild animals, left to their own devices to scavenge and go without clothing in the harshness of a desert environment to stress the dire straits of those who are cast away and used up by society. In verse 8, the image of such ones who "cling to the rock for want of shelter" may be an ironic charge: "Rock" in Jewish Scripture is a frequent metaphor for God (for example, Psalm 18:2). Job does not specify whether this metaphor is meant as an indictment of God's failure to protect the ones who seek shelter. But in verse 12, Job does speak bluntly: "Yet God pays no attention to their prayer."

Job 24:13-17. Job uses the themes of light and darkness in these verses to depict the reversal of values that has come to pass. In Psalm 104:20-22, night and darkness form a time when predatory animals ("young lions") go out in search of food. Human community, on the other hand, follows a rhythm of night as a time of rest (104:22-23). In these verses in Job, the rhythm of creation—and its justice—is overturned by human predators for whom the night is their "shelter." Murderers and adulterers and house thieves ply their "trades"—and returning to Job's opening words in this chapter, God's time remains hidden and obscured by their violence.

Job 24:18-25. The grammar and meaning in this passage present difficulties for interpreters. In particular, as noted in *The New Interpreter's Study Bible*, the words and argument of Job resemble those of the three friends. However interpreted, Job ends in verse 25 on a note of clear defiance in the face of his friends' attempts to put him in the wrong for what his suffering: "If it is not so, who will prove me a liar?"

Psalm 55. The precise context of history or personal experience that underlies this psalm of lament is unknown. The opening two verses use a set of four imperative verbs by which the psalmist evokes God's attention and intervention. The degree of distress is conveyed in verses 4-5 by a series of powerful descriptions of what has befallen the psalmist: "terrors of death . . . fear and trembling . . . horror." Verses 12-14 underscore that such trouble owes not to the words and actions of enemies—but to betrayal by a once-trusted friend. The key verse for this session comes in verse 16, which offers the confession of God as the One who saves. The severity of the betrayal finds further expression in verses 20-21, with a pair of contrasting metaphors that illustrate the psalmist's charge of his friend having "violated a covenant with me." The psalmist closes with an appeal to others to likewise trust in God.

INTERPRETING THE SCRIPTURE

The Central Crisis

The opening chapters of Job depict a horrific series of losses he experiences. Enemies steal his animals and kill his servants. A powerful wind bears down on a house where his children were dining, causing the structure to collapse and kill his sons and daughters. Job's body is afflicted with a terrible skin disease from head to toe.

As awful as all these things are, however, the central crisis suffered by Job is articulated in Job 24:12. The devastating experiences he has endured do not numb Job to those who suffer around him, but rather draw him closer to them. And as he looks about at the innocent victims of the wicked, and listens to the cries of the wounded and dying, Job declares: "Yet God pays no attention to their prayer."

For those, like his three friends, who seem to view faith as primarily a series of propositions that may or may not conform to experience, Job's utterance here would be heresy. How dare he speak like that to God!

But Job speaks—and not simply in the pages of Scripture. For "Yet God pays no attention to their prayer" is not the exclusive protest and crisis of Job. It was the crisis in the midst of the Holocaust, when smoke rose up from ovens in Auschwitz. It was the crisis in the killing fields of Cambodia, and in the rubble of the Federal Building in Oklahoma City in 1995. It was the crisis in the dust billowing up as the World Trade Center towers collapsed—and more recently, it was the crisis in a darkened movie theater in Aurora, Colorado, the cries of children gunned down in the Newtown, Connecticut, elementary school, and the anguish of spectators injured by an explosion at the Boston Marathon. When the innocent perish by violence or neglect, when the righteous suffer due to no fault of their own, one is led to wonder with Job why God pays no attention to prayers.

It is not sufficient in such times to sugarcoat the quandary, to say God needed another flower in the heavenly garden or any other such rationalization. It could be argued that the most faithful thing to do in the wake of such times and questions is to give them voice rather than keep silence. Job's bluntness may seem on the surface disrespectful or even offensive. But the point is this: Job does not cease the conversation with God, even when the conversation takes an unflattering turn. Job does not, like his friends, provide simplistic answers and formulaic faith to that which is anything but simple or formulaic. Job will not let go of the central crisis he experiences—and indeed, the crisis that looms before anyone who lives with eyes and ears and hearts wide open in this world—not in spite of his faith, but because of his faith. Job will not let God go.

Times and Timing

"Timing is everything," so the proverb goes. Or, to turn to another Old Testament passage of wisdom about times and timing: "For everything there is a season, and a time for every matter under heaven" (Ecclesiastes 3:1).

The complaint of Job in chapter 24 opens with a protest regarding time. The grammar of verse 1 is unclear, making translation difficult. In essence, Job wonders why the God who knows the time of judgment keeps those matters hidden—and not only hidden, but why that time never seems to arrive. It does not take the weight of tragedies that land on Job to make one wonder that same thing. Perhaps that is why one of the earliest prayers of the church takes the form of a two ancient Aramaic words: *marana tha*, meaning "Our

Lord, come" (1 Corinthians 16:22; see also the Greek equivalent in Revelation 22:20b). Even more pointedly, that request underlies the very first petition of the Lord's Prayer: "Your kingdom come" (Matthew 6:10). If we were satisfied with the times as they are, if the realm of God had fully come upon the earth, if the sort of violence and injustice that Job saw all around him and the same manner of incongruities with God's promised reign are the same that you and I can attest to, what need would we have of praying *marana tha*: Our Lord, come! Or to play upon the words of Bob Dylan: While it may seem that the times they are *not* a-changin, we confess with Job that they truly need to be changing—for the good, for the just, for the love of God.

Had we only possessed chapter 24 of Job, we might conclude that Job sees no hope. The confident trust of Psalm 55:16—"But I call upon God, and the LORD will save me"—seems far removed from the complaint(s) of Job 24. Two things need to be remembered. First, there is more to Job than this chapter, and like the psalms of lament (for example, Psalm 22), Job's complaints to God about the "times" and "timing" are ultimately concluded by Job's confession of trust (Job 42:2-6). But second, we do no service to God by rushing immediately to avow confidence and too easily assert a world where evil inevitably falls and good inevitably triumphs. In one sense, that is the failing of Job's friends. They want faith's affirmations without its struggles: They want safe formulas rather than trust that emerges out of the kiln of contradictory experience.

What do we want . . . and what do we seek?

How Do We Respond?

It is possible to engage the Book of Job in purely philosophical and theological terms. We can argue the fine points of Job's complaints and his friend's assertions. But in the light of chapter 24's complaint, more is sought from us than our opinions or even our creeds. For if Job is right in the lament of injustice still holding the day far too often, and if we indeed trust God's promises of times of justice and steadfast love on the way, just what are we going to do in the meantime (or in Job's perception, mean times) that witness to *and* usher in that promised justice and steadfast love?

And here is where, in the words borrowed by one of my seminary professors from tire advertisements, Scripture's "rubber meets the road." For in the end, beyond the safety of pure speculation, Job 24 serves as a summons and challenge to mission and ministry. For if Job is right, then and now, that "they thrust the needy off the road" (24:4), what will we do as persons and communities of faith to help the vulnerable get "back on track"? If Job is right, then and now, that the poor of the earth go without clothing, exposed to the elements (be they physical or economic elements that ravage the unprotected), what will we do as persons and communities of faith to give shelter and justice to those trampled by power and wealth untroubled with ethics and compassion?

Job does make this startling accusation that God pays no attention to the prayers of those who so suffer. But beyond our astonishment at the statement's brashness, let us remember: As the body of Christ, we are called to be the hands and feet, voice and ears, of Christ in this world. If we pay no attention to such cries for help and justice, then Job's accusation is not only against God—but perhaps more accurately, against those charged with bearing the presence and love of God into this world.

Job—and the God of justice and steadfast love—awaits our response.

SHARING THE SCRIPTURE

PREPARING TO TEACH

Preparing Our Hearts

Meditate on this week's devotional reading from Jeremiah 14:14-22. What connections might you make between verses 19-22 to today's lesson from Job? Are there times that you feel God has "completely rejected" you, that you can find no healing or peace? How would you describe such times? What do you need to "acknowledge" before God today?

Pray that you and the students will "set your hope" on God and live as faithful disciples.

Preparing Our Minds

Study the background Scripture from Job 5; 24; and Psalm 55:12-23. The lesson Scripture is from Job 24:1, 9-12, 19-25.

Consider this question as you prepare the lesson: *How can we stop wicked people from doing terrible things?*

Write on newsprint:
❏ information for next week's lesson, found under "Continue the Journey."
❏ activities for further spiritual growth in "Continue the Journey."

Review the "Introduction," "The Big Picture," "Close-up," and "Faith in Action," which all precede the first lesson of this quarter. Consider how you might use any of this material in today's lesson.

LEADING THE CLASS

(1) Gather to Learn

❖ Greet the class members and introduce guests.

❖ Pray that those who have come today will be aware that while evil ones seem to be in charge at times, God will save the needy and give hope to the poor.

❖ Read this comment by Robert Bellarmine (1542–1621): **"Because the designs of God's providence are deeply hidden and his judgment as great deeps, it happens that some, seeing that all the evils which men do go unpunished, rashly conclude that human affairs are not governed by God's providence or even that all crimes are committed because God so wills. 'Both errors are impious,' says St. Augustine, especially the latter."**

❖ Ask: **What role do you believe God plays in the affairs of humanity?**

❖ Read aloud today's focus statement: **Sometimes it seems as though the wicked people in the world get all the breaks and cannot be stopped from doing terrible things. How can this picture be changed? Job 24 complains that God supports the evil ones, but only for a while; however,**

Job 5 and the psalmist affirm that, even so, God saves the needy and gives the poor hope in the battles they are waging.

(2) Goal 1: Explore Job's Complaint about the Appearance that God Does Nothing to Call Wicked People to Account

❖ Choose one volunteer to read Job 24:1, 9-12, 19-25.
   ❖ Discuss these questions:
     1. **What are Job's major complaints?** (Use information from the portions on Job 24 in Understanding the Scripture and "The Central Crisis" in Interpreting the Scripture as you find it useful. Emphasize that Job is concerned that God's time to judge the wicked has not yet arrived [24:1] and that God seemingly pays no attention to the prayers of those who are poor and oppressed [24:12].)
     2. **How does Job view the actions of the wicked?**
     3. **What injustices have been wrought upon the powerless by those whom Job describes as "the mighty" (24:22)?**
     4. **Do you perceive Job's complaints to be valid today? Why or why not?**
     5. **What complaints would you like to bring before God right now?**
❖ Conclude this portion of the lesson by calling on four volunteers to read today's background Scripture from Psalm 55:12-23, which includes our key verse, 55:16. One volunteer will read verses 1-3 to introduce this individual lament; a second volunteer will read verses 12-15; a third, verses 16-19; and a fourth, verses 20-23. Ask: **How might the picture of God presented in this psalm encourage Job?**

(3) Goal 2: Appreciate that Although the Timing of God's Justice Is Often Mysterious to Us, It Is Certain

❖ Read or retell "Times and Timing" from Interpreting the Scripture.
   ❖ Post a sheet of newsprint and invite the adults to answer this question: **What injustices can you recall that have ultimately been put right?** Encourage the class to think of wrongs that have historically affected large numbers of people. Here are some examples: *slavery* (though this horrific practice still exists in parts of the world); *treatment of women as second-class citizens or property* (the United States has made great strides, but many countries have a long way to go); *totalitarian regimes* (the Berlin Wall fell and the Union of Soviet Socialist Republics has split, but many oppressive governments still control numerous people).
   ❖ Discuss these questions:
     1. **What role do you think God played in ending these injustices?**
     2. **What injustices are you eager to see God end soon?**
     3. **What injustices exist in our country right now?**
     4. **How will we as Christians work to reverse these injustices?**

(4) Goal 3: Determine Ways to Help God Bring Justice to the Poor and Weak

❖ Read "How Do We Respond?" from Interpreting the Scripture.
   ❖ Form several small groups and

give each one a sheet of newsprint and a marker. Challenge each group to identify types of people in your community who are crying out for justice. Children who receive school lunches, for example, may have no access to food during the summer and school holidays. Unscrupulous contractors may be cheating vulnerable homeowners after a disaster. Schools may have lowered expectations for students of particular racial or ethnic groups. Once the groups have identified those who seek justice, encourage them to identify one group that they believe the class could assist. Invite them to brainstorm actions they could take.

❖ Bring everyone together to hear reports from the groups. See if there are one or two ideas that the class wants to pursue together, perhaps with assistance from other church members. Create a task force to begin to work on this project and report back to the class.

(5) Continue the Journey

❖ Pray that as the learners depart they will remain faithful, despite the presence of evil persons who seem to be able to continue to get away with injustice.

❖ Post information for next week's session on newsprint for the students to copy:

- **Title: Hope Satisfies**
- **Background Scripture: Job 42; Psalm 86**
- **Lesson Scripture: Job 42:1-10**
- **Focus of the Lesson: People**

often wonder who or what controls the final outcomes in life's many challenges. Where can people find answers to life's ultimate questions? Job declares that God can do all things and ultimately will prevail over all obstacles, restoring the fortunes of those who are faithful; and the psalmist illustrates how God's people can pray that God will be gracious to them and preserve their lives.

❖ Challenge the adults to grow spiritually by completing one or more of these activities related to this week's session, which you have posted on newsprint for the students to copy:

(1) **Become involved with whatever group project the class has agreed on to assist those who are crying out for justice.**

(2) **Memorize today's key verse, Psalm 55:16. Call this verse to mind, especially in difficult circumstances.**

(3) **Offer daily prayers for people around the world who are suffering due to injustices.**

❖ Sing or read aloud "God Will Take Care of You."

❖ Conclude today's session by leading the class in this hope-filled benediction from Psalm 55:16, which is today's key verse: **I call upon God, and the LORD will save me.**

UNIT 2: DARK NIGHTS OF THE SOUL
HOPE SATISFIES

PREVIEWING THE LESSON

Lesson Scripture: Job 42:1-10
Background Scripture: Job 42; Psalm 86
Key Verse: Job 42:2

Focus of the Lesson:
People often wonder who or what controls the final outcomes in life's many challenges. Where can people find answers to life's ultimate questions? Job declares that God can do all things and ultimately will prevail over all obstacles, restoring the fortunes of those who are faithful; and the psalmist illustrates how God's people can pray that God will be gracious to them and preserve their lives.

Goals for the Learners:
(1) to explore the satisfactory conclusion of Job and God's conversation.
(2) to affirm that God will answer their questions in ways that are best for them.
(3) to become involved in an active and hopeful prayer life.

Pronunciation Guide:
Bildad (bil´ dad)   Shuah (shoo´ uh)
Eliphaz (el´ i faz)   Shuhite (shoo´ hite)
mezimmah (mez im maw´)   Teman (tee´ muhn)
Naamah (nay´ uh muh)   Temanite (tee´ muh nite)
Naamathite   Zophar (zoh´ fahr)
   (nay´ uh muh thite)

Supplies:
Bibles, newsprint and marker, paper and pencils, hymnals

READING THE SCRIPTURE

NRSV
Lesson Scripture: Job 42:1-10
¹Then Job answered the LORD:
²**"I know that you can do all things,**

CEB
Lesson Scripture: Job 42:1-10
¹Job answered the LORD:
²**I know you can do anything;**

---

and that no purpose of yours can be thwarted.

3'Who is this that hides counsel without knowledge?'
Therefore I have uttered what I did not understand,
  things too wonderful for me,
  which I did not know.
4'Hear, and I will speak;
  I will question you, and you declare to me.'
5I had heard of you by the hearing of the ear,
  but now my eye sees you;
6therefore I despise myself,
  and repent in dust and ashes."

7After the LORD had spoken these words to Job, the LORD said to Eliphaz the Temanite: "My wrath is kindled against you and against your two friends; for you have not spoken of me what is right, as my servant Job has. 8Now therefore take seven bulls and seven rams, and go to my servant Job, and offer up for yourselves a burnt offering; and my servant Job shall pray for you, for I will accept his prayer not to deal with you according to your folly; for you have not spoken of me what is right, as my servant Job has done." 9So Eliphaz the Temanite and Bildad the Shuhite and Zophar the Naamathite went and did what the LORD had told them; and the LORD accepted Job's prayer.

10And the LORD restored the fortunes of Job when he had prayed for his friends; and the LORD gave Job twice as much as he had before.

no plan of yours can be opposed successfully.

3You said, "Who is this darkening counsel without knowledge?"
I have indeed spoken about things I didn't understand,
  wonders beyond my comprehension.
4You said, "Listen and I will speak;
  I will question you and you will inform me. "
5My ears had heard about you,
  but now my eyes have seen you.
6Therefore, I relent and find comfort on dust and ashes.

7After the LORD had spoken these words to Job, he said to Eliphaz from Teman, "I'm angry at you and your two friends because you haven't spoken about me correctly as did my servant Job. 8So now, take seven bulls and seven rams, go to my servant Job, and prepare an entirely burned offering for yourselves. Job my servant will pray for you, and I will act favorably by not making fools of you because you didn't speak correctly, as did my servant Job."

9Eliphaz from Teman, Bildad from Shu'ah, and Zophar from Na'amah did what the LORD told them; and the LORD acted favorably toward Job. 10Then the LORD changed Job's fortune when he prayed for his friends, and the LORD doubled all Job's earlier possessions.

UNDERSTANDING THE SCRIPTURE

Introduction. After the series of speeches between Job and his three friends (chapters 3–31), and after the upbraiding of all four by one called Elihu (chapters 32–37), the poetic section of the Book of Job ends with God speaking "out of the whirlwind" (38:1; chapters 38–41).

The passage comprises a remark-able series of questions posed to Job (and, by some accounts, to the friends who could also be indicted by 38:2's charge of "darkens counsel by words without knowledge"). The question-ing focuses on matters that exceed human knowledge and/or control. The passage is also remarkable in that it provides no answers to the hard issues raised by Job's innocent suffer-ing (see chapters 1–2). The whirlwind speech of God is not an explication of the human condition, but a witness to the mystery of God in a world not always fair or just.

Job 42:1-6. Having received God's "answers" via questions in the whirl-wind, Job now answers God. Job's words, however, may not be as clear and single-minded as traditional readings of this passage presume. It is clear that Job has listened to God's words from the whirlwind. Verses 3a and 4 quote or closely paraphrase words spoken to Job from the whirl-wind. The affirmation of verse 2 acknowledges God's sovereignty that had been central to the whirlwind questions. But in verse 2, as in verse 6, not all may be as settled as it seems. Many interpreters view Job's overall response in 42:1-6 as elusive or lay-ered with meanings. The Hebrew word *mezimmah*, translated in verse 2 as "purpose" ("no purpose of yours can be thwarted"), is the same word translated as "schemes" in 21:27. *Mezimmah* carries in its connotation a sense of "mischievous" (Psalm 21:11) or even "evil," as is certainly implied in Job's accusatory reply to Zophar (21:27). Verse 2 thus may provide one indicator that Job's earlier defiant mood has not been totally subsumed in resignation. Others see that possi-bility in the ambiguities of Hebrew grammar and meaning in verse 6. "Myself" does not appear in the Hebrew original. As a result, what is despised could refer to "dust in ashes"—as in Job's rejection of these symbols of mourning and humilia-tion. Similar variations on the verb rendered here as "repent" present multiple interpretative possibilities of Job's words and stance.

Job 42:7-9. With verse 7, the Book of Job returns to a prose narrative. Some scholars view the opening two chapters (also written in prose) and this concluding verse of chapter 42 to have been a single older folk tradi-tion of an innocent man who suffers but receives restoration—with the intervening chapters coming from a later period that take up in poetic form the underlying questions of innocent suffering and the mystery of God in such situations. In Job 42:7-9, God addresses one of the three "friends" of Job with words that not once but twice take the three friends to task for not speaking "of me what is right" (42:7, 8). (The absence of the fourth friend—Elihu, whose speech in chapters 33–37 rebukes Job and the other three—is taken by some interpreters as an indication that the Elihu material was added at a later date.) What is even more intrigu-ing about the twofold rebuke of the friends by God is that the likewise twofold statement that they have not spoken what is right "as my servant Job has done." Is this in reference to Job's concluding words in 42:1-6? Or is this in reference to Job's positions all throughout his dispute with his friends: that he has suffered inno-cently? In the end, the restoring of relationship of these three to God is linked not simply to traditional acts of sacrificial offerings but also to the prayers of Job on their behalf (42:8-9).

Job 42:10-17. This final section makes note of the restoration of wealth and family Job receives—and in doing so, perhaps raises more questions than answers. Consider, first of all, the narrator's assessment of the underlying cause for the family's comforting of Job: "for all the evil that the Lord had brought upon him" (42:11). The Hebrew word translated as "evil" carries no ambiguous connotations that might find a softer interpretation. What is casually attributed to God in this verse equals or exceeds any of the protests Job raised in the earlier cycle of speeches and responses. And consider, second, the less than satisfying indication that Job received twice as much as he had before (42:10). Do twice as many children make up for the death of the first children? One final intriguing detail: Verse 15 indicates Job gave his daughters an inheritance along with his sons. Daughters had no such right of inheritance. Does Job simply defy tradition, or has his previous suffering made him more aware of those who were vulnerable—and thus chooses to treat them with empathy as his friends earlier failed to do for him?

Psalm 86. This psalm of lament sandwiches a hymn of praise between two petitions for help in the face of unidentified enemies. Verses 1-7 recount the first cry for God's saving intervention. The desperation of the situation as well as the psalmist's trust in God may be heard in the series of imperative verbs spoken by the psalmist: "incline your ear . . . preserve my life . . . gladden the soul . . . give ear, O Lord, to my prayer" (86:1-4, 6). The cause for the psalmist's confidence in God's power to deliver comes in the hymn of praise in verses 8-13. God's sovereignty above all other powers is celebrated, as is God's steadfast love. It is unclear whether the deliverance attested to in verse 13 remembers past experiences, or the confidence of deliverance in this situation leads the psalmist to frame it in past tense. The concluding cry for help includes in verse 15 the archetypal confession of God's merciful and gracious nature that basically quotes the words spoken by God to Moses in the cloud when he ascended Mount Sinai (Exodus 34:6).

INTERPRETING THE SCRIPTURE

"Now My Eye Sees You"

A series of commercials for a particular cell phone service is predicated on the tagline: "Can you hear me now?" The implication is that with other providers there are places where their users are "out of touch"— whereas the customers of the advertised service can always be heard.

"Can you hear me now?" can also be taken as a double-edged interpretation of the whole of the Book of Job—and particularly its close. Only now, the euphemism in play is not simply hearing, but seeing: "Can you see me now?"

In Job 42:4-5, "can you see me now?" relates to Job's confession that, up until this point (namely, in the wake of the whirlwind speeches), Job has not really "seen" God. "Seen," not in the sense of Moses ascending Mount Sinai to catch a glimpse of the Almighty (Exodus 33:18-23), but "seen" in terms of personal experience of God's presence and working rather than mere hearsay. "Now my eyes see you" declares Job in verse 5. But is this a self-emptying and humiliating acknowledgment by Job of his past failings on this point? Or is this more of an assertion that now Job understands there are no direct answers to his earlier laments and cries for justice? For in those times of suffering, Job's prayers and protests were, in one sense, his asking of God: "Can *you* see me now?" It is quite possible that what Job affirms in "now my eye sees you" (4:5) is the sight revealed in the whirlwind: the mystery of God, who exceeds human comprehension or control, who cannot be reduced to pat theological formulas or easy explanations as to the why of evil and suffering.

Is this a satisfactory conclusion to Job's earlier protestations and God's awe-inducing soliloquy in chapters 38–41? That will depend on the definition of "satisfactory" that the particular reader of or listener to this book will hold. If "satisfactory" implies God provides clear-cut answers to the sort of questions Job has raised regarding innocent suffering, then satisfaction will be only illusory. For God never does address Job's situation, or even broader matters of justice or theodicy (defined as a vindication of God's goodness and justice in the face of the existence of evil). But if "satisfactory" suggests that God's responses are in keeping with rather than denying of the realities of this world and its

all-too-often harsh experiences, then satisfaction may be taken. For when God speaks from the whirlwind, all that is asserted is the inscrutable mystery that God is present in this world even and especially when that presence defies our understanding or grasp. "Now my eye sees you" becomes, in that case, a faith-filled perception of God's sovereignty and grace, even when those assertions are tested to their utmost.

With Friends Like These . . . (Redux)

If this subtitle sounds familiar, it will likely be because it appeared in Interpreting the Scripture just two sessions ago. Then, it introduced a reflection upon the way in which Job's friends were, in truth, no friends at all in terms of any extension of understanding or empathy.

In this session, however, "with friends like these" arises from another relationship that has gone awry: that of the three friends of Job and their relationship with God. In their previous speeches to Job, all three presumed to speak out of knowledge of God and what God purposed in Job's situation. Thus can Eliphaz declare with self-righteous certainty in his arguments beginning in 5:17 that Job should be happy that God is disciplining him: "See, we have searched this out; it is true" (5:27). Or Zophar can impugn guilt with the pious tones of: "Know then that God exacts of you less than your guilt deserves" (11:6b).

"With friends like these . . ." Job could surely lament. But the final lament of "friends like these" does not issue from the mouth of Job, but from the voice of God in 42:7-10. God is angry with such "friends" who would speak on God's behalf, for they do not speak that which is right. Only Job, God confesses, has spoken what is right.

"With friends like these" might easily be taken as an ongoing lament of God in any number of contemporary situations. When those who claim to speak on behalf of God pepper their words and attitudes with hatred of others; when those who claim to speak on behalf of God ignore the cries of poor and vulnerable ones because their ears (and pockets) are filled by the siren songs of the rich and powerful in our time; when those who claim to speak on behalf of God make inane statements in the face of death that impart the rationale of a child's dying to "God wanting another flower in heaven's garden," God might well lament, with friends like these—and you fill in the ending.

At the close of today's passage, God links the restoration of relationship with these three "friends" with their going first to Job and making sacrifice—perhaps the ritual equivalent of making amends. It will be the prayers of Job that restore these friends not simply to him, but to God. Then again, Jesus offers a similar teaching in Matthew 5:23-25. Relationship, friendship, with God does not void relationship with others. Indeed, as both Jesus and God in Job make clear: Keeping covenant with God is evidenced in relationship with others. Or to put the matter in more graphic terms, as in 1 John 4:20: Those who say they love God but hate a brother or sister are liars.

In a New Place

"Eye for eye, tooth for tooth" (Exodus 21:24). In a positive sense, this ancient law and others like it sought to balance offense and punishment, in order to especially avoid feuds so that one retaliation was even greater than the one that preceded it. But in a negative sense, such traditions ultimately prove empty. Or, as some commentators have noted, they ultimately pave the way for a world full of blind and dentured folk.

A similar "arithmetic" is used in the close of Job. Job 42:10 informs that God gave Job twice as much as he had before. As if to underscore that point, verse 12 asserts that God "blessed the latter days of Job more than his beginning," at which point, we find an enumeration of the number of Job's livestock and children. And as if that were not enough, we find the detail in verse 15 that "in all the land there were no women so beautiful as Job's daughters."

All that is well and good.

But in the life of Job, and in our own experience we must ask: Does what gets restored take the place of what has been lost? When it comes to sheep and camels, oxen and donkeys, perhaps the case can be made that things are better. But what of Job's daughters—not the three who were the fairest in all the land, but the three upon whom the house collapsed and they died (1:18-19). Do three more make up for it; do they take their place?

Job is in a new place from where the story began. What accounts for the difference is not that he has more "stuff" at the end, but that he has endured suffering and accusation— and in his lament and in his silence, Job has come to see God. Perhaps that is why he can pray for the three friends. Perhaps that is how this story can be an encouragement to us in our times of testing. For when we can stand with Job in awe and in hope before God, we find the means to stand in community with and prayer for others.

SHARING THE SCRIPTURE

PREPARING TO TEACH

Preparing Our Hearts

Meditate on this week's devotional reading from Galatians 1:11-19. Throughout the book that bears his name, Job tried to defend himself against false allegations. What comparisons can you draw between Job and Paul, based on verses 11-19? What has God called you to do? How are you relying on God to fulfill this calling?

Pray that you and the students will recognize and proclaim the revelations of Jesus that you have discerned.

Preparing Our Minds

Study the background Scripture from Job 42 and Psalm 86. The lesson Scripture is from Job 42:1-10.

Consider this question as you prepare the lesson: *Where can people find answers to life's ultimate questions?*

Write on newsprint:

❏ information for next week's lesson, found under "Continue the Journey."
❏ activities for further spiritual growth in "Continue the Journey."

Review the "Introduction," "The Big Picture," "Close-up," and "Faith in Action," which all precede the first lesson of this quarter. Consider how you might use any of this material in today's lesson.

LEADING THE CLASS

(1) Gather to Learn

❖ Greet the class members and introduce guests.
❖ Pray that those who have come today will recognize that God can do all things.
❖ Read this quotation from Erwin W. Lutzer (1941–): "**Whenever we are faced with a crucial decision, our generation has been taught to ask, What's in it for me? Will it give me pleasure? Profit? Security? Fulfillment? We are not necessarily opposed to God; we just fit him in wherever he is able to help us. The idea that our wills should be subject to his control, even when our personal ambitions are at stake, is not easy to accept. We can assent mentally to God's control, but in practice, we might still spend our lives pleasing ourselves.**"
❖ Invite the adults to ponder these questions: **When you are faced with a major decision, who do you allow to control the final outcome? Why do you put your trust here?**
❖ Read aloud today's focus statement: **People often wonder who or what controls the final outcomes in life's many challenges. Where can people find answers to life's ultimate questions? Job declares that God can do all things and ultimately will prevail over all obstacles, restoring the fortunes of those who are faithful; and the psalmist illustrates**

how God's people can pray that God will be gracious to them and preserve their lives.

(2) Goal 1: Explore the Satisfactory Conclusion of Job and God's Conversation

❖ Recall with the class that during the first three weeks of the second unit, we have seen that Job's so-called friends attributed his suffering and punishment to his sin. In contrast, Job insisted that this suffering was morally wrong because he had done nothing to deserve such treatment from God. Job wanted to present his case directly to God. In today's session we hear Job's reaction to God's response to him out of the whirlwind in chapters 38–41. Point out that these chapters are filled with questions that God asks Job, as opposed to God's answers to Job's questions.

❖ Select three volunteers to read the words of Job (42:2-6), the words of the Lord (42:7b-8), and the words of the narrator (42:1, 7a, 9-10) from Job 42:1-10.

❖ Discuss these questions:
1. Based on Job's response to God in verses 1-6, what lessons would you say he has learned?
2. Why is the Lord so angry with Job's friends?
3. Verse 9 records that, as God commanded, Job prayed for his friends and God accepted his prayer. This prayer is not recorded. What do you suppose Job might have said to prompt God not to deal with the friends "according to [their] folly" (42:8)?
4. The story of Job is often seen as a challenge to the view of

Wisdom Literature, which claims that the good are rewarded and the evil are punished. Job loses everything, but according to verse 10 God restores what has been lost and does so twofold. Read the final two paragraphs of "In a New Place" in Interpreting the Scripture and ask: **How do you interpret the ending of this story?**

(3) Goal 2: Affirm that God Will Answer the Learners' Questions in Ways that Are Best for Them

❖ Read or retell "'Now My Eye Sees You'" in Interpreting the Scripture.

❖ Note that God never really answered Job's questions and ask:
1. **How do you respond when something occurs that prompts you to demand answers of God and those answers do not seem to be forthcoming?**
2. **What props up your faith when God does not seem to be responding?**
3. **Where do you find assurance that God is acting in your best interest?**

❖ Form several small groups. Read this unfinished story and invite the adults to talk through ideas to complete it:

The Taylors had attended a family reunion in another state. They were on their way home when a terrible accident occurred, killing all four family members. At the viewing, which you attended out of respect for these friends who belonged to your church, one of Mr. Taylor's cousins buttonholed you. He wanted to know why God had allowed such a vibrant, giving family to be snuffed out—and how the rest of the Taylor family could ever hope to recover from such a tragedy.

❖ Bring the groups together to hear their ideas.

(4) Goal 3: Become Involved in an Active and Hopeful Prayer Life

❖ Turn to this quarter's "Faith in Action: Finding Hope." Use this activity as suggested.

❖ Follow up the activity with these questions:

1. **What other psalms can serve as model prayers for those who seek hope?** (Invite participants to page through their Bibles to locate psalms that speak to them.)

2. **Who can I enlist as a prayer partner to help me strengthen my prayer life? How will I be accountable to this person?**

(5) Continue the Journey

❖ Pray that as the learners depart they will "see" God in their own way and recognize that God's presence may be found in even the most difficult of circumstances.

❖ Post information for next week's session on newsprint for the students to copy:

■ **Title: God's Divine Glory Returns**

■ **Background Scripture: Ezekiel 40:1–43:12**

■ **Lesson Scripture: Ezekiel 43:1-12**

■ **Focus of the Lesson: People look for a place where**

they can experience some sense of release and orderliness, away from the chaos that sometimes surrounds us. Where can such a place be found? Ezekiel's vision, given to him by God, revealed to the Israelites that God's calming presence and merciful glory could be felt in sacred places where God is truly worshiped.

❖ Challenge the adults to grow spiritually by completing one or more of these activities related to this week's session, which you have posted on newsprint for the students to copy.

(1) **Identify someone who may have reasons to feel despondent. Pray that he or she will find hope in God. Do whatever you can to support and encourage this person.**

(2) **Research biblical instances of people "seeing" God in Exodus 24:9-18 and 33:12-23. Ponder how the people involved may have been changed by their encounter with God. Compare these events with Job's report of seeing God in 42:5.**

(3) **Recall the words to Edward Mote's nineteenth-century hymn "My Hope Is Built." Consider how this hope brings you peace even in life's storms.**

❖ Sing or read aloud "Sweet Hour of Prayer."

❖ Conclude today's session by leading the class in this hope-filled benediction from Psalm 55:16, which is the key verse for October 19: **I call upon God, and the Lord will save me.**

UNIT 3: VISIONS OF GRANDEUR
God's Divine Glory Returns

PREVIEWING THE LESSON

Lesson Scripture: Ezekiel 43:1-12
Background Scripture: Ezekiel 40:1–43:12
Key Verses: Ezekiel 43:4-5

Focus of the Lesson:
People look for a place where they can experience some sense of release and orderliness, away from the chaos that sometimes surrounds them. Where can such a place be found? Ezekiel's vision, given to him by God, revealed to the Israelites that God's calming presence and merciful glory could be felt in sacred places where God is truly worshiped.

Goals for the Learners:
(1) to comprehend the vision of God's holy and merciful glory in the temple.
(2) to associate a sense of holiness of place with the presence and mercy of God.
(3) to grow in respect for the sacredness of worship settings.

Pronunciation Guide:
Chebar (kee´ bahr)   Torah (toh´ ruh)
Tel Abib (tel uh beeb´)

Supplies:
Bibles, newsprint and marker, paper and pencils, hymnals, pictures of sacred spaces

---

READING THE SCRIPTURE

NRSV
Lesson Scripture: Ezekiel 43:1-12
¹Then he brought me to the gate, the gate facing east. ²And there, the glory of the God of Israel was coming

CEB
Lesson Scripture: Ezekiel 43:1-12
¹Then he led me to the East Gate, ²where the glory of Israel's God was coming in from the east. Its sound

---
102

from the east; the sound was like the sound of mighty waters; and the earth shone with his glory. ³The vision I saw was like the vision that I had seen when he came to destroy the city, and like the vision that I had seen by the river Chebar; and I fell upon my face. **⁴As the glory of the Lord entered the temple by the gate facing east, ⁵the spirit lifted me up, and brought me into the inner court; and the glory of the Lord filled the temple.**

⁶While the man was standing beside me, I heard someone speaking to me out of the temple. ⁷He said to me: Mortal, this is the place of my throne and the place for the soles of my feet, where I will reside among the people of Israel forever. The house of Israel shall no more defile my holy name, neither they nor their kings, by their whoring, and by the corpses of their kings at their death. ⁸When they placed their threshold by my threshold and their doorposts beside my doorposts, with only a wall between me and them, they were defiling my holy name by their abominations that they committed; therefore I have consumed them in my anger. ⁹Now let them put away their idolatry and the corpses of their kings far from me, and I will reside among them forever. ¹⁰As for you, mortal, describe the temple to the house of Israel, and let them measure the pattern; and let them be ashamed of their iniquities. ¹¹When they are ashamed of all that they have done, make known to them the plan of the temple, its arrangement, its exits and its entrances, and its whole form—all its ordinances and its entire plan and all its laws; and write it down in their sight, so that they may observe and follow the entire plan and all its ordinances. ¹²This is the law of the temple: the whole territory

was like the sound of a mighty flood, and the earth was lit up with his glory. ³What appeared when I looked was like what I had seen when he came to destroy the city, and also like what I saw at the Chebar River, and I fell on my face. **⁴Then the Lord's glory came into the temple by way of the East Gate. ⁵A wind picked me up and brought me to the inner courtyard, and there the Lord's glory filled the temple.** ⁶A man was standing next to me, but the voice that I heard came from inside the temple. ⁷He said to me, Human one, this is the place for my throne and the place for the soles of my feet, where I will dwell among the Israelites forever. The house of Israel will never again defile my holy name, neither they nor their kings, with their disloyalties and with their kings' corpses at the shrines. ⁸When they set their plazas with mine and their doorposts next to mine, the wall was between us. They defiled my holy name with their detestable practices, so I consumed them in my anger. ⁹Now let them remove their disloyalties and their kings' corpses from me, and I will dwell among them forever.

¹⁰You, human one, describe the temple to the house of Israel. Let them be humiliated because of their guilt when they think about its design. ¹¹When they feel humiliated by all that they have done, make known to them the shape of the temple and its adornment, its exits and its entrances, its entire plan and all of its regulations. Write them down in their sight so that they may observe all of its entire plan and all its regulations and perform them.

¹²These are the instructions for the temple: the top of the mountain, as well as its boundaries all around, are

on the top of the mountain all around shall be most holy. This is the law of the temple.

most holy. These are the instructions for the temple.

UNDERSTANDING THE SCRIPTURE

Introduction. Four of this unit's five "visions of grandeur" draw their passages from the Book of Ezekiel. In his first chapter, Ezekiel's chariot vision of "a wheel within a wheel" (1:16) envisioned the mobility of God—a mobility demonstrated in a later vision of God's glory leaving the Jerusalem Temple prior to its destruction by the Babylonian armies (chapters 10–11). But neither of those visions is taken up in this session and the three that follow. Rather, the grand vision at center stage in these studies concerns the restored temple that forms the basis of the exiles' hope. Ezekiel 40–47 depicts hope in meticulous if not exhaustive details of sacred spaces of the envisioned temple and its environs.

Ezekiel 40:1-47. Chapter 1 had opened with a dating reference that placed its opening vision in 593 B.C.—meaning, among other things, that Ezekiel had been among the first group of deportees to Babylon, before the final exile in 587 B.C. Chapter 40 opens with a reference indicating that the prophet had lived in exile for twenty-five years (40:1)—almost an entire generation has passed in captivity. This vision is dated to April 28, 573 B.C. The "hand of the LORD" brings the prophet to a mountaintop location in Israel, where he is met by an unidentified man who holds a cord and a reed, both instruments used for measuring. The description in verse 3 of the man as having the appearance of bronze parallels the description

of the creatures in the chariot vision (1:7), making it clear the individual is some type of heavenly being. His role in this passage and beyond is to guide Ezekiel in a "tour" of the temple's exterior and interior. The first explorations are of the gates that separate the outer and inner courts. City gates were places where judgments were rendered as well as where access to the city was gained. Similarly, temple gates served as access points to the settings and rituals that took place within. The measuring of the temple gates and all their trappings underscores the significance of starting with the places of entry into holy space.

Ezekiel 40:48–42:20. With 40:48, the vision and "guided tour" move into the temple building per se. "Vestibule" (40:48) is more literally translated as "porch." "Nave" (41:1) is another older term that corresponds to what would be the "sanctuary" in a church. Interestingly, "nave" is a word that grows out of Christian architectural traditions, where the sanctuary was conceived as a "boat" (*navis* being the Latin derivative of "navy"). The "inner room" (41:3), which Ezekiel himself does not enter, is identified as the "most holy place" in 41:4 (the same word is used in 43:12, and references what is otherwise termed the "holy of holies," which only the high priest could enter on limited occasions). The remaining material in chapters 41–42 consists almost entirely of itemized descriptions of temple areas and furnishings that are often accompanied by *mostly* precise measurements. "Mostly" reflects the fact that almost all the measurements are length and width—but rarely are heights given. This has led some scholars to conclude that chapters 40–48 are not architectural blueprints for construction purposes, but a "vision and an ideal society."

Ezekiel 43:1-5. The detail of the gate facing east has two important undertones. First, from Jerusalem, Babylon would have been to the east. The image suggests that the God who accompanied the people of Israel into exile will return to the temple mount. Another possibility—or does this text partly account for its development?—is that the so-called Golden Gate that leads into the temple from the east is held by Judaism to be the gate through which the Messiah will enter Jerusalem. The association of sound and light with God's "glory" in verse 3a parallels details used earlier to depict the chariot vision (1:24). Chebar (43:3) provides the setting of Ezekiel's first vision (1:1). Chebar was a river or canal by the village of Tel-Abib, where apparently Ezekiel and other of the original exiles had been settled (3:15). "Glory of the Lord" references God's holy presence. In the Exodus narratives, "glory of the Lord" appears not only as an expression of God's presence but also as a metaphor for the cloud that led Israel by day (Exodus 16:10), the fire on the mountain (Exodus 24:17), and even for the gift of manna (Exodus 16:4-7). Thus, already in the stories of Exodus, as in the hopes of Ezekiel, the revealing of God's glory was for the sake of leading the people.

Ezekiel 43:6-9. The King James Version translates the word rendered in verse 7 of the NRSV by "mortal" as "Son of man." "Son of Man" is used many times in Ezekiel in reference to the prophet, while the phrase in Daniel 8:17 refers cryptically to a messianic figure. "Son of Man" serves as Jesus' most frequent self-reference in the Synoptic Gospels. The hope in verse 7a (repeated in verse 9b) that God will "reside among the people of Israel forever" bears close ties in phrase and meaning to the hope affirmed by Revelation 21:3 of God's dwelling among mortals. "Whoring" may reference past idolatry (Jeremiah 10:1-11) and/or pursuing foreign alliances rather than trusting in God (Isaiah 31:1-3), both of which are understood in the Prophets as what led to God's judgment of exile.

Ezekiel 43:10-12. The "missional" character of Ezekiel's vision is now revealed. The prophet is to share what he has seen, for the sake of bringing transformation to the exiles. The purpose of all the previous (and impending) details regarding the temple is linked to an "orderliness" of life and liturgy to be followed by the exiles. In verse 12, this connection is made even more explicit by the twofold statement: This is the law (*torah*) of the temple. *Torah* refers not simply to the first five books of the Hebrew Bible but to the way covenant is kept. And at the heart of Ezekiel's covenant renewal, as at the heart of verse 12, is the "most holy" that encompasses the whole temple mount, that is, the glory of God's presence. Such presence makes possible not only sacred encounter but also covenantal living.

INTERPRETING THE SCRIPTURE

"Mine Eyes Have Seen the Glory"

Julia Ward Howe wrote the famous words of the heading as the opening line for "The Battle Hymn of the Republic." Her lyrics mingled imagery of the Last Judgment with what she saw at stake in the American Civil War. She later wrote that the lyrics came to her during the night, and that she wrote them down early the next morning. Thus the "vision" in her opening line was that she has "seen the glory of the coming of the Lord."

"Mine eyes have seen the glory of the coming of the Lord" could also be applicable to the temple vision of Ezekiel. Only in Ezekiel's case, the coming was a homecoming—God's return from exile and reentry into the temple.

It must be remembered that what Ezekiel writes is a vision. At the time of its writing, long before the return from exile and even longer before the rebuilding of the Temple in Jerusalem, there was no temple standing in Israel. But what Ezekiel "sees" is the promise and hope of return—not only of God to the temple one day but also of the exiles to their long-lost homeland. The title of the unit begun in this session sets the tone for Ezekiel's words: "Visions of Grandeur." Grandeur" can mean "magnificence" or "something very impressive and amazing." Ezekiel's vision qualifies, and not simply because it is a vision of things not yet in place. More striking, the grandeur of Ezekiel's vision is its stark contrast to the exiles' present experience: twenty-five years, and hundreds of miles,

removed from the land and its now destroyed Temple. Grandeur is not always easy to accept. How in the world was return possible, at such a distance of time and space—and while Babylon's empire still firmly held the exiles as subjects?

It is likely that more than a few exiles would have considered Ezekiel's vision as misguided wishful thinking. Indeed, when the time and opportunity eventually did come for return, apparently only a minority, and perhaps a small one at that, returned. Life had grown more comfortable over time in Babylon. The exiles had developed their own contemporary institutions of religious life in captivity. Most notably, it is believed that the synagogue became an institution during this time.

But for exiles like Ezekiel, Babylon was not home—and the core and center of Jewish life and faith remained in the temple. Where Ezekiel had opened his book with God's judgment symbolized in a vision of God's glory taking flight from Jerusalem, now the time of hope is signified by this vision of God's return: "the glory of the LORD entered the temple by the gate facing east . . . and the glory of the LORD filled the temple" (43:4, 5). Ezekiel's eyes had foreseen the glory of the (home)coming of the Lord. The question now became, would the exiles now have hope in their own homecoming?

Holy Place

National Geographic published an article on "Vanishing Languages." Among the examples was a Mexican dialect known as *Seri*, spoken by fewer than one thousand persons. The article gives examples of unusual words or phrases in each such language—and one of the examples for *Seri* was a phrase that literally means "Where is your placenta buried?" Its meaning, dating to ancient traditions of burying a newborn's placenta at his or her place of birth, was "where do you come from?"

Place is an important concept in life. One's place of birth still can have enormous consequences. If you doubt that, read a week's worth of articles on the debate around immigration policies in the United States. *Place* can also become a descriptive term of where one finds vocation (place of work) or home (*I'm going back to my place*). Place figuratively and at times literally expresses our sense of grounding in life.

Ezekiel devotes large amounts of material not only to the details of sacred space regarding the temple but also to a more basic understanding of *place* that is holy. That may be a strange concept to modern ears. We have become so accustomed to "sacred is where you find it" (*I can worship God on the golf course, or on the fishing boat, or in the cathedral of ancient forests*) that we may have lost track of particular places that intentionally evoke remembrances and present experiences of the Holy in life. For Ezekiel, the envisioned temple was such a "place." Indeed, in Ezekiel's presentation, it is God who declares the particularity of sacred place: "Mortal, this is the place of my throne and the place for the soles of my feet" (43:7). We often link the recognition of the sacred as a human act, but here, as in Moses' encounter at the burning bush, it is God who decisively acts to

make a place holy, not because of how such a place looks in terms of architectural style (or the lack thereof), but rather because such a place brings to us encounter with the Holy.

So what is a holy place for you and why? Sanctuaries may have those characteristics. Their furnishings of crosses and candles and windows depicting scenes from the Bible may enhance that sense of sacred, but not necessarily, for in the end, what makes such places holy is the gracious presence of God conveyed through them, a presence often made recognizable by the experiences and stories by which we have come to know that gracious presence in the gift of community, through times of transition, and by the hope to which such places point us. A holy place reveals not only where and from whom we have come but also where and to whom we are headed.

Transformative Worship

Worship is not static but dynamic. That is, the holiness of sanctuaries and other such places in our lives is not only to bring us into holy presence but also to lead us into living lives responsive to the Holy One we encounter.

That is clearly the link Ezekiel points to in today's passage. The prophet's focus there is not simply on the many and varied details of the envisioned temple. As today's passage closes, the emphasis is upon how this holy place ("law of the temple" in verse 12) intends to transform the way Israel conducts its life as well as its liturgies.

Ezekiel's purpose poses a challenge to contemporary worship and worshipers. When we gather, the reason for doing so can never be reduced to "that's what we do on Sundays" or "didn't the preacher have a nice talk today?" When we gather, we stand on holy ground, which, in the context of Ezekiel 43, means to say we open ourselves and our lives to God's presence and transformative purposes. In Ezekiel 43, that opening evoked a call to repentance from what had been done that led to exile (43:11a). Transformative worship still beckons worshipers to make breaks with pasts that are destructive, whether of self or of others. And make no mistake, the prophetic critique of Israel's political and religious leaders (Ezekiel 34:10) and society as a whole (Jeremiah 5:31) means that worship's transformation aims not only at individual hearts but also societal turnings toward that which is just and good, the very qualities of the Holy One in whose presence we gather. For in those turnings, God's transformational presence flows through our worship and out into our lives and into the world.

SHARING THE SCRIPTURE

PREPARING TO TEACH

Preparing Our Hearts

Meditate on this week's devotional reading from Psalm 138. Why does the psalmist give thanks to God? What reasons do you have to be thankful today? The psalmist imagines "all the kings of the earth" (138:4) praising the Lord. Who will you ask to join you in praise of God?

Pray that you and the students will catch a glimpse of the glory of God and give thanks.

Preparing Our Minds

Study the background Scripture from Ezekiel 40:1–43:12 and the lesson Scripture from Ezekiel 43:1-12.

Consider this question as you prepare the lesson: *Where can people find a place to experience some sense of release and orderliness, away from the chaos that sometimes surrounds them?*

Write on newsprint:

❏ information for next week's lesson, found under "Continue the Journey."
❏ activities for further spiritual growth in "Continue the Journey."

Review the "Introduction," "The Big Picture," "Close-up," and "Faith in Action," which all precede the first lesson of this quarter. Consider how you might use any of this material in today's lesson.

Locate pictures of sacred spaces in books or online. If your Sunday school has a picture file, this would also be a good place to check.

Option: Consider holding the session in the church's sanctuary or worship space if no other groups meet there during the Sunday school time and if the class members can easily walk to that space.

LEADING THE CLASS

(1) Gather to Learn

❖ Greet the class members and introduce guests.

❖ Pray that those who have come today will find within the group a place where they can experience rest from the chaos of the world.

❖ Prior to the class, find the lyrics to Ralph Carmichael's hymn "There Is a Quiet Place" (http://www.hymnlyrics.org/requests/there_is_a_quiet_place.php). You can also find this music performed on YouTube. Read the lyrics or play the song. Invite the students to comment on places they go that are "far from the rapid pace" to quiet their minds and spirits. Also comment on why these places are so soothing.

❖ Read aloud today's focus statement: **People look for a place where they can experience some sense of release and orderliness, away from the chaos that sometimes surrounds them. Where can such a place be found? Ezekiel's vision, given to him by God, revealed to the Israelites that God's calming presence and merciful glory could be felt in sacred places where God is truly worshiped.**

(2) Goal 1: Comprehend the Vision of God's Holy and Merciful Glory in the Temple

❖ Distribute paper and pencils prior to reading Ezekiel 43:1-12. Encourage the adults to jot down anything this passage prompts them to see, hear, taste, touch, or smell.

❖ After you read these verses, discuss the sensory responses the adults noted.

❖ Invite the students to imagine themselves as Ezekiel and then ask:

1. **How would this vision, which seemed so very real, have affected you?**

2. **What questions would you have wanted to ask God?**
3. **What would this vision have suggested to you about God's plans for you and the other exiles in Babylon?**
4. **When you described the temple as God had commanded (43:10), how do you think other exiles would have responded?**

❖ Conclude this portion by reading or retelling "Mine Eyes Have Seen the Glory" in Interpreting the Scripture and soliciting questions or comments.

(3) Goal 2: Associate a Sense of Holiness of Place with the Presence and Mercy of God

❖ Read the third and fourth paragraphs of "Holy Place" from Interpreting the Scripture.

❖ As you go around the room, invite each person to complete this sentence: **I am most aware of God's presence when I am in a place that . . .** Encourage each person to answer; the same answer may be used multiple times.

❖ Continue the discussion by inviting the students to comment on things or actions that detract from their sense of God's holiness within a sacred space. For example, some may find that a praise band set up in front of the altar is distracting; others may find ornate art or carvings create a "busy" atmosphere that makes it difficult for them to concentrate. Others may find that a very plain space is too sterile. Remind the students that there are no right or wrong answers here, but people do need to be aware of how a worship setting affects their ability to connect with God and with other worshipers.

(4) Goal 3: Grow in Respect for the Sacredness of Worship Settings

❖ Read or retell "Transformative Worship" in Interpreting the Scripture. Notice that worship in holy space calls us to live as God's holy people.

❖ Read aloud this paragraph: **Whether people worship in a school gymnasium or a grand cathedral, the most important thing about the space, according to Ezekiel's vision, is that God resides in this place, provided the people feel "ashamed of their iniquities" (43:10). In other words, within holy space people feel called to repent. They are not just to feel sorry for what they have done or left undone but should make an honest effort, with God's help, to turn from their sinful ways.**

❖ Provide time for the adults to examine their hearts and silently repent of wrongdoings. If the group is meeting in the sanctuary, invite any who wish to come to the altar rail to pray there.

❖ Conclude with these words of assurance from *The United Methodist Hymnal*: **"If we confess our sins, God is faithful and just and will forgive our sins and cleanse us from all unrighteousness. Thanks be to God."**

(5) Continue the Journey

❖ Pray that as the learners depart they will seek and find sacred spaces where they can renew their relationship with God.

❖ Post information for next week's session on newsprint for the students to copy:
- **Title: The Altar: a Sign of Hope**

- **Background Scripture: Ezekiel 43:10–46:24**
- **Lesson Scripture: Ezekiel 43:13-21**
- **Focus of the Lesson: Sometimes people seek space in which they can find direction for making the most of life. Where can such space be found? The Israelites could hope for release from their iniquities by making sin sacrifices in the sacred space of the altar that stood before the Temple.**

❖ Challenge the adults to grow spiritually by completing one or more of these activities related to this week's session, which you have posted on newsprint for the students to copy.

(1) **Arrive early for worship next week. Walk around the sacred space, noting anything (for example, stained glass windows, carvings, paintings, candles, Bibles) that makes this space holy and God-filled for you.**

(2) **Create in your home a sacred space where you might have a Bible, candles, cross, and other items that are special to you. Regularly spend some time in this space communing with God.**

(3) **Talk with several other Christians about the characteristics of the places where they find God. If possible, interview someone who worships in an ornate church; someone else who worships in a simpler place, such as a clapboard church; and someone else whose**

church meets in a school or commercial building. What similarities and differences did you hear?

❖ Sing or read aloud "God Is Here."

❖ Conclude today's session by leading the class in this hope-filled benediction from Psalm 55:16, which is the key verse for October 19: **I call upon God, and the LORD will save me.**

UNIT 3: VISIONS OF GRANDEUR

THE ALTAR:
A SIGN OF HOPE

PREVIEWING THE LESSON

Lesson Scripture: Ezekiel 43:13-21
Background Scripture: Ezekiel 43:10–46:24
Key Verse: Ezekiel 43:27

Focus of the Lesson:
Sometimes people seek space where they can find direction for making the most of life. Where can such space be found? The Israelites could hope for release from their iniquities by making sin sacrifices in the sacred space of the altar that stood before the Temple.

Goals for the Learners:
(1) to review the instructions Ezekiel received for building a new altar and making offerings.
(2) to reflect on the value of finding personal sacred spaces for atonement and renewal.
(3) to identify and use personal sacred spaces for atonement and renewal.

Pronunciation Guide:
levitical (li vit´ i kuhl)   Zadokite (zay´ duh kite)
Zadok (zay´ dok)

Supplies:
Bibles, newsprint and marker, paper and pencils, hymnals, Bible dictionaries

---

READING THE SCRIPTURE

NRSV
Lesson Scripture: Ezekiel 43:13-21
    13These are the dimensions of the altar by cubits (the cubit being one cubit and a handbreadth): its base shall be one cubit high, and one cubit wide, with a rim of one span around

CEB
Lesson Scripture: Ezekiel 43:13-21
    13These are the dimensions of the altar, according to a twenty-one-inch unit of measure. The base is twenty-one inches high and twenty-one inches wide, with an outer curb measuring

its edge. This shall be the height of the altar: [14]From the base on the ground to the lower ledge, two cubits, with a width of one cubit; and from the smaller ledge to the larger ledge, four cubits, with a width of one cubit; [15]and the altar hearth, four cubits; and from the altar hearth projecting upward, four horns. [16]The altar hearth shall be square, twelve cubits long by twelve wide. [17]The ledge also shall be square, fourteen cubits long by fourteen wide, with a rim around it half a cubit wide, and its surrounding base, one cubit. Its steps shall face east.

[18]Then he said to me: Mortal, thus says the Lord GOD: These are the ordinances for the altar: On the day when it is erected for offering burnt offerings upon it and for dashing blood against it, [19]you shall give to the levitical priests of the family of Zadok, who draw near to me to minister to me, says the Lord GOD, a bull for a sin offering. [20]And you shall take some of its blood, and put it on the four horns of the altar, and on the four corners of the ledge, and upon the rim all around; thus you shall purify it and make atonement for it. [21]You shall also take the bull of the sin offering, and it shall be burnt in the appointed place belonging to the temple, outside the sacred area.

Key Verse: Ezekiel 43:27

[27]**When these days are over, then from the eighth day onward the priests shall offer upon the altar your burnt offerings and your offerings of well-being; and I will accept you, says the Lord GOD.**

one and a half inches all around. This is the altar's height. [14]From the base at ground level to the lower ledge is forty-two inches; the lower ledge is twenty-one inches wide. The distance from the lower to the upper ledge is seven feet; the upper ledge is twenty-one inches wide. [15]The hearth is seven feet high, with four horns projecting upward from the hearth. [16]The hearth is twenty-one feet square; each side is equal to the others. [17]The ledge around the hearth is twenty-four and a half feet long by twenty-four and a half feet wide, a square. Its outer rim is ten and a half inches, and its base all around is twenty-one inches. Its ramp faces east.

[18]He said to me, Human one, the LORD God proclaims: These are the regulations established for the altar on the day when it is prepared for making entirely burned offerings and dashing blood on it. [19]You will provide a young bull as a purification offering to the levitical priests who are descendants of Zadok, the ones who may draw near to minster to me. This is what the LORD God says. [20]You will take some of its blood and set it on the four horns of the altar and on the four sides of the ledge and on the curb all around. So you will purify it and purge it. [21]Then you will take the bull selected as the purification offering, and the priests will burn it in a designated place of the temple outside of the sanctuary.

Key Verse: Ezekiel 43:27

[27]**When the seven days are completed, the priests will offer your entirely burned offerings and your well-being sacrifices on the altar from the eighth day on, and I will accept you with pleasure. This is what the LORD God says.**

UNDERSTANDING THE SCRIPTURE

Introduction. Today's Scripture passage, and the remaining verses in chapter 43 that extend beyond it, are entirely devoted to details about the Temple's altar. While the area known as the Holy of Holies represented the most set apart section of the Temple where the very presence of God was said to reside, the altar serves as the Temple's primary intersection for divine/human encounter. "Altar" translates a Hebrew word whose root word means "to slaughter or kill for sacrifice." Although the Holy of Holies was only to be entered once a year, and then only by the high priest, sacrifices took place at the altar on a daily basis. Thus, the altar served as the most regular place of liturgy for the sake of sacrifice offered for sin or other acts of restoration and healing.

Ezekiel 43:10-12. Please refer to the commentary on these verses in the previous session.

Ezekiel 43:13-17. All these verses consist entirely of detailed measurements of the dimensions of the altar. Verse 13 clarifies that the length of the cubit used in this section is "a cubit and a handbreath." Two types of cubits (the cubit is thought to have derived from the length between the elbow and the fingertips) existed in ancient measurements. Ezekiel references here the "long" cubit (estimated at 20.5 inches, or seven handbreadths), while the normal cubit was approximately 17.7 inches, or 6 handbreadths). The other measurement that appears in verse 13 is a "span," which approximates the distance (about 8.75 inches) between the thumb and the little finger of a hand spread out. While Ezekiel elsewhere in his final four chapters pays little attention to matters of height, here he is explicit on the height of the altar (43:13b and following). The exact role played by the animal horns on the altar is unknown. Horns were a symbol of power—and 1 Kings 2:28-34 recalls the tradition that they afforded some measure of safety or asylum. In this particular story, that tradition was not honored.

Ezekiel 43:18-27. Once again addressing the prophet as "Mortal" (or "Son of Man"; see last week's comments on Ezekiel 43:6-9), Ezekiel's "guide" (40:3-4) now gives the prophet instruction on how the consecration is to take place in a week-long ritual. The mention in verse 19 of the role of the priests of the "family of Zadok" sets up a later contrast with the levitical priests, beginning in 44:10. Unblemished animals (goats, bulls, and rams) are to be used for these sacrifices.

Ezekiel 44:1-31. The east gate of the temple had earlier (11:1) been the setting of Ezekiel's vision of Jerusalem that culminates in the "glory of the LORD" departing Israel (11:23). In 43:1-2, the east gate had been the setting for Ezekiel's vision that the "glory of God of Israel was coming from the east." That return explains the declaration in 44:2 that the east gate is to remain shut. Verse 3 does allow for a slight exception. A figure identified only as "the prince" (see also 46:16-18) is allowed to sit and eat "in" the gate, but apparently not even he can go through it. Exactly who Ezekiel has in mind with this prince is unknown. The symbolism of the closed east gate may be seen in contemporary Jerusalem, where the east-facing Golden Gate remains walled up since the sixteenth century. In other Jewish tradition, this gate is also the place where the Messiah is expected to enter the city. Some commentators also see the shutting of that gate as a rejection of a ritual used in the Babylonian observance of New Year that included a ritual opening of a gate otherwise closed throughout the rest of the year. Verses 4-9 outline those who are to be excluded from admission to the temple, particularly foreigners. Ezekiel somewhat tempers this language by speaking of those excluded as "uncircumcised in heart and flesh" (perhaps leaving the door cracked open for foreigners whose heart is in the right place, as the "Godfearers" of New Testament times). The language is hard, and may have been one of the "proof texts" for exclusionary attitudes and practices that marked the postexilic community upon return to the land. The remaining two-thirds of Ezekiel 44 is given over to an extended distinction between the priestly Levites who "went astray" (44:10) and the levitical priests descended from Zadok (a high priest in the time of David and later Solomon) who kept faith (44:15). The Levites are assigned more ordinary work, while the Zadokites are charged with higher duties. The historical origin of these divisions between Levites and Zadokites is sketchy at best.

Ezekiel 45:1–46:24. The concluding two chapters of today's background Scripture contain a variety of instructions regarding marking off territory outside the Temple in order to protect sacred space (45:1-9); weights and measures that are to be used (ostensibly both within and without the Temple, 45:10-12); details regarding the elements used in offerings for both the people of the land and the "prince" (45:13-17); instructions on observing Passover and other festivals including sabbath (45:18–46:15); and further territorial details regarding inheritance (46:16-18) along with places of cooking and eating for the priests who serve at the Temple (46:19-24). While much of this section seems devoid of connection to contemporary life, it is worth noting that woven into these obscure injunctions are clear calls to justice. Ezekiel 45:9 is a strongly worded command to the "princes" to not engage in acts of violence or oppression, but rather to do what is just and right. Its ensuing charge to "cease your evictions of my people" resonates not only with 46:18 but also with contemporary occurrences where persons (or institutions) of wealth and power evict those without means at the moment to secure themselves. The section on weights and measures (45:10) is prefaced that these are to be "honest"—that is, not "weighted" in favor of those who have the upper hand (see Leviticus 19:36 and Micah 6:11).

INTERPRETING THE SCRIPTURE

Sizing It Up

Cubits and handbreadths and spans. Does that sound a little like "lions and tigers and bears. Oh my!"? On first reading of this passage, and in particular its opening five verses, it might seem we are so far from connection from contemporary faith and its practices as to be in as strange a land as Oz was to Dorothy.

But in with the minutia of measurement details, there is something going on here as Ezekiel "sizes up" the altar of God—as he has done in previous chapters and will do again in chapter 47.

Part of what lies beneath the surface of his measurements are the very standards used. Cubits and handbreadths and spans might seem distant, but do you know where they originate? The human body. Cubits roughly corresponded to the length of an adult's forearm. Handbreadths are basically equivalent to, well, the width of a hand. And spans? Hold your hand out and stretch out your fingers: the distance between the tip of your thumb and the tip of your little finger is a span.

So to begin with, Ezekiel does not use scientific exactitudes that can be calibrated down to the thousandth of an inch. He describes the temple using terms that are, literally, corporal—bodily. The temple's dimensions are not an obscure mathematical equation related to the value of *pi*: They are seen, even as they are experienced, by the human senses.

Second, when Ezekiel sizes up the altar using these numbers and measures, it is something like the way any one of us might "measure" a child or a spouse. That is, we could close our eyes and, by the touch of our hands, recognize the dimensions of face, the rounding of shoulders, and the feel of hands that are intimately related to our own. Ezekiel describes what he knows . . . what he loves . . . what he hopes.

Scholars tell us, and correctly so, that Ezekiel's precision on the measurements is to ensure in such careful ways the setting apart of a holy place unlike any other. But Ezekiel's devotion to those numbers is not abstract. The measurements of the holy place are given with such care and detail as to reveal Ezekiel's devotion to the One to be encountered there—the One who is the hope of his people in exile.

By what measures, through what stories, might we "size up" the holy place(s) in our lives? Where have we experienced, as Ezekiel before us, the place where God's voice thunderously whispers: "I will accept you" (Ezekiel 43:27, today's key verse)?

*What Transforms Space
into Sacred Place*

The second parish I served had recently completed a major building renovation before I arrived. A new office and education wing had been added. In the euphoria of the finished task, along with the way the project had fused the congregation together, it was determined that another Building Committee venture should be started to chart out the next building plan. The committee was formed, and it invited a minister in our conference well acquainted with building projects and, in particular, the fundraising programs that accompany them. My respect for John multiplied when the sole issue he pressed—and impressed upon—the committee was not "tell me what you want to build" but "tell me what you want to *do*." That is, what purpose will be served and what work will be made possible by whatever edifice gets constructed? Or, as I recall him directly saying to us, form follows function, not the other way around. Because there was really no clearly identified purpose for such expansion beyond "Wasn't it exhilarating when the annex was getting built?" the committee ended up disbanding with no new proposal.

I take this experience as a parable of sorts for the issue that forms this section's title, an issue that arises out of Ezekiel 43. What makes ordinary space into sacred place? You might think with all the emphasis Ezekiel places upon measurements and exhaustive descriptions, that everything has to do with precision of appearances and "building codes." But in Ezekiel 43:18-21, the prophet reveals that even those carefully laid plans need something more. In the immediate context he addresses, the "more" comes in a ritual for consecrating the new altar. And beyond that the reason for consecrating the altar is not simply that it be a sacred space, but rather that it be a place where sacred acts take place: namely, the rituals related to sin offerings and experiences of restoration. For what makes a place sacred, to return to my minister mentor John, is that form follows function. The holiest looking of places, whether churches or retreat sites or personal prayer closets, will not be a holy "form" unless what takes place there engages holy "function" of encounter with God.

The purpose of Ezekiel's vision of a restored temple was not to construct a grand but sterile monument to the past, but rather a living entryway into the promised future. The carefulness of Ezekiel's details of the temple's form simply yet profoundly express his grasping of the truth of its restorative function: the restoration of people to God, the restoration of people to home, the restoration of people to one another. Such are the functions of the forgiveness and grace that constitute the foundations of this temple—and of any sacred place we might hope to construct today.

Constructing Sacred Places Today

The temple Ezekiel envisioned, and in particular its altar, signified a place where sacrifices were made (remembering that in Hebrew, the word for altar derives from a root that literally means "slaughter"). The function of those sacrifices was essentially the restoration of relationship—with God, with others, and in the hope of Ezekiel with the land (the place where one dwells).

Clearly, Christian and Jewish faith and practice no longer engage in blood sacrifice. But that does not mean we no longer stand in need of seeking, or extending, restoration—which is to say, we still benefit from sacred places that continue to serve as the setting for that function in our lives and spiritual journey today. Communally, our places of worship often serve as the settings where we engage in restorative worship and community life. The way we furnish those setting intends to provide us with symbols and images that point to the promise and experience of restoration. Recall for a moment everything that is inside of your church's worship space. What purpose does each of those items serve in communicating or enabling the restorative work your congregation regularly observes in your liturgy?

A church's sanctuary need not, and in fact should not, be the sole "sacred place" in your practice of faith where the restorative nature of God's love and Christ's grace and Spirit's power is encountered. Is there a place, or a time, that you set aside in your daily routine for encounter with the Holy: for prayer, for some practice of a spiritual discipline, for simply pausing and taking note of the holiness of life all around . . . and within? In other words, where and when are your "altars": places not of slaughter, but rather places of holy encounter, where you find relationship with God and others and even your "place" in life renewed and refreshed with the gift of God's presence and the hope of God's enduring companioning of your life?

SHARING THE SCRIPTURE

PREPARING TO TEACH

Preparing Our Hearts

Meditate on this week's devotional reading from Psalm 130:1–131:3. What relationship do you see between the lament of Psalm 130 that cries to God for help and the prayer of trust in Psalm 131? What are you waiting for God to do in your life at this moment? How do your actions and attitudes reflect your trust in God?

Pray that you and the students will worship God in a spirit of trust that God will care for you.

Preparing Our Minds

Study the background Scripture from Ezekiel 43:10–46:24 and the lesson Scripture from Ezekiel 43:13-21.

Consider this question as you prepare the lesson: *Where can people find space for making the most of life?*

Write on newsprint:
❏ list of words for "Review the Instructions Ezekiel Received for Building a New Altar and Making Offerings."
❏ information for next week's lesson, found under "Continue the Journey."
❏ activities for further spiritual growth in "Continue the Journey."

Review the "Introduction," "The Big Picture," "Close-up," and "Faith in Action," which all precede the first lesson of this quarter. Consider how you might use any of this material in today's lesson.

Gather several Bible dictionaries to bring to class.

LEADING THE CLASS

(1) Gather to Learn

❖ Greet the class members and introduce guests.

❖ Pray that those who have come today will find in your classroom a sacred space where they can encounter God.

❖ Read this information: **A survey conducted by the National Association of Realtors of home buyers' preferences in 2013 revealed that although geography and the age and relationships of purchasers were influential, certain spaces were highly valued by a substantial number of buyers. For example, 78 percent of buyers chose a home with a garage. Other important features included central air-conditioning, a walk-in closet in the master bedroom, and an en suite master bathroom. Basements and in-law suites were also in demand, as were laundry rooms and** rooms that could be used as a study/home office/library.

❖ Ask: **How does having or not having a particular space that you value influence how you live?**

❖ Read aloud today's focus statement: **Sometimes people seek space where they can find direction for making the most of life. Where can such space be found? The Israelites could hope for release from their iniquities by making sin sacrifices in the sacred space of the altar that stood before the Temple.**

(2) Goal 1: Review the Instructions Ezekiel Received for Building a New Altar and Making Offerings

❖ Retell "Sizing It Up" in Interpreting the Scripture to help the students understand what the measurements mean.

❖ Select a volunteer to read Ezekiel 43:13-21.

❖ Form several groups and give each one a dictionary. Post this list of words that you wrote on newsprint prior to the session. Assign each group at least one of these words: *atonement, horns of the altar, levitical priests (or Levites), Zadok.*

❖ Reunite the class and ask a speaker for each group to discuss its assigned word.

❖ Ask: **How does greater familiarity with these words enable you to better envision the altar itself and what went on there?**

(3) Goal 2: Reflect on the Value of Finding Personal Sacred Spaces for Atonement and Renewal

❖ Read aloud the following:
• Imagine yourself standing before the altar that Ezekiel

envisioned. What are you seeing, hearing, or smelling? (Pause)
• What emotions well up in you as you envision the priests burning the sacrifice and smearing its blood on the altar as God directed? (Pause)
• How do you understand the idea of the sacrifice to "make atonement" for the altar (43:20)? (Pause)

❖ Invite the participants to comment on any insights they had as they did this visioning activity.

❖ Encourage the adults to name silently a sacred space where they can find assurance of Christ's atoning sacrifice on their behalf. Break the silence with these words: **Thanks be to you, O God, for spaces in our lives where we can feel your loving, saving presence in unmistakable ways.**

(4) Goal 3: Identify and Use Personal Sacred Spaces for Atonement and Renewal

❖ Read this information from "Moving Prayers" by Emily Snell, which appeared in the July/August 2013 edition of *Interpreter:* **Some people have found that they can create meaningful time with God as they exercise in particular spaces. Professor emeritus of spiritual formation at Garrett-Evangelical Theological Seminary, the Reverend Dwight Judy, used his time while jogging and walking to pray and intercede for others. He knew of a woman who led nature walks that included time for participants to stop at times to appreciate what was around them, and even write a poem. Judy also reports that some swimmers say the Jesus prayer or another prayer phrase** as they do their laps. Another man takes breaks from his regular walk to read and meditate on a psalm. Judy believes that any movement that prompts us to "pause from our very busy lives . . . and (get) back in touch just with ourselves and with God is good for us."

❖ Form small groups and give each one a sheet of newsprint and marker. Encourage the students to identify spaces where they can pray and renew their spirits. The list may include church, but challenge them to think of places such as a walking path or pool where they can commune with God.

❖ Bring everyone together and ask each group to report on its ideas.

❖ Suggest that each student identify one new space where he or she will try to meet God this week.

(5) Continue the Journey

❖ Pray that as the learners depart, they will feel a sense of hope because they are able to come apart for a time with God.

❖ Post information for next week's session on newsprint for the students to copy:

- Title: A Transforming Stream
- Background Scripture: Ezekiel 47:1, 3-12
- Lesson Scripture: Ezekiel 47:1, 3-12
- Focus of the Lesson: Sometimes people feel as if they are stranded on a high cliff, forced to leap into dangerous and unknown waters. Where can they find what they need to make the plunge? The life-giving water in Ezekiel's vision is a symbol of God's presence and blessings,

which flow from God's sanctuary and are available to the earth and its people.

❖ Challenge the adults to grow spiritually by completing one or more of these activities related to this week's session, which you have posted on newsprint for the students to copy.

(1) Recall that in Romans 12:1 Paul urges his readers to present their bodies as a holy, living sacrifice unto God. What can you do this week to begin to improve the condition of your "sacrifice"—your body—which the apostle also refers to as "a temple of the Holy Spirit" (1 Corinthians 6:19)?

(2) Go to the website of a religious supplier, such as www.Cokesbury.com. Use the word "paraments" to search for cloths that are used to adorn the altar, pulpit, and lectern. Scroll through the pictures. Think about how the changes in the altar cloths across the seasons may affect your worship. Also consider how cloths that are plainer/more ornate or traditional/modern may have a bearing on how you experience God's presence.

(3) Research offerings found, for example, in Leviticus 22 and 23. Compare God's instructions concerning these offerings to the offerings that people in your church bring, particularly in regard to their time, treasure, and talent. What similarities do you note between the

Temple offerings and those given today?

❖ Sing or read aloud "Take My Life, and Let It Be."

❖ Conclude today's session by leading the class in this hope-filled benediction from Psalm 55:16, which is the key verse for October 19: **I call upon God, and the LORD will save me.**

UNIT 3: VISIONS OF GRANDEUR
A Transforming Stream

PREVIEWING THE LESSON

Lesson Scripture: Ezekiel 47:1, 3-12
Background Scripture: Ezekiel 47:1, 3-12
Key Verse: Ezekiel 47:9

Focus of the Lesson:
Sometimes people feel as if they are stranded on a high cliff, forced to leap into dangerous and unknown waters. Where can they find what they need to make the plunge? The life-giving water in Ezekiel's vision is a symbol of God's presence and blessings, which flow from God's sanctuary and are available to the earth and its people.

Goals for the Learners:
(1) to become familiar with Ezekiel's vision of life-giving water.
(2) to appreciate covenant with God as an ever-deepening river of blessings.
(3) to commit to communing with God daily.

Pronunciation Guide:
Arabah (air´ uh buh)　　　　　　En-gedi (en ged´ i)
En-eglaim (en eg´ lay im)

Supplies:
Bibles, newsprint and marker, paper and pencils, hymnals

READING THE SCRIPTURE

NRSV

Lesson Scripture: Ezekiel 47:1, 3-12

¹Then he brought me back to the entrance of the temple; there, water was flowing from below the threshold of the temple toward the east (for the temple faced east); and the water

CEB

Lesson Scripture: Ezekiel 47:1, 3-12

¹When he brought me back to the temple's entrance, I noticed that water was flowing toward the east from under the temple's threshold (the temple faced east). The water was

was flowing down from below the south end of the threshold of the temple, south of the altar.

3Going on eastward with a cord in his hand, the man measured one thousand cubits, and then led me through the water; and it was ankle-deep. 4Again he measured one thousand, and led me through the water; and it was knee-deep. Again he measured one thousand, and led me through the water; and it was up to the waist. 5Again he measured one thousand, and it was a river that I could not cross, for the water had risen; it was deep enough to swim in, a river that could not be crossed. 6He said to me, "Mortal, have you seen this?"

Then he led me back along the bank of the river. 7As I came back, I saw on the bank of the river a great many trees on the one side and on the other. 8He said to me, "This water flows toward the eastern region and goes down into the Arabah; and when it enters the sea, the sea of stagnant waters, the water will become fresh. 9**Wherever the river goes, every living creature that swarms will live, and there will be very many fish, once these waters reach there. It will become fresh; and everything will live where the river goes.** 10People will stand fishing beside the sea from En-gedi to En-eglaim; it will be a place for the spreading of nets; its fish will be of a great many kinds, like the fish of the Great Sea. 11But its swamps and marshes will not become fresh; they are to be left for salt. 12On the banks, on both sides of the river, there will grow all kinds of trees for food. Their leaves will not wither nor their fruit fail, but they will bear fresh fruit every month, because the water for them flows from the sanctuary. Their fruit will be for food, and their leaves for healing."

going out from under the temple's facade toward the south, south of the altar. . . . 3With the line in his hand, the man went out toward the east. When he measured off fifteen hundred feet, he made me cross the water; it was ankle-deep. 4He measured off another fifteen hundred feet and made me cross the water; it was knee-deep. He measured off another fifteen hundred feet and made me cross the water, and it was waist-high. 5When he measured off another fifteen hundred feet, it had become a river that I couldn't cross. The water was high, deep enough for swimming but too high to cross. 6He said to me, "Human one, do you see?" Then he led me back to the edge of the river. 7When I went back, I saw very many trees on both banks of the river. 8He said to me, "These waters go out to the eastern region, flow down the steep slopes, and go into the Dead Sea. When the flowing waters enter the sea, its water becomes fresh. 9**Wherever the river flows, every living thing that moves will thrive. There will be great schools of fish, because when these waters enter the sea, it will be fresh. Wherever the river flows, everything will live.** 10People will stand fishing beside it, from En-gedi to En-eglayim, and it will become a place for spreading nets. It will be like the Mediterranean Sea, having all kinds of fish in it. 11Its marshes and swamps won't be made fresh (they are left for salt), 12but on both banks of the river will grow up all kinds of fruit-bearing trees. Their leaves won't wither, and their fruitfulness won't wane. They will produce fruit in every month, because their water comes from the sanctuary. Their fruit will be for eating, their leaves for healing."

UNDERSTANDING THE SCRIPTURE

Introduction. In the ancient Near East, "waters" served as a powerful metaphor for life. In the regions of the Tigris/Euphrates and the Nile Rivers, the prevalence of water surrounded by desert spoke of life's abundance in the midst of threatening environs, while the rivers' floods each spring provided a metaphor for life's renewal. In the regions of the Middle East devoid of dependable water sources, water in its scarcity offered a potent image of its preciousness. In today's passage addressed to the exiles, Ezekiel envisions a stream flowing from under the threshold of the temple. In their captivity in Babylon, the exilic community faced an empire whose wealth and power were largely attributable to its plentiful source of water. The exiles also faced the obstacle to hope that loomed in the form of expansive deserts stretching between them and their former home. Ezekiel's vision engages those symbolic experiences of water—even as he draws upon the formative imagery of Genesis 2:8-14, where a river flowing out of Eden watered the idyllic garden and watered its abundant trees. Ezekiel's use of water's imagery to affirm the hope of new creation and homecoming reflects other prophetic soundings of this same imagery: Isaiah 35:6 and its anticipation of "streams in the desert," and Joel's even closer parallel hope of a "fountain [that] shall come forth from the house of the Lord" (Joel 4:18).

Ezekiel 47:1. The "he" of "he brought me back" in this verse references the unnamed figure who has guided the prophet throughout the temple vision (40:2-4; 41:1; and so on).

Beginning at 45:10, the vision of the temple had taken a slight detour from emphasis upon its precincts and their measurements to various instructions and liturgical regulations. In 47:1, however, the temple vision resumes its focus on the places of the temple— even as the movement outward in this and succeeding verses prepares the audience for the ensuing expansion of the vision far beyond the temple into the promised restoration of the lands of Israel and the allotment to be made to the tribes (47:13–48:35). The narrative here details the water flowing (or trickling) "toward the east": a direction that may be indicative both of the exile's current location as well as the expectation of from whence God will return to the temple (43:2).

Ezekiel 47:3-5. The narrative continues with Ezekiel's guide proceeding with a cord or line in hand that allows for measurements to be made by it. The length of the cord/line is apparently substantial, for in each case the guide is able to mark off in these verses the length of one thousand cubits. As indicated in the CEB, this equates to approximately fifteen hundred feet—or slightly more than a quarter of a mile. The ensuing coupling of measurements of distance traveled with increasing depth of water is impressive. With each segment of fifteen hundred feet traveled, the depth goes from ankle-deep to knee-deep to waist-deep to deep enough to swim in. There are no accompanying measurements of how wide the stream is at each juncture, although at the end the text does imply growth in width as well ("it was a river that I could not cross").

In either case, in a space of little over a mile, the "trickle" has become "a river that could not be crossed" (47:5).

Ezekiel 47:6-7. Once again addressing the prophet as "Mortal" (in the CEB, "Human one"—perhaps an insinuation that the guide is neither mortal nor human), the guide asks whether Ezekiel has seen this. Clearly, by the prophet's description in verses 3-5, he has seen the expanding stream flowing from beneath the temple. The question seems more of an implicit invitation to the prophet to take his eyes off this already astounding sight and to take in another equally remarkable (and hopeful) one. That change in direction and focus takes explicit form as the guide leads the prophet further along (up?) the bank of the river. "Have you seen this" thus becomes the prelude to the sight of the many trees growing on either side of the river. That in itself would have been an ordinary sight to persons familiar with desert environs. Unbroken stretches of parched wasteland could be broken by meandering lines of thick vegetation and trees that grew up within rooting distance of rivers or even intermittent streams, as in the Jordan Valley (especially in the days when its waters flowed unimpeded by the water diversion projects that have arisen in our times). It would have been a familiar sight to exiles in Babylon, where the waterways of the Tigris and Euphrates and their tributaries would likely have been lined with growth, in stark contrast to the surrounding land that was not irrigated.

Ezekiel 47:8-12. Dominating this portion of the passage is the theme of water that brings life to places otherwise dead and stagnant. The leading example of that comes in verse 8, which depicts the effect of this stream as it brings its waters into the Dead Sea. In a stark image of renewal and restoration, the passage speaks of the result of this flow into the Dead Sea as follows: "the water will become fresh." The word translated as "become fresh" literally means "to heal." The springing forth of life made possible by these waters (47:9) closely parallels in word and theme Genesis 1:20, where the fifth day of creation is ushered in by God's command to "let the waters bring forth swarms of living creatures." Creation and human vocation (Ezekiel 47:10) will be renewed by these waters—as will be the case for the continuing abundance of salt, once the Dead Sea's almost sole attribute. Verse 12 closes this portion of the vision with an affirmation of both the fruitfulness of the trees so watered as well as the healing function of their leaves. That detail of "leaves for healing" appears in a much later vision of hope (Revelation 22:1-5) where trees in the city of God, watered by a stream flowing from the throne of God, will have leaves "for the healing of the nations" (22:2).

INTERPRETING THE SCRIPTURE

The Deepening

Samuel Taylor Coleridge's poem "The Rime of the Ancient Mariner" contains the memorable line: "Water, water, everywhere, nor any drop to drink." The setting is of a ship that has been first blown off-course, and now is stalled without wind in hot weather. The dwindling supply of water is magnified by the presence of water all around that is too salty to drink.

The exiles to whom Ezekiel wrote lived in a land enriched and indeed empowered by the plentiful waters supplied by the Tigris and Euphrates Rivers. "Water, water, everywhere" was their sight, too—but in many ways, it was water that was not theirs to drink. Its control, as their captivity, remained under the authority of the empire.

So when Ezekiel seeks to break the mold of captivity's despair—and its seduction to "go along to get along"— he turns to an alternate water source. To this point, the temple vision has served as a vehicle to convey the hope not only of return to the land but also of return to the liturgy and life centered on the temple. Now Ezekiel lifts up the promise of waters connected to that temple whose very flowing promises the hope of freedom and healing and renewal.

As with all hopes, Ezekiel portrays its beginning in the mere trickling of a stream. Hopes do not typically arise fully formed or irrefutable. Hopes must be first approached with trust more than absolute certainty. But the trickle that is first measured as ankle deep soon rises to the knees. Hope has that transforming effect, in terms of growing expectations and acting in response. By the time hope as in the waters reach the waist, there is a flow and power to hope that energizes and invites risk to step into its current. And then, as hope becomes water too deep to cross, it becomes evident that hope, like these waters, is not ours to conquer, but rather to be carried in and by.

The deepening of Ezekiel's stream that flows from beneath the threshold of the temple serves as a marvelous parable to the way hope can gain momentum and depth as we allow ourselves to step into its flow. In the end, for us as for Ezekiel's exiles, hope becomes that which carries us more than we carry it. Ezekiel's tracing of this irresistible flow to the temple further emphasizes that our deepest hopes originate in God, whose purposes and promises will not be turned away—not by an empire in Babylon, and not by any of its current incarnations. Hope will triumph eventually, because God will triumph inevitably.

Freshening and Healing

Years ago, my son and I fished the Paradise River in Mount Rainier National Park just above where it flows into the Nisqually River. At that time of year, the waters of the Paradise ran crystal clear. The Nisqually, on the other hand, flowed a cloudy milk-tan from the slurry of glacial rocks and powder. When we walked to the mouth of the Paradise, where it flowed into the far larger Nisqually, we saw the results. Extending slightly into the flow of the Nisqually was a small arc of clear water from the Paradise. For a few yards downstream of the arc, the waters of the Nisqually briefly ran lighter above the Paradise before settling back into the milk-tan slurry.

That image I take as one of hope— and about hope—that mirrors something of Ezekiel's promise of waters that would freshen ("heal") the Dead Sea and issue in the growth of trees whose leaves are for healing. Ezekiel's promise of freshening waters rely on an ever-growing stream whose purity and clarity will transform waters that only generate salt and stagnation into waters that stimulate swarms of living creatures.

Does that happen in an instant? Ezekiel gives no time frame. But experience and faith teach us the discipline of time required for hope to take hold and renew what has, for too long, been unhopeful and unviable. I take that struggle and transformation over time not simply to be the norm in life, but the context of Christian mission and discipleship. If we labor to see our hopes in the promises of God come to fulfillment in an instant, we are liable to be disappointed at best. Jesus did not give one sermon, and love and grace suddenly held the upper hand from that point forward. That did not even happen upon the cross. Hope remains a discipline as much as a gift. It is like the clear waters of the Paradise that continually flow into the glacial slurry of the Nisqually. There is not a single moment where that arc of clarity at their intersection goes from nonexistence into clear all the way downstream. In fact, in our lifetime, unless something dramatic happens, the expansion of the arc will always be slow and miniscule.

But I take Ezekiel's promise of waters that freshen and heal to be a long-term vision. The freshening of our lives in spiritual renewal, the healing of our spirits, is not a once-and-for-all event where afterward all is clear. The freshening and healing qualities of God's working in our lives are ongoing—and continually in need of renewal. To me, this is not a laborious cycle of "not there yet"—rather, it is living and serving with the realization that even the stream of grace is "a river that could not be crossed" (47:5). That is, the grace of God and the hope it instills are matters that, in the final word, carry us in their flow far more than we "construct" or control them. Empire, including imperial religion, relies on controlling the waters—and who gets to enjoy them. Prophetic faith and the gospel summon trusting ourselves and the whole of who we are and ever will be into the stream of hope that carries us in ministry and service, in worship and devotion—and eventually, from life through death into new life.

Have You Seen This?

Ezekiel's guide asks him this question when they are about to pivot from the sight of the deepening waters to the sight of those same waters bringing life, freshening stagnant waters, and supporting growth that brings healing.

But let me end these comments by turning the question upon you, the reader: "Have you seen this?" The question is not simply, have you seen what the prophet saw by way of waters and trees? Rather, the question more profoundly is this: Have you seen the hope and call to hopeful living to which this vision calls you in particular?

Have you seen that hope can build momentum in your life, growing from a trickle to an irresistible stream—if only you entrust who you are and who you would become into its flow, and thus into the way you live and speak and act in this world? Have you seen the freshening and healing possibilities of God's presence and hope in your life: freshening those places that have grown stagnant, healing those places that have experienced (or inflicted) hurt? Have you seen the transformative possibilities of trusting such waters as these to bring growth and renewal to your experience of God and to your relationship with others?

Have you seen this? For how you see life will become how you live.

SHARING THE SCRIPTURE

PREPARING TO TEACH

Preparing Our Hearts

Meditate on this week's devotional reading from Psalm 1. What metaphors or word pictures does the psalmist use to draw a sharp contrast between the wicked and the righteous? How does this psalm challenge or assure you? What do you do to show your own delight in God?

Pray that you and the students will choose the life of the righteous.

Preparing Our Minds

Study the background Scripture and the lesson Scripture, which are both from Ezekiel 47:1, 3-12.

Consider this question as you prepare the lesson: *Where can people find what they need to take a leap of faith?*

Write on newsprint:
❏ quotation for "Commit to Communing with God Daily."
❏ information for next week's lesson, found under "Continue the Journey."
❏ activities for further spiritual growth in "Continue the Journey."

Review the "Introduction," "The Big Picture," "Close-up," and "Faith in Action," which all precede the first lesson of this quarter. Consider how you might use any of this material in today's lesson.

Prepare a brief lecture from Understanding the Scripture for "Become Familiar with Ezekiel's Vision of Life-giving Water" to help class members better understand Ezekiel's vision.

LEADING THE CLASS

(1) Gather to Learn

❖ Greet the class members and introduce guests.

❖ Pray that those who have come today will experience the presence of God that will enable them to step out in faith.

❖ Read: **What began as a trip to visit friends in Philadelphia turned into a story of incredible survival. College student Morgan Lake had just begun to cross the 4.3-mile Chesapeake Bay Bridge when she was rear-ended by a tractor-trailer. The force sent her vehicle to the top of the jersey wall, where it teetered before plunging twenty-seven feet into the Bay. Morgan said she was falling for what "felt like an eternity." Once under water she thought she would drown, but she quickly made the decision to remain calm. She was able to unbuckle her seat belt, get out through a shattered window, and swim several hundred feet to a jetty. Airlifted to Shock Trauma Center in Baltimore with** uncertain injuries, Morgan miraculously suffered only "bumps and bruises." She commented that she felt "blessed to be alive."

❖ Ask: **What enables people to fight to survive when they take a literal (or figurative) plunge into dangerous waters?**

❖ Read aloud today's focus statement: **Sometimes people feel like they are stranded on a high cliff, forced to leap into dangerous and unknown waters. Where can they find what they need to make the plunge? The life-giving water in Ezekiel's vision is a symbol of God's presence and blessings, which flow from God's sanctuary and are available to the earth and its people.**

(2) Goal 1: Become Familiar with Ezekiel's Vision of Life-giving Water

❖ Call on a volunteer to read Ezekiel 47:1, 3-12. Post a sheet of newsprint so that as the volunteer is reading, you (or someone you designate) can make a simple sketch showing the rise of the water. Lines that are drawn higher on the page will signify deeper levels of water. Draw a squiggly line for the riverbank and add trees; use a large circle for the sea. Sketch some fish; add swamps and marshes, perhaps delineated with reeds.

❖ Read in unison the key verse, Ezekiel 47:9. Refer to the sketch to point out how the fresh waters of the river spawn and support life.

❖ Help the adults better understand Ezekiel's vision by giving the brief lecture that you have prepared using information from Understanding the Scripture. As an alternative, read "The Deepening" in Interpreting the Scripture.

❖ Conclude by asking: **What** connections do you draw between abundant life and the water of the temple as Ezekiel envisioned it flowing?

(3) Goal 2: Appreciate Covenant with God as an Ever-deepening River of Blessing

❖ Read "Have You Seen This?" from Interpreting the Scripture.

❖ Invite participants to give examples of things they have seen that demonstrate God's power to transform and bless.

❖ Comment that believers are in a covenant relationship with God as a result of their relationship with Jesus Christ. Suggest that half of the class turn to John 4:7-15 and the other half look at John 7:37-39. In both of these passages Jesus speaks about water. After allowing time for students to read silently, ask these questions:

1. **How might Jesus' words about "living water" be interpreted?** (A reader could think literally of "spring water" or metaphorically as "water of life.")

2. **What are the benefits of this water?**

3. **What does Jesus mean when he talks about "rivers of living water" in John 7:38?** (This is a metaphor for the new life that Jesus gives to those who enter into covenant with him.)

4. **What connections can you draw between Jesus' remarks on living water and Ezekiel's vision?**

5. **What connections can you draw between the living water, the life-giving river in Ezekiel's vision, and your own baptism?**

(4) Goal 3: Commit to Communing with God Daily

❖ Post on newsprint and read this quotation from the well-known German Protestant theologian Helmut Thielicke (1908–86): "**Wherever the Son of God goes, the winds of God are blowing, the streams of living water are flowing, and sun of God is smiling.**"

❖ Tell the students to talk with a partner or threesome about this quotation. Note that it speaks of certain things following Jesus on his journey. Invite the groups to talk about ways in which they join Jesus on the journey so as to experience the wind, living water, and smile of God on a daily basis.

❖ Reconvene and challenge the adults to make a commitment to commune with God every day.

(5) Continue the Journey

❖ Pray that as the learners depart they will give thanks for the river of blessings that flows from their relationship with God.

❖ Post information for next week's session on newsprint for the students to copy:

- Title: Transformation Continued
- Background Scripture: Ezekiel 47:13-23; Acts 2:37-47
- Lesson Scripture: Ezekiel 47:13-23
- Focus of the Lesson: Sometimes life leaves people needing a new beginning. What is available to everyone to make that happen? Ezekiel tells us that God

restored Israelites and the aliens among them with an inheritance of new land, signifying a new start. Peter says that God through Jesus Christ can redeem and give those who believe in God a new beginning, with the Temple as a place in which people can gather and support one another.

❖ Challenge the adults to grow spiritually by completing one or more of these activities related to this week's session, which you have posted on newsprint for the students to copy.

    (1) Write three of God's blessings you experience each day this week. Try to end with a total of twenty-one blessings, and give thanks for them.

    (2) Discover some other sacred river images by looking at Joel 3:18; Zechariah 14:8; and Revelation 22:1-5. Consider how these images broaden your understanding of God's ever-increasing bounty of provision.

    (3) Write a prayer, psalm, or litany in which you thank God for the blessings of life-giving water, in both the literal and figurative sense.

❖ Sing or read aloud "Shall We Gather at the River."

❖ Conclude today's session by leading the class in this hope-filled benediction from Psalm 55:16, which is the key verse for October 19: **I call upon God, and the Lord will save me.**

UNIT 3: VISIONS OF GRANDEUR
TRANSFORMATION CONTINUED

PREVIEWING THE LESSON

Lesson Scripture: Ezekiel 47:13-23
Background Scripture: Ezekiel 47:13-23; Acts 2:37-47
Key Verse: Acts 2:38

Focus of the Lesson:

Sometimes life leaves people needing a new beginning. What is available to everyone to make that happen? Ezekiel tells the people that God restored the Israelites and the aliens among them with an inheritance of new land, signifying a new start. Peter says that God through Jesus Christ can redeem and give those who believe in God a new beginning, with the Temple as a place in which people can gather and support one another.

Goals for the Learners:

(1) to receive God's Word on sharing their inheritance with all those who live among them.
(2) to affirm and appreciate one another as children of God who have made, or can make, new beginnings together.
(3) to embrace new beginnings as a gift from God to be shared with others.

Pronunciation Guide:

agape (ah gah´ pay)
Berothah (bi roh´ thuh)
Edomite (ee´ duh mite)
Hamath (hay´ math)
Hauran (haw´ ruhn)
Hazar-enon (hay´ zuhr ee´ nuhn)
Hazer-hatticon
  (hay´ zuhr hat´ uh kon)

Hethlon (heth´ lon)
Lebo-hamath (lee´ boh hay´ muhth)
Meribath-kadesh
  (mer´ i buhth kay´ dish)
Sibraim (sib´ ray im)
Tamar (tay´ mahr)
Wadi (wah´ dee)
Zedad (zee´ dad)

Supplies:

Bibles, newsprint and marker, paper and pencils, hymnals, optional map

READING THE SCRIPTURE

NRSV

Lesson Scripture: Ezekiel 47:13-23

[13]Thus says the Lord GOD: These are the boundaries by which you shall divide the land for inheritance among the twelve tribes of Israel. Joseph shall have two portions. [14]You shall divide it equally; I swore to give it to your ancestors, and this land shall fall to you as your inheritance.

[15]This shall be the boundary of the land: On the north side, from the Great Sea by way of Hethlon to Lebo-hamath, and on to Zedad, [16]Berothah, Sibraim (which lies between the border of Damascus and the border of Hamath), as far as Hazer-hatticon, which is on the border of Hauran. [17]So the boundary shall run from the sea to Hazar-enon, which is north of the border of Damascus, with the border of Hamath to the north. This shall be the north side.

[18]On the east side, between Hauran and Damascus; along the Jordan between Gilead and the land of Israel; to the eastern sea and as far as Tamar. This shall be the east side.

[19]On the south side, it shall run from Tamar as far as the waters of Meribath-kadesh, from there along the Wadi of Egypt to the Great Sea. This shall be the south side.

[20]On the west side, the Great Sea shall be the boundary to a point opposite Lebo-hamath. This shall be the west side.

[21]So you shall divide this land among you according to the tribes of Israel. [22]You shall allot it as an inheritance for yourselves and for the aliens who reside among you and have begotten children among you. They shall be to you as citizens of Israel;

CEB

Lesson Scripture: Ezekiel 47:13-23

[13]The LORD God proclaims: These are the boundaries of the portions of land that will be distributed as an inheritance to the twelve tribes of Israel. Joseph will receive two portions. [14]What I swore to give to your ancestors, you will distribute as an inheritance equally. This land is given to you as an inheritance. [15]This is the boundary of the land. The northern limit begins at the Mediterranean Sea and goes in the direction of Hethlon toward Lebo-hamath, Zedad, [16]Berothah, Sibraim (which is between the boundary of Damascus and the boundary of Hamath), and Hazer-hatticon (that is on the boundary of Hauran). [17]So the boundary from the Mediterranean Sea to Hazar-enon will run north of the boundary of Damascus, with the boundary of Hamath to the north. This is the northern limit. [18]For the eastern limit, you will measure continuously between Hauran and Damascus and between Gilead and the land of Israel, along the Jordan River as far as the Dead Sea. This is the eastern limit. [19]The southern limit runs from Tamar to the waters of Meribath-kadesh and from there along the border of Egypt to the Mediterranean Sea. This is the southern limit. [20]For the western limit, the Mediterranean Sea is the boundary up to Lebo-hamath. This is the western limit. [21]You will apportion this land among yourselves according to the tribes of Israel. [22]When you distribute the land as an inheritance, the immigrants who reside with you and raise families among you are considered full citizens along with

with you they shall be allotted an inheritance among the tribes of Israel. ²³In whatever tribe aliens reside, there you shall assign them their inheritance, says the Lord GOD.

Key verse: Acts 2:38

³⁸Peter said to them, "Repent, and be baptized every one of you in the name of Jesus Christ so that your sins may be forgiven; and you will receive the gift of the Holy Spirit."

the Israelites. They will receive an inheritance along with you among the tribes of Israel. ²³You will assign the immigrants' inheritance with the tribe with whom they reside. This is what the LORD God says.

Key verse: Acts 2:38

³⁸Peter replied, "Change your hearts and lives. Each of you must be baptized in the name of Jesus Christ for the forgiveness of your sins. Then you will receive the gift of the Holy Spirit.

UNDERSTANDING THE SCRIPTURE

Ezekiel 47:13-14. Ezekiel's temple vision begun in chapter 40 had largely focused on measurements and regulations related to the area defined by the boundaries of the temple. Beginning in 47:13, the vision shifts to an expansive vision of the borders of the land itself that still was a matter of promise for the exiles. The certainty of this landed vision comes in the opening words of verse 13: "Thus says the Lord GOD." The boundaries about to be delineated in the succeeding verses echo a similar command given by God to Moses in Numbers 34:1-15. In this and the next chapter of Ezekiel, the significance of "boundaries" and "borders" can be seen in the repeated use of these words. "Inheritance" suggests the promissory history of the land over generations, tracing back to the promise given to Abram at the very outset of his journey (Genesis 12:1, 7). Ezekiel indicates that the "twelve" tribes are each to be given allotments. But how is this possible when verse 13 indicates "Joseph" (through his two children) will receive two portions (based on

Genesis 48:8-22), thus seemingly making the tribal number to be thirteen? In Ezekiel 45:5, the "tribe" of Levi—the priests—is assigned territories in so-called "holy districts." Thus, their holdings are not counted among the twelve.

Ezekiel 47:15-20. In Numbers 34:3-14, the boundaries of the land to be allotted were listed in order of directions of the compass: south, west, north, and east. Similarly, these verses in Ezekiel delineate the boundaries by direction, going from north to east to south to west. The northern boundaries/borders identified in these verses have by far the greatest number of references. The eastern borders are perhaps the most interesting, especially when compared to the tribal allotments noted in Joshua 13–19. In Joshua 13, territories east of the Jordan are included—whereas in Ezekiel 47:18, no land east of the Jordan is allotted to the tribes (an intriguing counterpoint to contemporary folks who argue that modern-day Israel is entitled to lands east of the Jordan by biblical fiat). The southern boundary stretches not to the Nile, but to a wadi (intermittent stream) that stretches from Meribath-Kadesh to the Great Sea (Mediterranean) (on modern maps, at the northeastern edge of the Sinai Peninsula, quite distant from Egypt proper). The western border is the most clearly defined boundary of all, comprising the Mediterranean Sea. Ezekiel 48 specifies the tribal allotments made within these boundaries.

Ezekiel 47:21-23. These concluding three verses continue the theme of division of land and inheritance. They add to them a critical element that traces back to the Deuteronomic protection of strangers and sojourners (aliens). The principle for protecting these nonlanded noncitizens is made clear in Deuteronomy 10:19: Strangers and sojourners are to be protected because *you* (Israel) were strangers and sojourners in Egypt. An even more pointed reference that underscores such protection comes in Deuteronomy 23:7. There, concerning two groups that would have been most despised by the Israelites, the Edomites and Egyptians, Israel is forbidden from hating them. The commandment there anticipates Jesus' teaching about loving one's enemies (Matthew 5:43-48), and makes clear why Ezekiel 47:21-23 goes to such pains to include the outsiders (and their children) as those who are to receive "their inheritance" within the tribal borders. Indeed, Ezekiel goes so far as to say that these folks "shall be to you as citizens of Israel"— again, an interesting counterpoint for those in our time for whom national borders justify suspicions and worse toward noncitizens among us.

Acts 2:37-41. At the beginning of chapter 2, the author of Acts (traditionally attributed to Luke) has already established the setting for what unfolds. The place is Jerusalem, and the day is Pentecost—one of the three major pilgrimage festivals of Judaism mandated in Exodus 23:14-19, which accounts for the number of foreign visitors who have come to worship at the Temple. It is unclear how close in proximity to the Temple this event takes place, though clearly the Temple's function as serving as the symbol of God's dwelling place looms large as the signs of God's presence are displayed in rushing wind, "tongues" as of fire, and the disciples' speaking in tongues that gathers the crowd. Immediately preceding verses 37-42 is Peter's sermon to the diverse crowd. Our passage opens with the crowd asking, in response to that sermon, "What should we do?" Peter's response links baptism and repentance, hearkening back not only to Jesus' initial preaching of repentance and belief (Mark 1:15)—but even further back to John the Baptizer's prior proclamation of a baptism of repentance (Mark 1:4). Peter's sermon begins with the promise of the gift of the Holy Spirit, which was prophesied by Joel and fulfilled John the Baptizer's expectation (Luke 3:16). By the end of these verses, those who respond to Peter's call swell the Christian community from the 120 or so who gather after Jesus' ascension (Acts 1:15) to more than three thousand (2:41).

Acts 2:42-47. The transformation of the early Christian community is not merely measured in numbers. These verses describe the appearance of a community whose essential mark was sharing life in common. The word translated as "fellowship" in verse 42 comes from a root word that literally means "common" (as in verse 44). The distribution and sharing of goods has served as a frequent cause for conversation—and argument—as to how this communitarian ethic of community life might (or should) be replicated among us. The basic motive for their actions is identified as the ability to address "need" within the community. Some see in the reference to "broke bread at home and ate their food with glad and generous hearts" as a veiled reference either to some commemorative meal that evolved into Communion and/or the community meals that were sometimes termed as *agape* or "love" feasts. One detail that connects this overall passage from Acts with that of Ezekiel comes in verse 46: "they spent much time together in the temple." For the early Christian community—as for the earlier community of exiles Ezekiel sought to prepare for their eventual return home—life and ritual at the Temple were central to the community's life and transformation.

INTERPRETING THE SCRIPTURE

Inheritances

What "inheritances" do you most value? A collection of old family pictures? An heirloom piece of furniture? A family Bible? In a small garden in front of our home is a rock formed from small round crystals on the outside with a hollow interior. It originally came from my godparents' farm in St. Francois County, Missouri. My parents had it at their home, and now it is at ours, and one day will be at our son's.

Inheritances connect us to our past through the stories of how and why they came to us. But perhaps just as important, inheritances have a definite forward and future thrust as well. For the one who bestows the inheritance, the future becomes the repository of what is passed on from his or her belongings. And for the ones who receive, an inheritance serves as a reminder that there are elements of our lives that came to us as gifts—and that we, in turn, may keep and pass on to others. Surely that connection of inheritance of past and future are at work in Ezekiel's opening and recurring words in this passage regarding inheritance, and its particular connection to the land once promised to Abram.

But there is yet another significant meaning to the theme of inheritance here: ownership. The exiles in Babylon technically owned nothing, for they were landless. For some, if not most, that fact served as a hurdle to hope. But the message Ezekiel brings is that imperial Babylon is not the arbiter and owner of all. "The earth is the LORD's," as the psalmist confesses (Psalm 24:1), is an inherently subversive word, for it declares where ownership truly resides. And to landless exiles, the Sovereign God declares there will be an inheritance. There will be hope. And just in case Babylon (or any of its contemporary embodiments in our time) protests such an arrangement, Ezekiel plays the trump card at the very beginning of verse 13: "thus says the Lord GOD." This is not idle talk or wishful thinking.

This is the resolve of the Holy One, who scoffs at pretenders even and especially when they sit on thrones or manipulate markets. "Thus says the Lord GOD." There will be hope, because there will be inheritance that is totally beyond the control of any and all who would say otherwise.

The Geography of New Beginnings

It has been noted by biblical scholars that the promise of land in the Old Testament serves the same purpose as the promise of the kingdom or sovereign realm of God in the New Testament. Both anchor the community in hope, and in the anticipation of a place devoted to extraordinary new beginnings.

So it should not be surprising that Ezekiel, in illustrating the exiles' cause for hope, essentially provides a primer in geography for those exiles. Ezekiel 47:15-20 contains a host of place names that locate where the new beginnings of this people are to take root. Keep in mind, though, that all these places—some of which are known to us and some not—would have never been seen by those born in exile. And depending on how late this passage in Ezekiel came, it may be that only a few graybeards would have recognized the names, and been able to tell the young ones where these places were, and what they were like.

Hope always needs interpreters, those who are able to connect memory of things and places past with the promises directed toward the future. That is one of the critical values for ministries of Christian education and faith formation. New beginnings do not arise in a vacuum. New beginnings, in terms of the faith we hold and proclaim, have origins that run deep. Prophets like Ezekiel and Isaiah understood this. They framed their "gospel" of new beginnings in the language and imagery of Exodus and even creation. It is not as if God suddenly appears on the stage for the first time with this promise of land and inheritance. The trustworthiness of God and those promises brought by Ezekiel and others are grounded in God's history of engagement with and on behalf of God's people. And for those born into exile in Ezekiel's day, or for those in our day who have no connection with the stories and traditions that form us, it is critical to have individuals and communities who connect the promise of new beginnings with the gracious actions of God that form us from of old. Why? So that the hope of new beginnings can be grounded, and be trusted, and empower folks to journey in their light.

Ezekiel provides this primer in promissory geography to those long separated from those lands, so that they may take heart. What do we provide those in our time who yearn for a reason to take heart, to have hope, to see that new beginnings are possible?

Transformation: Making New by Making Room

In chapter 47, Ezekiel frames the hope of transformation and new beginnings in the language of boundaries and borders. On the surface, it is a curious choice. Boundaries and borders typically delineate limits. Often, they are seen in exclusive and excluding ways. Boundaries and borders suggest not only *places* that do not belong "inside," but at times they evoke judgments of *people* who do not belong inside. When Israel did return from exile and rebuild, the time that followed was marked by exclusionary policies. Indeed, many argue that the books of Ruth (whose namesake hero is a Gentile woman from Moab—Ruth 1:4) and Jonah (who flees from God's gracious character exhibited toward the hated Ninevites—Jonah 4:1-2) were written in this era to contest the exclusionary spirit that had arisen.

It might have been possible for those in favor of such exclusionary policies to have hearkened back to Ezekiel's words of boundaries and borders as a rationalization for such limits as justifying their "circling of the wagons." But that would have been a serious misjudgment, because at the end of today's passage, Ezekiel announces an extraordinary spirit of openness that is commanded within those very boundaries and borders. Those who are aliens—that is, non-Jewish and noncitizens—are to be treated not only with respect but also as citizens. More astounding, Ezekiel declares not once but twice that they are to be "allotted an inheritance" (47:22). And as if to underscore the point, the passage and these commands end not with the prophet saying, "take it from me" but "says the Lord GOD."

Gracious inclusion of strangers and sojourners (or "immigrants") is not an optional alternative if you want to be polite. Rather, inclusion is a directive that reflects God's purposes for the justice and equity that are to hold forth within those promised boundaries and borders. As noted in the comments on verses 21-23 in Understanding the Scripture, Ezekiel is not inventing a new idea here. The protection of strangers and sojourners traces back to the covenant commands of Deuteronomy.

How does Ezekiel anticipate transformation taking place in these promised lands? Making new occurs by making room: making room for others, making room for outsiders who would otherwise have no place.

And how does transformation take place in our own churches and communities? Not by erecting boundaries and borders that serve as walls to fence others out. God's transformative work of making new occurs by our making room for others: in our pews, in our dining halls, in our council rooms, and in our missional concerns and partnerships.

SHARING THE SCRIPTURE

PREPARING TO TEACH

Preparing Our Hearts

Meditate on this week's devotional reading from Psalm 51:1-13. Note that the heading of this penitential psalm attributes it to David after he had committed adultery with Bathsheba. How did David go about seeking a new beginning with God? How might praying this psalm help you to make a new beginning after you have sinned? What do you desire to hear from God?

Pray that you and the students will recognize that even after catastrophic failure, new beginnings are possible with God.

Preparing Our Minds

Study the background Scripture from Ezekiel 47:13-23 and Acts 2:37-47. The lesson Scripture is from Ezekiel 47:13-23.

Consider this question as you prepare the lesson: *What is available to help people make a new beginning?*

Write on newsprint:

❏ information for next week's lesson, found under "Continue the Journey."

❏ activities for further spiritual growth in "Continue the Journey."

Review the "Introduction," "The Big Picture," "Close-up," and "Faith in Action," which all precede the first lesson of this quarter. Consider how you might use any of this material in today's lesson.

Option: Locate a map showing the Promised Land, Assyria, and Babylon in the period between 721 B.C. (fall of the Northern Kingdom, Israel) and 586 B.C. (fall of the Southern Kingdom, Judah). Prior to the session, locate as many places named in Ezekiel 47:13-23 as possible. Use this map to give the class a general idea of the land to which Ezekiel refers.

LEADING THE CLASS

(1) Gather to Learn

❖ Greet the class members and introduce guests.

❖ Pray that those who have come today will hear good news that will help them to make a new beginning.

❖ Brainstorm answers to this question: **What kinds of situations may cause people to yearn for a new beginning?**

❖ Follow-up by answering this question for several situations the class has identified: **What help is available for making a new beginning?** (For example, if a new beginning is needed after a devastating storm, insurance, funds from being declared a disaster area, and donations from churches and other non-profits may be available.)

❖ Read aloud today's focus statement: **Sometimes life leaves people needing a new beginning. What is available to everyone to make that happen? Ezekiel tells the people that God restored Israelites and the aliens among them with an inheritance of new land, signifying a new start. Peter says that God through Jesus Christ can redeem and give those who believe in God a new beginning, with the Temple as a place in which people can gather and support one another.**

(2) Goal 1: Receive God's Word on Sharing the Learners' Inheritance with All Those Who Live Among Them

❖ Set the stage for today's passage by reading or retelling "Inheritances" from Interpreting the Scripture.

❖ Read Ezekiel 47:13-23. (You may want to read this passage yourself or provide a volunteer with the Pronunciation Guide, since there are many unfamiliar place names here.)

❖ **Option**: If you located a map with some of the place names prior to the session, show the map now to the class so they can visualize the extensive land mass to which Ezekiel refers. Note that the "Great Sea" is another name for the Mediterranean Sea.

❖ Discuss how this land is to be divided and among whom. (Refer to Ezekiel 47:13-14, 15-20, 21-23 in

Understanding the Scripture. Also see "The Geography of New Beginnings" in Interpreting the Scripture.)

❖ Ask: **What does this land and the way that God says it is to be parceled out reveal about who God is and how God works?** (Note, especially, the directions in verses 21-23.)

(3) Goal 2: Affirm and Appreciate One Another as Children of God Who Have Made, or Can Make, New Beginnings Together

❖ Point out that these land boundaries are part of Ezekiel's vision for a new beginning of God's people after they return from exile in Babylon. In an equally impressive, though different, way the early church provided a means for new beginnings, first among the Jews but soon to include Gentiles. Read in unison today's key verse, Acts 2:38, which provides the basis for this new beginning.

❖ Invite the adults to turn in their Bibles to Acts 2:41-47 to see how the first converts made a new beginning together.

❖ Discuss these questions:

1. **How does our congregation provide new beginnings for those who have heretofore not been part of the church?**
2. **How does our congregation provide new beginnings when trouble or dissension has split apart members?**

(4) Goal 3: Embrace New Beginnings as a Gift from God to Be Shared with Others

❖ Read "Transformation: Making New by Making Room" in Interpreting the Scripture.

❖ Focus on the final paragraph by creating a list of ways that your congregation makes room for others. Write the ideas on newsprint.

❖ Ask: **What else could we as a church (or class) do to welcome and make room for others?** Here is an example: Encourage everyone to speak to all the people within ten feet of them. Make a special effort to seek out newcomers. Invite them to sit with you, get a bulletin or hymnal for them, introduce them to others, invite them to lunch after the service or class, or invite them to come with you to a nonbusiness church activity that is coming up soon.

❖ Challenge the students to put some of these ideas into practice as a means of sharing God's gifts with others.

(5) Continue the Journey

❖ Pray that as the learners depart, they will be aware of new beginnings in their lives and the lives of others and give thanks for these new opportunities.

❖ Post information for next week's session on newsprint for the students to copy:

- **Title: Let Zion Rejoice**
- **Background Scripture: Psalm 33; Isaiah 52:1-2, 7-12**
- **Lesson Scripture: Isaiah 52:1-2, 7-12**
- **Focus of the Lesson: All people need to hear words of hope. Where will they find hopeful words? The psalmist and Isaiah tell God's people that God, who reigns above, is their help, shield, and salvation, and that they can put their hope in God and rejoice.**

❖ Challenge the adults to grow spiritually by completing one or more of these activities related to this week's session, which you have posted on newsprint for the students to copy.

(1) Do some genealogical research to get an idea of what you have inherited from your ancestors. Property and material goods are one form of inheritance, but a picture of an ancestor may reveal that you have this person's facial features or body build. Stories passed down through the family or found in old publications may suggest that you have similar values or interests. Share this research with other family members.

(2) Reach out to someone who is new to the community. Do whatever you can to make this person feel welcomed and at home here.

(3) Go to your local historical society to investigate the beginnings of your community. Who settled here? Why did these people leave their former home? What did they hope to find here? Were any indigenous people displaced by the settlers?

❖ Sing or read aloud "Spirit of the Living God."

❖ Conclude today's session by leading the class in this hope-filled benediction from Psalm 55:16, which is the key verse for October 19: I call upon God, and the LORD will save me.

UNIT 3: VISIONS OF GRANDEUR
LET ZION REJOICE

PREVIEWING THE LESSON

Lesson Scripture: Isaiah 52:1-2, 7-12
Background Scripture: Psalm 33; Isaiah 52:1-2, 7-12
Key Verse: Isaiah 52:7

Focus of the Lesson:
All people need to hear words of hope. Where will they find hopeful words? The psalmist and Isaiah tell God's people that God, who reigns above, is their help, shield, and salvation, and that they can put their hope in God and rejoice.

Goals for the Learners:
(1) to encounter Isaiah's words of hope, good news, and rejoicing.
(2) to express great joy through heartfelt worship for the Lord's salvation.
(3) to share the good news of God with others.

Supplies:
Bibles, newsprint and marker, paper and pencils, hymnals, construction paper, markers, scissors

---

READING THE SCRIPTURE

NRSV
Lesson Scripture: Isaiah 52:1-2, 7-12
¹Awake, awake,
  put on your strength, O Zion!
Put on your beautiful garments,
  O Jerusalem, the holy city;
for the uncircumcised and the
    unclean
  shall enter you no more.
²Shake yourself from the dust, rise
    up,
  O captive Jerusalem;

CEB
Lesson Scripture: Isaiah 52:1-2, 7-12
¹Awake, awake,
  put on your strength, Zion!
  Put on your splendid clothing,
  Jerusalem, you holy city; for the
    uncircumcised and unclean will
    no longer come into you.
²Shake the dust off yourself;
  rise up; sit enthroned, Jerusalem.
Loose the bonds from your neck,
  captive Daughter Zion!

loose the bonds from your neck,
  O captive daughter Zion!
**7How beautiful upon the mountains
  are the feet of the messenger who
    announces peace,**
who brings good news,
  who announces salvation,
  who says to Zion, "Your God
    reigns."
8Listen! Your sentinels lift up their
  voices,
  together they sing for joy;
for in plain sight they see
  the return of the Lord to Zion.
9Break forth together into singing,
  you ruins of Jerusalem;
for the Lord has comforted his
  people,
he has redeemed Jerusalem.
10The Lord has bared his holy arm
  before the eyes of all the nations;
and all the ends of the earth shall see
  the salvation of our God.
11Depart, depart, go out from there!
  Touch no unclean thing;
go out from the midst of it, purify
  yourselves,
  you who carry the vessels of the
    Lord.
12For you shall not go out in haste,
  and you shall not go in flight;
for the Lord will go before you,
  and the God of Israel will be your
    rear guard.

**7How beautiful upon the mountains
  are the feet of a messenger
  who proclaims peace,
  who brings good news,**
  who proclaims salvation,
  who says to Zion, "Your God
    rules!"
8Listen! Your lookouts lift their voice;
  they sing out together!
  Right before their eyes they see the
    Lord returning to Zion.
9Break into song together, you ruins
  of Jerusalem!
The Lord has comforted his people
  and has redeemed Jerusalem.
10The Lord has bared his holy arm in
  view of all the nations;
  all the ends of the earth have seen
    our God's victory.
11Depart! Depart! Go out from there!
  Unclean! Don't touch!
  Get out of that place; purify
    yourselves,
  carriers of the Lord's equipment!
12You won't go out in a rush,
  nor will you run away,
  because the one going before you
    is the Lord;
  your rear guard is the God of
    Israel.

UNDERSTANDING THE SCRIPTURE

Introduction. The final focus passage under consideration in this unit, previously taken up with Ezekiel's visions, is from Isaiah. Today's verses come from that portion of the book that is often designated as Second Isaiah (chapters 40–55). Biblical scholars place these writings immediately prior to the Israelites' return from exile in Babylon. Like Ezekiel, they are visionary portrayals in poetry and metaphor concerning what the future holds in terms of God's imminent deliverance of the exiles.

Psalm 33. Like the hopeful vision in Isaiah's passage, the "new song" this psalm invites Israel to sing (33:3) is grounded in God's sovereignty over all creation. This Sovereign, unlike the imperial reign experienced by the exiles, "loves righteousness and justice" (33:5). That contrast with the power claimed by Babylon is further drawn in verses 13-17. The psalmist portrays God in verses 13-14 as "looking down"—a phrase that can be spatial as well as derisive—upon such imperial presumptive claims of might. The conventional wisdom is that the power of empire, ancient and contemporary, draws upon the weaponry and forces that can be mustered for battle. The psalmist declares that understanding of sovereignty to be wrong. The God who has brought forth creation holds ultimate sway (33:10-11). Genuine power resides in acts of deliverance, and hope rests not in military prowess but in God's steadfast love (33:18-19). The final verses of the psalm reprise that theme of God's steadfast love, and the covenantal bond of trust in God that generates hope.

Isaiah 52:1-2. These two verses are structured by a series of imperative verbs that call upon the exiles to engage in the following actions: awake (twice), put on (twice), shake yourself, rise up, loose the bonds. The summons to "awake" was earlier sounded in Isaiah 51:9—although there, it was aimed at God ("the arm of the Lord"). The call in verse 1 to put on "beautiful garments" may contrast with the stripping of clothing (symbolic or literal) that accompanied exile (3:18-24). "Shake yourself from the dust" (52:2) reverses the act of mourning (for exile) that involved sitting in or covering oneself with dust. Loosing bonds from the neck may suggest neck chains

used on captives, or the image of a yoke on animals harnessed to do the owner's work—as the Jewish captives no doubt performed for the benefit of their Babylonian overseers. Also dominating these two verses are the repeated references to Jerusalem and Zion (Zion being the name of the hill in the city upon which the Temple had once stood—and would stand again, per the previous sessions' visions from Ezekiel). With these references, hope and homecoming were not vague but grounded—literally.

Isaiah 52:7-8. The scene shifts, in the prophet's vision, from Babylon to Jerusalem. While still addressed to the exiles, it is as if they are transported to see and hear how this word of hope unfolds in the land to which they would have opportunity to return. The passage begins with a celebration of the (unnamed) messenger who has brought this news to Jerusalem—or what remains of it. Focusing on the "feet" of the messenger not only underscores the journey that has been taken but also gives honor to what is typically viewed as one of the most humbling parts of the body (the lowest of the household servants would be the ones responsible for washing the feet of guests—a meaning that lends Jesus' foot washing of the disciples its power and humility). The Hebrew word translated here as "brings good news" appears also in 61:1. Jesus reads Isaiah 61:1 as he announces his own mission in Luke 4:16-21. In the Greek translation of 61:1, we find the word that has become the root of the English word "evangelize." "Sentinels" is a synonym for "watchmen," typically set on walls or high places, who serve as lookouts and "town criers" who called out what they saw. In verse 8 the prophet has them "sing for joy" in response to the closing declaration of the messenger in verse 7: "Your God reigns."

Isaiah 52:9-10. The voices of the sentinels lifted up in joyful response now spills out into the singing of the very ruins of Jerusalem, destroyed by Babylon's siege. God's comforting the people recalls the opening declaration of Second Isaiah (40:1-2), where God's call to the prophet to comfort and speak tenderly to the exiles is joined to the announcement that the time of exile has come to a close ("she has served her term"). God's "baring the arm" (52:10) is the act of a warrior preparing for battle. The sight of this redemptive intervention will not be limited to the exiles, but rather will be witnessed by "all the nations" and "all the ends of the earth."

Isaiah 52:11-12. Verse 11 mirrors verse 1: only now, the call to "awake, awake" is echoed by "depart, depart." The parallelism is even clear in Hebrew, as those verbs rhyme. The admonishment to "touch no unclean thing" likewise parallels the announcement in verse 1 ("the unclean shall enter you no more") in addition to serving as a preparatory act for entering into God's presence (contact with unclean things left one unable to enter the Temple for a period of time). "Go out" sounds the earlier call to depart Egypt at the time of the Exodus, thus connecting that previous act of God's deliverance to freedom with this current promise. Unlike the departure from Egypt, however, which was done in haste (Exodus 12:11; Deuteronomy 16:3), the departure from Babylon will not be in flight but more in the form of a procession. At the head of those returning to the land will be God—and to ensure their safety from any who might pursue, God will also bring up the rear of the advancing column.

INTERPRETING THE SCRIPTURE

Getting Out of Bed

We all know the struggle. The bed is so comfortable; sleep feels so good. Let's just roll over, hit the snooze button, and stay under the covers a little longer. Getting up can be all the more of an effort when what the day ahead promises (or threatens) to bring is more of the same routine, or the labor that wearies, or the relationships that aren't quite right. Sleep can be a seductive form of escape from the world.

To exiles lulled to sleep by presumptions that things would never change, that Babylon was now there home, that a land once promised was finally and forever lost, the prophet says, *wake up!* In fact, Isaiah repeats that summons twice to make sure no one sleeps through it. Moreover, Isaiah tells the Israelites to put on the clothing not of slave labor, or hopeless resignation, but fine garments—Sunday clothes, as we used to speak of them. Clothing suitable for entering into the presence of God, for God has come to deliver them.

Persons and communities of faith still stand in need of such rousing from time to time. We get bogged down in routines that reduce the life of faith from an adventure to a slugfest between who is right and who is wrong over this matter or that. We lose sight of hope when promises seem too long in coming, or when nothing ever seems to change, or when we feel powerless in the face of dominant cultural and political forces that seem destined to be entrenched forever. In other words, we reach the point where we might be tempted to pull the ecclesiastical covers over our heads and find escape from the world. Years ago I came across a poster that had the following quotation from *Don Quixote* that illustrates this same point . . . and danger: "so long as I am asleep I have neither fear nor hope, trouble nor glory."

That is why prophets arise like Isaiah, who trouble us by saying "wake up"; who call on us to put on a new life; who rouse us to shake off the dust of fearful inactivity and to rise up as servants of God.

Rejoicing in God's Saving Reign

Today is the first Sunday in Advent. In the calendar of the church year, we do not wait until January 1 to begin a new year. Today is that new day; Advent begins our new year. And Advent brings, as does today's passage, a message of extraordinary hope and promise: of good news, of salvation . . . and of the assurance that God reigns.

The coming reign of God has been portrayed, and expected, in varying ways. In some Old Testament passages—and in some hellfire-and-brimstone preaching—the coming reign of God ("the day of the Lord") takes shape in ominous terms. Fear becomes its predominant bludgeon, as the prophets of old sought to shake a people who had grown not merely complacent but also complicit in wrongdoing. To tyrants and to those entrenched in systems that rely on injustice and greed, the coming reign of God does indeed sound a note that such things cannot and will not continue. But to exiles who long for hope, to individuals and communities in our own time who yearn for justice and the practice of mercy, the coming reign of God brings saving anticipation and motives for engaging those hopes in daily living.

And so the linkage of this vision of Isaiah with this first day of the new year in the church's calendar is not only fitting, it is imperative. For its announcement of peace is to be our proclamation and our agenda. Its sounding of good news is to be our call to live lives that are not only good but that also seek God's good purposes for those around us and for all of creation. Its proclamation of salvation is to strike the chord that is to sound through all of our words and actions as a people not simply saved *from* sin, but saved *for* life in covenant with God and community. And its declaration that "God reigns" (52:7) is to be the foundation for all of the above. For the reign of God is what delivers us from mere wishful thinking about what might be, and sends us on the way of what God promises to be. The reign of God is what delivers us from fears that *nothing will ever change around here*, from despairing that the future will never be as good as the past.

For we take heart and rejoice in the promised reign of God, whose way and hope of life begins even now on the way to its sure transformation of all creation.

Moving—and Worshiping—Forward

The bulletin in my home church almost always had these words printed at the end: "Enter to worship, depart to serve." Church doors are meant to allow movement in and to encourage movement out.

Where today's passage began with a call to "awake," so it ends on the note of "depart." To the exiles in Babylon, "getting out" was a word of hope. Decades of confinement behind the closed doors of captivity now took a turn: The doors were opened. Exile could be safely left behind. Life and hope beckoned forward. The people could now choose.

Such possibilities and hope do not reside with sixth century B.C. exiles alone. When we gather as communities in worship, we celebrate the news and promise that the previous section detailed. We pass among us the peace of Christ. We attend to the reading and preaching of good news. We rejoice in God's salvation. We find ourselves commissioned by God's reign to be God's present-day messengers and servants. Such worship ought to fill us with joy and exuberance.

But life is not lived in sanctuaries. "Liturgy," which literally means "work of the people," is not exhausted in calls to worship and stirring anthems and fervent prayers and ascending hopes. Like Isaiah's advice in verse 11, like the words on those old bulletins of mine, getting out and departing is every bit as much an act of faith as gathering and celebrating. Like the exiles, we have to choose. We have to choose whether we will take all of those grand words spoken and uplifting feelings celebrated in worship into the lives we lead and the attitudes we carry and the priorities we make outside of the comfort zone of sanctuary. For God does not reign only in the sanctuary. Good news needs sounding not just from pulpits. Peace needs experiencing and sharing beyond circles of family and friends. Faithful worship, the very vision of faith entrusted to us, requires that we depart from where all those things are taken for granted—and where they are put to the test in the conduct of our lives, for the sake of the world that God so loved.

For then, and only then, will the gospel find its way into the places where it is most needed, into the corners where justice and mercy and steadfast love are most in jeopardy. In other words, only then will the gospel find modern-day incarnation, so that the visions of prophets and Christ may continue to pave the way for the coming reign of God.

SHARING THE SCRIPTURE

PREPARING TO TEACH

Preparing Our Hearts

Meditate on this week's devotional reading from Psalm 42:5-11. When have you felt like the psalmist who in the midst of deep distress longs for God? What does this psalm reveal about the writer's beliefs about God? What gives you hope to praise God even in the midst of trouble?

Pray that you and the students will continue to place your hope and trust in God for a brighter future.

Preparing Our Minds

Study the background Scripture from Psalm 33 and Isaiah 52:1-2, 7-12. The lesson Scripture is from Isaiah 52:1-2, 7-12.

Consider this question as you prepare the lesson: *Where can people find words of hope?*

Write on newsprint:

❏ questions for "Express Great Joy Through Heartfelt Worship for the Lord's Salvation."

❏ information for next week's lesson, found under "Continue the Journey."

❏ activities for further spiritual growth in "Continue the Journey."

Review the "Introduction," "The Big Picture," "Close-up," and "Faith in Action," which all precede the first lesson of this quarter. Consider how you might use any of this material in today's lesson.

LEADING THE CLASS

(1) Gather to Learn

❖ Greet the class members and introduce guests.

❖ Pray that those who have come today will be attentive to words of hope concerning God.

❖ Read: **Today is the first Sunday in Advent. During this first season of the church year believers look backward to the coming of the incarnate Jesus as a baby in Bethlehem who came to bring hope and reconciliation with God for all people. Believers also look forward in hope to the coming again of Christ.**

❖ Ask: **How does news of Jesus' coming and coming again give you hope?**

❖ **Option:** Distribute hymnals and invite the students to look at "Hail to the Lord's Anointed" to identify hoped-for changes that Jesus will bring, such as setting captives free.

❖ Read aloud today's focus statement: **All people need to hear words of hope. Where will they find hopeful words? The psalmist and Isaiah tell God's people that God, who reigns above, is their help, shield, and salvation, and that they can put their hope in God and rejoice.**

(2) Goal 1: Encounter Isaiah's Words of Hope, Good News, and Rejoicing

❖ Choose a volunteer to read Isaiah 52:1-2, 7-12. Suggest that the listeners imagine themselves as exiles in Babylon who are being called to awaken from the despair they have experienced during the exile and get ready to celebrate their return home.

❖ Ask: **Had you been an exile in Babylon, how would you have responded to Isaiah's good news?**

❖ Form small groups. Invite the adults to turn to today's passage from Isaiah in their Bibles and with their group identify the action words (verbs). Each group is to answer the question: **What are those who hear these words called to do?**

(3) Goal 2: Express Great Joy Through Heartfelt Worship for the Lord's Salvation

❖ Look more closely at some possible ways that people can express their joy through worship by reading this list. Pause after each item and invite students who find this aspect of worship especially meaningful for them to raise their hands:

1. Sing hymns or praise songs with the congregation.
2. Participate in or observe a liturgical dance.
3. Give a word of witness about how God has been working in your life.
4. Partake of Holy Communion.
5. Greet church members.
6. Welcome guests and newcomers.
7. Serve as a liturgist or Scripture reader.
8. Sing in the choir.
9. Serve as an usher.
10. Become engaged in the sermon.
11. Read or chant a psalm.
12. Play the organ, keyboard, or other instrument.
13. Enter into the instrumental music, perhaps by clapping hands or tapping feet.
14. Focus on the Scripture passages as they are being read.
15. Experience the presence of God in a way that is meaningful for you.

❖ Distribute paper and pencils and post the following questions. Suggest that the students ponder them and jot down any ideas that come to mind. Tell them that they will not be asked to share their answers with anyone.

1. If you do not find great joy in worship, what changes need to occur in the service?
2. If you do not find great joy in worship, what changes need to occur within you?
3. If you do find great joy in worship, how do you share this joy so that others may know of and experience the Lord's salvation?

Wrap up this portion of the lesson by again reading Isaiah 52:7, which is today's key verse.

(4) Goal 3: Share the Joyous Good News of God with Others

❖ Distribute construction (or unlined) paper, markers (or pencils), and scissors. Ask the adults to work in pairs to trace one foot of their partner and cut out the tracing. Then write the owner's name on the footprint and either Isaiah 52:7 or the entire verse, which is today's key verse.

❖ Direct the adults to turn over the footprint and write the names of two or three people with whom they will talk this week about God's salvation and how that was made manifest to humanity in the coming of Jesus at Christmas.

❖ Suggest that class members keep these footprints in a place where they will see them and remember to share God's good news, particularly with the people whom they have identified.

(5) Continue the Journey

❖ Pray that as the learners depart they will recognize that even in exile God's people rejoiced and that they, too, are called to celebrate and share good news.

❖ Post information for next week's session on newsprint for the students to copy:

- **Title: Worship Christ's Majesty**
- **Background Scripture: Hebrews 1:1-9**
- **Lesson Scripture: Hebrews 1:1-9**
- **Focus of the Lesson: Some people do seemingly miraculous**

things with their gifts and talents. How do Christians respond? For the true miracle of Jesus Christ, the gift of salvation, God's people respond with worship.

❖ Challenge the adults to grow spiritually by completing one or more of these activities related to this week's session, which you have posted on newsprint for the students to copy.

(1) Read Psalm 33, part of this week's background Scripture, each day this week. Let these words of praise and rejoicing help you to prepare during this season of Advent as you await the Lord's coming.

(2) Reflect on all of the lessons of the fall quarter. In what areas of your life do you need to sustain hope?

How might the Scripture passages we have studied empower you to continue to hope and trust that God will be present with you and meet your needs?

(3) Plan to help a family that may be feeling hopeless to celebrate Christmas. Perhaps your church will sponsor an angel tree, where you can gather information about gifts (often clothing) requested by children whose families cannot provide for them.

❖ Sing or read aloud "Marching to Zion."

❖ Conclude today's session by leading the class in this hope-filled benediction from Psalm 55:16, which is the key verse for October 19: **I call upon God, and the LORD will save me.**

SECOND QUARTER
Acts of Worship

DECEMBER 7, 2014—FEBRUARY 22, 2015

The twelve lessons of the winter quarter's study, "Acts of Worship," look primarily at New Testament texts to consider humanity's worshipful responses to God. The first unit, which includes a Christmas lesson, explores the awesomeness of God. The second unit focuses on prayer. The final unit examines aspects of stewardship.

Unit 1, "In Awe of God," begins on December 7 with a study of Hebrews 1:1-9 that will help us to consider why Jesus is worthy of adoration and worship. "Make a Joyful Noise," the session for December 14, explores Psalm 95:1-7a to recognize that God, who is the creator of the earth and maker of humankind, is truly worthy of praise. The beloved Nativity story from Luke 2:1-20 will be our focus on December 21 as we study the events that led the angels to sing "Glory to God in the Highest" and prompted the shepherds to journey to Bethlehem. This unit concludes on December 28 as we look at the response of the disciples who are "In Awe of Christ's Power" according to Matthew 14:22-36.

The second unit, "Learning to Pray," begins on January 4 with a study of the Lord's Prayer as found in Luke 11:1-13, which is "A Model for Prayer" of various kinds. On January 11 we turn to John 17:1-26 to overhear Jesus' praying for unity among all believers in a session titled "Jesus Prays for the Disciples." Hebrews 4:14–5:10 demonstrates how Jesus fulfills the role of intercessor for God's people as we will discover in "Jesus Intercedes for Us" on January 18. In a session titled "We Pray for One Another" on January 25 we will study how James urges us to pray for healing for one another in chapter 5.

Unit 3, "Stewardship for Life," starts on February 1 with "Feasting and Fasting," a lesson rooted in Daniel 1:5, 8-17 and Matthew 6:16-18; 9:9-17. To examine Jesus' teachings about the connection between compassionately "Serving Neighbors, Serving God," we will explore the familiar parable of the good Samaritan from Luke 10:25-34 on February 8. In "Serving the Least," the lesson for February 15 from Matthew 25:31-46, we hear Jesus' teachings about our obligations to meet the needs of those who are hungry, strangers, in need of clothing, or otherwise living on the fringes of society. This unit ends on February 22 with a study of Ephesians 6:10-20, "Clothed and Ready," which examines this epistle's teaching about putting on the whole armor of God.

MEET OUR WRITER

REV. JANICE CATRON

Janice Catron is a Christian educator and ordained minister in the Presbyterian Church (USA) currently pastoring at John Knox Presbyterian Church in Louisville, Kentucky. Prior to moving to this congregation, she served on the national staff of the Presbyterian Church (USA) for fourteen years in various positions related to education and publication. In conjunction with her publishing work, Rev. Catron was a member of the Committee of the Uniform Series. She also taught as adjunct faculty at Louisville Presbyterian Theological Seminary.

A native of Mississippi, Rev. Catron received her B.S. from Millsaps College, her M.A. from Emory University, her M.Div. from Louisville Presbyterian Theological Seminary, and did her doctoral work at the University of Chicago. In addition to writing for *The New International Lesson Annual*, Catron is the author of *Job: Faith Remains When Understanding Fails*; *God's Vision, Our Calling: Hope and Responsibility in the Christian Life*; *God's Abiding Presence: Studies in Exodus and Deuteronomy*; and the Immersion Bible Study on *Isaiah, Jeremiah, and Lamentations*.

Catron and her husband, Gordon Berg, live in Louisville, where he provides information technology support for a nonprofit educational and counseling facility for emotionally challenged teenage girls. When not working, they enjoy watching movies together, playing on the computer, and spoiling their cats.

THE BIG PICTURE: WORSHIPING AS GOD'S PEOPLE

Praise, prayer, song, Scripture, and commitment—these elements have formed the core of worship for centuries. This quarter we will look at several biblical texts that add to our understanding of worship as God's people.

A Biblical Assumption

Looking at the Bible from start to finish, it is easy to see that worship runs throughout the whole of it. Genesis 2:1-3 tells how God built the sabbath into creation because rest and renewal (via worship) were part of the divine plan from the beginning. Revelation 20–21 closes our Scriptures with a glorious image of the ongoing worship that will infuse the new heaven and new earth when God's realm comes at last. In between these accounts, we find a lot of instruction, guidance, and reflection on acts of worship. At the core is this: Worship is not just *commanded* by Scripture, it is *assumed*. The biblical writers cannot imagine people with hearts thankful for God's good gifts not joining in praise and gratitude, both spontaneously as individuals and liturgically as a community. The same holds true in darker times; Scripture assumes we will seek God's presence for aid and comfort, both individually and together.

Throughout the Bible, we see that God is worthy of our worship for many reasons. First is *power*. As the One who gives and sustains life, God deserves our respect and awe. This appropriate response to God is often translated in our Bibles as "fear of the Lord," an unfortunate holdover from a time when "fear" meant "awe" in English.

There is more to our worship than God's power and transcendence, however. God deserves our praise and thanksgiving for unceasing acts of divine mercy, compassion, and care. As people of faith, we see God's hand moving in even the smallest details of our life. As human beings, we also know how much we need forgiveness and love—and how much help we sometimes need to extend the same to others. In worship, the barriers between ourselves and God come down, along with the barriers between ourselves and others. We are given the chance to reorient ourselves and reground ourselves in a perspective based on humility and gratitude. Thus worship opens us to the blessings of trust, comfort, and the peace that passes understanding.

For many, this last element may be the most meaningful. We come to worship during times of severe hardship or sadness and find ourselves unexpectedly strengthened by the living presence of God. We are able to go back into life with a renewed sense of hope and the certainty that we are not alone. In those times when we cannot yet sing a joyous song of praise, we find comfort in the quiet gratitude that slowly fills our hearts.

Worship in the Psalms

The Bible records many acts of worship performed by individuals and the community of faith. In addition, certain legal texts describe the "rules" related to proper worship. These cover such details as what the priest shall wear, what sacrifices are appropriate for which occasions, and the schedule for the liturgical year. These laws also include instruction designed to help the poor or uneducated who may not have the means or knowledge to worship as others do.

The Psalms, however, provide our best insight into the corporate worship practiced by the Jewish community up to and including the time of Jesus. We see there that worship included a time of gathering (often associated with formal processionals on special days), prayer, singing, dancing, and offerings. In addition, materials for worship range from laments to praises, enthronement hymns to prayers for healing, thanksgivings to recitations of sacred history.

As we move through the collection of holy songs, we also catch a glimpse of the theology underlying these acts of worship. Psalm 34, for example, says we can come to God when we are "brokenhearted," "crushed in spirit," and suffering "afflictions" (34:18-19), finding a reason to hope even in the midst of great hardship because God will act to redeem the situation (34:4, 19, 22). Worship restores us to this encouraging position of trust.

Psalm 40 is a great example of this same theme. It maintains that we express our trust that God is with us in the present by celebrating God's faithful actions in the past. Even in the midst of trouble we sing praise and express gratitude now, confident that in the future we will sing a "new song" (40:3). One of the great gifts of Psalm 40 is how it affirms that personal deliverance has implications for the community as a whole. The thanksgiving song of one becomes the trust of many.

Trust in God's mercy allows us to bring our confessions to God, both individually and corporately. One of the best-known examples of this is Psalm 51, which occurs relatively often as a lectionary reading throughout the Christian year. Tradition says this psalm was written by David after his abuse of Bathsheba and murder of Uriah (2 Samuel 11). Here we find the amazing promise of worship—that if we approach God in true repentance, seeking forgiveness, we will find a God who stands ready to heal our brokenness and restore the joy of salvation (Psalm 51:12).

Psalm 96 reminds us, however, that worship is about God's divine glory, rather than just what God does for us. Its focus on the call to celebrate God's greatness in worship then points to another important connection. Worship is a time to express our faith, but it is also a time to testify to God's power and glory. Indeed, God's glory is such that it calls for a joyful witness beyond that offered by human lips. Psalm 96:11-12 describes how every element of creation takes up the cry of God's reign, because all are included in the joy summoned by the new song celebrating God's reign.

Of course, no worship service would be complete without some reference to or reading from God's Word. Psalm 119, the longest psalm in the Hebrew Scriptures, focuses exclusively on the delight to be found in studying and following God's teaching. Out of genuine love for Scripture, the psalmist celebrates the freedom (119:45), light (119:105), and wonder (119:129) of God's Word—and invites us to do the same.

The Book of Psalms closes with a glorious call to praise both in the sanctuary and in the heavens (Psalm 150). Accompanied by an orchestra of various instruments, the people are to express their delight and joy in God without reservation. Through singing and dancing, they lead all creation in praising God. What a wonderful image for worship this is!

Worship Through Living Rightly

The prophets also have a lot to say about worship, but their focus is more on attitude than practice. Time and again, we read that true worship involves reflecting God's compassion and love in our lives, not just showing up at church or following "the rules." The prophets consistently denounce empty worship rituals that are performed with no meaning and without any connection to ethical living. Consider, for example, these better-known references:

I hate, I despise your festivals,
   and I take no delight in your solemn assemblies.
Even though you offer me your burnt-offerings and grain-offerings,
   I will not accept them;
and the offerings of well-being of your fatted animals
   I will not look upon.
Take away from me the noise of your songs;
   I will not listen to the melody of your harps.
But let justice roll down like waters,
   and righteousness like an ever-flowing stream. (Amos 5:21-24)

For I desire steadfast love and not sacrifice,
   the knowledge of God rather than burnt-offerings. (Hosea 6:6)

What to me is the multitude of your sacrifices?
   says the LORD;
I have had enough of burnt-offerings of rams
   and the fat of fed beasts;
I do not delight in the blood of bulls,
   or of lambs, or of goats. . . .
Your new moons and your appointed festivals
   my soul hates;
they have become a burden to me,
   I am weary of bearing them. . . .
Wash yourselves; make yourselves clean;
   remove the evil of your doings

from before my eyes;
cease to do evil,
    learn to do good;
seek justice,
    rescue the oppressed,
defend the orphan,
    plead for the widow. (Isaiah 1:11, 14, 16-17)

"With what shall I come before the LORD,
    and bow myself before God on high?
Shall I come before him with burnt-offerings,
    with calves a year old?
Will the LORD be pleased with thousands of rams,
    with tens of thousands of rivers of oil?
Shall I give my firstborn for my transgression,
    the fruit of my body for the sin of my soul?"
He has told you, O mortal, what is good;
    and what does the LORD require of you
but to do justice, and to love kindness,
    and to walk humbly with your God? (Micah 6:6-8)

These sentiments find reflection in New Testament writings as well. Paul's instruction on the right attitude to bring to the Lord's Supper comes to mind (1 Corinthians 11:17-22), as does James's connection of faith to good deeds (James 1:19-27). Clearly worship involves more than coming to church to sing, pray, and hear a sermon. According to Scripture, true worship consists of both gathering with the body of faith to praise and honor God publicly and showing our witness and devotion to God in how we live outside of the sanctuary.

Worship in the New Testament

Because the earliest Christians were Jews, it is not surprising that the elements of worship we find in the Hebrew Bible carry over into the New Testament. There we find the same themes of liturgy, prayer, Scripture, and right living. Matthew, in particular, lifts up the common Jewish practices of fasting, prayer, and charity as acts of worship to be expressed in Christian living (see Matthew 6:1-18).

By way of a brief overview of worship in the Gospels and Epistles, it might be helpful to look at general language instead of specific verses. There are several Greek words associated with worship throughout the New Testament, and each shows a bit about how worship was viewed and practiced.

The most common word forms the root of *doxology* in English and refers to "glory." Occurring more than 150 times, this word grounds worship in the glory of God and Jesus Christ—the best reasons we have to lift our voices in awe and praise. In Romans 11:36, for example, Paul says, "For from him and through him and to him are all things. To him be the glory forever. Amen."

Another word associated with worship means "to kneel" but also "to kiss in reverence." This is the word used by the magi in Matthew 2:2 when they ask, "Where is the child who has been born king of the Jews? For we observed his star at its rising, and have come to pay him homage." This word carries the element of humility that we are to show before God.

A third word associated with worship carries the sense of ministering or serving. It is the word Paul uses in Romans 12:1 when he appeals to his brothers and sisters in Christ "to present your bodies as a living sacrifice, holy and acceptable to God, which is your spiritual worship." Once again we see the theme that worship is more than what happens in church on Sunday morning; it is intimately bound up in how we live.

Other words for worship express more of what we might expect. There are expressions related to praising, singing, magnifying, exalting, giving thanks, and rejoicing. Clearly these were—and still are—vital elements of worship for our life as a community of faith. What a wonderful challenge the Bible presents, though, to see God's relationship with us as being built on even more.

The Quarter in Review

Our texts for this quarter will touch on all the aspects of worship mentioned thus far. Given that this unit begins in Advent and ends in Lent, this seems a particularly appropriate time to consider worship and what it means for us.

Unit 1 begins with the theme of worship done "In Awe of God." The first three lessons are set in Advent and reflect themes appropriate to the season. Lesson 1, for example, starts us off by looking at the Letter to the Hebrews and how we are to worship Christ's majesty. A study on Psalm 95 then invites us to "make a joyful noise." We end the Advent season with Luke's narrative of the angels' appearance to the shepherds in the field and our own reasons to give glory to God. Lesson 4 rounds out this unit (and closes our year) with one account of Jesus walking on the water. We are invited to join the disciples in worship that spontaneously comes in awe of Christ's majesty.

Unit 2 focuses more specifically on "Learning to Pray." We begin with the Lord's Prayer, which is our model for prayer, on the Sunday that some of you will celebrate Epiphany. How wonderful that on the day we celebrate Jesus as the light to the world, we also get to read his instruction on drawing near to God in prayer! Then, looking at texts from John and Hebrews, we will see how Jesus prayed for the disciples before he died and how he intercedes for us still. The unit closes with practical instruction from James as to how we are to pray for one another.

Unit 3, "Stewardship for Life," then explores the way in which spiritual disciplines can become acts of worship within our daily living. Lesson 9 starts with the time-honored rituals of both feasting and fasting by focusing on texts from Daniel and Matthew. Following this, the parable of the good Samaritan in Luke challenges us to consider how we serve God by serving our neighbor—a theme that continues through the subsequent study of the parable of the sheep and the goats from Matthew's Gospel. Lesson 12, which falls on the first Sunday of Lent, ends our study with Ephesians' call to put on the whole armor of God so that we might be prepared and ready to face any challenges to actions dedicated to God as a form of worship.

In Closing

As you go through this quarter, my hope is that you may encounter God along the way and thus experience worship in the process. To that end, I offer these words from the Letter to the Ephesians as both blessing and prayer for the weeks ahead:

> I pray that you may have the power to comprehend, with all the saints, what is the breadth and length and height and depth, and to know the love of Christ that surpasses knowledge, so that you may be filled with all the fullness of God. Now to him who by the power at work within us is able to accomplish abundantly far more than all we can ask or imagine, to him be glory in the church and in Christ Jesus to all generations, forever and ever. Amen (Ephesians 3:18-21).

CLOSE-UP: RESOURCES FOR FURTHER STUDY

Since the theme of this quarter's study is worship, you may find it helpful to have a list of "editor's choice" resources to recommend to class members. The books are categorized according to the focus of each of the three units. To conserve space, only the bibliographical citation is given. As of this writing, they are all in print (or available on Kindle), so you will be able to check the Internet for information about their contents, reviews, and prices. Perhaps you can borrow books from your church library or pastor's study, or your community library.

Worship

Mitman, F. Russell. *Worship in the Shape of Scripture.* Cleveland: Pilgrim, 2001.

Saliers, Don E. *Worship as Theology: Foretaste of Divine Glory.* Nashville: Abingdon Press, 1994.

Stookey, Laurence Hull. *Calendar: Christ's Time for the Church.* Nashville: Abingdon Press, 1996.

Van Dyk, Leanne, ed. *A More Profound Alleluia: Theology and Worship in Harmony.* Grand Rapids: Eerdmans, 2005.

White, James F. *A Brief History of Christian Worship.* Nashville: Abingdon Press, 1993.

Prayer

Barry, William A. *God and You: Prayer as Personal Relationship.* Mahwah, N.J.: Paulist, 1987.

———. *Seek My Face: Prayer as Personal Relationship in Scripture.* Mahwah, N.J.: Paulist, 1989.

Foster, Richard J. *Prayer: Finding the Heart's True Home.* New York: Harper Collins, 1991.

Renovare Resource. *Prayer and Worship: A Spiritual Formation Guide for Individuals and Groups.* New York: Harper One, 2007.

Smith, Martin L. *The Word Is Very Near You: A Guide to Praying with Scripture.* Boston: Cowley, 1989.

Stewardship

Hall, Douglas John. *The Steward: A Biblical Symbol Come of Age.* Rev. ed. Grand Rapids: Eerdmans, 1990. (Earlier and later editions are also in print.)

Nouwen, Henri J. M. *The Wounded Healer: Ministry in Contemporary Society*. New York: Image, 1979.

Valet, Ronald E. *Stepping Stones of the Steward: A Faith Journey Through Jesus' Parables*. 2nd ed., rev. and enl. Grand Rapids: Eerdmans, 1994.

———. *The Steward Living in Covenant: A New Perspective on Old Testament Stories*. Grand Rapids: Eerdmans, 2001.

Witherington, Ben, III. *Jesus and Money: A Guide for Times of Financial Crisis*. Grand Rapids: Brazos, 2010.

FAITH IN ACTION: LIVING AS A BELIEVER

This quarter's sessions have focused on worship as a response to God. The selected Scriptures have demonstrated that worship encompasses far more than spending an hour each week in church, as important as that is. Worship is really a lifestyle. Worshipers stand in awe of God, practice spiritual disciplines such as prayer to draw closer to God, and use all of the resources God has entrusted to them as wise stewards.

Write the first idea on newsprint. Each week add one more idea until all twelve have been posted by the end of the quarter. As you close the session each week, note the new idea and encourage the adults to do several of these activities over the course of this study.

1. View a painting, sculpture, mural, fiber creation, or other art work that depicts Jesus. Use this art as a means to experience and give thanks for the majesty of Christ.
2. Page through a hymnal or book of carols. Sing or play an instrument so as to make a joyful noise to God in praise of Jesus.
3. Write a poem or short essay in which you give glory to God for sending Jesus into the world.
4. Be alert this week for miracles in your midst. Give thanks to God for the awesome power that you experience through Jesus.
5. Read the Lord's Prayer each day from a different translation of the Bible. Use the versions in Matthew 6:9-13 and Luke 11:2-4. How do these two versions, found in a variety of translations, enable you to more fully enter into Jesus' model prayer?
6. Focus one of your prayers each day on the church, your community, or an enemy.
7. Offer intercessory prayers each day for those who are hungry, homeless, victims of crime or abuse, and refugees.
8. Visit someone who is sick at home or in a hospital. Be prepared to read comforting words of Scripture to this person. Offer prayers for comfort and healing.
9. Plan a fast from food, television, electronic devices, or a hobby that you particularly enjoy. Use the time that you would spend preparing and eating food, watching television, doing nonessential tasks on an electronic device, or pursuing a hobby to interact with God through prayer, meditation, or journaling.
10. Look for opportunities this week to help someone, preferably a stranger, in need. Do whatever you can to help, but do not take anything in return.
11. Do some hands-on work this week with a church or community program that serves those in need. Consider becoming a regular volunteer with this organization.

12. Make a commitment to engage regularly in a spiritual discipline. Possible choices include worshiping, devotional Bible reading, praying, fasting, meditating, journaling, serving others, and living simply. Consult books such as Richard J. Foster's *Celebration of Discipline: The Path to Spiritual Growth* or Marjorie J. Thompson's *Soul Feast: An Invitation to the Christian Spiritual Life* for information about implementing different types of disciplines.

UNIT 1: IN AWE OF GOD
WORSHIP CHRIST'S MAJESTY

PREVIEWING THE LESSON

Lesson Scripture: Hebrews 1:1-9
Background Scripture: Hebrews 1:1-9
Key Verse: Hebrews 1:3

Focus of the Lesson:
Some people do seemingly miraculous things with their gifts and talents. How do Christians respond? For the true miracle of Jesus Christ, the gift of salvation, God's people respond with worship.

Goals for the Learners:
(1) to consider why Jesus is worthy of adoration and worship.
(2) to affirm that Jesus' superiority and God's anointing of him with "the oil of gladness" lead to their response of worship.
(3) to practice meaningful worship.

Pronunciation Guide:
Septuagint (sep´ too uh jint)

Supplies:
Bibles, newsprint and marker, paper and pencils, hymnals

READING THE SCRIPTURE

NRSV
Lesson Scripture: Hebrews 1:1-9
¹Long ago God spoke to our ancestors in many and various ways by the prophets, ²but in these last days he has spoken to us by a Son, whom he appointed heir of all things, through whom he also created the worlds. ³He is the reflection of God's glory

CEB
Lesson Scripture: Hebrews 1:1-9
¹In the past, God spoke through the prophets to our ancestors in many times and many ways. ²In these final days, though, he spoke to us through a Son. God made his Son the heir of everything and created the world through him. ³The Son is the light of

and the exact imprint of God's very being, and he sustains all things by his powerful word. When he had made purification for sins, he sat down at the right hand of the Majesty on high, [4]having become as much superior to angels as the name he has inherited is more excellent than theirs.

[5]For to which of the angels did God ever say,

"You are my Son;
today I have begotten you"?

Or again,

"I will be his Father,
and he will be my Son"?

[6]And again, when he brings the firstborn into the world, he says,

"Let all God's angels worship him."

[7]Of the angels he says,

"He makes his angels winds,
and his servants flames of fire."

[8]But of the Son he says,

"Your throne, O God, is forever and ever,
and the righteous scepter is the scepter of your kingdom.

[9]You have loved righteousness and hated wickedness;
therefore God, your God, has anointed you
with the oil of gladness beyond your companions."

God's glory and the imprint of God's being. He maintains everything with his powerful message. After he carried out the cleansing of people from their sins, he sat down at the right side of the highest majesty [4]And so, the Son became so much greater than the other messengers, such as angels, that he received a more important title than theirs.

[5]After all, when did God ever say to any of the angels:

You are my Son.
Today I have become your Father?

Or, even,

I will be his Father,
and he will be my Son?

[6]But then, when he brought his firstborn into the world, he said,

All of God's angels must worship him.

[7]He talks about the angels:

He's the one who uses the spirits for his messengers
and who uses flames of fire as ministers.

[8]But he says to his Son,

God, your throne is forever
and your kingdom's scepter is a rod of justice.

[9]You loved righteousness and hated lawless behavior.
That is why God, your God, has anointed you with oil
instead of your companions.

UNDERSTANDING THE SCRIPTURE

Introduction. The Letter to the Hebrews first appears in Christian records in A.D. 95, when it was quoted by Clement of Rome somewhat extensively. Beyond that, it is difficult to date the letter precisely. Most scholars suggest a range anywhere from A.D. 60 to 95.

The content of the letter, which is structured like a sermon, seems to address second-generation Jewish Christians (see Hebrews 2:3). We know the intended audience spoke Greek, because the author uses the Greek translation of Hebrew Scriptures (the Septuagint) when quoting the Old Testament. If the information in Hebrews 13:24 is correct that fellow Italian Christians were sending greetings back to the home congregation, then the letter's recipients might have lived in Rome. Beyond this, we know only that the congregation had suffered persecution (10:32-34), which many scholars think may refer to Roman emperor Claudius's nonviolent temporary expulsion of Jews and Jewish Christians in A.D. 49.

Clues to the letter's author are also sparse. Scholars have debated since the third century whether Paul wrote it, and John Calvin and Martin Luther continued the argument centuries later. The best evidence seems to point away from the apostle, however. The author does not claim to be either an apostle or an eyewitness to Christ (2:3), although Paul frequently makes that claim for himself. The writing style and theological content does not match that of Paul's known letters. Perhaps most telling, the letter does not include a personal address from Paul that states he is the author—a feature we find in his known letters.

We know only that the writer was concerned with believers who were losing heart and beginning to drift away from the faith (see 2:1-3; 6:1-6; 10:23-25; 12:12). These Christians had started strong, full of confidence and zeal (10:32-36), but somehow stalled along the way in their faith development (5:11-14). Thus, the author wants to encourage them by reminding them of all God has done for them in Christ, and thereby motivate and strengthen them in faith.

To this end, the writer uses two key themes: priesthood and pilgrimage. Jesus is central to both. As the ultimate high priest, he has permanently opened direct access to God for us by eliminating all that previously stood in our way—sin, guilt, and impurity. Moreover, he has shown us the path to follow in order to reach our new home in God, thus acting as a "pioneer" (12:2) for those of us who follow in his path as pilgrims.

It is also helpful to put this passage within the larger context of Christian theology. Many Christians, reading the Book of Hebrews in tandem with other New Testament passages, see there an affirmation of Jesus as the fulfillment of three Old Testament offices: prophet, priest, and king.

Hebrews 1:1-2. The opening verses of Hebrews show that it is not a typical letter. There is no greeting or salutation, no statement identifying the author. Instead, the text begins with the writer's initial concern: to establish continuity between what God has revealed in the past and what God has revealed through Jesus Christ, while also pointing to Jesus as being more than a prophet. Unlike former messengers of God, Jesus is God's own Son—bonded with God in such a way that he is both heir and cocreator of all things.

Hebrews 1:3-4. The next verses elaborate on the Son's nature and role. He is the reflection of God's own "glory," a word that can mean "radiance" but usually refers to God's full character and presence in Scripture. He is the stamp ("exact image") or likeness of God's own substance ("very being"). The first image is that of the sun's own brilliance shining back in our eyes from a mirror, while the second is that of a carved seal pressed into hot wax. Both are meant to convey that Jesus not only shows us God's self but also carries God's own power and authority as well.

This understanding is underscored by the next affirmation in verse 3—that the Son sustains all creation by "his powerful word." The One who participated in the beginning of creation and who will stand at its end as the "heir" (1:2) is also the One who maintains its existence in the meantime. The author may have intended us to hear a connection to the opening verses of John's Gospel here.

The Son's role is personal as well as transcendent, though. He is the One who has freed humankind by purifying us from sin. By implication, he is thus our redeemer, high priest, and lord. Certainly the Son's majesty is affirmed by his place at God's right hand—an affirmation made by quoting Psalm 110:1. The verses end with praise of the Son's superiority over the "angels," a word that also means "messengers." Whether the author refers to human prophets or heavenly beings, the Son's superiority is undeniable.

Hebrews 1:5. In order to show that the Son's name is above all others throughout eternity, the author uses a series of quotations from the Hebrew Scriptures. These quotations are from the Greek translation of these Scriptures, known as the Septuagint, which was commonly used by the writers of the New Testament. Verse 5 quotes Psalm 2:7 and 2 Samuel 7:14 to show that God has never called an angel "son."

Hebrews 1:6-7. The next two quotations are from Deuteronomy 32:43 and Psalm 104:4. As applied by the author, they are meant to show that the angels worship the Son, but they never rise higher than servitude to God as messengers. Moreover, the angels are compared to the changeable element of the wind in contrast to the Son who is ever "the same" (1:12). "Firstborn" in verse 6 is a title of familial preeminence and does not imply that Jesus was a created being.

Hebrews 1:8-9. The final quotation in our passage is from Psalm 45:6-7. Originally describing a human king, here it speaks of the Son's eternal and righteous rule, which God has ordained with joy. Hebrews 1:10-14, which is outside of our selection, continues this theme with quotations from Psalm 102:25-27 and 110:1.

INTERPRETING THE SCRIPTURE

The One We Worship

As we begin this new quarter of study, it is inevitable that our thoughts will be shaped by the season of Advent. Whether we are holding services in sanctuaries or homes, we are surrounded by "the signs of the time"—wreaths, holly, candles, and crèches abound. With all the colorful decorations and joyful Christmas music, Advent is a great time to begin a discussion on worship. The text for this first lesson, which we are studying on the second Sunday of Advent, invites us to consider carefully whom we worship—and why.

Part of why we love Christmas is the story of the baby Jesus. God comes among us as a helpless, tiny infant—warming our hearts with the gift of divine presence and love. There is also something comforting, although misleading, in the idea of God as a newborn human child. The picture of a God who is cute and cuddly is much more appealing to some people than the reality of a God who is all powerful, all knowing, and infinitely above us. Our passage from Hebrews calls us to remember just who Jesus really is. We do not gather in Advent to worship a regular human being, but the Son of God— he who is both fully human and fully divine.

According to the author of Hebrews, Jesus provides us with insight into God's own self. Our key verse from Hebrews 1:3 uses three particular phrases to expand this concept: "reflection of God's glory," "the exact imprint of God's very being," and One who "sustains all things."

First, Jesus is the "reflection" (NRSV) or "light" (CEB) of God's glory. The root of the Greek word used here means "radiance." This image brings to my mind an experience that sometimes occurs during plane travel. From up high, one can look down on rivers or lakes to see the sun's reflection more directly than is possible on land. The effect is dazzling and blinding—just as if you were to look at the sun itself. The author of Hebrews calls us to look beyond a tiny human child to the awesome glory of God's own self that abides within the infant. Part of the gift Jesus brings is that now we *can* see that glory instead of being overwhelmed by it.

Early Jewish Christians would have understood the magnitude of this gift as they thought back to the one time a human being asked to look directly on the face of God. Moses made this request while traveling in the wilderness after the Exodus event (Exodus 33:18-23). God replied that no mortal could look directly at the divine glory and survive. As a compromise, Moses was allowed to see God's back instead. Even a brief glimpse of the deflected glory was enough to transform him, however. Moses's face glowed with residual light from then on. As a result of this encounter he had to wear a veil in order to move among the people. This is the context for the gift we have received from Jesus—in him we can now encounter and experience God face-to-face and live.

Hebrews 1:3 then speaks of Jesus as "the exact imprint of God's very being." A very literal translation of the Greek says that Jesus is "the character of God's substance." In other words, Jesus' very nature not only *reflects* but *is* the essence of God. Do you want to know who God is in the simplest, most direct form? Then look at Jesus, says the writer of Hebrews.

Finally, the key verse tells us that Jesus "sustains" (NRSV) or "maintains" (CEB) the whole created order with his power, which is connected to speech (just as creation itself came from God's words—Genesis 1:3; John 1:1-3). The underlying Greek verb has two core meanings. The first is to "carry" or "bear." In other words, the small infant we see in the manger is actually bearing all of creation, actively willing (as God) to continue its existence moment by moment. The Greek word also means to "lead," though, which adds a glorious element to the picture. Jesus is not just carrying us along; he is leading us into God's plan for the future.

The One on High

For the writer of Hebrews, Jesus' role is not bound by time. He was present at creation and played a key role in that event (Hebrews 1:2), and he is certainly part of God's plan for the future. The phrase "in these last days" (1:2) is meant apocalyptically. That is, the writer sees a new age beginning with Jesus' birth.

Clues to the divine plan are scattered throughout the passage. Sins are forgiven (1:3), Jesus is elevated in majesty to God's right hand (1:3), and righteousness is established at last (1:8-9). Building on Old Testament concepts of righteousness, the passage speaks of a day to come in which every member of society will experience justice, wholeness, and well-being.

Traditional Advent services celebrate the hope we have in this promise. Our liturgy and hymns speak of Jesus' birth, but they also anticipate his return. The great joy of Christmas lies in the ongoing presence of the One who was and is and is to come.

The One Superior to the Angels

The author of Hebrews points to the exalted position of Christ, in part, by speaking of Jesus' superiority to the angels. In the Christmas season, we often see angels depicted as winged women with flowing hair or as small children wearing tinselly halos in a church pageant. This is not what our passage has in mind.

Throughout the Old Testament, angels appear as messengers of God. When interacting most directly with humans, they take the form of human males, yet somehow represent God's own presence. It is possible, then, that our Hebrews author wanted to make clear that Jesus himself is not an angel. He is something more.

The author quotes from two psalms to expand on this idea— Psalm 2:7 in Hebrews 1:5 and Psalm 110:1 in Hebrews 1:13 (which is not included in today's reading). These are both "enthronement psalms," written originally on the occasion of the coronation of an ancient Israelite king. The writer applies them to Jesus, both to show him as the king of all earthly kings and to establish him as being higher than the angels in the heavenly hierarchy.

Our passage leaves us with much to ponder. Jesus is both the human child whose birth we eagerly wait to celebrate and the One who shares in God's divine majesty. Hebrews invites us to consider this paradox during the Advent season in order to deepen our understanding of and gratitude for the incomparable work of God's gift of salvation in the Son.

As commentator Frances Taylor Gench puts it: "It is highly appropriate that the church's lectionary [list of weekly Scripture readings] holds this passage before us at Christmas, when we contemplate a baby in a manger. Christians who do not attend church regularly, making an appearance only at Christmas and Easter, may envision Christ only in diapers or nailed to a cross! Hebrews, however, encourages a broader perspective. It fills out the big picture, thereby laying the groundwork for a more mature understanding of the One who stands at the beginning and end of God's purposes for the world, and who makes available to us God's own life."

SHARING THE SCRIPTURE

PREPARING TO TEACH

Preparing Our Hearts

Meditate on this week's devotional reading from 1 Timothy 1:12-17. What reasons do you have to be grateful to God? How has God shown mercy to you? How might your life be an example for those who do not yet know Jesus to come into a loving relationship with him?

Pray that you and the students will live so as to demonstrate through your lives that you worship God through Jesus.

Preparing Our Minds

Study the background Scripture and the lesson Scripture, which are both from Hebrews 1:1-9.

Consider this question as you prepare the lesson: *How do Christians respond to miraculous gifts and talents?*

Write on newsprint:

❏ directions for "Practice Meaningful Worship" if you choose to work in groups.

❏ information for next week's lesson, found under "Continue the Journey."

❏ activities for further spiritual growth in "Continue the Journey."

Review the "Introduction," "The Big Picture," "Close-up," and "Faith in Action," which all precede this first lesson of the quarter. Consider how you might use any of this material in today's lesson.

LEADING THE CLASS

(1) Gather to Learn

❖ Greet the class members and introduce guests.

❖ Pray that those who have come today will be aware of the gifts in their midst and ready to respond to them.

❖ Read these stories of people who were child prodigies:

■ **Gregory Smith's first of four nominations for a Nobel Peace Prize was made when he was just twelve years old. The founder of International Youth Advocates, Gregory travels the world to promote peace and understanding. He has addressed the United Nations and met with Bill Clinton and Mikhail Gorbachev.**

■ **Alma Deutscher is a seven-year-old pianist, violinist, and composer whom some have compared to Mozart. Receiving her first violin at the age of three, this grade-school student has performed her own music on both the piano and violin. Alma has even written a short opera, *The Sweeper of Dreams*.**

■ **Fabiano Luigi Caruana became a chess Grandmaster in 2007 at the age of fourteen years, eleven months, twenty days. He was the youngest Grandmaster in the history of both countries where he holds citizenship: Italy and the United States. By April**

2009 he held the world's highest ranking of any player under the age of eighteen.

❖ Ask: **How do you respond when you hear stories of such talents?**

❖ Read aloud today's focus statement: **Some people do seemingly miraculous things with their gifts and talents. How do Christians respond? For the true miracle of Jesus Christ, the gift of salvation, God's people respond with worship.**

(2) Goal 1: Consider Why Jesus Is Worthy of Adoration and Worship

❖ Lead into today's session by reading "Introduction" from Understanding the Scripture.

❖ Select a volunteer to read Hebrews 1:1-4.

❖ Discuss these questions. Add information from Understanding the Scripture and "The One We Worship" from Interpreting the Scripture as appropriate.

1. **How is the Son similar to and different from the prophets?**
2. **How is the Son described in verses 1-4?** (You will find seven different descriptions here. Look at each one carefully.)
3. **If someone who is not a believer were to ask you why Jesus is worthy of worship, how could the writer of Hebrews help you to reply?**

❖ Form several groups of three students. Within each group one person is to be a skeptic who does not currently believe in Jesus but is willing to listen and raise questions; one, a believer who talks with the skeptic about why Jesus is worthy of worship; the third, an observer. The observer is to comment on the positive points made by the believer and suggest any other points that could have been made to help the nonbeliever. As time permits, encourage the students to change roles.

❖ Reconvene the class and invite the adults to identify comments and attitudes that seemed most helpful in encouraging the skeptic to believe in Jesus.

(3) Goal 2: Affirm that Jesus' Superiority and God's Anointing of Him "with the Oil of Gladness" Lead to the Learners' Response of Worship

❖ Invite a volunteer to read Hebrews 1:5-9.

❖ Read or retell "The One Superior to the Angels" from Interpreting the Scripture.

❖ Explore the quotations from Psalm 2:7 in Hebrews 1:5; Psalm 104:4 in Hebrews 1:7; Psalm 45:6-7 in Hebrews 1:8-9 by turning to these psalms and choosing readers.

❖ Ask these questions:

1. **Why do you think the writer of Hebrews chose to use these quotations?**
2. **How do these quotations help you to understand that the Son is superior to the angels?**
3. **What other Bible quotations can you think of that also make clear Jesus' superior position in relation to the angels?**

(4) Goal 3: Practice Meaningful Worship

❖ Choose one or more of these activities to help the students to engage in meaningful worship. If you want to do more than one activity, consider assigning the students to groups.

Write directions on newsprint prior to the session. Give each group a sheet of newsprint and a marker.

Activity 1: Locate and read hymns that praise Jesus or describe who Jesus is. Some Advent and Christmas hymns may be useful for this purpose. Record what you find on newsprint.

Activity 2: Ask one group member to read Revelation 19:1-9. Discuss and record on newsprint what you learn about heavenly worship from this vision.

Activity 3: Look at a church bulletin to discern the different actions your congregation takes during a worship service. Record ideas on newsprint.

❖ Bring the groups together to report their findings and then ask:

1. **What insights have you gleaned about why Jesus is worthy of worship?**
2. **What have you discovered about how Jesus is worshiped?**
3. **How might you and other members of your congregation worship Jesus so that you may truly experience his presence?**

(5) Continue the Journey

❖ Pray that as the learners depart, they will be better prepared to worship Christ's majesty and will go forth to do so.

❖ Post information for next week's session on newsprint for the students to copy:

- **Title: Make a Joyful Noise**
- **Background Scripture: Psalm 95:1-7a**

- **Lesson Scripture: Psalm 95:1-7a**
- **Focus of the Lesson: Many people realize that a power beyond them gives meaning to their lives. How do they respond to this knowledge? The psalmist declares that God is the rock of their salvation and is worthy of praise and worship.**

❖ Challenge the adults to grow spiritually by completing one or more of these activities related to this week's session, which you have posted on newsprint for the students to copy.

(1) **Look for books, art, media references or other depictions of angels. How does society portray angels? How do these portraits confirm or challenge your own beliefs about angels?**

(2) **Make spiritual preparations during this season of Advent to celebrate the coming of Jesus. What does it mean to you to say that Jesus came in the flesh as "the exact imprint of God's very being" (Hebrews 1:3)? Be ready to tell someone how Jesus' coming changed the world—and you.**

(3) **Review your church's worship schedule for upcoming weeks of Advent, Christmas, and Epiphany. Also check for ecumenical events where members of the Christian community are invited to come together. Make plans to attend as many of these services as possible. Invite friends or family members to join you.**

❖ Sing or read aloud "Majesty, Worship His Majesty."

❖ Conclude by leading the class in this benediction, adapted from the key verse for the session on December 21 from Luke 2:20: **May we go forth to worship as the shepherds, glorifying and praising God for all we have heard and seen.**

UNIT 1: IN AWE OF GOD
MAKE A JOYFUL NOISE

PREVIEWING THE LESSON

Lesson Scripture: Psalm 95:1-7a
Background Scripture: Psalm 95:1-7a
Key Verse: Psalm 95:1

Focus of the Lesson:
Many people realize that a power beyond them gives meaning to their lives. How do they respond to this knowledge? The psalmist declares that God is the rock of their salvation and is worthy of praise and worship.

Goals for the Learners:
(1) to discern that God, who is the creator of the earth and of humankind, is truly worthy of praise.
(2) to experience the enthusiasm, power, and excitement that comes when believers praise God as their divine King.
(3) to shed inhibitions in worship so as to praise God exuberantly.

Pronunciation Guide:
Pentateuch (pen´ tuh tyook)
Shiggaion (shuh gay´ on)

Supplies:
Bibles, newsprint and marker, paper and pencils, hymnals

READING THE SCRIPTURE

NRSV
Lesson Scripture: Psalm 95:1-7a
¹O come, let us sing to the LORD;
  let us make a joyful noise to the
  rock of our salvation!
²Let us come into his presence with
    thanksgiving;
  let us make a joyful noise to him
    with songs of praise!

CEB
Lesson Scripture: Psalm 95:1-7a
¹Come, let's sing out loud to the
    LORD!
  Let's raise a joyful shout to the
    rock of our salvation!
²Let's come before him with thanks!
  Let's shout songs of joy to him!
³The Lord is a great God,

³For the LORD is a great God,
and a great King above all gods.
⁴In his hand are the depths of the
earth;
the heights of the mountains are
his also.
⁵The sea is his, for he made it,
and the dry land, which his hands
have formed.
⁶O come, let us worship and bow
down,
let us kneel before the LORD, our
Maker!
⁷For he is our God,
and we are the people of his
pasture,
and the sheep of his hand.

the great king over all other gods.
⁴The earth's depths are in his hands;
the mountain heights belong to
him;
⁵the sea, which he made, is his
along with the dry ground,
which his own hands formed.
⁶Come, let's worship and bow down!
Let's kneel before the LORD, our
maker!
⁷He is our God,
and we are the people of his
pasture,
the sheep in his hands.

UNDERSTANDING THE SCRIPTURE

Introduction. The Psalms represent some of the oldest worship material in the Judeo-Christian tradition. Written as hymns, these texts reflect the troubles, pain, joy, and hope of individuals who, joined together with the whole community of faith, return time and again to their confidence in God and the reasons they have to praise the Holy One.

Indeed, there is evidence that the collection, known as the Psalter, was used by the ancient Israelites as a form of hymnal. Many of the psalms contain superscriptions indicating the instrument to be used (see Psalm 4), some now-forgotten technical instruction (for example, the "Shiggaion" of Psalm 7), or perhaps the name of a tune (such as "Lilies" for Psalms 45 and 69). In studying Psalm 95, try to hear it in its original liturgical setting: as an act of praise summoning the congregation to worship and offer honor and thanksgiving to God.

Early tradition ascribes nearly half of the Psalms to David, and this authorship is often indicated in titles or superscriptions. Other clues within the collection of Psalms show that many psalms were written long after David lived, stretching even into the time of exile (see Psalm 137, for example). A much later tradition attributing *all* the Psalms to David does injustice to the wealth of experiences that contributed to these songs throughout Israel's history.

Mirroring the Pentateuch (the first five books of the Bible), the Psalms are also divided into five books. Scattered across the divisions, scholars lift up at least eight different types:

There are *psalms of praise*, including those that celebrate God's rule (called *enthronement hymns*) and Jerusalem as God's holy city (*hymns of Zion*). These psalms generally call people to praise and offer reasons for the praise. Psalm 95 falls in this general category.

Wisdom psalms, which come from the same tradition as Proverbs, focus on the intersection of God's ways and human choices.

Royal psalms were written for specific court occasions, such as a coronation or a royal wedding, and they often seek God's guidance and blessing for the king. Psalms in this category, which are scattered throughout the five books, are linked by their interest in the monarchy.

Sacred history psalms retell the story of God's mighty acts on behalf of the nation throughout time.

Psalms of trust express confidence in God's willingness to give aid.

Psalms of thanksgiving express gratitude for deliverance that God has already provided from a particular cause of distress.

Psalms of lament, which may be individual or national, come from such times of trouble and are pleas for God's intervention. After describing the problem, the psalmist pleads for God's help, citing reasons why God should act. The supplicant then promises to praise God or offer sacrifice.

Finally, some psalms contain *liturgies* that were written for special worship services, such as the renewal of the covenant.

While these basic categories run throughout the collection known as Psalms, there are also sections where similar hymns are placed together. Psalm 95, for example, belongs to a larger group that encompasses Psalms 93 and 95–99. (Psalm 94 is a personal lament that has been injected among the others.) The six related psalms highlight God's "kingship" over creation and over all nations, Israel in particular. Given the emphasis on God's reign, scholars think these six

psalms of this group may have been written for use during the Jewish Festival of Booths, which highlights the same theme. This is a seven- or eight-day-long harvest celebration observed in the fall. It recalls Israel's days of wandering in the wilderness, when the people lived in tents and sought shelter in makeshift booths. This festival is a time of great rejoicing. Community celebrations are marked by processions, music, dancing, and the reciting of special psalms. One of the customs essential to the ritual is a daily procession to the Pool of Siloam, just outside Jerusalem. In ancient times, a pitcher of water was drawn and then ceremoniously delivered to the Temple for use as a drink offering. This water symbolized the water that sprang from the rock in the desert as part of God's provision for Israel (Exodus 17:1-7). Inherent in the festival and its symbolism is the religious conviction that God cares for the people, provides for their needs, and continues to lead and inspire them. It may open new insights to read Psalm 95 in this context.

Psalm 95:1-2. The hymn opens with a call to worship. God's people are summoned to sing praises to God and to enter into the divine presence "with thanksgiving." Why? Because God is "the rock of our salvation"— the solid and unmovable source of the people's safety and deliverance. "Rock" is a favorite metaphor for God in the Psalms, being used more than twenty times.

The verbs in these first two verses describe the heart of a worship service in the psalmist's time. The congregation is to come (that is, gather), sing, and make a joyful noise.

Psalm 95:3-5. These verses describe God as the creator of all that is. As the creator, God is above not only all human beings but also all heavenly beings ("gods"). There is no place on earth that God did not make, from the highest mountain to the deepest valley; therefore, there is no geographical territory that does not belong to God.

Psalm 95:6-7a. A second call to worship closes out the section on God's reign. Verse 6 adds to the visual image of worship in the psalmist's time—the people are to kneel and bow down before God. Verse 7a then recites one of the oldest statements of the covenant relationship: "For he is our God, and we are the people of his pasture, and the sheep of his hand." This may bring to mind John 10, in which Jesus describes himself as the Good Shepherd who knows and takes care of his sheep.

INTERPRETING THE SCRIPTURE

To Praise or Not to Praise

While our first lesson from Hebrews reminds us of who Jesus is and the reasons we have to give thanks in his name, today's focuses on the reasons we have to praise God. Together the lessons lift up two critical aspects of worship: gratitude and praise.

Psalm 95 especially lifts up the goodness of God, creator of all and our divine king. The same God who made the seas and the dry land cares intimately for the people, just as a shepherd cares for the flock. Moreover, the psalmist affirms that, in keeping with this love and care, God uses the divine power to bring salvation to the community of faith. Each of these themes runs throughout our Advent season, along with the good news of Jesus Christ. No wonder we too have reason to make a joyful noise!

The writer of Psalm 95 calls on the faith community to join in singing praise to God. Without intending to, the psalmist thus raises a somewhat touchy issue for today. To what extent should "praise" be an element in worship?

Different congregations have resolved this in various ways. Some have informal services with no printed liturgy. Music is offered by "praise bands" who sing upbeat contemporary Christian music. The focus of sermons in such services tends to be more on God's good gifts than on life's challenges. Other congregations follow a more traditional church model in which praise is offered to God in quieter, less exuberant ways.

Regardless of worship style, however, praise is a hallmark of all our worship services—and not just during Advent! If you listen carefully to the prayers and music of any service, you will hear praise there. God's goodness, majesty, and grace are always highlighted at various points in the service.

Psalm 95's enthusiastic call to praise reminds me of special visits in my childhood to a small church when I visited out-of-town family. My great-aunt never missed church, and she made sure the rest of us went too. A tall, full-figured woman, she had a booming voice that was more operatic in volume than in pitch—and she sang every hymn robustly.

She once commented, "I know I don't sing well, but the Lord said to make a joyful noise, and so I do!"

Why We Sing

As countless congregations this Advent join in singing "Joy to the World"—on pitch or otherwise—Psalm 95 lifts up for us four reasons we have to rejoice and praise God.

First is that God is "the rock of our salvation" (95:1). God is the unshakable, immutable, indestructible source of our life and well-being. The word translated "salvation" also means "deliverance" or "rescue." We can picture God, then, as a secure boulder to which we cling in order to avoid being swept away by a dangerous flood of impure emotions, attitudes, or actions. God saves us from sin, from the world, and from ourselves.

Another reason for praise lies in God's sovereignty. "Hear the good news!" cries the psalmist, in essence. "God is the One in control—not some other deity, prone to caprice or whim." Our lives, indeed all created things, rest in the hands of a God of love and mercy, a God whose power extends beyond anything we have previously imagined. There is no other god who can threaten or overcome our God's power.

This brings us to a third reason to give thanks. The powerful God who provides our salvation cares for us on an intimate and personal level, because this God is our creator. The same divine will that shaped the earth and the sea—the highest land and the deepest ocean—also formed us in care and love. We are not mere "things" to God; we are cherished treasures.

All of which leads to the fourth and best reason for praise—out of love, God our creator seeks a covenantal partnership with us. God invites us into a relationship that both affirms our value and opens us to blessings beyond measure. In the simple declaration that God is our God and we are God's people, we find our identity and our purpose. Named and claimed by God, we are sent forth to be a blessing to the world.

The Psalms as a whole teach us that our response to God's presence takes form not only in praise but also in attitude and conduct. God is the One who deserves our total trust. We participate in God's presence by conducting our lives according to the word and way that God reveals. Only in this way do we become living sanctuaries for God—a people whose lives reflect worship of the Holy One.

Celebrating God's Presence Then—and Now

Psalm 95 calls on people of faith to praise God, particularly through worship. This worship begins with God's greatness and glory, but it also assumes God's presence or nearness. Along with the rest of the Psalter, Psalm 95 thus stands as an eloquent testimony to the Holy Presence in the whole of life. As such, it is a fitting study for Advent, when we celebrate the incarnation of God in Jesus Christ.

While the form of the psalms varies in their address of this immanent and indwelling God—from praise to lamentation, from petition to confession—they all agree on one common foundation: God is present among and concerned for those whom the Holy One of Israel has fashioned and called. They emphasize this both through reviewing Israel's history and through personal reminiscences of the psalmists.

The Psalms do more than celebrate God's past presence in historical events, though; they also affirm that God is with us now in the daily routine of life. We may feel alienated and cut off from God at times but, nonetheless, God is with us. The Creator God of infinite power is also the "rock" who, out of intimate love and constant care, protects and saves us.

No wonder thankfulness over God's good gifts finds first expression in song! Think about this for a moment. Psalm 95's call to "sing out loud to the LORD" (95:1, CEB) reflects an understanding that worship is an expression of the whole person. Song comes from the body and the emotions, not just the mind. Singing also affirms something of the nature of communities at worship. Whether voices flow in unison or diverge in harmony, singing binds people together and carries them forward. Sometimes individual voices improve and take on strength when linked with others. The message of community may indeed be embodied and even formed in a song given voice by a community.

What's more, such wonder calls for a joyful witness beyond that offered by human lips. Psalm 96:11-12, for example, describes how every element of creation takes up the cry of God's reign. Heavens and earth, sea and land and all that inhabit them—no corner of creation remains outside of the chorus, because no corner of creation lives outside the scope of God's rule. Those two verses use four different verbs ("be glad," "rejoice," "exult," "sing for joy") to express the overwhelming sense of joy abounding in creation. The language itself testifies to the breadth of joy summoned by the new song celebrating God's reign.

In this Advent season, we too join in the song that all nature sings. Christ is coming; God's salvation draws near. Thanks be to God!

SHARING THE SCRIPTURE

PREPARING TO TEACH

Preparing Our Hearts

Meditate on this week's devotional reading from 1 Kings 8:54-62. How do these words of King Solomon as he blesses the worshipers who have gathered for the dedication of the Temple in Jerusalem speak to you? How do they express your beliefs about God and your desire for God's presence? Are you willing to say "amen" to verse 61 and act on that command?

Pray that you and the students will always walk hand-in-hand with God.

Preparing Our Minds

Study the background Scripture and the lesson Scripture, which are both from Psalm 95:1-7a.

Consider this question as you prepare the lesson: *How do people respond to the knowledge that there is a power beyond them that gives meaning to their lives?*

Write on newsprint:

❏ information for next week's lesson, found under "Continue the Journey."

❏ activities for further spiritual growth in "Continue the Journey."

Review the "Introduction," "The Big Picture," "Close-up," and "Faith in Action," which all precede the first lesson of this quarter. Consider how you might use any of this material in today's lesson.

LEADING THE CLASS

(1) Gather to Learn

❖ Greet the class members and introduce guests.

❖ Pray that those who have come today will be prepared to praise and worship God.

❖ Note that today is the Third Sunday of Advent. Encourage the class members to discuss ways that they are preparing for Christmas. Be sure to include comments concerning special events, such as concerts or plays, as well as seasonal church services. Discuss how these special events have helped them to worship God, even if they were not in a sacred space. Also discuss how the class members are worshiping God as they decorate a tree or write notes in Christmas cards or prepare food for guests.

❖ Read aloud today's focus statement: **Many people realize that there is a power beyond them that gives meaning to their lives. How do they respond to this knowledge? The psalmist declares that God is the rock of their salvation and is worthy of praise and worship.**

(2) Goal 1: Discern that God, Who Is the Creator of the Earth and of Humankind, Is Truly Worthy of Praise

❖ Read or retell "Why We Sing" in Interpreting the Scripture.

❖ Ask half of the class to read the even-numbered verses and the other half to read the odd-numbered ones from verse 1 to 7a of Psalm 95. If your hymnal includes a Psalter, use that so that everyone will have the same translation.

❖ Ask: **What reasons does the psalmist give for singing praise to God?** (Be sure to include the four reasons in "Why We Sing" in Interpreting the Scripture. Also note the portions in Understanding the Scripture for Psalm 95.)

❖ Invite the students to point out images used to describe God. (These include "rock of our salvation" [95:1], "great King" [95:3], "our Maker" [95:6]. In verse 7 God is also depicted as the shepherd, for the readers are described as "the people of his pasture.")

❖ Ask: **Do these images prompt you to worship God? If so, why? If not, what other images would be more appealing or familiar to you?**

(3) Goal 2: Experience the Enthusiasm, Power, and Excitement that Comes When Believers Praise God as Their Divine King

❖ Encourage the adults to share stories of worship services that were especially meaningful for them. Their comments may relate to a "regular" Sunday morning service, a funeral, a special service such as an Easter sunrise gathering, or a wedding. Urge the speakers to say specifically why the service was so meaningful and how this experience constituted a special encounter with God.

❖ Observe that people experience God in different ways, in part depending upon the space in which they worship. Read these incomplete sentences and call on volunteers to fill in the blanks. Not all participants will be able to answer all questions.

1. When I go on a mission trip and worship God in an unfamiliar space, perhaps in an unfamiliar language, I feel . . .
2. The power of God is most present for me when I worship . . .
3. I feel most connected to God when I worship in my family's church because . . .
4. When I worship in a space that is also used for other purposes, such as a school cafeteria, I find that my experience with God . . .
5. When I worship in one of the great cathedrals of Europe, my encounter with God . . .
6. I prefer a simple clapboard structure because . . .

❖ Provide quiet time for the adults to think about where they feel most able to worship God most freely and experience God most fully. If they do not currently worship in such a space, suggest that they also think about how they can mentally adapt the space where they worship to meet their needs.

(4) Goal 3: Shed Inhibitions in Worship so as to Praise God Exuberantly

❖ Distribute paper and pencils. Tell the students that you will read a list of words or phrases commonly associated with worship. They are to number their papers from 1 to 12 and write a word or phrase that comes to mind as you read. If they have no specific response, they may use a plus or minus sign to indicate how they generally respond to whatever is being described.

1. **Choir anthem**
2. **Sermon**
3. **Praise band**
4. **Prayer and praise time**
5. **Reciting of a historic creed**
6. **Reading of Scripture**
7. **Offering**
8. **Organ**
9. **Prayer of confession by the congregation**
10. **Communion**
11. **Liturgical dancing**
12. **Reading a psalm responsively**

❖ Go through the list and hear some responses. You may find that most people are in agreement or, conversely, that a wide variety of opinion exists. Make sure that everyone understands that there is no correct answer, but rather, that different people are drawn to different styles of worship. Some people are very exuberant and emotional, whereas others who are just as close to God are more reserved and introspective. All authentic worship has in common a focus on experiencing God and a heart that longs to praise God.

❖ Conclude this activity by reading "To Praise or Not to Praise" from Interpreting the Scripture.

(5) Continue the Journey

❖ Pray that as the learners depart they will seek opportunities to praise God.

❖ Post information for next week's session on newsprint for the students to copy:

- Title: Glory to God in the Highest
- Background Scripture: Luke 2:1-20
- Lesson Scripture: Luke 2:8-20
- Focus of the Lesson: Sometimes there is an event in people's lives that causes spontaneous celebration. What might cause people to be wild with joy? Angels announced the birth of the Savior and a multitude of heavenly host praised God.

❖ Challenge the adults to grow spiritually by completing one or more of these activities related to this week's session, which you have posted on newsprint for the students to copy.

(1) Read the accounts of creation in Genesis 1 and 2, as well as God's response to Job in Job 38 and 39 concerning creation. Write words of praise for all that God the Creator has made.

(2) Recall that in Psalm 95 people are called to praise and worship God. Look through the Book of Psalms. Where else do you see psalms of praise? Read at least one of these psalms of praise each day.

(3) Praise God by singing, dancing, drawing or painting a picture, or in some other creative way. Invite others to join you in praise.

❖ Sing or read aloud "Let All the World in Every Corner Sing."

❖ Conclude by leading the class in this benediction, adapted from the key verse for the session on December 21 from Luke 2:20: **May we go forth to worship as the shepherds, glorifying and praising God for all we have heard and seen.**

UNIT 1: IN AWE OF GOD
GLORY TO GOD
IN THE HIGHEST

PREVIEWING THE LESSON

Lesson Scripture: Luke 2:8-20
Background Scripture: Luke 2:1-20
Key Verse: Luke 2:20

Focus of the Lesson:

Sometimes there is an event in people's lives that causes spontaneous celebration. What might cause people to be wild with joy? Angels announced the birth of the Savior and a multitude of heavenly host praised God.

Goals for the Learners:

(1) to explore the events that led to the angels' spontaneous joy and the shepherds' pilgrimage to see Jesus.
(2) to feel the unrestrained joy that comes with the good news of the Savior's birth.
(3) to identify ways to worship God during Christmas and Epiphany.

Pronunciation Guide:

Quirinius (kwi rin´ ee uhs)

Supplies:

Bibles, newsprint and marker, paper and pencils, hymnals, optional refreshments

---

READING THE SCRIPTURE

NRSV

Lesson Scripture: Luke 2:8-20

[8]In that region there were shepherds living in the fields, keeping watch over their flock by night. [9]Then an angel of the Lord stood before them, and the glory of the Lord shone

CEB

Lesson Scripture: Luke 2:8-20

[8]Nearby shepherds were living in the fields, guarding their sheep at night. [9]The Lord's angel stood before them, the Lord's glory shone around them, and they were terrified.

around them, and they were terrified. [10]But the angel said to them, "Do not be afraid; for see—I am bringing you good news of great joy for all the people: [11]to you is born this day in the city of David a Savior, who is the Messiah, the Lord. [12]This will be a sign for you: you will find a child wrapped in bands of cloth and lying in a manger." [13]And suddenly there was with the angel a multitude of the heavenly host, praising God and saying,
[14]"Glory to God in the highest
　　　heaven,
and on earth peace among those
　　　whom he favors!"

[15]When the angels had left them and gone into heaven, the shepherds said to one another, "Let us go now to Bethlehem and see this thing that has taken place, which the Lord has made known to us." [16]So they went with haste and found Mary and Joseph, and the child lying in the manger. [17]When they saw this, they made known what had been told them about this child; [18]and all who heard it were amazed at what the shepherds told them. [19]But Mary treasured all these words and pondered them in her heart. **[20]The shepherds returned, glorifying and praising God for all they had heard and seen, as it had been told them.**

[10]The angel said, "Don't be afraid! Look! I bring good news to you—wonderful, joyous news for all people. [11]Your savior is born today in David's city. He is Christ the Lord. [12]This is a sign for you: you will find a newborn baby wrapped snugly and lying in a manger." [13]Suddenly a great assembly of the heavenly forces was with the angel praising God. They said, [14]"Glory to God in heaven, and on earth peace among those whom he favors."

[15]When the angels returned to heaven, the shepherds said to each other, "Let's go right now to Bethlehem and see what's happened. Let's confirm what the Lord has revealed to us." [16]They went quickly and found Mary and Joseph, and the baby lying in the manger. [17]When they saw this, they reported what they had been told about this child. [18]Everyone who heard it was amazed at what the shepherds told them. [19]Mary committed these things to memory and considered them carefully. **[20]The shepherds returned home, glorifying and praising God for all they had heard and seen. Everything happened just as they had been told.**

UNDERSTANDING THE SCRIPTURE

Introduction. Three of our lessons this quarter come from Luke's Gospel. Not much is known about this man, who also wrote the Acts of the Apostles, but tradition associates him with "the beloved physician" named in Colossians 4:14. Luke is also mentioned in 2 Timothy 4:11, Philemon 24, and parts of Acts concerned with the travels of Paul (16:10-17; 20:5-16; 21:1-18; 27:1–28:16). In Acts, we learn that Luke often accompanied the apostle, which gave him opportunity to meet people who knew Jesus before the Crucifixion and after the Resurrection. Because of his fluency in Greek and his name, many scholars think Luke might have been a Gentile convert to Christianity.

Perhaps because he was a physician—and certainly because he was a man of compassion—Luke lifts up the poor and the marginalized more than the other Gospel writers do. He speaks directly to the good news for people who are poor, ill, or suffering from disabilities. He even lifts up Gentiles and women as those who receive God's grace in Jesus Christ!

For Luke, it was fitting to announce God's good news to the lowly and unimportant members of society first, as a foretaste of the message to come. Perhaps this is why there are no "wise men from the East" (Matthew 2:1) in this account.

Luke 2:1-2. Writing as a historian, Luke sets his narrative in a specific time and place. Writing as a follower of Christ, he also injects some irony into the story at the outset. Luke and most of his readers would have known that the stable period of Emperor Augustus's reign was called the "Pax Augusta" (or "peace of Augustus") on inscriptions across the Roman Empire. Other inscriptions called Augustus "the savior of the whole world." Thus Luke mentions this ruler not only to give us a point in time but also to underscore Jesus' role as the true peacemaker and savior of the world.

Luke 2:3-5. Although Luke provides names of historical figures, scholars note discrepancies in the accuracy of Luke's dates. For example, Luke 1:5 dates the time of the pregnancies of Elizabeth and subsequently Mary to "the days of King Herod of Judea," who ruled until his death in A.D. 4. Quirinius became governor of Syria in A.D. 6 and conducted a census of Judea (not "all the world," 2:1). Luke's concerns are to show that Jesus was born in Bethlehem; that his parents were not rebels but abided by the law of the land; and that Joseph was a descendant of David.

Luke 2:6-7. The birth of Jesus is covered in two brief verses. The phrase "the time came" may intentionally point to the fullness of God's time—especially since Jewish tradition expected the Messiah to be born in Bethlehem (see Micah 5:2). The term translated "inn" in Luke 2:7 could also be translated as "guest room," as it is in 22:11 in connection with the place of the Last Supper.

Later Christian tradition has also focused on three other elements in this text:

- The phrase "firstborn son" has been taken by some denominations as an indication that Mary and Joseph later had children of their own. Other denominations see the phrase merely as an expression and maintain that Jesus was an only child.
- The fact that there was no room in the inn is meant to foreshadow Jesus' rejection by the world at large.
- Some theologians see the manger, which was a feeding trough for animals, as a symbol of God's intention to nourish the world through Jesus.

To these may be added a final consideration. Although it was common to wrap newborns in bands of cloth, Luke may intend a reference here to Solomon, the son who followed David as king. Solomon says in Wisdom of Solomon 7:4, "I was nursed with care in swaddling cloths."

Luke 2:8-14. According to this text, the first announcement of the birth comes to shepherds in a field, rather than to priests or rulers. For Luke, this fit God's new age of redemption. In the first century, shepherds were on the low end of the social strata. They were often poor and rarely able to participate in normal community life because they lived and worked outside of town. Shepherds had such a low reputation, in fact, that their testimony was not recognized in court. Yet it is to this group—not the rich or powerful—that the good news comes first. God has sent the Redeemer at last to usher in a whole new system.

An angel comes to herald the birth, and the shepherds are "terrified" (2:9). Maybe they are overwhelmed by the names given to the child: Savior, Messiah, and Lord (2:11). Maybe the "glory of the Lord" (2:9) around them or the sudden appearance of the heavenly choir is enough to shock them.

The angels sing of the glory of the Lord—but, even more important, that "glory" accompanies them. Here Luke builds on Old Testament imagery in which "glory" represents the presence of the divine, frequently manifested in the form of a bright light, a cloud, or a burning fire (see Exodus 16:10; 24:17; Ezekiel 1:28; Revelation 21:23).

Luke 2:15-20. The shepherds' response is one of curiosity, hope, and faith. Having been told of a sign—a baby in a manger (2:12)—they go to see for themselves. In excitement and trust, they go "with haste" (2:16) to seek the miracle. Once they find the child, they spread the good news to all they met.

In the midst of everyone else's wonder and amazement, we read of Mary's own quiet reaction as she "treasured all these words and pondered them in her heart" (2:19). According to Luke, Mary knew that her child was to be the Messiah (1:32-35) and that he would be recognized as "Lord" (1:43). To say that she pondered these things in her heart means she kept them to herself and tried to figure out what it all meant. Through her, Luke invites all readers to discern what this Child's coming means for them and for the world. The story of Christ's birth is meant to inspire us to follow in the steps of the shepherds—"glorifying and praising God" for all we have been told (2:20).

INTERPRETING THE SCRIPTURE

A Night of Joyous Surprises

As we move closer to Christmas, the tone in most church services becomes increasingly joyous. Bells ring out, candles sparkle, and beloved carols fill the air. If your congregation or choir has recently sung "Angels We Have Heard on High," you are well on the way to sharing the joy we find in this week's Scripture lesson!

Luke 2:1-20 is likely one of the most familiar texts from this Gospel. Shepherds keeping watch over their flocks, angels singing in the night sky over the fields near Bethlehem, an infant wrapped in bands of cloth and lying in a manger—all these images come to us solely from Luke's work. In these stories that we sometimes take for granted, Luke introduces other themes that are hallmarks of this Gospel: the inclusion of women (Mary) and outcasts (shepherds) in Jesus' ministry. The words of the angels about this birth carry a refrain that will be oft-repeated in Luke's Gospel: "good news of great joy for all the people" (2:10).

Typical for Luke's Gospel, this good news bursts in where it is most unexpected. The shepherds are in the midst of a routine daily task; they are tending their sheep. Indeed, Luke 2:8 tells us that the shepherds actually live in the fields so they can watch their sheep around the clock. Some of the shepherds are probably asleep, while others are designated to stay on guard. No doubt all wake up quickly once "an angel of the Lord stood before them" (2:9).

Part of why this heavenly appearance would not be expected to come to the early recipients of the Gospel lies in the general view of shepherds as a group. Later Rabbinic literature describes shepherds with disdain as thieves and sinners, and they may have been equally scorned in the first century. At any rate, for Luke they represent the humble and lowly segment of society, which fits his emphasis on God's concern precisely for such people.

The angel and the Lord's glory appear to the shepherds, who are filled with fear. Reassuring them, the angel gives the good news about the birth and the child's future role. Perhaps at this moment some recall Isaiah's words about a child to come: "a son given to us" (Isaiah 9:6). It is a wondrous message! The Messiah—the Prince of Peace, the One promised and predicted in Scripture—has come at last. It is almost too good to be true.

Before the shepherds have a chance to question or doubt the truth of the message, the angel reassures them that there will be a sign (Luke 2:12). They will find the child wrapped in bands of cloth and lying in a manger. The "bands of cloth" are not unusual; it was customary in that time to wrap infants in strips of cloth designed to hold their bodies straight. Finding the child in a manger, however, is quite unusual. Odd as this would be under normal circumstances, imagine how odd it must seem to the shepherds. They have just been told of the birth of the Savior, the Messiah, only to find that the child is housed in very humble conditions indeed.

Reason to Rejoice

"And suddenly there was with the angel a multitude of the heavenly host" (2:13). The occasion for this, of course, is the birth itself. In ancient tradition, townspeople often celebrated the birth of a child by going from house to house and singing songs of joy and welcome. In the case of a royal child, larger and more formal singing groups often went through the streets of the towns and cities. In the Roman Empire, in particular, it was customary for poets and other public speakers to declare peace and prosperity at the birth of the new ruler.

Luke's scene separates these experiences from normal life, however. Here, all the heavenly host join together to celebrate the birth of God's child, and the peace they foretell goes beyond regular earthly boundaries. Moreover, their celebration and their song have at heart the praise of God. The ultimate source of their celebration is God's activity in the birth of this child.

The Shepherds' Response

Carrying the Message Forward

When we read the rest of the shepherds' story, one thing is clear: Ignoring the message is not an option. Having been confronted by the good news, it is impossible for them to go back to their normal lives as if nothing has happened. Surely none of them is sleepy at this moment!

Once the angels leave, the shepherds immediately decide to go to Bethlehem "and see this thing that has taken place" (2:15). In other words, the shepherds take the message seriously. They show us that part of receiving God's Word is believing it. Beyond believing, however, they also act on the message. They let the good news become a factor in their decision-making process. Indeed, Luke almost implies that they cannot help themselves because of the urgency of the moment. Overall, the shepherds' single greatest response to the good news is excitement. They are amazed at what the angels said and eager to see the child who waits in the manger. Thus they go "with haste" to find Mary, Joseph, and the Child (2:16).

The shepherds' response to God's message does not end after seeing the baby. They begin to tell others "what had been told them about this child" (2:17). In this statement, Luke implies that the shepherds tell more people than just Mary and Joseph. The excitement from their experience spills over. It is not enough to receive the good news and see evidence of its truth; the shepherds want to share the good news with others.

After these events, the shepherds return to their flocks. They go back to the normal, perhaps boring, routine of their daily lives. Yet Luke shows us that life is no longer normal or boring for these people. The shepherds return "glorifying and praising God for all they had heard and seen, as it had been told them" (2:20). As a result of this good news, all of life is holy and wondrous for the shepherds. Their workplace is now a sanctuary, and their daily lives become a form of worship to God. Surely they will talk about the event among themselves for a long time.

Luke gives another picture of how people respond to God's message. When Mary first heard the story of the shepherds' experience, she "treasured all these words and pondered them in her heart" (2:19). Mary makes a point to remember the words and to keep thinking about them. In this way she always keeps the message fresh in her heart. Moreover, she never quits seeking to gain better understanding of what she heard. For Mary, responding to God's message is a lifelong process that involves heart, mind, and spirit. She stands as a reminder to us that even though the insight into God's good news may come in a moment, as it did when the angels spoke to the shepherds in the field, responding to that message with appropriate worship that glorifies God is a lifelong process.

SHARING THE SCRIPTURE

PREPARING TO TEACH

Preparing Our Hearts

Meditate on this week's devotional reading from Psalm 19. You may recognize these words of an anthem, "The Heavens Are Telling," from Joseph Haydn's oratorio, *The Creation*. What does this psalm tell you about God? How is creation described here? What do you learn about God's law? How do creation and the law seem to be connected?

Pray that you and the students will give glory to God the Creator who also provided instruction so that we might live according to divine precepts.

Preparing Our Minds

Study the background Scripture from Luke 2:1-20 and the lesson Scripture from Luke 2:8-20.

Consider this question as you prepare the lesson: *What might cause people to spontaneously break into a joyous celebration?*

Write on newsprint:
- ❏ questions for "Identify Ways to Worship God During Christmas and Epiphany."
- ❏ information for next week's lesson, found under "Continue the Journey."
- ❏ activities for further spiritual growth in "Continue the Journey."

Review the "Introduction," "The Big Picture," "Close-up," and "Faith in Action," which all precede the first lesson of this quarter. Consider how you might use any of this material in today's lesson.

Be aware that some regular attendees may be away and other members may bring guests with them today. Also be aware of any special events, such as a choir cantata, that may alter the morning schedule for everyone or necessitate some students leaving class early or arriving late.

Contact helpers early in the week to bring food and paper products if you plan to serve special refreshments today.

⟩ LEADING THE CLASS

(1) Gather to Learn

❖ Greet the class members and introduce guests.

❖ Pray that those who have come today will joyously praise God as they anticipate the celebration of the Savior's birth.

❖ Ask participants to name types of events in people's lives that usually call for a celebration. Examples could include graduation, marriage, birth of a child, baptism, new job, or retirement.

❖ Call on several volunteers to tell brief stories of one such celebration in their own lives and how they shared the news of this event with others.

❖ **Option:** This would be an appropriate time to serve refreshments if you plan to do so.

❖ Read aloud today's focus statement: **Sometimes there is an event in people's lives that causes spontaneous celebration. What might cause people to be wild with joy? Angels announced the birth of the Savior and a multitude of heavenly host praised God.**

(2) Goal 1: Explore the Events that Led to the Angels' Spontaneous Joy and the Shepherds' Pilgrimage to See Jesus

❖ Read Luke 2:8-20 as a drama by selecting volunteers to read parts of a narrator, an angel (2:10-12), and the shepherds (2:15b). Encourage the class to read in unison the praise of the heavenly host in verse 14.

❖ Discuss these questions. Add information from "Luke 2:8-14" in Understanding the Scripture as needed.

1. **What do you know about the work of the shepherds and their place in the first-century social hierarchy?**

2. **Why, in your opinion, would this news be announced to shepherds in the middle of a field, rather than to the religious leaders at the Temple in Jerusalem?**

3. **What, exactly, was the good news that the angel announced?** (See Luke 2:10-12.)

4. **What meaning would the phrases "city of David" and "a Savior, who is the Messiah, the Lord" have suggested?**

5. **Why is this news "great joy for all the people" (2:10)?**

❖ Wrap up this portion of the lesson by reading "A Night of Joyous Surprises" in Interpreting the Scripture.

(3) Goal 2: Feel the Unrestrained Joy that Comes with the Good News of the Savior's Birth

❖ Invite the adults to look at the shepherds' response in verses 15-20.

❖ Discuss these questions, using "The Shepherds' Response" in Interpreting the Scripture and information

from "Luke 2:8-14," and "Luke 2:15-20" in Understanding the Scripture to expand the discussion.

1, **The shepherds were going about their ordinary business when God's announcement pierced the darkness of the night. What words would you use to describe their emotional response to what they had seen and heard?**

2. **Luke 2:15 provides us with one sentence about the shepherds' decision to go to Bethlehem to check out what the angel had reported. What else might the shepherds have said before deciding to leave their flocks and head for Bethlehem?**

3. **The shepherds reported the angel's news to Mary and Joseph—and to "all who heard" them (2:18). Given that the testimony of shepherds was suspect, how might their words and demeanor have convinced people that this incredible news was actually true?**

(4) Goal 3: Identify Ways to Worship God During Christmas and Epiphany

❖ Lead the class in a unison reading of today's key verse, Luke 2:20.

❖ Point out that because of their encounter with the Child in a manger, the shepherds were changed people. They leave this encounter worshiping and praising God.

❖ Form small groups so that everyone can participate in the discussion. Post these questions, which you will write on newsprint prior to the session.

1. **What regular and special**

services do you plan to attend during this glorious season? (for example, special musical performances, Christmas pageants, and Christmas Eve services)

2. **What carols do you most enjoy singing? Why do these empower you to worship God joyously?** (for example, the tune, the meaning of the words, association of a carol with a family member or family tradition)

3. **What special decorations do you use to aid you in personal and family worship at home?** (for example, a crèche, Advent wreath to which a white candle is added at Christmas, Advent calendar)

4. **How do you extend your worship of God to other people?** (for example, sharing food and gifts with those who have few resources, caroling in the community; visiting those who are homebound or living in an institution)

❖ Challenge the students to choose several ways to worship God during this season of holy days.

(5) Continue the Journey

❖ Pray that as the learners depart they will celebrate and share with others the great news of the birth of the Lord and Savior.

❖ Post information for next week's session on newsprint for the students to copy:

■ **Title: In Awe of Christ's Power**
■ **Background Scripture: Matthew 14:22-36**
■ **Lesson Scripture: Matthew 14:22-36**

■ **Focus of the Lesson: Many things inspire awe in people. How do Christians know what is truly worth their reverence? Matthew tells about the times when Jesus miraculously walked on water to meet his disciples in a boat, which led them to worship him as truly the Son of God, and also when he healed the sick.**

❖ Challenge the adults to grow spiritually by completing one or more of these activities related to this week's session, which you have posted on newsprint for the students to copy.

(1) **Observe the ways in which retailers are encouraging people to celebrate Christmas. What strategies do they use? In what ways do the retailers' reasons and methods of celebration differ from those of the church?**

(2) **Sing and listen to Christmas carols. How do different carols describe the words and actions of both the angels and the shepherds?**

(3) **Read Matthew's account of Jesus' birth (1:18-25). Note the similarities and differences between Matthew's account and Luke's account (2:1-20). What specifics in each story prompt you to celebrate the good news of Jesus' birth?**

❖ Sing or read aloud "Angels We Have Heard on High."

❖ Conclude by leading the class in this benediction, adapted from the key verse for today's lesson from Luke 2:20: **May we go forth to worship as the shepherds, glorifying and praising God for all we have heard and seen.**

UNIT 1: IN AWE OF GOD
IN AWE OF CHRIST'S POWER

PREVIEWING THE LESSON

Lesson Scripture: Matthew 14:22-36
Background Scripture: Matthew 14:22-36
Key Verses: Matthew 14:32-33

Focus of the Lesson:

Many things inspire awe in people. How do Christians know what is truly worth their reverence? Matthew tells about the times when Jesus miraculously walked on water to meet his disciples in a boat, which led them to worship him as truly the Son of God, and also when he healed the sick.

Goals for the Learners:

(1) to explore the disciples' response to Jesus' miracles.
(2) to be inspired by the miracles of Jesus and yearn to become faithful worshipers.
(3) to believe in the miracles of Jesus and commit to be prayerful encouragers of others.

Pronunciation Guide:

Gennesaret (gi nes´ uh ret)

Supplies:

Bibles, newsprint and marker, paper and pencils, hymnals

READING THE SCRIPTURE

NRSV
Lesson Scripture: Matthew 14:22-36
²²Immediately he made the disciples get into the boat and go on ahead to the other side, while he dismissed the crowds. ²³And after he had dismissed the crowds, he went up the mountain by himself to pray. When

CEB
Lesson Scripture: Matthew 14:22-36
²²Right then, Jesus made the disciples get into the boat and go ahead to the other side of the lake while he dismissed the crowds. ²³When he sent them away, he went up onto a mountain by himself to pray. Evening came

evening came, he was there alone, [24]but by this time the boat, battered by the waves, was far from the land, for the wind was against them. [25]And early in the morning he came walking toward them on the sea. [26]But when the disciples saw him walking on the sea, they were terrified, saying, "It is a ghost!" And they cried out in fear. [27]But immediately Jesus spoke to them and said, "Take heart, it is I; do not be afraid."

[28]Peter answered him, "Lord, if it is you, command me to come to you on the water." [29]He said, "Come." So Peter got out of the boat, started walking on the water, and came toward Jesus. [30]But when he noticed the strong wind, he became frightened, and beginning to sink, he cried out, "Lord, save me!" [31]Jesus immediately reached out his hand and caught him, saying to him, "You of little faith, why did you doubt?" [32]**When they got into the boat, the wind ceased.** [33]**And those in the boat worshiped him, saying, "Truly you are the Son of God."**

[34]When they had crossed over, they came to land at Gennesaret. [35]After the people of that place recognized him, they sent word throughout the region and brought all who were sick to him, [36]and begged him that they might touch even the fringe of his cloak; and all who touched it were healed.

and he was alone. [24]Meanwhile, the boat, fighting a strong headwind, was being battered by the waves and was already far away from land. [25]Very early in the morning he came to his disciples, walking on the lake. [26]When the disciples saw him walking on the lake, they were terrified and said, "It's a ghost!" They were so frightened they screamed.

[27]Just then Jesus spoke to them, "Be encouraged! It's me. Don't be afraid."

[28]Peter replied, "Lord, if it's you, order me to come to you on the water." [29]And Jesus said, "Come."

Then Peter got out of the boat and was walking on the water toward Jesus. [30]But when Peter saw the strong wind, he became frightened. As he began to sink, he shouted, "Lord, rescue me!"

[31]Jesus immediately reached out and grabbed him, saying, "You man of weak faith! Why did you begin to have doubts?" [32]**When they got into the boat, the wind settled down.** [33]**Then those in the boat worshipped Jesus and said, "You must be God's Son!"**

[34]When they had crossed the lake, they landed at Gennesaret. [35]When the people who lived in that place recognized him, they sent word throughout that whole region, and they brought to him everyone who was sick. [36]Then they begged him that they might just touch the edge of his clothes. Everyone who touched him was cured.

UNDERSTANDING THE SCRIPTURE

Introduction. The author of Matthew's Gospel appears to be a Jewish Christian writing to other Jewish Christians at a time when Gentiles

had begun to join the church. Dating probably around A.D. 85–90, the account draws on the Gospel of Mark and other sources to tell the story of

Jesus. More particularly, Matthew seeks to show that Jesus was the Messiah by pointing out how Old Testament prophecies are fulfilled in his birth, life, and death. Most scholars agree that the writer is not the former tax collector who became a disciple, but the Gospel could contain some of his memories.

There are a few other characteristics we can note, in addition to the frequent use of Old Testament quotations designed to show how Jesus fulfilled prophecy. For example, throughout Matthew's Gospel the Pharisees are presented as the opposite of the apostles, especially in being legalistic and unforgiving. Matthew condemns them for their pride, hypocrisy, and lack of compassion. In contrast, Jesus is the perfect religious leader. He is the faithful shepherd who cares deeply for each member of the flock. This care is highlighted in the Gospel by Jesus' healing ministry, which tends to both physical and spiritual wounds. Jesus seeks to heal the whole person, often doing so with a mere word or touch.

As with all of Jesus' miracles, healing is a sign of his power, which is the very power of God. Matthew balances such scenes of Jesus' power with accounts of his need for solitude and prayer, which are aspects of his human nature. This week's text is set in this context.

The account also begins in progress. Chapter 14 starts with the death of John the Baptist and Jesus' need to withdraw after hearing the news (14:1-13a). The crowds follow him, however, and he subsequently feeds them with five loaves and two fishes (14:13-21).

Matthew 14:22-23a. Following this incident, verse 22 tells us that Jesus "immediately" (a term that occurs often in Matthew as well as Mark) sends the disciples away by boat to "the other side" of the Sea of Galilee. Following this, he dismisses the crowds as well. Alone at last, Jesus goes up the mountain to pray, as he had hoped to do earlier (14:13).

Some people see a parallel to Moses in the way these verses precede the rest of the story. Jesus goes up the mountain and later masters the sea in the same way that Moses went up a mountain and parted the sea during the Exodus. Others find this interpretation a stretch, in that the Exodus event is about delivering God's people, while this account is about showing Jesus' power and authority.

Matthew 14:23b-24. These verses set the stage for the drama to come. The disciples spend a storm-tossed night out on the sea, far from shore. The Greek literally says they were "many stadia" from land; there were about eight stadia in a mile.

Matthew 14:25. Jesus' power is shown in his ability to walk on water—and storm-tossed waves at that! He appears to the disciples in the early morning, roughly between 3 A.M. and 6 A.M. according to the Greek, which places the time as "in the fourth watch of the night." (Most English translations convert the Greek into time designations that are easier for modern readers to understand.)

Matthew 14:26. Seeing Jesus, the disciples become terrified at the thought they are seeing a ghost. Luke records the same reaction among the disciples when the resurrected Christ appears in their midst (Luke 24:37).

Matthew 14:27. "Immediately" Jesus reassures them and tells them not to be afraid. This is the classic response throughout Scripture when people encounter God directly or through a messenger. We might think of the angelic appearances to Joseph (Matthew 1:20) and Mary (Luke 1:30) before Jesus' birth, in which they are also told not to be afraid. In Matthew's Gospel, Jesus will say those words three more times: to the disciples at their commissioning (Matthew 10:31); to Peter, James and John during the Transfiguration (17:7); and to the women outside the empty tomb (28:10).

Matthew 14:28-31. The account of Peter walking on the water shows both his exuberance and his frailty. The fact that he actually accomplishes the miracle, at least at first, points both to Jesus' power and to Peter's potential as a believer. His subsequent fright and doubt may be a foreshadowing of his behavior when Jesus is arrested. On that night, Peter will first flee from Gethsemane (Matthew 26:56b), then follow at a distance (26:58), and ultimately deny Jesus three times (26:69-75). The current account ends with Peter wet from the sea; the latter ends with him wet from his own bitter tears.

Matthew 14:32-33. Jesus' power is clear to all when he walks on the water, enables Peter to do so, and then assists the disciple back to the boat. As if to add extra emphasis, the winds then miraculously cease. Verse 33 says that all in the boat worship him, which may include sailors in addition to the disciples themselves. They praise Jesus with the name "Son of God," a term often associated in Hebrew Scripture with the Messiah. This is the only time in Matthew that the disciples address Jesus by this title.

It is interesting to note that Mark ends his account of this event by saying the disciples do not understand what just happened—any more than they understand about the loaves and fishes—and so they do not worship Jesus as in Matthew's telling (Mark 6:51-52).

Matthew 14:34-36. Chapter 14 ends with the continued theme of Jesus' power and renown. Gennesaret was a district on the northwest shore of the Sea of Galilee, and even here word of his power has spread and crowds seek him out. Indeed, Jesus' power is so great that all who touch the hem of his garment are healed.

INTERPRETING THE SCRIPTURE

The Messiah Through the Eyes of Matthew

This is the last Sunday of 2014. The holidays are almost over. We may party on New Year's Eve, but then it is back to the same old routine. Only the calendar has changed. The one prediction one can make with certainty about the new year is that the lives of most of us will be very much as they were in the old year. We will be the same old persons up against the same old world.

For you that may be a happy prospect, but it is not for millions of others. I think particularly of a friend who has been recently overwhelmed by tragedy after tragedy. "I feel like I am drowning," he said.

For moments when you too may feel overcome by "a sea of troubles," as *Hamlet* puts it, we end the year (and Unit 1) with this encouraging account from Matthew 14. It speaks of Jesus' power to quell all storms, literal and figurative, and to bring us peace. Trusting in the Messiah's power is part of what brings depth and meaning to our worship.

But who is this Jesus the Messiah that Matthew portrays? Matthew was a Jew, clearly writing for a Jewish audience. The intent of the book is to convince Jews that Jesus is in fact the Messiah. Matthew goes about this task by repeatedly pointing out that Old Testament prophecies are fulfilled in Jesus, beginning with Jesus' birth (see 1:21-23) and on through the passion stories. Matthew 27:9 makes an explicit connection to the Prophets, whereas verse 35 assumes that readers know Psalm 22:18.

After Jesus' death and resurrection, the term "Messiah" took on new meaning. We see signs of this through each of the Gospels. In Matthew, Jesus' role as the Messiah specifically includes teaching, power, and kingship. Moreover, Jesus as a kingly Messiah belongs specifically to Israel (1:16) and comes at the beginning of a new age (1:17). Despite the elements of kingship and power, however, Jesus' own teachings associate his messiahship with suffering and death. He explicitly speaks with his disciples about his suffering and death three times in Matthew (16:21-23; 20:17-19; and 26:1-2).

Matthew also shows Jesus withdrawing from the hectic demands that surround his life and ministry (see 14:13, 23; 26:36-46). Jesus uses those times of quiet meditation and prayer to keep himself centered and focused on God's call. This is part of his personal worship life.

The Disciples Through the Eyes of Matthew

Matthew gives us a good feel for what it was like to be a disciple of Jesus. We should note that in Matthew's day it was common for rabbis to have followers or disciples. These disciples lived in intimate daily contact with the rabbi, learning from his teaching and his example. Typically, however, such disciples (or would-be scholars) sought out a teacher who was known to be particularly learned. The disciples pursued the rabbi and asked permission to be a follower.

This process differs significantly from the way Jesus gets special disciples, or apostles. In the few cases where we have any information about how a person comes to be one of the twelve disciples, it is always Jesus who initiates the relationship. The Twelve are chosen, or called, specifically to be disciples of Jesus. We have no indication that any of them are looking for a rabbi to follow before they meet Jesus.

Our passage for this week also shows how very human the disciples are. Ordinary people, just like us, they are prone to fears and concerns. When the storm arises, they become afraid—perhaps because they are fishermen by trade and so know better than most people how dangerous the Sea of Galilee can become.

Matthew invites us to see ourselves in the disciples and to join in their release from fear to worship and give thanks. We all can point to moments when Jesus brought unexpected peace or a sense of safety, perhaps even moments of deliverance, so we have as much reason to rejoice as our forerunners in the faith.

Peter's Faith

Various commentators point out that the way Matthew presents this week's passage allows it to serve as a kind of metaphor for disciples today. Our "boat" is the church, which is being "battered by the waves" (14:24) as we seek to follow Jesus' commands in difficult times. Our trust and hope, like that of the original Twelve, is in the One who has the power to overcome all that threatens to destroy us.

In this sense, then, Peter is a model for each of us when he joins Jesus on the waves. For one brief moment, Peter is able to move toward Jesus in confidence, sharing in Christ's power and ability beyond his own limits. Peter inspires us to seek and embrace similar moments in our own lives. Likewise, his failure to maintain the miracle reminds us that when we waver or weaken, Jesus will be there to lift us up.

From Worship to Ministry

Back in the boat, Peter joins with the others in worshiping Jesus, whose power over the sea is clear. Our passage does not end with this acclamation and awe-inspired act, however, but with Jesus' own return to healing and ministry. For Matthew, the Messiah is definitely not someone who sits around, basking in the worship and adoration of others when there is work to be done!

In this, Matthew reminds us that disciples are not to spend all our time in worship either. We are to praise God through our ongoing ministries as well. In John 14:12, Jesus promises that those who follow him will do the same works he does and even greater works. Matthew takes that promise seriously. Writing in the decade of the 80s, the Gospel writer knows that Jesus began a movement that had already existed for about fifty years after his resurrection. The call to bring healing and wholeness to broken people is still the mandate of the church.

Today the church carries out ministries of counseling and medical healing, speaks out on behalf of the poor and oppressed, preaches good news to the spiritually hungry and lost, and reconciles people of different races and cultures. Despite all of our shortcomings in the church, we struggle to carry on the work of our Lord. We are still in ministry to heal the sick, to restore the outcast, to comfort the bereaved, and to offer new life in the name of Christ.

On this last Sunday of 2014, we may wonder what stormy seas lie ahead in 2015. Paul writes to the church at Rome that they might face "hardship, or distress, or persecution, or famine, or nakedness, or peril, or sword." He also assures them: "In all these we are more than conquerors through him who loved us" (Romans 8:35, 37). As John puts it in his letter: "This is the victory that conquers the world, our faith" (1 John 5:4). Matthew tells us that what lies ahead is victory through our faith in the One who calms the storm.

Matthew 14 brings us to the end of our four December studies on the reasons we have to stand in awe of God. We have discussed God's gift of salvation in Jesus Christ, the immeasurable power of God the Creator, the message of good news offered to all people, and the power of Christ to overcome all threats and heal all wounds. Great reasons, all, for our awe and our worship. Praise be to God!

SHARING THE SCRIPTURE

PREPARING TO TEACH

Preparing Our Hearts

Meditate on this week's devotional reading from Mark 9:15-24. What connections can you draw between the boy's healing and faith? How do Jesus' miracles, such as the exorcism recounted here, affirm or challenge your faith? Are there situations in your own life where you could cry out to God, "I believe; help my unbelief!" (Mark 9:24)?

Pray that you and the students will believe by faith in Christ's power.

Preparing Our Minds

Study the background Scripture and the lesson Scripture, which are both from Matthew 14:22-36.

Consider this question as you prepare the lesson: *How do Christians know what is worth their reverence?*

Write on newsprint:

❏ information for next week's lesson, found under "Continue the Journey."

❏ activities for further spiritual growth in "Continue the Journey."

Review the "Introduction," "The Big Picture," "Close-up," and "Faith in Action," which all precede the first lesson of this quarter. Consider how you might use any of this material in today's lesson.

LEADING THE CLASS

(1) Gather to Learn

❖ Greet the class members and introduce guests.

❖ Pray that those who have come today will seek awe-inspiring signs of God that prompt them to worship.

❖ Invite the students to think about the true meaning of worship by reading these quotations and then asking: **How does this quotation express, deny, or challenge your own understanding of worship?**

▪ **"If worship does not change us, it has not been worship. To stand before the Holy One of eternity is to change. Worship begins in holy expectancy; it ends in holy obedience."** (Richard J. Foster, 1942–)

▪ **"More spiritual progress can be made in one short moment of speechless silence in the awesome presence of God than in years of mere study."** (A. W. Tozer, 1897–1963)

▪ **"Whatever is outward in worship must come as a direct result of what is inward— otherwise, it will be form without power."** (Howard Brinton, 1884–1973)

❖ Read aloud today's focus statement: **Many things inspire awe in people. How do Christians know what is truly worth their reverence? Matthew tells about the times when Jesus miraculously walked on water to meet his disciples in a boat, which led them to worship him as truly the Son of God, and also when he healed the sick.**

(2) Goal 1: Explore the Disciples' Response to Jesus' Miracles

❖ Invite two volunteers to read, one, Matthew 14:22-33; and the other, Matthew 14:34-36.

❖ Discuss these questions:

1. **How would you describe the disciples, particularly in verses 22-33?** (Use information in "The Disciples Through the Eyes of Matthew" in Interpreting the Scripture to help answer this question.)

2. **How is Peter a model for our own faith?** (See "Peter's Faith" in Interpreting the Scripture.)

3. **Jesus said that Peter was "of little faith," but he did not say that Peter had no faith (14:31). What hope does that give you in terms of your own relationship with Jesus, especially when the storms of life buffet you about?**

4. **How does Peter's experience on that stormy night strengthen his faith in Jesus?** (Note the key verses in Matthew 14:32-33.)

5. **When the boat reached shore, Jesus could have said they had had a difficult night and he needed a break, but he did not do that. What did he do?** (See Matthew 14:34-36.)

6. **What does Jesus' behavior suggest about how believers are to respond once they recognize the awesomeness of Christ's power?** (See "From Worship to Ministry" in Interpreting the Scripture.)

(3) Goal 2: Be Inspired by the Miracles of Jesus and Yearn to Become Faithful Worshipers

❖ Form four small groups. Assign the Gospel of Matthew to one group; Mark to another; Luke to the third group; and John to the final group. Direct them to page through their assigned Gospel to find references to other miracles of Jesus. Group members are to tell one another why they feel drawn to a certain miracle story.

❖ **Option:** If time permits, suggest that each group choose one miracle story to tell to the class and explain why this story is so inspiring to them.

❖ Call the groups together and ask: **How do Jesus' miracles inspire you to be a more faithful worshiper?**

(4) Goal 3: Believe in the Miracles of Jesus and Commit to Be Prayerful Encouragers of Others

❖ Read: **Eerdmans Dictionary of the Bible defines "miracles" as "extraordinary events that manifest divine power, that are wonders to human understanding, and therefore what human beings perceive as signs from God." Examples of miracles can be found in both Testaments. In the Gospels, about thirty-five miracles are credited to Jesus, but other people, such as Peter and John, are also depicted as performing miracles, particularly in Acts. The power to perform these miracles comes from God. From the biblical record it is clear that many people sought out Jesus because of his ability to perform miracles, but in our post-Enlightenment, rational age, many people are skeptical about the entire notion of miracles.**

❖ Ask these questions:

1. **Do you know people who scoff at the idea of miracles? If so, why do they refuse to accept the possibility that miracles can happen?**

2. **What do you believe about miracles? If you affirm that miracles can and do happen,**

what undergirds your belief? If you do not believe in Jesus' miracles, what prompts you to set them aside even though they are recorded in the Bible? (Please be careful not to let this discussion get out of hand with people insisting that others must accept their viewpoint. Note that we are all on a spiritual journey and different people are at different places on the journey. Indicate that we need to prayerfully encourage one another as we struggle with our respective beliefs.)

❖ Wrap up by reading this quotation from Louis Cassels (1922–74) and inviting the students to say how this idea puts the issue of miracles in perspective for them: "**Virtually all the miracles attributed to Jesus are directly associated with some lesson he was trying to teach or some insight he wanted to give to his disciples. The real question to be asked about any miracle is not how it happened but why: What was God saying to us in this significant act?**"

(5) Continue the Journey

❖ Pray that as the learners depart, they will continue to stand in awe of Christ's power, especially as it is displayed through the miracles he performs.

❖ Post information for next week's session on newsprint for the students to copy:
- **Title: A Model for Prayer**
- **Background Scripture: Luke 11:1-13**
- **Lesson Scripture: Luke 11:1-13**
- **Focus of the Lesson: People**

build intimate, trust-filled relationships by having open communication with one another. How do people maintain open communication? Jesus teaches that nurturing a relationship with God requires persistent prayer.

❖ Challenge the adults to grow spiritually by completing one or more of these activities related to this week's session, which you have posted on newsprint for the students to copy.

(1) **Develop a list of Scriptures that depicts Jesus healing or performing a miracle. Read and meditate on one of these stories each day in the coming week. Consider how each story enlarges your faith.**

(2) **Offer intercessory prayers for persons who seem to be "at the end of their rope" and in need of a miracle. Keep a list of those for whom you are praying. When answers come, make a note of them and offer thanks to God.**

(3) **Try talking with someone who cannot accept that Jesus actually performed miracles. Listen to this person's reasons. Help this person view the miracles through the lens of faith. If possible, tell a story from your own experience that you believe represents a miracle.**

❖ Sing or read aloud "Come, Christians, Join to Sing."

❖ Conclude by leading the class in this benediction, adapted from the key verse for the session on December 21 from Luke 2:20: **May we go forth to worship as the shepherds, glorifying and praising God for all we have heard and seen.**

UNIT 2: LEARNING TO PRAY
A MODEL FOR PRAYER

PREVIEWING THE LESSON

Lesson Scripture: Luke 11:1-13
Background Scripture: Luke 11:1-13
Key Verse: Luke 11:2

Focus of the Lesson:

People build intimate, trust-filled relationships by having open communication with one another. How do people maintain open communication? Jesus teaches that nurturing a relationship with God requires persistent prayer.

Goals for the Learners:

(1) to understand the Lord's Prayer as a model for various kinds of prayers.
(2) to accept the need for constant prayer.
(3) to develop a more disciplined prayer life as a means of developing a growing relationship with God.

Pronunciation Guide:

abba (ah´ buh) or (ab´ uh)

Supplies:

Bibles, newsprint and marker, paper and pencils, hymnals, resources related to prayer

---

READING THE SCRIPTURE

NRSV
Lesson Scripture: Luke 11:1-13

¹He was praying in a certain place, and after he had finished, one of his disciples said to him, "Lord, teach us to pray, as John taught his disciples." ²He said to them, **"When you pray, say:**

CEB
Lesson Scripture: Luke 11:1-13

¹Jesus was praying in a certain place. When he finished, one of his disciples said, "Lord, teach us to pray, just as John taught his disciples." ²Jesus told them, **"When you pray, say:**

Father, hallowed be your name.
Your kingdom come.
[3]Give us each day our daily bread.
[4]And forgive us our sins,
    for we ourselves forgive everyone
      indebted to us.
And do not bring us to the time of
    trial."

[5]And he said to them, "Suppose one of you has a friend, and you go to him at midnight and say to him, 'Friend, lend me three loaves of bread; [6]for a friend of mine has arrived, and I have nothing to set before him.' [7]And he answers from within, 'Do not bother me; the door has already been locked, and my children are with me in bed; I cannot get up and give you anything.' [8]I tell you, even though he will not get up and give him anything because he is his friend, at least because of his persistence he will get up and give him whatever he needs.

[9]"So I say to you, Ask, and it will be given you; search, and you will find; knock, and the door will be opened for you. [10]For everyone who asks receives, and everyone who searches finds, and for every- one who knocks, the door will be opened. [11]Is there anyone among you who, if your child asks for a fish, will give a snake instead of a fish? [12]Or if the child asks for an egg, will give a scorpion? [13]If you then, who are evil, know how to give good gifts to your children, how much more will the heavenly Father give the Holy Spirit to those who ask him!"

'Father, uphold the holiness of your
    name.
Bring in your kingdom.
[3]Give us the bread we need for today.
[4]Forgive us our sins,
    for we also forgive everyone who
      has wronged us.
And don't lead us into temptation.'"

[5]He also said to them, "Imagine that one of you has a friend and you go to that friend in the middle of the night. Imagine saying, 'Friend, loan me three loaves of bread [6]because a friend of mine on a journey has arrived and I have nothing to set before him.' [7]Imagine further that he answers from within the house, 'Don't bother me. The door is already locked, and my children and I are in bed. I can't get up to give you anything.' [8]I assure you, even if he wouldn't get up and help because of his friendship, he will get up and give his friend whatever he needs because of his friend's brash-ness. [9]And I tell you: Ask and you will receive. Seek and you will find. Knock and the door will be opened to you. [10]Everyone who asks, receives. Whoever seeks, finds. To everyone who knocks, the door is opened.

[11]"Which father among you would give a snake to your child if the child asked for a fish? [12]If a child asked for an egg, what father would give the child a scorpion? [13]If you who are evil know how to give good gifts to your children, how much more will the heavenly Father give the Holy Spirit to those who ask him?"

UNDERSTANDING THE SCRIPTURE

Introduction. Luke has more mention of prayer than the other Gospels. Only Luke says that Jesus was in prayer as the Spirit descended upon him in the form of a dove (3:21-22), and as he asked the question leading to Peter's confession of faith: "Who do the crowds say that I am?"

(9:18). In Gethsemane, Jesus told the disciples with him to pray (22:40, 46). At least three times, where Luke parallels other Gospels he adds to the account that Jesus prayed (5:16; 6:12; 11:1). Luke shows us that in prayer, we, too, have access to God who can help us to overcome all obstacles to participation in joyous and thankful lives within God's kingdom today.

Luke 11:1. All four Gospels mention how Jesus went away to pray, often to a mountain. Sometimes he went alone; sometimes he took some or all of the disciples. Matthew in particular lifts up prayer as one of the three great expressions of Jewish piety (the other two being almsgiving and fasting—see Matthew 6:1-18).

The Lord's Prayer itself is mentioned only in Luke and Matthew, and they each present it differently. Here in Luke, Jesus has apparently gone away from the crowds to pray, although the disciples are with him. One asks him to teach them how to pray, because John has done that for his disciples. In Matthew's Gospel, Jesus offers the prayer as part of the general teachings given in the Sermon on the Mount (Matthew 5:1–7:27; see especially 6:9-13).

Luke 11:2a. God's name encompasses the very nature of God, and long ago the sharing of God's name began the special covenant relationship in which the community of faith still remains. Some scholars believe Jesus may be using the familial Aramaic term "Abba" to open the prayer. This is a less formal, more intimate term for a father—something like "Daddy" or "Papa." This term of familiarity is followed by praise due a deity, however. "Hallowed" means both that God's name is holy and

that, accordingly, we are to honor and praise God's name.

Luke 11:2b. In Luke, verses 2b-4 are an alternate version of the Lord's Prayer, which is traditionally recited from the version found in Matthew 6:9-13. As the prayer unfolds, Jesus teaches that after praising God, we are to acknowledge and welcome God's kingdom. This first petition serves multiple purposes. It acknowledges God's sovereignty and rule, orients our desire toward God's divine plan, and opens our awareness to the realities around us. God's realm has not come yet, though, and this fact shapes the petitions still to come in the prayer. A comparison of the Lord's Prayer in Matthew shows he adds that we are also to pray for God's will to be done (6:10).

Throughout the prayer, starting in this verse, Luke uses first-person plural pronouns. This shows the Lord's Prayer is designed to be communal, rather than individual.

Luke 11:3. The prayer for daily bread is a reminder that it is God who provides for our needs. The language harkens back to the wilderness wanderings of the Exodus, when the people received manna each morning and quail each evening (see Exodus 16). Jesus may be evoking memories of that event as a way of affirming God's faithful provision in the past, which gives us reason to trust God in the present and the future.

Luke 11:4a. In Jewish tradition, sins create a barrier between humanity and God. The prayer of confession, in which we seek forgiveness, is necessary if we are to be able to come fully into God's presence. The statement about forgiving others is important because (1) not forgiving can become yet one more sin that keeps us from God and (2) we cannot in good conscience ask God for something we are not willing to extend to another.

Luke 11:4b. The final part of the prayer is a plea for protection from temptation (or testing or evil). Now that we have received forgiveness and been restored to God, we pray that this condition may last.

Some may wonder what happened to the doxology, found in Matthew 6:13 in some versions of the Bible, with which we expect to close the prayer: "for thine is the kingdom and the power, and the glory, forever. Amen" (KJV). The oldest manuscripts of the Lord's Prayer do not contain these words, which have roots in David's dying blessing (1 Chronicles 29:11-13). The shorter version recorded in Luke is likely to be closer to Jesus' original words.

Luke 11:5-8. Jesus' next words on prayer bring to mind the parable of the persistent widow in 18:1-5.

Luke 11:9-13. Building on the image of a persistent friend in need, Jesus teaches that God responds to persistent prayer. This reflects the Hebrew notion, found in such accounts as Abraham praying for Sodom (Genesis 18:16-33), that we can dialogue effectively with God. The ancient view is not that human beings can make God change the divine mind, but that we can hasten God's recollection of the divine self when God stands ready to lash out in anger because of being deeply hurt. Abraham, Moses, Jeremiah, Habakkuk, and others all remind God that the divine nature is one of compassion and mercy. In a way, each helps God "come to God's senses" even in the midst of grief. Thus Jesus suggests that through persistent prayer we too can remind God to be compassionate and merciful.

"Ask . . . search . . . knock" (Luke 11:9) occurs in another context in Matthew 7:7-11. Likewise, the overall view of prayer differs in that Gospel too. Matthew contends that we do not need to assault God with our needs, because God knows our needs before we ask (6:8; compare 6:32). Rooted as he is in the Old Testament, perhaps Matthew intends to connect this teaching of Jesus with Isaiah 65:24: "Before they call I will answer, while they are yet speaking I will hear."

INTERPRETING THE SCRIPTURE

A Proper Prayer

Prayer has always been central to worship. With this lesson, we begin a new unit that focuses on this vital way we connect to God.

The subject of today's lesson, the Lord's Prayer, is perhaps the best known of all Jesus' teachings. Countless believers have learned this prayer as part of their entry into the Christian community, and virtually all Christian churches use it as part of their corporate worship. While some of the words and phrases may change from denomination to denomination, the basic prayer taught by our Lord continues to provide a common heritage for Christians the world over.

The prayer taught by Jesus is short and to the point. It offers five petitions: two related to God and God's glory, followed by three related to our basic human needs. The prayer itself is very Jewish, as we might expect. Almost every phrase used in the prayer can be found in traditional Jewish literature and liturgy. Jesus takes the words and phrases dear to him from his own tradition, quite possibly phrases that he grew up hearing, and he shapes them into a heartfelt prayer of his own.

Addressing God

The Lord's Prayer begins by addressing the Creator God, the God of the cosmos, who has the power to grant all petitions. Jesus calls this God *abba*, an affectionate Aramaic term used by young children (and sometimes adult children) when addressing a respected older adult. The prayer invites us to call God our *abba* as well. The God of heaven is somehow immediate, near, and reachable—and that God is also loving and affectionate with us.

God is *abba* (intimate, inviting, and accepting) but God is also God (transcendent, holy, and awesome). Thus God's name is to be "hallowed," reverenced as holy. We do so through acts of worship and also by acts of love. Nothing shows more clearly the glory of God than the life of a faithful disciple.

In Jesus' prayer, the next two petitions focus on the end-time, when God's realm will be established, as some ancient manuscripts of Luke as well as Matthew put it, "on earth as it is in heaven" (Matthew 6:10). Jesus often teaches that the kingdom is already-but-not-yet. In other words, God's reign began on earth with the birth of Jesus, but we await its fulfillment at some future time.

Our life as believers exists in this "in-between time" during which we work to achieve "kingdom living" in the present moment. Accordingly, an inspired amendment to the Lord's Prayer I have heard in some worship services suggests that, in fact, we should pray, "Your kingdom come, beginning in me."

Prayers for Ourselves and Others

The next section of the Lord's Prayer begins the petitions related to human need. The first of these relates to physical sustenance, our "daily bread." For many of Jesus' original listeners, this verse carried a literal sense. Most of them existed on a day-to-day basis, earning just enough money one day to buy food for the next. Those of us who live with cupboards, refrigerators, and freezers stockpiled with enough food to last several days (or weeks) may have difficulty relating to just how pertinent this prayer was for first-century people.

At the same time, verse 3 teaches some basic truths that we can easily apply to our lives. First, we are physical beings and therefore we have certain physical needs. This is part of God's created order. Second, we can trust God to provide for those needs. This does not mean that God will provide all the material goods that we may want, but God will see that we do not go without what we have to have.

The text also teaches something more. The phrase "daily bread" can be also translated "our bread for tomorrow." Many scholars have seen in this a deliberate attempt to recall the story of God's daily provision of manna in the wilderness (Exodus 16).

What richness this adds to the text! We can trust God to provide for our daily needs because God has done so before. Moreover, God provides for us in the context of covenant faithfulness: The God who meets our daily needs is the caring and loving God who remains true to the covenant relationship no matter what.

The next petition, which concerns forgiveness, moves from physical concerns to emotional ones. Just as we are physical beings, we are also beings created to be in relationship with God and with one another. This petition addresses all things that threaten to break those relationships.

The petition also shows that God's action is related to our own. God stands ready to forgive us of whatever actions or attitudes may have caused a sense of separation between ourselves and our Creator. We have to be able to accept this forgiveness, however; in other words, we have to repent of our "debts." ("Debts" here is synonymous with "sins.") As long as we are unable to forgive others, then we are not truly repentant and we cannot receive God's gift of forgiveness.

The last petition is more commonly known from Matthew's version: "Lead us not into temptation, but deliver us from evil" (Matthew 6:13 KJV). While the previous two petitions may be understood to have a certain spiritual dimension to them, the emphasis on our spiritual needs is overt in this third request.

"And do not bring us to the time of trial," says Luke at the end of verse 4. The wording of the NRSV fits the intent of the original Greek better than the traditional translation with which we are more familiar. People have sometimes misunderstood "lead us not into temptation" to mean: (1) God is the source of all temptations in our life, and/or (2) believers can achieve temptation-free lives.

Still, it is unclear what "time of trial" Jesus has in mind. Perhaps he means the daily temptations we all face, or perhaps the great time of testing associated with the end of the age. Some have suggested he means both. Regardless, God is the One to whom we turn for protection and strength.

Further Instruction

Having taught us what to pray, Jesus now gives instruction on how to pray. We are to send our prayers to God confidently and boldly, trusting in God's love and attention. "Do not be afraid to approach God or to ask for what you want," Jesus says, in essence. "The One who loves you will not take offense or consider it a bother."

The three verbs found in response to the story of the persistent friend (11:5-13)—"ask," "search," and "knock"—cover all conditions of prayer life. Sometimes we know the need we are bringing to God, so we ask. Other times, we cannot see our way clearly and we come to God in confusion, seeking insight and guidance. In intense times of desperation, we pound on the very gates of heaven for help.

No matter the circumstances, Jesus reassures us that we can come to God as any child can come to a loving parent. We can pray, according to Thomas G. Long, "not as outsiders, but as God's children, tenderly, honestly, and confidently. In our secret, whispered prayers, we are known so well that God, like a mother listening with her heart to her children, can finish our sentences."

SHARING THE SCRIPTURE

PREPARING TO TEACH

Preparing Our Hearts

Meditate on this week's devotional reading from Psalm 103:1-13. How does the psalmist, who thanks God for divine goodness and forgiving love, describe who God is and what God does? Are you, like the psalmist, able to experience God as a compassionate father (103:13)? What blessings will you seek from God today? How will your life bless God today?

Pray that you and the students will give thanks for God's love, forgiveness, and mercy.

Preparing Our Minds

Study the background Scripture and the lesson Scripture, which are both from Luke 11:1-13.

Consider this question as you prepare the lesson: *How do people maintain open communication with others?*

Write on newsprint:
- ❏ list of suggested references for "Prayer" from "Close-up" for "Develop a More Disciplined Prayer Life as a Means of Developing a Growing Relationship with God."
- ❏ information for next week's lesson, found under "Continue the Journey."
- ❏ activities for further spiritual growth in "Continue the Journey."

Review the "Introduction," "The Big Picture," "Close-up," and "Faith in Action," which all precede the first lesson of this quarter. Consider how you might use any of this material in today's lesson.

Check the page near the beginning of this quarter titled "Close-up: Resources for Further Study." Prior to the session, list the resources for prayer on newsprint. Gather any of these resources that you can find. You may wish to add others.

LEADING THE CLASS

(1) Gather to Learn

❖ Greet the class members and introduce guests.

❖ Pray that those who have come today will open their hearts and minds to the voice of God.

❖ Brainstorm ideas to answer the following question. Record all responses on newsprint. **What suggestions would you give to people who want to build better relationships by communicating more effectively?** (Many answers are possible, but here are some to consider: listen carefully; focus on the issue at hand; try to see the situation under discussion from the other person's point of view; take responsibility for your words and actions; find ways to compromise; look for win-win solutions to problems.)

❖ Read aloud today's focus statement: **People build intimate, trust-filled relationships by having open communication with one another. How do people maintain open communication? Jesus teaches that nurturing a relationship with God requires persistent prayer.**

(2) Goal 1: Understand the Lord's Prayer as a Model for Various Kinds of Prayers

❖ Read "A Proper Prayer" from Interpreting the Scripture.

❖ Lead the class in praying the Lord's Prayer using whatever words are familiar to them.

❖ Direct the class to turn to Luke 11:1-4. Read verses 1-2a yourself and invite others to join you in reading the prayer itself.

❖ Engage the class in a comparative study of Luke's version (11:2-4) and Matthew's version (6:9-13) by asking: **How is Luke's version of the prayer similar to and different from the version that we usually pray.** (To begin, explain that most churches use a form of Matthew's version. Most also use a doxology that appears in manuscripts of Matthew that were available when the King James Version was written: "For thine is the kingdom, and the power, and the glory, forever. Amen." Since this doxology does not appear in earlier manuscripts that are now available to scholars, it is not included in the NRSV, CEB, or NIV.)

❖ Delve more deeply into Luke's version by asking these questions. Add to the discussion by using information in Understanding the Scripture (Luke 11:2a through 4b) and "Addressing God" and "Praying for Ourselves and Others," both from Interpreting the Scripture.

1. **How does Jesus teach us to address God?**
2. **What does Jesus teach us to pray for?**
3. **As you consider the versions from both Luke and Matthew, what would you say is the main message of this prayer?**

(3) Goal 2: Accept the Need for Constant Prayer

❖ Select a volunteer to read Luke 11:5-13.

❖ Look at the three verbs in verses 9-10: "ask," "search," "knock." Ask:
1. **What do these actions suggest to you about how to pray?**
2. **In a culture that expects instant results, how can Christians be taught and encouraged to pray persistently?**

❖ Read the final paragraph of "Further Instruction" in Interpreting the Scripture. Encourage the students to reflect on the Thomas G. Long quotation and silently consider their own approach to God. Do they pray as outsiders or as God's children? If they feel like outsiders, what changes do they need to make to pray as God's children?

❖ Bring everyone together, read aloud verse 13, and suggest that the adults review this verse, particularly at times when they believe that God is not answering prayer—or not answering it in ways they believe to be in their best interest.

Goal 3: Develop a More Disciplined Prayer Life as a Means of Developing a Growing Relationship with God

❖ Invite volunteers to tell of strategies they use to build a more intimate relationship with God through a disciplined prayer life.

❖ Post the prayer resources suggested in "Close-up" and display all of those that you have located. Encourage the adults to pass these books around. Perhaps you or some students will be familiar with one or more of the books and could comment on how they have inspired or challenged you. If possible, allow students to borrow the books, or suggest where they can find copies to borrow or buy.

❖ Distribute paper and pencils. Challenge the students to write one or two actions that they will take this week to strengthen their prayer lives.

(5) Continue the Journey

❖ Pray that as the learners depart they will recognize of the importance of communing regularly with God and commit themselves to doing so.

❖ Post information for next week's session on newsprint for the students to copy:

- Title: Jesus Prays for the Disciples
- Background Scripture: John 17:1-26
- Lesson Scripture: John 17:6-21
- Focus of the Lesson: Small intimate groups exist in the midst of a larger community. How can a small group impact the larger community? Jesus prayed that the disciples would be united and protected by God as they brought new people into their community in an unsafe world.

❖ Challenge the adults to grow spiritually by completing one or more of these activities related to this week's session, which you have posted on newsprint for the students to copy.

(1) Locate and read one of the resources suggested during the session. Use whatever ideas you find helpful to build a more disciplined prayer life.

(2) Scan entries for "pray," "prayer," and related words in a Bible concordance. Check out some of the many entries you will find. What do you learn from these verses about how to pray and why to pray?

(3) Begin or add to a prayer journal by listing the names of people or situations for which you are praying. Date each entry to show when you have offered a prayer for a particular person or situation. Also enter the date on which the prayer appears to be answered and lift a prayer of thanks to God for hearing and responding.

❖ Sing or read aloud "The Lord's Prayer." If your hymnal includes music based on a West Indian folk tune (see *The United Methodist Hymnal*, page 271), consider singing this rendition, which will provide a different "feel" to the words than the widely sung 1935 version by Alfred Hay Malotte.

❖ Conclude by leading the class in this benediction, adapted from the key verse for the session on December 21 from Luke 2:20: **May we go forth to worship as the shepherds, glorifying and praising God for all we have heard and seen.**

UNIT 2: LEARNING TO PRAY
JESUS PRAYS FOR THE DISCIPLES

PREVIEWING THE LESSON

Lesson Scripture: John 17:6-21
Background Scripture: John 17:1-26
Key Verse: John 17:21

Focus of the Lesson:
Small intimate groups exist in the midst of a larger community. How can a small group impact the larger community? Jesus prayed that the disciples would be united and protected by God as they brought new people into their community in an unsafe world.

Goals for the Learners:
(1) to study Jesus' prayer for the unity of all who believe in him.
(2) to experience intimacy with Jesus and God the Father through prayer.
(3) to unite in prayers for one another and for unity in Jesus Christ.

Supplies:
Bibles, newsprint and marker, paper and pencils, hymnals, basket or offering plate

---

READING THE SCRIPTURE

NRSV
Lesson Scripture: John 17:6-21
⁶"I have made your name known to those whom you gave me from the world. They were yours, and you gave them to me, and they have kept your word. ⁷Now they know that everything you have given me is from you; ⁸for the words that you gave to me I have given to them, and they have received them and know in

CEB
Lesson Scripture: John 17:6-21
⁶"I have revealed your name to the people you gave me from this world. They were yours and you gave them to me, and they have kept your word. ⁷Now they know that everything you have given me comes from you. ⁸This is because I gave them the words that you gave me, and they received them. They truly understood that I came

truth that I came from you; and they have believed that you sent me. ⁹I am asking on their behalf; I am not asking on behalf of the world, but on behalf of those whom you gave me, because they are yours. ¹⁰All mine are yours, and yours are mine; and I have been glorified in them. ¹¹And now I am no longer in the world, but they are in the world, and I am coming to you. Holy Father, protect them in your name that you have given me, so that they may be one, as we are one. ¹²While I was with them, I protected them in your name that you have given me. I guarded them, and not one of them was lost except the one destined to be lost, so that the scripture might be fulfilled. ¹³But now I am coming to you, and I speak these things in the world so that they may have my joy made complete in themselves. ¹⁴I have given them your word, and the world has hated them because they do not belong to the world, just as I do not belong to the world. ¹⁵I am not asking you to take them out of the world, but I ask you to protect them from the evil one. ¹⁶They do not belong to the world, just as I do not belong to the world. ¹⁷Sanctify them in the truth; your word is truth. ¹⁸As you have sent me into the world, so I have sent them into the world. ¹⁹And for their sakes I sanctify myself, so that they also may be sanctified in truth.

²⁰"I ask not only on behalf of these, but also on behalf of those who will believe in me through their word, **²¹that they may all be one. As you, Father, are in me and I am in you, may they also be in us, so that the world may believe that you have sent me.**

from you, and they believed that you sent me.

⁹"I'm praying for them. I'm not praying for the world but for those you gave me, because they are yours. ¹⁰Everything that is mine is yours and everything that is yours is mine; I have been glorified in them. ¹¹I'm no longer in the world, but they are in the world, even as I'm coming to you. Holy Father, watch over them in your name, the name you gave me, that they will be one just as we are one. ¹²When I was with them, I watched over them in your name, the name you gave to me, and I kept them safe. None of them were lost, except the one who was destined for destruction, so that scripture would be fulfilled. ¹³Now I'm coming to you and I say these things while I'm in the world so that they can share completely in my joy. ¹⁴I gave your word to them and the world hated them, because they don't belong to this world, just as I don't belong to this world. ¹⁵I'm not asking that you take them out of this world but that you keep them safe from the evil one. ¹⁶They don't belong to this world, just as I don't belong to this world. ¹⁷Make them holy in the truth; your word is truth. ¹⁸As you sent me into the world, so I have sent them into the world. ¹⁹I made myself holy on their behalf so that they also would be made holy in the truth.

²⁰"I'm not praying only for them but also for those who believe in me because of their word. **²¹I pray they will be one, Father, just as you are in me and I am in you. I pray that they also will be in us, so that the world will believe that you sent me.**

UNDERSTANDING THE SCRIPTURE

Introduction. The Gospel of John was written later than those of Matthew, Mark, and Luke—probably around A.D. 100. Writing in *The New Interpreter's Bible*, Gail R. O'Day asserts, "The Gospel of John was thus written by a Jewish Christian for and in a Jewish Christian community that was in conflict with the synagogue authorities of its day." The Gospel itself (20:31) explains that the purpose of the book is to help readers come to believe "that Jesus Christ is the Messiah, the Son of God, and that through believing you may have life in his name."

Tradition says that this Gospel was written in Ephesus, a once great city in what is now Turkey, and that John served there as a pastor. Another tradition, probably based on John 19:26-27, claims that John brought Mary, Jesus' mother, to Ephesus. We know that the Ephesus church faced difficulties, and there are hints of similar troubles in the Gospel. Jews who became Christians were expelled from the synagogue (John 9:22; 12:42; 16:2). The church itself had experienced a split (1 John 2:19). In addition, the long account of Christ before Pilate (John 18:28–19:16) hints that John's readers were already experiencing persecution from the Roman government.

The farewell words of Jesus in chapters 14–16 are permeated with his concern for his followers and his desire that they experience fullness of life as they fulfill their role as his successors. Throughout the passage, Jesus speaks of his departure (14:3, 28; 16:10, 17, 28; 17:11). His parting words call his disciples to a continuing relationship with God, to love one another, and to receive the promises of peace and joy. Their life will not be without risk, but it will also contain blessings. They will receive the Spirit of truth (14:16-17); they will be persecuted (15:20); they will be put out of the synagogue (16:2); they will be united with God the Father and with Jesus (17:24-26).

The address ends with a "high priestly prayer" that John 17 records in place of the prayer offered in Gethsemane that we find in the other Gospels. The disciples have shared the Last Supper and had their feet washed (13:1-38). Jesus has reassured them of their ongoing relationship with the glorified Christ and promised them the gift of the Holy Spirit (14:1-31). After outlining the pattern for a true believer's life (15:1-17), Jesus then addresses their relationship to the world (15:18–16:33). The prayer comes after these teachings and Jesus' words of reassurance to the disciples.

Overall, the farewell discourse serves an important function in John's Gospel. In terms of the plot, it allows for some narrative time to elapse in order for Judas (who departed from Jesus in 13:30) to work out his plan for Jesus' arrest. More important, this discourse reveals to the reader the absolute control that Jesus has over all the narrated events, indeed, even over his and their circumstances. Consider these highlights: The ruler of the world has no power over Jesus (14:30); the hatred of the world toward Jesus is but a fulfillment of Scripture (15:25); although the believers will have tribulation in the world, Jesus has conquered it (16:33); although the believers will be in the world, they are not a part of it (17:16).

To underscore Jesus' power and victory, the prayer in John 17 uses the word "world" eighteen times, more often than anywhere else in the Fourth Gospel. The prayer assures the reader that the presence of God has been invoked to guarantee the preservation of the believers in the world until the consummation of the ultimate mystical union of God the Father, Jesus, and all the believers (17:20-24).

John 17:1-5. In the first verses of John 17, Jesus prays for himself. At the beginning of his ministry, Jesus speaks of the "hour" when he will finally reveal himself and God's plan in full (2:4). In the fullness of God's time, that manifestation will be on the cross (7:30; 8:20; 12:23, 27; 13:1; 17:1). Now that the hour has come, Jesus prays that his pre-Incarnation glory will be restored and that God's plan to secure eternal life for all people will be accomplished through all that Jesus has done and is about to do.

John 17:6-19. Jesus next affirms that he has made God's name known (17:6). This involves more than assigning a mere label to God. Rather, it means that Jesus proclaims God's being, honor, and reputation.

Then Jesus prays for the disciples, who are to be left in the world after his ascension. He especially prays that they might be as united as he and God are, that they might have joy, that they might be protected from (and victorious over) evil, and that they might be holy and truthful representatives of Christ in the world.

Note that the unity for which Jesus prays is not an achievement gained by people who settle their differences. Rather, it is a gift of God to the church, and its essence is like that of the Son to the Father.

In addition, Jesus prays in verse 17 that the disciples might be sanctified in the truth. This is not simply truth that is described by verifiable facts, the kind of truth we might think of in scientific or propositional terms. This truth is evidenced by a quality of life that is marked by love and expressed in deeds consistent with the ministry of the Son.

In verse 12, "the one destined to be lost" is literally "the son of destruction," a term used in 2 Thessalonians 2:3 as a term for the "lawless one." Here it can be seen as a reference to Judas.

John 17:20-26. Jesus ends with a prayer for the church yet to come. He prays that its members might be united with God, himself, and one another—for only in such unity can they express perfect love, and only through love can they bring the world to believe. This might be a reference to rivalries among competing Christian groups in John's time.

INTERPRETING THE SCRIPTURE

A High Priestly Prayer

In chapter 13, John begins his account of Jesus in the upper room by describing how Jesus washed the disciples' feet. The subsequent upper room discourse of Jesus contains some of the most moving and hope-filled words in all the Bible. It is in this section of John's Gospel that Jesus promises the disciples that they will be with him forever, commands them to love as he has loved, and assures them of the coming of the Holy Spirit. This portion of Scripture also includes Jesus' teaching that he is the vine that gives life to the branches that bear fruit. Then, before facing the cross, Jesus offers what has come to be known as a "high priestly prayer." This prayer is unique to John's Gospel.

In the ancient world, almost all religions had priests and priestesses who served as the link between the people and their god. God's people in the Old Testament knew all about priests. It was through priests, they believed, that ordinary human beings had a way to get a hearing in heaven, and through them, heaven got a hearing with us.

As we will see in the next lesson, the Book of Hebrews calls Jesus a "great high priest" (4:14). What all the previous priesthood pointed toward, Hebrews tells us, has now become real in Jesus Christ. Our high priest, Christ, is continually making intercession for us, praying right now for us before the heavenly throne (Hebrews 7:23-25).

John 17 contains a special "high priestly prayer" offered by Jesus the night before he died. In John's Gospel, this is Jesus' last great recorded prayer to his Father, and it ends his last long address to his disciples. "Father, the hour has come," he says (John 17:1). Now Jesus is ready to die. Scholars, however, tell us that this prayer is not to be thought of as being simply for that single historical moment. It can be understood quite well as an ongoing prayer of the risen Christ, continuing down through the centuries.

If that is the case, then this is a prayer of enormous importance for us. In this lesson, we will be studying the prayer that Christ, our high priest in heaven, is right now praying for us.

The Gift of Glory

First, however, Christ prays for himself: "Glorify your Son so that the Son may glorify you" (17:1). Five times in the first five verses the words "glorify" or "glory" occur. Christ has "glorified" God on earth. Now he prays that God will "glorify" him.

What startles us is that Jesus talks about being "glorified" when he is on the way to a shameful death on the cross. Remembering Christ's sacrifice, however, we can now sing, "In the cross of Christ I glory" and "My glory all, the cross." It was not the cross alone, however, by which Jesus was glorified. Of the Resurrection, also, we sing, "The head that once was crowned with thorns Is crowned with glory now." It is in heaven that our glorious high priest is praying for us.

The first part of Christ's prayer has been, and still is being, wondrously answered. In his death, resurrection, and ascension, we see Christ's glory.

The Prayer for the Disciples

There is a sense, however, in which the answer to Christ's prayer depends on eleven men and a few women. At least, they are involved in it, because the next part of the prayer is prayed for the disciples: "I am asking on their behalf' (17:9). It is through them, in part at least, that Christ is to be glorified here on earth.

The followers are going to be left without him, and so Christ prays for the faithful disciples he must leave behind. Jesus prays "that they may have my joy made complete in themselves" (17:13). On the way to the cross, Christ prays that his disciples may share the joy he knows, even in this crisis.

Christ does not pray that his disciples be spared the troubles of this world (see 17:15). What Jesus does pray for is that they should be different. "Sanctify them," he begs (17:17), so "that they also may be sanctified in truth" (17:19). They are to be holy. That prayer is marvelously answered in the lives of the first disciples. None of them is perfect, of course, but they do glorify Christ by spreading the word he has given them.

Christ's Intercession for Us

The third part of the prayer, however, has not been fully answered yet. In a real sense its answer is up to us— for now Christ prays, "I ask not only on behalf of these [disciples], but also on behalf of those who will believe in me through their word" (17:20). In other words, the prayer is on our behalf.

In a way, Jesus is still praying for us the same things for which he initially prayed on behalf of the first disciples. There is, however, a special desire that he is now praying for the church: "That they may all be one" (17:21). Just to make sure no one can miss the point of the prayer, he repeats it: "That they may become completely one" (17:23). The night before he died, Jesus' great prayer for the church is that it will be united, never divided. That is what our great High Priest is still praying for us now in heaven, and this prayer is still a long way from being fully answered.

Of course, the church is united in many ways. Many other denominations, although they produce their own church school resources, use these same International Lesson Series, also know as Uniform Sunday School Lessons, Scripture passages each week. We are united in studying the same Bible.

In countless communities, individual congregations cross denominational lines to work together in evangelistic campaigns, Habitat for Humanity, food pantries for the poor, and other projects. Many congregations cross racial and ethnic lines in their membership and witness.

We are a long way, however, from being "completely one." There are several hundred different denominations in the United States and Canada, some even claiming that they alone are the "true church." It is still too sadly true, as Dr. Martin Luther King Jr. reminded us, that eleven o'clock on Sunday morning is the most segregated hour of the week. There is indeed a spiritual unity that binds these separate, and too often competing, denominations together, but it is often hard to see.

Thus Jesus prays to God that the church will be one spiritually, just "as we are one" (17:22). In effect, Jesus prays for a unity that those outside the church can see—a unity so visible that the world cannot only see it but be won by it.

Moreover, Jesus prays for unity "that the world may know that you have sent me" (17:23). What can turn the world away from the gospel more quickly than the spectacle of Christians who preach love and yet remain divided? And what can so *win* the world as a church united in service for Christ? Perhaps we need to join our great High Priest in the prayer he is praying for us at this moment, that his divided church will more and more become "completely one" (17:23).

SHARING THE SCRIPTURE

PREPARING TO TEACH

Preparing Our Hearts

Meditate on this week's devotional reading from John 15:1-11, which is the final "I am" saying of Jesus. How would you describe the relationship between a vine and its branches? What does it mean to "abide" in Jesus? What do you think Jesus would say to you about the quality and quantity of the fruit that you are bearing for him?

Pray that you and the students will be so enveloped in the love of Jesus that you will bear much excellent fruit.

Preparing Our Minds

Study the background Scripture from John 17:1-26 and the lesson Scripture from John 17:6-21.

Consider this question as you prepare the lesson: *How can a small group make an impact on the larger community?*

Write on newsprint:

❏ information for next week's lesson, found under "Continue the Journey."

❏ activities for further spiritual growth in "Continue the Journey."

Review the "Introduction," "The Big Picture," "Close-up," and "Faith in Action," which all precede the first lesson of this quarter. Consider how you might use any of this material in today's lesson.

Have on hand a basket, offering plate, or other container to collect prayer requests.

LEADING THE CLASS

(1) Gather to Learn

❖ Greet the class members and introduce guests.

❖ Pray that those who have come today will look for ways that they, as a small group, can make an impact on their community.

❖ Read: **Small groups are an important component of most churches. Groups exist for prayer, mission, study, and fellowship. They are often based on common interests, a particular goal, or an age level. In The United Methodist Church, Covenant Discipleship Groups meet weekly to hold members accountable to a mutually agreed upon covenant designed to strengthen their discipleship, to pray for one another, and to "watch over each other in love."**

❖ Ask: **What kinds of small groups do we have in our church and how do they impact the church as a whole?**

❖ Read aloud today's focus statement: **Small intimate groups exist in the midst of a larger community. How can a small group impact the larger community? Jesus prayed that the disciples would be united and protected by God as they brought new people into their community in an unsafe world.**

(2) Goal 1: Study Jesus' Prayer for the Unity of All Who Believe in Him

❖ Set the stage for today's lesson by reading "Introduction" from Understanding the Scripture.

❖ Call for two volunteers, one to read background Scripture from John 17:1-5 and another to read verses 6-21. Recommend that as this prayer is being read the participants close their eyes and listen for words, phrases, or ideas that strike them as especially meaningful.

❖ Invite volunteers to state the words that had special meaning and explain why these words captured their attention.

❖ Discuss these questions:

1. **How would you summarize Jesus' main concerns in this prayer to his Father?**
2. **What does Jesus say about his followers?**
3. **Verse 20 clearly includes a prayer for all "who will believe" in Jesus, which includes you. How does this intimate prayer influence your own relationship with Jesus?**
4. **How does this prayer influence your relationship with other members of the body of Christ?**

❖ Read in unison today's key verse, John 17:21, and ask: **Where do you see signs of unity among all who believe in Jesus?**

(3) Goal 2: Experience Intimacy with Jesus and God the Father Through Prayer

❖ Read: **In his book,** *God and You: Prayer as a Personal Relationship,* **Jesuit priest and pastoral psychologist William A. Barry discusses prayer as a personal, intimate relationship with God. God is always paying attention to us, but we need to learn how to be more attentive to God. Among the strategies Barry suggests for paying closer attention is contemplation of the Scriptures. We will look at Psalm 103:1-5 as a means of encountering God in the present.**

❖ Read Psalm 103:1-5 aloud as expressively as possible. Suggest that the adults follow along in their Bibles. Then ask these questions for quiet reflection, noting that whatever answers arise, this encounter with the Scripture has, in Barry's words, "opened a door to conversation with the Lord."

1. **What am I sensing or feeling as I hear these words?**
2. **If I have a positive response, such as gratitude, what reasons do I have to thank God today?**
3. **If I respond with discomfort, perhaps feeling that God has not blessed me, what do I need to ask God to do for me today?**

(4) Goal 3: Unite in Prayers for One Another and for Unity in Jesus Christ

❖ Read or retell "Christ's Intercession for Us" in Interpreting the Scripture.

❖ Point out that just as Jesus intercedes for us before the Father we are to offer prayers of intercession for others.

❖ Distribute paper and pencils. Suggest that the adults tear the paper in half or quarters. On each slip they are to write one prayer request. To protect confidentiality if the prayer is for an individual, please use only the first name or a generic identifier, such as "a friend." Pass around a basket and ask each person to drop all of the folded requests in the container. Pass the basket around again, perhaps more than once, and ask each person to take one request each time the basket comes around.

❖ Invite the class members to open the requests they have drawn from the basket, hold them in their hands, and pray silently for each one.

(5) Continue the Journey

❖ Break the silence by praying that as the learners depart they will continue to pray throughout the week for the names and situations that have been entrusted to them.

❖ Post information for next week's session on newsprint for the students to copy:

- Title: Jesus Intercedes for Us
- Background Scripture: Hebrews 4:14–5:10
- Lesson Scripture: Hebrews 4:14–5:10
- Focus of the Lesson: People often have someone who makes special efforts on their behalf. What qualifies and motivates a person to make that special effort? The writer of Hebrews informs us that God appointed Jesus, the high priest, as an intercessor on behalf of God's people.

❖ Challenge the adults to grow spiritually by completing one or more of these activities related to this week's session, which you have posted on newsprint for the students to copy.

(1) Offer an intercessory prayer each day for your congregation, your denomination (if applicable), and the church around the world. What are your major concerns about the church today for which you think prayer is needed?

(2) Recall that Jesus says in John 17:16 that his followers "do not belong to the world," but he is not asking the Father to "take them out of the world" (17:15). Rather, he is sending them "into the world" (17:18). Jesus prays that his followers will be sanctified in the truth of God's Word (17:17). What might be the outward signs of a sanctified follower who is in but not of the world? How might this person be different from nonbelievers, yet connected enough to encourage these nonbelievers to come to Christ?

(3) Form or join a small group for the purpose of praying for unity within the body of Christ and for a closer relationship among all Christians across the theological spectrum.

❖ Sing or read aloud "O Church of God, United."

❖ Conclude by leading the class in this benediction, adapted from the key verse for the session on December 21 from Luke 2:20: **May we go forth to worship as the shepherds, glorifying and praising God for all we have heard and seen.**

UNIT 2: LEARNING TO PRAY

JESUS INTERCEDES FOR US

PREVIEWING THE LESSON

Lesson Scripture: Hebrews 4:14–5:10
Background Scripture: Hebrews 4:14–5:10
Key Verse: Hebrews 4:15

Focus of the Lesson:
People often have someone who makes special efforts on their behalf. What qualifies and motivates a person to make that special effort? The writer of Hebrews informs us that God appointed Jesus, the high priest, as an intercessor on behalf of God's people.

Goals for the Learners:
(1) to discover how Jesus fulfills the role of intercessor with God for God's people.
(2) to appreciate that Christians do not stand alone before God with their sins.
(3) to pray with thanksgiving for their Intercessor with God and to tell others about him.

Pronunciation Guide:
Melchizedek (mel kis´ uh dek)

Supplies:
Bibles, newsprint and marker, paper and pencils, hymnals

READING THE SCRIPTURE

NRSV

Lesson Scripture: Hebrews 4:14–5:10

¹⁴Since, then, we have a great high priest who has passed through the heavens, Jesus, the Son of God, let us hold fast to our confession.

CEB

Lesson Scripture: Hebrews 4:14–5:10

¹⁴Also, let's hold on to the confession since we have a great high priest who passed through the heavens, who is Jesus, God's Son;

[15]For we do not have a high priest who is unable to sympathize with our weaknesses, but we have one who in every respect has been tested as we are, yet without sin. [16]Let us therefore approach the throne of grace with boldness, so that we may receive mercy and find grace to help in time of need.

[1]Every high priest chosen from among mortals is put in charge of things pertaining to God on their behalf, to offer gifts and sacrifices for sins. [2]He is able to deal gently with the ignorant and wayward, since he himself is subject to weakness; [3]and because of this he must offer sacrifice for his own sins as well as for those of the people. [4]And one does not presume to take this honor, but takes it only when called by God, just as Aaron was.

[5]So also Christ did not glorify himself in becoming a high priest, but was appointed by the one who said to him,
"You are my Son,
    today I have begotten you";
[6]as he says also in another place,
"You are a priest forever,
        according to the order of
            Melchizedek."

[7]In the days of his flesh, Jesus offered up prayers and supplications, with loud cries and tears, to the one who was able to save him from death, and he was heard because of his reverent submission. [8]Although he was a Son, he learned obedience through what he suffered; [9]and having been made perfect, he became the source of eternal salvation for all who obey him, [10]having been designated by God a high priest according to the order of Melchizedek.

[15]because we don't have a high priest who can't sympathize with our weaknesses but instead one who was tempted in every way that we are, except without sin. [16]Finally, let's draw near to the throne of favor with confidence so that we can receive mercy and find grace when we need help.

[1]Every high priest is taken from the people and put in charge of things that relate to God for their sake, in order to offer gifts and sacrifices for sins. [2]The high priest is able to deal gently with the ignorant and those who are misled since he himself is prone to weakness. [3]Because of his weakness, he must offer sacrifices for his own sins as well as for the people. [4]No one takes this honor for themselves but takes it only when they are called by God, just like Aaron.

[5]In the same way Christ also didn't promote himself to become high priest. Instead, it was the one who said to him,
You are my Son.
    Today I have become your Father ,
[6]as he also says in another place,
You are a priest forever,
        according to the order of
            Melchizedek.

[7]During his days on earth, Christ offered prayers and requests with loud cries and tears as his sacrifices to the One who was able to save him from death. He was heard because of his godly devotion. [8]Although he was a Son, he learned obedience from what he suffered. [9]After he had been made perfect, he became the source of salvation for everyone who obeys him. [10]He was appointed by God to be a high priest according to the order of Melchizedek.

UNDERSTANDING THE SCRIPTURE

Introduction. Hebrews 4:14–5:10 focuses on Jesus as our high priest. The writer compares and contrasts Jesus with the ancient Jewish priests, whose calling and instructions for work are found in Exodus, Leviticus, and Numbers.

Hebrews 4:14-16. The passage begins with a renewed call to faithfulness, founded on trust in what Jesus has accomplished—and continues to accomplish—for us. The author points to the gracious character of our "high priest" as a means of encouraging confidence, strength, and courage in the face of trials and downfalls. Two earlier passages (2:17-18 and 3:1) stressed Jesus' faithfulness in performing his role as high priest. To this the author now adds Jesus' compassion and sympathy with our weaknesses. Although Jesus remained without sin, he was genuinely tempted, as we are, and so understands when and why we succumb.

The reference to Jesus passing through the heavens (4:14) may intentionally parallel the high priest's actions on the Day of Atonement, when he went into the Holy of Holies at the Temple to make sacrifice and to pray for the people. The high priest would then come out to proclaim forgiveness to the people and to bless them. This seems to be Jesus' role, in part, in that he is the means by which we "receive mercy and find grace" (4:16). Because he is the perfect sacrifice, the action does not need to be repeated.

Hebrews 5:1-3. The author then turns to a description of earthly high priests. These special men, chosen from those who qualified, have responsibility to make gifts and sacrifices to redeem the people from their sin. Leviticus 16 describes how, on the Day of Atonement, the high priest is to offer a bull (16:11) and sprinkle its blood on the Holy of Holies, the inner sanctum of the Temple where the ark of the covenant was preserved. On that day in particular the high priest stands in for the people and acts to bring forgiveness and salvation to himself and them (Hebrews 5:3).

The human high priest is able to sympathize with the people because he knows both temptation and sin himself. This also makes him a true representative of the people before God—he stands alone, representing the failed humanity of all. Thus the high priest seeks mercy for himself, as well as others

These verses show a good familiarity with Jewish sacrificial law, which calls for both grain and animal sacrifices (Leviticus 2:1, 4; 7; 16:6). The two classifications of sinners—those who break the law unintentionally (Leviticus 4:2; 5:14, 17) and those who defy it knowingly (Numbers 15:30)—may be reflected in the author's reference to the "ignorant" and the "wayward" (Hebrews 5:2).

Hebrews 5:4. In Jewish tradition, Aaron was called by God to be the first high priest (Exodus 28:1). Subsequently, the high priest was elected from among Aaron's descendants in the tribe of Levi. By the time Hebrews was written, the selection of a new high priest had become tied with Roman politics. After the death of Herod, the governor of Jerusalem usually made the appointment. Thus the author suggests that a true high priest is somehow called and appointed by God, not by human institutions. Taken with Hebrews

5:1-3, this outlines the two criteria for a high priest: humanity and divine appointment.

Hebrews 5:5-6. The author now returns to quoting Hebrew Scripture as in prior chapters to make his point that Jesus is the perfect high priest on both counts. Both references are to royal psalms, written in honor of a king (Psalm 2:7; 110:4). The first quotation, which also appears in Hebrews 1:5, reminds us of the voice at Jesus' baptism (Mark 1:11)—and it reminds us that this is no ordinary human being, but God's own Son. Thus his priesthood will be eternal, a point that is also made in 1:10-12 and 7:16.

Melchizedek appears in Genesis 14:17-20 as the King of Salem and a priest of God Most High. The priest-king blesses Abraham, who in turn gives him a tithe (ten percent) of property from the spoils of a war to liberate his nephew Lot, who had been taken captive (Genesis 14:1-16). In Hebrews 7–10 the writer leads us through a somewhat convoluted deduction that the blessing and tithe combine to prove Melchizedek was "superior" to Abraham, and thus to Abraham's descendants, including the Levites (priests). By naming Jesus as being from "the order of Melchizedek" (5:6), the author of Hebrews is declaring Jesus to be of a higher order than any Jewish leader. Some scholars speculate that this whole section is meant to validate Jesus' role in spite of Jewish law, which held that only those of the tribe of Levi could become priests.

Hebrews 5:7-10. The final verses return to the theme of Jesus' humanity as high priest. The text speaks of his "prayers and supplications, with loud cries and tears," which could be a reference to the agony Jesus will undergo at Gethsemane (Matthew 26:36-46). If so, then the reference to God's listening because of Jesus' submission could point to the moment when Jesus prays for God's will and not his own to be done (26:39). Regardless, the author makes plain that Jesus' suffering will lead to results—from it, he "learned obedience" and was "made perfect" (Hebrews 5:8-9). In Greek, the word translated "made perfect" means that Jesus has reached a goal that was previously set. It can also mean he has matured. The whole image is that through his suffering Jesus has grown into (been shaped into) the ultimate high priest that God always intended him to be. In reaching this goal, Jesus fulfills God's larger plan, in that "he became the source of eternal salvation for all who obey him" (5:9).

Throughout this section, both Jesus' divinity and his human suffering are necessary components to his role as our heavenly high priest. He can truly lead us into God's presence only because he is the Son. Yet he can also empathize with us and effectively intercede for us only because he is truly human.

INTERPRETING THE SCRIPTURE

The Priestly Role

The role of Jesus as the great high priest is one of the primary images in Hebrews. The author introduces this idea in 2:17, where Jesus is called a "merciful and faithful high priest," and reiterates it in 3:1, where Jesus is referred to as the "high priest of our confession." Those verses stress Jesus' faithful service in carrying out the task God has given him. This week's passage from Hebrews 4:14–5:10, however, puts Jesus' role as high priest in the context of his experience and identity with humans and thus explores how this puts him in a unique position to intercede with God on our behalf.

In ancient Judaism, the priests were officials from the tribe of Levi who presided at ritual functions and sacrificial services. Aaron held a special position among priests; he and his sons were anointed and given the special clothing of priesthood (Exodus 28–29).

In the Bible, priests serve as the link between God and mortals, interceding with God on behalf of the people. Their special function in that task is the offering of "gifts and sacrifices for sin" (Hebrews 5:1). Sin upsets the relationship that should exist between people and God; sacrifices are meant to restore that relationship and bring those who repent into God's favor.

This work does not elevate the priests above others or give them cause for arrogance. The writer of Hebrews is careful to point out that priests, being human, have their own weaknesses. As a result, they are to "deal gently with the ignorant and wayward" (5:2), and they offer sacrifice for their own sins as well as the sins of others (5:3). The exception, of course, is Jesus. Because he is sinless, the sacrifice he offered is totally on behalf of the people.

The Day of Atonement

Special priestly duties and rituals occur on the Day of Atonement, which Israel celebrates ten days into their liturgical new year (Leviticus 23:27-32). Like our own season of Advent, this spiritual new year begins late in the calendar year—the seventh month (September–October), to be precise. The Day of Atonement is a day of fasting, when no work is done. The priest symbolically places the sins of the people on the head of a goat (called the "scapegoat"), and then drives the animal into the wilderness (Leviticus 16:10).

The writer of Hebrews has the Day of Atonement in mind when describing Jesus as the perfect high priest. Only on that day did the law allow the high priest to go beyond the curtain that led into the Temple's inner sanctuary, called the Holy of Holies, where the ark of the covenant rested. The ark, a symbol of God's presence and a reminder of the covenant relationship between God and Israel, was the most important object in the Temple. This gives us an image for understanding Jesus' passage from earth into the place of God's presence. Moreover, Jesus as the great and sinless high priest brings atonement to the people once and for all.

Our Sympathetic High Priest

The writer reminds us, however, that Christ's sinless state does not keep him from identifying with us. As proof, Hebrews 5:7 points to Jesus' suffering in the garden of Gethsemane. We get a vivid picture of his heartfelt prayers, offered "with loud cries and tears." These words convey the intensity of Jesus' suffering and the desperate nature of his pleas for help.

Having learned obedience through suffering (5:8), Jesus is able to accomplish his God-appointed task. As a final witness to the priesthood of Jesus Christ, the author says that Jesus is "the source of eternal salvation for all who obey him" (5:9). His place is assured as high priest, and thus we are assured of entry into the presence of God.

Throughout Hebrews, Jesus' divine nature is shown in combination with his human nature. The author has already made a strong case for Jesus' identity with humans, but he restates the case by reminding the readers that Jesus "in every respect has been tested as we are" (4:15). Because of this, Jesus is able to empathize with all human weaknesses. The weaknesses referred to here are not limited to specific sins or to suffering, but rather include all the shortcomings associated with human nature.

We know that Jesus faced temptations. In Matthew's account of the testing in the desert, for example, the temptations represent the things with the greatest potential for leading Jesus away from his appointed task (Matthew 4:1-11). Jesus has to face—and overcome—those temptations in preparation for his ministry.

Although Jesus is tested in all the ways we are, he remains "without sin" (Hebrews 4:15). That is why he is able to act as our high priest and to intercede on our behalf. (Compare 4:15 to 7:26, which describes what it means to be totally without sin.)

Our Priest Leads Us into God's Forgiving Presence

Jesus' identity with humans is so complete that he can empathize in a way no other high priest can. Jesus' human nature assures us of his empathy, just as his divine nature assures us of his power. Jesus, the great high priest, has opened the way for us to approach the throne of grace and come into God's presence with boldness and confidence. We no longer need the environment of the Temple, human priests, or animal sacrifices to connect us to God.

This is good news, indeed. Being guilty, and lacking the power to save ourselves, we need God's mercy. Even having received that mercy, we keep slipping back into our sinful ways, and are, therefore, in need of God's grace. The author of Hebrews says that now we can approach God with confidence, trusting we will receive the forgiveness and support we so desperately need. Grace comes to us—over and over—through Jesus Christ, our high priest.

Looking back, we see that almost two thousand years ago some of the children of Israel encountered One who seemed truly to embody the nature and will of God. What he expressed in word and action became recognized as the realities that accompany God's kingdom. Here was One who truly bore the nature and lived by the principles of the Heavenly Father. He could be none other than God's Son, the promised King who would express God's rule, not over physical territory but over the hearts and lives of believing, obedient servants.

Through the lens of the cross and the Resurrection, the truth of these perceptions becomes clear. This Jesus of Nazareth, the sinless One, has taken our place in regard to judgment and guilt. He knew our hearts then and he knows them today. He knows the ways in which we have abused power and manipulated others for our own advantage, and he knows the destruction this can bring into our lives and the lives of others. Yet, as he did when he walked the earth, our Savior reaches out in sorrow, in compassion, and in love. He calls to us still, "Confess. Repent. Receive forgiveness. Go and sin no more."

We are left to echo the glorious words of Paul: "Who is to condemn? It is Christ Jesus, who died, yes, who was raised, who is at the right hand of God, who indeed intercedes for us. . . . [Nothing] in all creation, will be able to separate us from the love of God in Christ Jesus our Lord" (Romans 8:34, 39). Hallelujah, and amen!

SHARING THE SCRIPTURE

PREPARING TO TEACH

Preparing Our Hearts

Meditate on this week's devotional reading from Psalm 107:1-15, which begins Book Five of the Psalms. What do you learn about God from this passage? What do you learn about how God deals with those in the midst of adversity? The psalmist begins by calling readers to "give thanks to the LORD, for he is good." What reasons do you have for giving thanks today?

Pray that you and the students will be aware that God is on your side and give thanks for God's steadfast love and forgiveness.

Preparing Our Minds

Study the background Scripture and the lesson Scripture, which are both from Hebrews 4:14–5:10.

Consider this question as you prepare the lesson: *What qualifies and motivates a person to make a special effort on behalf of someone else?*

Write on newsprint:
❏ information for next week's lesson, found under "Continue the Journey."
❏ activities for further spiritual growth in "Continue the Journey."

Review the "Introduction," "The Big Picture," "Close-up," and "Faith in Action," which all precede the first lesson of this quarter. Consider how you might use any of this material in today's lesson.

Familiarize yourself with information about priests and their duties by carefully reviewing the Understanding the Scripture portion.

LEADING THE CLASS

(1) Gather to Learn

❖ Greet the class members and introduce guests.

❖ Pray that those who have come today will consider the qualifications and motivations of those who make special efforts on behalf of others.

❖ Read this inspirational story: **The son of a preacher and beautician who worked hard, actor Denzel Washington recalls a mentor from the Boys Club who taught him how to focus on goals and recognize the consequences of his actions. As he grew, others helped him along the way. A teacher at the midtown campus of Fordham University not only encouraged Denzel but also believed that he had a talent worthy of nurture. Denzel acknowledges that he had had some luck, but he** also claims the he "had tremendous help along the way. That was a huge blessing from God. Behind every great *success* there's someone and often more than one person. A parent, teacher, coach, role model. It starts somewhere."

❖ Invite volunteers to tell brief stories of someone who made a special effort to help them.

❖ Read aloud today's focus statement: **People often have someone who makes special efforts on their behalf. What qualifies and motivates a person to make that special effort? The writer of Hebrews informs us that God appointed Jesus, the high priest, as an intercessor on behalf of God's people.**

(2) Goal 1: Discover How Jesus Fulfills the Role of Intercessor with God for God's People

❖ Read "The Priestly Role" in Interpreting the Scripture to introduce today's session.

❖ Enlist a volunteer to read Hebrews 4:14–5:10.

❖ Encourage class members to call out questions about who priests were and what duties they were expected to perform. Write the questions on newsprint.

❖ Form several groups and suggest that they review Leviticus 6, 7, 8, and 22 to learn more about the priests of Aaron's line and their responsibilities. Depending on time, you may wish to assign one chapter to each group.

❖ Bring the groups together and try to answer as many questions that were raised earlier as possible. Add information that you have studied from Understanding the Scripture.

❖ Conclude this portion by leading the class in reading today's key verse, Hebrews 4:15.

(3) Goal 2: Appreciate that Christians Do Not Stand Alone Before God with Their Sins

❖ Read "Our Priest Leads Us into God's Forgiving Presence" in Interpreting the Scripture.

❖ Encourage the participants to recall a time when they had to stand alone and do something that was going to be evaluated. Perhaps they had to take a test, which for many students creates a feeling of doom and judgment even before the exam questions are presented. Possibly they had to demonstrate a skill necessary to be hired for a job. Maybe they had to appear before a judge and argue why they should not have received a traffic ticket. Invite several volunteers to describe how they felt about their experience, though they need not discuss the specifics of the incident.

❖ Suggest that the students imagine for a moment how they might feel if called to stand alone before God with their sins. Likely, the feelings they previously expressed will be greatly magnified.

❖ Encourage the adults to close their eyes and imagine standing before God with their sins. This time, though, Jesus stands with them, interceding on their behalf. Ask: **What emotions now come to mind?**

❖ End this portion by reminding the students that as believers they have assurance that Jesus is on their side. They do not stand alone with their sins before God. Our great High Priest is right there with them.

(4) Goal 3: Pray with Thanksgiving for the Learners' Intercessor with God and Tell Others about Him

❖ Read these words of a giant of the Reformation, Martin Luther (1483–1546), in which he summarized the life, death, and work of Jesus: "In his life, Christ is an example, showing us how to live. In his death, he is a sacrifice, satisfying for our sins. In his resurrection, he is a conqueror. In his ascension, he is a king. In his intercession, he is a high priest."

❖ Ask: **What, if anything, would you add, subtract, or modify to bring Luther's description of Jesus in line with you own beliefs?**

❖ Suggest that each adult use a breath prayer to thank Jesus for his intercession. Breath prayers are short, generally prayed using one word or phrase to inhale and another word or phrase to exhale. Here are some examples: "My Jesus/I thank you." "Sinless Jesus/have mercy." "Lamb of God/take away my sin." Provide quiet time for the adults to discern a prayer and pray.

(5) Continue the Journey

❖ Break the silence by praying that as the learners depart they will continue to give thanks for Jesus, and share with others the good news that he is on their side and willingly intercedes for them before God.

❖ Post information for next week's session on newsprint for the students to copy:

▪ **Title: We Pray for One Another**

▪ **Background Scripture: James 5**

▪ **Lesson Scripture: James 5:13-18**

▪ **Focus of the Lesson: Illness is part of being human. How can believers overcome illness? The writer of James teaches that the prayer of faith brings healing and offers Elijah's prayer as an example of prayer's effectiveness.**

❖ Challenge the adults to grow spiritually by completing one or more of these activities, which you have posted on newsprint for the students to copy.

(1) **Set aside some time each day to confess your sins, remembering that Jesus our high priest will intercede for you.**

(2) **Learn more about Melchizedek by reading Genesis 14:17-24; Psalm 110:4; Hebrews 5:5-10; 6:19-20; 7:1-22. What relationship do you see between Jesus and Melchizedek?**

(3) **Offer forgiveness and intercessory prayer for someone who has wronged you in some way.**

❖ Sing or read aloud "My Faith Looks Up to Thee."

❖ Conclude by leading the class in this benediction, adapted from the key verse for the session on December 21 from Luke 2:20: **May we go forth to worship as the shepherds, glorifying and praising God for all we have heard and seen.**

UNIT 2: LEARNING TO PRAY

WE PRAY FOR ONE ANOTHER

PREVIEWING THE LESSON

Lesson Scripture: James 5:13-18
Background Scripture: James 5
Key Verse: James 5:16

Focus of the Lesson:
Illness is part of being human. How can believers overcome illness? The writer of James teaches that the prayer of faith brings healing and offers Elijah's prayer as an example of prayer's effectiveness.

Goals for the Learners:
(1) to explore James's admonitions for prayer for healing and its power to heal.
(2) to affirm that prayer is powerful and yields good results.
(3) to pray for the sick.

Pronunciation Guide:
orthodoxy (or´ thuh dok see)
orthopraxy (or´ tho prax y)

Supplies:
Bibles, newsprint and marker, paper and pencils, hymnals

READING THE SCRIPTURE

NRSV
Lesson Scripture: James 5:13-18

¹³Are any among you suffering? They should pray. Are any cheerful? They should sing songs of praise. ¹⁴Are any among you sick? They should call for the elders of the church and have them pray over

CEB
Lesson Scripture: James 5:13-18

¹³If any of you are suffering, they should pray. If any of you are happy, they should sing. ¹⁴If any of you are sick, they should call for the elders of the church, and the elders should pray over them, anointing them with

them, anointing them with oil in the name of the Lord. [15]The prayer of faith will save the sick, and the Lord will raise them up; and anyone who has committed sins will be forgiven. [16]**Therefore confess your sins to one another, and pray for one another, so that you may be healed. The prayer of the righteous is powerful and effective.** [17]Elijah was a human being like us, and he prayed fervently that it might not rain, and for three years and six months it did not rain on the earth. [18]Then he prayed again, and the heaven gave rain and the earth yielded its harvest.

oil in the name of the Lord. [15]Prayer that comes from faith will heal the sick, for the Lord will restore them to health. And if they have sinned, they will be forgiven. [16]**For this reason, confess your sins to each other and pray for each other so that you may be healed. The prayer of the righteous person is powerful in what it can achieve.** [17]Elijah was a person just like us. When he earnestly prayed that it wouldn't rain, no rain fell for three and a half years. [18]He prayed again, God sent rain, and the earth produced its fruit.

UNDERSTANDING THE SCRIPTURE

Introduction. The Letter of James is strongly identified with the statement, "Faith by itself, if it has no works, is dead" (2:17). Indeed, this emphasis led Martin Luther—in his introduction to the German translation of the New Testament—to describe this biblical book as an "epistle of straw" with "nothing of the nature of the Gospel about it." He is not the only one in the church's history who has had trouble with James's insistence on coupling faith with works.

In fairness to James, however, the letter clearly identifies certain concerns of the early Christian community. Believers confront the same concerns today: facing trials and temptations, caring for rather than hurting others, judging others with fairness and justice, and living by God's will and wisdom rather than by the wisdom of the world. The Letter of James was written to help us discover how we are called to put our faith into action.

In addition, we know from other biblical letters that the early Christians began to have problems as independent communities and started to follow different practices regarding leadership, ethics, and the sacraments. Doctrines varied depending on where one went. James appears to be a letter written to help bring guidance and uniformity to these various Christian churches, just as many of the other epistles were.

To this end, the letter sounds a clear call to the church and Christians in every time to live faithfully—which is to say, to live out faith in one's works. For those who call this letter to task for a so-called "works-righteousness" attitude, it is critical to remember that James does not argue that works apart from faith are sufficient. In the section on Abraham's serving as the model for enacted faith, the author of James makes this pronouncement: "Faith was active along with his works, and faith was brought to completion by the works" (2:22). Faith remains central and foundational: At issue is the nature of the faith that both "saves" and "does good." Faith without works is an illusion.

Throughout this letter, integrity serves as a keystone. Faith and deed, word and works, knowledge and practice—all are to be held in tandem. One cannot be omitted without loss of the other. For that reason, James's witness and value to the church remain critical. Individuals and communities of faith find a reminder in its texts that the pursuit of *orthodoxy* (right belief) cannot be separated from the embodiment of *orthopraxy* (right practice). Witness and work, liturgy and service, creed and program—faith requires enactment.

The very practicality of the book has shaped debates as to its origin. Some scholars suggest it had already existed within Judaism for a while in a slightly different form, serving as a kind of "book of wisdom." They think the author of the book as we have it added a few references to Jesus in order to make the text pertinent for Christians. Other scholars, however, see enough similarity to Jesus' own teachings to discount this idea. Pointing especially to the Sermon on the Mount and to parables about discipleship in action, they make the case that the Letter of James was originally written by a Christian for Christians. Either way, we do see that the author was aware of ethical traditions that spanned many sources. Apart from James 1:1 and 2:1, almost every teaching in the book can be found in some form in various other writings, including the practical sayings from Jewish tradition (for example, in Proverbs) and from Jesus himself as recorded in the Gospels.

James 5:1-6. In this final chapter of the book, James ends with admonitions to the community. First he addresses the rich and lifts them up as examples of the foolishness of chasing after wealth. He also points out how wealth leads people to deeds that are contrary to the wishes of God.

James 5:7-11. The rest of the chapter encourages the community of faith in various ways. Here we read that they are to wait patiently for the Lord's return. By the time this letter was written, some Christians had begun to doubt that Christ would come again and they were drifting away from the faith. James wants to reassure them and to strengthen both their hearts and their patience.

James 5:12. The second exhortation is not to swear oaths (compare Matthew 5:34-37). This is not a statement against "cussing" as much as it is a statement about integrity. Christians should always speak the truth and mean what they say, thus eliminating the need to swear as to the honesty of their words.

James 5:13-18. Instead of swearing oaths, God's people are to pray together. Elders of the community are to anoint the sick and pray over them, while all members of the community are to join together in prayers of confession and intercession. The link between forgiveness and healing is underscored by the Greek word translated as "save." It carries both the sense of "make well" and "save."

In addition, these verses may reflect the ancient belief that physical illness was a punishment for sin. Today we recognize that the stress of guilt or alienation can result in a negative emotional or spiritual condition. On this level, prayer can bring a type of healing that is most precious.

The process in verses 15-16 is confession, forgiveness of sins, then healing from sickness. Elsewhere in Scripture, especially in the Gospels, the order is rearranged or even reversed. Verse 16 is the only place in the New Testament where prayer for one another is explicitly mentioned. The story of Elijah, lifted up as a testament to the power of prayer, is found in 1 Kings 17–18.

James 5:19-20. The closing verses show the life-and-death importance of prayer and reconciliation in the church. They also show, as fits the rest of the letter, James's focus on the practical. One cannot imagine James saying we should pray in order to feel better or even because we are supposed to. Prayer, for James, is more important than that. It is tied to the function and goal of salvation itself.

INTERPRETING THE SCRIPTURE

Prayer and Piety

In the closing verse of chapter 4, James states the overriding theme of the whole letter: "Anyone then who knows the right thing and fails to do it commits sin" (4:17). In other words, *knowledge of right* requires *doing right*. This is the context in which James sets his teachings on prayer in chapter 5. As is true of other passages in this letter, James 5:13-18 considers specific needs within the community that require attention and response. Here, the writer addresses needs arising from suffering, illness, and sin. James then continues his practical bent by suggesting specific responses to these situations, ranging from prayer to anointing with oil to confession. Consistent with the earlier teachings in the letter, faith takes shape in actions done *with* and *for* one another.

This passage in particular resembles other instructions for practices of piety (prayer, song, anointing, confession) found in the early church. In the older traditions of Judaism, the practices of piety included (but were not limited to) such things as almsgiving, prayer, and fasting. The Letter of James builds on this heritage while presenting prayer as an action undertaken on behalf of the suffering and sick, as well as joining it to confession of sins and intercession for one another. For James, the traditional practices of praying, anointing, and fasting cannot replace other practical conduct taken on behalf of those who suffer or are cut off from community, but neither can they be divorced from it.

James's view of prayer has implications for our life together today as the people of God. Now, as then, we believers need to engage our minds and spirits in the discipline and gift of the heart's conversation with God. Our options for treating suffering have grown considerably beyond anointing with oil, yet the need remains for the community of faith to "touch" the lives (if not the very bodies) of those who face crises, to remind them of resources for healing beyond themselves. Various Christian traditions have developed ways to "confess [our] sins to one another" (5:16), yet the need remains constant to face not only our individual and corporate sin but also the estrangement it brings and the reconciliation it requires. Thus James's call to set piety into practice serves us well today.

A Spiritual Context for Prayer

When James writes about prayer, he taps into a rich spiritual tradition from the community of faith. Hebrew Scriptures record prayers that are now well over two thousand years old—prayers that were well known to James and his audience. These same texts, along with others in the New Testament, remain our prayers because they deal with the most basic elements of human existence. The prayers of the Bible reach across the boundaries of time and culture, and we can be immeasurably enriched by them.

These prayers remain meaningful for us, in part, because of their origin. Each grew out of the experience of what was happening between a human being and God. Feelings of passion, joy, anger, praise, or bewilderment are expressed honestly to God. Look, for example, at the Song of Moses, which expresses praise to God for deliverance from the Egyptians (Exodus 15), or the song of Hannah, which thanks God for a child (1 Samuel 2).

Over time, these prayers also were seen as more than expressions of the joys and concerns of a single person. They came to represent the prayers of the whole community of faith. Praying together, the members of the body are healed and comforted as the people of God.

James knows that we need to make communication with God the foundation of all our actions. Moreover, he reminds us that everything can be expressed in prayer—especially the fears and needs of our hearts. All that matters is that we are honest with God, trusting that God accepts us and loves us. Ultimately, James teaches us that God is concerned about all that happens. Life is not divided into compartments. There is no area that is beyond the concern of God. Rather, God is acting at the deepest level in all of life. *Everything* can be brought to God in prayer—and should be!

The Power of Prayer

James uses the example of miracles in Elijah's time as proof of the power of prayer. First Kings 17–18 describes how the prophet prayed that the life of a woman's son be restored and then asked for drought, and then prayed for rain to end a drought. In these cases, God acted in accord with the request.

While this example is meant to comfort and reassure us, it may have the opposite effect. After all, we are not prophets like Elijah—and we know all too well that prayers are not automatically answered the way we want, when we want, just because we ask.

What can we say when it seems our prayers are not answered? What about people, for example, who suffer in abusive relationships and see no end in sight? What of those who suffer hunger or homelessness, and who cry to God for help? What about patients with terminal illnesses who beg God for healing and do not receive it? The church has wrestled with the question of "unanswered" prayer for ages, and its own answers speak to the heart of the faithful life.

First, the church has always claimed that some prayers are appropriate and some are not. Sometimes God does not grant our prayers because we are asking for something that is not in God's great plan for the world or even in God's immediate plan for our own lives. This does not mean God doesn't care about human pain and suffering. It is a fundamental belief in the Christian church that God loves us and wants us to lead fulfilled lives. There is more to God's purpose and plan than we can ever see or understand, however. Sometimes, therefore, all we can ask for is God's presence, comfort, strength, and peace—gifts we will always receive.

Second, the church has always seen that God sometimes answers prayers in ways so unexpected that we do not recognize what is happening. We may pray to be more loving, for example, and find that we are asked to teach a church school class. God's answers are often not direct, quick-fix responses. Certainly, God answers prayers according to a divine timetable, not our own—and often God puts us in situations that give us the opportunity to develop our own answers to the prayers we have offered.

Finally, the church is continually challenging each of us to be the answer to other people's prayers. As the community of faith, we are called to enact God's love in the world. We can be part of God's answer to those who seem to pray in vain—to the abused, the hungry, the homeless, and the ill. If we do not care for those in need, then the reason their prayers go "unanswered" does not lie with God, but with us.

Today's passage provides a wonderful challenge for those times when our own prayers seem to go unanswered. If we can stay patient and faithful, as James calls us to be, then we too can see God's miracles come at last, even if they are not at all in the form that we expect.

SHARING THE SCRIPTURE

PREPARING TO TEACH

Preparing Our Hearts

Meditate on this week's devotional reading from Lamentations 3:52-58. How does the speaker (understood to be a personification of Judah/Jerusalem) feel that God responded to an ardent plea for help? How has God responded to you when you have cried out for help? What do you believe about God's willingness to help you in the future?

Pray that you and the students will confidently believe that God will answer when you call out in prayer.

Preparing Our Minds

Study the background Scripture from James 5 and the lesson Scripture from James 5:13-18.

Consider this question as you prepare the lesson: *How can believers overcome illness and find healing?*

Write on newsprint:

❏ information for next week's lesson, found under "Continue the Journey."

❏ activities for further spiritual growth in "Continue the Journey."

Review the "Introduction," "The Big Picture," "Close-up," and "Faith in Action," which all precede the first lesson of this quarter. Consider how you might use any of this material in today's lesson.

LEADING THE CLASS

(1) Gather to Learn

❖ Greet the class members and introduce guests.

❖ Pray that those who have come today will recognize that they can aid in the healing of others through prayer.

❖ Read this information from a 2011 article in *Science Daily*: **Accordinging to a study published by the American Psychological Association, prayer concerning health issues increased by 36 percent among American adults between 1999 and 2007. The article, which appeared in the journal *Psychology of Religion and Spirituality* (May 2011) stated that people whose health declined as well as those whose health improved reported praying more. Researchers suggest that those who "experience a progressive disease or an acute health change are more likely to use prayer to cope with changing circumstances." Although all groups included in the study showed an increase in prayer about health issues, women, African Americans, and those who were well educated were most likely to pray about their health. Thus, prayer is seen as a coping mechanism among those who face health concerns, but the study did not investigate whether prayer or the health concern came first. Nor did the study indicate what type of prayer(s) people offered.**

❖ Suggest that the students continue to think about the place and power of prayer when dealing with an illness as we study today's lesson from James 5.

❖ Read aloud today's focus statement: **Illness is part of being human. How can believers overcome illness? The writer of James teaches that the prayer of faith brings healing and offers Elijah's prayer as an example of prayer's effectiveness.**

(2) Goal 1: Explore James' Admonitions for Prayer for Healing and Its Power to Heal

❖ Introduce today's Scripture passage by reading or retelling "Prayer and Piety" in Interpreting the Scripture.

❖ Select a volunteer to read James 5:13-18.

❖ Discuss these questions:

1. **How do you think James would respond to Paul Ehrlich (1854–1915), who wrote, "Before you can cure the diseases of the body, you must cure the diseases of the soul—greed, ignorance, prejudice, and intolerance"?**

2. **Today we know that illness has many causes, some of which we cannot control, such as germs, bacteria, and genetics; and others of which we may be able to influence by the way we live, eat, exercise, and respond to stress. What impact do you think prayer has on these various diseases?**

❖ Note that in James 5:17-18, James lifts up Elijah as a model of one who prays fervently. Call on two volunteers, one to read 1 Kings 17:1-7 and the other to read 1 Kings 18:41-46, which concludes the story. Invite the students to talk with a partner or small group about the power of prayer.

(3) Goal 2: Affirm that Prayer Is Powerful and Yields Good Results

❖ Read "The Power of Prayer" in Interpreting the Scripture.

❖ Invite the adults to tell brief stories of illnesses that they—or those they know—have experienced and overcome. If they want to tell someone else's story, ask that they not mention the names of the ones who were ill. Affirm whatever part that medical intervention played in the healing but also note reliance on prayer.

❖ Discuss these questions:

1. **Were you aware that someone was praying for you while you were ill? If so, how did those prayers affect your mind and spirit?**
2. **What role do you think prayer played in your healing?**
3. **How did overcoming this illness affect your relationship with God?**
4. **Overall, how do you rate the power of prayer to bring about good results, whether these were the results you had hoped for or not?**

(4) Goal 3: Pray for the Sick

❖ Work with the class to create a litany of prayer for healing, which you will write on newsprint. Try to include prayers for people in these categories:

- for those who are ill

- for those who are dealing with a chronic disease
- for those who have a life-limiting disease and may be under hospice care
- for those facing surgery
- for physicians, nurses, and other medical personnel who tend the sick
- for caregivers of those who are ill
- for the family and friends of those who are ill

❖ Add a line that is repeated as a response throughout the litany, such as "Lord, in your mercy, hear our prayer."

❖ Prepare to read the litany by urging the participants not to say names aloud unless they are absolutely certain that the individual has requested prayer and is willing to have other people know he or she needs prayer. To further respect privacy, students should not identify the type of illness.

❖ Take the lead in reading the litany. Invite the students to pray silently for each person who falls into each category the class has used in the litany. After a few moments of silence after each category is read, begin the response. Then move to the next category.

(5) Continue the Journey

❖ Pray that as the learners depart they will offer intercessory prayers for one another, especially for those who are sick.

❖ Post information for next week's session on newsprint for the students to copy:

- **Title: Feasting and Fasting**
- **Background Scripture: Daniel 1:5, 8-17; Matthew 6:16-18; 9:9-17**

- Lesson Scripture: Daniel 1:5, 8-17; Matthew 6:16-18
- Focus of the Lesson: People often restrict their diets for both physical and spiritual reasons. What are some of the benefits of restricting a diet? The Scripture teaches that fasting is good stewardship that gives physical and spiritual benefits.

❖ Challenge the adults to grow spiritually by completing one or more of these activities related to this week's session, which you have posted on newsprint for the students to copy.

(1) Read 1 Kings 17:1-7 and the conclusion of the story in 18:41-46. Ponder the power of Elijah's prayer. Meditate on your own prayer life. What does the quality of your prayer life reveal about the depth of your relationship with God through Jesus?

(2) Recall prayers that seemingly went unanswered. Were any of these prayers answered in a different way than you had hoped? Could you recognize any of these answers as being better than what you had wanted?

(3) Scan the Gospels and Acts for stories of healing. What do you learn from them about God's desire and ability to heal? What hope do these stories give you?

❖ Sing or read aloud "Prayer Is the Soul's Sincere Desire."

❖ Conclude by leading the class in this benediction, adapted from the key verse for the session on December 21 from Luke 2:20: **May we go forth to worship as the shepherds, glorifying and praising God for all we have heard and seen.**

UNIT 3: STEWARDSHIP FOR LIFE
FEASTING AND FASTING

PREVIEWING THE LESSON

Lesson Scripture: Daniel 1:5, 8-17; Matthew 6:16-18
Background Scripture: Daniel 1:5, 8-17; Matthew 6:16-18; 9:9-17
Key Verses: Matthew 6:17-18

Focus of the Lesson:
People often restrict their diets for both physical and spiritual reasons. What are some of the benefits of restricting a diet? The Scripture teaches that fasting is good stewardship that gives physical and spiritual benefits.

Goals for the Learners:
(1) to understand what Jesus said about fasting and those who fast.
(2) to value being connected with God while fasting.
(3) to practice a regular discipline of seeking God by fasting.

Pronunciation Guide:
Antiochus Epiphanes
  (an ti´ uh kuhs i pif´ uh neez)
Ashpenaz (ash´ puh naz)
Azariah (az uh ri´ uh)
Hananiah (han uh ni´ uh)

Hasidic (hah sid´ ik)
Jehoiakim (ji hoi´ uh kim)
Mishael (mish´ ee uhl)
Nebuchadnezzar
  (neb uh kuhd nez´ uhr)

Supplies:
Bibles, newsprint and marker, paper and pencils, hymnals

READING THE SCRIPTURE

NRSV
Lesson Scripture: Daniel 1:5, 8-17

⁵The king assigned them a daily portion of the royal rations of food and wine. They were to be educated for three years, so that at the end of that time they could be stationed in the king's court.

CEB
Lesson Scripture: Daniel 1:5, 8-17

⁵The king assigned these young men daily allotments from his own food and from the royal wine. Ashpenaz was to teach them for three years so that at the end of that time they could serve before the king.

[8]But Daniel resolved that he would not defile himself with the royal rations of food and wine; so he asked the palace master to allow him not to defile himself. [9]Now God allowed Daniel to receive favor and compassion from the palace master. [10]The palace master said to Daniel, "I am afraid of my lord the king; he has appointed your food and your drink. If he should see you in poorer condition than the other young men of your own age, you would endanger my head with the king." [11]Then Daniel asked the guard whom the palace master had appointed over Daniel, Hananiah, Mishael, and Azariah: [12]"Please test your servants for ten days. Let us be given vegetables to eat and water to drink. [13]You can then compare our appearance with the appearance of the young men who eat the royal rations, and deal with your servants according to what you observe." [14]So he agreed to this proposal and tested them for ten days. [15]At the end of ten days it was observed that they appeared better and fatter than all the young men who had been eating the royal rations. [16]So the guard continued to withdraw their royal rations and the wine they were to drink, and gave them vegetables. [17]To these four young men God gave knowledge and skill in every aspect of literature and wisdom; Daniel also had insight into all visions and dreams.

Matthew 6:16-18

[16]"And whenever you fast, do not look dismal, like the hypocrites, for they disfigure their faces so as to show others that they are fasting. Truly I tell you, they have received their reward. **[17]But when you fast, put oil on your head and wash your face, [18]so that your fasting may be seen not by**

[8]Daniel decided that he wouldn't pollute himself with the king's rations or the royal wine, and he appealed to the chief official in hopes that he wouldn't have to do so. [9]Now God had established faithful loyalty between Daniel and the chief official; [10]but the chief official said to Daniel, "I'm afraid of my master, the king, who has mandated what you are to eat and drink. What will happen if he sees your faces looking thinner than the other young men in your group? The king will have my head because of you!"

[11]So Daniel spoke to the guard whom the chief official had appointed over Daniel, Hananiah, Mishael, and Azariah: [12]"Why not test your servants for ten days? You could give us a diet of vegetables to eat and water to drink. [13]Then compare our appearance to the appearance of the young men who eat the king's food. Then deal with your servants according to what you see."

[14]The guard decided to go along with their plan and tested them for ten days. [15]At the end of ten days they looked better and healthier than all the young men who were eating the king's food. [16]So the guard kept taking away their rations and the wine they were supposed to drink and gave them vegetables instead. [17]And God gave knowledge, mastery of all literature, and wisdom to these four men. Daniel himself gained understanding of every type of vision and dream.

Matthew 6:16-18

[16]"And when you fast, don't put on a sad face like the hypocrites. They distort their faces so people will know they are fasting. I assure you that they have their reward. **[17]When you fast, brush your hair and wash your face.**

others but by your Father who is in secret; and your Father who sees in secret will reward you.

[18]Then you won't look like you are fasting to people, but only to your Father who is present in that secret place. Your Father who sees in secret will reward you.

UNDERSTANDING THE SCRIPTURE

Introduction. This lesson weaves together texts from Daniel and Matthew to introduce biblical teachings on fasting as an element of worship. Since the lesson for December 28 provided background on Matthew and his Gospel, we will introduce the Book of Daniel here.

Many scholars believe the Book of Daniel was written during the time of Antiochus IV Epiphanes (175–164 B.C.), which was a time of crisis for Judaism, and the author may have been a Hasidic Jew. Members of this sect were fiercely loyal to God's law as recorded in the first five books of Hebrew Scripture, and they were willing to suffer martyrdom rather than be disloyal to God by breaking the law. Determined to force Jews to accept Greek culture, Antiochus committed atrocities against their religion by forbidding circumcision, destroying any Scripture scrolls he found, and sacrificing a pig on the altar in the Jerusalem Temple. Antiochus even named himself "Epiphanes" (or "the manifest god") and required all citizens, Jews included, to worship him as divine. This may be reflected in Daniel 3.

The Book of Daniel deliberately masks direct reference to contemporary historical events and persons by setting the tale in the ancient past. This way, the writer is able to address second-century Jews through a kind of coded message that purports to be looking forward from the past into the future, rather than speaking directly from the present. To lend weight to the tale, the author uses the name of Daniel deliberately because he was known as a traditional, pious Israelite (see Ezekiel 14:14, 20; and 28:3).

Daniel 1:5. The story begins in progress. Daniel has been selected, along with other young and handsome royal men, for service in the Babylonian court. They are taken aside to begin a three-year training program to this end, and they are assigned food and drink during this period from the king's own rations.

Daniel 1:8-17. Because the king's food is not kosher, Daniel cannot eat it without "defiling" himself. He chooses instead to impose a fast on himself. Traditionally, fasting within Judaism is observed in conjunction with mourning, repentance, or religious devotion, so this is fitting on several levels.

When the palace master refuses to allow a change of diet, lest it not go well and the king become angry, Daniel goes behind his back to the guard placed immediately in charge of him and his friends. This man agrees to a ten-day trial, although the text does not say whether this is in defiance or ignorance of his superior's ruling. At the end of ten days, the four young men appear "better and fatter" (1:15) than the rest, so the guard continues to allow them to keep their restricted diet. Perhaps as a reward for their faithfulness—but certainly as a result of it—the four young men grow in knowledge, skill, and wisdom. Daniel himself becomes able to interpret dreams and visions.

Matthew 6:16-18. By the time the Gospels are written, very pious Jews fast twice a week (see Luke 18:12). The standard days are Monday and Thursday. Jesus warns, however, against fasting for show. In Greek, the word *hypocrite* sometimes means "actor, particularly one wearing a mask, and that is what Jesus describes—persons who act far more affected than they are in order to be perceived as pious. Instead, Jesus says that fasting should be done with God alone as the audience. No one else should be aware of this act of devotion.

Matthew 9:9. The final passage of background Scripture connects following Jesus with a broad view of who is welcome at Jesus' table and a celebration of the feast to come. Verse 9 introduces the call of the tax collector, Matthew (called Levi in Mark 2:13-17 and Luke 5:27-32).

As a tax collector, Matthew is despised. He most likely is wealthy, which in this case does not mark him as blessed by God. At best, his wealth comes from collaborating with the hated Roman overlords. At worst, he has padded his pockets with income gouged from the people illegally.

Like the other disciples, Matthew is at his job when Jesus calls him. Unlike them, however, leaving to follow Jesus means he can never go back to this career. Collecting taxes is a form of oppression to the conquered Jews— one cannot serve Rome in that way and be loyal to Jesus at the same time.

Matthew 9:10-13. Verses 10-13 immediately jump to a picture of Jesus at dinner with "many tax collectors and sinners."

Table fellowship is a most serious matter among the ancient Jewish people. To eat with the unclean is to become unclean. To sit at table with sinners is to participate in their sinfulness. Even the early church will continue to struggle with this deep-rooted and divisive belief (see Galatians 2:11-12).

When the disciples later report to Jesus that the Pharisees have questioned them about this behavior, he quotes Hosea 6:6 as a means of challenging their restrictive views. In Matthew's Gospel, the Pharisees are opposite in nature to the disciples. Historically, the Pharisees were a group of Jews noted for their interpretation of the law, and they were highly influential. The Pharisees were especially concerned with purity, and table fellowship held an important place in their rituals. According to the view we get from Matthew, the Pharisees practice a kind of self-centered religion—one more concerned with their own holiness and salvation than with the needs or lives of others. They are quick to condemn and slow to empathize or forgive.

Matthew 9:14-17. This scene is followed by the disciples of John the Baptist asking why Jesus does not follow their own strict rules of fasting. Jesus is certainly not against the practice of fasting. His response to the inquirers, however, focuses on timing of the fast. While Jesus is with his disciples, they need not mourn or fast. When he is "taken away from them" (9:15) and crucified, that will be the right time for them to fast.

INTERPRETING THE SCRIPTURE

*Living as God's Stewards
in an Alien Culture*

This week we begin our final unit of study, which focuses on "Stewardship for Life." Today's lesson lifts up fasting as a spiritual discipline that can help deepen our sense of connection to God outside of regular worship services.

We begin with the Book of Daniel, which tells the story of one young Jewish man's attempt to stay faithful while captive in Babylon. We should note that Daniel's story is likely set in a time much earlier than its writing. The events described in the text date to the sixth century B.C., but many scholars agree that the text itself is probably written about four hundred years later. At the time the text was written, the Jews were suffering under the reign of Antiochus IV Epiphanes, an oppressive and unjust foreign ruler.

According to the text, Daniel is in one of the initial groups exiled after King Nebuchadnezzar overcomes Judah. "The third year of the reign of King Jehoiakim of Judah" (Daniel 1:1) dates the story to 606 B.C. Continued Judean rebellion prompts Nebuchadnezzar to bring key Jewish leaders to Babylon, including young men of noble blood who represent future leadership (1:3). Like others in this group, Daniel is young, handsome, strong, and educated.

Unlike later exiles, Daniel and his friends are treated well. The king supplies the best food and instruction available, for example. This favored status presents a problem, though. The training is specifically designed to prepare the young men for court positions (that is, for a life lived in the court), but this lifestyle involved practices contradictory to the Jewish religion.

The first conflict presents itself almost immediately. Daniel and his friends are to eat "the royal rations of food and wine" (1:5). These young Hebrew captives have no way of knowing whether this food and drink will adhere to Jewish dietary restrictions, such as those found in Leviticus 11 and 17. There is also a possibility that any meat might have been sacrificed to idols, thereby raising another issue for their faithfulness. Thus they speak out. With Daniel as their spokesperson, the young men win the favor of being served vegetables and water for a ten-day trial period. We should not take their food choices as any affirmation of vegetarianism or admonition against alcohol. Their preference is based on the law—as long as they do not break the Mosaic law, they will not "defile" themselves (1:8).

To the first Jews reading this story, Daniel and his friends represent a source of encouragement in the midst of difficult times. Remember that (based on the date you accept for the composition of Daniel) they themselves live under Greek control, with leaders who want to extend the Greek culture into every area of life. Antiochus carries this to an extreme when he ascends the throne. By the time the Book of Daniel is written, his acts of oppression actually threaten the Jewish religion. The writer uses Daniel as an example to encourage the Jews: "Don't give up too soon. Hold on to God in adversity."

Throughout their trial eating period, Daniel and his friends are strengthened by their observance of God's law. So much so, in fact, that "among them all, no one is found to compare . . . [and] therefore they were stationed in the king's court" (1:19). What a great testimony of support for the Jews who were struggling to stand up to a tyrannical king and the Hellenistic influence!

The early Christian church also drew strength from Daniel's story. By the end of the first century A.D., most Jewish Christians had already discontinued following dietary laws. After all, Jesus says, "It is what comes out of a person that defiles. For it is from within, from the human heart, that evil intentions come" (Mark 7:20-21). Nevertheless, the early Christians did not want to give in to the pressure to accept Roman customs in place of Christian practices. They were called to act like "a holy nation, God's own people" (1 Peter 2:9). Like the Jews in Daniel's time and beyond, they struggled to be distinctive in worship and in their lives.

Distinct in Spiritual Discipline

Daniel and his friends are not examples for us because they are different. They are examples because they are disciplined in their faith practices. Many Christians have found that similar discipline—whether expressed through prayer, meditation, fasting, or other means—brings vitality to faith. The onslaught of books on spiritual disciplines, and the number of Christians purchasing them, verify the desire for discipline in our faith journeys. Daniel serves us well as an example of one who is strengthened by his discipline.

One can argue that Daniel carries the ritualistic part of religion to an extreme. After all, Jesus criticizes unrighteous Pharisees who have lost their inspiration but still perform the priestly rituals. There is a difference between those men and Daniel, however. Daniel's obedience never takes the place of his faith. Rather, it is always a sincere expression of that faith. Genuine faith shows itself in the choices we make and the lives we lead. Daniel's spirituality and his relationship to God are strengthened by his observance of a faithful lifestyle. Following the rules is never the point. What matters is that Daniel remains steadfast in his faithfulness.

Jesus and Fasting

Although fasting has long been held as a necessary discipline for spiritual growth, it has fallen out of favor in our culture. Many Christians who are faithful, churchgoing people have never practiced the discipline of fasting, unaware that *not fasting* is a fairly recent development.

As Matthew 6:16-18 shows us, fasting is well known to Jesus and other religious people of his time. For faithful Jews, it is required on the Day of Atonement (Leviticus 23:26-32), and four other fast days are part of common Jewish practice (based on Zechariah 8:18-19). Throughout the Bible, fasting is also associated with mourning, and it is practiced as an outward response to inward repentance. Sometimes it serves as a sign of national penitence (see 1 Samuel 7:6; Nehemiah 9:1-2). Among many personal examples of fasting in the Bible, we see Jesus fasting and praying in the wilderness to gain strength to overcome temptations (Matthew 4:2).

In just seventeen days, we will begin this year's observance of Lent when it starts on Ash Wednesday. Some will associate this with a time to "fast" by giving up sweets or meat or other foods for forty days. Others will use this as a time to give up bad habits—a different kind of fast. Some will give up time watching TV or sitting at the computer, substituting time with God in prayer instead.

Through his example, Jesus encourages us to participate in a fast, in whatever form we choose that to be, as a means of emptying ourselves so that we can be filled instead with the presence and Spirit of God. To that end, may the following covenant prayer from John Wesley bless you now and through your Lenten journey:

Lord God, I am no longer my own, but thine.
Put me to what thou wilt, rank me with whom thou wilt.
Put me to doing, put me to suffering.
Let me be employed by thee, or laid aside for thee,
exalted for thee or brought low by thee,
Let me be full, let me be empty;
Let me have all things, let me have nothing.
I freely and heartily yield all things to thy pleasure and disposal.
And now, glorious and blessed God, Father, Son and Holy Spirit,
thou are mine, and I am thine. So be it.
And the covenant which I have made on earth,
let it be ratified in heaven.

SHARING THE SCRIPTURE

PREPARING TO TEACH

Preparing Our Hearts

Meditate on this week's devotional reading from 2 Chronicles 7:11-18, which recounts the Lord's second appearance to Solomon in a night vision. What does God call the people to do? How does God promise to respond if they obey? How can God's message to Solomon be a message to you as well?

Pray that you and the students will take seriously the call to repentance by humbling yourselves, praying, and seeking God.

Preparing Our Minds

Study the background Scripture from Daniel 1:5, 8-17; Matthew 6:16-18; 9:9-17 and the lesson Scripture from Daniel 1:5, 8-17; Matthew 6:16-18.

Consider this question as you prepare the lesson: *What are some of the spiritual and physical benefits of restricting your diet?*

Write on newsprint:

❏ information for next week's lesson, found under "Continue the Journey."

❏ activities for further spiritual growth in "Continue the Journey."

Review the "Introduction," "The Big Picture," "Close-up," and "Faith in Action," which all precede the first lesson of this quarter. Consider how you might use any of this material in today's lesson.

LEADING THE CLASS

(1) Gather to Learn

❖ Greet the class members and introduce guests.

❖ Pray that those who have come today will be open to the idea of fasting as a spiritual discipline.

❖ Choose a volunteer to read the story of Daniel and his friends at the Babylonian court from Daniel 1:5, 8-17.

❖ Ask: **What does this story suggest to you about the benefits of restricting your diet?** (Add information from "Living as God's Stewards in an Alien Culture" in Interpreting the Scripture as appropriate.)

❖ Read aloud today's focus statement: **People often restrict their diets for both physical and spiritual reasons. What are some of the benefits of restricting a diet? The Scripture teaches that fasting is good stewardship that gives physical and spiritual benefits.**

(2) Goal 1: Understand What Jesus Said about Fasting and Those Who Fast

❖ Introduce the Scripture passage by reading the first three paragraphs of "Jesus and Fasting" in Interpreting the Scripture.

❖ Select someone to read Matthew 6:16-18, which is part of the Sermon on the Mount.

❖ Add information from "Matthew 6:16-18" in Understanding the Scripture.

❖ Discuss these questions:
1. **When contemporary Americans talk about fasting, they are often observing such a practice as a means of weight loss. How do people of the biblical era define a "fast"?** (A fast involves voluntarily choosing to abstain from food as a sign of repentance or mourning or to devote time to God.)
2. **What does Jesus teach in Matthew 6 about how his followers are to fast?**
3. **How does the story of Daniel, which is set during the Babylonian exile, reflect the principles of fasting that Jesus will teach several hundred years later?**
4. **Look at Matthew 9:9-17, which is from our background Scripture. What does Jesus teach about when it is appropriate to fast?**

(3) Goal 2: Value Being Connected with God while Fasting

❖ Read these comments about spiritual disciplines from Richard J. Foster's Celebration of Discipline: The Path to Spiritual Growth: **"God has given us the Disciplines of the spiritual life as a means of receiving his grace. The Disciplines allow us to place ourselves before God so that he can transform us."** As Foster reminds us, **"biblical fasting always centers on spiritual purposes."** Although fasting is a discipline for all, it is noteworthy that many giants of the faith, both in the Bible (Moses, David, Elijah, Esther, Daniel, Anna, Paul, and Jesus) and throughout church history (Martin Luther, John Knox, John Wesley, Jonathan Edwards, Charles Finney) have fasted as a means of becoming more closely connected to God.

❖ Read: **In his sermon "Upon Our Lord's Sermon on the Mount:**

Discourse Seven," which is based on today's Scripture passage from Matthew 6, John Wesley states:

> A Fifth and more weighty reason for fasting is, that it is an help to prayer; particularly when we set apart larger portions of time for private prayer. Then especially it is that God is often pleased to lift up the souls of his servants above all the things of earth, and sometimes to rap them up, as it were, into the third heavens. And it is chiefly, as it is an help to prayer, that it has so frequently been found a means, in the hand of God, of confirming and increasing, not one virtue, not chastity only, (as some have idly imagined, without any ground either from Scripture, reason, or experience,) but also seriousness of spirit, earnestness, sensibility and tenderness of conscience, deadness to the world, and consequently the love of God, and every holy and heavenly affection.

❖ Discuss this question: **As you consider these words from Richard Foster and John Wesley, how do you think fasting might help you to become more connected with God and grow to greater spiritual maturity?**

(4) Goal 3: Practice a Regular Discipline of Seeking God by Fasting

❖ Read "Distinct in Spiritual Discipline" in Interpreting the Scripture.

❖ Remind the class that Lent, which will begin on February 18, is a time when Christians often fast from food, or at least give up some foods.

❖ Distribute paper and pencils. Read the following questions aloud

and challenge the adults to make a commitment to fast by writing their answers.

1. **Am I willing to participate in some kind of fast during Lent?**
2. **If so, will I abstain from a meal on a certain day of the week, give up a particular food, or give up something I regularly engage in that I truly enjoy if fasting from food is not appropriate for me?**
3. **How will I use the time that I would have spent shopping, preparing, and eating to grow closer to God?**
4. **What help do I need to get started?**

(5) Continue the Journey

❖ Offer John Wesley's "Covenant Prayer," found under "Jesus and Fasting" in Interpreting the Scripture. If you have access to *The United Methodist Hymnal*, invite participants to turn to page 607 and read this prayer in unison.

❖ Post information for next week's session on newsprint for the students to copy:

- **Title: Serving Neighbors, Serving God**
- **Background Scripture: Luke 10:25-37**
- **Lesson Scripture: Luke 10:25-37**
- **Focus of the Lesson: People of good will take care of and serve their neighbors. Why would they do this? The parable of the good Samaritan teaches that when the faithful serve their neighbors, they serve God.**

❖ Challenge the adults to grow spiritually by completing one or more of these activities related to this week's session, which you have posted on newsprint for the students to copy.

(1) **Make a commitment to fast, if it is medically safe for you to do so. Consider fasting for one meal per day to start. Locate information on the Internet or in books about how to fast and trust God to lead you to do whatever is appropriate for you.**

(2) **Consider fasting from things other than food. For example, turn off electronic gadgets for a period; refrain from watching television; stop engaging in a hobby or sport. Use the time that you would have devoted to these activities to develop your relationship with God.**

(3) **Read about fasting. Chapter 4, "The Discipline of Fasting" in Richard J. Foster's** *Celebration of Discipline,* **provides an excellent introduction to the purpose and practice of fasting.**

❖ Sing or read aloud "Seek Ye First."

❖ Conclude by leading the class in this benediction, adapted from the key verse for the session on December 21 from Luke 2:20: **May we go forth to worship as the shepherds, glorifying and praising God for all we have heard and seen.**

UNIT 3: STEWARDSHIP FOR LIFE
SERVING NEIGHBORS, SERVING GOD

PREVIEWING THE LESSON

Lesson Scripture: Luke 10:25-37
Background Scripture: Luke 20:25-37
Key Verses: Luke 10:36-37

Focus of the Lesson:
People of good will take care of and serve their neighbors. Why would they do this? The parable of the good Samaritan teaches that when the faithful serve their neighbors, they serve God.

Goals for the Learners:
(1) to examine Jesus' teaching about compassion for their neighbors.
(2) to reflect upon the connection between serving their neighbors and serving God.
(3) to expand their vision and application of service to neighbor and to God.

Pronunciation Guide:
denarii (di nair´ ee i)   Levite (lee´ vite)

Supplies:
Bibles, newsprint and marker, paper and pencils, hymnals

READING THE SCRIPTURE

NRSV

Lesson Scripture: Luke 10:25-37

²⁵Just then a lawyer stood up to test Jesus. "Teacher," he said, "what must I do to inherit eternal life?" ²⁶He said to him, "What is written in the law? What do you read there?" ²⁷He answered, "You shall love the Lord your God with all your heart, and

CEB

Lesson Scripture: Luke 10:25-37

²⁵A legal expert stood up to test Jesus. "Teacher," he said, "what must I do to gain eternal life?"

²⁶Jesus replied, "What is written in the Law? How do you interpret it? "

²⁷He responded, "You must love the Lord your God with all your heart,

with all your soul, and with all your strength, and with all your mind; and your neighbor as yourself." ²⁸And he said to him, "You have given the right answer; do this, and you will live."

²⁹But wanting to justify himself, he asked Jesus, "And who is my neighbor?" ³⁰Jesus replied, "A man was going down from Jerusalem to Jericho, and fell into the hands of robbers, who stripped him, beat him, and went away, leaving him half dead. ³¹Now by chance a priest was going down that road; and when he saw him, he passed by on the other side. ³²So likewise a Levite, when he came to the place and saw him, passed by on the other side. ³³But a Samaritan while traveling came near him; and when he saw him, he was moved with pity. ³⁴He went to him and bandaged his wounds, having poured oil and wine on them. Then he put him on his own animal, brought him to an inn, and took care of him. ³⁵The next day he took out two denarii, gave them to the innkeeper, and said, 'Take care of him; and when I come back, I will repay you whatever more you spend.' ³⁶**Which of these three, do you think, was a neighbor to the man who fell into the hands of the robbers?" ³⁷He said, "The one who showed him mercy." Jesus said to him, "Go and do likewise."**

with all your being, with all your strength, and with all your mind, and love your neighbor as yourself."

²⁸Jesus said to him, "You have answered correctly. Do this and you will live."

²⁹But the legal expert wanted to prove that he was right, so he said to Jesus, "And who is my neighbor?"

³⁰Jesus replied, "A man went down from Jerusalem to Jericho. He encountered thieves, who stripped him naked, beat him up, and left him near death. ³¹Now it just so happened that a priest was also going down the same road. When he saw the injured man, he crossed over to the other side of the road and went on his way. ³²Likewise, a Levite came by that spot, saw the injured man, and crossed over to the other side of the road and went on his way. ³³A Samaritan, who was on a journey, came to where the man was. But when he saw him, he was moved with compassion. ³⁴The Samaritan went to him and bandaged his wounds, tending them with oil and wine. Then he placed the wounded man on his own donkey, took him to an inn, and took care of him. ³⁵The next day, he took two full days' worth of wages and gave them to the innkeeper. He said, 'Take care of him, and when I return, I will pay you back for any additional costs.' ³⁶**What do you think? Which one of these three was a neighbor to the man who encountered thieves?"**

³⁷Then the legal expert said, "The one who demonstrated mercy toward him."

Jesus told him, "Go and do likewise."

UNDERSTANDING THE SCRIPTURE

Introduction. As stated in the lesson for December 21, Luke writes with an extraordinary compassion for those who are suffering or marginalized in any way. Indeed, Luke mentions weeping and tears, thereby showing remarkable sensitivity to the anguish caused by illness, grief, and shame.

Luke is very aware that people who are considered sinners by their society suffer greatly. We know that everyone sins, but we also know that each society judges certain sins as more despicable than others. Those who are accused (rightly or wrongly) of committing such sins are outcasts. For Luke, especially, the good news embodied in Jesus can lead such outcasts to forgiveness, acceptance, and restoration within the community. This is the context in which Luke sets the parable of the good Samaritan.

Luke 10:25-28. The passage begins with an exchange between Jesus and someone knowledgeable about religious law. That learned man asks, "Teacher, what must I do to inherit eternal life?" Jesus in turn asks, "What does the law say?" The man then quotes Deuteronomy 6:5 (adding, "and with all your mind") and Leviticus 19:18 as the greatest commandments, to which Jesus agrees.

This account corresponds to others that may spring to mind. Matthew 22:34-40 and Mark 12:28-34 record, respectively, how another legal expert and a scribe ask Jesus to name the greatest commandment, and he responds with these same Old Testament passages. Matthew 19:16-22, Mark 10:17-22, and Luke 18:18-23 tell of a man who asks Jesus what must be done to inherit eternal life. Matthew calls him "young" (19:20, 22), Luke calls him a "ruler" (18:18), and all three accounts mention his wealth—thus most of us know this figure as "the rich, young ruler." In these passages, Jesus does not ask a question, but replies by quoting several of the Ten Commandments.

Luke 10:29. The learned man then presents another question to Jesus, asking him to define "neighbor." The man no doubt assumes, as would others of his day, that "neighbor" means a fellow Jew, and he no doubt thinks he treats others in his society exactly as they deserve.

Luke states that the man asks because he wants "to justify himself." This phrase means that he wants to establish himself as righteous or acceptable before God—probably by being able to say he has done all that the law requires. The following passages are helpful for understanding the concept of "righteousness" throughout the Bible: the speeches of Job's friends (Job 11 and 25); the introduction to Elihu's speech (Job 32:1-5); Paul's treatise on justification (Romans 4–5); Jesus' teaching on prayer (Luke 18:9-14); and the dialogue concerning faith and works in James 2.

Based on the lawyer's words, some scholars suggest that this passage reflects two very different systems of ethics. For the lawyer, ethical actions are directed and specified by the law. He looks to the law for concrete examples of conduct pleasing to God. For Jesus, ethical actions are a natural response to God's love—a love to which the law testifies. Rather than dictating specific actions, the law inspires mercy. The setup for the parable, then, is a clash between the ethics of law (rigid guidelines and rules for living) and the ethics of love (conditions of and practices from the heart).

Luke 10:30. Jesus responds to the man's question with a parable. The setting is the desert road from Jericho to Jerusalem, which was notoriously dangerous in those days, much like the West Bank in Palestine is today. Traveling alone there, a man is robbed, beaten, and left for dead. Unlike the rest of the characters in the parable, we know nothing more about the man, although most scholars point out that he must have been Jewish for the rest of the parable to have real meaning to Jesus' listeners.

Luke 10:31-32. The first person to see the man is a priest, who represents the highest religious offices of Judaism. Next is a Levite, who represents all the rest. Both see the man but cross to the other side of the road and pass by him without offering to help. To interact with him will make them ritually impure according to Jewish law, so they opt not to take the chance. They choose to ensure their religious purity stays intact, even if it means the possibility of failing to aid a fellow Jew (which the law also calls for). Their ignorance of the man's religious affiliation—maintained by staying far enough away from him to see for sure—technically frees them from their obligation to the laws related to care and mercy.

Luke 10:33. The parable's surprise comes in this verse, when a Samaritan also passes by and is "moved with pity." This traveler is from a mixed race despised by the Jews and considered an ancient enemy. Relationships between Jews and Samaritans had been hostile for centuries (see 2 Kings 17). No one in Jesus' day would expect a Samaritan to show sympathy for a Jew, much less extend generous hospitality and care to one. Similarly, no one would expect a Samaritan to be lifted up as a model of neighborliness.

Luke 10:34-35. Pouring oil and wine on the wounds is certainly a medical act, and it may be a religious one as well. Alcohol in the wine would kill any germs breeding in open cuts, but the oil may have been poured on as an anointing while a prayer for healing is offered. The fact that the man has his own animal and is able to pay for an inn shows that he is not destitute. The two denarii paid to the innkeeper amount to a typical wage for two days' work.

Luke 10:36-37. In light of the parable, the answer is clear to the initial question, "Who is my neighbor?" The lawyer answers rightly, "The one who showed him mercy." Seeing that the lawyer understands, Jesus sends him on his way with the brief but powerful instruction, "Go and do likewise."

INTERPRETING THE SCRIPTURE

The Lawyer's Questions

Our second lesson in the "Stewardship for Life" unit focuses on serving our neighbor by looking at one of Jesus' best-known stories—the parable of the good Samaritan. Jesus tells the story in response to questions raised by a Jewish lawyer, an expert in the law. Not everyone recognizes the context or the blessing of this parable, though. The story illustrates the doctrine of justification and blesses believers with a present experience of God's coming reign.

Today's Bible passage begins with a conversation between Jesus, a rural rabbi from an area geographically and culturally remote from Jerusalem, and an educated "lawyer"—a man himself accustomed to answering legal questions on divine law. From the beginning, the audience waits to see how this will go.

The first question, "What must I do to inherit eternal life?" (10:25) is an impossible question. Logic suggests that if eternal life is an *inheritance*, then it is a gift given by one family member to another family member. An answer to the question might be, "Be born into the right family." That's impossible! Humans do not pick their parents nor do children determine how parents pass on an inheritance. Jesus, however, does not point out the impossibility. Rather, Jesus poses another question, "What does the law say?" Easily, the lawyer summarizes the law with Deuteronomy 6:5, "You shall love the Lord your God with all your heart, and with all your soul, and with all your might" (Luke 10:27) and Leviticus 19:18b, "You shall love your neighbor as yourself." Jesus commends his answer with the words, "Do this, and you will live" (Luke 10:28).

The conversation should be over, but there is something unsettled for the lawyer. His answer has failed to define the limits of the law. Without limits, the law is huge—so huge it cannot be fulfilled. Therefore, seeking the boundary lines in order to justify

himself through his actions, the lawyer poses a "point of clarification" question. The lawyer asks Jesus to define "neighbor." He does not get the judicious guideline he expects, however—the story he hears from Jesus shatters all categorical thinking.

A Disturbing Answer

Jesus' parable opens with a robbery. Tales about the robbers along the road from Jerusalem to Jericho often describe small-time bandits. These outlaws demanded a portion of the traveler's money or valuables but did not ordinarily use violence. In contrast to these thieves, known in Greek by a word from which we get the English word "kleptomaniac," Luke chose another Greek word that describes armed bandits who traveled in gangs and brutally set upon travelers to steal their property.

As chance would have it, a priest is in transit between Jerusalem and Jericho. The half-dead man poses a severe moral dilemma to the priest. On the one hand, if the man is a Jew, the priest owes him mercy. On the other hand, if the man is a Gentile or if he is really dead, the priest will be defiled by approaching and touching him. The dilemma is intensified by the lack of clues. The priest cannot talk to an unconscious man; therefore, he cannot discover by direct question nor discern by dialect the man's religious heritage. Moreover, he is naked. Without clothing, another reliable indicator of status and identity, the man could be anyone. The priest is in a bind: One duty demands he maintain his ritual purity, and another duty demands mercy. What does one do with an unidentified, half-dead person of unknown background? What does one do when faced with two duties? The priest opts for the clearer and, according to his profession, the more compelling duty. He passes by in order to protect the priestly office and his ceremonial purity.

Next comes the Levite. He follows the lead of the priest. When duty and duty sit side by side, a person of limited authority and responsibility ordinarily looks to a superior for guidance. The priest passed by; now the Levite does likewise. Some interpreters suggest that this man, confident that the priest was obedient, simply followed the pattern of the priest without any moral discernment.

Generally the words "priest," "Levite," and "Israelite" would be used to encompass all of Jewish society. Thus, if the story followed a logical pattern, the next person on the scene would be a Jewish layperson. Instead, a traveling Samaritan appears. This man is a signal to the audience that Jesus is about to teach a new truth. Old truths come in old forms, but a Samaritan starring in a Jewish story signals novelty. Not only had Jews no dealings with the ritually unclean Samaritans, but also irreconcilable hostilities existed between the two groups. A Samaritan would never be featured as "a good guy" in a Jewish parable—but Jesus is no ordinary Jewish storyteller.

The Samaritan comes near, sees the man, is moved to pity, and responds. His response is immediate: He provides first aid. His response is also practical: He moves the man to a more secure place. It is, as well, long range: He pays in advance for a place where the man can recover. The last response is as significant as the first. Without immediate first aid the man will surely die; yet a man with no resources to pay his bill at the inn could be sold as a slave, another kind of death.

Final Lessons

The Samaritan's rescue is both practical and thorough. He not only saves a life, he also ensures that the injured man will have a future. If it is difficult for you to imagine the lawyer's dismay over this story, just retell it to yourself and substitute for the Samaritan someone who might be regarded with loathing in your community. That may help to show how intensely the lawyer is offended, shamed, angered, moved to pity, chided, and confronted by Jesus' parable.

The "lesson" for the lawyer does not stop there, however. Jesus' final question confronts the man's heart and motivation, rather than his reputation and self-image. The lawyer wants to justify himself. He assumes once "the neighbor" is defined, he can satisfy the "duty" of loving the neighbor. Jesus directs the lawyer away from definitions and toward the distinguishing quality of mercy. The lawyer again answers correctly by defining the neighbor as "the one who showed mercy" (10:37), though he would not speak the word "Samaritan." Jesus still has yet another lesson to teach him.

"Go and do likewise" (10:37). To recognize mercy is insufficient. Mercy is to be lived not as a command, but as a joyful participation in God's will. Mercy is a response to a neighbor *as* a neighbor, but it is also an announcement of the nearness of God. The sign of this is in our own transformation through loving acts. We who follow Jesus experience a new and substantial life whenever we respond as neighbors in the world.

As mercy flows among Jesus' believers, all of our desire for self-justification dissolves. Disciples discover themselves freed from the drain of judging self and others. Instead of endless discussions on the definition and application of laws, those who side with Jesus learn to live from hearts filled by mercy. That's why Jesus commands: "Go and do likewise." The lawyer understands but is never mentioned again. The disciples understand, travel on with Jesus, and forever live as neighbors to the needy. Either response is possible, but only in one do we show ourselves to be good stewards and worship God through our way of living.

SHARING THE SCRIPTURE

PREPARING TO TEACH

Preparing Our Hearts

Meditate on this week's devotional reading from Matthew 22:33-40 where Jesus pronounces the greatest commandment in response to a lawyer's question posed to test him. What kind of answer do you think the Pharisees and Sadducees were expecting to hear? Why might they find Jesus' answer disturbing? How do these commandments, which Jesus quotes from Deuteronomy 6:5 and Leviticus 19:18, respectively, shape your Christian ethics and practice?

Pray that you and the students will seek constantly to love God and to love neighbor.

Preparing Our Minds

Study the background Scripture and the lesson Scripture, which are both from Luke 10:25-37.

Consider this question as you prepare the lesson: *Why do people care for and serve their neighbors?*

Write on newsprint:

❑ information for next week's lesson, found under "Continue the Journey."

❑ activities for further spiritual growth in "Continue the Journey."

Review the "Introduction," "The Big Picture," "Close-up," and "Faith in Action," which all precede the first lesson of this quarter. Consider how you might use any of this material in today's lesson.

LEADING THE CLASS

(1) Gather to Learn

❖ Greet the class members and introduce guests.

❖ Pray that those who have come today will open their hearts to neighbors everywhere.

❖ Read: **According to the Pew Research Center, beginning on January 1, 2001, and stretching over nineteen years, approximately ten thousand baby boomers will celebrate their sixty-fifth birthday each day. By 2030, 18 percent of the U.S. population will be at least sixty-five years of age. Of the challenges posed by aging, one of the most prominent is housing. Many homes in the United States are large, multistory dwellings that served families well. But these same homes cannot easily** accommodate an aging population. Although some people will make other arrangements, such as assisted living, many older adults want to remain in their beloved homes but need some help to do so. Enter Village to Village, a community-based group that promotes aging in place in one's own home by providing supportive services. Those who join pay a membership fee. Much of the work needed to keep these older adults in their homes, such as home maintenance, housekeeping, legal and financial assistance, and transportation, is provided by volunteers. By helping to meet the needs of their older neighbors, these volunteers are enabling them to remain in their homes.

❖ Read aloud today's focus statement: **People of good will take care of and serve their neighbors. Why would they do this? The parable of the good Samaritan teaches that when the faithful serve their neighbors, they serve God.**

(2) Goal 1: Examine Jesus' Teaching about Compassion for Neighbors

❖ Choose four volunteers to read the part of the narrator, the lawyer, Jesus, and the Samaritan. If possible, ask them to come to the front of the class to read Luke 10:25-37.

❖ Discuss these questions:
1. **Why might the lawyer have asked Jesus questions?** (See "The Lawyer's Questions" in Interpreting the Scripture and "Luke 10:29" in Understanding the Scripture.)
2. **Why might the lawyer and other listeners have been shocked or disturbed by Jesus' parable?** (See "A

Disturbing Answer" in Interpreting the Scripture and "Luke 10:33" in Understanding the Scripture.)
3. **What point does Jesus make about how God's people are to treat neighbors?** (See "Final Lessons" in Interpreting the Scripture.)

(3) Goal 2: Reflect upon the Connection Between Serving Neighbors and Serving God

❖ Read: **Oswald Chambers (1874– 1917) summed up the connection between our relationship with God and our relationship with neighbor in these words: "If my heart is right with God, every human being is my neighbor."**

❖ Talk together about how to handle these situations, which you will need to read aloud, as a good neighbor:
1. **You and a neighbor got into a heated exchange because his dog got loose and ruined some of your flowers. You see each other later outside. What do you do or say?**
2. **You were on duty last week during your church's good Samaritan day, when people from the community can come in to get food, clothing, and financial assistance for utilities and medicine. One woman became very demanding, so you decided not to honor her request for food. You see the same woman coming through the door again this week. How do you react?**
3. **An apparently homeless person approaches you to ask**

for some change for coffee. How do you respond?

4. **You see a motorist pulled to the side of the road with the hood up. You have tools in your truck and often stop to help others, but then you notice that driver's clothing reveals she is from a different ethnic or religious group. Will you stop to help? Why or why not?**

(4) Goal 3: Expand the Learners' Vision and Application of Service to Neighbor and to God

❖ Read: **Most Christians are willing to help those they know, including other church members. Jesus, however, calls us to serve neighbors who for some reason—perhaps racial or ethnic group, language, political leanings, sexual orientation, addictive behaviors, refugee or immigration status—we cannot identify with and would not choose to help.**

❖ Form small teams and distribute paper and pencils. Invite each group to rewrite Jesus' parable using contemporary people and situations. For example, the three passersby may include a pastor, a doctor, and a recently paroled convict. The injured party may be a Muslim whose car was forced off the road. Encourage the groups to be as creative as possible. The only boundary is that their story has to somehow illustrate service to one who would not normally be thought of as a neighbor.

❖ Bring the groups together to read their stories.

❖ **Option:** Suggest that the groups plan to act out, rather than read, their stories.

❖ Wrap up this activity by reading today's key verses, Luke 10:36-37, and encouraging the adults to hear Jesus' words as a call to action.

(5) Continue the Journey

❖ Pray that as the learners depart they will seek opportunities to serve others.

❖ Post information for next week's session on newsprint for the students to copy:

- **Title: Serving the Least**
- **Background Scripture: Matthew 25:31-46**
- **Lesson Scripture: Matthew 25:31-46**
- **Focus of the Lesson: Opportunities for serving others are all around us, although believers don't always recognize or respond to them. What are the consequences of their action or inaction? Matthew says that believers should serve others as if they were the Lord, and God will judge the believers accordingly.**

❖ Challenge the adults to grow spiritually by completing one or more of these activities related to this week's session, which you have posted on newsprint for the students to copy.

(1) **Be alert this week for opportunities to serve a neighbor, preferably a stranger, in need. Listen to his or her story. Offer this person not only food, money, or whatever else will satisfy the immediate need but also God's blessings.**

(2) **Contemplate your willingness to serve others,**

particularly those who are strangers or somehow different from you. If you find it challenging to serve others, make a list of your reasons. Pray about how you can overcome this fear, prejudice, or whatever else is holding you back.

(3) Research "Samaritans" to learn more about why Jesus' parable would have been so disturbing to his listeners. Think about those groups that are like "Samaritans" to you.

❖ Sing or read aloud "Jesu, Jesu."

❖ Conclude by leading the class in this benediction, adapted from the key verse for the session on December 21 from Luke 2:20: **May we go forth to worship as the shepherds, glorifying and praising God for all we have heard and seen.**

UNIT 3: STEWARDSHIP FOR LIFE
SERVING THE LEAST

PREVIEWING THE LESSON

Lesson Scripture: Matthew 25:31-46
Background Scripture: Matthew 25:31-46
Key Verse: Matthew 25:40

Focus of the Lesson:
Opportunities for serving others are all around us, although believers do not always recognize or respond to them. What are the consequences of their action or inaction? Matthew says that believers should serve others as if they were the Lord, and God will judge the believers accordingly.

Goals for the Learners:
(1) to understand Jesus' comments on the obligation of believers to serve those in need.
(2) to experience how God's love for all inspires them to meet the needs of others.
(3) to respond to God's call to serve others.

Pronunciation Guide:
apocalyptic (uh pok uh lip´ tik)

Supplies:
Bibles, newsprint and marker, paper and pencils, hymnals

READING THE SCRIPTURE

NRSV
Lesson Scripture: Matthew 25:31-46

31"When the Son of Man comes in his glory, and all the angels with him, then he will sit on the throne of his glory. 32All the nations will be gathered before him, and he will separate people one from another as a shepherd separates the sheep from the goats, 33and he will put the sheep at his right hand and the goats at the left. 34Then the king will say to those

CEB
Lesson Scripture: Matthew 25:31-46

31"Now when the Human One comes in his majesty and all his angels are with him, he will sit on his majestic throne. 32All the nations will be gathered in front of him. He will separate them from each other, just as a shepherd separates the sheep from the goats. 33He will put the sheep on his right side. But the goats he will put on his left.

at his right hand, 'Come, you that are blessed by my Father, inherit the kingdom prepared for you from the foundation of the world; [35]for I was hungry and you gave me food, I was thirsty and you gave me something to drink, I was a stranger and you welcomed me, [36]I was naked and you gave me clothing, I was sick and you took care of me, I was in prison and you visited me.' [37]Then the righteous will answer him, 'Lord, when was it that we saw you hungry and gave you food, or thirsty and gave you something to drink? [38]And when was it that we saw you a stranger and welcomed you, or naked and gave you clothing? [39]And when was it that we saw you sick or in prison and visited you?' [40]And the king will answer them, **'Truly I tell you, just as you did it to one of the least of these who are members of my family, you did it to me.'** [41]Then he will say to those at his left hand, 'You that are accursed, depart from me into the eternal fire prepared for the devil and his angels; [42]for I was hungry and you gave me no food, I was thirsty and you gave me nothing to drink, [43]I was a stranger and you did not welcome me, naked and you did not give me clothing, sick and in prison and you did not visit me.' [44]Then they also will answer, 'Lord, when was it that we saw you hungry or thirsty or a stranger or naked or sick or in prison, and did not take care of you?' [45]Then he will answer them, 'Truly I tell you, just as you did not do it to one of the least of these, you did not do it to me.' [46]And these will go away into eternal punishment, but the righteous into eternal life."

[34]"Then the king will say to those on his right, 'Come, you who will receive good things from my Father. Inherit the kingdom that was prepared for you before the world began. [35]I was hungry and you gave me food to eat. I was thirsty and you gave me a drink. I was a stranger and you welcomed me. [36]I was naked and you gave me clothes to wear. I was sick and you took care of me. I was in prison and you visited me.'

[37]"Then those who are righteous will reply to him, 'Lord, when did we see you hungry and feed you, or thirsty and give you a drink? [38]When did we see you as a stranger and welcome you, or naked and give you clothes to wear? [39]When did we see you sick or in prison and visit you?'

[40]"Then the king will reply to them, **'I assure you that when you have done it for one of the least of these brothers and sisters of mine, you have done it for me.'**

[41]"Then he will say to those on his left, 'Get away from me, you who will receive terrible things. Go into the unending fire that has been prepared for the devil and his angels. [42]I was hungry and you didn't give me food to eat. I was thirsty and you didn't give me anything to drink. [43]I was a stranger and you didn't welcome me. I was naked and you didn't give me clothes to wear. I was sick and in prison, and you didn't visit me.'

[44]"Then they will reply, 'Lord, when did we see you hungry or thirsty or a stranger or naked or sick or in prison and didn't do anything to help you?' [45]Then he will answer, 'I assure you that when you haven't done it for one of the least of these, you haven't done it for me.' [46]And they will go away into eternal punishment. But the righteous ones will go into eternal life."

UNDERSTANDING THE SCRIPTURE

Introduction. A basic introduction to Matthew's Gospel was given in the lesson for December 28, but a word should be said here about chapters 24–25 in particular. These two chapters contain teachings on the end of the current age in a style that is known as apocalyptic. The material is not original to Matthew, but he collected and included these writings for a specific reason: He wanted to offer comfort and hope to Christians in his day who were beginning to lose hope that Jesus would ever return. After all, for many years they had expected him to do so.

Matthew wants to reassure his contemporaries that the waiting will not go on forever. Although no one can predict the day or hour of Christ's return, those who stay faithful and joyful in anticipation will not be disappointed. The glorious day will come when Christ will usher in a new age and all will be made right.

As often occurs in apocalyptic writings, Matthew uses the theme of waiting to encourage both readiness and endurance. Since we cannot know when the end will come, we must stay ready by constant acts of faithfulness. Serving God and loving our neighbors must not be postponed but must continue. Likewise, we must be ready to suffer on behalf of our faith if necessary. Matthew knows that discipleship can lead to all kinds of struggles, so he emphasizes that God will prevail. The faithful will be preserved and rescued when the Messiah is revealed as the Lord of all creation.

This week's passage contains the last of four parables about Christ's return found in Matthew 24:45–25:46. Often referred to as the parable of the sheep and the goats, it does not read like a traditional parable—more like a royal pronouncement. It also has more symbolism (and, paradoxically, is also more direct) than a typical parable. Where these verses do fit the traditional parable is in the revelation of an unexpected truth.

Matthew 25:31. The parable begins with a classic setting right out of Jewish apocalyptic literature. The expected messianic figure, the "Son of Man," will come in glory to usher in God's new age. He will be accompanied by "all the angels," as befits his status, and will sit on a heavenly throne as a symbol of his power. The connection between this figure and God is inherent in Matthew's use of the word "glory"—a term that represents the presence and essence of God in both Testaments.

Matthew 25:32-33. The cosmic rule of the Son of Man puts all nations under his domain. Thus all people, Jew and Gentile alike, come before him to be judged. The scene rapidly switches to the mundane imagery that one expects in a parable, though. The grand setting of the ultimate judgment is described as the routine sorting of sheep and goats by a shepherd. In this visual description, the common use of "shepherd" to describe God or Jesus as one who cares takes on an unexpected tone of judgment.

Matthew 25:34. The Son of Man's initial address to the sheep echoes promises made elsewhere that God will give the heavenly kingdom to those whom the world would not expect, such as the poor in spirit (Matthew 5:3) or the disciples themselves (Luke 12:32). Moreover, it affirms that

God has intended this gift for them since the beginning of time.

Matthew 25:35-36. The good deeds performed by the sheep are lifted up throughout Scripture as part of the loving action God asks of us. Matthew may have had in mind Isaiah 58:6-7, which specifically mentions feeding the hungry, housing the homeless, and clothing the naked as true acts of worship desired by God. One may also think of James 1:27, which repeats the Old Testament call to care for widows and orphans, or James 2:15-16, which couples compassion with feeding and clothing those in need. The connection of acts of earthly kindness with heavenly repercussions occurs in Hebrews 13:2, where we are reminded that sometimes the recipients of our hospitality may, in fact, be angels! We may also recall Paul's prayer in 2 Timothy 1:16, when he asked for God's mercy on the household of one who had cared for him in prison.

Matthew 25:37-40. Many people remember this poignant scene of the sheep asking, "When did we do these things?" and Jesus' surprising answer—"Just as you did it to the least of these . . . you did it to me." Few realize, however, that Jesus is lifting up a concept found elsewhere in Scripture. Proverbs 19:17 maintains that whoever is financially kind to the poor actually gives to God, and "will be repaid in full." This same theology seems to lie behind Jesus' teaching that anyone who gives even a cup of water to the disciples will be rewarded (Matthew 10:42; Mark 9:41) and the affirmation in Hebrews 6:10 that God will remember and take notice of our care of others.

Matthew 25:41-46. The second part of the parable describes the punishment of the goats—those who did not engage in acts of kindness when they could have. Whereas the sheep will receive eternal life in God's kingdom, these will suffer forever in a place of fire. The image of an everlasting fire pit (Mark 9:48) or "lake of fire and sulfur" (Revelation 20:10) was late to Jewish thinking. For most all of the period during which the Old Testament was written, the place of the dead was pictured as a place of sleep. After the fall of the Babylonians, who had brought the Israelites into captivity, Persian theology added the concept of Satan or a devil and introduced the idea of a fiery pit. Other cultures contributed ideas concerning who Satan was and what he did. By Jesus' time, these ideas were fairly well developed. One of the earliest references to a reward of eternal life versus a punishment of eternal shame or contempt is in Daniel 12:12. Likewise, John 5:29 refers to a "resurrection of life" for the good and a "resurrection of condemnation" for the evil.

INTERPRETING THE SCRIPTURE

A Long Wait

Matthew 24–25 represents a style of literature called *apocalyptic*, a term that refers to writings about the end time. The stories recorded here had been preserved through the oral traditions for several years. Matthew includes them in his Gospel to continue to offer hope and comfort to Christians waiting for Jesus' return. For the people of Matthew's community, the wait had already lasted several long decades.

At first, the expectation of Jesus' return was great. No one understood why it had been delayed, except to say that no human fully understands God's plan or knows God's timing. As time went by, however, the early Christians began to lose hope. Matthew 24–25 reminds people that Jesus had warned them not to live careless or inattentive lives, because the exact time of his coming cannot be known for sure. Like the master who returns to see how the servant has fared, Christ "will come on a day when [we do] not expect him and at an hour that [we do] not know" (24:50).

If we read these chapters as a warning, they seem harsh and unrelenting. If, however, we read them as a promise, they become filled with hope and comfort. The waiting will not go on forever. Those who are found waiting with joyful anticipation, staying faithful to their calling, will find joy in Christ's return.

A Shepherd's Job

Unlike some of the parables Jesus told, this one is very dramatic. It paints a picture in our mind's eye: All the nations are gathered together, the Son of Man sits on a royal throne, angels attend him, glory surrounds. Then the shepherd's work of separating the sheep from the goats begins.

The metaphor of a shepherd at work resonates throughout the language of this passage. For example, "gathering together" and "separating" describe the shepherd's daily work. Picture this in first-century Palestine. Flocks of goats and sheep graze together during the day, but at night the shepherd separates the flock according to the needs of each. The goats, needing more warmth at night, are herded into small caves, while the sheep, preferring fresh air and not being as sensitive to cold, are penned in the open air. Shepherds stay with each flock throughout the night. The younger "shepherds-in-training" guard the goats, while the experienced shepherds sleep at the door of the sheep's pen.

Deepening the impact of the imagery, however, is the ancient hope for a true shepherd for the flock of Israel. In Ezekiel 34, the prophet describes God's displeasure with the "shepherds" of Israel, those who are to guide and protect the nation through education, ritual, and the promotion of righteousness. Then, Ezekiel shares a bold announcement: "For thus says the Lord GOD: I myself will search for my sheep, and will seek them out. As shepherds seek out their flocks when they are among their scattered sheep, so I will seek out my sheep" (34:11-12a). This image of the Good Shepherd is frequently applied to Jesus, who knows, guides, and grants salvation to the sheep of his flock (see John 10).

Surprises in the Story

Like most parables, this one includes a surprise twist or two. The first is the nature of the separation itself. In the religious system of Jesus' culture, the lines between members of the covenant and those outside the covenant were clear. In Jesus' parable, the lines are fuzzier. The group at the right hand is not restricted to those in a formal covenant relationship with God; rather, it includes merciful people from all nations (even Gentiles).

The second surprise is that the standard has only one criterion: deeds of mercy. Sins are not a part of this judgment! Breaking the commandments or doing actual harm to others is not mentioned. The basis for judgment is limited to good deeds. Either one acts mercifully toward others and is rewarded, or one ignores the needs of others and is punished. Surprisingly, nothing else matters.

So why does Matthew's Gospel include this scene, which by its dramatic detail invites speculation on earning salvation? Perhaps because it addresses an ancient concern regarding the Gentiles, namely, how will those outside the covenant, new and old, be judged?

Taking into account that the word translated as "nations" (25:32) refers to Gentiles, we see the parable affirms that *everyone* encounters and pleases God when they respond to the needy of the world. What an amazing surprise this is to most of us!

The final surprise is Jesus' identification with those who need and receive mercy. The idea of an ambassador—that is, a subordinate carrying authority on behalf of a superior—was a well-known principle of Roman rule and Jewish life in Palestine. Jesus transforms this ordinary idea. He does not name the needy as his "representative"—rather, he actually identifies himself with them.

Matthew lays the groundwork for this understanding in two previous passages in which Jesus says that he may be "discovered" in others. In Matthew 10:40-42, Jesus explains that whenever a disciple is welcomed or given a cup of water, he himself is welcomed and served. In Matthew 18:5, Jesus tells us that whoever welcomes a child welcomes him. Putting these two verses together, the surprise Jesus teaches is, in essence, "I am present in those who are vulnerable, needy, and dependent; as you respond to the child or the hungry or the thirsty or the stranger or the naked or the sick or the imprisoned, you respond to me."

The Gospel in Miniature

In many ways, this parable represents the whole of Matthew's Gospel, which seeks always to point to Jesus as the Messiah who has been raised to glory and who will return as king and judge at the end time. It is in this context, for example, that Jesus assures the disciples that their obedience to him not only secures them eternally but also gives them a position in the Last Judgment (Matthew 19:28-30). Likewise, it is as the king and judge to come that Jesus declares salvation cannot be achieved; it can only be received (19:25-26).

The parable of the sheep and the goats reminds us that our faith is naturally expressed in good deeds and merciful living—and that we meet and are nurtured by Jesus in just such moments. What's more, our gracious acts of kindness help others see and encounter Jesus as well. Every act of hospitality or charity has the potential to become an act of witness, a proclamation of the good news of the kingdom. As we think about what this means for our own "Stewardship for Life," it may help to consider these words, written by Thomas G. Long as a comment on Jesus' teaching in the parable:

> So, the Christian church is sent out to the world on a vital mission—to bear witness to the gospel of Jesus Christ. . . . The gospel, however, is more than mere words, and the church proclaims the gospel by living in the world as Jesus lived. The disciple is to be like the teacher

(Matt. 10:24); the church must become humble like a child and show hospitality to those in need (Matt. 18:1-5). In Matthew's Gospel, if you want to find Jesus, look among those who are "harassed and helpless, like sheep without a shepherd" (Matt. 9:36). The church that is faithful will be found in precisely the same place.

God grant that it be so!

SHARING THE SCRIPTURE

PREPARING TO TEACH

Preparing Our Hearts

Meditate on this week's devotional reading from Psalm 10:12-18, which is part of a prayer for deliverance from enemies. Which groups in your community need to find justice? Which of these groups or individuals would you be able to help? How will you do that? When will you start?

Pray that you and the students will be aware of those vulnerable people who need help and do all in your power to assist them.

Preparing Our Minds

Study the background Scripture and the lesson Scripture, which are both from Matthew 25:31-46.

Consider this question as you prepare the lesson: *Given that there are many opportunities to serve others, what are the consequences of believers' actions or inactions?*

Write on newsprint:

❏ information for next week's lesson, found under "Continue the Journey."

❏ activities for further spiritual growth in "Continue the Journey."

Review the "Introduction," "The Big Picture," "Close-up," and "Faith in Action," which all precede the first lesson of this quarter. Consider how you might use any of this material in today's lesson.

Create the chart for "Gather to Learn."

LEADING THE CLASS

(1) Gather to Learn

❖ Greet the class members and introduce guests.

❖ Pray that those who have come today will be ready to recognize and respond to the needs of others.

❖ Play a game with the adults by asking, **"How do you know what ____ needs?"** Fill in the blanks per the chart below. Once an answer has been given, ask two more questions: **"What happens when you meet ____'s needs?" "What happens if you ignore ____'s needs?"** You may wish to use the first question as an example.

How do you know what ____ needs?	What happens when you meet ____'s needs?	What happens if you ignore ____'s needs?
your dog He paws at the door.	Fido goes out, relieves himself, and returns to take a nap.	Fido urinates on the rug.
an infant		
a boss		
a friend		
a shabbily dressed person on the street		

❖ Point out that our actions and inactions always have consequences that are usually either positive or negative, though we do not necessarily perceive the consequences immediately.

❖ Read aloud today's focus statement: **Opportunities for serving others are all around us, although believers do not always recognize or respond to them. What are the consequences of their action or inaction? Matthew says that believers should serve others as if they were the Lord, and God will judge the believers accordingly.**

(2) Goal 1: Understand Jesus' Comments on the Obligation of Believers to Serve Those in Need

❖ Lead into today's session by reading "Introduction" in Understanding the Scripture.

❖ Choose one volunteer to read the part of the narrator and one to read the part of the king in Matthew 25:31-46. Choose two or three volunteers who have the same translation to read the part of the righteous in verses 37-39. Ask two or three other volunteers to read verse 44. If possible, have the readers stand together.

❖ Make a list on newsprint with a line drawn down the center. On the right side, write "Sheep" and on the left, write "Goats." Under each heading, note the actions that the sheep or goats did—or did not—take.

❖ Discuss these questions:
1. **How would you characterize the basis on which the king separated the sheep from the goats?** (Point out that deeds of mercy on behalf of vulnerable people make all the difference

as to whether one is labeled a sheep or a goat.)
2. **Did the basis for the separation between the sheep and goats surprise you? If so, how?** (See "Surprises in the Story" in Interpreting the Scripture.)
3. **How is our church fulfilling God's expectation that believers feed and clothe people in need, welcome the stranger, and visit the sick and imprisoned? What else could we do?**

(3) Goal 2: Experience How God's Love for All Inspires the Learners to Meet the Needs of Others

❖ Read or retell "A Shepherd's Job" from Interpreting the Scripture to remind the students that God loves and cares for us as a shepherd cares for his sheep.

❖ Post a sheet of newsprint with these words: "God's love is like . . ." Invite the students to finish the sentence. For some, images related to today's story may come to mind such as "a warm blanket enfolding me" or "a plate of comfort food."

❖ **Option:** Distribute hymnals and read in unison Brian Wren's hymn "How Can We Name a Love." Discuss how this hymn prompts us to see God in other people and to share God's love with others.

❖ Challenge the learners to remember God's love for them and let that love flow through them as they work to meet the needs of others.

(4) Goal 3: Respond to God's Call to Serve Others

❖ Recall that in the "Gather to Learn" portion we considered the needs of some people and the consequences of our action or inaction in meeting those needs.

❖ Note that Lent will begin this Wednesday. Distribute paper and pencils and challenge each student to think of at least one group of people or an agency that he or she could assist during Lent. For example, a student may forego a meal and donate nonperishable food to a food bank each week. Another student may commit to visiting a nursing home to see people who normally do not receive visitors.

❖ Encourage each person to state his or her plans. Perhaps several students who have similar ideas will want to work together.

❖ Conclude by reading "The Gospel in Miniature" in Interpreting the Scripture.

(5) Continue the Journey

❖ Pray that as the learners depart they will be attentive to the needs of others and ready to assist as they are able.

❖ Post information for next week's session on newsprint for the students to copy:
- Title: Clothed and Ready
- Background Scripture: Ephesians 6:10-20
- Lesson Scripture: Ephesians 6:10-20
- Focus of the Lesson: Proper preparation can give assurance that certain things are accomplished. What does one do to be prepared? In order to be ready to serve, Christians need to fortify themselves with the whole armor of God: truth, righteousness, peace, faith, salvation, the Word of God, and prayer.

❖ Challenge the adults to grow spiritually by completing one or more of these activities related to this week's session, which you have posted on newsprint for the students to copy.

(1) Identify a group of people for whom you could be an advocate. Lobby elected officials, send letters to the editor, or gather with grassroots groups to let the needs of these people be known. As an advocate, you are trying to change the system that enables an injustice to occur.

(2) Spearhead a drive to collect food and donate it to your church pantry, an ecumenical food pantry, or other place where those who need food can have access to it.

(3) Clean your closet. Donate any clothing that is still wearable to your church clothes cupboard or a nonprofit agency such as Goodwill or the Salvation Army that accepts clothing and sells it in thrift stores.

❖ Sing or read aloud "Cuando El Pobre (When the Poor Ones)."

❖ Conclude by leading the class in this benediction, adapted from the key verse for the session on December 21 from Luke 2:20: **May we go forth to worship as the shepherds, glorifying and praising God for all we have heard and seen.**

UNIT 3: STEWARDSHIP FOR LIFE
CLOTHED AND READY

PREVIEWING THE LESSON

Lesson Scripture: Ephesians 6:10-20
Background Scripture: Ephesians 6:10-20
Key Verse: Ephesians 6:11

Focus of the Lesson:
Proper preparation can give assurance that certain things are accomplished. What does one do to be prepared? In order to be ready to serve, Christians need to fortify themselves with the whole armor of God: truth, righteousness, peace, faith, salvation, the Word of God, and prayer.

Goals for the Learners:
(1) to examine the epistle's teaching to put on the whole armor of God.
(2) to value the feeling of being prepared to serve God.
(3) to prepare to serve God.

Supplies:
Bibles, newsprint and marker, paper and pencils, hymnals, props or pictures of armor

---

READING THE SCRIPTURE

NRSV
Lesson Scripture: Ephesians 6:10-20

¹⁰Finally, be strong in the Lord and in the strength of his power. **¹¹Put on the whole armor of God, so that you may be able to stand against the wiles of the devil.** ¹²For our struggle is not against enemies of blood and flesh, but against the rulers, against the authorities, against the cosmic powers of this present darkness, against the spiritual forces of evil in the heavenly places. ¹³Therefore take

CEB
Lesson Scripture: Ephesians 6:10-20

¹⁰ Finally, be strengthened by the Lord and his powerful strength. **¹¹Put on God's armor so that you can make a stand against the tricks of the devil.** ¹²We aren't fighting against human enemies but against rulers, authorities, forces of cosmic darkness, and spiritual powers of evil in the heavens. ¹³Therefore pick up the full armor of God so that you can stand your ground on the evil day and after you

up the whole armor of God, so that you may be able to withstand on that evil day, and having done everything, to stand firm. [14]Stand therefore, and fasten the belt of truth around your waist, and put on the breastplate of righteousness. [15]As shoes for your feet put on whatever will make you ready to proclaim the gospel of peace. [16]With all of these, take the shield of faith, with which you will be able to quench all the flaming arrows of the evil one. [17]Take the helmet of salvation, and the sword of the Spirit, which is the word of God.

[18]Pray in the Spirit at all times in every prayer and supplication. To that end keep alert and always persevere in supplication for all the saints. [19]Pray also for me, so that when I speak, a message may be given to me to make known with boldness the mystery of the gospel, [20]for which I am an ambassador in chains. Pray that I may declare it boldly, as I must speak.

have done everything possible to still stand. [14]So stand with the belt of truth around your waist, justice as your breastplate, [15]and put shoes on your feet so that you are ready to spread the good news of peace. [16]Above all, carry the shield of faith so that you can extinguish the flaming arrows of the evil one. [17]Take the helmet of salvation and the sword of the Spirit, which is God's Word.

[18]Offer prayers and petitions in the Spirit all the time. Stay alert by hanging in there and praying for all believers. [19]As for me, pray that when I open my mouth, I'll get a message that confidently makes this secret plan of the gospel known. [20]I'm an ambassador in chains for the sake of the gospel. Pray so that the Lord will give me the confidence to say what I have to say.

UNDERSTANDING THE SCRIPTURE

Introduction. Tradition says that Paul wrote this letter to the church in Ephesus. The earliest manuscripts do not mention the city, however, and the style of the epistle (represented by vocabulary and grammar) does not seem to match those of the apostle's known letters, although the themes do. Accordingly, scholars still debate whether the traditional view is accurate, but no clear consensus has been reached. For purposes of this study, we will assume Paul is the author.

The letter celebrates the life of the church, established by God to an eternal purpose with Christ at its head. Key themes include our spiritual blessings; new life in Christ; our unity and function as the body of Christ; and some of the "new rules" for living together as family, church members, and citizens that come as a result of our new lives.

In chapter 6, verses 10-24 comprise Paul's final words in Ephesians, summing up his letter. Here he deals with how Christians are to prepare for spiritual warfare (6:10-20) and adds a few personal words of parting (6:21-24).

Ephesians 6:10. "Be strong in the Lord," Paul urges at the start of this section. He does not mean we can acquire strength within ourselves, but that we can be made strong "in the strength of [Christ's] power" (6:10). Some translators prefer to rephrase this command in Greek into the passive voice: "Be made strong."

Ephesians 6:11a. "Put on the whole armor of God," says Paul. The whole armor means the complete set, with each piece of equipment made ready for use. Paul, no doubt, has seen Roman soldiers during his imprisonment and, thus, is acquainted with their battle dress. As a Roman citizen, he might also have seen soldiers in the streets of any major Roman city.

The description in these verses brings to mind the armor of God that Isaiah describes: "Righteousness shall be the belt around his waist, and faithfulness the belt around his loins" (Isaiah 11:5); and "He put on righteousness like a breastplate, and a helmet of salvation on his head; he put on garments of vengeance for clothing, and wrapped himself in fury as a mantle" (59:17).

Ephesians 6:11b-12. Thus equipped, the Christian "may be able to stand against the wiles of the devil" (6:11). The image is not of a march or a charge on the enemy, but of defending against attack, holding the fort. Heading the enemy forces is the devil, who is a wily tactician. Clearly, for Paul, there is a personal dimension to the forces that oppose God's love and power.

As Paul describes it, the Christian's struggle of faithfulness is not merely an inward battle or a conflict of interpersonal relationships. We contend "not against enemies of blood and flesh, but against the rulers, against the authorities, against the cosmic powers of this present darkness,

against the spiritual forces of evil" (6:12). Although these are the same powers Christ himself defeated (see 1:20-23), the Christian must contend with the remnants of this army whose defeat is a foregone conclusion.

Ephesians 6:13-17. Now Paul develops the metaphor of *God's armor* that he has begun. As before, the passage is not a call to arms, but a call to withstand assault (6:13).

The order of the pieces of armor described is the order in which a soldier would put them on. Before putting on armor, one must first, as the phrase in verse 14 of the KJV and NAB describe, "gird up one's loins," that is, gather up the flowing garments that must be tucked in before one can run a race, perform heavy work, or prepare for battle. The "belt" or "girdle" for fastening up the gathered garments is "truth." Probably this means integrity, the "truth in the inward being" of which Psalm 51:6 speaks.

Then comes the "breastplate of righteousness" reminiscent of the heavenly warrior (Isaiah 59:17) and of 2 Corinthians 6:7. Most commentators take this to mean uprightness of character and moral integrity, rather than the righteousness granted to us through faith in Jesus Christ. Next there is the footwear that makes one "ready to proclaim the gospel of peace" (Ephesians 6:15). The "shield of faith," the "helmet of salvation," and the "sword of the Spirit" complete the ensemble (6:16-17).

The Christian's one weapon is the sword, identified as the word of God (see Revelation 19:15). The Old Testament often speaks of speech as a sword, and Hebrews 4:12 reminds us that "the word of God is living and active, sharper than any two-edged sword, piercing until it divides soul from spirit, of joints from marrow; it is able to judge the thoughts and intentions of the heart."

Ephesians 6:18-19. The end of this week's passage adds to our picture of adequate Christian defense. "Pray in the Spirit at all times," says Paul in verse 18. This is how the Christian stays alert and ready for battle, preparing to face the forces that are not of God.

Moreover, Christians are to pray for one another, especially in times of trouble. Our prayers for one another add to our defense and to our ability to be strong in the Lord. Paul's own request is that his friends will pray for him, that he might be bold in proclaiming the gospel. This apostle, who has founded churches and converted untold numbers to the faith, wants to be even bolder in his efforts!

Ephesians 6:20. Faithfulness to the gospel message means everything to Paul. His preaching lands him in jail, yet his joy in serving Christ leads him to see imprisonment as an opportunity, rather than as a failure. He calls himself "an ambassador in chains" (6:20), a striking image. An ambassador is an authorized representative or messenger, as Paul is for God. Usually, an ambassador wanders unhindered, enjoying great freedom and many privileges. In contrast, Paul is a prisoner, either literally or figuratively "in chains." He does not deny the reality of his imprisonment, but neither does he lose sight of a higher reality. In essence, he is saying: "A prisoner is *what* I am, but God's ambassador is *who* I am."

INTERPRETING THE SCRIPTURE

"Be Strong"

Our final session in this unit's study looks at Paul's closing words to the Christian community. If we assume that this letter comes from Paul's final imprisonment (6:20) and that it was written to the church at large, then the words gain heightened energy. Here Paul grounds his vision of the new humanity in a strength willing to endure difficult challenges by standing against the current of personal and societal forces. This call to stand firm and be strong is a fitting topic for today, the first Sunday in Lent.

In the first verse of this passage, Paul lays down the bedrock affirmation on which all else rests: "Be

strong in the Lord and in the strength of his power" (6:10). By this, Paul does not mean that we are to be stoic or unmoved in emotional situations, such as grief. There are times we are moved deeply, even to tears, and this is natural. Rather, the Greek verb translated "be strong" also means "be made strong." Paul intentionally points to power outside of ourselves as reassurance that we can find strength beyond that which is normally, or even naturally, available to us.

That understanding becomes clear when Paul encourages us to be (made) strong "in the Lord and in the strength of his power" (6:10). As we live in Christ, his power becomes our own by God's gracious gift.

Moreover, our empowerment by God in Christ provides a clear hint about the purpose of ministry: We are to help strengthen others, just as Christ has strengthened us.

"The Armor of God"

Ephesians 6:11-12 describes the Christian's response to times and situations when we should not yield to that which we consider wrong. The imagery of warfare and battle takes center stage when Paul describes the armor we are to put on so that, once again, we may stand firm.

"The whole armor of God" (6:11) parallels Isaiah 59:17, where it is God who dons armor in a passage announcing judgment on God's adversaries. That spirit of confrontation fits well with the mood in this text from Ephesians. Five times in these two verses Paul uses the word *against* to identify those with whom the faithful will struggle: "Against the wiles of the devil . . . against the rulers . . . against the authorities . . . against the cosmic powers of this present darkness, against the spiritual forces of evil in the heavenly places" (Ephesians 6:11-12). These all provide reasons why the church needs to be made strong in Christ and put on the full armor of God.

Some might argue that Paul's imagery speaks solely to an older age when such powers were readily acknowledged. Yet Paul pushes us to confront the idea that evil forces exist in systemic ways that affect us all. Our modern world is full of examples: prejudice, genocide, and political dictatorships still stand as forces counter to the kingdom of God.

In Ephesians 6:14-17, Paul catalogs the items of spiritual armor with which we equip ourselves. This list of equipment reflects the standard armor worn by Roman soldiers. The purpose of this armor is far from an ordinary military use, however.

Paul writes of a spiritual armoring, rather than a literal one. Four of the pieces of armor—belt of truth, breastplate of righteousness, shield of faith, and helmet of salvation—serve as armor to protect the Christian from evil. In contrast, the word of God stands out as a weapon. It is the "sword of the Spirit" (6:17) with which evil can be attacked. Moreover, shoes are worn to proclaim the gospel of peace.

"Persevere and Pray"

We may feel that, despite the equipment God provides, the potential of those things standing against us is too much. The purpose of the lists of enemies is not to frighten us or to cause us to be discouraged, though. Rather, it is to remind us that, in Christ, God has won the eternal victory against all evil, however humans describe it. While the enemy is still here to harass us, the victory has already been won by Christ.

Given this assurance, we can confidently go to battle against all in the world that would deny God's love, goodwill, and mercy. In that confidence we can struggle against all that would deny us the freedom Jesus died to give us. In that confidence we can battle all that divides us against ourselves, all that pulls us down, all that depresses us, all that causes us to want to give up. Our confidence comes from the fact that we do not struggle alone.

Ephesians 6 shows us that we did not select these pieces of armor for ourselves. They are God-given gifts—as is God's own presence to comfort, forgive, and encourage us. Thus we can continue to "be strong in the Lord and in the strength of his power" (6:10).

Paul follows the description of the Christian's spiritual armor with a call to "pray in the Spirit at all times in every prayer and supplication" (6:18). The ability to stay strong in the fight, it would seem, depends on prayer.

Note the two objects of prayer that Paul mentions. First he seeks prayer "for all the saints" (6:18). Our prayers help the church, the body of Christ in the world, to stay strong in faith and action. Next Paul entreats, "Pray also for me" (6:19). In this appeal, Paul reveals himself to be part of the community, not above it. Even one who stands in a position to counsel the entire church does not outgrow the need of others' prayers.

The example Paul gives in this request for prayer can guide us in the difficult situations in which we may find ourselves. Our instinct is usually to ask for deliverance from such adversities, and for good reason. Yet Paul shows us a spirit striving to be faithful within life's precarious situations. We cannot always find escape. Deliverance does not always appear, at least not in the terms for which we might have hoped. In such circumstances, we are called to stand firm. We are called to live out the faith in whatever conditions may surround us. "Pray for me" is our appeal as well as Paul's.

"An Ambassador in Chains"

It seems, according to verse 20, that Paul was in prison when this letter was written. Nevertheless, those harsh life circumstances did not change his key sense of identity and purpose: "I am an ambassador [for Christ]."

In chains or out, we represent our Lord Jesus in everything we do, and never more so than when we are performing acts of ministry in his name. If we were to condense Paul's instructions in this week's passage into a simple poster showing "Seven Steps for Worshiping God with Our Lives," it might read something like this:

1. Trust God.
2. Stand prepared and firm in the faith.
3. Work for God's kingdom in all things.
4. Pray for others.
5. Ask others to pray for you.
6. Proclaim the gospel.
7. Be Christ in the world.

What do you say? Shall we give it a shot this Lenten season?

SHARING THE SCRIPTURE

PREPARING TO TEACH

Preparing Our Hearts

Meditate on this week's devotional reading from Colossians 3:12-17, which includes details on the traits with which Christians are to clothe themselves. Which of the traits in verses 12 and 14 are in your wardrobe? How do you experience "the peace of Christ" (3:15) dwelling in your heart? What will you thank God for today?

Pray that you and the students will be clothed and prepared to go forth as loving disciples.

Preparing Our Minds

Study the background Scripture and the lesson Scripture, which are both from Ephesians 6:10-20.

Consider this question as you prepare the lesson: *How does one prepare to serve God?*

Write on newsprint:

❏ the seven steps listed in "An Ambassador in Chains" in Interpreting the Scripture.

❏ information for next week's lesson, found under "Continue the Journey."

❏ activities for further spiritual growth in "Continue the Journey."

Review the "Introduction," "The Big Picture," "Close-up," and "Faith in Action," which all precede the first lesson of this quarter. Consider how you might use any of this material in today's lesson.

Prior to the session gather props that can be used to represent the whole armor of God: belt, shoes, hat (or helmet). Instead of, or in addition to, these props, check the Internet for pictures of the whole armor of God. Many websites have such pictures, some much more detailed than others.

LEADING THE CLASS

(1) Gather to Learn

❖ Greet the class members and introduce guests.

❖ Pray that those who have come today will prepare themselves to serve God.

❖ Invite the students to think of a task that they perform on a regular basis, such as cooking a meal, doing the laundry, washing the car, weeding a garden, or engaging in a particular sport or hobby. Form groups of two or three and ask each person to state the preparations necessary to perform the task, without mentioning what the task is. The other two members of the group are to guess what task is being performed.

❖ Read aloud today's focus statement: **Proper preparation can give assurance that certain things are accomplished. What does one do to be prepared? In order to be ready to serve, Christians need to fortify themselves with the whole armor of God: truth, righteousness, peace, faith, salvation, the Word of God, and prayer.**

(2) Goal 1: Examine the Epistle's Teaching to Put on the Whole Armor of God

❖ Select a volunteer to read Ephesians 6:10-20.

❖ Use "The Armor of God" in Interpreting the Scripture and "Ephesians 6:13-17" in Understanding the Scripture to help the learners envision the armor and its purpose. If you were able to bring representatives of this armor, such as a belt and shoes, place them on a table where everyone can see them. Or hold up any pictures you were able to find of the whole armor of God.

❖ Discuss these questions:

1. **Paul uses the metaphor of armor to discuss spiritual protection. What other metaphors or images—perhaps ones that better relate to contemporary life—might Paul use if he were writing today?**

2. Our writer makes the point that "the passage is not a call to arms, but a call to withstand assault." In other words, the armored "warrior" is not taking an offensive position but a defensive one. The only exception is the "sword of the Spirit, which is the word of God" (6:17). Why might a sword be so important to the believing "warrior"?

3. Notice that verse 15 calls believers to put on their feet "whatever will make you ready to proclaim the gospel of peace." Despite being dressed for battle, believers are called to proclaim peace. What do you think will make you ready to proclaim this peaceful gospel?

(3) Goal 2: Value the Feeling of Being Prepared to Serve God

❖ Read "Persevere and Pray" in Interpreting the Scripture.
 ❖ Discuss these questions:
1. When you need the strength and perseverance to do a task, what do you perceive to be the benefits of prayer?
2. How do you feel when you know that even in the face of challenging circumstances you have prayed with perseverance and are prepared by God's grace?
❖ Read these scenarios and invite the students to respond:
1. You have been asked to teach a Sunday school class. What training or resources will you need to feel that you are truly prepared to serve God through this ministry?

2. Your church is participating in a Habitat for Humanity build. You are not handy with tools, but feel called to do something. What encouragement do you need to feel that you are prepared to serve God?
3. You want to invite an unchurched neighbor to join you for class and worship. What do you need to do before issuing the invitation to feel that you are well prepared to host this neighbor at your church?

(4) Goal 3: Prepare to Serve God

❖ Encourage the students to discuss what it means to be "an ambassador." You may define the word this way: An ambassador is one who has been appointed and authorized to speak for and represent a country, organization, or person.
 ❖ Read "An Ambassador in Chains" in Interpreting the Scripture.
 ❖ Post the "Seven Steps for Worshiping God with Our Lives" on newsprint. Distribute paper and pencils so that the adults can copy the steps you have posted. Invite them to suggest other steps that could be added.
 ❖ Read the following questions and direct the students to write confidential answers.
1. Where do you feel called to serve?
2. What character traits do you have that equip you for this service?
3. What traits do you need to develop?

❖ Come together and ask two additional questions:

1. How can the church help you to develop whatever traits you feel you need?
2. What relationship do you see between worship and service?

(5) Continue the Journey

❖ Pray that as the learners depart they will stand ready to serve as God's ambassadors.

❖ Post information for next week's session on newsprint for the students to copy:

- **Title: The Lamb of God**
- **Background Scripture: John 1:29-34**
- **Lesson Scripture: John 1:29-34**
- **Focus of the Lesson: In a world of competing religious and political values, people are not always clear that one system is of any greater value than another. How can Christians know which set of beliefs carries more weight than all others? John testifies that the baptism of the Holy Spirit surpasses water baptism and that the Spirit bears witness that Jesus is God's Son.**

❖ Challenge the adults to grow spiritually by completing one or more of these activities related to this week's session, which you have posted on newsprint for the students to copy.

(1) Identify one or more spiritual disciplines—such as prayer, meditation, Bible study, journaling, or fasting—that you could turn to when you feel that your spirit and beliefs are being challenged. Commit yourself to practicing this discipline regularly.

(2) Teach a child about the whole armor of God by reading Ephesians 6:10-17 together and then drawing a picture of this armor or pretending to put the armor on. Note that actual armor would have been put on in the order in which it is mentioned in the Bible.

(3) Recall that Paul told the Ephesians to "persevere in supplication for all the saints" (6:18), and in the next verse asked for prayer for himself. Make a list of those who need prayer this week. Include those who are actively working for the church, but also think about the needs of all God's people. Pray persistently for them.

❖ Sing or read aloud "Soldiers of Christ, Arise."

❖ Conclude by leading the class in this benediction, adapted from the key verse for the session on December 21 from Luke 2:20: **May we go forth to worship as the shepherds, glorifying and praising God for all we have heard and seen.**

THIRD QUARTER
The Spirit Comes

MARCH 1, 2015—MAY 31, 2015

The fourteen lessons for the spring quarter focus on God's work through the Holy Spirit to empower disciples to live their faith. Four of the five sessions in Unit 1 focus on John's Gospel. The fifth lesson explores Mark's account of Jesus' entry into Jerusalem. The second unit, a five-study session for the Easter season, examines the work of the Holy Spirit within the community of faith as viewed through 1 Corinthians and 1, 2, and 3 John. The quarter ends with a four-session study of 1 Corinthians that makes the connection between loving one another and living as Christ's witnesses in the world.

Unit 1, "The Pledge of God's Presence," starts on March 1 with "The Lamb of God," an exploration of John's testimony concerning Jesus and his baptism as found in John 1:29-34. On March 8 we turn to John 14:15-26 to begin to understand the significance of the Holy Spirit in "Jesus Promises an Advocate." In "The Spirit of Truth," the session for March 15, John 16:4b-15 reports on Jesus' explanation as to how the Holy Spirit works on our behalf. "Receive the Holy Spirit," the lesson for March 22 that has background Scripture in John 20:19-23 and Acts 1:4-8 and 2:1-4, considers the importance of Jesus' post-resurrection appearance to his disciples. "The One Who Comes," which tells the story of Jesus' triumphal entry into Jerusalem on Palm Sunday, is found in our study for March 29 from Mark 11:1-11.

The second unit, "The Community of Beloved Disciples," begins on Easter, April 5, with "Resurrection Guaranteed," a session that explores the meaning of Christ's resurrection as explained by Paul in 1 Corinthians 15:1-22. "Love One Another," the session from 1 John 3:11-24 on April 12, sets forth John's message for how we are to love God and others. On April 19 we continue in 1 John with chapters 4 and 5 to learn what is required to live in unity with the community of faith in "Believe God's Love." In the session for April 26, "Watch Out for Deceivers!," 1 John 5:6-12, 18-20 and 2 John caution believers to beware of those who do not abide in Christ's teachings. In the fifteen verses of John's third letter, which we will explore on May 3 in a lesson titled "Coworkers with the Truth," we will learn about the importance of hospitality.

On May 10 as we begin Unit 3, "One in the Bond of Love," we will examine the purpose of the spiritual gifts as set forth in 1 Corinthians 12:1-11 in a lesson titled "Gifts of the Spirit." We will consider on May 17 how each member of the body supports other members in "The Spirit Creates One Body," based on 1 Corinthians 12:12-31. On May 24 "Gift of Languages" investigates how the Holy Spirit helped people communicate both in different native and spiritual languages as recorded in Acts 2:1-21 and 1 Corinthians 14:1-25. The unit ends on May 31 with the familiar poetry from 1 Corinthians 13 concerning the meaning of love in "The Greatest Gift Is Love."

MEET OUR WRITER

DR. JERRY L. SUMNEY

Dr. Jerry L. Sumney is a member of the Society of Biblical Literature and is past president for the Southeastern Region of the Society. At the national level, he also served as the chair of the steering committee for the Theology of the Disputed Paulines Group from 1996 through 2001 and currently serves as the chair of the steering committee for the Disputed Paulines Section. He is also currently chair for the Pauline Epistles and Literature Section of the International Meeting of the Society of Biblical Literature. He was elected to membership in the Studiorum Novi Testamenti Societas (SNTS) in 2005.

Dr. Sumney has written six books: *The Bible: An Introduction* (2010); *Colossians: A Commentary*, New Testament Library Series (2008); *Philippians: A Handbook for Second-Year Greek Students* (2007); *Servants of Satan, False Brothers, and Other Pauline Opponents* (1999); *Preaching Apocalyptic Texts* (coauthored with Larry Paul Jones (1999); and *Identifying Paul's Opponents* (1990). He is editor of *The Order of the Ministry: Equipping the Saints* (2002) and coeditor of *Theology and Ethics in Paul and His Interpreters* (1996), *Paul and Pathos (2001),* and *Romans* in the Society of Biblical Literature Bible Resources series (2012). Dr. Sumney has written more than thirty articles in journals and books. He also contributed entries to the *New Interpreter's Dictionary of the Bible* and the *Dictionary of the Later New Testament and Its Developments,* and the *Dictionary of Scripture and Ethics.* In addition, he is a contributor to *The College Study Bible* and the *CEB Study Bible.*

Prior to joining the faculty of Lexington Theological Seminary (LTS) where he is professor of biblical studies, he taught in the religion department at Ferrum College from 1986 through 1997. He received his B.A. from David Lipscomb University in 1978, his M.A. from Harding University in 1982, and his Ph.D. from Southern Methodist University in 1987.

Dr. Sumney has presented papers at regional, national, and international academic conferences. He has also led numerous workshops for elders and deacons; Bible study workshops and series, including in the Lay School of Theology at LTS and in the school for licensed ministers sponsored by the Kentucky region of the Christian Church. He is the regular teacher of an adult Sunday school class in his home church, Central Christian Church (Disciples of Christ) in Lexington.

Dr. Sumney and his wife, Diane, have three daughters: Elizabeth, Victoria, and Margaret.

THE BIG PICTURE:
THE EARLY CHURCH AND
THE HOLY SPIRIT

The readings for this quarter stretch across a number of different streams of the tradition of the early church. As distinctive as these groups are, they were all convinced of the importance of the Spirit. The Spirit was a visible and powerful force in the early church. The church expected manifestations of the Spirit that confirmed its presence and provided strength and guidance. Those believers felt the Spirit's movement in their worship together and in their private times. So powerfully was the Spirit present that there needed to be rules about how to use the gifts given so that they fulfilled their proper function, that is, to strengthen the church. While many in the church today do not experience such dramatic manifestations of the Spirit, the New Testament gives us assurance that we can be certain that God is present in the church and in the lives of Christians through the Spirit.

The Gospel of John

The Gospel of John is distinctive. While Matthew, Mark, and Luke share a great deal of material about the life of Jesus (and so are known as the Synoptic Gospels), John has different stories and teachings of Jesus. For example, in the Synoptics Jesus talks a lot about the kingdom of God, but John seldom mentions it, choosing instead to concentrate on the identity of Jesus as the One sent from God. Even the activities and travels of Jesus are different in John: John has Jesus go to Jerusalem regularly during his ministry, but the Synoptics have him go only once at the end. The writer of John has used a collection of traditions about Jesus in Jerusalem and Judea (the area around Jerusalem) that the other Gospel writers do not draw on.

The Gospel of John had a complicated origin. A first draft of it was written by a person known as the "Beloved Disciple," a person who is never given a name in the text. He does not appear in the story until 13:23, at the Last Supper. In 21:24, the text claims that this disciple is the author of the Gospel. But that verse also says, "we know his testimony is true." This "we" has added some things to the Gospel of John, at least 21:24-25. Most New Testament scholars think a good deal more has been added or rearranged, perhaps to include more in the text than the Beloved Disciple did in his first writing of the story. It seems likely that after the Beloved Disciple's death, those who were close to him reworked and completed his Gospel. Many of this quarter's readings from John come from a section that seems to have been added in such a reworking.

Within the Farewell Discourse (chapters 14–17, which includes the concluding prayer for the disciples) Jesus talks about the Spirit far more than what we find in the other Gospels. These chapters consist mostly of long speeches by Jesus that tell of the time after he is gone. They come at the end of the Last Supper, when Jesus is about to be arrested. Chapters 14–17 have Jesus preparing the disciples for his arrest and departure. In light of what is about to happen, Jesus offers comfort, assuring them that God will not leave them without God's presence. Indeed, Jesus will be present with them through the Spirit.

We do not know the identity of the Beloved Disciple. Tradition has identified him as John the son of Zebedee, but most scholars think that is incorrect. John was from Galilee, but there are few stories about Galilee in the Gospel of John—though there are many in the Synoptics. John is never mentioned in the Gospel of John and his brother has a much smaller role than in the other Gospels. For these and many more reasons, it seems unlikely that John wrote the Gospel of John. It was attached to John because the church attached the Gospels to apostles very early and so gave them apostolic authority. Further, the Gospel of John seemed associated with Ephesus and there were two known tombs related to a John in Ephesus. So the tradition made the connection. Recognizing that this Gospel does not come from the apostle John does nothing to reduce its place in the New Testament or as an authority for the church. The early Christians heard the voice of God here in a distinctive and authoritative way. The subsequent church has confirmed that judgment. We will continue to call the author John because that is the title by which we know this book.

John is also distinct in its theology. John is the only one of the Gospels that identifies Christ as a preexistent being (1:1-14). John emphasizes the identity of Jesus as the One Sent from God and has Christ possess a oneness with God in ways the other Gospels do not contemplate. Within the Farewell Discourse (chapters 14–17) Jesus talks about the Spirit far more than what we find in the other Gospels. In these and many other ways, John more directly addresses the needs and situation of his church, helping them understand the meaning of Christ's work on earth and his continuing presence in the church through the Spirit.

We must be very careful when we read one particular feature of John. John says many derogatory things about how "the Jews" reject Jesus. The first thing to remember is that the author of this Gospel is a Jew and so are most people in the church for which he writes. So when he says "the Jews" he does not mean all Jews. Many scholars think that the phrase really intends to designate only the leaders in Jerusalem. That is obviously its meaning in some uses. John speaks harshly of this group because his church has suffered at the hands of leaders of their local synagogue. Like so many early church members, most people in John's church continued to be law-observant Jews. They kept the sabbath and the food laws, they went to synagogue services; they did all those things that make Jews distinctive. But as members of John's church began to make claims about the identity of Jesus (probably particularly about his identity with God), the leaders of their synagogues banned them from attending. This is the equivalent of being banned from your home church. Interpreters find evidence for this in passages such as John 9:22, where it says that the parents of the man born blind are afraid to answer the questions about his healing because "the

Jews" had decided to put out of the synagogue anyone who said Jesus was the Messiah. Most interpreters think this statement reflects the experience of John's own church. John and his readers are feeling the sting of this rejection when this Gospel is written. But this is name-calling within the family. John still thinks it is a good thing to be a child of Abraham and an Israelite, but reserves the title "the Jews" to those who oppose Jesus. Unfortunately, this naming of Jesus' opponents has been used to promote anti-Semitism. This is a wrong understanding and use of John. Again, John himself is a Jew and he was not against Jesus. So we must not use John to make accusations against all Jews—not even all Jews of the first century, and certainly none in the twenty-first.

1, 2, 3 John

As a group, 1, 2, and 3 John are known as the Johannine Epistles because they are all attached to the same line of tradition as the Gospel of John. They share with John much of its distinctive language and theological emphases. Like the Gospel of John, the author is never named in any of these letters. But since they are so much like the Gospel of John, tradition has made John their author just as it did the Gospel. These letters probably come from about the year 100, a time after the death of John. While 1 John draws on the importance of eyewitness testimony about Jesus, the other letters more obviously come from a church leader of a later generation. The author of 2 and 3 John simply calls himself "the elder." He is well known and seen as a leader by multiple churches, but he is not an apostle. Still, he represents the apostolic teaching in the face of a dangerous alternative.

The problem that all three of these letters addresses is Docetism. Docetism is the belief that Jesus did not have a physical body. Those who held this view acknowledged that Jesus was divine, but not human. They envisioned the material world as evil and contaminating. They thought the material that this world is made of was automatically defiling. Touching it makes one immoral. The goal of salvation, then, was to get out of this defiling world and have a body-free existence. This teaching draws its way of viewing the world from some philosophical schools of the first century, but it makes them more radical. If this is one's understanding of the world, one clearly could not let the divine come into actual contact with it. Real contact would bring contamination. So they said that Jesus only seemed to have a physical body. (The word "Docetism" comes from the Greek word *dokeō*, which means "to seem.") They claimed that Jesus fooled people into thinking that he was a physical presence. That preserves the holiness of God while having God be present in Jesus. In addition, it allows God to send humans a message. On the other hand, since Docetism assumes that God's world is evil, it also says that humans, as a part of the creation, are by nature evil. Thus, it denies God's pronouncement of the world's goodness at creation. Beyond this, it means that Jesus was a deceiver. His whole ministry was in some senses a sham.

The writer(s) of these letters rejects Docetism vigorously, and sometimes rather harshly. He is willing to be so severe because of the damage this teaching does to the truth of the gospel and the lives of those who believe it. The author of 1 John declares this teaching untrue by drawing on the apostolic witness to the physical nature of the presence of Christ. The apostles saw and touched Jesus and testify that he was genuinely physical. All three letters say that being a Docetist puts a person out of the church. Holding to some beliefs is incompatible with being a Christian.

These three Johannine letters show the progression of the dispute. First John rejects the teaching at length, saying it is incompatible with the true faith. Second John encourages the church to be loving toward one another, but to reject Docetists. In 2 John, readers are told that they must believe that Jesus is the Christ (verse 7), that is, that the earthly Jesus is the Christ from heaven. Both 1 and 2 John see believing the right things about Jesus as a part of keeping God's commandments. Both also see morality as a necessary element of the Christian life. The guiding principle for all conduct is love for one another. For both letters, love is the most important command. By the time we get to 3 John, the Docetists seem to have gained powerful allies. At least one church leader, Diotrephes, has been won over. He has led his church to refuse support to teachers or missionaries that come from the author's church. This final letter of the group calls the faithful to remain in the faith and have love, even in the midst of difficulties.

1 Corinthians

Paul writes 1 Corinthians to a troubled church. They have let their previous and non-Christian understandings of spirituality overly influence their view of Christian spirituality. That has led to all sorts of problems, including misunderstandings about leadership, ethics, worship, and even the Resurrection. Paul tries throughout this letter to reorient their understanding of the Spirit and what it does for the believer. They thought spirituality was concerned largely with enhancing one's own life, especially through exciting experiences of God and through various manifestations that would make the spiritual person appear superior to others. Paul rejects this view. He argues that true spirituality imitates Christ's willingness to put the good of the other person ahead of one's own good. The most important thing the Spirit does in this letter is to enable believers to put the other person first. Paul neither denies nor rejects the power of personal experiences. He just wants them put in proper perspective. Seen through Christ's example, which is exemplified in his giving of himself on the cross, Christian leaders must not demand deference, but rather serve others. Leadership in worship does not exalt the person with impressive gifts; instead, it enables the gifted person to use them to benefit the church as a whole. All of chapters 12–14 are about how to use spiritual gifts properly for the good of the church, rather than as means to enhance one's own status. Love is the most important spiritual gift.

Some at Corinth also thought that bodily existence was something that needed to be overcome. They had not gone to the extreme we see in Docetists, but they are worried about the contaminating effects of embodiment. Thus, Paul also must discuss the Resurrection, assuring them that God created humans in an embodied form and called it good. When people are in their final form in

God's presence, they will be bodily and good—just as God intended them. The evidence for this understanding is the bodily resurrection of Christ. If spirituality meant overcoming embodied existence, Paul says, God would not have raised Christ to a bodily resurrection.

Acts

Some reading this quarter comes from Acts. This book is a selective telling of the church's founding and growth through its first three decades. The first half tells of the gospel spreading among Jews and those related to them ethnically and religiously (that is, Samaritans). The second half tells of the church's advance among Gentiles, ending with preaching in the capital of the empire. From its beginning, the story of the church is the story of the movement of the Spirit. The church begins when the Spirit comes on those believers gathered on Pentecost; it advances among Samaritans when the Spirit comes to them; and it is launched among Gentiles through a powerful coming of the Spirit on them. The Spirit also guides the important events in the life of the church, whether it is a question of how to take care of the needy or of where to preach next. The coming of the Spirit in Acts is a gift of God that is mediated through Christ. The Spirit is the means by which the apostles come to understand Christ and the one who demonstrates that the gospel is for the whole world by giving the church many languages on Pentecost. The Spirit is also a sign of the end times. It is through the Spirit that God is now living directly in and among God's people, just as the prophets had promised. In Acts, the Spirit provides the church the strength and ability to carry out God's work.

CLOSE-UP: WHO IS THE HOLY SPIRIT?

Christians have long accepted the Holy Spirit as one of the three persons of the Godhead, but this person is not as familiar to many believers as God the Father or God the Son. Let's explore what the Bible reveals about the work and person of the Holy Spirit.

We can discern information about the *nature* of the Spirit. God's Spirit is, in essence, "truth" (John 16:13), "holiness" (Romans 1:4), "life" (Romans 8:2), "eternal" (Hebrews 9:14), and "glory" (1 Peter 4:14).

Moreover, the Bible teaches that the Holy Spirit *is* God, for the Spirit has the attributes of God. Those attributes include omnipresence, meaning that the Spirit is everywhere (Psalm 139:7) and omniscience, meaning that the Spirit knows all things (1 Corinthians 2:10-11) and is, in fact, from God (1 Corinthians 2:12). In the story of Ananias and Sapphira, Peter asks why this couple has lied to the Holy Spirit (Acts 5:3) and then says that they have lied to God (5:4). Thus, Peter clearly equates the Holy Spirit with God.

Although the word "Trinity" is not found in the Bible, there are several places in which the Father, Son, and Holy Spirit are linked together. In the Great Commission of Matthew 28:19, the risen Christ commands his followers to baptize "in the name of the Father and of the Son and of the Holy Spirit." Another example is found in 2 Corinthians 13:14 where Paul's concluding blessing refers to "the grace of the Lord Jesus Christ, the love of God, and the communion of the Holy Spirit."

In addition to the divine connection, the Holy Spirit is also portrayed as a person. In Romans 8:27 Paul writes about the mind of the Spirit. In Acts 8:29, the Spirit speaks with an intelligible voice to direct Philip to join the chariot of the Ethiopian eunuch. The Spirit can be grieved, as attested to in Isaiah 63:10 and Ephesians 4:30. Being questioned by the high priest and council, Peter bore testimony to Jesus' death and resurrection, claiming that not only were he and the apostles witnesses to these events but so too was the Spirit a witness (Acts 5:32).

The Bible also describes various activities of the Holy Spirit. The Spirit intercedes for us, according to Romans 8:26, especially when we do not know how to pray. The Spirit leads us, even as the Spirit led Jesus into the wilderness to be tempted (Matthew 4:1). In John 14:26, Jesus refers to the Holy Spirit as the Advocate or Helper who will teach us everything and remind us what Jesus has said. Writing in 1 Corinthians 12:7, Paul asserts that God gives gifts through the Holy Spirit for the common good. One of the gifts given to the church by the Spirit is that of the "overseers" who are responsible for shepherding God's people (Acts 20:28). The Spirit who raised Christ from the dead dwells in us and gives us life (Romans 8:11).

Since the spring quarter is devoted to the Holy Spirit, you may wish to consult a concordance or topical Bible to find more information about the many names and titles given to the Spirit, each of which reveals more about who the Spirit is.

FAITH IN ACTION: EMPOWERED BY THE SPIRIT

Help the adults recall that this quarter's sessions focus on the coming and work of the Holy Spirit. Many of the biblical passages emphasize the importance of love, not as a noun that describes a feeling but as a verb that spurs believers to action. During intervals throughout March, April, and May, present several projects and work through the ideas with the class members.

Project 1: Identify a major decision that is facing your church. Suggest that some members of the class agree to pray daily, perhaps even at a specific time, for the Holy Spirit to guide those responsible for making this decision so that their choices will benefit the entire congregation.

Project 2: Review Jesus' words in John 20:21-23. Note that Jesus says he is sending out the disciples just as the Father sent him. Then he breathes on them and they receive the Holy Spirit. Discuss these questions with the class:

1. **What is God sending our congregation to do?**
2. **What spiritual gifts have our members received to do this work?**
3. **What action will we take to respond to God?**

Project 3: Form small groups to (a) discuss what the students believe about Jesus' resurrection and (b) role-play a conversation between a believer and someone who has doubts or does not believe at all in his resurrection. Challenge the participants to go forth, empowered by the Holy Spirit, to communicate their convictions to others.

Project 4: Brainstorm with the adults the names of agencies in your community that serve people who may feel unloved or rejected. Such agencies could include, for example, nursing homes, residential treatment centers, prisons, and shelters for victims of domestic violence. Form small groups based on interest in a particular facility that has been named. Challenge each group to formulate a short-term or long-term project that is designed to help those involved with the facility to feel unconditional love, to know that someone really cares about them.

Project 5: Suggest that the participants view their class as if they were visitors. What do they do to make people feel welcome? How does the class follow up with visitors to encourage them to return? Consider ways that the class could be even more welcoming. For example, could you provide a mentor or "buddy" for a newcomer? Put any suggestions into practice as soon as possible.

Project 6: Do a Bible study by forming groups and assigning one to Romans 12:6-8, another to 1 Corinthians 12:28-30, and a third group to Ephesians 4:11-13.

Ask each group to compare its list of gifts to the one in 1 Corinthians 12:8-11 from the lesson for May 10. Invite each group to present its findings. Distribute paper and pencils and prompt each participant to name at least one gift that he or she has received from the Spirit and explain how this gift is being used for the common good. Challenge the adults to use their gifts for the benefit of the church.

UNIT 1: THE PLEDGE OF GOD'S PRESENCE
THE LAMB OF GOD

PREVIEWING THE LESSON

Lesson Scripture: John 1:29-34
Background Scripture: John 1:29-34
Key Verse: John 1:34

Focus of the Lesson:
In a world of competing religious and political values, people are not always clear that one system is of any greater value than another. How can Christians know which set of beliefs carries more weight than all others? John testifies that the baptism of the Holy Spirit surpasses water baptism and that the Spirit bears witness that Jesus is God's Son.

Goals for the Learners:
(1) to explore John's account of Jesus' baptism.
(2) to relive emotions felt while observing or participating in a baptism.
(3) to assess how they live out their baptismal covenant.

Supplies:
Bibles, newsprint and marker, paper and pencils, hymnals

READING THE SCRIPTURE

NRSV
Lesson Scripture: John 1:29-34

²⁹The next day he saw Jesus coming toward him and declared, "Here is the Lamb of God who takes away the sin of the world! ³⁰This is he of whom I said, 'After me comes a man who ranks ahead of me because he was before me.' ³¹I myself did not know him; but I came baptizing with water for this reason, that he might be revealed to Israel." ³²And John testified, "I saw the Spirit descending

CEB
Lesson Scripture: John 1:29-34

²⁹The next day John saw Jesus coming toward him and said, "Look! The Lamb of God who takes away the sin of the world! ³⁰This is the one about whom I said, 'He who comes after me is really greater than me because he existed before me. ³¹Even I didn't recognize him, but I came baptizing with water so that he might be made known to Israel." ³²John testified, "I saw the Spirit coming down from heaven like

from heaven like a dove, and it remained on him. ³³I myself did not know him, but the one who sent me to baptize with water said to me, 'He on whom you see the Spirit descend and remain is the one who baptizes with the Holy Spirit.' **³⁴And I myself have seen and have testified that this is the Son of God."**

a dove, and it rested on him. ³³Even I didn't recognize him, but the one who sent me to baptize with water said to me, 'The one on whom you see the Spirit coming down and resting is the one who baptizes with the Holy Spirit. **³⁴I have seen and testified that this one is God's Son."**

UNDERSTANDING THE SCRIPTURE

Introduction. John the Baptist was a powerful figure. Long after his death, groups of disciples continued to follow his teachings (see Acts 19:1-7). The church of the Gospel of John's writer knows of John the Baptist and his disciples. This Gospel wants to make the distinction between John and Jesus very clear, making certain that Jesus is seen as superior to John. So the section that precedes our reading has John refuse titles that might be applied to a messiah and has John identify himself as the person who prepares the way for someone greater than himself. In 1:29-34, John identifies Jesus as that One who is greater.

John 1:29-30. These verses take up the story the day after John is questioned about his own identity. The Gospel does not tell us who John says this to because the important thing is that the readers of the Gospel hear it. The first thing John says about Jesus, beyond the vague affirmation that Jesus is greater than he, is that Jesus is "the Lamb of God who takes away the sin of the world" (1:29). The imagery of the lamb is drawn from Israel's preparation for their departure from Egypt. God commanded that an unblemished male lamb, taken from the sheep or the goats, be sacrificed

for the newly instituted Feast of Passover (Exodus 12, especially verse 5). Another connection is made between an animal sacrificed for sins and the Day of Atonement, when the high priest would offer a goat for the sins of the people (Leviticus 16:9). Blood, as the essence of life, was seen as the most precious gift the people could offer as a sign of their repentance. God accepted this offering as the people's way to maintain the covenant in spite of their shortcomings. This image also draws on the self-giving suffering servant in Isaiah 53:7. There Isaiah envisions a leader who is willing to suffer for the good of others. So John identifies Jesus as the One who willingly gives himself for the sins of the people. We should note that this Lamb gives himself not only for the sins of Israel but also for the sins of the whole world. So this Gospel has in mind the universal effectiveness of the death of Jesus from its very beginning. Since the Gospel writer does not see a need to explain what he means by this image of the lamb, we should assume that it is well known in the early church.

One other element of this identification of Jesus is also important. John says in verse 30 that Jesus is greater because "he was before me." This Gospel began with a notice that the "Word" was with God in the beginning, was God's agent in the creation of the cosmos. The Gospel writer has John the Baptist echo that understanding of Jesus here. "Before me" means that the One incarnated as Jesus existed before John the Baptist, who was born before Jesus in the Gospel of Luke and is assumed to be older. Thus, in these two verses, John affirms two important things about Jesus: As the Lamb of God he does away with sin and he is able to do this because he is also the One through whom God made the world.

John 1:31-33. While it may seem strange for John to say he did not recognize Jesus at first, this beginning emphasizes that John's knowledge of Jesus' identity comes through a revelation from God. John makes himself subordinate to Jesus again in these verses. First he says that the purpose of his ministry of baptizing with water is finally to make the identity of Christ known to others. John then says that he saw the Spirit descend on Jesus as a dove. The other Gospels tell us that the Spirit descended on Christ at his baptism. John does not speak explicitly of Jesus' baptism, only the coming of the Spirit that the other Gospels associate with Jesus' baptism. Some interpreters see this omission as a way to avoid the awkwardness of having one who is supposed to be inferior baptizing his superior. Whether the baptism is explicitly mentioned or not, the point is that Jesus has the Spirit of God in ways that others do not. Readers do not need to depend on John's interpretation of this sign. John says God told him that when he sees the Spirit descend in this way, he will know

that this is the One for whom John has been preparing.

Now Jesus is not only the Lamb of God and greater than John but he is also the One who baptizes with the Spirit. This gives Jesus a role in the unfolding of God's plan that prophets such as Joel had looked forward to. Joel saw the day of God's deliverance of God's people as the time when God would be present with God's people in a new and intimate way (see Joel 2:28-29; these verses are quoted in Acts 2:17-18 on the Day of Pentecost). John here identifies Jesus as the One through whom God will be with God's people in this new and personal way. So Christ is the mediator or the Spirit, of the presence of God in the lives of believers.

John 1:34. John gives his powerful testimony about one other thing in these verses. He says that what he has seen demonstrates that Jesus is the Son of God. This is an important title for Jesus in the Gospel of John. It speaks of the relationship between God and Christ and of the way that Christ represents God and God's will to the world.

This testimony about Christ is made all the more powerful because it comes from John who is recognized as a prophet by the church and by an even wider group of people. If that were not enough for it to be convincing, our passage has made clear that this identification of Jesus came to John as direct revelation from God. So Jesus as God's Son, who was God's agent in creation, is the Lamb who brings forgiveness and the One who mediates the presence of the Spirit in the lives of believers. These powerful affirmations about who Jesus is and about how God is with us through him stand at the beginning of John's story of the ministry of Jesus. Thus, these understandings of Christ are to influence all else that we hear about him in John.

INTERPRETING THE SCRIPTURE

Who Is Jesus?

The main topic of our reading today is the identity of Jesus. One of the first things the text wants to make clear is not an issue for us. That is, it wants to make sure readers see Jesus as superior to John the Baptist. While we do not worry about that comparison, we do face many kinds of claims that compete for our allegiance. We hear claims made about who we are as human beings and what our world should be like; we hear claims about what God wants and about whether God should be considered in various kinds of decisions; and we hear claims about which spiritual powers we should listen to. These competing claims come from politicians, scientists, and other religions (including those "spiritual" movements such as are found in the New Age movement). John says he grounds his claims in a direct revelation from God. God revealed to him the true identity of Jesus. While we would not claim such a direct word from God, we have Scripture and the witness of the church as grounds for believing in Christ. We also have the experience of God in our lives that is mediated to us in Christ. So we are not without good reasons for the claims the church makes about Christ.

John claims several things for the identity of Jesus in this passage. When it is read in connection with the beginning verses of John's Gospel, Christ, as the One who "was before me" (1:30), is identified as the One through whom God made all things. Christ is also the mediator of the Spirit, the One who brings the presence of God to us. Christ is able to mediate this intimate presence of God because he is also the Lamb, the One who willingly gives himself for the forgiveness of others. Once forgiven and so purified, we are prepared to have the Spirit live in us. Finally, John identifies Jesus as the Son of God. That title signals both an unequaled relationship with God and a status in the cosmos that is above all others. As God's Son, Christ is the only one who has seen God and so knows God fully. With this full knowledge, Christ as the Son represents God to us and does God's will, showing us what God wants for our lives.

What Does Jesus Give Us?

What we see about the things believers receive through Christ is perceived largely through the things said about the identity of Jesus. Since he is the Lamb of God, he gives believers forgiveness; since he is the one who "was before," he is the giver and sustainer of life; and since he is the Son of God, he can offer us entrance into the household of God. But the emphasis in this text falls on Christ as the One who brings us into contact with the Spirit of God. Indeed, Christ "baptizes with the Holy Spirit" (1:33). The contrast with John's baptism is sharp. John baptizes with water, not the Spirit. This does not suggest that John's baptism was without value or ineffective. It was a sign of repentance, a demonstration of the person's commitment to live for God. John says that the baptism that comes from Jesus is quite different. Rather than being an act that primarily signals something that the person who is being baptized does, Jesus brings a baptism in which God is a primary actor. Christ baptizes believers with the Holy Spirit. While the baptism of John was a way for people to express their commitment to God and receive forgiveness (see Mark 1:4), the baptism of Jesus adds the giving of the Spirit. This baptism brings the presence of God into our lives at the deepest levels.

sends the Spirit into a believer. This also seems to be the view of Paul and the author of Acts. Whatever the precise timing, baptism itself is a symbol of the beginning of a new life lived in the presence of God and with the help of God.

This baptism with the Spirit that Christ gives us does not suggest that extraordinary manifestations are required. While some groups use the language of baptism of the Spirit to express things such as speaking in tongues, that is not what John has in mind here. John uses the language of baptism to make the contrast with the work of John the Baptist as clear as possible. John's meaning is that through Christ, believers receive the presence of God in their lives.

Baptism and the Spirit

Biblical scholars have often debated the relationship between the Christian's reception of the Spirit and their baptism. Some have argued that the Spirit comes to the person before baptism, others that it comes after baptism (perhaps when the baptized person is anointed with oil following baptism), and others that it comes at the moment of baptism. One thing is clear: New Testament writers expect that everyone who has joined the Christian community through baptism will have the Spirit living in them. As the Gospels tell the story of the baptism of Jesus, the Spirit comes upon him at his baptism. That is explicit in the story in the first three Gospels and is implicit in John. If they intend the baptism of Jesus to serve as some type of paradigm for Christian baptism, which seems likely, then they probably think of baptism at the point at which God

The Spirit as the Presence of God

Once we hear that Christ brings us the Spirit, we may well wonder what that does for us. I have already noted that there is no single dramatic gift that all receive. We will see this affirmed in the course of this quarter (particularly when we look at 1 Corinthians). The less dramatic things the Spirit imparts are even more important for our Christian lives. The Spirit brings us assurance of our salvation and of our relationship with God. This coming of God into our lives is not dependent upon us being sufficiently worthy, but on Christ. Christ is the One who baptizes us with the Spirit. God has determined to live in us because we trust in Christ. This is an act of grace, just as forgiveness is. We can know with certainty that God is with us because that is the promise of God in Christ. In addition, the Spirit enables us to live for God. Without God's help we are not able to live as we should, but with the Spirit we can begin to embody those virtues that Paul calls the fruit of the Spirit (Galatians 5:22-23). As our lives begin to conform to the will of God through the help of the Spirit, we can begin to better discern the will of God in our lives and in our churches.

Thus, the Spirit helps us to live up to the commitments made in baptism to live according to the will of God. This promise of the Spirit, then, means that God does not leave us on our own to strive to live for God in a world that would lead us to value things that are outside the will of God.

SHARING THE SCRIPTURE

PREPARING TO TEACH

Preparing Our Hearts

Meditate on this week's devotional reading from Joel 2:23-27. What does God promise to the people through the prophet? How do these promises speak to you? How does the way you live reflect your belief that God is with you—and that there is no other God? For what reasons will you praise God today?

Pray that you and the students will be in awe of the glorious presence of God in your life.

Preparing Our Minds

Study the background Scripture and the lesson Scripture, which are both from John 1:29-34.

Consider this question as you prepare the lesson: *In a world of competing religious and political values, how can Christians know which set of beliefs carries more weight than all the others?*

Write on newsprint:

❏ questions for "Assess How the Learners Live Out Their Baptismal Covenant."

❏ information for next week's lesson, found under "Continue the Journey."

❏ activities for further spiritual growth in "Continue the Journey."

Review the "Introduction," "The Big Picture," "Close-up," and "Faith in Action," which all precede this first lesson of the quarter. Consider how you might use any of this material in today's lesson.

LEADING THE CLASS

(1) Gather to Learn

❖ Greet the class members and introduce guests.

❖ Pray that those who have come today will be ready to hear and evaluate the testimony of John the Baptist.

❖ Discuss these questions with the class:

1. **Have you ever served on a jury or watched a television show involving a trial?**

2. **If so, how did you as a juror or an observer evaluate the evidence to determine whether the testimony of the prosecution's witnesses or those of the defendant carried greater weight?**

❖ Note that today we will be examining the testimony of John the Baptist concerning the identity of Jesus.

❖ Read aloud today's focus statement: **In a world of competing religious and political values, people are not always clear that one system is of any greater value than another. How can Christians know which set of beliefs carries more weight than all others? John testifies that the baptism of the Holy Spirit surpasses water baptism and that the Spirit bears witness that Jesus is God's Son.**

(2) Goal 1: Explore John's Account of Jesus' Baptism

❖ Select a volunteer to read John 1:29-34.
  ❖ Discuss these questions:
  1. **What does John report about who Jesus is?** (See "Who Is Jesus?" in Interpreting the Scripture.)
  2. **According to John, what do we receive from Jesus?** (See "What Does Jesus Give Us?" in Interpreting the Scripture.)
  3. **According to John, when does one receive the Spirit?** (See "Baptism and the Spirit" in Interpreting the Scripture.)
  4. **According to John, what can believers do as a result of the presence of the Spirit?** (See "The Spirit as the Presence of God" in Interpreting the Scripture.)
  5. Look again at John 1:32-34. Discuss what John actually reports about Jesus' baptism. **Having baptized Jesus, what is John's testimony about the relationship among the Father, Jesus, and the Spirit?**

(3) Goal 2: Relive Emotions Felt While Observing or Participating in a Baptism

❖ Encourage the students to recall a baptism they have participated in, perhaps their own or that of a child or godchild, or one that they have witnessed, perhaps as a member of a congregation. Invite them to call out words that describe their emotions in the midst of this sacrament. List these words on newsprint.
  ❖ Review the list and ask:
  1. **Which of these emotions concerns (1) cuteness of the child, (2) the joy of the parents, and (3) the spiritual dimension of welcoming a new life into the community of faith? Write the appropriate number next to each word.**
  2. **If most of the emotions concern the baby or the parents, how can we help our members recognize the importance of the spiritual dimension of the sacrament of baptism?**

(4) Goal 3: Assess How the Learners Live Out Their Baptismal Covenant

❖ Distribute copies of your church's baptismal covenant(s), which are often found in denominational hymnals. Invite the adults to turn to the covenant, or to page through the different baptismal services that are approved by their denomination. Discuss what the candidate for baptism or parents of this candidate are promising to do.
❖ Read these words from "Baptismal Covenant II," found on page 43 of *The United Methodist Hymnal*:

Through baptism
you are incorporated by the Holy Spirit
　into God's new creation
and made to share in Christ's royal priesthood.
We are all one in Christ Jesus.
With joy and thanksgiving we welcome you
　as *members* of the family of Christ.

❖ Distribute paper and pencils. Ask the students to choose one or two of these questions, which you will post on newsprint, and comment on it.

1. What do you understand to be the role of the Holy Spirit in your life?
2. In what ways are you living out your baptismal covenant by participating in Christ's royal priesthood?
3. How do you reach out to non-believers to invite them into the church community, and to believers to demonstrate that all are one in Christ Jesus?
4. In sum, how would you say that your life is a testimony to Jesus?

❖ Bring everyone together and call on volunteers to share one of their responses. Wrap up the discussion by encouraging everyone to recognize the depth of the baptismal covenant and the way that they do live out—or could live out—the promises made at their baptism.

(5) Continue the Journey

❖ Pray that as the learners depart, they will make a commitment to live out their baptismal covenant and offer reliable testimony about Jesus to others.

❖ Post information for next week's session on newsprint for the students to copy:
- Title: Jesus Promises an Advocate
- Background Scripture: John 14:15-26
- Lesson Scripture: John 14:15-26
- Focus of the Lesson: There are times when people know what is right, but struggle to follow through as they should. What motivates one to make the right choices? Jesus said that he would send the Holy Spirit to help his followers to love God and live according to God's commandments.

❖ Challenge the adults to grow spiritually by completing one or more of these activities related to this week's session, which you have posted on newsprint for the students to copy.

(1) Consider the vows you made or that were made in your name at baptism. How are you living out these promises? What changes might you need to make to be more faithful to these vows?

(2) Write a journal entry concerning a baptism you have participated in or witnessed. Who was present? What happened? What was your perception of this event? How did your involvement with the sacrament of baptism enable you to grow spiritually?

(3) Share you testimony about how God has worked and is working in your life with

someone who needs to ex-
perience the love, saving
grace, and forgiveness of
God.

❖ Sing or read aloud "When Jesus
Came to Jordan."

❖ Conclude today's session by
leading the class in this benediction
adapted from 1 Corinthians 12:13,
which is the key verse for the lesson
for May 17: **Let us go forth rejoicing
that in the one Spirit we were all
baptized into one body—Jews or
Greeks, slaves or free—and we were
all made to drink of one Spirit.**

UNIT 1: THE PLEDGE OF GOD'S PRESENCE
JESUS PROMISES AN ADVOCATE

PREVIEWING THE LESSON

Lesson Scripture: John 14:15-26
Background Scripture: John 14:15-26
Key Verse: John 14:26

Focus of the Lesson:

There are times when people know what is right, but struggle to follow through as they should. What motivates one to make the right choices? Jesus said that he would send the Holy Spirit to help his followers to love God and live according to God's commandments.

Goals for the Learners:

(1) to understand the significance of the Holy Spirit.
(2) to recognize the power available through the Holy Spirit.
(3) to pray for the guidance of the Holy Spirit in making decisions.

Pronunciation Guide:

Paraclete (pair´ uh kleet)   *parakletos* (par ak´ lay tos)

Supplies:

Bibles, newsprint and marker, paper and pencils, hymnals

READING THE SCRIPTURE

NRSV

Lesson Scripture: John 14:15-26

¹⁵"If you love me, you will keep my commandments. ¹⁶And I will ask the Father, and he will give you another Advocate, to be with you forever. ¹⁷This is the Spirit of truth, whom the world cannot receive, because it neither sees him nor knows him. You

CEB

Lesson Scripture: John 14:15-26

¹⁵"If you love me, you will keep my commandments. ¹⁶I will ask the Father, and he will send another Companion, who will be with you forever. ¹⁷This Companion is the Spirit of Truth, whom the world can't receive because it neither sees him

know him, because he abides with you, and he will be in you.

¹⁸"I will not leave you orphaned; I am coming to you. ¹⁹In a little while the world will no longer see me, but you will see me; because I live, you also will live. ²⁰On that day you will know that I am in my Father, and you in me, and I in you. ²¹They who have my commandments and keep them are those who love me; and those who love me will be loved by my Father, and I will love them and reveal myself to them." ²²Judas (not Iscariot) said to him, "Lord, how is it that you will reveal yourself to us, and not to the world?" ²³Jesus answered him, "Those who love me will keep my word, and my Father will love them, and we will come to them and make our home with them. ²⁴Whoever does not love me does not keep my words; and the word that you hear is not mine, but is from the Father who sent me.

²⁵"I have said these things to you while I am still with you. ²⁶But the Advocate, the Holy Spirit, whom the Father will send in my name, will teach you everything, and remind you of all that I have said to you.

nor recognizes him. You know him, because he lives with you and will be with you.

¹⁸"I won't leave you as orphans. I will come to you. ¹⁹Soon the world will no longer see me, but you will see me. Because I live, you will live too. ²⁰On that day you will know that I am in my Father, you are in me, and I am in you. ²¹Whoever has my commandments and keeps them loves me. Whoever loves me will be loved by my Father, and I will love them and reveal myself to them."

²²Judas (not Judas Iscariot) asked, "Lord, why are you about to reveal yourself to us and not to the world?" ²³Jesus answered, "Whoever loves me will keep my word. My Father will love them, and we will come to them and make our home with them. ²⁴Whoever doesn't love me doesn't keep my words. The word that you hear isn't mine. It is the word of the Father who sent me.

²⁵"I have spoken these things to you while I am with you. ²⁶The Companion, the Holy Spirit, whom the Father will send in my name, will teach you everything and will remind you of everything I told you.

UNDERSTANDING THE SCRIPTURE

Introduction. Chapters 14–17 of John are known as the "Farewell Discourse." The material in these chapters is primarily a series of monologues by Jesus. Although there are some questions by the disciples, these serve only to allow Jesus to expand on the topics he has already introduced. The Farewell Discourse is part of John's story of the Last Supper. At the end of the supper and just before they all leave to go to Gethsemane, Jesus explains to the disciples that he is about to leave them. They will no longer have him in their midst as they have had during his ministry, but this long speech intends to assure them that they will not be alone. God will be with them and so will Christ, though in a different way. Jesus speaks of the connection between himself and the disciples in various ways. The most prominent way Jesus talks about this continuing presence among them is his promise to send the Spirit. Our passage today is the first explanation of the coming of the Spirit in the Farewell Discourse.

John 14:15-17. Having just told the disciples he is leaving them but assuring them that he will be an advocate for them before God, Jesus now tells the disciples how they must respond. Jesus says that if they love him they will keep his commandments. Here and three more times in this reading (14:21, 23, 24) John links loving Christ and living as he commands. John emphasizes that believers must live as Christ commands if they expect to continue to receive the blessings described in this section. So the presence of Christ in believers' lives demands that the persons live the proper kind of life. If they live in this way, Christ promises them *another* comforter. Whatever John says the Spirit will do here, Jesus has been doing for the disciples while he is with them. In essence, the Spirit fills the void left by the presence of Jesus.

The NRSV translation says that Jesus will send another "Advocate," while the CEB says he will send another "Companion." The Greek word that appears here in John can mean a number of things. It may describe one who encourages others or give them comfort. But it may also designate someone who advocates for others. The CEB translates the term as it does because the Spirit keeps the disciples from being left alone. The Spirit serves as the continuing presence of God among the disciples. In place of the presence of Jesus, the Spirit brings comfort and encouragement, and advocates for their good.

But the Spirit does yet more because it is the Spirit of truth. The rest of the world does not recognize or accept the Spirit because it does not recognize the truth about Christ and the knowledge of God he brings. This Spirit, Jesus says, will embrace the community of believers so that they will understand Christ and experience the presence of God.

John 14:18-21. Jesus again emphasizes that his departure (his death and resurrection) does not mean that he will desert his disciples. But his presence with them will not be in a way that the rest of the world can perceive. Though he will have been killed, he will be alive and "in the Father" (14:20). In this position, his life will infuse believers because they are "in him," that is, identified with him and drawn into his life. This promise of the presence of God renews Jesus' call for the disciples to obey his commands. The stakes are even raised a bit as Jesus says not only that they show their love for him by keeping the commands but also that the person who shows love for Christ in this way will be loved by God. Further, the people who obey these commands are the ones Christ will continue to be with. The promise of the continuing presence of Christ, then, is contingent on the proper response to the gift of salvation.

John 14:22-24. When we remember that this teaching of Jesus comes while he is standing among the disciples, we will not be surprised at Judas's response. He wants to know how it is possible for Jesus to be seen by them but not by everyone else. Jesus' response is not quite direct. He explains that he will come to and be present with only those who show their love for him by living as he commands. This is understandable only after Christ's death and resurrection. Only then does Christ possess a kind of life that makes it possible for him to be in the lives of some but not in those of others who are in the same physical location. After the Resurrection, he can be present with them in a nonphysical manner; he will be present through the Spirit. Jesus also assures them that what he is telling them comes from God.

John 14:25-26. Jesus tells the disciples these things while he is with them so they will not be overly discouraged when he leaves them in death. Jesus' departure makes way for the coming of the Spirit. Note that God remains the primary actor. God is the One who sends the Spirit. While in many ways the Holy Spirit is seen here as the Spirit of Christ, it is finally the Spirit sent by God, just as Christ has been the One sent by God throughout John's Gospel. The Spirit's purpose here is to teach and remind. Given that the Spirit "reminds," this aspect of the Spirit's presence seems to be addressed to the disciples rather than all believers. Yet John may well think that the Spirit continues to help the church discern the will of God. Some interpreters have gone so far as seeing this as an affirmation of the truth of church tradition. This seems unlikely for John, since that tradition had hardly begun to be recognizable when this Gospel was written. Still, he probably sees the Spirit as an aid in the church's deliberations about the will of God. He may even think that this aid in discernment extends to helping the church remember the most appropriate teaching of Jesus to address a particular question or situation.

INTERPRETING THE SCRIPTURE

The Spirit as Assurance

As Jesus tells the disciples that he is leaving them, he also tells them he will not be absent from their lives. Through the Spirit he will be with them as another Paraclete (*paraletos*). In this role the Spirit gives believers assurance of the presence of Christ in their lives. In this place in John's story, the most immediate cause for discouragement will be the death of Jesus. John, however, expects readers to experience the seeming absence of Christ in various ways. The original readers of this Gospel were ostracized from the religious community of their birth and from their social and economic contacts. They know what it is like to feel forsaken. This word from Jesus provides important encouragement. He says that despite what the outward circumstances look like, or even feel like, believers are not alone. God has not abandoned them. If they remain faithful, God promises to be with them. This presence does not take away the difficult situation or remove the pain that comes with it. It does, however, offer assurance that God remains faithful. Suffering does not mean that God is absent. God suffers with us and for us. The Spirit in our lives helps to renew and strengthen this confidence. And not only is God now present with us but the Spirit also assures believers of continuing and future life with God. However difficult the present is, the Spirit is with us and in us. The Spirit assures us that God loves us and that God will complete the work of salvation that the gift of the Spirit shows has already begun.

The Spirit as Advocate

In addition to offering comfort and assurance, the Spirit serves as an Advocate for believers, as one who takes up their cause. Just as Jesus works for the good of those who have faith, so the Spirit works for our salvation. The Spirit works for our good by revealing the truth. The Spirit brings us truth about who God is and what God has done for us in Christ. We may see this as a work that had its primary time of activity in the formation of Scripture and the early church, but the Spirit continues this work by confirming the truth of that earlier revelation in the hearts of believers. The Spirit, then, works for our good by helping us to recognize the truth of God's will.

Beyond this work in our own hearts, the Spirit's work as Advocate extends to aiding us in bringing our deepest needs to God. In Romans 8:26-27 Paul says we do not know how we ought to pray or how to pray in accordance with God's will. We find ourselves unable to discern God's will because we live in a world that lures us to desire things that are harmful to ourselves or our neighbors. Even with the Spirit in us, we are drawn to destructive and injurious thoughts and actions. The indwelling Spirit searches our inner selves for our true needs and brings those to God for us. So God both acts to save us in Christ and enables us to want what is best for us and what keeps us in the proper relationship with God. Through the Spirit, then, God continues to work on our behalf so that the salvation already begun will bear its full fruit at the end.

The Necessity of Obedience

This passage emphasizes the importance of obedience. In these twelve verses, Jesus says four times (14:15, 21, 23, 24) that the way to show love for him is by obeying his commands. Jesus does not have a simple list in mind. John does not want you to search back through the Gospel to find particular commands; rather, he wants you to orient your life toward the will of God as it is seen in Christ. This word of Jesus is a call to conduct the whole of your life in the way Christ lived his life. Both the words and the life of Jesus set this pattern of living that we can identify as the "commands" of Jesus.

It is difficult at first to think about obeying commandments as an expression of love. But if we set this expectation within the context of our own relationships, it may begin to make better sense. We know that relationships come with expectations. These expectations sometimes impose a burden, but one we find acceptable because of our love for the other person. Those expectations may come in the form of avoiding certain behaviors or taking up new ways of acting. Adhering to these expectations becomes a way of showing respect and love for the other person. Over time, those new things even become part of who we are. The commands of Jesus are expectations that come from One who loves us. But these expectations are not just what Jesus wants;

they are also best for our lives. These commands enhance our lives. More than being expectations of Christ, these commands make our lives fuller and more meaningful. The Spirit not only reminds us of these expectations but also enables us to live up to them. We should neither set the demand to obey these commands in a legal context nor should we think of it in legalistic terms. Instead, setting this demand in the context of an ongoing relationship changes how the demand sounds and what it means. Just as a failure to live up to certain expectations in our marital relationship amounts to unfaithfulness to our pledge of love, so in our relationship with Christ a failure to live by his commands is a breech in our relationship with him. We show faithful love for Christ through proper living.

The Spirit as an Aid in Discernment

When John calls the Spirit the "Spirit of truth" (14:17), he means that the Spirit not only possesses God's truth but also that the Spirit conveys that truth to believers. While John has in mind the active work of providing the originating and authoritative interpretation of Jesus' life, death, and resurrection, that is not all he means. This promise of the presence of the Spirit of truth extends beyond that immediate circle of disciples; this is a promise to the church. Of course, it does not mean that the church always hears the voice of the Spirit clearly. The church has often claimed divine authorization for ungodly decisions. But Jesus promises that the Spirit will remain to continue to help the church discern the word and will of God. This seems to be what verse 26 has in view when it says that the Spirit will teach them "everything" and will remind Jesus' followers of what he taught. Again, the original statement gave authority to the apostles. But since John seems to have the broader church in mind when he speaks of the other functions of the Spirit in this passage, he also expects the Spirit to help the church discern the will of God in each successive era. While this is obviously no guarantee that the church will hear the Spirit's word, it can be encouragement that God continues to work within and among us.

SHARING THE SCRIPTURE

PREPARING TO TEACH

Preparing Our Hearts

Meditate on this week's devotional reading from Psalm 23. What memories or special associations come to mind when you think of this beloved psalm? In what ways does the Shepherd express love and care for the flock? How do you experience the Shepherd as a comforter in your life?

Pray that you and the students will be aware of and give thanks for the comforting Shepherd.

Preparing Our Minds

Study the background Scripture and the lesson Scripture, which are both from John 14:15-26.

Consider this question as you prepare the lesson: *What motivates people to make the right choices?*

Write on newsprint:

❑ information for next week's lesson, found under "Continue the Journey."

❑ activities for further spiritual growth in "Continue the Journey."

Review the "Introduction," "The Big Picture," "Close-up," and "Faith in Action," which all precede the first lesson of this quarter. Consider how you might use any of this material in today's lesson.

LEADING THE CLASS

(1) Gather to Learn

❖ Greet the class members and introduce guests.

❖ Pray that those who have come today will recognize the work and power of the Holy Spirit in their lives.

❖ Note that today we will be considering how we are guided to make sound choices. Read: **Psychologist Lawrence Kohlberg developed a theory of moral reasoning that includes six stages that people may progress through, though some people may remain fixed in a particular stage and not move further. In Stage 1 rules are viewed as rigid; people choose to obey them in order to avoid punishment. In Stage 2, people make moral decisions on the basis of rewards they hope to gain, rather than punishments that they hope to avoid. By the teen years, most people are concerned about conforming to social norms that enable them to enjoy good relationships with others and so move to Stage 3. In Stage 4, people look beyond their own needs and base moral judgments on attempts to maintain the social order and show** respect for authority. **People at Stage 5 recognize that there are competing values and so may disobey the rules in order to bring about change, if they find them to be inconsistent with their values. In Stage 6, which is seldom achieved on a continuing basis, people put themselves in the shoes of others and follow a universal ethical principle, regardless of the laws.**

❖ Read aloud today's focus statement: **There are times when people know what is right, but struggle to follow through as they should. What motivates one to make the right choices? Jesus said that he would send the Holy Spirit to help his followers to love God and live according to God's commandments.**

(2) Goal 1: Understand the Significance of the Holy Spirit

❖ Begin by asking: **What do you know about the Holy Spirit?** (Use all or part of "Close-up: Who Is the Holy Spirit?" found at the beginning of this quarter to help the students understand the nature and work of the Holy Spirit.)

❖ Choose a volunteer to read John 14:15-26.

❖ Discuss these questions, adding information from Understanding the Scripture as you find it helpful:

1. **What does Jesus tell the disciples about the Holy Spirit?**

2. **What connections does Jesus make between obedience and love?**

3. **How would you have felt had you been present to hear Jesus' words?**

❖ Read or retell "The Spirit as Advocate" in Interpreting the Scripture.

(3) Goal 2: Recognize the Power Available Through the Holy Spirit

❖ Read in unison today's key verse, John 14:26.

❖ Note that in verse 26, Jesus refers to the Holy Spirit as the Paraclete, from a Greek word that can be translated as "Advocate," "Comforter," "Counselor," or "Helper." Ask: **How does each of these words enable you to better understand and appreciate the relationship that the Spirit desires to have with you?**

❖ Point out that in John's Gospel Jesus makes reference to the coming of the Holy Spirit not only in 15:26-27 but also in 14:16-17, 26; and 16:7. Invite the learners to look at the two verses in chapter 15 to discern Jesus' promises about the Spirit, what the Spirit will do, and how believers are to respond.

❖ Ask: **Given that the Paraclete is the link between the ministry of the incarnate Jesus and the church as it exists after his death, why do you think that in many churches the Spirit is often the overlooked member of the Trinity?**

(4) Goal 3: Pray for the Guidance of the Holy Spirit in Making Decisions

❖ Read or retell "The Spirit as an Aid in Discernment" in Interpreting the Scripture.

❖ Ask: **What means might the Spirit use to help Christians make decisions?** Write on newsprint ideas that may include the Scriptures, circumstances that clearly favor one course of action, inspiration received through a sermon or prayer, or the words of a friend.

❖ Encourage the adults to be in an attitude of prayer and meditation as they softly sing or read "Spirit of the Living God." Prior to singing, suggest that as the song concludes, they close their eyes and pray for the Spirit's help in making a decision that they are facing. If they have no personal decisions to make, suggest that they offer prayer for whoever needs to make a decision that will have an impact on the church or a group of people.

(5) Continue the Journey

❖ Break the silence by praying that as the learners depart, they will continue to seek the guidance of the Holy Spirit, trusting that the Spirit will stand with them as they make a decision and act.

❖ Post information for next week's session on newsprint for the students to copy:

- **Title: The Spirit of Truth**
- **Background Scripture: John 16:4b-15**
- **Lesson Scripture: John 16:4b-15**
- **Focus of the Lesson: It may be difficult to maintain a direction in life when a mentor is lost. How do people find the resources to carry on when the strength and vision of someone close to them is no longer available? Jesus promised his disciples that the Holy Spirit would be as real a presence to them as his physical presence was while he lived with them on earth.**

❖ Challenge the adults to grow spiritually by completing one or more of these activities related to this week's session, which you have posted on newsprint for the students to copy.

(1) Make a conscious effort to recognize how you are being guided to make decisions, especially those that affect other people or are important to your own life. What role does the Holy Spirit play?

(2) Identify an important decision that your church, family, community, or country must soon make. Pray that those in positions of authority will be led by the Holy Spirit to make a decision that reflects the moral and ethical teachings of Jesus.

(3) Stand at the side of someone who is ill, grieving, or in the midst of a crisis. Serve as a comforter and advocate for this person. Call upon the Holy Spirit in prayer to guide you both.

❖ Sing or read aloud "Holy Spirit, Come, Confirm Us."

❖ Conclude today's session by leading the class in this benediction adapted from 1 Corinthians 12:13, which is the key verse for the lesson for May 17: **Let us go forth rejoicing that in the one Spirit we were all baptized into one body—Jews or Greeks, slaves or free—and we were all made to drink of one Spirit.**

UNIT 1: THE PLEDGE OF GOD'S PRESENCE
THE SPIRIT OF TRUTH

PREVIEWING THE LESSON

Lesson Scripture: John 16:4b-15
Background Scripture: John 16:4b-15
Key Verse: John 16:7

Focus of the Lesson:
It may be difficult to maintain a direction in life when a mentor is lost. How do people find the resources to carry on when the strength and vision of someone close to them is no longer available? Jesus promised his disciples that the Holy Spirit would be as real a presence to them as his physical presence was while he lived with them on earth.

Goals for the Learners:
(1) to learn what Jesus says about how the Holy Spirit works on our behalf.
(2) to express feelings about loss of those close to them and the subsequent support received.
(3) to tell others about how the Holy Spirit works on their behalf.

Supplies:
Bibles, newsprint and marker, paper and pencils, hymnals

READING THE SCRIPTURE

NRSV
Lesson Scripture: John 16:4b-15
"I did not say these things to you from the beginning, because I was with you. ⁵But now I am going to him who sent me; yet none of you asks me, 'Where are you going?' ⁶But because I have said these things to you, sorrow has filled your hearts. ⁷Nevertheless **I tell you the truth: it**

CEB
Lesson Scripture: John 16:4b-15
"I didn't say these things to you from the beginning, because I was with you. ⁵But now I go away to the one who sent me. None of you ask me, 'Where are you going?' ⁶Yet because I have said these things to you, you are filled with sorrow. **⁷I assure you that it is better for you that I go away. If I**

is to your advantage that I go away, for if I do not go away, the Advocate will not come to you; but if I go, I will send him to you. ⁸And when he comes, he will prove the world wrong about sin and righteousness and judgment: ⁹about sin, because they do not believe in me; ¹⁰about righteousness, because I am going to the Father and you will see me no longer; ¹¹about judgment, because the ruler of this world has been condemned.

¹²"I still have many things to say to you, but you cannot bear them now. ¹³When the Spirit of truth comes, he will guide you into all the truth; for he will not speak on his own, but will speak whatever he hears, and he will declare to you the things that are to come. ¹⁴He will glorify me, because he will take what is mine and declare it to you. ¹⁵All that the Father has is mine. For this reason I said that he will take what is mine and declare it to you.

don't go away, the Companion won't come to you. But if I go, I will send him to you. ⁸When he comes, he will show the world it was wrong about sin, righteousness, and judgment. ⁹He will show the world it was wrong about sin because they don't believe in me. ¹⁰He will show the world it was wrong about righteousness because I'm going to the Father and you won't see me anymore. ¹¹He will show the world it was wrong about judgment because this world's ruler stands condemned.

¹²"I have much more to say to you, but you can't handle it now. ¹³However, when the Spirit of Truth comes, he will guide you in all truth. He won't speak on his own, but will say whatever he hears and will proclaim to you what is to come. ¹⁴He will glorify me, because he will take what is mine and proclaim it to you. ¹⁵Everything that the Father has is mine. That's why I said that the Spirit takes what is mine and will proclaim it to you.

UNDERSTANDING THE SCRIPTURE

Introduction. Chapter 16 is a part of the Farewell Discourse, as have been the readings of the previous two Sundays. There is some repetition throughout this section as John has Jesus go over the same points in multiple ways so that the readers understand the points as clearly as possible. In this reading, we return to and give greater attention to the role of the Spirit as the One who helps the disciples understand God's will and also to the meaning of Christ's ministry and death.

John 16:4b-7. Jesus tells the disciples that he has not taught them

all they need to know. One of the recurring literary devices in John's Gospel is that Jesus says something confusing and then explains what he means when his hearer does not understand. Not only does this serve John's purposes in individual stories (for example, Nicodemus in chapter 3 and the woman at the well in chapter 4), but here it also seems to be a way to understand Jesus' ministry as a whole. John does not just want the people in the stories to seem dull or dimwitted. Instead, he wants a chance for Jesus to explain the topic, not just for the person in the story but also for the reader. But at this point in John we hear that there are things Jesus has not even told the disciples. Given the point in Jesus' life where we are in this Gospel, the main thing they do not know is how to understand his death and resurrection. This unexpected and troubling turn of events seems to defy any reasonable explanation. Jesus here assures the readers that the interpretation that the disciples, and especially the Beloved Disciple, give to his death and resurrection is correct.

John assumes that no one, including the disciples, can understand who Jesus is or what he means for the world until after the crucifixion and Resurrection. This is why Jesus must go. Earlier in this Gospel, John provided readers with an aside that tells them that the disciples did not, and will not, understand a particular act of Jesus until after his resurrection (see, for example, 12:16). The implication is that you cannot fully understand Jesus and his teachings until after that event. The Spirit comes to guide the disciples into the new truth that the death and resurrection of Christ make it possible for believers to know.

John 16:8-11. While assuring the disciples that they understand Christ correctly, the Spirit also functions to convict outsiders of three things. The first is about sin. They are convicted about, perhaps even by, their sin because they refuse to believe in Jesus and so accept God's forgiveness. Second, they are convicted about righteousness because Christ has shown them what real righteousness is, and that way of living is validated by the Resurrection. Third, they are convicted about judgment because the "ruler of this world" (16:11) is judged.

John seems to see Christ's death and resurrection as a demonstration that the powers that govern the present have been rejected and defeated by God in that death and resurrection. As did all early Christians, John sees the world as a place that has been taken over by evil powers. Sometimes they are assigned particular names (such as Satan); other times they are just referred to by a title as they are here. Either way, John sees a contest between God and other beings for control of the world. The world has been given over to these evil powers in the present. But God's resurrection of Christ is the clear evidence that God has more power. In addition, that resurrection is the promise that God will use that superior power to set things right. So while the Resurrection is a sign of hope for believers, it is also a sign to the powers of evil that God will triumph and that they will be held accountable for their evil deeds. The Spirit reveals both of these meanings.

John 16:12-15. It seems important at this point for Jesus to repeat that the disciples do not have all they need to understand what is about to happen to him. Jesus says they are not yet able to understand, but that they will be. The central function Jesus assigns to the Spirit in this reading is that of helping the disciples understand his death and resurrection. Once they see these events, they will be ready to understand the full truth about Christ. Jesus offers another bit of assurance about what they receive through the Spirit when he tells them that the Spirit does not act apart from the word and will of Christ. The Spirit speaks only what Christ says. The fullness of the truth that the Spirit will provide comes from the resurrected Christ who is with God. Indeed, Christ is more than with God. God has given all things to Christ. Thus, the fullest possible understanding of God is the understanding that is open to believers and comes through Christ and his sending of the Spirit to reveal those things to the disciples. What the Spirit reveals is from God, mediated through Christ.

Readers need to recognize what Jesus identifies as the purpose of the Spirit's work of revealing the truth: The Spirit will glorify Christ (16:14). The Spirit's purpose is to show believers the fullness of who Jesus is and what he has accomplished. When those things are understood clearly, believers will honor Christ as they should because they will recognize his splendor. So the Spirit's work is to point to Christ as the Spirit brings revelation about who Christ is and who God is. At the same time, the Spirit assures God's people of their future with God and shows them what God expects of them. All things from God come to God's people through the Spirit. But all of this must await the death and resurrection of Christ because those are the central events that reveal who God and Christ are. The Spirit ensures that the disciples understand those crucial events properly.

INTERPRETING THE SCRIPTURE

The Spirit as Interpreter for the Church

This week's Scripture passage sets out some important functions of the Spirit. In its most immediate meaning, Jesus assures the disciples that they will not be left on their own when he is gone. Of course, the first questions that would come to their minds is why Jesus was gone and what that means about who he was and what his life meant. This passage offers assurance not only to the disciples but also to the church. The presence of the Spirit does something essential for the whole church. Jesus says that the Spirit will show the disciples the meaning of the death and resurrection of Christ. We may be accustomed to knowing about the Crucifixion as the conclusion of the ministry of Christ, but the early church found it to be profoundly difficult to understand or explain. How could it be that the will of God is accomplished through the execution of the messenger of God? Everyone expected God to be seen in power, not in death. These verses assure the church that the disciples, who are now the apostles, have understood the life, ministry, death, and resurrection correctly. The church can trust what the apostles say because Jesus promises that this interpretation of his life and death comes from Jesus himself. The Spirit speaks what Christ gives it to speak.

The message John has about Christ can only be complete after his telling of the Crucifixion and Resurrection. Jesus could not tell the disciples the meaning of his death with any thoroughness. They had to experience that death before they were able to understand it. So while Jesus assures the disciples that they will understand, the church is also assured that what it says his death means comes from God, through Christ, by means of the Spirit. This is powerful affirmation of the truth of the Gospel of John and of all the apostolic teaching that the church receives through Scripture.

The Spirit Speaks to the Church

The most immediate meaning of Jesus' words to the disciples in this passage applies to the disciples themselves and their teaching about the meaning of Jesus. But the promise of the giving of the Spirit goes beyond those who were immediately present to hear these words. Scripture continues to reveal the word of God and to mediate the will of God to the church. Even beyond the word of God we hear in Scripture, the Spirit continues to speak to the church. Some of that guidance we recognize as the traditions that make up the creeds we recite and the confessions that shape our various churches. We recognize in these traditions formulations of the truths about God that the church continues to receive through its reading of Scripture and its attempts to interpret that word for a new day. As times change, how we need to express our beliefs about God needs to develop so that we speak in language that is meaningful both within the church and among those outside it. This does not mean that the truth of God changes or that the character of God changes. It simply means that the church needs ways to communicate those truths that speak to the world in which it lives. We rely on the Spirit to help us remain faithful to the gospel while we find those new ways to deepen our understanding and offer the gospel to others.

This revealing presence of the Spirit is not, then, limited to the past.

The Spirit continues to be with the church today as the church seeks to discern the will of God. The church continues to face questions that are difficult to respond to. The new cultural contexts in which the church finds itself often call for a reassessment of what God would have us do. In past decades the church wrestled with whether women should be leaders. It was with the help of the Spirit that the church read its Scriptures and thought about what their message means for a new day. As we face difficult and even divisive issues today, we can ask the Spirit to lead us in our deliberations, to be with us as we see the ways God is moving in the lives of the people around us. We can move forward with less fear when we recognize that God is still among us through the Spirit, moving us toward what God wants for God's people and the world.

The Spirit as Presence of God in Our lives

This passage can also bring us assurance that God is with us in all the times of our lives. The Spirit is not only with the gathered church, it is always with each of us. New Testament writers see the presence of the Spirit as one of the new gifts that Christ gives to believers. Because of Christ, God dwells with and in every believer. This is so certain that Paul says that if you do not have the Spirit, you are not a Christian (Romans 8:9). As the presence of God in our lives, the Spirit can bring us comfort and assurance. It can let us know that we do not face the difficulties of our lives alone. However desperate or difficult the experience may be, God is with us. This will not take the problem away, but we can be certain that God is with us, suffering with us and wanting the best for us. Christians are never without that gift of the presence of God, even when we do not feel it. This is the promise of the Spirit in our lives. This indwelling of the Spirit also gives us strength to face our problems and challenges. God does not promise that we can overcome every challenge, but God does promise to remain a constant and loving presence in us and with us even when challenges are so great that they seem to overcome us.

The Spirit Enables Believers to Live for God

The gift of the Spirit also supports us as we strive to live for God. One of the promises that comes with the indwelling Spirit that Jesus promises is that God will enable us to live as we should. We all know how difficult

it is to resist adopting attitudes and behaviors that do not reflect the love and justice of God. We are constantly drawn to seek our own good rather than that of others. We are pulled to accept the values that shape our world. Resisting things such as greed and self-centeredness is difficult. In fact, the New Testament teaches that it is impossible to resist the pull of sin on our own. One of the great gifts of having the indwelling Spirit is that it enables us to live for God more fully. The revelation of who God is helps us to see what is truly good for us and those around us. Then it enables us to resist things that diminish our lives, even though they look appealing. The Spirit helps us want those things that bring fullness and meaning to life. So while helping us live as God calls us to live, the Spirit simultaneously brings us a richer experience of life.

SHARING THE SCRIPTURE

PREPARING TO TEACH

Preparing Our Hearts

Meditate on this week's devotional reading from 1 Samuel 3:1-10, which tells the story of the priest Eli mentoring the young Samuel, who was called by God. How does Samuel help Eli? Who has been a spiritual mentor in your life? How has this person helped you to grow in your relationship with God?

Pray that you and the students will give thanks for all who have inspired and mentored you.

Preparing Our Minds

Study the background Scripture and the lesson Scripture, which are both from John 16:4b-15.

Consider this question as you prepare the lesson: *How do people find the resources to carry on when one who has been a mentor and advocate is no longer available?*

Write on newsprint:
❏ information for next week's lesson, found under "Continue the Journey."
❏ activities for further spiritual growth in "Continue the Journey."

Review the "Introduction," "The Big Picture," "Close-up," and "Faith in Action," which all precede the first lesson of this quarter. Consider how you might use any of this material in today's lesson.

Prepare a lecture based on the information in Understanding the Scripture for "Learn What Jesus Says about How the Holy Spirit Works on Our Behalf."

LEADING THE CLASS

(1) Gather to Learn

❖ Greet the class members and introduce guests.

❖ Pray that those who have come today will seek the presence of the Holy Spirit.

❖ Read this quotation from Bob Mumford: **"When Christ's abiding presence becomes our guide, then guidance becomes an almost unconscious response to the gentle moving of the Holy Spirit within us."**

❖ Invite the adults to think silently about how they are able to experience Christ, even though he is no longer physically present on the earth. Call on several volunteers to share any insights they may have.

❖ Read aloud today's focus statement: **It may be difficult to maintain a direction in life when a mentor is lost. How do people find the resources to carry on when the strength and vision of someone close to them is no longer available? Jesus promised his disciples that the Holy Spirit would be as real a presence to them as his physical presence was while he lived with them on earth.**

(2) Goal 1: Learn What Jesus Says about How the Holy Spirit Works on Our Behalf

❖ Solicit a volunteer to read John 16:4b-15 as if Jesus is speaking to the class.

❖ Present the lecture you have prepared from the Understanding the Scripture portion to help the students understand what Jesus says about the Holy Spirit in this passage from John 16.

❖ Read or retell "The Spirit Speaks to the Church" in Interpreting the Scripture.

❖ Discuss these questions:
1. **Where do you see evidence that the Spirit is working in the church at large today?**
2. **Where do you see evidence that the Spirit is at work in your congregation?**

(3) Goal 2: Express Feelings about the Loss of Those Close to Them and the Subsequent Support Received

❖ Invite each student to talk with a partner about someone who has been important to him or her in terms of faith formation. This person may be a pastor, Sunday school teacher, coach, coworker, friend, or family member. Suggest that the partners share information about these people's character and how they provided guidance.

❖ Bring everyone together and ask: **If the person you identified is no longer in your life, how did you feel when you lost this person's counsel?**

❖ Distribute paper and pencils. Encourage the adults to write a letter to this person (living or deceased) expressing gratitude for the role he or she played in the learner's life. Call on several volunteers to read their letters, or briefly tell the content. Suggest that these letters be edited at home and then sent to the person if possible. If the person is deceased or contact information has been lost, keep this letter as a remembrance.

(4) Goal 3: Tell Others about How the Holy Spirit Works on Their Behalf

❖ Read: **In a 1953 letter to Sheldon Van Auken, C. S. Lewis wrote, "Think of me as a fellow patient in the same hospital who, having been admitted a little earlier, [could] give some advice." This statement summarizes a facet of the role of a mentor. In addition to giving advice, mentors also model behavior for and develop relationships with the one being mentored. We just recalled how our own mentors had an impact on our lives. Let's think now about how we can have an impact on the lives of others by serving as mentors for them.**

❖ Suggest that the adults write the name of at least one person to whom they could be a mentor in the faith. This may be a young person, perhaps a child or grandchild, but it could also be an adult who is new to the faith. The thought of being a spiritual mentor may be daunting, so ask: **What reasons can you give for not wanting to assume the responsibility of mentoring someone else?** (Answers may include a lack of time, a lack of knowledge to share, a lack of experience because they have not had faith mentors of their own, or feelings that "I'm not a mature enough Christian to help anyone else.")

❖ Provide assurance that the students are able to mentor others by reading these statements:

- **You are not alone; the Spirit is with you.**
- **You have had experiences with Jesus, and the Spirit will give you words to help others understand how he has worked in your life.**
- **The basic tenets of the Christian faith are found in "The Apostles' Creed," which you likely know well.**
- **You are currently in a class that studies the Scriptures and have probably studied the Bible for years.**
- **Most of you can rearrange your schedules to make room for important priorities, such as mentoring.**

❖ Conclude by reading "The Spirit Enables Believers to Live for God" in Interpreting the Scripture.

(5) Continue the Journey

❖ Pray that as the learners depart, they will give thanks for the Holy Spirit and do all in their power to let others know the good news of the Spirit's comforting presence.

❖ Post information for next week's session on newsprint for the students to copy:

- **Title: Receive the Holy Spirit**
- **Background Scripture: John 20:19-23; Acts 1:4-8; 2:1-4**
- **Lesson Scripture: John 20:19-23**
- **Focus of the Lesson: A charismatic speaker can often lift and inspire an attentive audience. What is done and said to bring about such an effect? Jesus speaks peace to and empowers the disciples with the gift of the Holy Spirit.**

❖ Challenge the adults to grow spiritually by completing one or more of these activities related to this week's session, which you have posted on newsprint for the students to copy.

(1) **Act as a mentor for a young person or new Christian. Help this person to recognize the role that the Holy Spirit plays in one's spiritual life.**

(2) **Name and give thanks for those who have been mentors for you.**

(3) **Talk with other believers about their understanding of the person and work of the Holy Spirit.**

❖ Sing or read aloud "Spirit of Faith, Come Down."

❖ Conclude today's session by leading the class in this benediction adapted from 1 Corinthians 12:13, which is the key verse for the lesson for May 17: **Let us go forth rejoicing that in the one Spirit we were all baptized into one body—Jews or Greeks, slaves or free—and we were all made to drink of one Spirit.**

UNIT 1: THE PLEDGE OF GOD'S PRESENCE
RECEIVE THE HOLY SPIRIT

PREVIEWING THE LESSON

Lesson Scripture: John 20:19-23
Background Scripture: John 20:19-23; Acts 1:4-8; 2:1-4
Key Verse: John 20:22

Focus of the Lesson:

A charismatic speaker can often lift and inspire an attentive audience. What is done and said to bring about such an effect? Jesus speaks peace to and empowers the disciples with the gift of the Holy Spirit.

Goals for the Learners:

(1) to explore the importance of Jesus' appearance to the disciples.
(2) to describe feelings from times when the words of others calmed their fears.
(3) to fulfill the mission God has for their lives as empowered by the Holy Spirit.

Pronunciation Guide:

Docetism (doh´ suh tiz uhm)   Docetist (do ce´ tist)

Supplies:

Bibles, newsprint and marker, paper and pencils, hymnals

READING THE SCRIPTURE

NRSV

Lesson Scripture: John 20:19-23

¹⁹When it was evening on that day, the first day of the week, and the doors of the house where the disciples had met were locked for fear of the Jews, Jesus came and stood among them and said, "Peace be with you." ²⁰After he said this, he showed them his hands and his side. Then

CEB

Lesson Scripture: John 20:19-23

¹⁹It was still the first day of the week. That evening, while the disciples were behind closed doors because they were afraid of the Jewish authorities, Jesus came and stood among them. He said, "Peace be with you." ²⁰After he said this, he showed them his hands and his side. When

the disciples rejoiced when they saw the Lord. [21]Jesus said to them again, "Peace be with you. As the Father has sent me, so I send you." **[22]When he had said this, he breathed on them and said to them, "Receive the Holy Spirit.** [23]If you forgive the sins of any, they are forgiven them; if you retain the sins of any, they are retained."

the disciples saw the Lord, they were filled with joy. [21]Jesus said to them again, "Peace be with you. As the Father sent me, so I am sending you." **[22]Then he breathed on them and said, "Receive the Holy Spirit.** [23]If you forgive anyone's sins, they are forgiven; if you don't forgive them, they aren't forgiven."

UNDERSTANDING THE SCRIPTURE

Introduction. All of today's readings deal with the initial coming of the Spirit. You may notice that they are not entirely consistent in the details. These differences did not bother the authors of these texts because they are both making important points by the way they tell their stories. They are completely consistent in saying that the Spirit comes to believers through Christ. The Spirit is a gift that Christ gives to the church.

John 20:19-23. This is the first appearance of the risen Christ to the disciples in John's Gospel. It is Sunday, the first day of the week, the day of Jesus' resurrection. Mary Magdalene has told the disciples that she had seen Jesus, but they are still in hiding. Since their leader had just been executed by the authorities, they seem to have good reason for hiding until the situation calmed down. Suddenly the risen Christ appears in their midst, even though the door was locked. Jesus' first words are intended to calm them: "Peace be with you" (20:19). After he demonstrates that he is not a ghost by showing them his hands and side, he repeats his blessing of peace. It is disturbing to see the dead raised! Jesus gives them no time for questions or thanksgiving. He immediately

commissions them. They are sent into the world as emissaries for Christ, just as God had sent Christ as God's emissary. But Christ does not send them out on their own; he gives them the Spirit to strengthen them in the fulfilling of their commission.

Christ imparts the Spirit by breathing on them. This is reminiscent of God breathing on the face of the waters and breathing life into Adam in Genesis. As God gave life to the world and to Adam, now Christ gives new life to the disciples. But this is no ordinary giving of the Spirit. While the Spirit is a gift that every believer receives, Christ empowers the disciples with an extraordinary measure of the Spirit to fulfill their apostolic tasks. Christ also invests them with extraordinary authority: They have authority to forgive sins, or even to keep sin bound to a person. In this context, this power is primarily exercised through their preaching of the gospel. Because they have seen and been commissioned by Christ, they now have the authority to take the good news to the world. At the same time, this passage implies that they are the ones who have the true interpretation of Christ and his death and resurrection.

Acts 1:4-8. Luke begins Acts by telling readers that Jesus continued to appear to the disciples for forty days. At the end of this period, he tells them to remain in Jerusalem until they receive what God had promised them. From what follows, we see that this promise is the baptism of the Holy Spirit. The initial installment of the fulfillment of this promise comes on the Day of Pentecost when the Spirit comes on all those followers of Christ who are gathered in the upper room. The contrast with John the Baptist here at the beginning of Acts reminds us that the coming of the Spirit is something new. John had a valid baptism of repentance. The baptism Jesus brings, however, is greater; it is a baptism that brings the Spirit into the life of the baptized. The disciples then ask if the kingdom of Israel is about to be restored. They understood the coming of the Spirit to be a sign that the new time of the kingdom of God had arrived. Jesus says the time of the end will remain a mystery known only to God, but that the Spirit will empower them to become witnesses to what God has done in Christ. God will empower them to take this message to the entire world. Some interpreters see verse 8 as a minioutline of the whole of Acts because it foresees the spread of the gospel in the order of locations that the book subsequently has the church expand (Jerusalem, Judea, Samaria, then all the way to Rome). If this is right, then in Luke's account the Spirit is what enables that amazing spread of the church.

Acts 2:1-4. This text begins the story of the Day of Pentecost, the story of the birth of the church. Importantly, the church comes into existence through the power of the Spirit. The disciples have done as Jesus had told them and stayed in Jerusalem. It has been a bit over a week since the Ascension. The disciples are all gathered to celebrate the Feast of Pentecost. This sacred time is a remembrance of the ways God cared for the people of Israel in the wilderness, as well as an agricultural festival that marked the beginning of the wheat harvest. Instead of the usual festivities, however, the Spirit descends on those gathered. With a dramatic entrance, the Spirit distributes gifts to those disciples of Christ who had gathered that morning. And they were all given something to say through the Spirit. In this case, all received the same gift: speaking in tongues. This speaking in tongues was different from all others in the New Testament. In all other cases, what is said in "a tongue" can only be understood by someone who has the gift of interpretation. But here, people hear their native languages. This way of presenting tongues, though unusual in the New Testament, stresses two things: that all receive a gift and that the message of the gospel is for the whole world. The following verses show that the gospel is for the whole world when they say that people from all over the world understood what was said in their native languages. This coming of the Spirit marks the beginning of the church's mission to proclaim the gospel to the whole world.

This story unfolds in a different way than our John text. In John the disciples are given the Spirit in a way that sets them apart, even if the rest of the church will receive the Spirit. On Pentecost, all believers are given the Spirit and so share in that presence of God in their lives and are given a gift to participate in the mission of the church.

INTERPRETING THE SCRIPTURE

The Risen Christ Appears

The appearance of the risen Christ is disturbing. We sometimes see the disciples and other people in the ancient world as fairly gullible and so seeing miracles everywhere. But having someone rise from the dead was more than unusual. And having someone rise without the intervention of some wonderworker was unheard of. So the appearance of Christ to the disciples is troubling, just as it is hard for us to understand. And so the first thing Jesus says is, "Peace be with you." And he has to repeat this after he shows them his hands and side. But more is going on than calming the nerves of people who have seen a person raised from the dead. The Resurrection is a validation of the ministry and death of Jesus. Things have gone according to the plan of God. Jesus has taught and healed. He has revealed who God is and promised a continuing presence among his disciples through the Comforter. Then he gave himself up to death.

The disciples have not understood that death is to be part of God's plan or part of what should happen to One sent from God. They see it as a defeat that makes them doubt what they had thought about Jesus. And it made them afraid; they are hiding in a locked room. Then Christ appears and grants them peace, peace from the shock of seeing him and peace from their troubled thoughts. The appearance of the resurrected One demonstrates that Jesus is in fact the One sent from God. What Jesus had told them about his identity and about God and living for God are all validated by the Resurrection. With this proof in view, Jesus reminds them in John 20:21 that he is the One sent by God. The significance of the Resurrection is not just assurance that God can raise a dead person; it also assures us that Christ is the sure revelation of God and God's will. At the same time, the Resurrection also brings with it a task. As the risen Christ, Jesus now gives the disciples the task of going into the world to continue his work and offer salvation to those they reach.

The Resurrection Validates Bodily Existence

Beyond serving as validation of the message and identity of Jesus, the Resurrection also assures us that God values bodily existence. Jesus proves he is not a ghost (after appearing in a locked room as though he were immaterial) by showing the disciples his hands and side. They see that he is still an embodied person. This and other strange descriptions of the risen Christ in the Gospels combined with the discussion of the Resurrection in 1 Corinthians 15 show that the early church saw the resurrection of Christ as bodily. But this was no resuscitation of a corpse—something much more important happened. In Christ's resurrection, a new kind of existence is born. It is bodily existence and recognizable, but this is not a body like any other body people had ever seen. As Paul describes it in 1 Corinthians 15, it is a body made of better material, material that is "imperishable" (15:42). But it is a body.

The risen Christ is the promise and

demonstration of what believers will receive from God when they enjoy the fullness of their salvation in the presence of God. Affirmation of the bodily nature of Christ's resurrection is important for John. His churches faced a teaching known as Docetism. This doctrine asserted that Christ was fully divine but only seemed to have a body. Docetists said Jesus did not have a body because the holiness of God would be defiled by genuine contact with the material world. The letters of 1 John and 2 John argue against this view explicitly. The Gospel of John rejects it with what it affirms about Jesus, here about the risen Jesus. Jesus shows the disciples his hands and side so they can see the marks left by the Crucifixion. Thus they see that he is genuinely Jesus and truly bodily. While we do not face Docetists, this recognition of the bodily nature of the Resurrection assures us of the significance of our bodily lives. God loves and cares about our bodily selves, not just our souls. The bodily resurrection invests our bodily living with meaning as we see that God made us bodily creatures and affirms the goodness of our whole selves, body and soul.

The Spirit Signals the Coming of the Kingdom

The resurrection of Christ and the giving of the Spirit are end-time events. When Jesus tells the disciples that they will receive the baptism of the Spirit (that is, a baptism that consists of having the Spirit live in them), they ask if this is the end-time, if this is when God restores the kingdom to Israel (Acts 1:6). The restoration of the independence of Israel was seen as at least the beginning of the end-times

for many within Judaism. Now the resurrection of the dead has begun with Christ and the Spirit is coming. Both of these occurrences are signs of the end times. But Jesus shifts the conversation. They will have to come to a new conception of what the "kingdom" is. Further, before the kingdom comes in its fullness they will receive power through the Spirit. That comes at Pentecost.

It is hard for us to think about the time we live in as "the last days." After all, the Resurrection occurred two thousand years ago. But the New Testament's talk about the "last days" is not really about how many days are left before the end of the world. Rather, the New Testament sees the end times as the time after Christ's resurrection and so as the time when former promises are fulfilled. Because of what Christ has done, God now dwells among God's people in new and more intimate ways. The Spirit of God now lives within the heart. It is now that God calls all people into this close relationship. The gift of the Spirit is an end-time gift because it is something that God's people as a whole did not enjoy before it was given to them through Christ. The church is an institution of the last days. It is the community in which the Spirit resides and one of its important duties is to be a sign of what God wants for all the world.

The Spirit Empowers the Church for Its Mission

According to the account in Acts 2, when the Spirit falls on believers at Pentecost, it falls on all of them, not just Peter and the apostles. In this outpouring of the Spirit, every believer received a gift from God. That gift was used to advance the mission of the church. Here on the first day of the church's existence, every believer contributes to the spreading of the gospel. They all participate in sharing the gospel because the Spirit gives them the gifts they need to do this work.

Although we no longer expect tongue-speaking as the evidence of the Spirit, the Spirit does give every Christian a gift to share that contributes to the life and growth of the church. Importantly, we are not left on our own to do God's work in the church and the world; the Spirit empowers us to accomplish that work and to live for God. So the Spirit of God not only brings us comfort in difficult and frightening circumstances; the Spirit also enables us to live for God and to further the church's mission.

SHARING THE SCRIPTURE

PREPARING TO TEACH

Preparing Our Hearts

Meditate on this week's devotional reading from Romans 14:13-19. According to Paul, what constitutes the kingdom of God? What actions can believers take to build up others and live in peace? What steps will you take this week to share the joy and peace of the Holy Spirit with others?

Pray that you and the students will be mindful of the Spirit's presence.

Preparing Our Minds

Study the background Scripture from John 20:19-23 and Acts 1:4-8; 2:1-4. The lesson Scripture is from John 20:19-23.

Consider this question as you prepare the lesson: *What can one say or do to lift and inspire an attentive audience?*

Write on newsprint:
❏ information for next week's lesson, found under "Continue the Journey."
❏ activities for further spiritual growth in "Continue the Journey."

Review the "Introduction," "The Big Picture," "Close-up," and "Faith in Action," which all precede the first lesson of this quarter. Consider how you might use any of this material in today's lesson.

LEADING THE CLASS

(1) Gather to Learn

❖ Greet the class members and introduce guests.

❖ Pray that those who have come today will be open to the inspiration of the Holy Spirit.

❖ Point out that throughout the course of history some speakers, often presidents or other influential leaders have captured the imagination of their audiences with several memorable words. Here are three examples:

- **Abraham Lincoln's 1863 "Gettysburg Address" emphasized "that government of the people, by the people, for the people, shall not perish from the earth."**
- **John F. Kennedy's 1961 "Inaugural Address" challenged**

the American people to "ask not what your country can do for you—ask what you can do for your country."

- During the 1963 March on Washington, DC, Martin Luther King Jr. laid out a vision for the future when he said, "I have a dream that one day this nation will rise up and live out the true meaning of its creed: 'We hold these truths to be self-evident, that all men are created equal.'"

❖ Ask the students: **Why do these lines and those of other memorable speeches remain etched in the memories of those who heard them?**

❖ Read aloud today's focus statement: **A charismatic speaker can often lift and inspire an attentive audience. What is done and said to bring about such an effect? Jesus speaks peace to and empowers the disciples with the gift of the Holy Spirit.**

(2) Goal 1: Explore the Importance of Jesus' Appearance to the Disciples

❖ Choose a volunteer to read John 20:19-23.

❖ List on newsprint the events that occur in these five verses and any meaning that the students can attach to them. Begin by noting that although Mary Magdalene had testified earlier in the day that Jesus had risen (20:18), the fearful disciples are huddling behind locked doors on Easter evening when this encounter occurs. Be sure to include these events:

- Jesus appeared to the disciples. His body must have been transformed, since he could enter despite the locked doors.
- Jesus offered the disciples peace, thereby fulfilling his promise in 14:27 to give peace.

- He showed the disciples evidence of his brutal death.
- The disciples rejoiced when they realized that Jesus was among them.
- Jesus again offered his peace.
- He commissioned the disciples to go forth, just as God had commissioned and sent him.
- He breathed on the disciples, as God had breathed on Adam in the garden (Genesis 2:7), that they might receive the Holy Spirit, which he had promised before his death (John 14:15-17).
- "Sin," which in John's Gospel means failing to recognize God's revelation in Jesus, will be forgiven as the faith community, now empowered by the Spirit, continues Jesus' work in the world.

❖ Summarize this passage by reading "The Risen Christ Appears" in Interpreting the Scripture.

(3) Goal 2: Share Feelings of Times When the Learners' Fears Were Calmed Through the Words of Others

❖ Read aloud this guided imagery:

- **Recall a time when you felt frightened. Envision the circumstances. How old were you? Was there a particular place that prompted fear? Were there particular people who caused you to be afraid? (Pause)**
- **Remember how your fears were alleviated. Did your dad take action by searching under the bed for monsters? Did Grandma hold you in her lap and reassure you? Did a coworker talk with**

you and explain that news of a shutdown was simply a rumor? (Pause)

- Concentrate on things people said to you. Was there anything that someone said that allayed your fears and gave you peace? (Pause)

❖ Bring everyone together and encourage volunteers to recount feelings they had when their fears were calmed, particularly by gentle words. They need not explain what caused the fear; they are only being asked to share feelings about the fear once it was relieved.

(4) Goal 3: Fulfill the Mission God Has for the Learners' Lives as Empowered by the Holy Spirit

❖ Read again Jesus' words of commissioning from John 20:21.

❖ Distribute paper and pencils. Invite the students to write the following words and then complete the sentence: God is calling me to . . . Next, they are to identify ways that they may go about fulfilling the missions to which they are called, knowing that they are not working alone but are empowered by the Holy Spirit.

(5) Continue the Journey

❖ Pray that as the learners depart, they will be open to receiving a new breath of wind from the Holy Spirit to fulfill the missions to which they have been called.

❖ Post information for next week's session on newsprint for the students to copy:

- **Title: The One Who Comes**
- **Background Scripture: Mark 11:1-11**
- **Lesson Scripture: Mark 11:1-11**

■ **Focus of the Lesson: People want to be in the presence of and pay homage to important people. Why are celebrity events important to us? The people celebrated Jesus' arrival in Jerusalem as the coming of God's kingdom.**

❖ Challenge the adults to grow spiritually by completing one or more of these activities related to this week's session, which you have posted on newsprint for the students to copy.

(1) Play a game beginning with the word "fear" and then changing only one letter in each word until you reach the word "fire." (Here is one possible solution: *fear, pear, peas, pens, pins, pine, fine, fire.*) If you are feeling afraid, what steps can you take to move from fear to the zealous fire of the Holy Spirit?

(2) Spend time daily meditating on these questions: How do you experience the peace of Christ in your life? How do share that peace with others? Act on your answers to the second question.

(3) Offer words of God's peace to someone who is responding with fear to life situations.

❖ Sing or read aloud "Breathe on Me, Breath of God."

❖ Conclude today's session by leading the class in this benediction adapted from 1 Corinthians 12:13, which is the key verse for the lesson for May 17: **Let us go forth rejoicing that in the one Spirit we were all baptized into one body—Jews or Greeks, slaves or free—and we were all made to drink of one Spirit.**

UNIT 1: THE PLEDGE OF GOD'S PRESENCE
THE ONE WHO COMES

PREVIEWING THE LESSON

Lesson Scripture: Mark 11:1-11
Background Scripture: Mark 11:1-11
Key Verse: Mark 11:9

Focus of the Lesson:
People want to be in the presence of and pay homage to important people. Why are celebrity events important to us? The people celebrated Jesus' arrival in Jerusalem as the coming of God's kingdom.

Goals for the Learners:
(1) to survey the story of Jesus' triumphal entry into Jerusalem.
(2) to share feelings about the kingdom of God.
(3) to find creative ways to pay homage to Jesus.

Pronunciation Guide:
Bethphage (beth´ fuh jee)

Supplies:
Bibles, newsprint and marker, paper and pencils, hymnals

READING THE SCRIPTURE

NRSV

Lesson Scripture: Mark 11:1-11

¹When they were approaching Jerusalem, at Bethphage and Bethany, near the Mount of Olives, he sent two of his disciples ²and said to them, "Go into the village ahead of you, and immediately as you enter it, you will find tied there a colt that has never been ridden; untie it and bring it. ³If anyone says to you, 'Why are you doing this?' just say this, 'The Lord

CEB

Lesson Scripture: Mark 11:1-11

¹When Jesus and his followers approached Jerusalem, they came to Bethphage and Bethany at the Mount of Olives. Jesus gave two disciples a task, ²saying to them, "Go into the village over there. As soon as you enter it, you will find tied up there a colt that no one has ridden. Untie it and bring it here. ³If anyone says to you, 'Why are you doing this?' say, 'Its

needs it and will send it back here immediately.'" 4They went away and found a colt tied near a door, outside in the street. As they were untying it, 5some of the bystanders said to them, "What are you doing, untying the colt?" 6They told them what Jesus had said; and they allowed them to take it. 7Then they brought the colt to Jesus and threw their cloaks on it; and he sat on it. 8Many people spread their cloaks on the road, and others spread leafy branches that they had cut in the fields. **9Then those who went ahead and those who followed were shouting,**

"Hosanna!

Blessed is the one who comes in the name of the Lord!

10 Blessed is the coming kingdom of
　·our ancestor David!
Hosanna in the highest heaven!".

11Then he entered Jerusalem and went into the temple; and when he had looked around at everything, as it was already late, he went out to Bethany with the twelve.

master needs it, and he will send it back right away.'"

4They went and found a colt tied to a gate outside on the street, and they untied it. 5Some people standing around said to them, "What are you doing, untying the colt?" 6They told them just what Jesus said, and they left them alone. 7They brought the colt to Jesus and threw their clothes upon it, and he sat on it. 8Many people spread out their clothes on the road while others spread branches cut from the fields. **9Those in front of him and those following were shouting, "Hosanna! Blessings on the one who comes in the name of the Lord!** 10Blessings on the coming kingdom of our ancestor David! Hosanna in the highest!" 11Jesus entered Jerusalem and went into the temple. After he looked around at everything, because it was already late in the evening, he returned to Bethany with the Twelve.

UNDERSTANDING THE SCRIPTURE

Introduction. The story of Jesus' triumphal entry is a joyous one in all four Gospels. But in Mark it is also very ironic. Beginning with 8:31, Jesus has been trying to prepare the disciples for what is coming in Jerusalem. He tells them again in chapters 9 and 10 that when they get there, he will be arrested, abused, and killed, and then he will rise. Every time Jesus says this, Mark says that the disciples cannot understand what he is talking about. He has told them this as late as 10:33-34. They simply cannot comprehend the idea that Jesus will suffer humiliation at the hands of the Romans

(see 8:32-33; 10:33-34). They think that if he is from God he will stand up against them and perhaps defeat them immediately. Of course, this is not the mission of Jesus. He will do nothing so small as defeat the Roman Empire; his mission has cosmic goals. So after all this misunderstanding of what Jesus will do, rather than being distraught at what is about to happen to him, the disciples participate in a sort of victory parade. On the other hand, in ways they do not comprehend, Jesus is about to win a greater victory than they can imagine.

Today's passage from chapter 11

begins a major section in Mark, that of the Jerusalem ministry of Jesus. Once Jesus gets to the city, he will never return to Galilee in the narrative of Mark. In this section Jesus confronts the religious and civil leaders of Judea and so, by implication, the power of Rome. He will question their authority as they will question his. Eventually Jesus will withdraw and tell his disciples of the coming end of things. One of the important functions of the whole section is to prepare the readers of Mark for the destruction of the Temple that occurs in A.D. 70. In chapter 13, the end of this section, Jesus predicts that fall so that it is not as devastating to the later church.

Mark 11:1-3. As this narrative begins, Jesus is nearing Jerusalem for the one and only time he goes there in the story Mark tells of Jesus' ministry. The villages of Bethphage (whose precise location is uncertain) and Bethany are very near Jerusalem, and one can see the Temple from the Mount of Olives. So they are very close. When Jesus sends the disciples to get the donkey, he intends to set up the scene that follows. The scheme is reminiscent of Zechariah 9 in which the triumphant warrior of the Lord has defeated Israel's enemies. His riding into town on a donkey, rather than a war horse, symbolizes his peaceful intentions. He defeats Israel's enemies, but brings peace to the people of God. This scene intentionally evokes that image so that readers understand Jesus as the One who defeats the enemies of God's people and brings them peace. It may be that Mark makes a point of mentioning that the animal had not been ridden so that it is like the animals consecrated to the Lord in earlier biblical texts. Those animals were also untamed and had not been used for work. What Jesus tells the disciples to say is also interesting. The CEB rightly translates the instructions of Jesus here. He says to tell bystanders that "its master" [or even better, "owner"] needs it. This is an interesting claim that Jesus makes. The word "master" is that same word as "Lord." The NRSV has "Lord," but omits the pronoun "its." However we interpret the word "Lord," Jesus is claiming to be the true owner of this donkey.

Mark 11:4-6. Things go exactly as Jesus had told the disciples. They go to the village and find a donkey tied up to a "gate" (11:4 CEB). As they untie it and begin to take it, people who are there ask them what they are doing. They respond as Jesus had told them and are allowed to take it. This element of the story demonstrates Jesus' foreknowledge as he heads into Jerusalem. Thus, it shows that things are going as he plans, even if those plans are not what he might wish for.

Mark 11:7-11. The heart of the story is the reception and praise Jesus receives as he enters Jerusalem. First the disciples put their cloaks on the donkey. Cloaks were outer garments that might be our equivalent to a jacket, though of course their cloaks would have been longer and less fitted. After Jesus sits on the donkey, others in the crowd who had been following him spread their cloaks on the road, while still others cut leafy branches and do the same thing. (Only John says they are palm branches.) This reception of Jesus reminds one of the royal processions or the festival processions of Israel. Their acclamations are based in part on Psalm 118:26. So Jesus is being received as royalty in a festive atmosphere.

As Jesus rides by, the crowd shouts "Hosanna," which means "save us now." The crowd recognizes him as one who represents the will and authority of God. He is coming in the name of the Lord. Then the crowd's commentary becomes overtly political. They call for the establishment of "the coming kingdom of our ancestor David" (11:10). This is a dangerous statement because it implies the overthrow of the Romans as the nation of Israel is established as an independent and secure state. This statement is so inflammatory that the other three Gospels leave it out. It is true that Jesus will establish the long-awaited kingdom, but it will not be what anyone at this procession expects. They speak something that Mark's readers know is true, yet those in the scene itself have no idea what their words will mean. The parade and celebration ends at the Temple. It will be the center of Jesus' ministry in Jerusalem. For now, he only looks around and leaves for Bethany. When he returns it will be for confrontation and will signal the beginning of the final days of his life. The proclamation of his identity as the One who brings God's kingdom combined with his actions at the Temple could only lead to Good Friday.

INTERPRETING THE SCRIPTURE

Christ as Lord of All

This text leads us to think about who Jesus is and how we respond to that. The people Mark envisions at the procession are looking forward to a mighty act of God, one that brings freedom and comes through the One who comes in the name of the Lord, Jesus. With the image of the donkey, they see a successful warrior against God's enemies coming to them in peace. But the crowd and even the disciples fail to see the fuller meaning Mark wants readers to grasp as he tells the story. Jesus here fills an even larger role than those at the procession hope for.

We see this role even in the instructions Jesus gives the disciples about bringing the donkey. In telling them what to do if someone asks why they are taking the animal, Jesus claims ownership of it by saying they should tell the bystanders that "its master" (11:3 CEB) or "the Lord" needs it. Since Jesus has not been to this area during his ministry, he clearly does not hold the title to this animal. Yet he is its master. This simple statement implies that Christ is the Lord of all things. It is a brief intimation of what will be said soon in the Temple about all possessions. When asked about paying taxes Jesus responds by telling the questioners that they should give to Caesar what is Caesar's and to God what is God's (12:13-17). If we ask about what belongs to God, the clear answer is everything. Jesus' ownership of the donkey is a fleeting example of this way of thinking and designates Jesus as God's representative in the world. As the One who comes in the name of the Lord, Christ is the Lord not just of this donkey but also of every person and the whole world. Thus, he is the One who should receive the praise we hear on the road to Jerusalem.

*The One Who Brings
the Coming Kingdom*

The crowd going to Jerusalem for Passover both underestimates who Jesus is and misconstrues what he will accomplish. These onlookers are able to say the right things about him, but they do not know what those statements really mean. When Mark writes about these acclamations from the crowd, he expects the church to see different meanings in them than those that the crowd originally meant. When the crowd looks for the "coming kingdom," they want an earthly kingdom that will free them from the domination of Rome and all other foreign powers. When Mark's church reads about the "coming kingdom," they know that it has already begun to be present in the church and they look forward to a cosmic coming that will change all of reality. They look for the kingdom that will establish God's reign everywhere.

Mark's church also sees this new act of God as something that is consistent with what God has always wanted for the world. Christ comes as the One who brings that will of God into reality. The political meaning that the crowd gives the proclamation is simply too small to capture what God is accomplishing in the coming, death, and resurrection of Christ. Like the disciples in the preceding chapters of Mark, those in the crowd expect mighty displays of power and immediate victory. What they will get in the week to come is incomprehensible, completely out of line with what they think they are proclaiming about Jesus. Like them, it is hard for us to see clearly what God does for us and the world through Christ. Like them, we often misconstrue what the Kingdom is about. This reading provides a moment for us to think carefully about what the coming of the Kingdom means, especially what it means about how to live in the present. Only as we examine our ideas about the Kingdom will we be able to align our lives with the will of God.

Save Us

As the triumphal procession began, the people called out for salvation. The salvation those in the original setting had in mind was rescue from domination by the Romans. Once again, the crowd did not understand fully what it meant to ask for salvation. Mark wants his readers to see another, deeper understanding of the person and mission of Jesus. Jesus is, indeed, the One who will bring the salvation from God, but that salvation is fuller and more far-reaching than the crowd imagines. The salvation Mark envisions goes beyond who is in political control; this salvation reaches into all aspects of life.

As we hear their plea for salvation, we also know the need for salvation that goes beyond resolving political struggles. It is not that salvation has nothing to do with what we work for in the world, but rather that the arenas of government and politics are only a part of what is affected. The salvation we need is wider than such matters. We know the brokenness that is evident in the world, the church, and ourselves. We need a salvation that brings healing within and among ourselves, as well as restoration of our relationship with God. We yearn for this fuller salvation as we call out "Hosanna," which means "save now." As Mark wants his readers to understand it, this parade of palms and cloaks acknowledges that Jesus is the One through whom God acts to bring this larger salvation. Because we know the lengths to which Christ went to secure this salvation, we can ask for it with the joyous confidence those on the road to Jerusalem expressed as Jesus rode into town.

Praising Christ

In their praise of Christ, the crowd said things that were not true in the ways they meant them. Yet Mark takes these acclamations and uses them to proclaim to his readers things about Christ that he knows are true. As often happens in Mark, people say something about the identity of Jesus or about the purpose of his mission that they do not fully understand. In fact, it is only after the death and resurrection of Christ that the full meaning could be known. Yet those statements of praise are worth preserving because they express a truth that we can now see more fully.

We must also admit that our praise of Christ and our statements about the meaning of what he accomplished for our salvation are often (perhaps always) inadequate. Our praise always falls short of expressing the fullness of the truth about Christ. This should not, however, silence our praise. We should regularly seek ways to express our love for Christ and our gratitude for the salvation we receive in him. These moments of praise and thanks should go beyond the formulations we know from our traditions. They will draw on our traditions and Scripture, but our praise should give expression to the experience of God's grace that we know in our lives. Such heartfelt praise will produce new ways of expressing our thanks. These acclamations (whether in word or deed) will not convey everything that ought to be said about Christ. Even so, such praise can glorify God and build up the church. Just as the people on the road to Jerusalem offered up their best understanding of praise and request for God's presence, so we should offer our praise to God, knowing that our efforts express pleasing thanks to God.

SHARING THE SCRIPTURE

PREPARING TO TEACH

Preparing Our Hearts

Meditate on this week's devotional reading from Isaiah 45:20-25. What does the prophet declare about God? Notice that verse 23b is quoted by Paul in Romans 14:11 and echoes again in Philippians 2:10-11. What connections would you say that Paul is making between God and Jesus? Where are you seeking salvation?

Pray that you and the students will give glory and honor to the one God who offers salvation to all.

Preparing Our Minds

Study the background Scripture and the lesson Scripture, which are both from Mark 11:1-11.

Consider this question as you prepare the lesson: *Why are we drawn to events that feature important people?*

Write on newsprint:

❏ information for next week's lesson, found under "Continue the Journey."

❏ activities for further spiritual growth in "Continue the Journey."

Review the "Introduction," "The Big Picture," "Close-up," and "Faith in Action," which all precede the first lesson of this quarter. Consider how you might use any of this material in today's lesson.

LEADING THE CLASS

(1) Gather to Learn

❖ Greet the class members and introduce guests.

❖ Pray that those who have come today will be eager to pay homage to Jesus.

❖ Read the following "headlines" and discuss what they have in common. (Help the adults see that many people are drawn to events that feature celebrities or other important people.)

• Media from around the world camp out at St. Mary's Hospital in London for days in July 2013 awaiting the birth of Prince George, the son of Prince William and the Duchess of Cambridge.

• Football fans press together as the Super Bowl champs return home for a triumphant parade.

• Crowds line the streets of Washington, D.C., on Inauguration Day to catch a glimpse of the president.

• Film aficionados hope for a peek at the stars as they make their grand entrance along the red carpet.

❖ Read aloud today's focus statement: **People want to be in the presence of and pay homage to important people. Why are celebrity events important to us? The people celebrated Jesus' arrival in Jerusalem as the coming of God's kingdom.**

(2) Goal 1: Survey the Story of Jesus' Triumphal Entry into Jerusalem

❖ Set the stage for today's lesson by reading or retelling "Introduction" from Understanding the Scripture.

❖ Call on a volunteer to read Mark 11:1-11, except for verses 9b-10, which the class will read in unison.

❖ Discuss these questions. Check Understanding the Scripture and Interpreting the Scripture for ideas to add to the discussion.

1. **Had you been one of the disciples, what would you have thought when bystanders allowed you to take the colt you were untying? (See "Christ as Lord of All.")**

2. **Had you been along the "parade route," where might you have been standing? What would you have shouted? What might you have believed about Jesus?**

3. **What did the people apparently mean when they shouted "hosanna" or "save us"? (See "Save Us.")**

4. **What did the onlookers believe about who Jesus was? In what ways were they right? In what ways had they misunderstood Jesus and his kingdom? (See "The One Who Brings the Coming Kingdom.")**

5. **What do you believe about the Kingdom that the people**

who welcomed Jesus could not have known until after his death and resurrection?

(3) Goal 2: Share Feelings about the Kingdom of God

❖ Read this quotation from Charles Colson (1931–2012): "**While human politics is based on the premise that society must be changed in order to change people, in the politics of the kingdom it is the people who must be changed in order to change society."**

❖ Ask these questions:

1. Do you think the people who witnessed Jesus' entry into Jerusalem would have agreed with Colson? Why or why not?

2. How do you think that Mark's early readers in about A.D. 70, who were being politically persecuted or faced the threat of persecution, would have thought of Colson's comments?

3. Do you agree with Colson's understanding of the kingdom of God? Why or why not?

4. In what other ways would you talk about the kingdom of God?

5. How has being part of the kingdom of God had an impact on your life?

(4) Goal 3: Find Creative Ways to Pay Homage to Jesus

❖ Invite the students to consider how they might welcome Jesus into their own city or town by answering these questions:

1. What parade route in our city or town would give Jesus maximum exposure to our community?

2. How would Jesus enter our town—on foot, mounted on an animal, riding in a car, standing on a parade float?

3. What would we wave as a sign of welcome and homage to Jesus?

4. What words or phrases or Bible verses might we shout to let Jesus know what we think of him?

5. Where would the parade route end?

6. What kind of special event might we host for Jesus after the parade ended?

❖ Recognize that although you cannot actually hold a parade for Jesus, class members can use their gifts and talents to pay homage to him. Distribute paper and pencils. Encourage each person to list one means of paying homage, such as writing a psalm, singing a hymn of praise, talking to someone about Jesus, assisting needy persons in Jesus' name. Collect the papers, shuffle them, redistribute them, and ask the students to read whatever is on the paper he or she is holding. Give thanks for the ways the class can pay homage to Jesus. Challenge the adults to do whatever they listed and, if possible, to use other ideas they have heard read today.

(5) Continue the Journey

❖ Pray that as the learners depart, they will give glory and honor to the One who comes in the name of the Lord.

❖ Post information for next week's session on newsprint for the students to copy:

- Title: Resurrection Guaranteed
- Background Scripture: 1 Corinthians 15:1-22
- Lesson Scripture: 1 Corinthians 15:1-11, 20-22
- Focus of the Lesson: People need to be reminded of important events that shape their identities and actions. What kind of event can make such an influence on their lives? Jesus' resurrection provided tangible evidence of the possibility of resurrection for those whose identity is formed by Christ Jesus.

❖ Challenge the adults to grow spiritually by completing one or more of these activities related to this week's session, which you have posted on newsprint for the students to copy.

(1) Compare the story of Palm Sunday as recorded in Mark 11:1-11 with the story in Matthew 21:1-11; Luke 19:28-40; and John 12:12-19. How are the details similar and different?

(2) Use your talents to do whatever you can to pay homage to Jesus during this Holy Week.

(3) Attend special church services that recall the Last Supper on Holy Thursday and Jesus' crucifixion on Good Friday. Invite others to join you.

❖ Sing or read aloud "All Glory, Laud, and Honor."

❖ Conclude today's session by leading the class in this benediction adapted from 1 Corinthians 12:13, which is the key verse for the lesson for May 17: **Let us go forth rejoicing that in the one Spirit we were all baptized into one body—Jews or Greeks, slaves or free—and we were all made to drink of one Spirit.**

UNIT 2: THE COMMUNITY OF BELOVED DISCIPLES
RESURRECTION GUARANTEED

PREVIEWING THE LESSON

Lesson Scripture: 1 Corinthians 15:1-11, 20-22
Background Scripture: 1 Corinthians 15:1-22
Key Verse: 1 Corinthians 15:22

Focus of the Lesson:
People need to be reminded of important events that shape their identities and actions. What kind of event can make such an influence on their lives? Jesus' resurrection provided tangible evidence of the possibility of resurrection for those whose identity is formed by Christ Jesus.

Goals for the Learners:
(1) to explore the meaning of Christ's resurrection.
(2) to value and appreciate one's identity in Jesus Christ.
(3) to witness personally and corporately to the resurrection of Jesus Christ.

Pronunciation Guide:
Cephas (see´ fuhs)

Supplies:
Bibles, newsprint and marker, paper and pencils, hymnals

READING THE SCRIPTURE

NRSV
Lesson Scripture: 1 Corinthians 15:1-11, 20-22

¹Now I would remind you, brothers and sisters, of the good news that I proclaimed to you, which you in turn received, in which also you stand, ²through which also you are

CEB
Lesson Scripture: 1 Corinthians 15:1-11, 20-22

¹Brothers and sisters, I want to call your attention to the good news that I preached to you, which you also received and in which you stand. ²You are being saved through it if you

being saved, if you hold firmly to the message that I proclaimed to you—unless you have come to believe in vain.

³For I handed on to you as of first importance what I in turn had received: that Christ died for our sins in accordance with the scriptures, ⁴and that he was buried, and that he was raised on the third day in accordance with the scriptures, ⁵and that he appeared to Cephas, then to the twelve. ⁶Then he appeared to more than five hundred brothers and sisters at one time, most of whom are still alive, though some have died. ⁷Then he appeared to James, then to all the apostles. ⁸Last of all, as to one untimely born, he appeared also to me. ⁹For I am the least of the apostles, unfit to be called an apostle, because I persecuted the church of God. ¹⁰But by the grace of God I am what I am, and his grace toward me has not been in vain. On the contrary, I worked harder than any of them—though it was not I, but the grace of God that is with me. ¹¹Whether then it was I or they, so we proclaim and so you have come to believe.

²⁰But in fact Christ has been raised from the dead, the first fruits of those who have died. ²¹For since death came through a human being, the resurrection of the dead has also come through a human being; ²²**for as all die in Adam, so all will be made alive in Christ.**

hold on to the message I preached to you, unless somehow you believed it for nothing. ³I passed on to you as most important what I also received: Christ died for our sins in line with the scriptures, ⁴he was buried, and he rose on the third day in line with the scriptures. ⁵He appeared to Cephas, then to the Twelve, ⁶and then he appeared to more than five hundred brothers and sisters at once—most of them are still alive to this day, though some have died. ⁷Then he appeared to James, then to all the apostles, ⁸and last of all he appeared to me, as if I was born at the wrong time. ⁹I'm the least important of the apostles. I don't deserve to be called an apostle, because I harassed God's church. ¹⁰I am what I am by God's grace, and God's grace hasn't been for nothing. In fact, I have worked harder than all the others—that is, it wasn't me but the grace of God that is with me. ¹¹So then, whether you heard the message from me or them, this is what we preach and this is what you have believed.

²⁰But in fact Christ has been raised from the dead. He's the first crop of the harvest of those who have died. ²¹Since death came through a human being, the resurrection of the dead came through one too. ²²**In the same way that everyone dies in Adam, so also everyone will be given life in Christ.**

UNDERSTANDING THE SCRIPTURE

Introduction. Among the problems that Paul addresses as he writes 1 Corinthians is the issue of what happens to believers when they die. Some within the diverse congregation at Corinth have begun saying that there is no resurrection from the dead. They do not deny that Christ was raised but do deny that believers are raised. Paul brings up Christ's resurrection as proof that there is such a thing as the resurrection. These people do not deny that there is an afterlife, only that it takes the form of the resurrection of the body. They seem to believe in the immortality of the soul rather than the resurrection of the body. They believe that the essential part of humans is only the soul and that the body simply weighs down the goodness of the soul as it seeks to be in the presence of God. Paul rejects this because he believes that bodily existence is what God intends for humans and therefore is good. His proof of this view is that Christ was raised bodily. All of chapter 15 argues that since Christ was raised bodily, that is the kind of existence believers should expect as they enjoy their final salvation in the presence of God. This form of the afterlife affirms the significance of our lives both now and hereafter.

1 Corinthians 15:1-11. These verses contain some of the oldest and most important teaching of the church. Paul first identifies what he is about to remind them of as the gospel by which they are saved. Then in verse 3 he says that what he is about to say is the "most important" (CEB) element of the gospel. The language he uses to introduce this statement of the faith suggests that he is passing on tradition, and he explicitly says that this is what was passed to him as the heart of the gospel. Then in verses 3-4 he quotes a confession that has three central affirmations: (1) Christ died for our sins (according to the Scriptures), (2) he was buried, and (3) he was raised on the third day. This is a tradition that served as the kernel of the gospel before Paul was in the church because this is what was passed on to him. So within the first few years

of the church's life, this confessional summary was recognized as the very core of the church's faith. Thus, Paul can use these assertions as evidence in his argument about the nature of the afterlife for believers. Verses 5-7 provide a list of witnesses who vouch for the reality of Christ's resurrection. These witnesses include Cephas (Peter), the apostles, the leader of the Jerusalem church (James), and a large group of ordinary believers. So in addition to the foundational confession, these various witnesses, including those who are acknowledged as authorities, confirm that Christ had a bodily resurrection, not just a rising of his spirit or soul. In verses 8-11 Paul adds his personal testimony. He has also experienced the risen Christ and so can testify to the nature of his existence. He notes that this experience radically changed his life. He went from being a persecutor of the church to being its hardest working advocate. That sort of radical change is further evidence for the understanding of the resurrection he advocates because it demonstrates its power to change lives. Paul concludes the passage by reminding the Corinthians that this belief in the death and resurrection of Christ is the common message of the whole church and it is what had brought them salvation.

1 Corinthians 15:12-19. Having reminded the Corinthians of what they had already confessed, Paul draws out some implications of that confession. Paul argues that the resurrection of the dead is a reality because the resurrection of Christ was a reality. The logic Paul presses is that if you deny that there is a resurrection of the dead, then you necessarily deny that Christ was raised. Conversely, if you accept that Christ was raised, then you admit that a resurrection of the dead is a logical possibility. Paul has those who believe only in the immortality of the soul between a rock and a hard place. If they continue to deny that there is a resurrection, then they deny a central and essential part of the faith. But if they admit that Christ was raised, then they must admit that they are wrong about whether there is such a thing as a resurrection of the body. He presses the point hard, forcing them to acknowledge that if Christ was not raised then their faith in Christ and consequently the church are built on a lie. Given this alternative, they must acknowledge the Resurrection or deny their own salvation and experience of God.

1 Corinthians 15:20-22. These verses introduce the paragraph that runs through verse 28. This section talks about the relationship between Christ's resurrection and that of believers. Paul says the resurrected Christ is the "first fruits" (15:20) from the dead. According to the Mosaic law, Jews dedicated the first produce of the crop each year as a sacrifice to God (Leviticus 23:9-14). That sacrifice was the "first fruits." The first fruits were the sample of the rest of the crop and the assurance that the rest would be coming in. Christ's resurrection serves these purposes. It is the sample of what the resurrection of believers will be and God's promise that such a blessing awaits those who are faithful. Paul introduces another kind of logic here. He says that just as the sin of Adam had implications for all who came after him, so the faithfulness of Christ has implications for all who come after him. While Adam's actions brought death, Christ's resurrection brings life. We do not yet see that life in its fullness, but because of Christ's resurrection believers can rest assured that God is able and will raise them from the dead. The remainder of this paragraph assures the Corinthians that even though they do not see the resurrection of those who have died yet, things are moving forward according to the plan of God. In the end death will be conquered and the will of God will shape all of existence. This will of God includes the continuing bodily existence of the saved.

INTERPRETING THE SCRIPTURE

The Heart of the Gospel

For Paul the resurrection of Christ is an absolute necessity for the Christian faith, and as far as he knows there are no believers at Corinth or elsewhere in the church who question its reality. Some in Corinth do question the resurrection of believers. Some Corinthians want to leave bodily existence behind so that they can live as spirits and not be held back by a body. Paul argues that they have misunderstood the nature of humans and what God has in store for them after this life. He begins this argument by pointing them to the earliest confession of the church that we possess. This confession comes to us from a time before Paul was in the church. While Paul was still a persecutor, the church had already given its faith expression by confessing that the death of Christ was for sins and that he was raised—and that all of this was in accord with the Scripture and so in continuity with whom God is known to be there.

Some interpreters speculate that after the death of Jesus, some of his followers gave no significant place to his death and resurrection, but only looked to him as a teacher. Besides the absence of evidence for such groups, this confession indicates that Paul knows of no one he considers a member of the church who does not confess that Jesus' death and resurrection were the means by which God dealt with the sin of humanity. Without these things, the institution that is left is not the church. Note that there is no explanation about how the death of Christ deals with sin or about the exact form of the Resurrection. The essential core of the faith is set forth in as few words as possible. All other Christian theology is an explication of the assertions found in the few words of the confession in verses 3-4. This understanding of the death and resurrection of Christ is the bedrock to the church's faith.

The Nature of Christ's Resurrection

The resurrection of Christ is not, however, the resuscitation of a corpse. It is something much greater. As Paul talks about it, Christ's resurrection is the initiation of a new kind of life, a kind of reality that had never existed before that moment. As he describes it in the latter parts of 1 Corinthians 15, the resurrection body of Christ is composed of material that is different from "flesh and blood" (15:50). The matter that makes up the resurrection body of Christ is different from the matter of which our present bodies are composed. In the ancient world

people saw the cosmos as layered. The higher one went, the better the material the inhabitants were made of. Paul's explanation of the resurrection body seems to be that it is composed of matter from one of those higher realms. Thus it can be immortal and incorruptible.

If this sounds strange, think of the stories the Gospels tell about the appearances of the resurrected Christ. He can appear in locked rooms, but also eat. He can be mistaken for a ghost, but then invite people to touch him to prove otherwise. The Gospel writers are trying to describe a kind of body, really a kind of existence, that no one had seen before. This is a resurrection into a life that never ends. Its existence proclaims the coming end of death because death cannot overcome this life. Christ's resurrection is the demonstration of the power of God over the worst that the forces of evil can do to us. The resurrection of Christ promises that it is not just pain and suffering that will end, but death itself will be defeated. Christ's resurrection is the assurance that the will of God cannot be overcome by evil and that life will win out over death. This resurrection is necessary for Christian hope to have any firm foundation.

*The Connection Between Christ's
Resurrection and that of Believers*

Today's reading begins Paul's discussion of the relationship between Christ's resurrection and that of believers. He gives two ways to think of this relationship. When he compares Christ to Adam, he compares their effects. As the sin of Adam changed everything and touched everyone; so does the resurrection of Christ. But Christ's resurrection brings cosmos-changing life that more than counteracts the death that came through Adam. Calling Christ's resurrection body the "first fruits" of the resurrection of the dead (15:20) means that the resurrection of the believer will be like that of Christ's. Christ's resurrection is the sample of what resurrection life will be for believers. Paul is saying that believers will have the same kind of body as the resurrected Christ. It will be made of the same kind of immortal and incorruptible matter. We sometimes wonder if we will look the same as we do now or if we will have the infirmities that afflict us now. Paul would assure us of fullness of life in the presence of God.

As he tries to explain how our bodily selves of the present are related to those of the future, he resorts to an analogy. He says our future existence and our present are related as a seed and plant are related (15:37-38). You plant a seed and what comes up looks nothing like what was planted, but there is an essential relatedness and continuing identity between them. So it will be with us. What is raised in the future is essentially related to and has continuous identity with who we are now. All of this is demonstrated and guaranteed in the resurrection of Christ. So the resurrection of Christ is not simply an event of the past; it remains a promise about our future with God and about God's final defeat of death. This understanding of what is to come can ease our fear of death because Christ's resurrection assures us that it includes our whole selves and a full life with God.

An Affirmation of Human Life

This talk of resurrection may seem speculative and somewhat removed from the ordinary conduct of our lives, but Paul does not think so. He does not insist on the bodily nature of the afterlife just because of some doctrinal purity. He understands humans to be a psychophysical unity. A person is not a full human being with only a soul or only a body. You must have both to be all that God intends humans to be. Being human is a good thing in the eyes of God, and God intends us to be fully human in our existence in God's presence. This understanding of our lives grants a deep significance to the way we conduct ourselves now. How we live in this world as bodily beings matters deeply.

Paul concludes his long discussion of the Resurrection in 1 Corinthians 15:58 with an exhortation. Since you know you will be raised bodily, the apostle says believers should abound in the work of the Lord, knowing that their work is not for nothing. God cares how we live in the present because God cares about our whole selves, not just some hidden part of us. The bodily resurrection invests current life with meaning and significance. To proclaim the resurrection of Christ and our resurrection through him is to assert that our present embodied life is meaningful. It is to insist that present life should be lived for God, just as our future will be with God.

SHARING THE SCRIPTURE

PREPARING TO TEACH

Preparing Our Hearts

Meditate on this week's devotional reading from John 11:20-27. Jesus asked Martha, whose brother Lazarus had died, whether she believed that those who lived in him, "even though they die, will live" (11:25). How would you have answered Jesus' question? Especially as the church celebrates Easter, what do you believe about his resurrection? What do you believe about the possibility of your own resurrection?

Pray that you and the students will celebrate Christ's resurrection and the meaning it holds for you.

Preparing Our Minds

Study the background Scripture from 1 Corinthians 15:1-22 and the lesson Scripture from 1 Corinthians 15:1-11, 20-22.

Consider this question as you prepare the lesson: *What kinds of events can shape people's actions and identities?*

Write on newsprint:

❏ Scripture passages for "Value and Appreciate One's Identity in Jesus Christ."

❏ information for next week's lesson, found under "Continue the Journey."

❏ activities for further spiritual growth in "Continue the Journey."

Review the "Introduction," "The Big Picture," "Close-up," and "Faith in Action," which all precede the first lesson of this quarter. Consider how you might use any of this material in today's lesson.

LEADING THE CLASS

(1) Gather to Learn

❖ Greet the class members and introduce guests.

❖ Pray that those who have come today will celebrate Jesus' resurrection.

❖ Distribute paper and pencils. Invite the class members to list events of great importance in their own lives. These may include significant milestones, such as attending school, graduating, getting married, being present at the birth of a child, getting a promotion at work, or becoming a naturalized citizen. They may also include major events in their faith journeys.

❖ Call on two or three volunteers to read their lists. As each event is read, invite others who have experienced a similar event to raise their hands. Identify those events that seem most common to the group and ask: **How did [name of event] shape your identity?**

❖ Read aloud today's focus statement: **People need to be reminded of important events that shape their identities and actions. What kind of event can make such an influence on their lives? Jesus' resurrection provided tangible evidence of the possibility of resurrection for those whose identity is formed by Christ Jesus.**

(2) Goal 1: Explore the Meaning of Christ's Resurrection

❖ Use "Introduction" in Understanding the Scripture to lead the students into this lesson.

❖ Select a volunteer to read 1 Corinthians 15:1-11, 20-22.

❖ Discuss these questions:

- **What teachings of the church, which Paul had received and passed on to the Corinthian believers, do you find in these verses?** (See "1 Corinthians 15:1-11" in Understanding the Scripture.)

- **What are believers to understand about Christ's resurrected body?** (See "The Nature of Christ's Resurrection" in Interpreting the Scripture.)

- **Why might Paul have included the biographical information in verses 5-8?**

- **What did Paul mean when he wrote that the resurrected Christ was "the first fruits of those who have died" (15:20)?** (See the first paragraph of "The Connection Between Christ's Resurrection and that of Believers" in Interpreting the Scripture.)

(3) Goal 2: Value and Appreciate One's Identity in Jesus Christ

❖ Read "An Affirmation of Human Life" from Interpreting the Scripture.

❖ Ask: **If "the bodily resurrection invests current life with meaning and significance," then what does that say to you about how you are to live as a believer right now?**

❖ Point out that those who live in Christ value and appreciate their identity in him. Post the following list of Bible passages, which you will have written prior to the session, that provides scriptural evidence about believers' identities in Christ:

Psalm 139:13-16

Jeremiah 29:11
Matthew 5:13-14
John 1:12-13
John 15:15
Romans 6:18
1 Corinthians 3:16
2 Corinthians 1:21-22
2 Corinthians 5:17-21
Galatians 3:26-27
Galatians 4:6-7
Ephesians 1:4-5
Ephesians 2:6
Ephesians 2:10
Ephesians 2:19
Philippians 3:20
Colossians 3:12
1 Peter 2:5
1 Peter 2:9
1 John 5:18

❖ Go around the room and ask each person to read one passage. (You may need to go around more than once, depending on the number of students present.) Those who do not wish to read may say "pass."

❖ Invite the students to turn to a partner or small group and name at least one facet of their own identity in Christ for which they are especially grateful.

❖ Conclude this activity by affirming that as Easter people our identities are shaped by the resurrected Christ.

(4) Goal 3: Witness Personally and Corporately to the Resurrection of Jesus Christ

❖ Form small groups and give each one a sheet of newsprint and a marker. Encourage each group to write a brief creed about what they believe about Jesus and his resurrection, based on Paul's words to the Corinthian church that we have studied from chapter 15.

❖ Bring everyone together and ask

one person from each group to read the creed the group has crafted.

❖ Challenge the adults to use the ideas from these creeds to bear witness to Christ's resurrection. Remind them that since "all will be made alive in Christ" (15:22), it is important for them to share the good news with anyone they can.

❖ Option: Write a class creed based on the ones the groups have created. Ask someone to make a poster, either by hand or with a computer, that can be displayed on a bulletin board or other prominent place as the class's corporate witness about Christ's resurrection. Submit this creed to the editor of the church newsletter so that others can read and reflect on the witness of this creed.

(5) Continue the Journey

❖ Pray that as the learners depart, they will give thanks that Christ is alive and because he lives, they too will live.

❖ Post information for next week's session on newsprint for the students to copy:

- **Title: Love One Another**
- **Background Scripture: 1 John 3:11-24**
- **Lesson Scripture: 1 John 3:11-24**
- **Focus of the Lesson: People wonder if life is a random sequence of events or has an ordered purpose. How do believers measure meaning in life? John's letter indicates that the measure of people's lives is calculated by their**

faith in Christ and their love for one another.

❖ Challenge the adults to grow spiritually by completing one or more of these activities related to this week's session, which you have posted on newsprint for the students to copy.

(1) **Witness to someone this week about your own beliefs concerning the resurrection of Jesus. Include a story to illustrate your personal experiences with him. Think of this as your "eyewitness account."**

(2) **Create or review your last will and testament. Have you distributed your worldly goods in a way that honors your love and commitments to family, friends, your church, and organizations important in your life?**

(3) **Pray for those who do not know Jesus. Ask the Lord to work in their hearts so that they might come into a personal relationship with the One whom God resurrected from the dead.**

❖ Sing or read aloud "Sing with All the Saints in Glory."

❖ Conclude today's session by leading the class in this benediction adapted from 1 Corinthians 12:13, which is the key verse for the lesson for May 17: **Let us go forth rejoicing that in the one Spirit we were all baptized into one body—Jews or Greeks, slaves or free—and we were all made to drink of one Spirit.**

UNIT 2: THE COMMUNITY OF BELOVED DISCIPLES
LOVE ONE ANOTHER

PREVIEWING THE LESSON

Lesson Scripture: 1 John 3:11-24
Background Scripture: 1 John 3:11-24
Key Verse: 1 John 3:11

Focus of the Lesson:
People wonder whether life is a random sequence of events or has an ordered purpose. How do believers measure meaning in life? John's letter indicates that the measure of people's lives is calculated by their faith in Christ and their love for one another.

Goals for the Learners:
(1) to understand John's message about loving one another.
(2) to affirm the fundamental discipleship principle of love for God and others.
(3) to express unconditional love to others.

Supplies:
Bibles, newsprint and marker, paper and pencils, hymnals

READING THE SCRIPTURE

NRSV
Lesson Scripture: 1 John 3:11-24

¹¹**For this is the message you have heard from the beginning, that we should love one another.** ¹²We must not be like Cain who was from the evil one and murdered his brother. And why did he murder him? Because his own deeds were evil and his brother's righteous. ¹³Do not be astonished, brothers and sisters, that the world hates you. ¹⁴We know that we have passed from death to life

CEB
Lesson Scripture: 1 John 3:11-24

¹¹**This is the message that you heard from the beginning: love each other.** ¹²Don't behave like Cain, who belonged to the evil one and murdered his brother. And why did he kill him? He killed him because his own works were evil, but the works of his brother were righteous.

¹³Don't be surprised, brothers and sisters, if the world hates you. ¹⁴We know that we have transferred

338

because we love one another. Whoever does not love abides in death. [15]All who hate a brother or sister are murderers, and you know that murderers do not have eternal life abiding in them. [16]We know love by this, that he laid down his life for us—and we ought to lay down our lives for one another. [17]How does God's love abide in anyone who has the world's goods and sees a brother or sister in need and yet refuses help?

[18]Little children, let us love, not in word or speech, but in truth and action. [19]And by this we will know that we are from the truth and will reassure our hearts before him [20]whenever our hearts condemn us; for God is greater than our hearts, and he knows everything. [21]Beloved, if our hearts do not condemn us, we have boldness before God; [22]and we receive from him whatever we ask, because we obey his commandments and do what pleases him.

[23]And this is his commandment, that we should believe in the name of his Son Jesus Christ and love one another, just as he has commanded us. [24]All who obey his commandments abide in him, and he abides in them. And by this we know that he abides in us, by the Spirit that he has given us.

from death to life, because we love the brothers and sisters. The person who does not love remains in death. [15]Everyone who hates a brother or sister is a murderer, and you know that no murderer has eternal life residing in him. [16]This is how we know love: Jesus laid down his life for us, and we ought to lay down our lives for our brothers and sisters. [17]But if a person has material possessions and sees a brother or sister in need and that person doesn't care—how can the love of God remain in him?

[18]Little children, let's not love with words or speech but with action and truth. [19]This is how we will know that we belong to the truth and reassure our hearts in God's presence. [20]Even if our hearts condemn us, God is greater than our hearts and knows all things. [21]Dear friends, if our hearts don't condemn us, we have confidence in relationship to God. [22]We receive whatever we ask from him because we keep his commandments and do what pleases him. [23]This is his commandment, that we believe in the name of his Son, Jesus Christ, and love each other as he commanded us. [24]The person who keeps his commandments remains in God and God remains in him; and this is how we know that he remains in us, because of the Spirit that he has given to us.

UNDERSTANDING THE SCRIPTURE

Introduction. First John is written for a community that has endured strife because of false teaching, particularly a teaching about the nature of Christ's presence in the world. This dispute has led to tensions even among those who have remained faithful to the apostolic teaching. These tensions move John to speak about the importance of love. In the verses that immediately precede our reading, John has talked about how to distinguish between the children of God and those of the devil. Our reading continues that discussion by talking about the characteristics of children of God. John will make dramatic contrasts with no room for compromise. Each individual must decide whether to be a child of God or of the devil. John makes his point in this strident way so that his readers know how important it is to love one another even in the midst of dissension.

1 John 3:11-14. Verse 11 begins with an intentional echo of the first verse of 1 John. Both verses talk about what was "from the beginning." Chapter 1 talks about the teaching about Christ that has been in the church since the beginning; chapter 3 reminds readers of the command that has been with the church just as long. The command is that they are to love one another. At this point, John has in mind loving other members of the church who have remained faithful to the apostolic teaching. Beyond believing the right things about Christ, those who are children of God must also love their fellow Christians. From verse 11, it seems that all of Christian righteousness can be summed up with this one command. After John recites the command to love one another, he emphasizes its importance by making the alternative to keeping it being like Cain, the one who murdered his brother in Genesis 4. If this were not bad enough, Cain is "from the evil one" (3:12), that is, from the devil. Perhaps there was already a tradition that associated Cain with the devil because this accusation appears in some second-century writings of other Jewish Christians. A second reason John gives as motivation for Cain's act of murder is that his deeds were wicked while Abel's were righteous. Thus Cain hated Abel for showing how evil Cain's deeds were. John sees this as a pattern that plays itself out in the life of the church. When the church lives righteously and lovingly, the outside world will hate it. So believers should be prepared. In spite of this opposition, they must cultivate love among themselves because that is the sign that they now possess God's life in them. Those without love remain "in death" (3:14), that is, they have not received the life of salvation.

1 John 3:15-18. John stresses the necessity of love even more strongly by saying that the alternative is being guilty of murder—and murderers face God's condemnation. This threat is followed by another reason for having love for one another: Christ loved us. Christ's love for us was so deep that it led him to die for us. This is the kind of love believers are to have. They are to love one another in the same radical way that Christ loved us. John then gives a primary way believers should show this love. They are to share their possessions with those who have need. This seems especially addressed to the wealthy, those who have "riches." John finds it unthinkable that those who have the love of God in their hearts would neglect their duty to share with their fellow Christians who need economic help. The love John sees as a necessary mark of Christians is that they share their financial means with those who need help. The command sums up the duty: Do not love in word only, but in "action and truth" (3:18 CEB).

1 John 3:19-24. John says that if we keep the love command in both what we say and how we respond to the needs of others, we can have a clear conscience before God. Even if we are worried about standing before God, keeping this command is sufficient evidence to assure us that we are of the light, that we are counted among the people of God. Living out the love seen in Christ by sharing one's possessions is ample evidence that the person is one of God's children. This is the judgment of God, who transcends our consciences and so makes the proper judgments. John refers to his readers as "beloved" (3:21). This description provides assurance of their standing with God while at the same time reminding them that they should show love by meeting the needs of others because they are the recipients of a love that meets their needs. John encourages these "beloved" readers, who can have a clear conscience because they love others, to bring their needs to God. God will meet those needs because they keep God's commands and so have lives that are pleasing to God. With all of this emphasis on love, John does not forget that it is also important to believe the right things. As he summarizes his instructions in verse 23, they come down to two things: believe in Christ and love one another. These are related commands because he has said that we know how to love because of the example Christ has given us. John says that those who obey these commands live in God and God lives in them. So Christians are not simply required to show love on their own. They are empowered by the Spirit of God to be loving people. This indwelling Spirit is also a sign that God loves them because God chooses to live in them. As John expresses it, this also means that believers live within the realm that is characterized by the presence of God. This presence of God is not something that is only with them at times; it is the environment in which they live. They are surrounded by the presence of God that keeps them aware of God's love, even as it enables them to show love.

INTERPRETING THE SCRIPTURE

Love in the Midst of Strife

Our reading today reminds us of the importance of loving our fellow Christians. This can be difficult even in the best of times. We always find it easier to love those who are distant. We know the faults and weaknesses of those we see regularly. Such foibles often make our fellow church members harder to love. But John is not addressing a church where all is going well. The church John addresses has experienced a painful split. Even though the split was necessary, it has left this church hurting.

Those who remain know and care about those who left. They are worried about whether those people who advocate a harmful view of the nature of Christ's presence in the world still have a relationship with God. The decision to reject that teaching and those who advocate it must have been controversial. (See "The Big Picture: The Early Church and the Holy Spirit" for discussion of the debated teaching.)

Now the church that remains must come together. It is not enough to believe the correct things about God and Christ, being the church also demands that believers treat one another in ways that reflect who they know God to be. The church must reflect the character of God in its life. In this passage, John calls the members to reflect the love of God in the ways they see and treat one another. John says this is a core command; it has been with the church "from the beginning" (3:11). Love for one another should be a distinguishing attribute of the church, always. Remember that this command comes to this church at the worst possible moment. Tempers have been hot, debate has been vehement, lines have been drawn. It is precisely in this moment that John says the central characteristic of their relations with one another must be love. Without this, being right does not matter. The only alternative to manifesting love that John allows is that they hate their brothers and sisters. Those who hate, he says, belong in the same category as murderers, even among those who murder their own brothers. Such a stark contrast impresses upon them the centrality of the demand to love one another, precisely now when it is the hardest. To fail at this task, he says, is to put oneself outside the sphere of salvation.

Following the Example of Christ's Love

As John's church hears this demand to love and as they consider the harshness of the alternatives, they may feel overwhelmed. How can anyone be expected to do what John demands? Perhaps anticipating their need for a way to move toward complying with such a demand, John reminds them that they have been recipients of just the kind of love he calls them to embody. The love to which John calls this church has been exemplified for them in Christ. Christ loved them so much that he gave his life for them. John and those who remain in this church have insisted that Christ had a genuine bodily form. Thus to say he died for them means that he experienced real death. Christ agrees to follow this path out of love "for us" (3:16). There can be no more extreme example of love.

John has already interpreted the death of Christ as the act that makes it possible for people to have a relationship with God (2:1-2). So they know they have received great benefits from the love Christ has shown them. Given that they have been loved in this way, they should respond by showing the same kind of love to one another. In 3:16, John goes so far as to say they should be willing to die for one another. As John sees it, standing for the truth about Christ is a show of love because that helps keep people within the sphere of God's salvation. But now they must show love in other ways as they relate to one another within the church. Love must overcome the hurt feelings and tensions. Following the example of Christ means that they must show love even before the other person signals a desire to restore a relationship.

A Central Manifestation of Love

John has demanded that the church, in the midst of conflict, must live out the kind of love seen in Christ. Then the discussion takes an unexpected and uncomfortable turn in verse 17. Suddenly the subject becomes how the rich should treat the poor within the church. This could be a very difficult topic in their church. If it is like other early churches, it included slaves and slave owners, fairly wealthy business people and people whose children who went to bed hungry. What does love look like in such a church? John demands that the wealthy share what they have to relieve the hardships of the poor.

So insistent is John about this that he makes this the command that immediately follows his reference to Christ being willing to die for us. This sharing of monetary resources is the way the church is to live out its willingness to die for one another. The radical nature of the demand to be willing to die for fellow Christians is exemplified centrally by sharing one's wealth. As challenging as this is, John suggests that the love of God is not in those who fail to show love in this way. This aspect of loving others is among the most difficult for us to hear in our culture in which each person is expected to fend for himself or herself. John rejects that cultural outlook, identifying unearned sharing as a central way Christians express love.

Abiding in God

The task of showing love properly now seems nearly out of reach. But we must remember that John writes about showing love in this way because that church needed to hear it. It is because they were not living out this love as they should have that he needs to direct and encourage them to begin to do so. Fortunately, John concludes this demanding section with a reminder that God's Spirit continues to live within believers even as they struggle to live as they should. God does not withdraw from us when we neglect our duties to God and fellow Christians. Even when we fail to love, the Holy Spirit is with us.

John says not only that God abides or remains in us but also that we live within God. That is, God remains the atmosphere within which we live our lives. God's presence surrounds us, even as God lives within us. God does not desert us when we fall short; God is committed to being with and in us. This embrace of God is what strengthens us to live for God. It is with this immersion in the presence of God that we can begin to live out the love command. It is from the assurance of the love of God seen in Christ's willingness to die that we can gain the strength to love one another. Still there is reciprocity here. The generous love of God must evoke a response from us. The gift of love demands that we enter a relationship with God. As it is with all relationships, this one has expectations for each party. A central expectation for those who accept God's love is that they love others. Failing to show such love is evidence that a person has not accepted the gift and has decided not to live in the sphere of God's saving presence.

SHARING THE SCRIPTURE

PREPARING TO TEACH

Preparing Our Hearts

Meditate on this week's devotional reading from John 13:31-35. What connections can you draw between the commandment Jesus gives in verses 34-35 and what he says in Mark 12:29-31? What are some appropriate ways that believers can express their love for other people? With whom will you share God's love today?

Pray that you and the students will lovingly work through any differences you may have with others in the church.

Preparing Our Minds

Study the background Scripture and the lesson Scripture, which are both from 1 John 3:11-24.

Consider this question as you prepare the lesson: *How do you measure meaning in life?*

Write on newsprint:

❑ information for next week's lesson, found under "Continue the Journey."

❑ activities for further spiritual growth in "Continue the Journey."

Review the "Introduction," "The Big Picture," "Close-up," and "Faith in Action," which all precede the first lesson of this quarter. Consider how you might use any of this material in today's lesson.

Prepare the suggested lecture for "Understand John's Message about Loving One Another."

LEADING THE CLASS

(1) Gather to Learn

❖ Greet the class members and introduce guests.

❖ Pray that those who have come today will take stock of the sources of meaning in their lives.

❖ Read this excerpt from Kurt Vonnegut's novel, *Cat's Cradle.*

In the beginning, God created the earth, and he looked upon it in his cosmic loneliness.

And God said, "Let Us make living creatures out of mud, so the mud can see what We have done." And God created every living creature that now moveth, and one was man. Mud as man alone could speak. God leaned close to mud as man sat, looked around, and spoke. "What is the purpose of all this?" he asked politely.

"Everything must have a purpose?" asked God.

"Certainly," said man.

"Then I leave it to you to think of one for all this," said God.

And He went away.

❖ Ask: **What does this quotation suggest about the meaning of life and how humanity is supposed to find it? Do you agree?**

❖ Read aloud today's focus statement: **People wonder whether life is a random sequence of events or has an ordered purpose. How do believers measure meaning in life? John's letter indicates that the measure of people's lives is calculated by their faith in Christ and their love for one another.**

(2) Goal 1: Understand John's Message about Loving One Another

❖ Introduce today's Scripture by giving your prepared lecture to help the students understand the challenges John's community faced. Use the section titled "1, 2, 3 John" in "The Big Picture: The Early Church and the Holy Spirit," which is found at the beginning of the spring quarter. Also use information from "Love in the Midst of Strife" in Interpreting the Scripture.

❖ Choose a volunteer to read 1 John 3:11-24.

❖ Discuss these questions:

- **Look at today's key verse, 3:11. Why do you think that John specifies that the message of love was one that the community had heard "from the beginning"?**
- **What is John's point in using Cain as an example of one who is unloving?** (See "1 John 3:11-14" in Understanding the Scripture.)
- **What is John's point in using Jesus as the premier example of love?** (See "Following the Example of Christ's Love" in Interpreting the Scripture.)
- **What does John say about how believers are to love, particularly in the midst of conflict?** (See "A Central Manifestation of Love" in Interpreting the Scripture.)
- **How does the Holy Spirit figure into John's teachings on love?** (See "Abiding in God" in Interpreting the Scripture.)

(3) Goal 2: Affirm the Fundamental Discipleship Principle of Love for God and Others

❖ Compare 1 John 3:16-17 with James 1:22 and 2:14-17. Encourage the adults to comment on any connections they see between hearing, loving, and taking action.

❖ Brainstorm the names of church members who are in the military or away at college. Form several teams and ask each team to take one name. Suggest that they plan to put together a "care package" for this person as a means of affirming their love for God and for others.

(4) Goal 3: Express Unconditional Love to Others

❖ **Option:** Do "Project 4" on the page at the beginning of the quarter titled "Faith in Action: Empowered by the Spirit."

❖ Distribute paper and pencils. Read these statements and ask each student to respond. Allow time for the adults to write their responses. Tell them that they will not be asked to share their responses.

- **List three talents that you have.**
- **For each talent, write one action you could take that would show someone else that you cared about him or her.**
- **Write the name of at least one member of your family, church, or community who needs to experience God's love this week. Perhaps this person does not know Jesus, or perhaps life is especially challenging and the person needs to be reassured that God does care.**
- **Look at your talents, the actions you could take using those talents, and the name(s) you have listed. Complete this sentence:** *I will use my talent of ____ in order to ____ (action you will take) for ____ (name of person).*

❖ Conclude this activity by suggesting that the students put their papers in their Bibles and refer to them throughout the week until they have completed the actions they have promised to take on behalf of someone who needs to feel unconditional love.

(5) Continue the Journey

❖ Pray that as the learners depart they will share the love of God with everyone they meet.

❖ Post information for next week's session on newsprint for the students to copy:

- **Title: Believe God's Love**
- **Background Scripture: 1 John 4–5**
- **Lesson Scripture: 1 John 4:13–5:5**
- **Focus of the Lesson: Community is built on unity and mutuality. What holds the members of a community together? The writer of 1 John says believers are made complete when as a community they abide in God's love and the Spirit of God's love abides in them.**

❖ Challenge the adults to grow spiritually by completing one or more of these activities related to this week's session, which you have posted on newsprint for the students to copy.

(1) **Recall that John's community was so divided by internal conflict that some had separated from the church.** What issues threaten to divide your own congregation or denomination? Do whatever you can to serve as a mediator and peacemaker by showing love to all.

(2) **Review 1 John 3:18 where we are told to love "in truth and action." What action can you take to show unconditional love to someone who needs to experience God's love?**

(3) **Visit a member of your congregation who is sick or homebound. Let this person know how much he or she is valued and missed. Offer to do something for this person, such as run an errand.**

❖ Sing or read aloud "Help Us Accept Each Other."

❖ Conclude today's session by leading the class in this benediction adapted from 1 Corinthians 12:13, which is the key verse for the lesson for May 17: **Let us go forth rejoicing that in the one Spirit we were all baptized into one body—Jews or Greeks, slaves or free—and we were all made to drink of one Spirit.**

UNIT 2: THE COMMUNITY OF BELOVED DISCIPLES
BELIEVE GOD'S LOVE

PREVIEWING THE LESSON

Lesson Scripture: 1 John 4:13–5:5
Background Scripture: 1 John 4–5
Key Verse: 1 John 5:1

Focus of the Lesson:
Community is built on unity and mutuality. What holds the members of a community together? The writer of 1 John says believers are made complete when as a community they abide in God's love and the Spirit of God's love abides in them.

Goals for the Learners:
(1) to comprehend what is required to live with unity in community.
(2) to share experiences of love within the community that exemplify faith in and love for God.
(3) to celebrate the community's contribution to their formation as disciples of Jesus.

Supplies:
Bibles, newsprint and marker, paper and pencils, hymnals

READING THE SCRIPTURE

NRSV
Lesson Scripture: 1 John 4:13–5:5

¹³By this we know that we abide in him and he in us, because he has given us of his Spirit. ¹⁴And we have seen and do testify that the Father has sent his Son as the Savior of the world. ¹⁵God abides in those who confess that Jesus is the Son of God, and they abide in God. ¹⁶So we have known and believe the love that God has for us.

CEB
Lesson Scripture: 1 John 4:13–5:5

¹³This is how we know we remain in him and he remains in us, because he has given us a measure of his Spirit. ¹⁴We have seen and testify that the Father has sent the Son to be the savior of the world. ¹⁵If any of us confess that Jesus is the God's Son, God remains in us and we remain in God. ¹⁶We have known and have believed the love that God has for us.

God is love, and those who abide in love abide in God, and God abides in them. ¹⁷Love has been perfected among us in this: that we may have boldness on the day of judgment, because as he is, so are we in this world. ¹⁸There is no fear in love, but perfect love casts out fear; for fear has to do with punishment, and whoever fears has not reached perfection in love. ¹⁹We love because he first loved us. ²⁰Those who say, "I love God," and hate their brothers or sisters, are liars; for those who do not love a brother or sister whom they have seen, cannot love God whom they have not seen. ²¹The commandment we have from him is this: those who love God must love their brothers and sisters also.

¹Everyone who believes that Jesus is the Christ has been born of God, and everyone who loves the parent loves the child. ²By this we know that we love the children of God, when we love God and obey his commandments. ³For the love of God is this, that we obey his commandments. And his commandments are not burdensome, ⁴for whatever is born of God conquers the world. And this is the victory that conquers the world, our faith. ⁵Who is it that conquers the world but the one who believes that Jesus is the Son of God?

God is love, and those who remain in love remain in God and God remains in them. ¹⁷This is how love has been perfected in us, so that we can have confidence on the Judgment Day, because we are exactly the same as God is in this world. ¹⁸There is no fear in love, but perfect love drives out fear, because fear expects punishment. The person who is afraid has not been made perfect in love. ¹⁹We love because God first loved us. ²⁰If anyone says, I love God, and hates a brother or sister, he is a liar, because the person who doesn't love a brother or sister who can be seen can't love God, who can't be seen. ²¹This commandment we have from him: Those who claim to love God ought to love their brother and sister also.

¹Everyone who believes that Jesus is the Christ has been born from God. Whoever loves someone who is a parent loves the child born to the parent. ²This is how we know that we love the children of God: when we love God and keep God's commandments. ³This is the love of God: we keep God's commandments. God's commandments are not difficult, ⁴because everyone who is born from God defeats the world. And this is the victory that has defeated the world: our faith. ⁵Who defeats the world? Isn't it the one who believes that Jesus is God's Son?

UNDERSTANDING THE SCRIPTURE

Introduction. Throughout 1 John, we see a pattern of alternating between calls for love and refutations of false teaching. These stand in an important tension. It is important to believe correct things and to argue for them powerfully, but those debates must be conducted in love. We find it hard to hold together having a dispute and having love for the other person. But 1 John demands that readers do both. John is insistent about proper teaching because he knows that what we believe conditions how we act.

The alternating pattern appears in chapters 4–5. Chapter 4 begins with a harsh rejection of the other teaching, then moves to a section that advocates love for fellow believers. It shifts back to arguing against the other view at verse 13, but back to emphasizing love in 4:16. Then at 5:6 we move back to a milder refutation of the other teaching. John is convinced that the church must both maintain its teaching and be loving.

1 John 4:1-6. John sees a great deal at stake in the argument about the humanity of Christ. The early church was open to a good bit of diversity, but what John rejects here crosses the line. Some church members have argued that the material world was too evil for the divine to actually touch. Thus, the divine Christ must not have truly had a physical body. John emphatically rejects this idea. Those who hold such a view are the anti-Christ, he says in verse 3. The issue is not just about the nature of Christ but about the nature of the world God made and so also of human nature. Their view implies that humans are inherently evil because of the material of which they are made. John sees the world, and so humans, as the creation of a good God who made a good world. Saying that Christ had not actually come into the world suggests that he did not love the world enough to come into genuine contact with it. That diminishes the gospel to an extent that John says is unacceptable.

1 John 4:7-12. These verses shift the focus to the need to love one another, but maintain a current of rejection of the false teaching. We must love because God loves us, a love seen in the sending of the Son into the world to be the means of forgiveness of sins. This way of stating the point both urges readers to respond to God's love and affirms the bodily nature of Christ's presence in the world. This love of God is not just something God exercises on occasion; John says that "God is love" (4:8). Love is a defining characteristic of God's nature. As people of God, then, Christians must reflect who God is and so make love a defining characteristic of their lives. Thus, God's love comes to expression in God's children.

1 John 4:13-16a. John asserts that God's Spirit resides in those who confess that Jesus, the bodily person, is the Son of God and Savior of the world. Remaining in God and retaining God's Spirit in one's life is dependent upon confessing these things about Jesus. These elements of the gospel are so important because they are the central demonstrations of God's love; God loves the world so much that God sends the Son to bring salvation. In various places in 1 John, the author speaks as though he is a witness to the physical appearance of Jesus. We find that implied at the very beginning of the book and again here in 4:14 where John says "we have seen" that God has sent the Son. While 1 John is written after the time of such witnesses, it calls on that apostolic witness of the nature of Christ to validate the church's beliefs about him. Relying on this work of Christ gives believers the intimate relationship they have with God: God remaining in them and they in God.

1 John 4:16b-21. John opens the renewed discussion of love by reasserting that "God is love" (4:16b). Thus, those who have love enjoy the presence of God in their lives. The love spoken of here is not just love of other people; it is primarily love for God. This love for God leads believers to want to live for God, just as loving another person leads you to want to please him or her. Love that shapes one's life is the mature love that John wants his church to strive for. When believers live to please God because they love God, fear of judgment dissipates. Again, just as fear of rejection diminishes as love grows in human relationships, so it is with God, the One who is perfect love. And since we have seen the extent of God's love in Christ, we have good reason to move beyond fear of judgment. Even so, our love for God must be manifested in the ways we love others, particularly fellow Christians.

1 John 5:1-12. As John begins the closing section of the book, he returns to the double theme of believing in the bodily Jesus as the Christ and Savior and of the necessity of having love. Possessing these two things means that a person has life with God. John emphasizes the physical nature of Jesus by talking about "water and blood" (5:6). The primary referents of the water and the blood through which Christ comes are Jesus' baptism and death. But many interpreters think that the following mention of the Spirit indicates that John wants the readers to hear a secondary reference to the Eucharist (Holy Communion) as a reminder of the saving work that the death of Christ accomplishes. In any case, these words refute those who say Christ did not have a physical body.

1 John 5:13-21. John closes with encouragement. He acknowledges the readers' faithfulness and assures them that God hears their prayers. He also calls on them to pray for one another's faults. Some sins are worse than others. All sin is evil, but some can be forgiven through the prayers of others. He does not name which sins are "unto death" (5:16 KJV) and which are not, but we may assume that a lack of love is a sin "unto death." He finally exhorts them generally to keep themselves holy and not be like the world. Rather, they are to reflect the truth of God in their lives.

INTERPRETING THE SCRIPTURE

God Is Love

One of 1 John's best-known sayings is "God is love." John says it twice in chapter 4 (4:8, 16). By saying this, John identifies love as one of the central features of God's character, indeed as a defining element of who God is. This means that we can always depend on God to behave in ways that give expression to love. All of God's interactions with the world are governed by love. Even when God acts in judgment (and John is certain that God does act in judgment), what God does is shaped by love. Everything God does is loving because love is such a fundamental part of who God is. Such love is not simply fondness; it is an active devotion to the good of the one loved. It includes a constant commitment to do what is in the best interest of the beloved. "God is love" is the lens through which much of 1 John should be read. God as love is the source of the manner in which God interacts with the world to bring salvation and to remain present with believers. This characterization of God is also the ground for thinking about how to treat fellow Christians.

God's Love Seen in Sending the Son into the World

The most important way God's love is manifested is in the sending of Christ. This act of reaching out to a world that had turned away from God is something that flows completely out of God's love. Those who rejected God (that is, all of us) had been given all good things by God and yet chose not to honor God. Because of God's great love, God refuses to allow that rejection to be the defining moment in humanity's relationship with God. In love, God tries to reestablish that relationship with us. The astonishing level of commitment on God's part is seen in sending Christ to become a full participant in this world. The bodily existence of Christ is so important to John in part because it demonstrates the extent to which God is determined to show love to humanity. God is willing to engage the world by being fully identified with it, by becoming one of us. The salvation believers enjoy in Christ is a product of God's love. John says that God sent "the Son to be the savior of the world" (4:14 CEB). This full engagement and participation in the world show how valuable the world and material existence are to God.

Whatever it is about us that makes us need salvation, it is not that we have a material or bodily existence from which we need to be freed. All of John's talk about the genuinely bodily nature of Jesus indicates that there is nothing wrong with embodiment. We must keep that in mind when we hear John say that believers have "overcome the world" (5:4-5 KJV). John does not mean believers have overcome bodily existence. Here, as it often is in the New Testament, "the world" stands for the standards of values and commitments that dominate the outlook of economic and social systems. The values on which all cultural systems rest are not consistent with God's will for the world; none operate with love for the other as a central value. Conquering this "world" means that believers escape those understandings of how to value and treat others. As the church, believers can live in relation to one another by the standards set by recognizing that God is love and seeing how to live in that love by looking at Christ.

Loving Our Brothers and Sisters

John clearly stresses the importance of love as a characteristic of God and of God's people. Love appears as the most important virtue for believers, the one thing that guides all other behavior. The real focus of the expression of this love is the community, that is, the church. It is not that John does not care about how the church shows love to those outside, just that his focus as he writes here is on how Christians relate to one another. We should remember that he urges them to be loving in difficult circumstances. There has been a contested debate about proper beliefs and the church to which John writes has split. Hard feelings must exist not just between the groups but also within each of the groups. It is in the midst of such trying times that John calls for love. He is not emphasizing the need for love for those who left this church, but among those who remain. The exposed nerves of various members no doubt make getting along more difficult. But John does not call the church to love those who are easy to get along with or who are not offended easily. He calls believers to love everyone in their church.

While this may sound like a difficult task, John gives them good reason to behave in this way. He reminds them in 4:19 that God loved us before we loved God. It was while we had turned our backs to God that God extended love to us. Thus, as we have seen in other places, John asks believes to treat one another as they have already been treated by God. That is, they are not being asked to do anything that God has not already done for them. In what seems in some ways counterintuitive, John says it should be easier to love those we see than it is to love God whom we cannot see. Acknowledging that trying to love someone you have never seen may be difficult, John emphasizes the necessity of acting in love toward fellow Christians. Not loving them denies in reality what you might claim by saying that you love God. True love for God must show itself in love for others.

We Are Children of God

In 5:1-5, John constantly describes believers as children of God, or those who have been born by God. He makes being born by love a synonym for being born of God. This reinforces the importance of having love. In addition, the responsibility of loving fellow Christians is given another angle. In the preceding verses, believers are to love their "brothers and sisters" (4:21). Now these siblings are seen to be children of God. We are then to show them the same kind of love God has shown us because they hold this high status of being children of God. If we love God, John says we show that by loving fellow Christians.

Showing this love is also how we keep God's commands. But being a child of God also means that we should love God. If we have this love, we will recognize that God's commands are actually good for us. What God tells us to do really makes for the best life. As our love for God grows, we trust more and more that those commands are for our good. Then we can begin to keep them because we love God rather than because we fear judgment. John says that mature love for God alleviates fear of judgment. We obey God because we know God wants the best for us, not because we fear condemnation. Furthermore, we trust that God's love, because we love God and obey, will be so dominant in any evaluation of us that we have nothing to fear.

SHARING THE SCRIPTURE

PREPARING TO TEACH

Preparing Our Hearts

Meditate on this week's devotional reading from Romans 8:31-39. Who or what seems to be working against you right now? How do Paul's words of assurance that nothing can separate you from the God who loves you help you put the conflict you are experiencing into perspective? What evidence do you have that God is truly for you?

Pray that you and the students will recognize and give thanks for the constant love of God.

Preparing Our Minds

Study the background Scripture from 1 John 4–5 and the lesson Scripture from 1 John 4:13–5:5.

Consider this question as you prepare the lesson: *What holds the members of a community together?*

Write on newsprint:

❏ information for next week's lesson, found under "Continue the Journey."

❏ activities for further spiritual growth in "Continue the Journey."

Review the "Introduction," "The Big Picture," "Close-up," and "Faith in Action," which all precede the first lesson of this quarter. Consider how you might use any of this material in today's lesson.

LEADING THE CLASS

(1) Gather to Learn

❖ Greet the class members and introduce guests.

❖ Pray that those who have come today will seek to live in unity with this community of believers.

❖ Read: **In his mid-nineteenth-century novel, *The Three Musketeers*, Alexandre Dumas's character d'Artagnan immortalized the motto "All for one, one for all." His point was to show that he and the three musketeers of the title—Athos, Porthos, and Aramis—stood together as a unified team. Similarly, the phrase has been the unofficial motto of Switzerland since it was used in an appeal for donations that went out to all regions following widespread flooding in the Alps in the fall of 1868. Here, too, the point was to emphasize solidarity among** people who, in this case, shared a common homeland, though had only come together as a country in 1847. Although the motto appears in no legal Swiss documents, it is acknowledged throughout the country and was even written in the cupola of the Federal Palace of Switzerland in 1902.

❖ Ask: **Why motivates people to stick together?**

❖ Read aloud today's focus statement: **Community is built on unity and mutuality. What holds the members of a community together? The writer of 1 John says believers are made complete when as a community they abide in God's love and the Spirit of God's love abides in them.**

(2) Goal 1: Comprehend What Is Required to Live with Unity in Community

❖ Introduce the theme of today's lesson by reading "God Is Love" in Interpreting the Scripture.

❖ Solicit one volunteer to read 1 John 4:13-21 and another to read 1 John 5:1-5.

❖ Discuss these questions:

1. **How does knowing that God first loved you (4:19) affect the way that you relate to other people?**

2. **First John 4:20-21 teaches that if one truly loves God then one must also love brothers and sisters in the community of faith. Yet there are often disagreements and conflicts within congregations and denominations. Why do you think Christians are unable to live in unity?**

3. **The early church soon recognized diversity when**

Gentiles were allowed to be included with Jewish believers. How is it possible to experience unity when the people of the church are so diverse?

4. Contemporary Christians often think of love as a noun, but 1 John 5:2 makes clear that love is a verb. One's love for God is directly linked to one's obedience to God's commands. Do you think it is more difficult to love others when active obedience, rather than simple assent, to God's commands is expected? Why or why not?

(3) Goal 2: Share Experiences of Love Within the Community that Exemplify Faith in and Love for God

❖ Read or retell "Loving Our Brothers and Sisters" in Interpreting the Scripture.

❖ Form small groups. Encourage each person to tell the group about an experience that he or she had within the church that truly exemplified God's love.

❖ Remain in groups to consider ways that love can be shared within the community. What faith-filled actions can the group members do in order to show others within the congregation (including those who are visitors) that God's love is real and present in this church?

(4) Goal 3: Celebrate the Community's Contribution to the Learners' Formation as Disciples of Jesus

❖ Post a sheet of newsprint on which you will write the learners' answers to this question: **How has** this congregation helped you and your family members become more faithful disciples of Jesus? (Try to think here of worship, mission and outreach projects, age-level activities, and special programs that assist in spiritual formation, but do not limit discussion to these. Include ideas about the way members greet and care for newcomers and current members, the way they resolve conflicts, and their attitudes to those who are in need or are in some way different from most of the congregation.)

❖ Review the list. Make note of any programs that may have been helpful in the past that are no longer in existence. Ask if there is any interest in revamping them. If so, pass that information along to the appropriate committees.

❖ Create a simple litany of thanksgiving by inviting half of the class to read each item on the list in turn and the other half to respond by saying, **"For this and for all the blessings of your love, we give you thanks, O God."**

(5) Continue the Journey

❖ Pray that as the learners depart, they will give thanks for God's love and its impact on their lives.

❖ Post information for next week's session on newsprint for the students to copy:

■ **Title: Watch Out for Deceivers!**
■ **Background Scripture: 1 John 5:6-12, 18-20; 2 John**
■ **Lesson Scripture: 2 John**
■ **Focus of the Lesson: People who do not share their community's life-sustaining beliefs are a threat to the community. How does the**

community deal with this threat? The writer of 1 John suggests that those who remain faithful in their belief in Christ will have eternal life; the writer of 2 John warns them to beware of deceivers lest they corrupt the community of believers.

❖ Challenge the adults to grow spiritually by completing one or more of these activities related to this week's session, which you have posted on newsprint for the students to copy.

(1) Be aware of the Spirit's prompting to be reconciled with someone with whom you have had a falling out. Recognize that God loves both you and the person from whom you are estranged.

(2) Identify a fear that currently holds you in its grip. Memorize these words from 1 John 4:18: "Perfect love casts out fear." Say this verse whenever you feel yourself beset by fear.

(3) Explore the Bible to find examples of how love and obedience are related, particularly in the teachings and actions of Jesus.

❖ Sing or read aloud "Where Charity and Love Prevail."

❖ Conclude today's session by leading the class in this benediction adapted from 1 Corinthians 12:13, which is the key verse for the lesson for May 17: **Let us go forth rejoicing that in the one Spirit we were all baptized into one body—Jews or Greeks, slaves or free—and we were all made to drink of one Spirit.**

UNIT 2: THE COMMUNITY OF BELOVED DISCIPLES
WATCH OUT FOR DECEIVERS!

PREVIEWING THE LESSON

Lesson Scripture: 2 John
Background Scripture: 1 John 5:6-12, 18-20; 2 John
Key Verse: 2 John 8

Focus of the Lesson:
People who do not share their community's life-sustaining beliefs are a threat to the community. How does the community deal with this threat? The writer of 1 John suggests that those who remain faithful in their belief in Christ will have eternal life; the writer of 2 John warns them to beware of deceivers lest they corrupt the community of believers.

Goals for the Learners:
(1) to research John's caution to beware of those who do not abide in Christ's teachings.
(2) to reflect on the emotional response to teachings that are contrary to what they have been taught previously.
(3) to testify that walking in Jesus' commandment to love protects the faith community from deceivers and corruption.

Supplies:
Bibles, newsprint and marker, paper and pencils, hymnals

READING THE SCRIPTURE

NRSV

Lesson Scripture: 2 John

¹The elder to the elect lady and her children, whom I love in the truth, and not only I but also all who know the truth, ²because of the truth that abides in us and will be with us forever:

CEB

Lesson Scripture: 2 John

¹From the elder.

To the chosen gentlewoman and her children, whom I truly love (and I am not the only one, but also all who know the truth), ²because of the truth that remains with us and will be with us forever.

³Grace, mercy, and peace will be with us from God the Father and from Jesus Christ, the Father's Son, in truth and love.

⁴I was overjoyed to find some of your children walking in the truth, just as we have been commanded by the Father. ⁵But now, dear lady, I ask you, not as though I were writing you a new commandment, but one we have had from the beginning, let us love one another. ⁶And this is love, that we walk according to his commandments; this is the commandment just as you have heard it from the beginning—you must walk in it.

⁷Many deceivers have gone out into the world, those who do not confess that Jesus Christ has come in the flesh; any such person is the deceiver and the antichrist! ⁸**Be on your guard, so that you do not lose what we have worked for, but may receive a full reward.** ⁹Everyone who does not abide in the teaching of Christ, but goes beyond it, does not have God; whoever abides in the teaching has both the Father and the Son. ¹⁰Do not receive into the house or welcome anyone who comes to you and does not bring this teaching; ¹¹for to welcome is to participate in the evil deeds of such a person.

¹²Although I have much to write to you, I would rather not use paper and ink; instead I hope to come to you and talk with you face to face, so that our joy may be complete.

¹³The children of your elect sister send you their greetings.

³Grace, mercy, and peace from God the Father and from Jesus Christ, the Son of the Father, will be ours who live in truth and love.

⁴I was overjoyed to find some of your children living in the truth, just as we had been commanded by the Father. ⁵Now, dear friends, I am requesting that we love each other. It's not as though I'm writing a new command to you, but it's one we have had from the beginning. ⁶This is love: that we live according to his commands. This is the command that you heard from the beginning: live in love.

⁷Many deceivers have gone into the world who do not confess that Jesus Christ came as a human being. This kind of person is the deceiver and the antichrist. ⁸**Watch yourselves so that you don't lose what we've worked for but instead receive a full reward.** ⁹Anyone who goes too far and does not continue in the teaching about Christ does not have God. Whoever continues in this teaching has both the Father and the Son. ¹⁰Whoever comes to you who does not affirm this teaching should neither be received nor welcomed into your home, ¹¹because welcoming people like that is the same thing as sharing in their evil actions.

¹²I have a lot to tell you. I don't want to use paper and ink, but I hope to visit you and talk with you face-to-face, so that our joy can be complete.

¹³Your chosen sister's children greet you.

UNDERSTANDING THE SCRIPTURE

1 John 5:6-12. John is insistent that there are some things that people must believe to be members of the church. In these verses John argues for the physical nature of the presence of Christ in the world. It is particularly clear in 2 John 7 that this is the issue at stake. The evidence that John gives for the reality of the bodily nature of Jesus is the "water and blood" (5:6). These seem to be a reference to the baptism and death of Jesus, moments when John sees the full humanity of Jesus demonstrated very clearly. But he also adds the testimony of the Spirit. This mention of the Spirit may refer to multiple moments of the Spirit's work. It may point to the story of Jesus' baptism when the Spirit descends and so gives witness to the identity of Jesus. It may also point to the Spirit's presence in worship or the Eucharist, where the Spirit confirms the proper understanding of Christ. Finally, it may also point to the testimony of the Spirit in the hearts of believers. Whether one or all of these is correct, John sees the Spirit as a powerful witness from God that proves that his teaching about Jesus is correct. You can see the importance John puts on this issue in verses 11-12: Those who believe it have eternal life, whereas those who do not believe have neither life nor God.

1 John 5:18-20. As John concludes this letter, he reminds the readers of the importance of living a moral life. This also means that they will be different from those around them. John sees the world outside the church as one that is dominated by evil. But those in the church have been rescued from that tyranny by God through Christ. John finally reminds them again of the importance of believing the right things about Christ. Believing that Jesus had a genuine physical body is connected with this concern about ethics. The bodily nature of Jesus confirms the goodness and importance of our bodily existence. The realm of our physical world matters to God. Thus, we must live in a way that acknowledges the importance of bodily existence. Those who have the truth about Christ and act in accord with it through ethical living are the ones who have the truth and so have eternal life.

2 John 1-3. The short letter of 2 John has one purpose: to tell its recipients not to accept the teaching of those who say Jesus did not have a physical body. It is addressed to "the elect lady" (verse 1). Most interpreters recognize that this does not refer to a specific individual, but to the church. Her children are the members of the church. Calling her "elect" means that she has been chosen by God. This does not imply a doctrine of some people being foreordained for salvation and others for damnation. Her chosenness is seen in her faithfulness to God. This is especially clear when we remember that she is a church rather than an individual. This is probably a congregation that John's church started.

John writes as "the Elder," that is, as a recognized leader in his church. As such a leader in the church that sponsored the beginnings of the addressed congregation, he is someone to whom they should listen. Plus, 2 John says he and his whole church love this church. In no place does this letter identify its author with anyone named John, just as was the case with 1 John. We refer to the author of these texts as John because they have so much in common with the Gospel of John and because some traditions connected John and these writings. We continue to refer to the author as John even though we do not know who actually wrote them (see "The Big Picture: The Early Church and the Holy Spirit" for more). John stresses truth as this letter begins. Those in his church know the truth, the truth remains with them forever, he loves them in truth, and wished God's blessing on them in truth and love. With this start, there is no doubt that correct belief is important for this letter.

2 John 4-11. The same combination of ethics and doctrine that we saw in 1 John reappears in 2 John. When John says he is pleased about their manner of life he means both their conduct and what they believe. He renews the central commandment we saw in 1 John: Love one another. He again says this command has been with the church since its beginning as an essential expectation and guide for all behavior. John says that the way one shows this love is by keeping God's commandments. The commandments help us to see what love for our neighbor looks like it. Without this kind of guidance, we would be able to say and even think we were acting in loving ways but really be working for goals that benefit ourselves rather than our neighbor. So John reminds this church of the guidance we have been given in Scripture. He also sets up those who teach false doctrine as

the opposite of those who show love. The "deceivers" are those who deny that Jesus came "in the flesh" (verse 7). This belief is so dangerous that it will take away their salvation. It is so dangerous that they must not do anything to support the ministry of those who teach it. John identifies anyone who advocates this teaching as "the antichrist" (verse 7). Clearly, this is not some figure whose appearance will signal the end of the world. Rather, an antichrist here is one who advocates false beliefs in the church. John uses this dramatic language to stress how dangerous this teaching is. The one who is an antichrist does the opposite of the presence of Jesus; Jesus brings salvation, the antichrist deprives people of salvation.

2 John 12-13. The closing of this letter stresses the importance of the message with the author saying that he wishes he could see them in person so he could make his case in that setting. In person he thinks he could convey more clearly and thoroughly why the recipients must avoid this false teaching about Christ.

INTERPRETING THE SCRIPTURE

False Teaching

Many of us today are reticent to talk about "false teaching." We shy away from saying that some beliefs are so dangerous that they deprive people of salvation. We have seen the damage that can be done to people when they are condemned for what they believe. We may know of people driven from the church by those who claim to uphold the truth. Often we think of those who talk about false teaching as

the narrow-minded, perhaps as those who care more about details on paper than they do about people.

John, however, is convinced that many truths are worth fighting for. They are worth arguing about because what we say about the question shapes how we think of ourselves and one another. What we think about God determines how we think we should relate to one another. Beliefs matter. In the case of 1 and 2 John, the belief worth arguing about and even worth excluding people from the church has to do with the nature of Christ. This sounds like one of those esoteric topics that we should be able to agree to disagree about, but John does not think so. He rejects this live-and-let-live approach because what we say about the appearance of Christ has implications for how we think about ourselves and the importance of life in the world. It is important to John to affirm the bodily nature of Christ because that affirms the goodness of creation. A real bodily Christ means that God cares about our lives here and now, not just our souls in some other reality. A bodily Jesus affirms God's desire to be related to us and this world. So even when it seems that some teaching is removed from what matters in life, we need to think about it carefully. It may have more to say than first meets the eye.

Love and the Commandments

Just as we avoid talk about false teaching, we often also want to avoid talk of commandments. We associate talk of commandment with legalism. We like to think of ourselves as mature enough not to need rules; we will just reason our way to what is right. John is not so confident in us. As we have seen, the most important command for John is the love command. No command is more a part of the core of the faith than this. John says it has been part of the faith from the beginning. The Gospel of John has it as an important element of the teaching of Jesus (13:31-35). It is an inescapable part of what it means to be a Christian. But it is insufficient by itself. We need help discerning what the loving thing to do really is. We know that our own motives can inadvertently shade

our reasoning so that we do things that we claim (maybe even think) are for the good of others but are actually what we want. That is why John adds that the way to show love is to keep the commandments.

The church struggled with how its Gentile members should relate to the Mosaic law, and Jews of the first century discussed how to keep old laws in new situations, although those difficulties are not sufficient reason to disregard the commandments. John wants his church to think about how to keep the commandments because they chart a path that helps us to honor God. The commandments reflect the character of God and so give us a pattern of life that pleases God and is consistent with our identity as children of God. We do not need to be literalists in order to "live according to his commands" (verse 6 CEB). While we live in a different time that requires a different way of living out what God wants, the commands can serve as a guide. We can see what God expected then and discern how that was a demonstration of love. Then we must determine how to use that pattern to determine how we should show love today.

Beliefs and Ethics

John is concerned about how Christians live and about what they believe—and he thinks the two are connected. One of the reasons John is so insistent that his readers reject the false teaching is that he is convinced that it will change for the worse the way they live. In this case, he believes that denying that Jesus had a body will lead to neglect of how we live our lives in this world. If our bodily and material existence is too polluting for God to have real contact with, then there is no reason for us to try to live as we should. Such efforts are doomed to dismal failure because of our very nature.

While John would not fool himself about the possibility that we will live perfect lives or about the world suddenly beginning to conform itself to the will of God, he refuses to break the connection between God's good will and the world. Our bodily existence is within the scope of things that God cares about. All of this is at stake in this debate about doctrine. This is not a strange exception. What we believe should and does affect how we live. We generally agree that Christians should be concerned about justice. That is the case because of what we believe about God. We believe that justice is a part of the identity of God, so we work for justice, which shows by example of that characteristic of God. The same is true for love. In 1 John 4:7, John makes the connection directly. We are to love because God is love. We need to be clear and careful about what we believe because it will shape how we live.

Love and Right Teaching

We find it a bit strange to have a book that emphasizes both love and the necessity of believing the right thing. We usually envision the loving person as the one who is not insistent on agreement, but is open to all views. John sees love as something that searches for the deeper good for others. That deeper good is not always simple acceptance. In this case, John sees vehement arguments about right teaching and even refusal to recognize others as Christian as the loving thing. Such actions show love because they keep others from falling prey to beliefs and practices that damage the life and faith of those who hold them. He may even see this as showing love to those rejected because that action shows how damaging he thinks their teaching is.

We should see John's actions here are an extreme. We should remember that the early church accepted a great deal of diversity in many things. But there were matters that were seen to violate the faith, and those could not be tolerated without harming the church and its members. John is not alone in this view. It is the consistent one in the New Testament (see, for example, 2 Timothy 3:14). Believers are to remain or abide in the teaching that reflects truly who God is and what God wants for God's people. They will pursue that clarity of thought and teaching in a loving spirit. Only by doing both will we be what God wants of us and for us.

SHARING THE SCRIPTURE

PREPARING TO TEACH

Preparing Our Hearts

Meditate on this week's devotional reading from Galatians 6:6-10. What instructions does Paul provide for how believers are to live in community with one another? How could these instructions, if followed, help your congregation? Which of these instructions could you implement right now?

Pray that you and the students

will assist one another and also take responsibility for yourselves.

Preparing Our Minds

Study the background Scripture from 1 John 5:6-12, 18-20 and 2 John, and the lesson Scripture from 2 John.

Consider this question as you prepare the lesson: *How does a community deal with threats to its core beliefs?*

Write on newsprint:

❏ information for next week's lesson, found under "Continue the Journey."

❏ activities for further spiritual growth in "Continue the Journey."

Review the "Introduction," "The Big Picture," "Close-up," and "Faith in Action," which all precede the first lesson of this quarter. Consider how you might use any of this material in today's lesson.

LEADING THE CLASS

(1) Gather to Learn

❖ Greet the class members and introduce guests.

❖ Pray that those who have come today will be on guard against those who attempt to deceive them.

❖ Read: **A deceiver by any other name—con artist, liar, fraud, cheat, fake, betrayer, crook, charlatan, trickster, impostor, snake in the grass—is still someone who misleads people into believing something that is not true. E. R. Beadle insightfully claims, "half the work that is done in the world is to make things appear what they are not."** Often the deceiver perpetrates a scam in order to prosper financially. But a deceiver can also spin the

truth to urge people to accept ideas, beliefs, and accounts of events that are untrue. We see many examples of deception in our day, but deliberately misleading others is not a new phenomenon. In fact, we hear about deceivers in our Bible passage for today.

❖ Read aloud today's focus statement: **People who do not share their community's life-sustaining beliefs are a threat to the community. How does the community deal with this threat? The writer of 1 John suggests that those who remain faithful in their belief in Christ will have eternal life; the writer of 2 John warns them to beware of deceivers lest they corrupt the community of believers.**

(2) Goal 1: Research John's Caution to Beware of Those Who Do Not Abide in Christ's Teachings

❖ Select one volunteer to read the salutation of the letter (2 John 1-3), a second to read the body of the letter (verses 4-11), and a third to read the final greetings (verses 12-13).

❖ Discuss these questions:

1. **What do verses 1-3 tell you about the recipients of this letter?** (See "2 John 1-3" in Understanding the Scripture.)

2. **What do verses 1-3 tell you about the sender of this letter?** (See "2 John 1-3" in Understanding the Scripture.)

3. **What does the writer suggest in verses 4-6 about the relationship between what Christians believe and how they conduct themselves?** (See "Beliefs and Ethics" in Interpreting the Scripture.)

4. **What does the writer suggest about the connection**

between the command to love and the need to follow right teachings? (See "Love and Right Teaching" in Interpreting the Scripture.)

5. Why might the writer want to see the recipients in person, rather than communicate further information with them by letter? (See "2 John 12-13" in Understanding the Scripture.)

(3) Goal 2: Reflect on the Emotional Response to Teachings that Are Contrary to What the Learners Have Been Taught Previously

❖ Suggest that the students imagine themselves as very young children who had been taught to believe in Santa Claus, the Easter Bunny, the Tooth Fairy, or some other figure that they later learned did not truly exist. Ask each person to respond to this question using just a few words: **How did you feel when you learned that your beloved figure was not actually real—did not deliver presents on Christmas Eve or hide eggs for discovery on Easter morning or pay cash for lost baby teeth?**

❖ Form small groups and encourage everyone to talk about other teachings that they learned as children that they later discovered were either false or did not include the entire truth.

❖ Bring the groups together and ask:

1. **What were your feelings when you encountered teachings that challenged, perhaps even disproved, something you had been taught earlier?**

2. **How did this discovery** alter your relationship with or trust in the person whom you now feel had deliberately conveyed inaccurate information? (Note that in some instances feelings will not change because the "teacher" was stating what was accepted as truth at that time. For example, Pluto is no longer designated a planet, but that does not mean that a teacher who decades ago claimed that Pluto was a planet was being deceitful or dishonest.)

3. **If you think that you received inaccurate teaching about the Bible or God, how did you feel when you made discoveries that challenged what you learned earlier?**

❖ Read or retell "False Teaching" in Interpreting the Scripture.

❖ Conclude by reading in unison today's key verse, 2 John 8.

(4) Goal 3: Testify that Walking in Jesus' Commandment to Love Protects the Faith Community from Deceivers and Corruption

❖ Read or retell "Love and Right Teaching" in Interpreting the Scripture.

❖ Read again: **"Believers are to remain or abide in the teaching that reflects truly who God is and what God wants for God's people. They will pursue that clarity of thought and teaching in a loving spirit."**

❖ Invite the students to discuss (a) the beliefs they think are essential in terms of who God is and what God wants and (b) how they can convey and stand up for these beliefs in loving ways.

(5) Continue the Journey

❖ Pray that as the learners depart, they will be aware of challenges to their beliefs and be ready to lovingly speak up for those beliefs.

❖ Post information for next week's session on newsprint for the students to copy:

- Title: Coworkers with the Truth
- Background Scripture: 3 John
- Lesson Scripture: 3 John
- Focus of the Lesson: Most people really appreciate the kindness and generosity they have experienced as a result of good hospitality. What is it about receiving hospitality that makes it so important? Third John says that hospitality is one way that Christians express their faith in Christ to others, thereby making the faithful coworkers with the truth.

❖ Challenge the adults to grow spiritually by completing one or more of these activities related to this week's session, which you have posted on newsprint for the students to copy.

(1) Recall that 2 John was written in response to a threat to the church posed by "deceivers" who denied that Jesus had come in the flesh. Do you perceive any current threats to the church? If so, what are they? How can you stand against these threats and alert others to them?

(2) Speak to someone in person about how you experience the presence of Jesus in your life.

(3) Demonstrate your love for God and neighbor by showing hospitality to someone.

❖ Sing or read aloud "I Want to Walk as a Child of the Light."

❖ Conclude today's session by leading the class in this benediction adapted from 1 Corinthians 12:13, which is the key verse for the lesson for May 17: **Let us go forth rejoicing that in the one Spirit we were all baptized into one body—Jews or Greeks, slaves or free—and we were all made to drink of one Spirit.**

UNIT 2: THE COMMUNITY OF BELOVED DISCIPLES

COWORKERS WITH THE TRUTH

PREVIEWING THE LESSON

Lesson Scripture: 3 John
Background Scripture: 3 John
Key Verse: 3 John 8

Focus of the Lesson:
Most people really appreciate the kindness and generosity they have experienced as a result of good hospitality. What is it about receiving hospitality that makes it so important? Third John says that hospitality is one way that Christians express their faith in Christ to others, thereby making the faithful coworkers with the truth.

Goals for the Learners:
(1) to learn the importance of hospitality as described in 3 John.
(2) to tell experiences of hospitality and reactions to it.
(3) to practice acts of hospitality.

Pronunciation Guide:
Demetrius (di mee´ tree uhs)   Docetism (doh´ suh tiz uhm)
Diotrephes (di ot´ ruh feez)   Gaius (gay´ yuhs)

Supplies:
Bibles, newsprint and marker, paper and pencils, hymnals

READING THE SCRIPTURE

NRSV
Lesson Scripture: 3 John
¹The elder to the beloved Gaius, whom I love in truth.

²Beloved, I pray that all may go well with you and that you may be in good health, just as it is well with

CEB
Lesson Scripture: 3 John
¹From the elder.

To my dear friend Gaius, whom I truly love.

²Dear friend, I'm praying that all is well with you and that you enjoy

your soul. ³I was overjoyed when some of the friends arrived and testified to your faithfulness to the truth, namely how you walk in the truth. ⁴I have no greater joy than this, to hear that my children are walking in the truth.

⁵Beloved, you do faithfully whatever you do for the friends, even though they are strangers to you; ⁶they have testified to your love before the church. You will do well to send them on in a manner worthy of God; ⁷for they began their journey for the sake of Christ, accepting no support from non-believers. **⁸Therefore we ought to support such people, so that we may become co-workers with the truth.**

⁹I have written something to the church; but Diotrephes, who likes to put himself first, does not acknowledge our authority. ¹⁰So if I come, I will call attention to what he is doing in spreading false charges against us. And not content with those charges, he refuses to welcome the friends, and even prevents those who want to do so and expels them from the church.

¹¹Beloved, do not imitate what is evil but imitate what is good. Whoever does good is from God; whoever does evil has not seen God. ¹²Everyone has testified favorably about Demetrius, and so has the truth itself. We also testify for him, and you know that our testimony is true.

¹³I have much to write to you, but I would rather not write with pen and ink; ¹⁴instead I hope to see you soon, and we will talk together face to face. ¹⁵Peace to you. The friends send you their greetings. Greet the friends there, each by name.

good health in the same way that you prosper spiritually.

³I was overjoyed when the brothers and sisters arrived and spoke highly of your faithfulness to the truth, shown by how you live according to the truth. ⁴I have no greater joy than this: to hear that my children are living according to the truth. ⁵Dear friend, you act faithfully in whatever you do for our brothers and sisters, even though they are strangers. ⁶They spoke highly of your love in front of the church. You all would do well to provide for their journey in a way that honors God, ⁷because they left on their journey for the sake of Jesus Christ without accepting any support from the Gentiles. **⁸Therefore, we ought to help people like this so that we can be coworkers with the truth.**

⁹I wrote something to the church, but Diotrephes, who likes to put himself first, doesn't welcome us. ¹⁰Because of this, if I come, I will bring up what he has done—making unjustified and wicked accusations against us. And as if that were not enough, he not only refuses to welcome the brothers and sisters but stops those who want to do so and even throws them out of the church! ¹¹Dear friend, don't imitate what is bad but what is good. Whoever practices what is good belongs to God. Whoever practices what is bad has not seen God.

¹²Everyone speaks highly of Demetrius, even the truth itself. We also speak highly of him, and you know that what we say is true.

¹³I have a lot to say to you, but I don't want to use pen and ink. ¹⁴I hope to see you soon, and we will speak face-to-face.

¹⁵Peace be with you. Your friends here greet you. Greet our friends there by name.

UNDERSTANDING THE SCRIPTURE

Introduction. The letter of 3 John follows the conventions of first-century letter writing more closely than most other New Testament letters. Some conventional elements that are replaced or radically changed in other New Testament letters return to their more common form in 3 John. For example, the wish for the good health of the recipient in verse 2 is a standard part of friendly letters that is missing in other New Testament letters, but it resurfaces here. Perhaps this is also why the final exchange of greetings is among friends rather than brothers and sisters as is usually the case in the New Testament.

This letter addresses a serious rift in the relations among the churches that were related to the community from which we get the Gospel of John, as well as the Epistles of John. The break probably developed in the midst of the argument about Docetism, that belief that Jesus only *seemed* to have a physical body. This letter shows that a leader in some church (Diotrephes) had rejected the authority of the leader of the church that had been the source from which the others had come. In addition he has refused to receive representatives of the founding church. The doctrinal dispute has turned into personal attacks and produced rivalry. This letter addresses a church with serious problems.

3 John 1-4. The author introduces himself only as "the Elder." He apparently has enough of a reputation as a leader that he needs no other identification. Like 1 and 2 John, this letter comes from a time after the death of the apostles. Still, there are recognizable leaders in the church. Elder has been a church office from quite an early time in the church. The writer of Acts has Paul address elders at Ephesus when he was on his way to Jerusalem for the last time (20:17-24). We do not know the identity of this Elder in John, except to say that he was a known and recognized leader of an important church. It also seems clear that he was also the writer of 2 John, and perhaps of 1 John. The letter directly addresses Gaius, who is called "beloved." Gaius is a leader of a congregation who seems to be in a position to influence his congregation and perhaps others to remain faithful to the Elder's church and its teaching. The Elder considers the members of Gaius's church "my children" (verse 4) and so believers for whom he has some responsibility. These opening verses renew the emphasis on truth that we have seen in both 1 and 2 John. So the Elder remains concerned about right teaching.

3 John 5-12. The central reasons the Elder writes this letter are to thank Gaius and his church for supporting the work of representatives of the Elder's church and to encourage them to continue that practice. The mission of those sent by the Elder seems to have included being missionaries. The practice of the early church was to support traveling missionaries by taking them in and providing for them while they were in town. This practice was open to abuse, so the church soon developed rules. An example is that a true prophet would not stay more than two days; a longer stay shows he is a false prophet.

Relying on churches for hospitality

meant that the missionaries could preach their message without taking money from their most recent converts. This practice goes all the way back to Paul and Barnabas who had refused to accept support from people on their initial mission trip to a city (see 1 Corinthians 9). The Elder sees teachers willing to sacrifice in this way to be the kinds of people the church should support. This is one of the few mentions of mission work that we find in the Johannine letters, but the form it takes sounds much like Paul's missionary method.

Verse 9 introduces Diotrephes, another leader in the church. He is the leader of a faction that is rejecting the Elder, his teaching, and his representatives. He is probably not in the same congregation as Gaius, but has become a rival. He will not take in or provide food for the mission workers from the Elder's church. This refusal is evidence of the deep division between the Elder and Diotrephes. Basically, Diotrephes does not recognize these missionaries as Christian teachers. He is so insistent about this that he threatens others within his church with exclusion if they provide support. Given this letter's relationship with 1 and 2 John, the theological argument about Jesus' bodily existence has probably led to this situation. In 1 John, we saw the author being willing to exclude others if they held the wrong teaching. Now Diotrephes is doing the same thing from the other direction. Perhaps this rejection of the Elder's teaching is the slander he mentions.

The bad example of Diotrephes is balanced with the good example of Demetrius. He has behaved as he should toward the Elder's representatives and he has remained faithful to correct teaching. Perhaps he is a member of the same church as Diotrephes. If so, they are vying for leadership there.

3 John 13-15. The closing of this letter is very much like that of 2 John. Again the author wants to be present to discuss matters rather than having to rely on written communication. The closing of 3 John is distinctive because it calls fellow Christians "friends" rather using familial language (for example, brother, children). The NRSV veils this distinctiveness because it is very inconsistent in the way it translates the Greek word for "brothers." It sometimes translates this word as "friends" (though generally refers to "brothers" in the textual footnote). This translation is a disservice because it does not include the closeness that the family language conveys. The term "brothers" in New Testament texts usually intends to refer to all church members, so it is properly rendered "brothers and sisters." That is what the authors who used the word meant. Thus the CEB does a better job of conveying the meaning of this language throughout 3 John (and the rest of the New Testament). In any case, after calling the missionaries "brothers [and sisters]," the Elder calls the other church members "friends."

INTERPRETING THE SCRIPTURE

Strife in the Church

John's church is experiencing something most of us know: strife. We know how difficult disputes can become. This one has gotten about as bad as it can. Each side refuses to cooperate with the other; each side denounces the other and perhaps accuses the other side of things they deny. We do not know anything about Diotrephes other than what the Elder tells us. John makes him out to be arrogant and assuming: He likes to "put himself first" (verse 9). This means he both looks out for his own good and likes to be in charge. We have all had experiences with people who try to dominate discussions and silence those who may take a different view. John wants readers to see Diotrephes as that sort of person. He presents Diotrephes as a person who oversteps his or her authority to speak for the church and dares others to defy him. John has nothing good to say about Diotrephes. He simply accuses him of arrogance and falsehood and says he is a bad example. The Elder sees him as the kind of person who must be overcome.

Meanwhile, there is another example the readers should imitate: Demetrius. The only thing we know about him is that he maintains the truth. John is certain that the gospel must not be compromised to please a strong personality who wants to attain power. In a sense, the opposite of the arrogance of Diotrephes is the preservation of the truth. This contrast allows us to see some exaggeration in the Elder's description of his opponent. Perhaps the arrogance of Diotrephes consists in his rejection of the Elder's teaching. In later times, those who write against heretics will say they hold errant views because of pride or arrogance. This text calls us both to uphold healthy teaching and to refuse to allow people to dominate our churches through the strength of their personalities. At the same time, it sends us looking for ways to navigate through strife while keeping the value of all members in view.

Credible Mission Work

The Elder's comments about traveling teachers open a window into the practices of the early church. We know from Paul's writings that there were debates in the early church about how missionaries and teachers should receive support. Their debates were part of a larger debate among philosophers about how teachers should be paid. The fundamental question was about having freedom to speak the truth. Some thought that taking pay from students would mean that the teacher would have to say what the students wanted to hear; others thought that having a wealthy patron would limit telling the truth that might violate his interests. Paul refused money from recent converts so they would not think he was preaching for personal gain and so they could not call on him to alter his teaching to suit their desires (1 Corinthians 9; 2 Corinthians 11:7-15).

The wider church seemed to adopt a practice similar to this. Traveling preachers and missionaries moved from town to town relying on the hospitality of churches that were already there. They seem to have stayed in the houses of church members and to have received their meals from them. Accepting these teachers was expected. But soon the church imposed some clear rules about how the system should work to ensure that teachers were not taking advantage of fellow believers. This allowed missionaries to live in a way that made their message credible to outsiders. It was clear that the missionary was not serving his or her own good. They did not seek converts to get money and they did not take advantage of their hosts' generosity. Mission work in every setting must find ways to ensure that it appears in a credible guise to those it would reach and lives up to that credible image in its relations with its sponsors as well as its converts. Closer to home, the church must be certain it lives its faith in ways that make that faith credible to those in the immediate community.

Hospitality

The Elder says that the beloved Gaius has demonstrated his love through his treatment of the church's representatives. He has treated them with the care and respect they should have. He has done for them what we talked about above; he has taken them into his home, fed them, and met whatever needs they had. By acting in this way Gaius has lived up to being one of the people of God and so has honored God. That is what it means when John says he has acted in "a manner worthy of God" (verse 6). This is all the more noteworthy because these were strangers. While John does not use the term, the word for "hospitality" in Greek is a combination of the words "stranger" and "love." So it expresses the idea of hospitality by referring to extending love to the stranger. Think of how difficult it would be to invite strangers into your home to spend a day or two—and you do this just because they are members of your denomination or have been recommended by a church leader in another city. We do such things for youth groups, but it would be a different thing if some adults just showed up at church. John says that such radical hospitality shows we have love.

John is speaking directly of showing hospitality to fellow Christians. Supporting God's people in this way makes one a coworker in the truth (verse 8). As previously noted, taking traveling teachers in as boarders was seen as proper behavior by the time 3 John was written. That it was proper does not mean it was easy. John provides needed encouragement to help believers continue to show this kind of hospitality.

Hospitality remains an important Christian virtue, one shown to both members and nonmembers. For us, hospitality usually refers to how we treat outsiders, how we make our church accepting of visitors, and how we welcome them. But we need to consider how to expand that understanding so that our hospitality extends love to people who do not come into our comfortable spaces. Our hospitality should be seeking ways to show love to strangers and so draw them into our fellowship.

Celebrating Faithfulness

For all of the turmoil and problems facing the churches involved with 3 John, we also see the Elder giving thanks for the good things happening in their midst. The Elder is very glad to hear of the steadfastness of Gaius, but even happier to hear how "my children" live in truth (verse 4). He celebrates their faithfulness even as he worries about what others are doing. He does not give thanks solely to encourage those he is writing to; rather, such thanksgiving is part of their worship. John notes that those who had been treated so well had returned home and told not just John but the whole church about the love they had been shown. He celebrates the commitment of those missionaries by saying they are just the sort of people you should treat well.

One way this church gives thanks to God is to recount the blessings God has given. Such a practice helps church members draw closer to one another and to God as they hear of God's presence in the lives and deeds of fellow members. Maybe it also begins to attune others to see how God blesses their lives, perhaps through something as simple as receiving hospitality.

SHARING THE SCRIPTURE

PREPARING TO TEACH

Preparing Our Hearts

Meditate on this week's devotional reading from 2 Timothy 2:14-19. What are the characteristics of sound teaching that Paul identifies for Timothy? What are you doing to show yourself to God as an approved worker? How does Paul describe the actions of false teachers?

Pray that you and the students will be well prepared to offer sound teaching.

Preparing Our Minds

Study the background Scripture and the lesson Scripture, which are both from 3 John.

Consider this question as you prepare the lesson: *What is it about receiving hospitality that makes it so important?*

Write on newsprint:
❑ list of Scriptures concerning biblical hospitality for "Tell

Experiences of Hospitality and Reactions to It."
❑ information for next week's lesson, found under "Continue the Journey."
❑ activities for further spiritual growth in "Continue the Journey."

Review the "Introduction," "The Big Picture," "Close-up," and "Faith in Action," which all precede the first lesson of this quarter. Consider how you might use any of this material in today's lesson.

LEADING THE CLASS

(1) Gather to Learn

❖ Greet the class members and introduce guests.

❖ Pray that those who have come today will offer and experience gracious hospitality during this session.

❖ Invite participants to tell brief stories of hospitality that has been extended to them, perhaps by a church, by strangers, or by good Samaritans who assisted them. Encourage them to say what this hospitality meant to them at the time and why it is so warmly remembered now.

❖ Read aloud today's focus statement: **Most people really appreciate the kindness and generosity they have experienced as a result of good hospitality. What is it about receiving hospitality that makes it so important? Third John says that hospitality is one way that Christians express their faith in Christ to others, thereby making the faithful coworkers with the truth.**

(2) Goal 1: Learn the Importance of Hospitality as Described in 3 John

❖ Read or retell "Strife in the Church" in Interpreting the Scripture. This information will help the learners to see that the divisive problems that prompted the Elder to write also motivated him to commend Gaius.

❖ Call on one volunteer to read the salutation and final greetings of 3 John (verses 1, 13-15); ask another to read John's commendation of Gaius (verses 2-8), and a third to read John's comments about Diotrephes and Demetrius (verses 9-12).

❖ Discuss these questions:
1. Why does the writer commend Gaius, who is presumably the leader of the church to whom John writes? (See first paragraph in "3 John 5-12" in Understanding the Scripture.)
2. How does hospitality figure into the work of the church? (See second paragraph in "3 John 5-12" in Understanding the Scripture.)
3. What does the writer have to say about Diotrephes? (See

third paragraph in "3 John 5-12" in Understanding the Scripture.)
4. What does the writer have to say about Demetrius? (See fourth paragraph in "3 John 5-12" in Understanding the Scripture.)
5. In our age of social media and electronic communications, what do you think the writer's closing remarks say to us about personal interaction within the church?

(3) Goal 2: Tell Experiences of Hospitality and Reactions to It

❖ Read "Hospitality" from Interpreting the Scripture.

❖ Form three groups and assign each group to one of the sections of Scripture passages, which you will have written on newsprint prior to the session. Provide paper and pencils for each student. Tell the groups to read their assigned passages to determine: (1) who was showing hospitality, (2) how hospitality was shown, and (3) how the recipient of the hospitality responded or likely would have felt.

• **Group 1: Examples of Hospitality in the Old Testament—Genesis 18:1-15; 1 Kings 17:1-16; 2 Kings 4:8-16**
• **Group 2: Examples of Hospitality Shown to Jesus—Matthew 8:14-17; Luke 7:36-50; Luke 24:28-35**
• **Group 3: Examples of Hospitality Shown to Paul and His Coworkers—Acts 16:11-15; Acts 16:25-34; Acts 28:1-6**

❖ Gather the groups together and have each one report to the class. After each report ask:

1. How did the hospitality shown in the passage(s) seem similar to and different from the hospitality for which John commended Gaius?
2. How would you have felt in the same situation?

(4) Goal 3: Practice Acts of Hospitality

❖ Read these examples of concerning newcomers to a church and encourage the class to say, first, how they think their congregation would react to each opportunity to practice hospitality and then how they personally would hope to respond:

- a young mother who begins breastfeeding her fussy child during the service
- a woman in very stylish attire, who is over six feet tall and clearly transgender
- a young man who speaks out of turn, holds his hymnal upside down, and seems too agitated to participate, perhaps because of mental illness
- a homeless man who has not had a bath or fresh clothes in some days
- a woman with a guide dog
- a soldier back from Afghanistan, in uniform, visiting with his aunt and uncle who are church members

❖ Ask these questions:
1. What characteristics do the people we believe our church would welcome share with one another?
2. If there are groups of people whom we do not believe would be welcomed, what can we do to change the congregational mind-set?

❖ Conclude by reading "Celebrating Faithfulness" from Interpreting the Scripture.

(5) Continue the Journey

❖ Pray that as the learners depart, they will actively seek situations in which they can practice hospitality on behalf of Jesus.

❖ Post information for next week's session on newsprint for the students to copy:
- **Title: Gifts of the Spirit**
- **Background Scripture: 1 Corinthians 12:1-11**
- **Lesson Scripture: 1 Corinthians 12:1-11**
- **Focus of the Lesson: Most humans seek opportunities to become loyal contributing members of their societies. What motivates and empowers them to work together? Paul says that since one person does not possess all of the spiritual gifts, believers must work together for the church's common good.**

❖ Challenge the adults to grow spiritually by completing one or more of these activities, which you have posted on newsprint for the students to copy.

(1) Invite a new church member to attend Sunday school with you. Ask other classmates to work with you in preparing a special welcome for this newcomer.

(2) Talk with your pastor and worship committee to see if your congregation and another congregation in the community could work together for a common cause.

(3) Extend hospitality on behalf of your congregation

by staffing a church food pantry, assisting needy persons in receiving monetary donations from the church, or serving a free lunch. Get to know the people who use these outreach services that the church provides.

❖ Sing or read aloud "Blest Be the Tie That Binds."

❖ Conclude today's session by leading the class in this benediction adapted from 1 Corinthians 12:13, which is the key verse for the lesson for May 17: **Let us go forth rejoicing that in the one Spirit we were all baptized into one body—Jews or Greeks, slaves or free—and we were all made to drink of one Spirit.**

UNIT 3: ONE IN THE BOND OF LOVE
GIFTS OF THE SPIRIT

PREVIEWING THE LESSON

Lesson Scripture: 1 Corinthians 12:1-11
Background Scripture: 1 Corinthians 12:1-11
Key Verse: 1 Corinthians 12:7

Focus of the Lesson:
Most humans seek opportunities to become loyal contributing members of their societies. What motivates and empowers them to work together? Paul says that since one person does not possess all of the spiritual gifts, believers must work together for the church's common good.

Goals for the Learners:
(1) to explore the purpose of spiritual gifts according to 1 Corinthians 12:1-11.
(2) to appreciate individual spiritual gifts and ways they are used.
(3) to discover the spiritual gifts of the faith community and how they can be used for its benefit.

Pronunciation Guide:
charisma (kuh riz´ muh)   *pneumatikos* (pnyoo mat ik os´)

Supplies:
Bibles, newsprint and marker, paper and pencils, hymnals

READING THE SCRIPTURE

NRSV
Lesson Scripture: 1 Corinthians 12:1-11

¹Now concerning spiritual gifts, brothers and sisters, I do not want you to be uninformed. ²You know that when you were pagans, you were enticed and led astray to idols

CEB
Lesson Scripture: 1 Corinthians 12:1-11

¹Brothers and sisters, I don't want you to be ignorant about spiritual gifts. ²You know that when you were Gentiles you were often misled by false gods that can't even speak. ³So

that could not speak. ³Therefore I want you to understand that no one speaking by the Spirit of God ever says "Let Jesus be cursed!" and no one can say "Jesus is Lord" except by the Holy Spirit.

⁴Now there are varieties of gifts, but the same Spirit; ⁵and there are varieties of services, but the same Lord; ⁶and there are varieties of activities, but it is the same God who activates all of them in everyone. **⁷To each is given the manifestation of the Spirit for the common good.** ⁸To one is given through the Spirit the utterance of wisdom, and to another the utterance of knowledge according to the same Spirit, ⁹to another faith by the same Spirit, to another gifts of healing by the one Spirit, ¹⁰to another the working of miracles, to another prophecy, to another the discernment of spirits, to another various kinds of tongues, to another the interpretation of tongues. ¹¹All these are activated by one and the same Spirit, who allots to each one individually just as the Spirit chooses.

I want to make it clear to you that no one says, "Jesus is cursed!" when speaking by God's Spirit, and no one can say, "Jesus is Lord," except by the Holy Spirit. ⁴There are different spiritual gifts but the same Spirit; ⁵and there are different ministries and the same Lord; ⁶and there are different activities but the same God who produces all of them in everyone. **⁷A demonstration of the Spirit is given to each person for the common good.** ⁸A word of wisdom is given by the Spirit to one person, a word of knowledge to another according to the same Spirit, ⁹faith to still another by the same Spirit, gifts of healing to another in the one Spirit, ¹⁰performance of miracles to another, prophecy to another, the ability to tell spirits apart to another, different kinds of tongues to another, and the interpretation of the tongues to another. ¹¹All these things are produced by the one and same Spirit who gives what he wants to each person.

UNDERSTANDING THE SCRIPTURE

Introduction. One of the central issues of the whole of 1 Corinthians is how to understand spirituality. The Corinthians misunderstood Christian spirituality in multiple ways—what it means for leadership, for ethics, and for life together as the church. All of chapters 1–4 are devoted to redefining spirituality. Beginning in chapter 5, Paul addresses specific questions about how to live as believers in Christ. Chapters 11–14 are all about how to conduct worship; there are questions about how to dress for worship (11:2-16) and about how to

serve the Lord's Supper (11:17-34). Chapter 12 takes up the question of how to use spiritual gifts in worship. Some members have been exercising their gifts in ways that disrupt worship and the wider life of the church. This is such a big problem that Paul devotes the whole of chapters 12–14 to this question. The reading today opens this discussion of the meaning of gifts and how to use them.

1 Corinthians 12:1-3. As he does in several places in 1 Corinthians, Paul begins a new topic by saying, "Now concerning" (12:1). (Unfortunately, the CEB omits this important expression.) When he uses this phrase, he is probably responding to questions the Corinthian church members had sent him. The first time he uses it, he mentions a letter from them that contained questions for him (7:1). So the ways spiritual gifts were being used in their worship services and in their church were enough of a problem that they had asked Paul to talk about how to use them. Paul starts by reminding them of how little they know about such things. He says in verse 2 that they were so foolish not long ago that they worshiped idols that cannot speak at all. The implication is that it seems ridiculous that some of them think they are now experts about how the Spirit works when they were that ignorant that recently. He then goes on to give some basic rules. First, the Spirit will never lead a person to say Jesus be cursed. Some interpreters have argued that some Corinthians have said "Jesus be cursed" to deny the bodily nature of Christ in the world. But this seems unlikely since Paul does not take up this matter in 1 Corinthians. This statement does serve as a way to put some Corinthians in their place. That is, they are so ignorant of spiritual matters that they do not even know that the Spirit would not inspire such speech. In stronger language, Paul says that no one can confess that "Jesus is Lord" (12:3) except by the Spirit. Even faith is a gift given by God through the Spirit. This also means that all people in the church have the Spirit because the only way to make the confession is through the Spirit. So no one can claim that he or she has the Spirit and others do not. This way of phrasing the confession of Jesus as Lord may also oppose allegiance to the Roman Empire. While others proclaimed Caesar as Lord, the alternative community of the church gave this title to Jesus. This confession signaled that the church embraced different values and commitments.

1 Corinthians 12:4-11. After introducing the topic, Paul changes his terminology. In verse 1 he said the topic was "spiritual things," usually translated "spiritual gifts," which is the correct understanding of the topic. In verse 1 he uses a word that has "spirit" as its root (*pneumatikos*). But as Paul begins the fuller discussion, he changes his terminology and uses the word "gifts" (*charisma*), a word related to grace. This shifts the focus so that he can introduce the idea that every manifestation of the Spirit is a gift from God, rather than allow the Corinthians to think of manifestations as things a person attains through merit or effort. Some in Corinth had been asserting that their gifts were superior to others. There seems to be some dispute about which gifts were best, with some claiming speaking in tongues as superior, and others saying the superior gift was wisdom. Paul wants to put an end to this bickering. First he says all such abilities are gifts. Then, through a repetition of a "different"/"the same" formula, Paul asserts that all kinds of gifts have the same source, the Spirit. The repetition of the formula in verses 4-6 emphasizes that all workings of the Spirit come from the same place, so none can claim superiority. Paul is not thinking of different persons of the Trinity when he says the gifts have their source in the same Spirit, Lord, and God. He is simply giving his repetition some stylistic variety as he drives home the point that all gifts have the same origin. Now in verse 7 he tells the Corinthians the real purpose of all spiritual gifts: They are intended to be used to contribute to "the common good." While some in Corinth wanted to use them as demonstrations of superiority, Paul says that their real purpose is to serve the good of the church, not that of the person who has the gift. This is the central claim of this section and of much of 1 Corinthians as a whole. The Christian life is to be oriented toward doing what is good for the community, particularly fellow Christians. To make sure his readers do not miss the point, Paul lists spiritual gifts present in the Corinthian church. Perhaps because speaking in tongues has been such a problem, he waits until late in the list to mention it, indicating that it is not so important. Paul concludes the paragraph by reminding them that all gifts have the same origin. He says that they are distributed just as God wants them and that each church member has the gift God wants the person to have. What gift someone has is dependent on God's will, not the person's effort or desire. God gives each person the gift he or she has because that is the gift the church needs; that is, the gift that contributes to the common good. So both the individual gifts and their distribution are designed to serve the good of the community rather than that of the individual.

INTERPRETING THE SCRIPTURE

Defining Spirituality

The Corinthians had great difficulty in trying to understand Christian spirituality. The world around them defined spirituality as an individualistic experience of the presence of a god that brought assurance and comfort to the person. Such an experience would make the person more secure and help him or her to be a more powerful and successful person. This is the view Paul must overcome if he is to help this church enjoy what the Spirit supplies.

Much about first-century spirituality sounds familiar. There is little difference between what it sought and what we might read in many current books on spirituality and in the spiritual self-help section of bookstores. What the Corinthians want is something like what those who say they are spiritual but not religious seek. In truth, it sounds too much like what most Christians mean when they talk about spirituality. We commonly see spirituality as an individualistic matter between the person and God. We look to mountaintop experiences (whether our own or those of others) as the real moments of spirituality. Spirituality, we think, is about contemplation and moments between God and the individual.

Paul would say that we have much to learn about true spirituality. Christian spirituality is not simply between God and the individual; it is about life in the community in which all share the Spirit and what it gives to all. When Paul finally gets to this topic in 1 Corinthians, he has already spent pages explaining how the Christian life must be oriented toward doing what is in the best interest of the other person. Christians shape their lives in this way because they follow a crucified Lord. Christ's acceptance of crucifixion is the pattern for the lives of his followers. They are to accept disadvantage for the good of others, just as he did. The Spirit that comes to those who confess Jesus as Lord helps believers conform their lives to this pattern. The Spirit does not come just for the well-being of the individual. A Christian spirituality will be a spirituality that is more concerned with contributing to the lives of others than it is about the inner life of the individual. It is not that experiences of God and attainment of inner well-being are unimportant. But they are not the focus of a spirituality that Paul recognizes as Christian or that follows the example of Christ.

Defining Spiritual Gifts

We have a hard time relating to the problems Paul addresses at Corinth because the spiritual gifts he mentions are unfamiliar. The overt manifestations he discusses seem at odds with the more contemplative practices we identify with spirituality. But the Corinthians are not so different from us. The feelings they attain in meditation are just what some Corinthians claim. Others claim gifts of knowledge and wisdom that seem to be abilities to present and argue persuasively for particular practices or ideas in the church. Since these skills are gifts of God, some say they should be listened to. The gift of faith may be an initial reference to the ability to work miracles of some sort, a gift mentioned again in the list. The Corinthians believed also that some were given the ability to heal diseases. After mentioning those gifts

that work outside of worship, Paul returns to gifts used in the assembly. The gift of prophecy was not predicting the future so much as it was bringing an authoritative word from God, being able to say what the church should do or think in a particular moment. Discerning spirits is largely a counterpart to prophecy; it is the ability to decide whether what a prophet says is really from God. Speaking in tongues was an ecstatic experience as it is in some churches today. It is an experience of the presence of God that seizes individuals and causes them to say things they do not understand. The gift of interpretation is the ability to translate what the tongue speaker said.

While many of us do not have such manifestations in our churches, what we have may be closer than we recognize. Part of the reason these seem so foreign is that we do not label people's abilities as gifts of the Spirit. Culturally, we attribute talents and skills to the person or one's genes rather than to the Spirit. Paul would have us recognize that in the context of the church those things we call talents are gifts of the Spirit. Paul does not give a complete list of spiritual gifts here. Elsewhere in 1 Corinthians he will add gifts of teaching, administration, helping, and leadership, among others (12:27-31). Paul wants both the person who has them and the church to know that these skills and capabilities are gifts of the Spirit. One of the notions Paul combats in 1 Corinthians is the idea that the best spiritual gifts are the flashy gifts. So the absence of ecstatic gifts, such as speaking in tongues, must not lead us to the mistaken notion that we do not have spiritual gifts.

The Purpose of Spiritual Gifts

The way the Corinthians understood spiritual gifts led them to misuse them. Since they thought such gifts were given primarily to enhance the life of the person who got them, they were using their gifts to advance their position and status in the church (and perhaps the wider community). Paul must convince them to reorient their understanding of the purpose of spiritual gifts. Our own understanding of such gifts is often not much different from that of the Corinthians. When we adopt the cultural understanding of spirituality as something about self-fulfillment, we fall into the same trap the Corinthians did. Paul says that the purpose of spiritual gifts is to help the church, to contribute to its good. When we long for a kind of gift or the experiences that others have, Paul would encourage us to look outward to the good of the church rather than to our desires. That orientation uses the spiritual gifts we possess in the ways God intended. Although looking to the good of the church may not put an end to our desires to have other experiences, that orientation can bring a kind of spiritual fulfillment within the life of the whole community. Church members receive the benefits of the exercise of other members' gifts even as they each contribute their own.

Identifying Spiritual Gifts

We may still be tempted to dismiss this discussion of spiritual gifts as not relevant to us in the twenty-first century. But to do so is to miss the ways that God is active within our churches. Paul is convinced that every member has a gift to share; a gift that strengthens the church. When we recognize that various kinds of leadership are not the only manifestations of the Spirit, we can begin to see in others and ourselves talents and abilities that would contribute to the good of the church. No contribution of this type is inconsequential. When we exercise these gifts for the church and encourage others to use their gifts for the common good, we are being truly spiritual.

SHARING THE SCRIPTURE

PREPARING TO TEACH

Preparing Our Hearts

Meditate on this week's devotional reading from Romans 12:1-8. How have you been transformed from one who "goes along to get along" in the world to a disciple who is wholly devoted to Jesus Christ? What gifts do you believe God has entrusted to you for the common good of the body of Christ? How are you using these gifts?

Pray that you and the students will identify the gifts God has bestowed on you and use them for the benefit of the community of faith.

Preparing Our Minds

Study the background Scripture and the lesson Scripture, which are both from 1 Corinthians 12:1-11.

Consider this question as you prepare the lesson: *What motivates and empowers people to work together for their common good?*

Write on newsprint:

❏ information for next week's lesson, found under "Continue the Journey."

❏ activities for further spiritual growth in "Continue the Journey."

Review the "Introduction," "The Big Picture," "Close-up," and "Faith in Action," which all precede the first lesson of this quarter. Consider how you might use any of this material in today's lesson.

Prepare a brief lecture to begin this unit's study of 1 Corinthians by using "Introduction" in Understanding the Scripture and "1 Corinthians" in "The Big Picture: The Early Church and the Holy Spirit" article found at the beginning of this quarter.

LEADING THE CLASS

(1) Gather to Learn

❖ Greet the class members and introduce guests.

❖ Pray that those who have come today will discern ways to work together with other members of the faith community.

❖ Mention two types of groups known for working together: a sports team and a symphony orchestra. Ask these questions:

1. **What motivates a team or orchestra to work together as a unit?**

2. **What expectations does one member have of the other teammates or musicians?**

3. **What role does a coach or conductor play in these groups?**

4. **What happens when individual athletes or musicians decide to put their own needs**

first or do things their own way?

5. **What is the end result when everyone works together?**

❖ Read aloud today's focus statement: **Most humans seek opportunities to become loyal contributing members of their societies. What motivates and empowers them to work together? Paul says that since one person does not possess all of the spiritual gifts, believers must work together for the church's common good.**

(2) Goal 1: Explore the Purpose of Spiritual Gifts According to 1 Corinthians 12:1-11

❖ Use the lecture you have prepared to help the students understand the issues Paul was addressing as he wrote to the church in Corinth.

❖ Choose a volunteer to read 1 Corinthians 12:1-11.

❖ Ask: **What role does the Holy Spirit play in Paul's discussion of spiritual gifts?**

❖ Read "1 Corinthians 12:4-11" from Understanding the Scripture to help the students understand what Paul is saying about spiritual gifts.

❖ Form four groups, give each one a sheet of newsprint and marker, and assign each group one of the following headings: Romans 12:6-8; 1 Corinthians 12:8-10; 1 Corinthians 12:28; Ephesians 4:11. Each group is to list the gifts shown in its assigned passage.

❖ Call the groups together and have them display their newsprint. Post the four sheets next to one another for easy comparison. Words may vary due to Bible translations, but here are possible answers:

Romans 12:6-8	1 Corinthians 12:8-10	1 Corinthians 12:28	Ephesians 4:11
Prophecy	Word of wisdom	Apostles	Apostles
Ministry	Word of knowledge	Prophets	Prophets
Teaching	Faith	Teachers	Evangelists
Exhortation	Gifts of healing	Miracles	Pastors
Giving	Miracles	Gifts of healing	Teachers
Leading	Prophecy	Assistance	
Compassion	Discernment of spirits	Leadership	
	Tongues	Tongues	
	Interpretation of tongues		

❖ Note that some items on the list refer to offices held by specific people, whereas others refer to gifts that the Spirit may bestow on anyone, regardless of office. Also observe that a specific gift may be found in more than one list.

❖ Read in unison today's key verse from 1 Corinthians 12:7. Compare that with Ephesians 4:12-13 to discern the purpose of the Spirit's gifts.

❖ Conclude by reading or retelling "The Purpose of Spiritual Gifts" in Interpreting the Scripture.

(3) Goal 2: Appreciate Individual Spiritual Gifts and How They Are Used

❖ Distribute slips of paper and pencils. Invite the students to review the posted lists of gifts and write each gift that he or she has, using a single slip of paper for each gift. No names are to be written on the papers.

❖ Collect the papers. Ask two or three students to sort them into piles representing the same gift. Then they are to tally the number of people with the same gift, for example, eight with the gift of leadership; six with the gift of teaching. While the counters are working, read "Defining Spiritual Gifts" from Interpreting the

Scripture. Invite comments on these ideas.

❖ Ask the counters to announce their tally to the class. Write each gift and its totals on newsprint. After each gift and the number of students with that gift are read, the students are to respond by saying, "Thanks be to God."

(4) Goal 3: Discover the Spiritual Gifts of the Faith Community and the Ways They Can Be Used for Its Benefit

❖ Review the newsprint that shows the particular gifts these class members have. Ask: **What kinds of ministry opportunities do we have—or could we have—to use the gift of [fill in the blank]?** (For example, a Sunday school class or Bible study group may need a teacher; a committee may need a leader; compassionate persons may be needed to visit those who are sick or homebound.)

❖ Challenge the students to make a commitment to use their spiritual gifts in ways that benefit the common good.

(5) Continue the Journey

❖ Pray that as the learners depart, they will recognize and give thanks for the spiritual gifts within their congregation that the Holy Spirit has given for the common good.

❖ Post information for next week's session on newsprint for the students to copy:

- Title: The Spirit Creates One Body
- Background Scripture: 1 Corinthians 12:12-31
- Lesson Scripture: 1 Corinthians 12:12-31
- Focus of the Lesson: Organizations are composed of several interrelated, interdependent functional parts. Why is it important to value all the parts? In his letter, Paul tells the Corinthian church that all spiritual gifts are necessary for its efficient operation.

❖ Challenge the adults to grow spiritually by completing one or more of these activities related to this week's session, which you have posted on newsprint for the students to copy.

(1) Visit another faith community, perhaps one in the Pentecostal or Assemblies of God tradition. Observe how the gifts of the Spirit are used in these communities. What did you learn from this experience?

(2) Pray for discernment about your own spiritual gifts. What are your gifts? How are you using them for the common good? Are there opportunities for ministry that would allow you to make better use of your gifts? If so, what steps will you take to become involved with those ministries?

(3) Take a spiritual gifts inventory to determine and understand your own spiritual gifts. Books such as *Your Spiritual Gifts Inventory* by Charles Bryant and *Rediscovering Our Spiritual Gifts* by John I. Penn, both of which are available through Cokesbury.com, will be helpful to you.

❖ Sing or read aloud "Many Gifts, One Spirit."

❖ Conclude today's session by leading the class in this benediction adapted from 1 Corinthians 12:13, which is the key verse for the lesson for May 17: Let us go forth rejoicing that in the one Spirit we were all baptized into one body—Jews or Greeks, slaves or free—and we were all made to drink of one Spirit.

UNIT 3: ONE IN THE BOND OF LOVE

THE SPIRIT CREATES ONE BODY

PREVIEWING THE LESSON

Lesson Scripture: 1 Corinthians 12:12-31
Background Scripture: 1 Corinthians 12:12-31
Key Verse: 1 Corinthians 12:13

Focus of the Lesson:
Organizations are composed of several interrelated, interdependent functional parts. Why is it important to value all the parts? In his letter, Paul tells the Corinthian church that all spiritual gifts are necessary for its efficient operation.

Goals for the Learners:
(1) to learn how each member of the body supports the other members.
(2) to value the different gifts operating within the church.
(3) to use spiritual gifts in cooperation with others for building up the body of Christ.

Supplies:
Bibles, newsprint and marker, paper and pencils, hymnals

READING THE SCRIPTURE

NRSV
Lesson Scripture: 1 Corinthians
12:12-31

¹²For just as the body is one and has many members, and all the members of the body, though many, are one body, so it is with Christ. **¹³For in the one Spirit we were all baptized into one body—Jews or Greeks, slaves or free—and we were all made to drink of one Spirit.**

CEB
Lesson Scripture: 1 Corinthians
12:12-31

¹²Christ is just like the human body—a body is a unit and has many parts; and all the parts of the body are one body, even though there are many. **¹³We were all baptized by one Spirit into one body, whether Jew or Greek, or slave or free, and we all were given one Spirit to drink.**

[14]Indeed, the body does not consist of one member but of many. [15]If the foot would say, "Because I am not a hand, I do not belong to the body," that would not make it any less a part of the body. [16]And if the ear would say, "Because I am not an eye, I do not belong to the body," that would not make it any less a part of the body. [17]If the whole body were an eye, where would the hearing be? If the whole body were hearing, where would the sense of smell be? [18]But as it is, God arranged the members in the body, each one of them, as he chose. [19]If all were a single member, where would the body be? [20]As it is, there are many members, yet one body. [21]The eye cannot say to the hand, "I have no need of you," nor again the head to the feet, "I have no need of you." [22]On the contrary, the members of the body that seem to be weaker are indispensable, [23]and those members of the body that we think less honorable we clothe with greater honor, and our less respectable members are treated with greater respect; [24]whereas our more respectable members do not need this. But God has so arranged the body, giving the greater honor to the inferior member, [25]that there may be no dissension within the body, but the members may have the same care for one another. [26]If one member suffers, all suffer together with it; if one member is honored, all rejoice together with it.

[27]Now you are the body of Christ and individually members of it. [28]And God has appointed in the church first apostles, second prophets, third teachers; then deeds of power, then gifts of healing, forms of assistance, forms of leadership, various kinds of tongues. [29]Are all apostles? Are all prophets? Are all teachers? Do all

[14]Certainly the body isn't one part but many. [15]If the foot says, "I'm not part of the body because I'm not a hand," does that mean it's not part of the body? [16]If the ear says, "I'm not part of the body because I'm not an eye," does that mean it's not part of the body? [17]If the whole body were an eye, what would happen to the hearing? And if the whole body were an ear, what would happen to the sense of smell? [18]But as it is, God has placed each one of the parts in the body just like he wanted. [19]If all were one and the same body part, what would happen to the body? [20]But as it is, there are many parts but one body. [21]So the eye can't say to the hand, "I don't need you," or in turn, the head can't say to the feet, "I don't need you." [22]Instead, the parts of the body that people think are the weakest are the most necessary. [23]The parts of the body that we think are less honorable are the ones we honor the most. The private parts of our body that aren't presentable are the ones that are given the most dignity. [24]The parts of our body that are presentable don't need this. But God has put the body together, giving greater honor to the part with less honor [25]so that there won't be division in the body and so the parts might have mutual concern for each other. [26]If one part suffers, all the parts suffer with it; if one part gets the glory, all the parts celebrate with it. [27]You are the body of Christ and parts of each other. [28]In the church, God has appointed first apostles, second prophets, third teachers, then miracles, then gifts of healing, the ability to help others, leadership skills, different kinds of tongues. [29]All aren't apostles, are they? All aren't prophets, are they? All aren't teachers, are they? All don't perform miracles, do

work miracles? ^{30}Do all possess gifts of healing? Do all speak in tongues? Do all interpret? ^{31}But strive for the greater gifts. And I will show you a still more excellent way.

they? ^{30}All don't have gifts of healing, do they? All don't speak in different tongues, do they? All don't interpret, do they? ^{31}Use your ambition to try to get the greater gifts. And I'm going to show you an even better way.

UNDERSTANDING THE SCRIPTURE

Introduction. Chapter 12 begins an extensive discussion of the use of spiritual gifts. Paul starts by reminding the Corinthians of their ignorance about spiritual matters (12:1-4) and then asserts that all spiritual powers have the same source: God's Spirit. In this introductory section in verses 1-11 Paul reiterates the theme of all of his discussion of spirituality in 1 Corinthians. That theme is that the primary purpose of all spiritual gifts is working for the common good of all the church. (See the more extensive discussion of these verses in the lesson for May 10.)

1 Corinthians 12:12-21. Some church members at Corinth were arguing that the ecstatic gifts like speaking in tongues were the best gifts. Such gifts were a clear demonstration of closeness to God. After all, in those moments God seems to take over your inner self so that you are one with God. How could there be any clearer sign of spirituality? Paul directs the Corinthians' attention away from what gifts do for the person and toward what they do for the church. The gifts that build up the church, he says, are really the ones that demonstrate spirituality and closeness to God. To help the Corinthians think about the proper way to use spiritual gifts, Paul introduces the metaphor of the body. He says that the church is the body of Christ. In 1 Corinthians, this metaphor applies primarily to the local congregation rather than to the universal church. In later writings (for example, Ephesians) authors see the church as the cosmic body of Christ, but in 1 Corinthians it remains a metaphor for local congregational life. The only place where something larger than the local church may be in view is verse 13, where he says all have received the same Spirit, without regard for ethnicity or social status. Paul borrows the image of the body to illustrate how society, from philosophers to politicians, should operate. They had already used the image of the body to maintain the status quo in a hierarchical society. People were encouraged to recognize which part of the body they were (for example, a foot or a head) and to fulfill their role in the sustaining of society by living out their proper roles. In this way, the subordinate classes were encouraged to see meaning in the roles they filled and so be willing not to disrupt the functioning of the body, that is, not upset the social order.

Paul takes this image, but uses it to make just the opposite kinds of points. He argues that by virtue of baptism all are members and so are needed members of the body. He contends further that the diversity of gifts is precisely what is needed, just as the body needs to be composed of many different kinds of parts (ears, eyes, hands, feet, and so on). The functioning of the body depends on these diverse parts all working together in unity, with each part depending on and needing the others. Paul says that this diversity and interdependence come from God. In fact, each person has just the gift God wants him or her to have. Thus, each person should be happy with the gift he or she has and give up trying to get the gift someone else has been given. So far, Paul's use of the body analogy sounds the same as others who had used this familiar image.

1 Corinthians 12:22-26. Then Paul's argument takes a radically different turn. Rather than saying that the superior parts need to be in charge and the inferior need to do as they are told, Paul says that the parts we consider less valuable are really those that are most necessary. Paul develops the metaphor in this unexpected direction by comparing the church with the ways that we clothe our bodies. Those parts that we are embarrassed to show, we give honor to by covering them with clothing. But it is just those parts that are among the most necessary for a good life. Without those parts we cover there would be no continuation of the species and we would soon die if we could not, for example, eliminate waste from the body. So those parts make life possible. Paul asserts that the same is true for the way the church works. He says that the gifts we often do not honor in the church, those that may seem unimportant,

are the most important for the continuing life of the church. Without those gifts, the church could not continue to live. He is encouraging the church members to see that every gift is valuable and to recognize that they have exalted the wrong gifts. In addition, the diversity of gifts in the church is not only valuable, it is what God intends. It is only when there are multiple kinds of gifts that the church can function as it should. Thus, members should see how they are all interconnected and interdependent.

1 Corinthians 12:27-31. Paul concludes this section by reminding the Corinthians that the different gifts assign people specific places in the life of the church. Just as different parts of the body have different functions, so it is with different gifts of the Spirit. Paul then provides a kind of ranking of gifts. While every member is necessary, the differences assign members different places within the body. Paul arranges the list as he does to drive home the points he has been making. The gifts that he ranks the highest are nonecstatic, but those that bring a word from God. Then he moves to healing, helping, and leading. The lowest manifestations on the list, speaking in tongues and interpreting them, are among the gifts that some in Corinth had ranked highest and perhaps as necessary for all who want to claim to be truly spiritual. Paul makes those more sensational gifts least important. He will explain that ranking in chapter 14, but from what we have already read in chapter 12, it is clear that they are lowest because they do the least to build up the whole church.

INTERPRETING THE SCRIPTURE

Diversity of Gifts Is a Necessity

As we look around our churches, we see differences among the members. At times, those differences create difficulties. Differences in ages, income levels, cultural backgrounds, and a host of other things can make church life complicated. It makes us wish everyone could be like us. But that would be worse than having people who are different. If everyone in a church had accounting skills but no one could sing, that would be a problem. And if everyone could sing but no one could teach Bible classes, that would be a problem. The truth is that we need diversity, even though it complicates life.

Paul is trying to convey the necessity of diversity to the Corinthians. They think everyone should be alike in at least one aspect: They should all have the same spiritual gift, or at least recognize that those who have the same gift that they have are superior to others. Paul says that such uniformity would be damaging to the church. He argues that diversity is as necessary in the church as it is in the body. The church *needs* differences. The church needs these differences for its survival. Without these differences the church would not be able to function as it should, just as the body cannot function without its different parts. As a body could not function or live if the whole of it were an eye, so the church cannot carry out its mission if everyone is the same, if everyone is an eye or a tongue (as some Corinthians wanted it).

Diversity of Gifts Is a Blessing

Paul goes beyond arguing that diversity is necessary; he says it is a blessing. The various parts of a body need one another. Eyes need hands just as hands need eyes. In the body there is a clear interdependence of one part upon the others. This diversity of parts helps all parts function better. It is the same way in the church. The different parts need one another. It is often hard for us to recognize interdependence rather than see more one-sided relationships. We often see the one better off economically giving to the less advantaged, with no real benefit being given by the less advantaged to the well-off. The one who gives more in the offering is seen to be carrying the ones who cannot contribute financially at that level. Or we may think of those gifted at preaching or leading as the ones who do the real work of the church that others support, so that the majority do not have a real ministry but only a secondary role.

Paul would call us to look again, both to recognize the gifts of others and to encourage everyone to recognize the gifts they have and to use them for the good of the church. This may mean that we need to expand what we see as a spiritual gift. We all recognize the gifts of those who lead worship, but we are less inclined to mention the gift of visiting the sick or the dying as a gift that is important for the church. We should recognize that those who chair committee meetings are sharing a spiritual gift. So are those who greet visitors at the door. The person who makes children feel welcome and the one who locks the building after everyone leaves are exercising spiritual gifts. So is the person who serves at church dinners and prays for those experiencing difficult times.

Each of us needs to think about the abilities we use in the rest of our lives and make them a gift to the church. God has given us those talents and expects us to use them to strengthen the church and advance God's will in the world. We may want to develop some abilities to be able to use them more effectively. In that process we need to be sure that we are not seeking someone else's gift rather than building on what God has given us. When Paul says that some gifts are more vital than others, he does not mean that the church can do without any of them. All are important to the life of the church. Paul also acknowledges that some spiritual gifts serve primarily to strengthen the felt connection between the person and God. But he says these are the least important because they do the least for the church. Still, these are real and important gifts.

church. The most important gifts are those that are less flashy, those gifts that we do not put on display. Gifts of helping and serving, welcoming and comforting are the greater kinds of gifts. These are demonstrations of the love of God that is the foundation of the life of the church. These are the gifts that most clearly demonstrate the kind of love for others that we see in the ministry and death of Jesus.

Paul has spent the first four chapters of 1 Corinthians persuading the church that the way they must evaluate all things is through the cross. He has argued that they must see helping others at one's own expense as the Christian manner of life. Now he applies that pattern to evaluating spiritual gifts. The important gifts are not those that get the person attention and accolades, but those that give to others without expectation of return or recognition. Those gifts and the way they are used are compared to those parts of the body that we cover with clothes; they may not be the most presentable, but they are the most important for the life and success of the church.

The Surprising Value of Different Gifts

More surprising than seeing all those kinds of service as spiritual gifts is the way they are to be valued in relation to one another. In Paul's body metaphor, he stands on their heads the ways the Corinthians and we usually value things. We expect that the best spiritual gifts are those that look impressive. The person who can give a moving sermon must have the greatest gift; likewise with the one who can sing beautifully. Paul says that these gifts are good, but not the ones that are vital for the life of the

Cooperation and Interdependence as the Body of Christ

One of the central points Paul wants to make with the body metaphor is that every gift is needed in the church and should be used for the good of the whole. This means that the church needs to seek ways to help those with differences and different gifts work together. Some kinds of gifts may seem at first incompatible with others. Paul would call on the whole church to find ways that enable each person to use his or her gift for the good of all. A part of this is the recognition that the strength of one gift leaves a weakness that the other gift may fill. So there is a necessary interdependence. Each gift needs the others. Recognition of this need can help us move toward better coordination. The very different (and perhaps irritating) gift provides something for the church that our gift does not. This can be difficult to acknowledge in the midst of church life, but that is what Paul calls the church to do in this text. The Spirit creates one body out of many parts, and the sum of this body is greater than its individual parts.

SHARING THE SCRIPTURE

PREPARING TO TEACH

Preparing Our Hearts

Meditate on this week's devotional reading from Galatians 3:23-29. Who may be included in the body of Christ? How are individuals melded into this body? Where do you see yourself within the body?

Pray that you and the students will recognize that as each person takes his or her place that the whole of the body of Christ will become greater than the sum of its individual parts.

Preparing Our Minds

Study the background Scripture and the lesson Scripture, both of which are from 1 Corinthians 12:12-31.

Consider this question as you prepare the lesson: *Why is it important to value all parts of an organization, especially within the church?*

Write on newsprint:
❑ information for next week's lesson, found under "Continue the Journey."
❑ activities for further spiritual growth in "Continue the Journey."

Review the "Introduction," "The Big Picture," "Close-up," and "Faith in Action," which all precede the first lesson of this quarter. Consider how you might use any of this material in today's lesson.

LEADING THE CLASS

(1) Gather to Learn

❖ Greet the class members and introduce guests.

❖ Pray that those who have come today will see the importance and value of the contributions that everyone in the church can make to its well-being.

❖ Invite the students to focus on the structure of a corporation. Identify the different departments that one might find, such as research and development, manufacturing, marketing, order fulfillment, and human resources. Talk briefly about what each department is expected to contribute to the whole. Think about what would happen if, for example, a product were designed and manufactured, but no one was marketing it, even though people were standing by to fill orders. Mention that the church, though more than a human organization, shares some characteristics with organizations such as a corporation.

❖ Read aloud today's focus statement: **Organizations are composed of several interrelated, interdependent functional parts. Why is it important to value all the parts? In his letter, Paul tells the Corinthian church that all spiritual gifts are necessary for its efficient operation.**

(2) Goal 1: Learn How Each Member of the Body Supports the Other Members

❖ Help the class to begin to think about how parts of the human body support one another by reading author and radio host Joni Eareckson Tada's description of how the human body works: **"The human body is probably the most amazing example of teamwork anywhere. Every part needs the other. When the stomach is hungry, the eyes spot the hamburger. The nose smells the onions, the feet run to the snack stand, the hands douse the burger with mustard and shove it back into the mouth, where it goes down to the stomach. Now that's cooperation!"**

❖ Select one or more volunteers to read 1 Corinthians 12:12-31.

❖ Discuss these questions:
   1. **In what ways is Paul's comparison between the human body and the body of Christ helpful to believers in understanding how church members are to relate to one another and to Christ?**
   2. **How do you think Paul might respond to this comment: "The diversity of gifts you describe, Paul, is interesting, but are all these gifts really necessary?" (See "Diversity of Gifts Is a Necessity" in Interpreting the Scripture.)**

3. **Does Paul give you the impression that he values all gifts? Explain your answer. (See "The Surprising Value of Different Gifts" in Interpreting the Scripture.)**

(3) Goal 2: Value the Different Gifts Operating Within the Church

❖ Read or retell "Diversity of Gifts Is a Blessing" in Interpreting the Scripture.

❖ Note that in 1 Corinthians 12:22-25 Paul gives as much weight to so-called "inferior" gifts as he does to those that are "respectable." In other words, although gifts differ, they are all to be valued. Ask:
   1. **What kinds of gifts does our congregation seem to value most highly? What behaviors or attitudes suggest that these gifts we have named are more highly valued than others?**
   2. **What kinds of gifts do we take for granted, perhaps even ignore? What behaviors or attitudes suggest that these gifts are of lesser value?**
   3. **What changes can we as a congregation make to show everyone that whatever gifts they have to offer are needed and valuable?**

(4) Goal 3: Use Spiritual Gifts in Cooperation with Others for Building Up the Body of Christ

❖ Read or retell "Cooperation and Interdependence of the Body of Christ" in Interpreting the Scripture. Take note of the last sentence concerning the body being greater than the sum of its parts.

❖ Encourage the adults to think of the activities that go on during a typical Sunday morning, such as one or more worship services, Sunday school, and a coffee hour. List on newsprint each activity and underneath name the gifts that are necessary for this activity to be of real value to the body of believers. Include not only "public" gifts, such as pastor, but also gifts such as giving, which everyone can exercise. Continue to list activities and their associated gifts until you have what is needed to conduct the program on Sunday morning.

❖ Discuss these questions:

1. **How would Sunday mornings at our church be different if we did not have members willing to use their gifts and work with others?**

2. **What other gifts could help us to expand our Sunday morning ministry?**

3. **Who appears to have such gifts? How will we approach these people and encourage them to volunteer?**

(5) Continue the Journey

❖ Pray that as the learners depart, they will recognize the importance of each individual gift working in concert with all other gifts to build up the body of Christ.

❖ Post information for next week's session on newsprint for the students to copy:

- **Title: Gift of Languages**
- **Background Scripture: Acts 2:1-21; 1 Corinthians 14:1-25**
- **Lesson Scripture: Acts 2:1-7, 12; 1 Corinthians 14:13-19**
- **Focus of the Lesson: Communication is important as groups implement programs that will affect the lives of others. What is needed to achieve the best communication possible? Finding a common understanding is necessary whether people are speaking in different native languages as in Acts 2 or unknown spiritual languages as in 1 Corinthians 14.**

❖ Challenge the adults to grow spiritually by completing one or more of these activities related to this week's session, which you have posted on newsprint for the students to copy.

(1) **Encourage other members of the church to use their spiritual gifts by being a role model in terms of the way you use your own gifts.**

(2) **Care for a member of the body that is suffering.**

(3) **Express your gratitude to people in the church who are exercising their spiritual gifts. Let them know how much their gifts help everyone. Be especially mindful of those who feel they have "lesser" gifts, so that they will know they are needed and that their gifts are valuable.**

❖ Sing or read aloud "They'll Know We Are Christians by Our Love" from *The Faith We Sing*.

❖ Conclude today's session by leading the class in this benediction adapted from 1 Corinthians 12:13, which is the key verse for today's lesson: **Let us go forth rejoicing that in the one Spirit we were all baptized into one body—Jews or Greeks, slaves or free—and we were all made to drink of one Spirit.**

UNIT 3: ONE IN THE BOND OF LOVE

GIFT OF LANGUAGES

PREVIEWING THE LESSON

Lesson Scripture: Acts 2:1-7, 12; 1 Corinthians 14:13-19
Background Scripture: Acts 2:1-21; 1 Corinthians 14:1-25
Key Verse: 1 Corinthians 14:15

Focus of the Lesson:
Communication is important as groups implement programs that will affect the lives of others. What is needed to achieve the best communication possible? Finding a common understanding is necessary whether people are speaking in different native languages as in Acts 2 or unknown spiritual languages as in 1 Corinthians 14.

Goals for the Learners:
(1) to discover how the Holy Spirit helped people communicate both in different native and spiritual languages.
(2) to empathize with persons in situations where language inhibits communication.
(3) to find ways to communicate with diverse people and have common understanding.

Supplies:
Bibles, newsprint and marker, paper and pencils, hymnals

READING THE SCRIPTURE

NRSV
Lesson Scripture: Acts 2:1-7, 12

¹When the day of Pentecost had come, they were all together in one place. ²And suddenly from heaven there came a sound like the rush of a violent wind, and it filled the entire house where they were sitting. ³Divided tongues, as of fire, appeared

CEB
Lesson Scripture: Acts 2:1-7, 12

¹When Pentecost Day arrived, they were all together in one place. ²Suddenly a sound from heaven like the howling of a fierce wind filled the entire house where they were sitting. ³They saw what seemed to be individual flames of fire alighting on each

among them, and a tongue rested on each of them. ⁴All of them were filled with the Holy Spirit and began to speak in other languages, as the Spirit gave them ability.

⁵Now there were devout Jews from every nation under heaven living in Jerusalem. ⁶And at this sound the crowd gathered and was bewildered, because each one heard them speaking in the native language of each. ⁷Amazed and astonished, they asked, "Are not all these who are speaking Galileans? . . ."¹²All were amazed and perplexed, saying to one another, "What does this mean?"

1 Corinthians 14:13-19

¹³Therefore, one who speaks in a tongue should pray for the power to interpret. ¹⁴For if I pray in a tongue, my spirit prays but my mind is unproductive. ¹⁵**What should I do then? I will pray with the spirit, but I will pray with the mind also; I will sing praise with the spirit, but I will sing praise with the mind also.** ¹⁶Otherwise, if you say a blessing with the spirit, how can anyone in the position of an outsider say the "Amen" to your thanksgiving, since the outsider does not know what you are saying? ¹⁷For you may give thanks well enough, but the other person is not built up. ¹⁸I thank God that I speak in tongues more than all of you; ¹⁹nevertheless, in church I would rather speak five words with my mind, in order to instruct others also, than ten thousand words in a tongue.

one of them. ⁴They were all filled with the Holy Spirit and began to speak in other languages as the Spirit enabled them to speak.

⁵There were pious Jews from every nation under heaven living in Jerusalem. ⁶When they heard this sound, a crowd gathered. They were mystified because everyone heard them speaking in their native languages. ⁷They were surprised and amazed, saying, "Look, aren't all the people who are speaking Galileans, every one of them? . . ."¹²They were all surprised and bewildered. Some asked each other, "What does this mean?"

1 Corinthians 14:13-19

¹³Therefore, those who speak in a tongue should pray to be able to interpret. ¹⁴If I pray in a tongue, my spirit prays but my mind isn't productive. ¹⁵**What should I do? I'll pray in the Spirit, but I'll pray with my mind too; I'll sing a psalm in the Spirit, but I'll sing the psalm with my mind too.** ¹⁶After all, if you praise God in the Spirit, how will the people who aren't trained in that language say "Amen! " to your thanksgiving, when they don't know what you are saying? ¹⁷You may offer a beautiful prayer of thanksgiving, but the other person is not being built up. ¹⁸I thank God that I speak in tongues more than all of you. ¹⁹But in the church I'd rather speak five words in my right mind than speak thousands of words in a tongue so that I can teach others.

UNDERSTANDING THE SCRIPTURE

Acts 2:1-4. Acts 2 tells the story of the beginning of the church. Jesus has told the apostles to remain in Jerusalem until the Spirit comes on them (1:4). This coming of the Spirit is the sign that the church has begun, that God has begun to live among God's people in a new and more intimate way. There is a large crowd in Jerusalem this day because Pentecost is a pilgrimage feast within Judaism (see Exodus 23:16-17). It is a harvest festival that comes fifty days after Passover. It also celebrates the way that God took care of the Israelites while they were in the wilderness. The church's birth comes at the time of this festival. Acts says that the Spirit comes on those who have remained committed to Jesus, and it comes dramatically. Its presence is symbolized by fiery tongues over the heads of each person. It is important to note that this gift of the Spirit comes to all who confess Christ as risen, not just to the apostles. That presence of the Spirit in all of God's people was the sign of the new time of God's action in the world. God is doing a new thing through Christ. The ability of each one to speak in tongues is the evidence that each one has the Spirit.

Acts 2:5-13. There were thousands of pilgrims in Jerusalem for the feast. While they are all Jews and proselytes (2:10), their coming from all over the world is a sign that the gospel is for the whole world. This is portrayed vividly by the nature of the gifts of speaking in tongues on this occasion. Here in Acts, when those first people received the Spirit, they were enabled to speak in known languages they had never studied. In other places in the New Testament, speaking in tongues involves uttering sounds that are not a language known to anyone present. So this manifestation of the Spirit at Pentecost is extraordinary. Its distinctiveness enables all who have it to share the gospel. Some who hear this are amazed, but others scoff, thinking it is nonsense.

Acts 2:14-21. In response to the crowd, Peter rises to give the first Christian sermon. In it he interprets the coming of the Spirit as an end-time event. The prophets had said that in the last days the Spirit would come upon all of God's people, not just prophets and kings. Peter proclaims that this time has arrived. God's Spirit is now given to men and women, all races and ethnicities, and all social classes. The upheaval of earth and sky spoken of here is the way the prophets talked about what we might call "earth-shaking events." God is reshaping the world. God's intimate presence in the church changes everything. When Acts says this is an end-time event, it does not imply that the world will end soon. Most important, the "last days" are the new time when God will be present in this new way. It matters little how many last days there are. What the church needs to hear is that it is now empowered to do the will of God by having God's Spirit in and among them. This new presence of God comes through Christ and is a sign of God's determination to bring salvation to the whole world.

1 Corinthians 14:1-12. Paul begins his final instructions on how to use spiritual gifts in worship by reminding the Corinthians of the guiding principle of the entire discussion: Gifts are to be used to build up the church. He compares the gifts of prophecy and tongues to make the point. In 1 Corinthians and most of the New Testament, "speaking in tongues" means uttering things that neither the speaker nor the hearers understand. This is different from Acts 2, where the tongues enabled people of various languages to understand. At Corinth, tongues is a gift that enables the speaker to sense a closeness to God; it is a sort of mystical encounter in which the believer feels God take control of his or her speech. Thus, it enhances a person's experience of God. This is a good thing, but Paul says it is not the most important thing when the church is gathered as a community because it only benefits the person having the experience. Paul says prophecy is superior because it provides something that benefits others. The cognitive content of prophecy conveys a message that builds up the whole church by bringing it a word from God. So in worship services, prophecy is superior to tongues. Verses 6-11 provide examples of how clarity of meaning is important in other contexts. Then in verse 12 Paul repeats the central point: Do what benefits the church rather than yourself.

1 Corinthians 14:13-19. Paul does not, however, tell the Corinthians never to exercise the gift of tongues in worship. He does mention its limitations. Only part of the self is engaged in speaking in tongues; the mind is idle in that experience. Since Paul wants the whole person engaged, he tells the Corinthians to pray to receive the interpretation of what they say in the tongue. Even more important, if the tongue speaker can interpret, then the whole church can participate in the worship of God. Paul is not against personal and private encounters with God. He says he is glad he has them more often than any of the Corinthians, but in the assembled church the good of the whole takes precedence over the good of the individual.

1 Corinthians 14:20-25. Paul calls the Corinthians to use wisdom to discern how best to use spiritual gifts in worship services. Tongues can serve a function. They may show some nonbelievers that there is a presence of God within the church, but they may also lead people to think that church people are just crazy. Prophecy may build up the church by directing it where God wants it to go. It may also bring people in as God reveals to the prophet things that will lead nonbelievers to acknowledge the presence and word of God and so repent and become a part of the church. So each gift has its place. The church must discern how to use each to build up the church and witness to the world.

INTERPRETING THE SCRIPTURE

The Spirit Empowers the
Church for Its Mission

The giving of the Spirit is an end-time event. It is hard for us to think about the time we live in as "the last days." After all, the Resurrection occurred two thousand years ago. But the New Testament's talk about the "last days" is not really about how many days are left before the end of the world. Rather the New Testament sees the end times as the time after Christ's resurrection and so as the time when former promises are fulfilled. Because of what Christ has done, God now dwells among God's people in new and more intimate ways. The Spirit of God now lives within the heart. It is now that God calls all people into this close relationship. The gift of the Spirit is an end-time gift because it is something that God's people as a whole did not enjoy before it was given them through Christ.

The church is an institution of the last days. It is the community in which the Spirit resides and one of its important duties is to be a sign of what God wants for the entire world. When the Spirit falls on believers at Pentecost, it falls on all of them, not just Peter and the apostles. In this outpouring of the Spirit, every believer received a gift from God. That gift was used to advance the mission of the church. Here on the first day of the church's existence, every believer contributes to the spreading of the gospel as they speak in languages that are understood by people from many different places throughout the world. They all participate in sharing the gospel because the Spirit gives them the gifts they need to do this work. This speaking in many languages symbolizes the gospel's power to overcome differences and so bring salvation to all. It symbolically overcomes a formidable barrier to spreading the good news to the diverse world. While most of us no longer expect tongue speaking as evidence of the Spirit, the Spirit gives every Christian a gift to share that contributes to the life and growth of the church. Importantly, we are not left on our own to do God's work in the church and the world; the Spirit empowers us to accomplish that work and so further the church's mission.

Tongues and Prophecy

Our texts today talk a lot about speaking in tongues and prophecy. Prophecy does not refer to predicting the future as much as to giving

authoritative teaching. Early Christian prophets were people who brought God's word for that moment. They helped the church determine what it should do and teach in particular moments. The gift of tongues is described in two different ways. In Acts 2, it enables a person to communicate with someone whose language she does not know.

In 1 Corinthians, however, the only person who can understand what a tongue speaker says is a person who has the gift of interpretation. At Corinth, speaking in tongues is an ecstatic experience in which the speaker does not know what he or she is saying. Thus the one who speaks in tongues cannot explain it when it is over (unless that one also has the gift of interpretation). Neither does this utterance employ a language spoken elsewhere in the world. It is, rather, a manifestation of an experience of God that touches the emotional life of the person speaking. This experience assures one of the closeness of God and of the love of God because God cares enough to take a direct part in the person's life. God puts words in the person's mouth. For the person speaking in tongues, the content of the utterance is less important than the experience itself.

Interior Life and the Spirit

Paul seems rather critical of the gift of tongues in 1 Corinthians 14. He says that prophecy is a superior gift and that speaking in tongues does not engage the mind. On the other hand, he also says that he is glad he speaks in tongues more than anyone in the Corinthian church. Paul does not oppose the practice of speaking in tongues, but he does want to regulate its use in worship services. From his own experience, Paul sees tongues as a good and enriching encounter with God. Speaking in tongues is a type of mystical experience. While we think of mystical experiences in contemplative terms, the early church and ancient world saw more active ways to attain and experience that direct contact with a god. Paul believes such encounters can enhance one's experience of God. But he does not think those encounters are superior to other ways of communing with God. Study or song may also lead to closeness with God.

Paul is concerned that the Corinthians not require tongues or any one experience of all believers. The intense encounter with God that accompanies tongues can be good, but other experiences can be just as meaningful. Paul does not want tongues or any ecstatic or mystical manifestation to be the only kind of spiritual experience believers think about because they only engage a part of the human person. Paul says prophecy is superior because it engages the intellect as well as the spirit. Spirituality is not just about lofty moments of the soul's flight or oneness with God; it is also about clearheaded thought about God. Listening for the voice of God in logical discussion of an issue is a practice of Christian spirituality as Paul describes it. The mind should be engaged in worship and prayer, even as the spirit is. The full spiritual life does not focus exclusively on those desired quiet moments in the presence of God. It also expects God to be present in the midst of careful thought and in works done for the good of others.

Spiritual Gifts and the Church

One of the reasons Paul wants to be sure the Corinthians do not limit spirituality to personal, private experience is that such spirituality does not fully reflect the gospel. For Paul, true Christian spirituality seeks the good of the other person. Its exemplar is the self-giving love of Christ. Prophecy is a better gift because it can enhance the life of the church. Prophecy provides the church with intelligible content that the church then evaluates to discern whether it is a genuine revelation. Prophecy, the gift that engages the mind of both the prophet and the hearers, enhances worship because it helps the church honor God in appropriate ways.

We do not expect someone to have a direct word from God, but we may hope that a gift of discerning God's will is present among us as we seek to understand and conform to God's will today. Such discernment is a gift that may help us bring together those who begin with different understandings of God's will. Perhaps the Spirit will guide discussion and debate in ways that help people identify their common understandings of God and divine will so God's people can work together to make the world more of what God would have it to be. Paul wants all gifts, including the many abilities that members possess beyond tongues and prophecy, to contribute to the fuller life of the church. All gifts are put to their fullest purpose when they serve the good of the community rather than just the individual. When we see gifts used to enhance the church's life, we see the exercise of true Christian spirituality.

SHARING THE SCRIPTURE

PREPARING TO TEACH

Preparing Our Hearts

Meditate on this week's devotional reading from Deuteronomy 4:32-40. What reasons are given that lead you to believe that Israel is a privileged people? What do you learn about God? How does the image of fire in this passage relate to Acts 2?

Pray that you and the students will recognize the ways that people communicate with one another and with God.

Preparing Our Minds

Study the background Scripture from Acts 2:1-21 and 1 Corinthians 14:1-25. The lesson Scripture is from Acts 2:1-7, 12 and 1 Corinthians 14:13-19.

Consider this question as you prepare the lesson: *What is needed to achieve the best communication possible?*

Write on newsprint:
- ❏ list for "Find Ways to Communicate with Diverse People and Have Common Understanding."
- ❏ information for next week's lesson, found under "Continue the Journey."
- ❏ activities for further spiritual growth in "Continue the Journey."

Review the "Introduction," "The Big Picture," "Close-up," and "Faith in Action," which all precede the first lesson of this quarter. Consider how you might use any of this material in today's lesson.

LEADING THE CLASS

(1) Gather to Learn

❖ Greet the class members and introduce guests.

❖ Pray that those who have come today will recognize the role of the Holy Spirit in enabling people to communicate with understanding.

❖ Form several teams of four to six persons to play the Telephone Game, which many adults may remember from childhood. Begin the game by whispering this sentence just once in the ear of one person from each team: **Early Christians heard good news in their native language when the Holy Spirit came on Pentecost.** Each person is to whisper this sentence in the ear of a teammate until everyone on each team has heard it. Invite the last person on each team to say what he or she heard. Then read the statement as you said it to the first people.

❖ Ask: **What does this game teach us about communicating with one another?**

❖ Read aloud today's focus statement: **Communication is important as groups implement programs that will affect the lives of others. What is needed to achieve the best communication possible? Finding a common understanding is necessary whether people are speaking in different native languages as in Acts 2 or unknown spiritual languages as in 1 Corinthians 14.**

(2) Goal 1: Discover How the Holy Spirit Helped People Communicate Both in Different Native and Spiritual Languages

❖ Introduce the Book of Acts by reading or retelling "Acts" from the article, "The Big Picture: The Early Church and the Holy Spirit," found at the beginning of this quarter. Point out that today is Pentecost Sunday.

❖ Choose a volunteer to read Acts 2:1-7, 12 and discuss these questions:

1. How did the first Christians describe the coming of the Holy Spirit on Pentecost?
2. What is the reader told about the languages that the people heard?
3. What was the purpose of the disciples using languages that were unknown to them? (See "The Spirit Empowers the Church for Its Mission" in Interpreting the Scripture.)

❖ Select a volunteer to read 1 Corinthians 14:13-19 and discuss these questions:

1. What is the difference between the languages spoken on Pentecost and the languages that Paul refers to here? (See "Tongues and Prophecy" in Interpreting the Scripture.)
2. How might speaking in tongues, described in 1 Corinthians 14, enhance one's spiritual life? (See "Interior Life and the Spirit" in Interpreting the Scripture.)

(3) Goal 2: Empathize with Persons in Situations Where Language Inhibits Communication

❖ Read this story: A sailor from South Korea left his ship docked in Baltimore in search of oil paints so that he could pursue his hobby. He spoke no English but somehow found a hardware store that sold interior and exterior paints. The clerks tried hard to help this customer by making hand motions and holding cans of paint, but to no avail. The proprietor had a Spirit-inspired idea. She called the local Berlitz, a company that teaches global languages, and asked to speak to someone who taught Korean. The school receptionist said she would locate one of their Korean teachers whose business was not far from the hardware store and have him call. The teacher quickly called, and the proprietor explained the dilemma. She put the customer on the phone and he explained that he wanted artists' oil paint, which the teacher relayed to the proprietor, whose store did not carry such paint. But the teacher did more. He asked that an employee put the customer on the bus and give the driver the teacher's address so that the teacher could meet this newcomer at the bus stop, treat him to lunch, and take him to a nearby art supply store to find what he wanted. One of the clerks did as asked and even paid the bus fare. The teacher called back to report on a lovely afternoon with his new friend.

❖ Ask these questions:

1. Where in this true story do you see examples of empathy with someone who faced a language barrier?
2. What opportunities exist in your community to help persons who do not speak the native language?

(4) Goal 3: Find Ways to Communicate with Diverse People and Have Common Understanding

❖ Post this list of people who may experience barriers to communication within the church. Invite the students to add other groups.

- People who have been deaf or hard of hearing for most of their lives.
- Older people who have sustained hearing loss over the years.
- People who are not fluent in the native language of the rest of the congregation.
- People who cannot comprehend a wide vocabulary.
- Teens who may not be familiar with references to events or cultural icons that are well known to the adults in the congregation.
- Adults who may not be familiar with references familiar to teens.
- People who struggle to read words that they do know if spoken.

❖ Encourage the adults to comment on what their church could do to better communicate with these diverse people. Suggest ways to implement their ideas.

(5) Continue the Journey

❖ Pray that as the learners depart, they will seek to communicate the gospel clearly with everyone they meet.

❖ Post information for next week's session on newsprint for the students to copy:
- Title: The Greatest Gift Is Love
- Background Scripture: 1 Corinthians 13

- Lesson Scripture: 1 Corinthians 13
- Focus of the Lesson: Love is the primary requirement for societies attempting to make a dramatic influence on the world around them. What is it about love that makes it so indispensable? In 1 Corinthians 13, Paul says that love is needed to achieve fully the benefit of all spiritual gifts.

❖ Challenge the adults to grow spiritually by completing one or more of these activities related to this week's session, which you have posted on newsprint for the students to copy.

(1) Do whatever you can to help someone who is facing a language barrier.
(2) Talk with other members of your congregation about hosting ESL (English as a second language) classes.
(3) Practice being as precise in your meaning as possible when you speak to someone so as to avoid miscommunications.

❖ Sing or read aloud "O Spirit of the Living God."

❖ Conclude today's session by leading the class in this benediction adapted from 1 Corinthians 12:13, which is the key verse for the lesson for May 17: **Let us go forth rejoicing that in the one Spirit we were all baptized into one body—Jews or Greeks, slaves or free—and we were all made to drink of one Spirit.**

UNIT 3: ONE IN THE BOND OF LOVE

The Greatest Gift Is Love

PREVIEWING THE LESSON

Lesson Scripture: 1 Corinthians 13
Background Scripture: 1 Corinthians 13
Key Verse: 1 Corinthians 13:13

Focus of the Lesson:
Love is the primary requirement for societies attempting to make a dramatic influence on the world around them. What is it about love that makes it so indispensable? In 1 Corinthians 13, Paul says that love is needed to achieve fully the benefit of all spiritual gifts.

Goals for the Learners:
(1) to explore the meaning of love as seen in 1 Corinthians 13.
(2) to appreciate one another in love.
(3) to find a variety of ways to express love.

Supplies:
Bibles, newsprint and marker, paper and pencils, hymnals

READING THE SCRIPTURE

NRSV
Lesson Scripture: 1 Corinthians 13

¹If I speak in the tongues of mortals and of angels, but do not have love, I am a noisy gong or a clanging cymbal. ²And if I have prophetic powers, and understand all mysteries and all knowledge, and if I have all faith, so as to remove mountains, but do not have love, I am nothing. ³If I give away all my possessions, and

CEB
Lesson Scripture: 1 Corinthians 13

¹If I speak in tongues of human beings and of angels but I don't have love, I'm a clanging gong or a clashing cymbal. ²If I have the gift of prophecy and I know all the mysteries and everything else, and if I have such complete faith that I can move mountains but I don't have love, I'm nothing. ³If I give away everything that I

if I hand over my body so that I may boast, but do not have love, I gain nothing.

⁴Love is patient; love is kind; love is not envious or boastful or arrogant ⁵or rude. It does not insist on its own way; it is not irritable or resentful; ⁶it does not rejoice in wrongdoing, but rejoices in the truth. ⁷It bears all things, believes all things, hopes all things, endures all things.

⁸Love never ends. But as for prophecies, they will come to an end; as for tongues, they will cease; as for knowledge, it will come to an end. ⁹For we know only in part, and we prophesy only in part; ¹⁰but when the complete comes, the partial will come to an end. ¹¹When I was a child, I spoke like a child, I thought like a child, I reasoned like a child; when I became an adult, I put an end to childish ways. ¹²For now we see in a mirror, dimly, but then we will see face to face. Now I know only in part; then I will know fully, even as I have been fully known. ¹³And now faith, hope, and love abide, these three; and the greatest of these is love.

have and hand over my own body to feel good about what I've done but I don't have love, I receive no benefit whatsoever.

⁴Love is patient, love is kind, it isn't jealous, it doesn't brag, it isn't arrogant, ⁵it isn't rude, it doesn't seek its own advantage, it isn't irritable, it doesn't keep a record of complaints, ⁶it isn't happy with injustice, but it is happy with the truth. ⁷Love puts up with all things, trusts in all things, hopes for all things, endures all things.

⁸Love never fails. As for prophecies, they will be brought to an end. As for tongues, they will stop. As for knowledge, it will be brought to an end. ⁹We know in part and we prophesy in part; ¹⁰but when the perfect comes, what is partial will be brought to an end. ¹¹When I was a child, I used to speak like a child, reason like a child, think like a child. But now that I have become a man, I've put an end to childish things. ¹²Now we see a reflection in a mirror; then we will see face-to-face. Now I know partially, but then I will know completely in the same way that I have been completely known. ¹³Now faith, hope, and love remain—these three things—and the greatest of these is love.

UNDERSTANDING THE SCRIPTURE

Introduction. This chapter appears in the middle of Paul's discussion of spiritual gifts and how to use them in the church. He has argued that all spiritual gifts must be used to benefit the church rather than to make the one who has the gift look impressive or allow that person to gain some advantage. At the end of chapter 12

he lists gifts the Corinthians know, saying some are better than others. Then he tells them to seek the better gifts. Chapter 13 tells them what the best spiritual gift is.

1 Corinthians 13:1-3. Verses 1-3 are a dramatic introduction to the importance of having love for fellow Christians. All spiritual gifts are to be used to express love. It is the "more excellent way" Paul has said he will show them (12:31). The Corinthians seem especially proud of the gifts of speaking in tongues, prophecy, and being given knowledge from God. Paul asserts that these powers are meaningless unless the people who have them also have love for fellow believers. He pushes his point to the extreme of saying that giving away all of one's possessions and even dying for others mean nothing unless motivated by love. Of course, in the competition about spiritual gifts at Corinth, the thing all participants have lacked is love. Their arguing about this matter is a clear indication of the absence of love. Paul concludes this introduction by saying that any exercise of a spiritual gift that lacks love gains the person nothing: no legitimate status within the church and no closer relationship with God.

1 Corinthians 13:4-7. Once Paul has established just how important love is, he describes what it looks like in practice. In many respects, what Paul says about love here is the opposite of what he has heard about the way the Corinthians are behaving. They have been boastful and arrogant; they have put their own good before that of the other person and of the church as a whole. Paul responds by saying that their powerful and impressive gifts mean nothing unless they are used in love, used to exhibit the characteristics of patience, goodness, and willingness to put up with the faults of others. Among the ways he describes the embodiment of love is to say that it does not seek its own good (13:5). This characteristic is especially important because Paul has spent

the first four chapters of this letter showing how Christian spirituality must be shaped by the cross. As the determinative example for believers, it requires them to do what is in the best interest of others. All of the characteristics of love that Paul names are designed to help the Corinthians change how they behave toward one another.

1 Corinthians 13:8-13. To drive home his point, Paul compares having love with the three gifts they prize (tongues, prophecy, and knowledge). The Corinthians seem to think that these gifts are clear demonstrations of one's close relationship with God and of spiritual power. Paul says they are temporary and of only passing importance. While such gifts are important at the moment, they will cease. His second evaluation of them is that they are partial. Those with such gifts do not hear the whole message God has for the church. Their value and existence ceases when the "complete" or "perfect" (CEB) thing comes (13:10). There has been a great deal of discussion about what this "perfect thing" is. Some have said it is the full structure of the hierarchical church, others that it is the completion of the New Testament. In context, it is clear that neither of these is correct. Rather, the complete thing is more likely the Second Coming of Christ. It is only then that we will understand clearly, only then will our partial knowledge be made full.

Paul almost makes the three manifestations of the Spirit that the Corinthians treasure a sign of spiritual immaturity. He compares possessing these gifts with his behavior as a child. Certain behaviors were appropriate when he was a child, but only then. Just as he stopped behaving in those ways as he matured, so the church will not need these gifts when it matures. He does not envision a settled church that no longer needs spiritual gifts. The time of full maturity does not arrive until the Second Coming.

The second analogy Paul uses to discuss the partial knowledge of God that the church now has is a mirror. Mirrors were not as clear as those we have today, but even if you assume a good mirror, it can only give a one-dimensional and partial image. That partial understanding is what the church has now. The knowledge received through cherished gifts supplies only a dim reflection of the full knowledge of God that awaits the faithful when they are directly in the presence of God.

Finally, Paul names three things that will remain: faith, hope, and love. This triad appears elsewhere in Paul's letters (for example, 1 Thessalonians 1:3). After discussing what happens at the Second Coming, the "now" at the beginning of verse 13 returns to the present, to the time that the church exists between its beginning and the return of Christ. Throughout this period, the central gifts that are always most important for the church are faith, hope, and love. Faith refers to our trust and reliance on God. Hope is the church's confident expectation that the God who raised Christ will also raise its members. And love is our valuing of and commitment to God and fellow believers. Love is the greatest of these because it grounds all the others and lasts even past the Second Coming. When reliance upon God is easier in God's presence and hope is no longer necessary because we already enjoy God's blessings, love continues. Our love for God and God's love for us come even more fully to define our lives as we enjoy the immediate presence of God that comes without the interference of things that turn us away from God now. God's love for us is the basis for the love that we are to have and show to one another. Embodying that love in the church is the greatest spiritual gift.

INTERPRETING THE SCRIPTURE

Love Is the Most Important Spiritual Gift

We are accustomed to hearing this passage at weddings, but it is not really about the love between people who are about to get married. This passage appears in the middle of a discussion of how to use spiritual gifts *in the church*, and particularly when the church is gathered for worship. In the immediately preceding verse (12:31), Paul encouraged the Corinthians to seek the better gifts.

Then he says he will show them a "more excellent way," a way that is better than having any of the gifts he has mentioned. That more excellent way is having love. Just so they do not miss the point, Paul mentions the spiritual gifts they find most important and says that exercising them means nothing if the person who has them does not have love. This is like someone saying to the world's best preacher that his or her work is of no worth if she or he does not have love.

Paul is saying that the use of all talents and abilities in the church must flow out of love or they are not what God wants. He says that even giving oneself as a martyr is meaningless if it is done for self-aggrandizement. It may be hard for us to fathom how people could be so concerned about self-promotion that they would willingly die, but we have seen the kind of attitude Paul is describing. We know of talented people who go to great extents to accomplish things so that others will be impressed and praise them. We see it in the church when singing becomes performance rather than praise or when preaching becomes a garnering of admiration (or gaining adherents for a coming vote) rather than proclamation of the gospel. Using our gifts for the wrong reasons is no less of a temptation today than it was for the Corinthians. Paul would remind us that all we do in the church must grow from love. Every act of leadership, every deed of helping others, every effort to make things run smoothly, everything must be done in love. This love is a love for our fellow Christians as well as for God. In making this demand, Paul is giving some specifics to what Jesus means when he says that the greatest command is to love God and the second is to love one's neighbor as oneself (Matthew 22:34-40; Mark 12:28-34; Luke 10:25-28). The command to love one another is central in Paul's understanding of how Christians must relate to one another.

Love Is Not a Feeling

When we talk about love, we usually think of certain kinds of feelings that we have for another person. When we read 1 Corinthians 13, we think of these feelings in part because we are so used to hearing it read at weddings. If we look back at the text, however, there is no real attention to how we feel. Love is not described as a feeling or an emotional attachment, but as a way of behaving. Love is a decision to relate to others in particular ways and not in others. Love is manifested in the ways we act, not in how we feel. When Paul describes love, he tells about how it treats others: It is patient, kind, not jealous, not boastful, not proud, not rude.

Overall, love is seen as not seeking one's own good, but that of others. That is one of the central messages of all of 1 Corinthians, and it is a theme that appears in other Pauline Letters. It is so important because putting the good of others before our own good is the foundational way that we conform our lives to that of Christ. Paul sees Christ's incarnation and death as acts that put our good before Christ's own good. That manifestation of love becomes the pattern for the way all of Christian life is to be lived. Believers conform their lives to the self-giving love of Christ. Paul does not mention the cross in chapter 13, but it has been central to his correction of their understanding of spirituality throughout the letter, especially in chapters 1–4 where he talks about the cross as the standard for evaluating all things (see, for example, 1:18; 2:1-4). We would perhaps rather think about love as a feeling because deciding to put the good of others first makes so little sense in our world, just as it was the case in the ancient world. All of the ways Paul describes love in 13:4-7 require us to subordinate our desires, wishes, and gain to what is good for others. This kind of love makes mustering a certain kind of feeling for someone seem easy.

Actions and Attitudes

Paul, then, calls for a love that is defined by how we behave toward one another. The acts that manifest love may well, however, call for an inner transformation. But that inner transformation is a reforming of how we value others as human beings, as children of God. Love demands that we determine to hope the best for someone, not to hold a grudge, and not keep track of how others have wronged us (13:5-7). Consistently maintaining such treatment will require us to see fellow Christians as people who are loved by God and thus seen as valuable by God.

Our treatment of them will require that we acknowledge that extraordinary value and their relationship with God. Our relationships with them will reflect that recognition. Such love will manifest itself in reaching out to those suffering pain or loss. It may show itself in acts of service where we see need. It surely must govern our conduct in controversies and disputes within the church. We are not required to have warm feelings or to like every other Christian. Our attitude toward and valuing of everyone must, however, be shaped by love.

Faith, Hope, Love

Paul identifies faith, hope, and love as the most important gifts. First, note that none of these has the extraordinary or impressive manifestations the Corinthians (and perhaps we) desire. As Paul uses the word "faith," it is an orientation of life. It is our commitment not only to believe certain things but also to live in a particular manner. The belief and determination that constitute our response to God are also gifts of God. So God enables us to trust in and live for God. This makes the life of faith a gift rather than something we simply decide to do. The hope Paul refers to is our confidence in the future that God will bring to God's people. As a gift, it can remain strong in the face of difficult circumstances. Finally, the greatest gift is love. Again, love is not just a demand; rather, it is a gift. The central thing God requires us to do has been given to us.

Being loving may be difficult at times, but in its closing words this chapter, which imposes significant demands and calls into question our means of evaluating so much of life, assures us that love is a gift. We are not left on our own to gather the strength to love our fellow church members. Paul assures us that through the Spirit God enables us to live together as God's children, showing love to one another and so being a sign to the world of what God wants everywhere and for all.

SHARING THE SCRIPTURE

PREPARING TO TEACH

Preparing Our Hearts

Meditate on this week's devotional reading from Ephesians 3:14-21 in which Paul prays for his readers. What does it mean to you to be "rooted and grounded in love" (3:17)? How do you experience the love of Jesus? Memorize the doxology in verses 20-21.

Pray that you and the students will give glory and praise to Jesus, who loves you and all the church.

Preparing Our Minds

Study the background Scripture and the lesson Scripture, which are both from 1 Corinthians 13.

Consider this question as you prepare the lesson: *Why is love so indispensable?*

Write on newsprint:

❏ words for "Appreciate One Another in Love."

❏ Bible passages for "Find a Variety of Ways to Express Love."

❏ information for next week's lesson, found under "Continue the Journey."

❏ activities for further spiritual growth in "Continue the Journey."

Review the "Introduction," "The Big Picture," "Close-up," and "Faith in Action," which all precede the first lesson of this quarter. Consider how you might use any of this material in today's lesson.

LEADING THE CLASS

(1) Gather to Learn

❖ Greet the class members and introduce guests.

❖ Pray that those who have come today will reflect on love and its importance for all people.

❖ Read aloud the titles of these love songs and invite the students to recall the words:

• "Love Makes the World Go 'Round" (theme song written for the 1961 musical *Carnival!* by Bob Merrill)

• "Love Story" (from the 1970 movie *Love Story*)

• "She Loves You" (The Beatles, 1963)

• "This Guy's in Love with You" (Herb Alpert, 1968)

• "I Just Called to Say I Love You" (Stevie Wonder, 1984, heard in the Gene Wilder film *The Woman in Red*, for which it won the Academy Award for Best Original Song)

• "Love Will Keep Us Together" (Captain and Tennille, 1975)

❖ Ask: **When North Americans think of love, romantic songs often come to mind. What elements of love are missing when we confine ourselves to lyrics such as those we have discussed?**

❖ Read aloud today's focus statement: **Love is the primary requirement for societies attempting to make a dramatic influence on the world around them. What is it about love that makes it so indispensable? In 1 Corinthians 13, Paul says that love is needed to achieve fully the benefit of all spiritual gifts.**

(2) Goal 1: Explore the Meaning of Love as Seen in 1 Corinthians 13

❖ Use "Introduction" in Understanding the Scripture to set the stage for today's lesson.

❖ Select three volunteers to read these passages from 1 Corinthians 13: verses 1-3; verses 4-7; verses 8-13.

❖ Post a sheet of newsprint. Head the left side "LOVE IS" and head the right side "LOVE IS NOT." Invite the adults to call out words or phrases from 1 Corinthians 13 that fit under each heading.

❖ Form small groups and distribute paper and pencils so everyone can jot down ideas. Ask half of the groups to discuss this question: **How would you describe someone who lives according to Paul's description of love?** Ask the other half of the groups to discuss this question: **How would you describe someone who lives according to Paul's description of what is not love?** If students have copies of *The New International Lesson Annual,* direct their attention to Understanding the Scripture to explore Paul's teaching on love.

❖ Bring the groups together and hear their descriptions.

❖ Wrap up this portion by reading "Love Is Not a Feeling" in Interpreting the Scripture.

(3) Goal 2: Appreciate One Another in Love

❖ Write on newsprint these words adapted from 1 Corinthians 13:4: [NAME], you show us that love is patient and kind.

❖ Seat the students in circles of six to eight people. Select one person to start this affirmation activity. The first speaker will say to the person on the left: **[NAME], you show us that love is patient and kind.** The first speaker will then tell a brief story about the person on the left that illustrates his or her patience and kindness as expressions of love. The second person will then turn to the person on his or her left and repeat the process. Continue around the circle until everyone has heard words of affirmation and appreciation. (Be sure that stories are brief so that everyone will be included.)

(4) Goal 3: Find a Variety of Ways to Express Love

❖ Read or retell "Actions and Attitudes" in Interpreting the Scripture, which emphasizes that love is shown by how we behave toward one another.

❖ Recall that Jesus and the early church recognized people who needed to experience God's love and then acted to demonstrate that love in a variety of ways. List the following passages on a sheet of newsprint prior to the session. Invite volunteers to look up each passage and call out the kinds of people mentioned there. As they do, write the kinds of people next to the Bible passage, such as the hungry or the sick. (Add other passages as you choose.)

Matthew 25:34-40
Luke 7:1-10
Luke 8:40-42a, 49-56
Luke 8:42b-48
Acts 4:32-37
James 1:27

❖ Brainstorm ideas with the class as to how they could show love to similar people—the hungry, homeless, sick, imprisoned, poor, and so on. Write those ideas on newsprint. Challenge the students to select a group of people and consider what they will do—individually or as a class—to demonstrate God's love, not just in word but also in deed.

(5) Continue the Journey

❖ Pray that as the learners depart, they will be aware of opportunities to show God's love to others within the church—and beyond the church walls.

❖ Post information for next week's session on newsprint for the students to copy:

- Title: Judgment on Israel and Judah
- Background Scripture: Amos 2:4-16
- Lesson Scripture: Amos 2:4-8
- Focus of the Lesson: Even though they know right from wrong, some people treat others unjustly. What can unjust people expect will be the result of their misdeeds? God will not overlook injustice but will punish the unjust.

❖ Challenge the adults to grow spiritually by completing one or more of these activities related to this week's session, which you have posted on newsprint for the students to copy.

(1) Memorize 1 Corinthians 13:4-7. Call these verses to mind whenever you are tempted to lash out at someone. Allow Paul's message to reshape your response.

(2) Listen to comments in conversations and the media for different ways that the word "love" is used. Which of these uses concerns Christian love, as defined by Paul in 1 Corinthians? Such love, as theologian Georgia Harkness (1891–1979) reminds us, "links love of God and love of neighbor in a twofold Great Commandment from which neither element can be dropped, so sin against neighbor through lack of human love is sin against God."

(3) Be alert for someone who needs to see God's love in action. Do whatever you can to demonstrate this love.

❖ Sing or read aloud "The Gift of Love."

❖ Conclude today's session by leading the class in this benediction adapted from 1 Corinthians 12:13, which is the key verse for the lesson for May 17: Let us go forth rejoicing that in the one Spirit we were all baptized into one body—Jews or Greeks, slaves or free—and we were all made to drink of one Spirit.

FOURTH QUARTER
God's Prophets Demand Justice

JUNE 7, 2015–AUGUST 30, 2015

The three units of our summer quarter discuss justice and injustice from the perspective of seven Old Testament prophets. We will investigate the perpetrators of injustice and their victims, as well as the nature of injustice. We will also see how movement is possible from injustice to repentance, redemption, and restoration.

Eight centuries before Christ, a man from Tekoa, south of Jerusalem, prophesied against Israel's elite who oppressed the poor. Unit 1 explores four of Amos's prophecies against social injustice. The four lessons of the second unit examine prophecies of another prophet of the eighth century B.C., Micah, who also championed the cause of the poor and unjustly treated. Unit 3 considers the diverse prophecies of Isaiah, Jeremiah, Ezekiel, Zechariah, and Malachi in its five sessions.

Unit 1, "Amos Rails Against Injustice," opens on June 7 with a lesson from Amos 2:4-16 that will help us to understand God's "Judgment on Israel and Judah." We turn to Amos 5 on June 14 to learn how God establishes justice for the righteous and punishes deceivers, because "God Is Not Fooled." Amos 6 is the background Scripture for our lesson on June 21, "Rebuked for Selfishness," which investigates God's response to injustice as recorded by the prophet. This unit concludes on June 28 with a study of Amos 8 in which we will look at unjust practices and their consequences during Amos's time in a session titled "God Will Never Forget."

The second unit, "Micah Calls for Justice Among Unjust People," looks at Micah 2 on July 5 in a lesson titled "No Rest for the Wicked" to explore Micah's depiction of people who deny their wrongdoing. "No Tolerance for Corrupt Leaders and Prophets," the session for July 12, examines Micah 3 to determine how the prophet confronted corrupt leaders. Micah 6 is the background Scripture for "Justice, Love, and Humility," which we will study on July 19 to discover how to honor God by exhibiting the traits that God requires. "God Shows Clemency" proclaims Micah 7:11-20 in the final session of this unit on July 26.

Unit 3, "Advocates of Justice for All," begins on August 2 with an exploration of Isaiah 59 and Psalm 89:11-18 in "Our Redeemer Comes" to discern how God promises a renewed covenant relationship. Ezra 7:1, 6, 21-28 and Jeremiah 7:1-15 form the backdrop on August 9 for "A Choice to Be Just," a session that reviews messages of both doom and hope found in Jeremiah. "A Call for Repentance," the session for August 16 from Ezekiel 18 and Proverbs 21:2-15, delves into Ezekiel's message concerning personal responsibility for one's actions. On August 23 we will investigate Zechariah 7:8-14 and Isaiah 30:18-26 in "God Demands Justice" to study the punishment God metes out for those who reject God's requirements. This unit and the 2014–15 Sunday school year close on August 30 with "Return to a Just God," which considers Malachi 3:1-12 and Matthew 7:12 to investigate Malachi's prophecy about possessions, wealth, and hospitality in light of faithfulness and justice.

MEET OUR WRITER

DR. JEROME F. D. CREACH

Jerome F. D. Creach is the Robert C. Holland Professor of Old Testament at Pittsburgh Theological Seminary (PTS) where he has taught since 2000. Before accepting his current post he taught at Barton College in Wilson, North Carolina (1994–2000), the College of William & Mary (1993–94), and the Baptist Theological Seminary at Richmond (1991–92). In addition to his work at PTS, Dr. Creach preaches and teaches frequently in churches in the Pittsburgh area. He has also taught and lectured at many retreat centers, churches, and other academic institutions.

Dr. Creach earned his Ph.D. at Union Presbyterian Theological Seminary (Richmond, Virginia) in 1994. His work there focused on the Book of Psalms. He has published three books on the Psalter: *Yahweh as Refuge and the Editing of the Hebrew Psalter* (Sheffield: Sheffield Academic Press, 1996); *Psalms* (Interpretation Bible Studies; Louisville: Geneva, 1998); *The Destiny of the Righteous in the Psalms* (St. Louis: Chalice, 2008). He has also written a commentary on the Book of Joshua in the series *Interpretation: A Commentary for Teaching and Preaching* (Louisville: Westminster John Knox, 2003) and *Violence in Scripture: Interpretation: Resources for the Use of Scripture in the Church* (Louisville: Westminster John Knox Press, 2013). He is active in the Society of Biblical Literature.

Dr. Creach is a Minister of the Word and Sacrament in the Presbyterian Church (U.S.A.). He is married to Page L. D. Creach, who is pastor of the United Presbyterian Church of Freeport, Pennsylvania. They have two children. In his spare time Dr. Creach enjoys hiking, camping, and fishing. He is an avid fan of the Pittsburgh Steelers. He enjoys watching *The Andy Griffith Show* and listening to the music of Bruce Springsteen, Johnny Cash, and U2.

THE BIG PICTURE: PROPHETS CALL FOR JUSTICE

The main subject of this series of lessons is God's desire for justice and the consequences for not doing justice. The prophetic books of the Old Testament provide the primary material for addressing the subject. The first unit features passages from the Book of Amos, the prophet perhaps most closely associated with issues of justice and equity for the poor. Micah is very similar in his message, and passages from the book that bears his name make up the second unit. Both Amos and Micah prophesied during the same time period. A major problem they addressed was that the elite members of society were taking advantage of those who were less powerful and influential. Amos and Micah called for God's people to act fairly in the marketplace and in the court, both places where the rich could take advantage of the weak and vulnerable. The third unit addresses the concern for justice with passages from a variety of other prophets from different time periods: Isaiah, Jeremiah, Ezekiel, Zechariah, and Malachi. Despite the difference in time and circumstances, however, each of these prophets echoes the crucial message of Amos and Micah: God expects God's people to care for those who are weak and powerless. Throughout these lessons the background Scripture includes a number of complementary passages from Ezra, the Psalms, Proverbs, and the Gospel of Matthew. This variety of additional passages testifies to the fact that justice is at the heart of the Bible's theological and ethical agenda.

The Nature of Justice

The word "justice" is often associated with actions of judges and the court system. In such settings the term essentially means fairness. This understanding of justice is true for the prophets of the Old Testament, but the term has broader implications that are important to recognize. One clue to the larger significance of justice is that it is frequently paired with the term "righteousness" as in Amos 5:24: "But let justice roll down like waters, and righteousness like an ever-flowing stream." The prophets seem to understand justice as something that grows out of righteousness. For example, Amos 6:12 refers to justice as "the fruit of righteousness." Therefore, it is necessary to understand the biblical concept of righteousness in order to comprehend the meaning of justice.

Righteousness is often misunderstood as moral purity. But the word "righteousness" is a relational word that has to do with acting rightly in relation to others or to God. It is instructive to note that in the story of Abraham, Abraham "believed the LORD; and the LORD reckoned it to him as righteousness" (Genesis 15:6). That is, righteousness for Abraham—what God expected in relationship—was Abraham's trust in God. So when the prophets speak of justice as the fruit of righteousness they are essentially saying that justice is something that grows out of a right relationship with God and being right with God means living in humility and trust before God. To act in righteousness and justice is to imitate God and to participate in the work of God in the world. As Psalm 97:2 says, "righteousness and justice are the foundation of his [God's] throne."

The Nature of Prophecy

In addition to understanding the meaning of the terms "justice" and "righteousness," it is helpful also to explore the nature of prophecy in the Old Testament. What is a prophet, and what was the purpose of prophecy?

In ancient Israel, as in the ancient Near East in general, prophets were people thought to have the ability to receive messages from God and pass those messages on to humans. In general, prophets got the word of God from visions or related experiences. For that reason prophets were sometimes called "seers" (as in Amos 7:12). The notion that God spoke to the prophets through visions is stated directly in Numbers 12:6: "when there are prophets among you, I the LORD make myself known to them in visions; I speak to them in dreams." Therefore, God's revelation came to the prophets indirectly and it is easy to see how the role of prophets could be manipulated by members of society or how the prophets themselves might proclaim their messages for their own gain. Many Old Testament texts recognize that some prophets were unfaithful (see especially Micah 3:5-7). Nevertheless, the prophets whose sayings and actions were collected into books are remembered as heroic and courageous figures who spoke the plain truth. It is those prophets—the "cream of the crop"—who now appear in our Old Testament.

Prophets spoke in certain ways that helped people recognize their messages were revelation from God. They often introduced their oracles with the words "thus says the Lord." Or the written form of the prophetic message acknowledges that "the word of the LORD came to" the prophet (see Zechariah 7:8). These words indicated that the prophet was not just issuing an opinion but was speaking a message that came directly from God.

Judgment and Restoration

The prophetic message often featured an analysis of Israelite society as it related to God's expectations for the people. Each of the prophets in our study gives an evaluation of God's people, particularly in terms of their failure to do justice. That analysis frequently includes promises of judgment. In the prophetic passages in our lessons the theme of judgment will be abundantly clear. In fact, each of the prophets we are studying promises God's judgment in the form of major catastrophe or the complete downfall of God's people. Micah's prediction of the fall of Jerusalem is typical: "Zion shall be plowed like a field; Jerusalem shall become a heap of ruins, and the mountain of the house a wooded height" (Micah 3:12).

Despite this persistent message of judgment for lack of justice, however, the prophets do not leave their audience without hope. In fact, a key part of the prophetic message is that after judgment, God restores and revitalizes the people who were judged. Or perhaps a better way to put it is to say that God's judgment is always for the purpose of cleansing and renewal (see Isaiah 19:16-25 that even speaks of God's judgment on Egypt as being for the purpose of healing). So the prophetic prediction of destruction is almost always followed by words of hope. After Micah's prediction of Jerusalem's fall, for example, the prophet declares a glorious future for the city and its place of worship: "In days to come the mountain of the LORD's house shall be established as the highest of the mountains" (Micah 4:1; see the parallel passage in Isaiah 2:2). This pairing of judgment and restoration is important for understanding the theology of the prophetic books. The prophets call God's people to account for their lack of justice and their disobedience to God. But God's justice is characterized by God's mercy. God therefore does not leave the people in the rubble of their destroyed cities, but points the way to a brighter future. This message of hope is always the final word.

Time Periods

The prophets spoke to particular times and circumstances, so it is important to understand the various time periods of Israelite prophecy in order to appreciate their messages. Each period had its particular challenges. The concern for justice, however, applied to them all, as it continues to apply to our world. Three primary time periods are important.

The first prophets we will study (Amos and Micah) appeared in the eighth century B.C. After the time of David (1000–960 B.C.) and Solomon (960–930[?] B.C.), the United Monarchy those two kings led had broken into two kingdoms, Israel in the north and Judah in the south. During the ninth century both kingdoms were oppressed by major empires like Assyria, but the eighth century was a time of freedom from those empires (Assyria and Egypt were both weakened by internal conflicts) and Israel and Judah enjoyed economic prosperity. The wealth of the two kingdoms, however, came at a tremendous price. As some citizens became wealthy, they also found ways to gain more wealth at the expense of the poor. Israelite tradition tried to ensure that all people had access to economic opportunity by providing each family with land that was to be passed on through subsequent generations. But in the eighth century, wealthy members of society began to acquire the ancestral land of the poor as payment for debts. The problem was not the accumulation of wealth per se, but the acquisition of the inherited land, the only tie the poor had to the Promised Land. Without the ancestral land, the poor became poorer. They were destined to become indentured servants or slaves while the upper class became even wealthier. As the gap between rich and poor grew, there was also more temptation for the rich to take advantage of the poor through the court system. The prophets of the eighth century declared that God would not allow this circumstance to continue. They promised judgment. Judgment would come by the end of the century in the form of invasions by the rejuvenated Assyrians. The Assyrians destroyed the Northern Kingdom in 722 B.C. and destroyed many towns and villages in Judah, though Jerusalem was spared.

The next major time period for the prophets in our study comes about one hundred years after the prophecies of Amos and Micah. During this time the Babylonians were the major world power. They threatened the tiny kingdom of Judah and its capital, Jerusalem, and eventually destroyed the holy city in 587 B.C. The main prophetic voices during this time were Jeremiah and Ezekiel. Both of these prophets addressed the injustices of the people in relation to the worship of the Temple. For both prophets the issue was that worship had to be pure and worship had to urge people to justice if it was true worship. The people of Judah did not heed this word and the Babylonians destroyed Jerusalem and took away a large group of exiles. Both prophets continued to speak to the people of Judah about what the destruction and exile meant. They both pointed forward to a future God would make for God's people.

The exile at the hands of Babylon ended in 539 B.C. when the Persians conquered Babylon and released all the people Babylon had displaced. When it did, the people of Judah were free to return to Jerusalem and rebuild their city and their Temple. But the age of restoration brought fresh problems that the prophets Zechariah and Malachi would address. During this time the Temple became the center of everything; it was the hub of social, religious, and judicial activity. Thus, questions of true worship—worship that produces justice and righteousness—became more critical.

Portraits of the Prophets

As already noted, each of the prophets spoke to a particular time period, and each prophet's message about justice was addressed to the circumstances of his time. Before exploring the prophetic texts themselves, it would seem helpful to give a thumbnail sketch of the prophets spotlighted in the lesson Scriptures and their theological concerns.

Amos was a prophet to the northern kingdom of Israel. He prophesied during the eighth century when a major problem was the growing gap between rich and poor. The words "justice" and "righteousness" are perhaps the key terms in Amos's message. He called for justice for the poor, justice that grew out of righteousness (Amos 6:12). Amos indicted those in Israel who "trample on the needy" and brought "to ruin the poor of the land" (Amos 8:4). This prophet promised Israel would have a day of reckoning, the "day of the LORD" (Amos 5:18-20) that would bring punishment for injustice. Amos said this day would come as a surprise to those who thought they lived within God's favor despite their oppressive actions toward the weak and vulnerable.

Micah was a contemporary of Amos, but Micah prophesied to the southern kingdom of Judah. The issues of social justice were just as strong for Micah as for Amos. Micah spoke against those who added field to field as they confiscated the land of the poor (Micah 2:2). He was concerned that the most vulnerable members of society were being forced out of their homes to satisfy the greed of the wealthy (Micah 2:9). Like Amos, Micah cried out against Judah for assuming that no matter what they did "surely the LORD is with us" (Micah 3:11). But Micah also focused specifically on the injustice of the elite leaders of Judah: priests, prophets, rulers (Micah 3:9-11). These people who were supposed to care for the people and to deliver God's Word were like cannibals who devoured the people instead (Micah 3:1-3).

Jeremiah was closely linked to the Temple through the Levites, the ones who were responsible for the daily care of the holy place and for instructing the people in right ways to worship and right ways to treat fellow citizens (see the roles of the Levites in 1 Chronicles 15:16-24; Ezra 7:7-10). Jeremiah hailed from Anathoth, a levitical town in the territory of the tribe of Benjamin and was the son of Hilkiah, a well-known priest who helped reform Judah's worship (Jeremiah 1:1; see reference to Hilkiah in 2 Kings 23:4). Jeremiah was particularly concerned about justice for widows, orphans, and resident aliens—the three groups often identified as deserving special protection (Jeremiah 7:5-6). Paying attention to these groups and others who were vulnerable would ensure God's presence and God's protection. Many people in Judah, however, thought God would protect them simply because the Temple was in their midst.

Ezekiel was similar to Jeremiah in his concern for the Temple, except his connection to the Temple was through his role as one of the elite priests responsible for making sacrifices and performing the holiest acts of worship. For Ezekiel, ritual purity was of utmost importance. Only by adherence to dietary laws and other laws of holiness did Ezekiel think one could properly come before God to worship. These laws for him, however, stood alongside laws that focused on social justice. For Ezekiel, both types of laws showed that a person was aligned with the intentions of God. If the person was not, God would not continue to be present and the Temple in Jerusalem would not stand.

Zechariah and Malachi were prophets of the restoration era. They prophesied after the Jerusalem Temple was rebuilt. Both were concerned about the just treatment of the poor and needy as part of a larger concern for worshiping God in truth. True worship, as many of their predecessors said, produced compassion and concern for widows, orphans, aliens, and the poor (Zechariah 7:8-10). Malachi makes the specific point that such compassion would bring God's blessings to the people and to their newly restored place of worship. But failure to act in these ways would cause the people to languish in poverty and hardship (Malachi 3:5-7). The message of this prophet, and indeed of all the prophets, is that justice matters. If affects not only those who need justice to be done for them but also the entire people of God whose life together is diminished if justice is not the norm.

CLOSE-UP: OVERVIEW OF THE PROPHETS

During the summer sessions we focus on the prophecies of Amos, Micah, Isaiah, Jeremiah, Ezekiel, Zechariah, and Malachi.

Date	Prophet	Meaning of Name of Prophet	King(s) of Judah (fell 587 B.C.)	King(s) of Israel (fell 722/721 B.C.)	Prophecy to or About	Concerns and Assurances
760 – 750	Amos	Burden bearer	Uzziah	Jeroboam II	Israel (ruling classes); Judah; all nations	Oppression of poor; sexual immorality; luxury; corruption
722 – 701	Micah	Who is like God?	Ahaz Hezekiah	n/a	Samaria; Jerusalem; whole earth	Injustice; oppression of poor and powerless; failure to obey covenant
626 – 587	Jeremiah	God will elevate	Josiah Jehoahaz II (Shallum) Jehoiakim (Eliakim) Jehoiachin (Jeconiah)	n/a	Judah	Social ills; warnings of disasters caused by people's sin, not God's capriciousness or inability to ward off Babylonians
593 – 571	Ezekiel	Strength of God	Jehoiachin (Jeconiah) Zedekiah	n/a	Exiles in Babylon; (Ezekiel is exiled in Babylon); oracles against other nations	God's warnings due to Judah's faithlessness, injustice; in exile, calls for repentance
537	Third Isaiah (chapters 56–66)	God's salvation	n/a	n/a	Exiles returning from Babylon	God is sovereign and compassionate; injustice and oppression will end; God will bring redemption
520 – 518	Zechariah	God has remembered	n/a	n/a	Zerubbabel; Joshua; returned remnant	Wickedness; lack of judgment, mercy, and peace; rededication of Temple
500 – 450	Malachi	My messenger	n/a	n/a	Returned exiles	Neglect of covenant obligations; need for right sacrifice and return to God

FAITH IN ACTION: ACTING WITH JUSTICE

The summer quarter's lessons call us to recognize that "God's Prophets Demand Justice." As we explore the writings of Amos, Micah, Isaiah, Jeremiah, Ezekiel, Jeremiah, and Malachi, we will see that over a period of roughly three centuries each of these prophets called for justice in their respective situations. Broadly speaking, they all focused on injustices perpetrated against the most vulnerable members of society: the widow, the orphan, the alien, and the poor. Moreover, these prophets called God's people to repentance.

Although our current historical circumstances are different, the message of the prophets is still important for us to hear and heed. Form two groups (or multiples of two if the class is large) and assign one of the following key verses to each group. Write the key verses and the questions on two sheets of newsprint and post them where the group members can see them. Provide each group with a sheet of newsprint, a marker, and tape or tacks to post its paper after they have reported.

GROUP 1

He has told you, O mortal, what is good;
and what does the LORD require of you
but to do justice, and to love kindness,
and to walk humbly with your God? (Micah 6:8, key verse for July 19)

1. Where in your community, state, or nation do you see examples of injustice?
2. What can this class do to provide short-term assistance to those who are being treated unjustly?
3. How can the class members act as advocates to change public policies and attitudes that have enabled this injustice?
4. How might this class show God's kindness to people who long to experience it, particularly to those who are not connected with a church?
5. What activities (for example, spiritual disciplines, mission projects) can class members be encouraged to engage in so as to walk humbly with God?

GROUP 2

Thus says the LORD of hosts: Render true judgments, show kindness and mercy to one another; do not oppress the widow, the orphan, the alien, or the poor; and do not devise evil in your hearts against one another. (Zechariah 7:9-10, key verses for August 23)

1. What can the class do to show kindness and hospitality to one another and to those who come to this church, whether to participate in a service or other activity or to receive help from the church?
2. What groups might you add to Zechariah's list of those who are oppressed

(or "underdogs") in your community?
3. In addition to prayer and financial contributions, how can you offer tangible assistance to meet the needs of those who need help?
4. What activities (for example, spiritual disciplines, Bible study, prayer) can class members engage in so as to conform the attitudes of their hearts more closely to Christ's desire for love, justice, and mercy toward all people?

Call everyone together and invite a spokesperson for each group to report. Post the ideas and, if possible, allow them to remain on display until the end of the quarter. Urge the participants to take note of the ideas and do whatever they can to act with justice.

UNIT 1: AMOS RAILS AGAINST INJUSTICE
JUDGMENT ON ISRAEL AND JUDAH

PREVIEWING THE LESSON

Lesson Scripture: Amos 2:4-8
Background Scripture: Amos 2:4-16
Key Verse: Amos 2:4

Focus of the Lesson:
Even though they know right from wrong, some people treat others unjustly. What can unjust people expect will be the result of their misdeeds? God will not overlook injustice but will punish the unjust.

Goals for the Learners:
(1) to review God's judgment of Judah and Israel.
(2) to encourage sensitivity toward social injustice.
(3) to address issues of injustice in local and global communities.

Pronunciation Guide:

Ammonite (am´ uh nite)	Og (og)
Amorite (am´ uh rite)	Sihon (shi´ hon)
nazirite (naz´ uh rite)	torah (toh´ ruh)

Supplies:
Bibles, newsprint and marker, paper and pencils, hymnals, optional world map

---

READING THE SCRIPTURE

NRSV	CEB
Lesson Scripture: Amos 2:4-8	Lesson Scripture: Amos 2:4-8
⁴Thus says the LORD:	⁴The LORD proclaims:
For three transgressions of Judah,	For three crimes of Judah,
and for four, I will not revoke	and for four, I won't hold back
the punishment;	the punishment,

because they have rejected the law
    of the LORD,
and have not kept his statutes,
but they have been led astray by the
    same lies
after which their ancestors
    walked.
⁵So I will send a fire on Judah,
    and it shall devour the strong-
    holds of Jerusalem.
⁶Thus says the LORD:
For three transgressions of Israel,
    and for four, I will not revoke the
    punishment;
because they sell the righteous for
    silver,
    and the needy for a pair of
    sandals—
⁷they who trample the head of the
    poor into the dust of the earth,
    and push the afflicted out of the
    way;
father and son go in to the same girl,
    so that my holy name is profaned;
⁸they lay themselves down beside
    every altar
    on garments taken in pledge;
and in the house of their God they
    drink
    wine bought with fines they
    imposed.

because they have rejected the
    Instruction of the LORD,
and haven't kept his laws.
They have been led off the right
    path by the same lies
after which their ancestors
    walked.
⁵So I will send a fire on Judah,
    and it will devour the palaces of
    Jerusalem.
⁶The LORD proclaims:
For three crimes of Israel,
    and for four, I won't hold back the
    punishment,
because they have sold the innocent
    for silver,
    and those in need for a pair of
    sandals.
⁷They crush the head of the poor into
    the dust of the earth,
    and push the afflicted out of the
    way.
Father and son have intercourse with
    the same young woman,
    degrading my holy name.
⁸They stretch out beside every altar
    on garments taken in loan;
in the house of their god they drink
    wine bought with fines they
    imposed.

UNDERSTANDING THE SCRIPTURE

Introduction. The Book of Amos is set in the middle of the eighth century B.C. when Israel and Judah were experiencing great freedom and prosperity. As often happens in times of prosperity, however, some of the people of Israel and Judah prospered at the expense of others. Amos thus declared that the two nations neglected God's commands, particularly the divine instructions to care for the poor and vulnerable. The prophet addressed the sins of the two nations with the declaration that God would bring disaster on both Israel and Judah.

Amos 2:4-5. This kind of numerical pattern appears most often in the wisdom teachings of the Old Testament. The purpose of the formula is to organize a number of items into a list for consideration (as in Proverbs

6:16-19). Sometimes the focus is on the final item in the list (as Job 5:19-26), and this seems to be Amos's purpose. He assumes a list of offenses, but only names the final (fourth) one.

Amos 2:6-8. The indictment against Israel is structured just like the indictment against Judah. The crime Amos describes, however, is much more specific. He rails against Israel because of the way they mistreat the poor and powerless people in their midst. Amos lists four individual offenses, but each one seems to be a variation on the same theme of mistreatment of the poor.

The parallel terms "righteous" and "needy" indicate something of what both terms mean. "Righteous" refers to those who are innocent in a legal case. "Needy" connotes those without sufficient financial means. The statement that the rich are treating such persons unjustly may mean they are taking advantage of powerless people through the legal system (see Amos 5:10, 12, 15). Amos describes at least three particular crimes against the poor in these verses. First, the selling of the righteous refers to slavery. In the ancient Near East people often became slaves because they owed debt. Second Kings 4:1-7 tells the story of a widow who fears the creditor will take her children as slaves. As horrible as such scenarios were, Amos 2:6 implies some Israelites were enslaving their fellow Israelites even though they did not owe a debt. "For a pair of sandals" may refer to selling people as slaves for very little money. More likely, however, it refers to the way property was transferred, namely, by passing a sandal from one person to another (see Ruth 4:7). Hence, Amos seems to be describing the sale of people as slaves in exchange for land. Second, "father and son go in to the same girl" in verse 7 likely refers to the mistreatment of a female slave. Exodus 21:7-11 carefully outlines how a young woman in such horrible circumstances must be treated. She may be taken as a wife by one man in the household, but father and son cannot both claim her as a sexual partner. Amos seems to indict the Israelites for breaking this tradition that was meant to protect powerless women whose families were poor. Third, Amos's statement in verse 8 that the Israelites lay down "on garments taken in pledge" seems to refer to a violation of laws against taking a poor person's cloak as collateral for a loan (Exodus 22:26). The outer garment could be taken "in pledge" but it had to be returned before sundown since it was the person's only cover at night. Amos seems to say the Israelites not only break this provision regularly but they also take the garments of the poor to religious festivals and gloat over their exploits ("they lay themselves down beside every altar," 2:8).

Amos 2:9-11. Israel's crimes seem even more shocking in light of God's goodness to them. God "destroyed the Amorite" so the Israelites could enter and possess the land of Canaan. "Amorite" refers to those people who lived east of the Jordan, led by kings Sihon and Og (see Deuteronomy 2:26–3:7). These people would not let the Israelites pass peacefully through their territory. So God defeated them in order to usher the Israelites into the land. God's defeat of the Amorite occurred just after God led the Israelites out of Egypt, which was the greatest sign of God's grace. Furthermore, Israel has no excuse for not recognizing God's acts for them since God appointed some of them as nazirites and prophets (Amos 1:11). Such persons were to keep in mind and proclaim the deeds of God to God's people so they would not forget what God had done for them.

Amos 2:12. A primary sign that the people of Israel were unfaithful in their relationship with God was that those who were supposed to represent and proclaim faithfulness encouraged individuals in the other direction. Nazirites took vows not to eat or drink anything that comes from grapes. They also pledged not to cut their hair and not to touch a dead body (Numbers 6). These disciplines were signs they were set apart for God's service. Amos charged the Israelites with thwarting the commitment of the Nazirites ("you made [them] drink wine"). Likewise, Amos

said the Israelites shut up the prophets so they could not declare God's truth, including the judgment that Israel was sinful.

Amos 2:13-16. The background Scripture concludes with Amos declaring judgment. The particular judgment comes immediately after the indictment of Israel, but it was perhaps intended for Judah as well. Amos 2:13 gives the basic message in a metaphor: Just as a cart gets overloaded with grain and cannot bear the weight, so also Israel will not be able to bear the weight of God's judgment. Verses 14-16 then list how this judgment will play out. All those who rely on their strength or military prowess will be overwhelmed when an enemy attacks. Military defeat will be the sign that God has brought judgment on God's people.

INTERPRETING THE SCRIPTURE

God's Law and Justice

Amos's indictment of Judah centers on the failure to keep the "law of the LORD" (2:4). This indictment may not resonate with some Christians who identify themselves strongly with the freedom that comes in Jesus Christ. The apostle Paul declares that we do not "rely on works of the law" for salvation or for how to direct our lives (Galatians 3:10). It is easy to think of "law" as legalism. But there are two crucial points about Amos's words against Judah that should bring empathy for the message. First, the English word "law" translates the Hebrew term *torah*, which really means instruction. Thus the word

refers to the whole of Scripture as well as other sources of God's wisdom. So for Amos to say that Judah rejected the law of the Lord said in part that Judah rejected its own story of God's salvation. The people of Judah ceased to recognize they were beneficiaries of God's grace, which God showed to them by rescuing them from slavery in Egypt and giving them the land of Canaan (as described in Amos 2:9-10). It also means they rejected the sources of truth God gave them in the people designated to speak God's Word (like Nazirites and prophets; see Amos 2:12).

Second, one of the most central parts of the law in the narrow sense of that term is the command to care for the poor and treat them justly. When Amos uses the term "statutes" in parallel to torah, it is not clear what specific matters the prophet has in mind. What is clear, however, is that the most commonly cited moral issue in the statutes Moses gave to God's people are those pertaining to doing justice for the vulnerable members of society. The poor have a special place in God's economy. It is no accident that the term "righteous" is a synonym for "poor" in Amos 2:6. As we have observed, "righteous" refers to innocence. But the word also refers to one who is in right relationship with God. To be properly related to God means to recognize how dependent we are on God. The poor are models of those who recognize their vulnerability. Hence, we have a special responsibility for the poor and particular lessons to learn from them about what it means to stand rightly before God.

Injustice Is Like War Crimes?

The message Amos delivered to Judah and Israel cannot be understood fully unless it is heard in the context of the prophet's indictment of Israel's neighbors in Amos 1:3–2:3. Amos's proclamation against God's people is cast in exactly the same form as the oracles against Israel's enemies that appear in Amos 1:3–2:3: "For three transgressions . . . and for four, I will not revoke the punishment" (Amos 1:3, 6, 9, 11, 13; 2:1). Since the form of his words to Judah and Israel is identical to that of his indictment of other nations, and since 1:3–2:8 proceed with no breaks between any of the oracles, this section seems intended to be read as a unit. In fact, we might imagine this section as a sermon Amos preached. This is not hard to imagine since we are told later in the book that Amos did deliver a sermon in the sanctuary at Bethel (7:10-17). The sermon was not well received, and the priest of Bethel asked Amos to leave and never return (7:12-13). Amos 1:3–2:8 might just be the sermon he delivered that got this reaction.

Amos begins his message by speaking against Damascus, the capital of Syria, one of Israel's rivals: "For three transgressions of Damascus, and for four, I will not revoke the punishment . . ." (1:3-5). We can imagine that the crowd reveled in this message. "That's right! Give it to 'em Amos." Furthermore, the crowd must have agreed totally with the judgment against Damascus. Amos charged Damascus with extreme cruelty in waging war with Gilead. Amos said they "threshed Gilead with threshing sledges of iron" (1:3). The Israelites perhaps had heard about this injustice. We can imagine those who listened to Amos erupting in cheers.

As Amos continued his sermon, he laid out similar crimes for others. The most shocking was the crime of the Ammonites. They "ripped open pregnant women in Gilead in order to enlarge their territory" (1:13). It seems clear that Amos was cataloging the atrocities of war the neighbors of Judah and Israel committed. The message must have been very popular.

But then Amos began to speak against God's own people with the same type of speech he used for Israel's enemies. The effect of Amos's sermon delivery is to charge Judah and Israel with crimes that were essentially equal in severity to the crimes of

Israel's enemies in Amos 1:3–2:3. It is striking that Judah's offense is simply disobedience to the law of the Lord (2:4). God's statutes, however, are not trivial or legalistic requirements. Rather, they encompass every aspect of relationship with God that, in turn, shapes how the people of God treat one another and how they relate to all people. The specific charge against Israel for mistreating the poor is particularly telling. Amos does not say the Israelites killed or tortured anyone (though Amos 2:7 might be interpreted as such). Furthermore, the wealthy Israelites might have understood their actions as shrewd business practices. They took advantage of the system for their own gain. But with his form of speech, Amos says these Israelites are guilty of crimes as severe as that of the Ammonites who "ripped open pregnant women in Gilead in order to enlarge their territory" (1:13). The message therefore is clear: God takes mistreatment of the poor as seriously as any crime against humanity.

Importance of Judgment

Amos's pronouncement of judgment on Judah and Jerusalem may be hard to hear and accept because we believe in a God who is loving. God wants good things for God's people, and God is not destructive toward God's creatures. While this sentiment is understandable, it misses the essential nature of God's judgment as part of God's love. It is important for our understanding of God to retain the belief in God's judgment for at least two reasons. First, as this section of Amos makes clear, God's judgment is intended in part to protect those who cannot protect themselves. It makes a strong statement that God is on the side of the poor and vulnerable and acts against anyone who would abuse them. This is essentially the same belief that underlies Jesus' prayer "your kingdom come" and Jesus' assurance that "the meek will inherit the earth" (Matthew 6:10; 5:5). That is, God's judgment against those who harm the poor and lowly in this world indicates that God's kingdom will bring equity for those who are victims of the powers of this world.

Second, God's judgment is important for us to understand God's love. When God's judgment is directed at us it is like the discipline of a parent. Imagine what a child's relationship with her parents would be like if there were never any consequences for wrong actions. It would be devastating for the child because she would never build character and would never develop a proper concern for those around her. The comparison of God's judgment to a parent's discipline is apt especially since God's judgment, like the discipline of a good father or mother, is never the last word. Even though Amos promises destruction for Judah and Israel, the last word in the Book of Amos is about restoration and new life (Amos 9:11-15).

SHARING THE SCRIPTURE

| PREPARING TO TEACH | LEADING THE CLASS |

PREPARING TO TEACH

Preparing Our Hearts

Meditate on this week's devotional reading from Psalm 75. Why does the psalmist give thanks to God? What does "cup" refer to in verse 8? (Compare Psalm 11:6; Isaiah 51:17; Jeremiah 25:15-17; Ezekiel 23:31-34.) What "wondrous deeds" (75:1) in your own life will you thank God for today?

Pray that you and the students will recognize and give thanks for God's justice.

Preparing Our Minds

Study the background Scripture from Amos 2:4-16 and the lesson Scripture from Amos 2:4-8.

Consider this question as you prepare the lesson: *When people treat others unjustly, what can they expect to be the result of their misdeeds?*

Write on newsprint:

❏ "Close-up: Overview of the Prophets" for "Gather to Learn."
❏ information for next week's lesson, found under "Continue the Journey."
❏ activities for further spiritual growth in "Continue the Journey."

Review the "Introduction," "The Big Picture," "Close-up," and "Faith in Action," which all precede this first lesson of the quarter. Consider how you might use any of this material in today's lesson.

Option: Locate a large map of the twenty-first century world.

LEADING THE CLASS

(1) Gather to Learn

❖ Greet the class members and introduce guests.

❖ Pray that those who have come today will recognize the importance of treating all people with justice.

❖ Introduce this quarter's study by posting "Close-up: Overview of the Prophets" where everyone can see this chart, which you have copied onto newsprint prior to the session. Talk with the students about the individual prophets, their messages, and their audiences. Look especially at Amos, whose prophecies we will focus on during the first unit. Point out that the prophets expected God to visit punishment upon those people who refused to turn aside from injustice.

❖ Read aloud today's focus statement: **Even though they know right from wrong, some people treat others unjustly. What can unjust people expect will be the result of their misdeeds? God will not overlook injustice but will punish the unjust.**

(2) Goal 1: Review God's Judgment of Judah and Israel

❖ Read "God's Law and Justice" in Interpreting the Scripture to help the class delve into the prophecies of Amos.

❖ Choose two volunteers, one to read God's judgment on Israel in Amos 2:4-5 and the other to read God's judgment on Judah in verses 6-16, which includes background Scripture.

❖ Discuss these questions:

1. **What are the main reasons that prompted God to judge Judah?** (List these reasons, found in verses 4-5, on the left side of a sheet of newsprint.)

2. **What are the reasons that prompted God to judge Israel?** (List these reasons, found in verses 6-16, on the right side of a sheet of newsprint.)

3. **How are these judgments similar—and different?** (Use any information you need from Understanding the Scripture to explain Amos's message.)

4. **How is God's judgment related to God's love?** (See "Importance of Judgment" in Interpreting the Scripture.)

❖ End this portion of the lesson by inviting the adults to ponder these words of the Anglican priest and poet George Herbert from his 1651 book of proverbs titled *Jacula Prudentum*: "God's mill grinds slow but sure." Ask: **What does this proverb suggest about God's justice and judgment?**

(3) Goal 2: Encourage Sensitivity Toward Social Injustice

❖ Refer to "Close-up: Overview of the Prophets," which you posted at the beginning of the session. Form several groups, distribute paper and pencils, and encourage each group to consider this question: **If any of these prophets were alive today, what messages about social injustice might they have for our country?**

❖ Come together and invite the groups to share their insights. List on newsprint any concerns that the groups raise.

❖ Return to small groups and challenge them to consider how they might increase general awareness about types of people who are experiencing social injustice. What steps could the church take to help people become more aware of these injustices?

❖ Bring the groups together to report their ideas. Agree as a class on at least one action that they can take to increase awareness of social injustice.

(4) Goal 3: Address Issues of Injustice in Local and Global Communities

❖ Brainstorm answers to these questions and write them on newsprint:

1. **What injustices plague the earth today?** (Think about injustices that affect large numbers of people, such as those who are victims of human trafficking, modern slavery, abusive treatment of women, mistreatment of immigrants, racial and ethnic discrimination, disparities in quality of education, denial of voting rights, lack of access to food and housing, economic injustice, violence.)

2. **Where in the world do you find such injustices?** (Either name the places, or as an option, post a current map of the world and pinpoint the locations. Be sure that the class not only notes injustices taking place around the globe but also right in their own community.)

❖ Determine how the class members can address one or more of these issues by taking the following steps. Distribute paper and pencils, and encourage the adults to jot down responses to each step as you read it.

Step 1: Choose an issue and rate your "passion level" about this issue on a scale of 1 to 10 with 10 being the most passionate. Those who are most likely to bring about change will be those who are most incensed about the damage that a particular injustice is doing. (Pause)

Step 2: Become educated about the issue. It is one thing to express concern about hunger in a community; it is another to know the statistics about who is hungry and why and where. Where might you seek information? (Pause)

Step 3: Identify and network with other advocates who share concern about fixing this problem. Some advocates may be in this class. Others may work with specific groups or agencies. With whom might you network? (Pause)

Step 4: Identify places where change needs to occur. Often laws and public policies are in need of change. People's individual sense of morality and ethics may also need to change. What steps can you take to bring about these changes? (Pause)

Step 5: Contact legislators, company owners, or others who can make decisions that will bring about change. Keep working until the injustice is righted. (Pause)

❖ Challenge the students to go forth to act on their ideas.

(5) Continue the Journey

❖ Pray that as the learners depart, they will be sensitive to the injustices around them and work to overcome them.

❖ Post information for next week's session on newsprint for the students to copy:

- **Title: God Is Not Fooled**
- **Background Scripture: Amos 5**
- **Lesson Scripture: Amos 5:14-15, 18-27**
- **Focus of the Lesson: Some people cover their evil ways with outward acts of goodness. Who will uncover their deceit and demand justice? The people learned through Amos that God will not be fooled by insincere offerings and will severely punish all sinners.**

❖ Challenge the adults to grow spiritually by completing one or more of these activities related to this week's session, which you have posted on newsprint for the students to copy.

(1) **Be on the lookout for people who are being treated unjustly in your community. Are there laws that need to be changed? Are their attitudes among the residents that need to be changed? What can you do to create a more just environment for those who have been treated unjustly?**

(2) **Talk directly to someone who is acting unjustly. Tell this person about God's expectations for justice. Help to change this person's actions and attitudes.**

(3) **Research the actions of Saint Nikolai Evangelical Lutheran Church in Leipzig, Germany, that led**

to the fall of the Berlin Wall. How could similar peaceful actions in your own community cause barriers to just treatment for all to fall?

❖ Sing or read aloud "I Want a Principle Within."

❖ Conclude today's session by leading the class in this benediction adapted from Micah 6:8, which is the key verse for July 19: **Let us depart to do justice, and love kindness, and walk humbly with our God.**

UNIT 1: AMOS RAILS AGAINST INJUSTICE
GOD IS NOT FOOLED

PREVIEWING THE LESSON

Lesson Scripture: Amos 5:14-15, 18-27
Background Scripture: Amos 5
Key Verse: Amos 5:24

Focus of the Lesson:
Some people cover their evil ways with outward acts of goodness. Who will uncover their deceit and demand justice? The people learned through Amos that God will not be fooled by insincere offerings and will severely punish all sinners.

Goals for the Learners:
(1) to learn how God establishes justice for the righteous and punishes deceivers.
(2) to recognize and reflect on actions of injustice within the community of faith.
(3) to identify unjust practices and commit to stop their participation in them and help others do the same.

Pronunciation Guide:
Beer-sheba (bee uhr shee´ buh)   Kaiwan (ki´ wuhn)
Bethel (beth´ uhl)   Sakkuth (sak´ uhth)
Gilgal (gil´ gal)

Supplies:
Bibles, newsprint and marker, paper and pencils, hymnals

READING THE SCRIPTURE

NRSV
Lesson Scripture: Amos 5:14-15, 18-27
[14]Seek good and not evil,
   that you may live;
and so the LORD, the God of hosts,
   will be with you,

CEB
Lesson Scripture: Amos 5:14-15, 18-27
[14]Seek good and not evil, that you
   may live;
and so the LORD, the God of heavenly forces, will be with you

just as you have said.
¹⁵Hate evil and love good,
  and establish justice in the gate;
it may be that the LORD, the God of
  hosts,
  will be gracious to the remnant of
    Joseph.
¹⁸Alas for you who desire the day of
  the LORD!
  Why do you want the day of the
    LORD?
It is darkness, not light;
    ¹⁹as if someone fled from a lion,
  and was met by a bear;
or went into the house and rested a
  hand against the wall,
  and was bitten by a snake.
²⁰Is not the day of the LORD darkness, not light,
  and gloom with no brightness in it?
²¹I hate, I despise your festivals,
  and I take no delight in your solemn assemblies.
²²Even though you offer me your
  burnt offerings and grain
  offerings,
  I will not accept them;
and the offerings of well-being of
  your fatted animals
  I will not look upon.
²³Take away from me the noise of
  your songs;
  I will not listen to the melody of
    your harps.
**²⁴But let justice roll down like
  waters,
  and righteousness like an
    ever-flowing stream.**
²⁵Did you bring to me sacrifices and offerings the forty years in the wilderness, O house of Israel? ²⁶You shall take up Sakkuth your king, and Kaiwan your star-god, your images, which you made for yourselves; ²⁷therefore I will take you into exile beyond Damascus, says the LORD, whose name is the God of hosts.

just as you have said.
¹⁵Hate evil, love good, and establish
  justice at the city gate.
Perhaps the LORD God of heavenly
  forces will be gracious to what
  is left of Joseph.
¹⁸Doom to those who desire the day
  of the LORD!
  Why do you want the day of the
    LORD?
It is darkness, not light;
    ¹⁹as if someone fled from a lion,
  and was met by a bear;
  or sought refuge in a house, rested
  a hand against the wall, and
  was bitten by a snake.
²⁰Isn't the day of the LORD darkness,
  not light;
  all dark with no brightness in it?
²¹I hate, I reject your festivals;
  I don't enjoy your joyous
  assemblies.
²²If you bring me your entirely
  burned offerings and gifts of
  food—I won't be pleased;
  I won't even look at your offerings
  of well-fed animals.
²³Take away the noise of your songs;
  I won't listen to the melody of
  your harps.
**²⁴But let justice roll down like
  waters,
  and righteousness like an
    ever-flowing stream.**
²⁵Did you bring me sacrifices and offerings during the forty years in the wilderness, house of Israel? ²⁶You will take up Sakkuth your king, and Kaiwan your star-god, your images, which you made for yourselves. ²⁷Therefore, I will take you away beyond Damascus, says the LORD, whose name is the God of heavenly forces.

UNDERSTANDING THE SCRIPTURE

Introduction. Amos 5 is a collection of oracles that vary in subject, style, and type of speech. The chapter is bound together, however, by two interrelated concerns: the lack of justice practiced in everyday life and worship that does not lead to right action. Although Judah was implicated in Amos 2:4-5, Amos 5 focuses solely on Israel.

Amos 5:1-3. The chapter opens with a dirge, literally. The word translated "lamentation" is a technical term that refers to the funeral song. Such songs had a distinct meter with three beats, followed by two beats in each line of poetry. A good example of the funeral song is the lament David raised over Saul and Jonathan in 2 Samuel 1:17-27. What is remarkable in Amos 5:1, however, is that Israel has not been defeated yet. Israel is not "dead," and yet the funeral is already taking place. After offering the lament in verse 2, "Fallen, no more to rise," Amos then explains in verse 3 that Israel's military forces will be decimated. A meager one-tenth of the troops will return from battle.

Amos 5:4-5. The funeral song is followed by commands to see the Lord and live. There is still hope! The dirge was a mock funeral song; if Israel turned from its ways the funeral would be called off. The key to the way out of the funeral is in the word "seek." In the Old Testament, this word usually means to go to a sanctuary where there are priests and prophets and ask them to inquire of God. For example, Psalm 27:8 speaks of seeking God's face in the context of the psalmist going to the Temple. But Amos says emphatically that Israel should seek the Lord but not through the typical means of the sanctuary. The prophet specifically mentions three important worship sites: Bethel, Gilgal, and Beer-sheba. In each of these places a system of worship was established by which worshipers could pray and make sacrifices. Through this organized worship at Israel's shrines worshipers were offered God's grace. But as James Luther Mays observes, Amos is saying that the grace offered to them in this manner was "cheap grace." It did not require them to change their lives.

Amos 5:6-7. Again Amos commands Israel to seek the Lord and live. The alternative is to have God break out like fire and devour Israel. "House of Joseph" is a synonym for Israel. The Joseph tribes (Ephraim and Manasseh) occupied most of the northern territory that made up the Northern Kingdom. Thus, Israel was sometimes known as Joseph. Bethel was the main sanctuary in this region and represented the "cheap grace" just discussed. Verse 7 lays out the main offense of these people that made them worthy of destruction: They perverted "justice" and discarded "righteousness." Justice refers to the basic activity of the court. Deuteronomy 25:1 describes justice by saying simply that when two people have a dispute, they take it to court to discover who is right. If the judgment of the court is followed, justice is done. Righteousness refers to right relationship to God that produces justice. Indeed, Amos 6:12 refers to justice as the "fruit of righteousness."

Amos 5:8-9. This section resembles

a hymn like those that praise God the creator in the Psalms (see Psalm 93). The message is twofold: First, God is powerful, as illustrated by God's creation of the world. This use of creation as illustration of God's ability to act appears often in Isaiah 40–55. Second, God who made the heavens also enters history to punish those who act contrary to the divine will.

Amos 5:10-13. The city gate was the place of commerce and court proceedings. Therefore, Amos identifies the gate as the main place Israel's offenses against the poor take place (offenses already laid out in Amos 2:6-8).

Amos 5:14-15. In 5:6 Amos called the Israelites to "seek the LORD." Now he gives the same charge except he replaces "the LORD" with "good." Good is the opposite of evil. Seeking good involves doing justice and acting rightly toward those who are not powerful. Amos follows this charge with another version of it that reverses the order: "Hate evil and love good" (5:15). "Hate" and "love" are covenant words. They have to do with that to which a person makes formal commitments. Amos thus tells the Israelites to declare their rejection of evil, but to proclaim their intent to do good.

Amos 5:16-17. The funeral dirge that began the chapter is here portrayed as taking place for real when the Israelites are defeated. "Alas! Alas!" is what mourners would cry out in formal expression of their grief (see also 1 Kings 13:30). Amos declares this cry will be heard everywhere. In fact, the mourning will be so great that everyone will be summoned to participate. As part of the typical funeral service, professional mourners were hired to wail and cry on behalf of the bereaved family (see Jeremiah 9:17-22). But Amos foresees a time when there will be such a need for mourners that even the farmers will be called to participate although they have no training in making lamentation.

Amos 5:18-20. This is one of the most famous passages in the Book of Amos. It declares what the day of the Lord will be like for Israel. The audience knows what the day of the Lord is; no introduction is necessary. It has to do with judgment and justice. But what Israel does not understand is that the judgment will be on them, not on an enemy. The impact of this message appears in part in the opening word, "Alas" that describes those who desire the day of the Lord. Again, this is the language of mourning one would use at a funeral. But like the funeral lament of Amos 5:1, the cry of lamentation here is raised over those still alive.

Amos 5:21-24. A natural follow-up to the declaration of the day of the Lord is a section about worship. The day of the Lord was probably something the Israelites celebrated and prayed for in worship. So it is appropriate that here Amos corrects the Israelites on the nature of their worship as well. The main issue is that the Israelites' elaborate rituals were not accompanied by right action.

Amos 5:25-27. Amos follows his charge to the Israelites to purify their worship with a question about whether they made sacrifices during the period of wilderness wandering. The wilderness epoch in some passages is considered the pristine time in Israel's history when Israel walked in humility with God (Jeremiah 2:1-3). Hence, the question Amos poses is rhetorical. It denies the usefulness of sacrifices by suggesting that sacrifices were not part of the wilderness experience.

INTERPRETING THE SCRIPTURE

What Is the Day of the Lord?

Amos is the first of the Old Testament writers to mention the day of the Lord, but as already noted he speaks of the concept as something that is known to his audience. His words indicate that the Israelites are anticipating the day. He declares, however, that they *should not be so anticipating it.* What is the day of the Lord? This, or similar expressions, appear many times in the prophetic books. Some references speak of the Lord's day as a time when God will bring vengeance on Israel's enemies (for example, Isaiah 24:21). This is perhaps what the Israelites were expecting. Psalm 118:24 speaks of a special day in a festival celebration ("the day that the LORD has made"). It is possible that on such a day in worship the Israelites celebrated God's victory over enemies. Hence, the day of the Lord may have been both a day of vindication Israel waited for and a day in Israel's worship in which they celebrated their assurance that such a day would come. Regardless of exactly what Amos thought about the day of the Lord, it was obviously something the Israelites thought was good for them.

In verses 18-19 Amos declares, however, that the day of the Lord will be bad news for Israel. Amos makes two key points about the nature of this day. First, he declares that no one will be able to escape the day of the Lord. To communicate this idea Amos uses a pair of scenarios about dangers in the animal kingdom: A man escapes from a lion only to be met by a bear; or a person goes inside the house and, thinking he is safe, rests his hand on the wall, and a snake bites him. The images suggest the day of the Lord is inevitable and comes upon Israel unsuspectingly. Second, Amos says the day of the Lord will be darkness, not light. To modern people this may seem like no more than another way of saying the day will be "evil, not good." But to ancient Israelites the expression probably had a deeper meaning. It suggests the day of the Lord will be marked by the absence of God's order and purpose. Darkness characterizes the world's precreation state. When the day of the Lord comes it will plunge Israel back into the chaos of the world before creation.

Should We Fear the Presence of the Lord?

What Amos describes under the title "day of the Lord" seems to be the intense presence of God among humans. It might seem this would be a good thing. Does God's presence not mean love and warmth? Indeed, it does. But God's nearness also brings God's holiness and expectations for humans to join in that holiness. Since humans cannot be holy as God is holy, God's nearness naturally produces judgment. In other words, the same fire that warms may also burn us if we get too close. In Amos 5:18-20 God's nearness on the day of the Lord is bad news for Israel because they have taken God too lightly; they have not followed the lead of God's holiness to produce their own holiness.

This idea of the intense presence of God in other parts of the Old

Testament is sometimes described as the shining of God's face on humankind. That God's gaze on humans can be an expression of God's anger and judgment is seen in the psalmist's plea for God to turn away. Indeed, Psalm 39:13 recognizes God not looking upon the human situation as a sign of God's grace. For God not to look upon human sin is part of God's mercy. For Amos, the concentrated presence of God occurs in the most severe way on the day of the Lord. Such a day might be too much for any human being to stand. But it will certainly be bad news—punishment and destruction—for Israel because they have taken too casually what being close to God's presence requires.

Let Justice Roll Down

Although Amos does not say it directly, he indicates indirectly that God requires justice of Israel for God's presence not to spell destruction. Interestingly, the word translated "justice" can also be rendered "judgment." Amos 5:24 is usually translated "let justice roll down" and it is assumed this line is a call for Israel to do justice. But it is possible that Amos 5:24 actually announces the coming of God's judgment. That is, God's justice will flow down like a mighty river upon Israel. The traditional understanding of this verse, however, has much to commend it.

The concern for justice throughout the Book of Amos is that the Israelites have a lack of justice in their lives together. Thus, it seems that Amos's declaration is a call for justice to flow down by the Israelites acting justly. Just as flowing water nourishes the earth, so also justice nourishes the ground of human society, and Israel

is called to supply that nourishment. Nevertheless, Amos makes clear that if Israel does not do justice, God will bring judgment. God will make sure justice is done. The question is whether Israel will participate in God's justice-making activities as a willing partner or as one who participates after being judged and punished.

The Case Against Formal Worship

Amos 5 contains some of the strongest statements against formal worship and places of worship in the Bible. Indeed, the prophet speaks against the sanctuaries at Bethel, Gilgal, and Beer-sheba (5:5). He also gives a series of declarations against certain worship practices: "I despise your festivals" (5:21); "I will not accept" "your burnt offerings and grain offerings" and "the offerings of well-being of your fatted animals" (5:22); "I will not listen to the melody of your harps" (5:23).

It may sound as though Amos is against institutional religion and its core rituals. This would be a misunderstanding, however, of Amos's message. Amos shares with other prophetic books and several psalms a critique of Israel's worship. But Amos and these other texts are not rejecting sacrifice or formal worship per se. Rather, they are arguing against ritual that is devoid of any moral imperative. True worship praises God, that is, it recognizes and expresses God's true nature. If we really acknowledge that God is our creator, that God is the ruler of the universe, and that God provides for us all we need to live, then we simply cannot act as though the world belongs to us. We cannot act in self-centered ways or take advantage of others for our own gain. We cannot act in these ways because we live with an awareness that we depend on God for our very lives and, in turn, we are called to be gracious to others. Amos criticized Israel's worship so much precisely because the Israelites attended and participated in worship and still acted in ways that displeased God.

SHARING THE SCRIPTURE

PREPARING TO TEACH

Preparing Our Hearts

Meditate on this week's devotional reading from Psalm 14. What does the psalmist declare about those who do not believe that God exists? Why will evildoers "be in great terror" (14:5)? Why will God's people rejoice? What does this psalm say to you about living under the reign of God?

Pray that you and the students will recognize that God is not fooled by injustice.

Preparing Our Minds

Study the background Scripture from Amos 5 and the lesson Scripture from Amos 5:14-15, 18-27.

Consider this question as you prepare the lesson: *Who will uncover the deceitful ways of evil people and demand justice?*

Write on newsprint:
❏ Scriptures for "Recognize and Reflect Upon Actions of Injustice Within the Community of Faith."
❏ information for next week's lesson, found under "Continue the Journey."
❏ activities for further spiritual growth in "Continue the Journey."

Review the "Introduction," "The Big Picture," "Close-up," and "Faith in Action," which all precede the first lesson of this quarter. Consider how you might use any of this material in today's lesson.

LEADING THE CLASS

(1) Gather to Learn

❖ Greet the class members and introduce guests.

❖ Pray that those who have come today will be ready to stand up and demand justice.

❖ Read this summary of an ABC news exclusive, which aired on October 11, 2013: **At age 11, Malala Yousafzai began blogging for the British Broadcasting Corporation (BBC) to let the world know about life in Pakistan under the repressive Taliban. Malala stood up for the rights of girls to be educated, despite death threats from the Taliban, which had issued an edict in 2009 that banned education for all girls. In October 2012, the Taliban tried to make good on their threat by boarding a school bus and shooting Malala in the head at point-blank range. The bullet should have killed her, but as Dr. Javid Kayani told ABC's Diane Sawyer, "The fact that she didn't die on the spot or very soon thereafter is to my mind nothing short of miraculous." Remaining in England** for treatment and attending school there, Malala still hopes to return to Pakistan one day. Despite her ordeal, Malala has continued to stand firm and undaunted in her fight to ensure that girls everywhere receive an education. She has been recognized around the world for her courage, including a nomination for the Nobel Peace Prize and an opportunity to address the United Nations on her sixteenth birthday about the importance of education. Malala's determination to find justice extends to the offer of forgiveness for her attackers, which she says "real Islam" teaches.

❖ Read aloud today's focus statement: **Some people cover their evil ways with outward acts of goodness. Who will uncover their deceit and demand justice? The people learned through Amos that God will not be fooled by insincere offerings and will severely punish all sinners.**

(2) Goal 1: Learn How God Establishes Justice for the Righteous and Punishes Deceivers

❖ Introduce today's lesson by reading "The Nature of Justice" and "The Nature of Prophecy" both from "The Big Picture: Prophets Call for Justice," found at the beginning of this quarter.

❖ Select a volunteer to read Amos 5:14-15.

❖ Use "Amos 5:14-15" in Understanding the Scripture to explain the meaning of these verses.

❖ Invite the volunteer to continue by reading Amos 5:18-27 and then discuss these questions:

1. **Verses 18-20 are the earliest references to the day of the LORD. To what does this day refer?** (See "What Is the Day

of the Lord?" and "Should We Fear the Presence of the Lord?" in Interpreting the Scripture.)

2. **In verses 21-24 Amos seems to speak against festivals and sacrifices. What is his point?** (See "Amos 5:21-24" in Understanding the Scripture and "The Case Against Formal Worship" in Interpreting the Scripture.)

3. **Read Amos 5:21-24 and Isaiah 1:10-17. How are the ideas of these two prophets similar and different?**

4. **Why might Amos remind the people of their days in the wilderness?** (See "Amos 5:25-27" in Understanding the Scripture.)

❖ Conclude this portion of the lesson by reading in unison today's key verse, Amos 5:24.

(3) Goal 2: Recognize and Reflect Upon Actions of Injustice Within the Community of Faith

❖ Post on newsprint these selected Old Testament Scriptures dealing with injustice within the community of faith. Invite volunteers to look up and read aloud these verses.

- Exodus 22:21-22
- Exodus 23:1-9
- Leviticus 19:35-36
- Psalm 82:2-4
- Proverbs 14:31
- Proverbs 20:10
- Proverbs 28:8
- Jeremiah 22:3
- Lamentations 3:34-36
- Amos 5:11-12

❖ Discuss these questions:

1. **How did the actions in a particular verse identify and**

address injustices among God's people?

2. Which of these injustices continue today within the church?

3. How can the church overcome injustices in whatever form they exist today?

(4) Goal 3: Identify Unjust Practices and Commit to Stop the Learners' Participation in Them and Help Others Do the Same

❖ Observe that members of the community of faith can be guilty of unjust practices. Read this list of practices and encourage the learners to think about whether they have ever engaged in any of them. They will not be asked to name any violations aloud.

1. Have you ever used "bait-and-switch advertising" to prod customers to buy a more expensive product?

2. Have you ever discriminated against someone because of race, creed, language, or sexual orientation?

3. Have you ever spread lies or gossip about someone?

4. Have you ever stolen office supplies or other items from your employer?

5. Have you ever knowingly cheated on your income tax return?

❖ Provide quiet time for the adults to reflect on any of these injustices (or others they can name) and ask themselves: What can I do to right this wrong? What steps will I take to ensure that I do not commit the same injustice again?

(5) Continue the Journey

❖ Break the silence by praying that as the learners depart, they will do all in their power to let justice roll down.

❖ Post information for next week's session on newsprint for the students to copy:

- **Title: Rebuked for Selfishness**
- **Background Scripture: Amos 6**
- **Lesson Scripture: Amos 6:4-8, 11-14**
- **Focus of the Lesson: Some persons care only about accumulating lavish possessions for themselves and care nothing for those who possess little. What happens to greedy and selfish people? God will dispossess the greedy and selfish and thus demonstrate God's justice.**

❖ Challenge the adults to grow spiritually by completing one or more of these activities, which you have posted on newsprint for the students to copy.

(1) **Research injustices in your denomination's history. Look especially for issues relating to racial and ethnic groups and the role of women. How have these injustices been righted? What issues currently need to be addressed?**

(2) **Consider how your expressions of worship are in keeping with the way you act to ensure that others are justly treated. How might God respond to your worship? What changes, if any, do you need to make?**

(3) Check labels on each product you purchase to see where it was made. Is it certified as a Fair Trade item? Is it made of sustainable materials? Do you believe that the workers who created the product are justly treated and fairly paid? Would you consider making changes in your buying habits?

❖ Sing or read aloud "For the Healing of the Nations."

❖ Conclude today's session by leading the class in this benediction adapted from Micah 6:8, which is the key verse for July 19: **Let us depart to do justice, and love kindness, and walk humbly with our God.**

UNIT 1: AMOS RAILS AGAINST INJUSTICE
REBUKED FOR SELFISHNESS

PREVIEWING THE LESSON

Lesson Scripture: Amos 6:4-8, 11-14
Background Scripture: Amos 6
Key Verse: Amos 6:12

Focus of the Lesson:
Some persons care only about accumulating lavish possessions for themselves and care nothing for those who possess little. What happens to greedy and selfish people? God will dispossess the greedy and selfish and thus demonstrate God's justice.

Goals for the Learners:
(1) to explore God's response to injustice as recorded by Amos.
(2) to reflect upon ways individuals practice greed and selfishness.
(3) to discover ways God does justice in the midst of injustice and how humans can join God in the fight against injustice.

Pronunciation Guide:
Baal (bay´ uhl) or (bay ahl´)   Karnaim (kahr nay´ im)
Calneh (kal´ neh)   Lebo-hamath (lee boh hay´ muhth)
Gath (gath)   Lo-debar (lo dee´ buhr)
Hamath (hay´ math)   Omri (om´ ri)
Jeroboam (jer uh boh´ uhm)   Wadi Arabah (wah´ dee air´ uh buh)

Supplies:
Bibles, newsprint and marker, paper and pencils, hymnals, magazine pictures

---

READING THE SCRIPTURE

NRSV
Lesson Scripture: Amos 6:2-8, 11-14
²Cross over to Calneh, and see;

CEB
Lesson Scripture: Amos 6:2-8, 11-14
²Cross over to Calneh and see;

from there go to Hamath the great;
   then go down to Gath of the
     Philistines.
Are you better than these kingdoms?
   Or is your territory greater than
     their territory,
[3]O you that put far away the evil day,
   and bring near a reign of violence?
[4]Alas for those who lie on beds of
     ivory,
   and lounge on their couches,
and eat lambs from the flock,
   and calves from the stall;
[5]who sing idle songs to the sound of
     the harp,
   and like David improvise on
     instruments of music;
[6]who drink wine from bowls,
   and anoint themselves with the
     finest oils,
   but are not grieved over the ruin
     of Joseph!
[7]Therefore they shall now be the first
   to go into exile,
   and the revelry of the loungers
     shall pass away.
[8]The Lord GOD has sworn by himself
(says the LORD, the God of hosts):
I abhor the pride of Jacob
   and hate his strongholds;
   and I will deliver up the city and
     all that is in it.
[11]See, the LORD commands,
   and the great house shall be shat-
     tered to bits,
   and the little house to pieces.
[12]Do horses run on rocks?
   Does one plow the sea with oxen?
But **you have turned justice into
    poison
   and the fruit of righteousness
    into wormwood—**
[13]you who rejoice in Lo-debar,
   who say, "Have we not by our
     own strength
   taken Karnaim for ourselves?"

from there go to Hamath the great;
   then go down to Gath of the
     Philistines.
Are you better than these kingdoms?
   Or is your territory greater than
     their territory?
[3]Doom to those who ignore the evil day
   and make violent rule draw near:
[4]who lie on beds of ivory,
   stretch out on their couches,
   eat lambs from the flock,
   and bull calves from the stall;
[5]who sing idle songs to the sound of
     the harp,
   and, like David, compose tunes on
     musical instruments;
[6]who drink bowls of wine,
   put the best of oils on themselves,
   but who aren't grieved over the
     ruin of Joseph!
[7]Therefore, they will now be the first
   to be taken away,
   and the feast of those who
     lounged at the table will pass
     away.
[8]The LORD God has solemnly sworn,
says the LORD, the God of heavenly
     forces:
I reject the pride of Jacob.
   I hate his fortresses.
   I will hand over the city and all
     that is in it.
[11]Look, the LORD is giving an order;
   he will shatter the great house into
     bits
   and the little house into pieces.
[12]Do horses run on rocks?
   Does one plow the sea with oxen?
But **you have turned justice into
    poison
   and the fruit of righteousness
    into bitterness—**
[13]you who rejoice in Lo-debar,
   who say, "Haven't we by our own
     strength taken Karnaim for
     ourselves?"

¹⁴Indeed, I am raising up against you
a nation,
O house of Israel, says the LORD,
the God of hosts,
and they shall oppress you from
Lebo-hamath
to the Wadi Arabah.

¹⁴Indeed, I will raise up against you a
nation, house of Israel, says the
LORD God of heavenly forces,
and they will oppress you from
Lebo-hamath to the desert
ravine.

UNDERSTANDING THE SCRIPTURE

Introduction. This chapter of Amos may be summed up by the first line of verse 1: "Alas for those who are at ease." The chapter pronounces lamentation over the Israelites who enjoy a luxurious lifestyle. Each individual section within the chapter expresses some version of the message that those who presently live at ease will experience woe. The reason for the impending downfall of Israel is not the Israelites' wealth per se, but the confidence the people place in that wealth. They act as though their lives are made secure by their own abilities and capacity. In reality, however, all they have is due to God's goodness. Failure to acknowledge that fact, in turn, leads to every other fault Amos identifies.

Amos 6:1-3. The chapter begins with a woe cry ("Alas") typical of the cries for the dead that appear other places in Amos (see Amos 5:18). "Those who are at ease" refers to the people who trust in their own resources rather than in the power of God. The self-confident people are identified with Zion and Samaria, the two main royal cities of the Israelites. Zion refers to the city of David. Sometimes the name Zion is simply synonymous with Jerusalem, but it can also refer more specifically to that part of the city where the palace and Temple were located. It was the capital of the United Monarchy of David and Solomon and of Judah after the kingdom split at Solomon's death. Samaria was the capital of Israel, the Northern Kingdom. Omri made Samaria the capital of Israel and it was particularly associated with his dynasty that included his son Ahab and Ahab's wife, Jezebel (1 Kings 16:24-34). It is somewhat surprising that Zion and Samaria are lumped together with no distinction since the Old Testament often associates Samaria and its kings with the worship of Baal (see 1 Kings 22:51-53). But Amos speaks of both cities as places whose people have forgotten their true God. Furthermore, Amos declares these cities are no better and have no more advantages than other cities outside Israel. Amos mentions Calneh and Hamath, city-states north of Israel, and Gath, a prominent Philistine city. The residents of Zion and Samaria are as susceptible to God's wrath as residents of these other cities because they deny their vulnerability and their dependence on God.

Amos 6:4-8. Amos depicts people who live in great luxury. Ivory was and is a sign of opulence. "Beds of ivory" refers to couches and other furniture that had inlaid ivory in their frames. Such furnishings were typically available only to royalty. In Amos's time, however, there was an expanded upper class that enjoyed this type of wealth. Eating lambs and calves may not sound outrageous to modern Western people who are accustomed to eating meat regularly. But most people in the ancient Near East rarely ate meat. As the story of the prodigal son illustrates, even a relatively wealthy family would fatten a calf to be eaten only during a grand celebration such as a wedding feast (Luke 15:23). Most people in that world ate meat once each year. But the wealthy of Israel in Amos's day were living large and enjoyed meat regularly. They also drank wine in excess and they had time to play musical instruments (Amos 6:5). This constant celebrating and feasting is set over against the disaster that is coming. God hates the "pride of Jacob" (6:8), that is, the self-reliant, overconfident attitude of the Israelites. Therefore, the fortifications the people trust to give them security will be overrun by enemies and the weakness of human protection will be revealed.

Amos 6:9-10. Verses 9-10 seem disconnected from what Amos has said thus far in this chapter. These verses portray a time of disaster and extreme reactions to that disaster. The verses are connected to Amos 6 for this reason: They illustrate what it will be like when God "delivers up" the Israelites to destruction (as Amos 6:8 says). The picture of verses 9-10 seems to be of a plague or disease that has struck the land and it is interpreted as a curse from the Lord. Verse 9 refers literally to "ten men" being in a house. This is an extremely large number for a single household. It is possible the "house" referred to is the palace that would have housed many soldiers and servants. Alternatively, the number could be an exaggerated but round number that simply illustrates how comprehensive God's judgment will be. The description of bodies being taken from the house and burned is striking. Burning was not a typical means of disposing of a body in Israel. This may indicate that the death came from some deadly disease that now prevents typical funeral practices. Whatever the situation, Amos implies it would be interpreted as a sign of God's disfavor. Indeed, the time will be marked by resistance to saying the name of the Lord, probably because the disaster is understood as something brought on by God's curse.

Amos 6:11-14. The final portion of the chapter begins in verse 11 with a declaration that the Lord will destroy the "great house" and "little house." This is a way of saying that the destruction will be complete. Then the prophet presents again the reasons for destruction. He does so first by asking ridiculous questions—do horses run on cliffs? or is the sea plowed with oxen?—and then answering that in fact the unbelievable has happened in Israel. Justice has been turned to poison. Justice is the "fruit of righteousness" (6:12). That is, it emerges from right relationship with God and right living according to God's standards. But in Israel in Amos's day the poor came to the courts as victims seeking justice and they encountered there the very injustice from which they had fled. Thus, justice has become like wormwood, a bitter plant. It is not good for any purpose for which it is sought.

INTERPRETING THE SCRIPTURE

God's Use of Agents for Judgment

Amos 6 speaks several times about impending disaster for Israel. Although Amos does not say it explicitly, the agent of God's wrath for Israel was the mighty Assyrian army. The Assyrians invaded Israel and destroyed Samaria, its capital, in 722 B.C. The reference to exile in Amos 6:7 anticipates this traumatic event. Amos 6:14 makes another general reference that expresses the idea: "I am raising up against you a nation . . . and they shall oppress you from Lebo-hamath to the Wadi Arabah." This pronouncement raises several questions about prophetic predictions of judgment and God's actions to discipline God's people: Did prophets like Amos predict precise events like the exile of 722 B.C.? Does God cause specific catastrophes to punish people for their sins? How should we think about God's judgment against Israel?

Concerning the first question, we should note that Amos and the other prophets in the Old Testament are not primarily predictors of events, but proclaimers of God's truth, including the divine critique of Israelite society. When they do mention a nation specifically as God's agent of punishment, the identification does not come out of the blue. The prophet observes the circumstances of the world, the possible tragedies that would likely come, and then interprets them for the Israelites as God's judgment on them. So for Amos the mention of exile in Amos 6:7 draws the connection between a well-known practice of the Assyrians and God's punishment of Israel. Amos did not need any special revelation to know that Israel would encounter the Assyrians and their wrath. It must have seemed inevitable. But Amos speaks of such events as a sign of something God is doing in the world. That is Amos's unique contribution to the observations of Assyrian action in his day.

Although Amos does not predict historical events that could not be seen by others, it is important nevertheless to recognize that he (and the other Old Testament prophets) believed firmly that God's judgment on Israel occurred in very tangible ways. Judgment came, Amos insists, by God using human agents who would attack Israel. Two points about this way of understanding God's actions are important: First, although God uses human agents, God does not micromanage the historical process. Perhaps the most troubling aspect of this conclusion for us is that the Assyrian assault hurt many people who were not guilty of the crimes Amos indicted Israel for committing. This is inevitable. Human lives are interrelated and any community or national disaster affects everyone. It should also be noted that some of God's judgment through human agents is a natural consequence of the moral order. The prophets proclaim that Israel reaps what it sows (see Obadiah 15-16). Thus, Amos 6 emphasizes that those who are "at ease" (6:1) will be surprised by the coming disaster. The implication is that the arrogance of the wealthy Israelites led naturally to their downfall. But unfortunately, many innocent people also suffer for their arrogance.

Second, the kind of judgment

Amos predicts for Israel is not an end in itself, but God's way of leading Israel to a new life. Although most of the Book of Amos dwells on Israel's faults and predictions of punishment, the book ends with promises of restoration (Amos 9:11-15). The prophets did not present simply a pattern of punishment and restoration. Rather, they presented punishment as part of the process of restoration. This is expressed in a most radical way by Isaiah 19:22, which speaks of the Lord punishing Egypt: "The LORD will strike Egypt, striking and healing; they will return to the LORD, and he will listen to their supplications and heal them." In other words, there is a big picture of God's judgment that is important to keep in view. As Terence Fretheim observes, God punishes in order to correct, purge, and restore.

On Appreciating Our Wealth

"Don't leave that food on your plate. Don't you know there are children starving in China!" This stereotypical parental admonition has been the brunt of many jokes and, indeed, the connections it draws are not altogether logical or helpful for moral formation. Nevertheless, the saying is intended to produce appreciation for the luxurious provisions most people in North America enjoy. Amos speaks to Israelites who also lack proper appreciation for what they have. But for Amos's audience the problem is greater than simply not recognizing the blessings in front of them. They are not just unaware of their fortune. They overindulge to the point they cannot see the problems around them. Indeed, the Israelites are like the rich man in Jesus' parable who ignored the poor beggar at his gate (Luke 16:19-31). The problem is not wealth in and of itself. Rather, it is the enjoyment of wealth to the neglect of human needs.

The portrait of the Israelites is similar to that given by Chrystia Freeland in a recent study of super-rich people in America. Most interesting was the attitudes of people who had attained their wealth by building a business rather than through inherited money. Almost to the person, Freeland reports, these people had little or no concern for others who had not succeeded or who faced financial challenges. They spoke with disdain about the lower classes while indulging themselves with the belief they deserved it and had gained it all by themselves.

Boasting in Our Ability

One of the main problems Amos identifies in the people of Israel is their supreme confidence in themselves. Amos 6:13 highlights the problem by pointing to two cities east of the Jordan River the Israelites recovered to help secure their borders. Damascus previously took control of these two towns from Israel, but now under the leadership of Jeroboam II they regained control of them. Amos mocks the Israelites who say, "Have we not by our own strength" captured these two cities?

The problem Amos addresses is not military or political, but theological. The Israelites think they have acted on their own when in fact everything they have ever accomplished was made possible by God's grace. Amos identifies the problem through sarcasm. He uses the names of the two towns to get the message across. The name of the first town is Lo-debar, known in other passages such as 2 Samuel 17:27. The name given in the Hebrew text of Amos 6:13, however, is Lo-dabar, a slight variation that means "No thing." The mispronunciation is a subtle declaration that Israel places its confidence in "nothing." The name of the second town, Karnaim, means "horns," which is a metaphor for strength. The name itself supplies the message: Israel thinks it has captured strength by its own strength.

According to the Old Testament, the problem Amos addresses here is one of the most fundamental problems human beings face. Over and over again the Old Testament speaks against those who place too much confidence in themselves and who do not recognize how dependent they are on God. In fact, this may be the most fundamental sin in the Old Testament. It is such a problem in part because this attitude of self-reliance inevitably leads to the mistreatment of others. Thus, Amos identifies the boastful Israelites as the same people who have "turned justice into poison and the fruit of righteousness into wormwood" (Amos 6:12).

SHARING THE SCRIPTURE

PREPARING TO TEACH

Preparing Our Hearts

Meditate on this week's devotional reading from Psalm 119:31-38, a psalm in the wisdom tradition that extols God's law. What do you need God to teach you at this point in your life? Are there areas in your life controlled by "selfish gain" (119:36)? If so, what help do you need in focusing your life on God?

Pray that you and the students will identify and eradicate any greed in your life.

Preparing Our Minds

Study the background Scripture from Amos 6 and the lesson Scripture from Amos 6:4-8, 11-14.

Consider this question as you prepare the lesson: *What happens to greedy and selfish people?*

Write on newsprint:
❑ information for next week's lesson, found under "Continue the Journey."
❑ activities for further spiritual growth in "Continue the Journey."

Review the "Introduction," "The Big Picture," "Close-up," and "Faith in Action," which all precede the first lesson of this quarter. Consider how you might use any of this material in today's lesson.

Collect pictures from magazines (or elsewhere) for "Reflect upon Ways Individuals Practice Greed and Selfishness." These pictures should show people who are in obvious need. Ideally, some pictures would also show people who appear to have plenty to share but are not offering assistance; others would show volunteers (perhaps at a shelter or soup kitchen) aiding those in need.

LEADING THE CLASS

(1) Gather to Learn

❖ Greet the class members and introduce guests.

❖ Pray that those who have come today will care about those for whom God demands justice.

❖ Read the following quotations and invite the adults to comment on how each one agrees with or challenges their understanding of greed.

- **"Earth provides enough to satisfy every man's needs, but not every man's greed."** (Mahatma Gandhi)
- **"We have always known that heedless self interest was bad morals, we now know that it is bad economics."** (Franklin D. Roosevelt)
- **"Our economy is based on spending billions to persuade people that happiness is buying things, and then insisting that the only way to have a viable economy is to make things for people to buy so they'll have jobs and get enough money to buy things."** (Philip Slater)
- **"You have succeeded in life when all you really WANT is only what you really NEED."** (Vernon Howard)

❖ Read aloud today's focus statement: **Some persons care only about accumulating lavish possessions for themselves and care nothing for those who possess little. What happens to greedy and selfish people? God will dispossess the greedy and selfish and thus demonstrate God's justice.**

(2) Goal 1: Explore God's Response to Injustice as Recorded by Amos

❖ Read "Introduction" in Understanding the Scripture to begin today's session.

❖ Select a volunteer to read Amos 6:4-8, 11-14 and then ask:

1. **How would you describe the lifestyle that Amos is taking to task in verses 4-8?** (See "Amos 6:4-8" in Understanding the Scripture.)
2. **How would you describe the concern that these people have for the future of their country?** (Note especially Amos 6:6.)
3. **How does God intend to deal with the injustice in Israel?** (See "God's Use of Agents for Judgment" in Interpreting the Scripture.)
4. **How does life in ancient Israel seem similar to life in the modern Western world, especially the United States?**
5. **What lessons might the people of the United States learn from Amos and the demise of ancient Israel?**

(3) Goal 2: Reflect upon Ways Individuals Practice Greed and Selfishness

❖ Read or retell "Boasting in Our Ability" in Interpreting the Scripture.

❖ Show whatever picture(s) you have brought. If you have several, form groups and give each group one picture. Otherwise, work with everyone to tell a story about the people in the picture and whatever greed and selfishness seems to be present. Invite each person to add a detail to the story. For example, someone may say that the woman on the right is forty-three-year-old Mary Jones, who is clutching the hand of her granddaughter, Lily. Someone else may add that Mary is raising Lily because her mother, Mary's daughter, was an innocent victim of violence during a drug deal. Continue until the students have created a story about at least one of the people.

❖ Encourage the adults to comment on the ways that the people in the picture(s) are victims of those who practice greed and selfishness.

(4) Goal 3: Discover Ways God Does Justice in the Midst of Injustice and How Humans Can Join God in the Fight Against Injustice

❖ Read "On Appreciating Our Wealth" in Interpreting the Scripture. Highlight the final paragraph and encourage the adults to comment on how the super rich—the 1 percent, as we often say—are acting toward those who are in need. Add to the discussion these words from Elizabeth Warren, a former professor of law at Harvard University and politician from Massachusetts: **"There is nobody in this country who got rich on their own. Nobody. You built a factory out there? Good for you. But I want to be clear: you moved your goods to market on the roads the rest of us paid for; you hired workers the rest of us paid to educate; you were safe in your factory because of police forces and fire forces that the rest of us paid for. You didn't have to worry that marauding bands would come and seize everything at your factory. . . . Now look, you built a factory and it turned into something terrific, or a great idea? God bless. Keep a big hunk of it. But part of the underlying social contract is you take a hunk of that and pay forward for the next kid who comes along."**

❖ Ask: **Keeping in mind our reading from Amos, the quotations we**

have explored, and the stories we have imagined, how do you think you—as an individual and as part of this class—can join God in the fight against injustice? List ideas on newsprint.

❖ Challenge the students to do whatever they can to identify injustice and work against it.

(5) Continue the Journey

❖ Pray that as the learners depart, they will repent of selfishness and greed.

❖ Post information for next week's session on newsprint for the students to copy:

- **Title: God Will Never Forget**
- **Background Scripture: Amos 8**
- **Lesson Scripture: Amos 8:1-6, 9-10**
- **Focus of the Lesson: Some people are so deep into deceit and cheating others that they ignore warnings and must live with the consequences of their wicked ways. What happens to those who do not heed a warning? Amos says that God will no longer overlook their misdeeds and will destroy them for all time.**

❖ Challenge the adults to grow spiritually by completing one or more of these activities related to this week's session, which you have posted on newsprint for the students to copy.

(1) **Investigate socially responsible investing. How can you support companies that share your ethical values, particularly concerning justice for all people?**

(2) Review your income and assets. How much truly is enough for you to live on? How are you acquiring whatever resources you have? What do you think Jesus would say to you about your lifestyle and your treatment of others, particularly in light of your lifestyle?

(3) Look around your community or region. Do you observe any unjust practices, such as toxic products being disposed of in a poor community, or poor communities lacking affordably priced groceries, or a lack of medical services? With whom can you work to change whatever unjust practices you observe?

❖ Sing or read aloud "Lord, Whose Love Through Humble Service."

❖ Conclude today's session by leading the class in this benediction adapted from Micah 6:8, which is the key verse for July 19: **Let us depart to do justice, and love kindness, and walk humbly with our God.**

UNIT 1: AMOS RAILS AGAINST INJUSTICE
GOD WILL NEVER FORGET

PREVIEWING THE LESSON

Lesson Scripture: Amos 8:1-6, 9-10
Background Scripture: Amos 8
Key Verse: Amos 8:2

Focus of the Lesson:
Some people are so deep into deceit and cheating others that they ignore warnings and must live with the consequences of their wicked ways. What happens to those who do not heed a warning? Amos says that God will no longer overlook their misdeeds and will destroy them for all time.

Goals for the Learners:
(1) to explore unjust practices and their consequences during Amos's time.
(2) to reflect upon how the church practices injustices and seems to be oblivious.
(3) to encourage the church to address injustices practiced within their community of faith.

Pronunciation Guide:
ephah (ee´ fuh)
qayits (kah´ yits)
qets (kates)

Supplies:
Bibles, newsprint and marker, paper and pencils, hymnals

READING THE SCRIPTURE

NRSV
Lesson Scripture: Amos 8:1-6, 9-10
  ¹This is what the Lord GOD showed

CEB
Lesson Scripture: Amos 8:1-6, 9-10
  ¹This is what the LORD God

me—a basket of summer fruit. ²**He said, "Amos, what do you see?" And I said, "A basket of summer fruit." Then the LORD said to me, "The end has come upon my people Israel; I will never again pass them by.**
³The songs of the temple shall become wailings in that day,"
says the Lord GOD;
"the dead bodies shall be many, cast out in every place. Be silent!"
⁴Hear this, you that trample on the needy,
and bring to ruin the poor of the land,
⁵saying, "When will the new moon be over
so that we may sell grain;
and the sabbath,
so that we may offer wheat for sale?
We will make the ephah small and the shekel great,
and practice deceit with false balances,
⁶buying the poor for silver
and the needy for a pair of sandals,
and selling the sweepings of the wheat."
⁹On that day, says the Lord GOD,
I will make the sun go down at noon,
and darken the earth in broad daylight.
¹⁰I will turn your feasts into mourning,
and all your songs into lamentation;
I will bring sackcloth on all loins,
and baldness on every head;
I will make it like the mourning for an only son,
and the end of it like a bitter day.

showed me: a basket of summer fruit. ²**He said, "Amos, what do you see?" I said, "A basket of summer fruit." Then the LORD said to me, "The end has come upon my people Israel; I will never again forgive them.**
³On that day, the people will wail the temple songs,"
says the LORD God;
"there will be many corpses, thrown about everywhere.
Silence."
⁴Hear this, you who trample on the needy and destroy
the poor of the land,
⁵saying,
"When will the new moon
be over so that we may sell grain, and the Sabbath
so that we may offer wheat for sale,
make the ephah smaller, enlarge the shekel,
and deceive with false balances,
⁶in order to buy the needy for silver
and the helpless for sandals,
and sell garbage as grain? "
⁹On that day, says the LORD God,
I will make the sun go down at noon,
and I will darken the earth in broad daylight.
¹⁰I will turn your feasts into sad affairs
and all your singing into a funeral song;
I will make people wear mourning clothes
and shave their heads;
I will make it like the loss of an only child,
and the end of it like a bitter day.

UNDERSTANDING THE SCRIPTURE

Introduction. Amos 8 is entirely about judgment. It appears in the middle of a series of visions about the downfall of Israel that began in Amos 7 and finished in Amos 9. Amos 8 begins with a vision that predicts Israel's "end" (8:1-3). Then Amos gives an indictment that explains why the end must come (8:4-6). The chapter concludes with three sayings that describe the effects of God's judgment (8:7-8, 9-10, 11-14). Together these sections of Amos 8 make clear that the end of God's people will be the result of their disobedience and sinfulness.

Amos 8:1-3. Amos reports a vision God gave him in which God declares a catastrophic end for Israel. Amos's report of the vision communicates its message by means of a word-play. After giving Amos the vision, God asks Amos what he sees. Amos responds, "a basket of summer fruit." In Hebrew the term for this late fruit is *qayits*. God then responds by·saying, "The end has come." The word "end" in Hebrew is *qets*, a word related to the term for summer fruit that has a very similar sound. After this declaration, God then describes a scene of death and destruction. The joyful songs Israel once enjoyed in worship will now be turned to songs of mourning.

Amos 8:4-6. The reason for Israel's end is the injustice of God's people in relation to the poor (Amos 8:7-8). The particular problem Amos identifies here is that those who are dishonest practice their dishonesty on the heels of worship! They observe the sabbath and other holy festivals (this is the meaning of "new moon" in Amos 8:5).

But worship has no effect on them. After the sabbath they go out to cheat their customers. They do so by means of dishonest weights and measures. The *ephah* was a unit of measure for grain. The merchants Amos speaks against declare their plans to "make the ephah small" (8:5). That is, they will give less than the buyer thinks he or she is getting. On the other hand, these merchants will exact more pay for their goods than is fair. The *shekel* was a weight used to determine the amount of silver or other currency accepted in the marketplace. These merchants would use a shekel that was heavier than it was supposed to be. Thus, they take more in pay than the buyer thinks the price tag asks. The picture Amos paints is of people who see only profit. They do not see the human beings who buy from them, nor do they consider the welfare of their customers. Amos sums up his indictment with two additional statements in the mouth of the rich that indicates the extent of their quest for money: (1) they buy and sell "the needy for a pair of sandals" (8:6), a charge Amos has made before (2:6); and (2) they sell "the sweepings of the wheat" (8:6). The final statement refers to selling a mix of chaff and refuse left over after winnowing the wheat for sale. It is the final sign that the only concern is for personal gain without care for the expense to others.

Amos 8:7-8. Now the Lord swears to act against what the merchants are doing. The meaning of "pride of Jacob" by which the Lord swears in verse 7 is difficult to understand. In Amos 4:2 and 6:8 God swore by himself.

Perhaps "pride of Jacob" is another name for the Lord, the One who rescued Israel from slavery in Egypt. God's action against Israel will cause the land itself to shake. The comparison to the Nile may be simply that the great river of Egypt fluctuated with no explanation; thus, punishment would come to Israel without warning.

Amos 8:9-10. The day of judgment for Israel will be marked by darkness. That is, the light God gave as a gift to creation in the beginning (Genesis 1:3) will be taken away. This condition of darkness will occur in conjunction with Israel's celebrations being changed to occasions of mourning. Just as Israel enjoyed its festivals and shallow worship, so now Israel will sing songs of lament. Such times were marked by putting on sackcloth, a rough material that was worn during times of penance. Shaving the head was a similar sign of grief. That day would be like the death of an only child that marked the end of hope for the future (see Jeremiah 6:26).

Amos 8:11-14. The final saying that describes "the end" of Israel (Amos 8:2) refers to the effects and results of God's punishment. Namely, God will be at such a self-imposed distance from Israel that they will not receive God's word. The famine of the word Amos describes may refer to the fact that the Israelites will not receive any answers to their laments and songs of mourning. Though they search all over their territory, they will find no one who will be able to explain God's actions to them or offer them hope for the future. This dire circumstance may be a veiled reference to the fact that the priest of Bethel essentially banished Amos from the land in Amos 7:10-17 and now there is no one to speak the word to them. Whether this is the intention or not, Amos 8:11-14 declares there will be no messenger of the Lord to give them the true word. The effect will be equal to that of famine. Indeed, the truth that "one does not live by bread alone" (Deuteronomy 8:3; Matthew 4:4) becomes obvious here. Without the word of God there is no hope for restoration or future. Without such hope even the strongest and most vibrant people will faint beneath the weight of their guilt. Verse 14 pokes fun at those Israelites who swore by and put confidence in other gods. Those gods will be useless to protect them or give them an answer to their dilemma when the Lord's judgment comes.

INTERPRETING THE SCRIPTURE

The End Has Come

Amos 8:1-3 reports the last of four visions the prophet had concerning God's punishment of Israel. As with Amos's oracles of judgment in 1:3–2:8, the form of the prophet's speech is an important part of his message. Amos 8:1-3 is nearly identical in form to the three vision reports that precede it. By paying attention to how this final vision report falls in relation to the three before it, we can discern its larger message. Namely, the sequence of visions declares that God's judgment is absolutely justified. Severe judgment is the only choice God has to deal with these rebellious people. When God declares "the end has come" (8:1) for Israel it has become obvious that God has tried everything to bring Israel back, but nothing has worked.

Amos 7:1-3, 4-6, 7-9 and 8:1-3 all report that "the Lord GOD showed" Amos something related to the disaster that was coming for Israel. But as the visions progress from one to another it becomes more and more evident that Israel has no chance of escaping the disaster because Israel has not heeded God's warnings to change its evil ways. In the first two visions Amos tells us what he saw (a swarm of locusts that will devour the crops [7:1]; a fire that will eat up the land [7:4]) and then Amos begs God not to let it come to pass. "How can Jacob stand? He is so small," Amos pleads (7:2, 5). In both cases God has mercy on Israel and does not let the disaster come.

In the third vision something new happens: God asks Amos a question, "Amos, what do you see?" (7:8). Amos sees a plumb line, which determines if Israel is square with God's requirements or not. It seems that God will make this decision by putting Amos in the midst of Israel to test them, for this is exactly what happens next. Amos 7:10-17 reports a story of Amos preaching and predicting that Israel will fall. The message is received with stubborn resistance rather than repentance. Indeed, the priest of Bethel sends Amos away and tells him never to prophesy again in Israel (7:12-13). The story of Amos's rejection at Bethel thus makes clear that God's charges of injustice have had no effect. But more important, this sequence of visions reveals something about how God works with rebellious creatures. God is gracious and gives them every opportunity for change. Thus, God responds

to Amos's pleas for mercy by not destroying Israel. Furthermore, God sends messengers to deliver the call to repentance in language the people can understand. The story in Amos 7:10-17 reports that Amos is that messenger. But when all else fails, God sends judgment.

In Amos 8:1-3 the final word comes. Just as in Amos 7:8, God asks Amos what he sees. Amos answers, "a basket of summer fruit" (8:1). As noted in the Understanding the Scripture portion (8:1-3), the sound of the word for summer fruit is related to the word "end." God's word to Amos works on a wordplay. But *what* Amos sees is also a symbol of what God says will happen to Israel. Just as the fruit is the last of the season, so also Israel has reached the end of its fruitfulness. There is no more opportunity for turning around. There is no more help Amos can give God's people. The end has come.

The picture of Israel in Amos 8:1-3, in light of the series of visions in Amos 7:1-9 and the story in Amos 7:10-17, is of a spoiled child who would not listen to the warnings of coming punishment. Israel had every opportunity to turn from its evil ways, but it did not. Now, for Israel's own good, God brings on the people the most severe punishment.

Never on Sunday

The reason for Israel's downfall is described in Amos 8:4-6. The message is similar to what Amos has charged before: Israel is "buying the poor for silver and the needy for a pair of sandals" (8:6; compare 2:6). But here Amos's indictment has a new twist. Amos relates Israel's injustice against the poor to the observance of the sabbath, or lack of such observance. The wealthy and powerful people who are oppressing the poor do observe the sabbath, but they only recognize the letter of the law and not its spirit. Amos says they cannot wait for the day of rest to be over so they can return to the marketplace to take advantage of people again. The picture of these greedy merchants is of people who are fastidious when it comes to the outward observance of the law. They do not open their shops on the sabbath; they abide by every requirement for the day's observance. But they miss completely what the day is meant to produce; namely, a strong sense that God has given all wealth to humanity and all those who enjoy wealth, in turn, must be kind and gracious to those who have not received as much.

The institution of sabbath was intended as a deterrent against the kind of injustice Amos rails against. The prohibition against work has the general goal of reminding God's people that the earth is not theirs to control. Although God gave humans dominion over the earth and God invited them to subdue it, human dominion exists within the context of God's ultimate dominion (as Genesis 1:26-31 suggests). Sabbath was to be a day to remember that lesson. If humans could remember God's reign by observing the sabbath, they might also remember that they did not own other people. By ceasing their work on the sabbath, they would practice placing limits on how much they tried to control the world and other people.

Creation Will Revolt

The picture Amos paints of the day of destruction has two prominent images: the image of mourning, as at a funeral, and the image of the cosmos responding. The first of these images has appeared before (see 5:16-17). The songs will be lamentation; the people will wear sackcloth; everyone will have a shaved head, a sign of shame and humiliation.

The second image, however, is of the nonhuman world responding to Israel's situation by the sun ceasing to light the earth: "the sun will go down at noon, and darken the earth in broad daylight" (8:9). It may well be that experiences with solar eclipses inspired this description. It must have been quite ominous for an ancient person to see the sky go completely dark in the middle of the day during such an event. But Amos likely has more in mind than just a natural phenomenon when he describes the absence of light on the day of judgment. Indeed, the message seems to be that the lights in the sky will work against the Israelites because of their sinfulness. Hence, Amos is probably saying more than just that Israel will be in the dark. They are, indeed, in spiritual darkness, as Amos has pointed out. But the judgment Amos pronounces at least hints that creation itself is working against the Israelites. Recall how God sent plagues on the Egyptians in Exodus 7–12. The nonhuman world acted against Pharaoh and his people: water turned to blood, flies swarmed over everything, and locusts destroyed the crops. The last plague before the death of all firstborn was darkness (Exodus 10). It was essentially a sign that God had rolled back the first day of creation when God made light and separated light from darkness (Genesis 1:3). Now Amos says the darkness of chaos and disorder will come to the Israelites because of their sins.

SHARING THE SCRIPTURE

PREPARING TO TEACH

Preparing Our Hearts

Meditate on this week's devotional reading from Hosea 11:1-7. How is God seen in relation to Israel as the people wandered in the wilderness in the days of Moses? What is the relationship between God and Israel as Hosea writes in the mid-eighth century B.C.? What evidence do you have that God will never give up on you?

Pray that you and the students will seek justice.

Preparing Our Minds

Study the background Scripture from Amos 8 and the lesson Scripture from Amos 8:1-6, 9-10.

Consider this question as you prepare the lesson: *What happens to those who do not heed warnings about the consequences of their wicked ways?*

Write on newsprint:

❏ list of words for "Reflect Upon How the Church Practices Injustices and Seems to Be Oblivious."

❏ information for next week's lesson, found under "Continue the Journey."

❏ activities for further spiritual growth in "Continue the Journey."

Review the "Introduction," "The Big Picture," "Close-up," and "Faith in Action," which all precede the first lesson of this quarter. Consider how you might use any of this material in today's lesson.

LEADING THE CLASS

(1) Gather to Learn

❖ Greet the class members and introduce guests.

❖ Pray that those who have come today will become sensitive to injustices and find ways to address them.

❖ Read: **Henry H. Crane reminds us, "Some of the finest cheating in the world has been done under the guise of honesty." Whom can you name that claimed to be dealing honestly but was later found to be cheating many, many people?** (Here are some examples: Bernie Madoff, who ran a Ponzi scheme that bilked people, who were hoping to make a large profit, out of huge sums of money. Kenneth Lay and Jeffrey Skilling spoke glowingly about Enron Energy Corporation, which collapsed in bankruptcy due to a serious auditing failure. Bicyclist Lance Armstrong not only insisted he had never used performance-enhancing drugs to win races, including the Tour de France seven times, but also seriously damaged the reputation of other cyclists who claimed that he had.)

❖ Read aloud today's focus statement: **Some people are so deep into deceit and cheating others that they ignore warnings and must live with the consequences of their wicked ways. What happens to those who do not heed a warning? Amos says that God will no longer overlook their misdeeds and will destroy them for all time.**

*(2) Goal 1: Explore Unjust
Practices and Their Consequences
During Amos's Time*

❖ Set the stage for today's lesson by reading "The End Has Come" in Interpreting the Scripture. This portion gathers up prior themes to show how the vision in Amos 8 relates to previous visions.

❖ Solicit a volunteer to read Amos 8:1-6 and then discuss these questions:

1. **What charges does God bring against Israelite merchants in Amos 8:4-6?** (See "Amos 8:4-6" in Understanding the Scripture.)
2. **How does the sabbath figure into God's concerns?** (See "Never on Sunday" in Interpreting the Scripture.)
3. **What does this passage from Amos say to the church and to its members today?**

❖ Invite a volunteer to read Amos 8:9-10. Discuss how creation will respond to the coming disaster and conclude by reading or retelling "Creation Will Revolt" in Interpreting the Scripture.

*(3) Goal 2: Reflect Upon How the
Church Practices Injustices and Seems
to Be Oblivious*

❖ Post these names of groups that you have listed on newsprint prior to the session:
Women
People of color
Gay, Lesbian, Bisexual, and Transgender people
Children
Poor people

❖ Form small groups, provide paper and pencils, and encourage the participants to discuss these questions. Make clear that their observations need not be limited to their own congregation or denomination. Allow each small group to determine which group of people they want to address.

1. **In what ways do you perceive [name of group] has been treated unjustly within the church?** (As an example, the issue of child sexual abuse, particularly within the Roman Catholic Church, had been hidden from the public.)
2. **How were the needs of [name of group] ignored or belittled?** (For example, the needs of children were ignored while perpetrators were moved to another parish. Children had often been told not to reveal the abuse and so much of it went unreported.)
3. **Have these injustices been righted? If so, how?** (For example, some victims of abuse have been paid as a result of lawsuits. Regardless of compensation, the damage done to a child who trusted an authority figure who supposedly represented God can never truly be righted.)

❖ Bring the groups together to report their ideas.

*(4) Goal 3: Encourage the Church to
Address Injustices Practiced Within
Their Community of Faith*

❖ Ask the class to identify injustices that they see in their own denomination or congregation. Encourage them to identify who is being treated unjustly and how this problem can be remedied so that righteousness is put into practice.

❖ Read this information: **Jesus called his disciples to live justly. One way that he demonstrated such righteous living was by including everyone in his circle. Let's take a look at our church. Who in our community might not feel welcome in our church? Why? Do we seem to shut people out because of their age, economic standing, gender, sexual orientation, marital status, level of education, or some handicapping condition that prohibits them from entering our building or participating in the service? What can we do to help these persons feel that they are welcome and belong here?**

(5) Continue the Journey

❖ Pray that as the learners depart, they will be aware of injustice wherever it may occur, including within the church, and do all in their power to end the injustice and bring healing to the victims.

❖ Post information for next week's session on newsprint for the students to copy:

- **Title: No Rest for the Wicked**
- **Background Scripture: Micah 2**
- **Lesson Scripture: Micah 2:4-11**
- **Focus of the Lesson: People do not want to be confronted with their social and moral abuse of others. What is the result of their failure to acknowledge their evil ways? Micah prophesied that God would give no rest to those who practice evil against God's faithful ones.**

❖ Challenge the adults to grow spiritually by completing one or more of these activities related to this week's session, which you have posted on newsprint for the students to copy.

(1) **Review Amos 8:4-6. If you are a business owner, are there practices that you need to change because they are dishonest? If you are an employee, what steps can you take when you recognize dishonest dealings within the company for which you work? What are the consequences of the moral choices you must make?**

(2) **Recall times when you felt cheated by merchants. What happened? Did the product not live up to its advertised performance or value? Were you shortchanged? Did the seller not stand behind the product? Was the situation resolved? How did you feel about dealing with this merchant—or any others?**

(3) **Ponder God's words to the Israelites spoken through Amos that we have studied so far this quarter. Where do you hear messages addressed to you?**

❖ Sing or read aloud "All Who Love and Serve Your City."

❖ Conclude today's session by leading the class in this benediction adapted from Micah 6:8, which is the key verse for July 19: **Let us depart to do justice, and love kindness, and walk humbly with our God.**

UNIT 2: MICAH CALLS FOR JUSTICE AMONG UNJUST PEOPLE

No Rest for the Wicked

PREVIEWING THE LESSON

Lesson Scripture: Micah 2:4-11
Background Scripture: Micah 2
Key Verse: Micah 2:7

Focus of the Lesson:

People do not want to be confronted with their social and moral abuse of others. What is the result of their failure to acknowledge their evil ways? Micah prophesied that God would give no rest to those who practice evil against God's faithful ones.

Goals for the Learners:

(1) to explore Micah's depiction of people who deny their wrongdoing in the community.
(2) to express feelings about people who attempt to justify the evil and harm they commit.
(3) to respond with appropriate opposition to those engaged in wrongdoing in the community.

Pronunciation Guide:

Moresheth (mor´ uh sheth)   Naboth (nay´ both)

Supplies:

Bibles, newsprint and marker, unlined paper and colored pencils or crayons, hymnals

---

READING THE SCRIPTURE

NRSV
Lesson Scripture: Micah 2:4-11
⁴On that day they shall take up a

CEB
Lesson Scripture: Micah 2:4-11
⁴On that day, a taunt will be raised

taunt song against you,
and wail with bitter lamentation,
and say, "We are utterly ruined;
the LORD alters the inheritance of
my people;
how he removes it from me!
Among our captors he parcels out
our fields."
⁵Therefore you will have no one to
cast the line by lot
in the assembly of the LORD.
⁶"Do not preach"—thus they
preach—
"one should not preach of such
things;
disgrace will not overtake us."
**⁷Should this be said, O house of
Jacob?
Is the LORD's patience exhausted?
Are these his doings?
Do not my words do good
to one who walks uprightly?**
⁸But you rise up against my people
as an enemy;
you strip the robe from the
peaceful,
from those who pass by trustingly
with no thought of war.
⁹The women of my people you drive
out
from their pleasant houses;
from their young children you take
away
my glory forever.
¹⁰Arise and go;
for this is no place to rest,
because of uncleanness that destroys
with a grievous destruction.
¹¹If someone were to go about uttering empty falsehoods,
saying, "I will preach to you of
wine and strong drink,"
such a one would be the preacher
for this people!

against you;
someone will wail bitterly:
"We are utterly destroyed!
He exchanges the portion of
my people; he removes what
belongs to me; he gives away
our fields to a rebel."
⁵Therefore, you will have no one to
set boundary lines
by lot in the LORD's assembly.
⁶"They mustn't preach!" so they
preach.
"They mustn't preach of such
things!
Disgrace won't overtake us."
**⁷(Should this be said, house of
Jacob?)
"Is the LORD's patience cut
short? Are these his deeds?"
Don't my words help the one
who behaves righteously?**
⁸But yesterday, my people, the LORD
rose up as an enemy.
You strip off the glorious clothes
from trusting passersby, those
who reject war.
⁹You drive out the women of my
people,
each from her cherished house;
from their young children you
take away my splendor forever.
¹⁰Rise up and go! This can't be the
resting place;
because of its uncleanness,
it destroys and the destruction is
horrific.
¹¹If someone were to go about
inspired and say deceitfully:
"I will preach to you for wine and
liquor,"
such a one would be the preacher
for this people!

UNDERSTANDING THE SCRIPTURE

Introduction. The prophet Micah came from Moresheth, a small town south of Jerusalem. He spoke against the ruling elite class in Jerusalem from the perspective of a small-town person. But his concerns were similar to those of Amos, namely, the injustice that was rampant in the marketplace and the mistreatment of the poor by the wealthy. Micah 2 presents the basic argument against the people of Judah in verses 1-3 and 6-11. Then the judgment that is coming is described in verses 4-5 and 12-13. Perhaps more clearly than any prophet of his day, Micah denounced the wealthy citizens of Judah for taking away ancestral land in order to enrich themselves. Their actions resembled the worst expressions of capitalism. God called these people, however, to share the land equally in recognition that they did not own it; it was a gift from God.

Micah 2:1-2. Micah begins with the word "alas." Amos also uses this term numerous times (Amos 6:1, 4). It is the word that introduced a funeral lament. In its most natural use, this word would be followed by the name of the deceased person. In this case, however, Micah speaks the words of lamentation over people who are very much alive. Their actions, however, will soon bring woe upon them. The objects of the prophet's lament are profiteers who cannot wait to cheat the next person. They devise evil schemes in their beds at night, just waiting for morning when they can carry them out. Such persons are like the merchants Amos describes who cannot wait for the sabbath to be over so they can take advantage of vulnerable people again (Amos 8:4-6). Their "evil deeds" are called "iniquity." This word refers to deeds that are destructive to the community, acts that go against God's work to establish well-being (see Jeremiah 4:14). Greedy people who lie awake at night devising schemes to exploit others are the type of people Micah cries against.

The exact nature of the iniquity mentioned in verse 1 is described in verse 2. Those who "devise wickedness . . . covet fields, and seize them." Thus, they break the direct command of God not to covet what belongs to one's neighbor (Exodus 20:17). The charge also implies that these devisers of wickedness steal, thus breaking another Commandment (Exodus 20:15). But perhaps the greatest injustice is that what they were stealing was the "inheritance" of their fellow citizens. Inheritance refers to property passed down in a family from one generation to the next. When the Israelites settled the land, each family received a portion of land as an inheritance that was to be passed down from generation to generation. Such land gave the family a basis for economic security. But for ancient Israelites, inheritance was more than economic wealth. It gave the person his or her place in society. Without the inheritance, a person essentially had no share in the Promised Land and became a slave, as their ancestors had been slaves in Egypt. This is the background to the story of Naboth's vineyard in 1 Kings 21 (see especially 21:3). King Ahab wanted land that was Naboth's inheritance. In Micah's time this system of family inheritance was breaking up as wealthy and powerful members of society were taking the land of those who were poor and less powerful.

Micah 2:3-5. Micah reports the words of God ("thus says the LORD," 2:3) concerning the people who do injustice. God promises to bring evil upon them. Then God describes the circumstances of the people of Judah when the evil comes. A song will be raised over them. The song is identified first as a "taunt song" (2:4). The language here is general. But the second word identifies the song as "lamentation," a term that refers to the funeral song used to mourn the dead. As we have seen numerous times in the Prophets, Micah speaks of a funeral for those still alive. The funeral in this case, however, seems to be for what the people have lost, not for the people themselves. They will cry out that God has given away their inheritance to those who defeat them. Thus, the people who took away the inheritance of others (2:2) will now have their inheritance taken away.

Micah 2:6-11. The prophet complains that the people of Judah reject his very calling and vocation. They deny the truth of the prophet's words because they cannot accept the idea that God might act against them. Micah suggests, however, that this should not be a surprise since they act as an enemy toward their own people

(2:8). The wealthy take advantage of the weakest people in society, those who represent faith and dependence on God (those who trust; 2:8).

Micah 2:12-13. The final portion of Micah 2 is difficult to understand because it is not clear if it is an oracle of judgment or a promise of salvation. Much of the language of the passage suggests it is a promise of salvation. It assumes God's people have been scattered (by defeat and exile) and now need to be gathered and restored. Indeed, the word "gather" (2:12) and the description of God bringing the people together like sheep in a fold sound like assurance that God protects the people like a shepherd protects his sheep. If this interpretation is right, then the reference to the king in verse 13 is a reference to God who *is* the rightful king of these people. He acts as all good kings did, as a protective shepherd who brings his flock to safety. This image is quite similar to Isaiah 40:11, which concludes the grand promise that God will bring the exiled people of Judah back to their homeland.

The lack of clarity as to whether this section is indeed a promise of salvation stems from the unusual appearance of a salvation oracle here. The rest of chapter 2 and all of chapter 3 are pronouncements of judgment and predictions of destruction.

INTERPRETING THE SCRIPTURE

Do Not Preach

One of the most striking responses of the people of Judah to Micah's preaching is "Do not preach!" That is, the people do not want to hear the criticism the prophet is giving (2:6).

Instead, they want to hear lies about how wonderfully they are doing. So, Micah declares, the one who would preach about something as frivolous as "wine and strong drink" would be the preacher for these people (2:11).

The problem Micah highlights

is a common theme among the Old Testament prophets. When Amos preached to the people in the sanctuary at Bethel, the priest there told him not to prophesy, but to go to Judah and proclaim his message (Amos 7:10-17). The prophet's words were not welcome because they predicted Israel's destruction. Jeremiah also said the people of Jerusalem listened to deceptive words about their security rather than the truth of the prophetic word about their impending downfall (Jeremiah 7; 26).

Perhaps the reason the Old Testament prophets' words were so often rejected is that such rejection of unwanted rebuke is a common human problem. It is certainly a problem for the church today as much as it was for the people of ancient Judah. The word of God often tells us what we do not want to hear about ourselves. If we are liberal and pride ourselves on open-mindedness, God's Word may call us to concerns about purity. If we are conservative and hold to strict theological and ethical views, God's Word may call us to greater compassion for those who are suffering and a greater capacity for forgiveness. The basic problem is that we have trouble being humble enough to allow the Word of God to direct us, correct us, and call us into question. Many pastors who have studied Scripture and theology and strive to guide their congregations by what they have learned report resistance to biblical principles in favor of business models or other approaches common to our society. Indeed, at every level of faith and in every aspect of the life of the church a common cry of us all is "Do not preach!" Our challenge is to open ourselves to what God's Word has to teach us,

whether through direct reading of it or through the messages of faithful people who have answered God's calling. To really hear the Word of God preached is a central concern for the church.

Robbing the Poor of Inheritance

Perhaps the main problem with the society Micah speaks against is that wealthy citizens are engaging in ruthless capitalistic business practices by taking land from ordinary people in order to satisfy debts. The reason such actions were so reviled is that inherited land was understood as God's gift. Therefore, it was a sign of God's grace. To take away this land was like removing the person from the covenant community. For the poor it was essential to know that God cared for them and provided for them.

As previously noted, the inheritance each Israelite received provided economic security *and* an identity among the people God rescued from slavery in Egypt. The latter feature of the inheritance is the one that is most shocking. God's gift of the land to the people, the most concrete sign of God's grace, was in danger of being lost to all but the wealthiest and most influential people of Judah.

Micah 2:9 describes the outcome of this taking away of inherited land: The most vulnerable members of society will suffer. Women, who depended on either father or husband for their economic well-being, would be expelled from their houses. They would be like Naomi and Ruth who, when in similar circumstances, cast themselves on the mercy of society. Perhaps even worse, the children of these women would also be homeless and hopeless. But their pitiful state would not be simply an economically impoverished condition. Micah says those who lost their land would also be separated from the glory of God. This does not mean that God would be absent. But the tangible signs of God's presence—a society in which all persons live in dignity, in which no one was enslaved to another—would be missing.

Abusing the Patience of the Lord

Much of the message of prophets like Micah seems to relate to God's impending judgment of God's people. This, in turn, leads some to conclude that God in the Old Testament is primarily wrathful and angry and that grace is secondary to God's character. Those who feel this way believe that somehow this came to be reversed in the New Testament through the ministry of Jesus. Two points are important, however, to correct this idea. First, as Micah 2:7 indicates, the Old Testament has no conception of God as primarily angry and vengeful. When Micah refers to the patience of the Lord he almost quotes from a common Old Testament creed. It appears first and perhaps most powerfully in the story of Israel making and worshiping the golden calf in Exodus 32–34. Moses was ready for God to destroy the Israelites, but God revealed to Moses God's essential character: "merciful and gracious, slow to anger, and abounding in steadfast love and faithfulness" (Exodus 34:6). Hence, God's wrath is certainly part of the Old Testament, but the accent is on God's patience and mercy. Second, the New Testament, despite its focus on God's grace, also gives much attention to

judgment. We need only remember Jesus' warning to the Pharisees (Matthew 23) or Paul's assurance that God brings judgment ultimately on the unrighteous (Romans 2:1-16) to confirm this New Testament interest in God's wrath. So while we affirm that God is gracious, God also has expectations for us. Indeed, God's mercy requires us to act with gratitude and faithfulness. Otherwise, we show no signs of experiencing God's grace.

Micah 2:6b-7a essentially give this same warning of God's grace and God's demands to people who have come to affirm the former without acknowledging the latter. That is, Micah seems to be quoting the Israelites who respond to Micah's predictions of judgment with "are these his doings?" They did not believe God would ever act against them. This belief then allowed them to continue in their injustice because they had no fear of God's justice. They took advantage of God's patience. Or, perhaps more accurately, they saw only part of God's character and therefore did not recognize God's true character.

This balance between God's grace and God's judgment is essential for Christians. It may seem preferable to think only of God's mercy. It is important, however, to maintain a healthy belief in God's judgment. God's judgment is directed at injustices such as human trafficking, mistreatment of the poor, and neglect of the elderly. Therefore, a belief in God's judgment about such things ensures that we take them seriously and work against them too. Belief in God's judgment also reminds us that God wants to be in close relationship with us. Any close relationship carries expectations, and so does our relationship with God. The problem with Micah's audience was precisely that they forgot the expectations of their relationship with the One who had saved them. They forgot that their place in the world was the result of God's grace.

SHARING THE SCRIPTURE

PREPARING TO TEACH

Preparing Our Hearts

Meditate on this week's devotional reading from Proverbs 11:1-10. What do you learn from these proverbs about the righteous? What do you learn about the wicked? What do you learn about the effect of the righteous and the wicked on the cities in which they live? Which of these proverbs seems to be a word from the Lord for you?

Pray that you and the students will recognize, repent of, and change any wicked ways in your own lives.

Preparing Our Minds

Study the background Scripture from Micah 2 and the lesson Scripture from Micah 2:4-11.

Consider this question as you prepare the lesson: *When people fail to acknowledge their wicked ways, what is the result?*

Write on newsprint:
❏ information for next week's lesson, found under "Continue the Journey."
❏ activities for further spiritual growth in "Continue the Journey."

Review the "Introduction," "The Big Picture," "Close-up," and "Faith in Action," which all precede the first lesson of this quarter. Consider how you might use any of this material in today's lesson.

LEADING THE CLASS

(1) Gather to Learn

❖ Greet the class members and introduce guests.

❖ Pray that those who have come today will recognize wrongdoing in their community and do all in their power to overcome it.

❖ Read the following list and invite the students to comment on whether they believe such action causes harm to the community and, if so, how people are hurt because of each action.

- **A merchant advertises cheap prices, but when buyers examine their receipts they find they have been overcharged.**
- **A jurisdiction auctions off property because a homeowner owes less than $1,000 in back taxes.**
- **A doctor in the community sexually abuses two patients.**
- **A teacher often yells at a class and puts down individual students.**
- **A lawyer takes a case knowing that the chances of winning a lawsuit are slim, but the accused will have to pay a lot to mount a defense.**
- **A pastor constantly preaches about moral and ethical standards that she secretly violates.**
- **A politician who claims to be**

working for his constituents is actually taking money from a company whose product is harming the community.

❖ Read aloud today's focus statement: **People do not want to be confronted with their social and moral abuse of others. What is the result of their failure to acknowledge their evil ways? Micah prophesied that God would give no rest to those who practice evil against God's faithful ones.**

(2) Goal 1: Explore Micah's Depiction of People Who Deny Their Wrongdoing in the Community

❖ Present the information in "Introduction," "Micah 2:1-2," and "Micah 2:3-5" in Understanding the Scripture to help the adults move into this first lesson on Micah.

❖ Choose a volunteer to read Micah 2:4-11.

1. **Why is Micah told not to preach?** (See "Do Not Preach" in Interpreting the Scripture.)
2. **Why is robbing the poor of their inheritance such a serious sin?** (See "Robbing the Poor of Inheritance" in Interpreting the Scripture.)
3. **What picture of God emerges from Micah's preaching?** (See "Abusing the Patience of the Lord" in Interpreting the Scripture.)
4. **How would you describe the evildoers portrayed in today's lesson?**

❖ Choose several volunteers to role-play this scenario, which you will need to read aloud, based on today's lesson Scripture: **You are standing together listening to Micah, the prophet of Moresheth, who speaks to the people of Judah. You hear him quote his opponents, who command him not to preach such a negative message. These naysayers insist that God would never take such terrible action. Not true, declares Micah! These people have violated God's justice, especially in regard to theft of people's property and possessions. Moreover, the people who are bearing the brunt of such evil are innocent women and children. Micah declares that God will not allow these wicked ones to continue in their evil ways. Micah stops speaking. You and your friends begin to walk away. What do you have to say about Micah and his message?**

(3) Goal 2: Express Feelings About People Who Attempt to Justify the Evil and Harm They Commit

❖ Distribute unlined paper and colored pencils or crayons. Suggest that the adults use color and perhaps shapes to express their feelings about people who try to justify the evil they do and the harm that results from their actions. Perhaps some adults will prefer to draw a picture, but try to focus on the color and intensity of the emotion, possibly shown by the pressure of the pencil and the speed with which the strokes are made.

❖ Gather everyone together to show their papers. Encourage the class to talk about the emotions that come through.

❖ Provide a few moments for the adults to reflect quietly on any harm committed against them and offer silent prayers for transformation on the part of those who have caused this harm. Then bring the group back together.

(4) Goal 3: Respond with Appropriate Opposition to Those Engaged in Wrongdoing in the Community

❖ Read these words of Dr. Martin Luther King Jr.: **"He who passively accepts evil is as much involved in it as he who helps to perpetrate it. He who accepts evil without protesting against it is really cooperating with it."**

❖ Brainstorm with the class answers to this question: **What historical and current examples can you give of people passively accepting—perhaps even welcoming—evil rather than actively protesting and working against it?** List examples of such behavior on newsprint. Do not name names, unless those involved are public figures. For example, many Germans supported Hitler. In the United States, racism was widely tolerated and accepted. Children were regularly exploited by factory and mine bosses.

❖ Ask: **How can we collectively and as individuals take a stand against each of the evils we have identified?**

(5) Continue the Journey

❖ Pray that as the learners depart, they will be equipped to confront those who are causing harm in the community.

❖ Post information for next week's session on newsprint for the students to copy:

- **Title: No Tolerance for Corrupt Leaders and Prophets**
- **Background Scripture: Micah 3**
- **Lesson Scripture: Micah 3:5-12**
- **Focus of the Lesson: Some leaders are corrupt, lie to the people they are charged to**

protect, and then find associates who will support their evil ways. What can be done to end this dishonesty? God will judge and punish corrupt leaders and prophets.

❖ Challenge the adults to grow spiritually by completing one or more of these activities related to this week's session, which you have posted on newsprint for the students to copy.

(1) **Focus on an injustice in your own community. How will you speak and act to bring about justice? What gives you hope that God is still in charge, even though this situation exists?**

(2) **Identify someone whose actions are causing harm in your church or neighborhood. Do what you can to confront this person and insist that these harmful actions be halted and restitution be made insofar as possible.**

(3) **Browse the Internet using these words: "those who deny wrongdoing." Select a few "hits" to read. What is the situation? Based on the article, would you agree that the accused is actually innocent, or simply trying to find community support? In what ways do these people sound like the people of Micah's day?**

❖ Sing or read aloud "God Be with You till We Meet Again."

❖ Conclude today's session by leading the class in this benediction adapted from Micah 6:8, which is the key verse for July 19: **Let us depart to do justice, and love kindness, and walk humbly with our God.**

UNIT 2: MICAH CALLS FOR JUSTICE
AMONG UNJUST PEOPLE

No Tolerance for Corrupt Leaders and Prophets

PREVIEWING THE LESSON

Lesson Scripture: Micah 3:5-12
Background Scripture: Micah 3
Key Verse: Micah 3:8

Focus of the Lesson:
Some leaders are corrupt, lie to the people they are charged to protect, and then find associates who will support their evil ways. What can be done to end this dishonesty? God will judge and punish corrupt leaders and prophets.

Goals for the Learners:
(1) to explore how Micah confronted corrupt leaders.
(2) to reflect on reactions to leaders who mislead and deceive people.
(3) to address corruption in leadership within the church and the broader community.

Pronunciation Guide:
shalom (shah lohm´)

Supplies:
Bibles, newsprint and marker, paper and pencils, hymnals, scarf or tie

---

READING THE SCRIPTURE

NRSV
Lesson Scripture: Micah 3:5-12
⁵Thus says the LORD concerning the
    prophets

CEB
Lesson Scripture: Micah 3:5-12
⁵The LORD proclaims concerning the
    prophets,

who lead my people astray,
who cry "Peace"
　when they have something to eat,
but declare war against those
　who put nothing into their
　　mouths.
⁶Therefore it shall be night to you,
　without vision,
　and darkness to you, without
　　revelation.
The sun shall go down upon the
　prophets,
　and the day shall be black over
　　them;
⁷the seers shall be disgraced,
　and the diviners put to shame;
they shall all cover their lips,
　for there is no answer from God.
⁸But as for me, I am filled with
**　power,**
**　with the spirit of the LORD,**
**　and with justice and might,**
to declare to Jacob his transgression
**　and to Israel his sin.**
⁹Hear this, you rulers of the house of
　Jacob
　and chiefs of the house of Israel,
who abhor justice
　and pervert all equity,
¹⁰who build Zion with blood
　and Jerusalem with wrong!
¹¹Its rulers give judgment for a bribe,
　its priests teach for a price,
　its prophets give oracles for
　　money;
yet they lean upon the LORD and say,
　"Surely the LORD is with us!
　No harm shall come upon us."
¹²Therefore because of you
　Zion shall be plowed as a field;
Jerusalem shall become a heap of
　　ruins,
　and the mountain of the house a
　　wooded height.

those who lead my people astray,
those who chew with their teeth
　and then proclaim "Peace!"
but stir up war against the
　one who puts nothing in their
　　mouths:
⁶Therefore, it will become night for
　you,
　without vision, only darkness
　without divination!
The sun will set on the prophets;
　the day will be dark upon them.
⁷Those seeing visions will be
　ashamed,
　and the diviners disgraced;
they will all cover their upper lips,
　for there will be no answer from
　　God.
⁸But me! I am filled with power,
**　with the spirit of the LORD,**
**　with justice and might,**
to declare to Jacob his wrong-
**　doing and to Israel his sin!**
⁹Hear this, leaders of the house of
　Jacob,
　rulers of the house of Israel,
you who reject justice and make
　crooked all that is straight,
¹⁰who build Zion with bloodshed
　and Jerusalem with injustice!
¹¹Her officials give justice for a bribe,
　and her priests teach for hire.
Her prophets offer divination for
　silver,
　yet they rely on the LORD, saying,
　　"Isn't the LORD in our midst?
　　Evil won't come upon us!"
¹²Therefore, because of you, Zion will
　be plowed like a field,
Jerusalem will become piles of
　rubble,
　and the temple mount will
　become an overgrown mound.

UNDERSTANDING THE SCRIPTURE

Introduction. The primary subject of Micah 3 is the injustices and leadership failures of the "heads of Jacob" (3:1). The label "heads" refers to leaders of all types. Presumably this includes those making legal decisions since verses 2-3 and 9-11 speak of perversions of justice. The "heads" in verse 11 are "rulers" who "give judgment for a bribe," probably a reference to legal judgments in favor of the rich. Hence, Micah here renders judgment in a way similar to Amos. The chapter also mentions priests (3:11), who give instruction for money. But the chapter reserves its harshest criticism for the prophets. The prophets he refers to are probably the prophets of Jerusalem. The prophets, who are charged with communicating God's word that will give direction to the people, instead speak falsely and take money in exchange for favorable words. Micah contrasts himself with them in that he speaks of Judah's injustice and sinfulness, a message the people do not want to hear.

Micah 3:1-4. Micah begins with the words "And I said." What follows is his own testimony, similar to that given by other prophets when they report their call by God to prophesy (Jeremiah 1:4-10, especially verse 6). He begins his indictment with a rhetorical question that indicts the leaders of Judah for not promoting justice. They are to "know" justice, that is, to have knowledge of the legal traditions of Israel that are to govern the courts. But their actions show no such knowledge. Instead, they take advantage of those who need an advocate in court. Thus Micah says in verse 2 that

they "hate" what is good and "love" what is evil. Hate and love are covenant words. They point to formal—even public—commitment, which makes the crime even greater. Micah describes the abuse of the leaders as cannibalism (3:2-3). The revolting images reveal how strong the prophet's feelings were about the officials' misuse of the helpless. The imagery is simply of eating human flesh, but it may be helpful to note that Ezekiel 34 portrays the "shepherds of Israel," those leaders who are to care for God's people, as those who kill the sheep and eat their flesh (see especially verses 1-3). Micah's indictment is similar. The ones who are supposed to feed and care for the sheep are feeding off them. As a result, the leaders will call out to God when they are in trouble but they will get no answer. Specifically, Micah says God will "hide his face from them" (3:4). This is an expression of divine disapproval, of God withholding blessings. The language of God making God's face to shine upon the people is best known from the priestly blessing in Numbers 6:24-26: "The LORD bless you and keep you; the LORD make his face to shine upon you, and be gracious to you; the LORD lift up his countenance upon you, and give you peace." Micah declares the leaders of Judah will have exactly the opposite of this blessing.

Micah 3:5-8. Micah now turns his attention specifically to the prophets. The problem is simply that they do not speak the truth. Their message is to be what is revealed by God, whether the news is good or bad. But these prophets are crafting their messages to suit those who pay them. Indeed, people in Micah's time assumed the words of a prophet came directly from God. The prophets often spoke in ways that indicated as much. They began their speeches with "thus says the LORD" or "this is what the Lord showed me." But Micah says the prophets in his time are speaking good news to those who give a reward and bad news to those who do not offer compensation. The good news is characterized by the word "peace." The Hebrew term here is *shalom*. It is a declaration that all is well, that a state of wholeness and health is present. Such is the message to those who pay the prophet. But they "declare war" (3:5) against those who do not feed them.

Micah sets himself over against the prophets. It may be helpful to note that Micah does not actually refer to himself as a prophet and he does not label his speech as prophecy. Micah clearly fits the character of what is commonly known as a prophet (see the discussion that follows). But it may be that the office of prophet had become so misused that now legitimate prophets did not actually call themselves by that label. Amos likewise seems to reject the label, at least as a prophet was commonly conceived (Amos 7:14). Micah declares that he speaks the true word of God and he is led by God's spirit (Micah 3:8). These actions should be evident in the life of God's prophets. Since Micah perceives that other prophets apparently are neither speaking God's truth nor following God's leading, he does not identify with this group.

Micah 3:9-12. In the final portion of the chapter Micah reiterates his message against the "heads" of the nation. As in verse 1, he refers to them again in verse 9 with the identifying names Jacob and Israel. These names remind those who hear them that the leaders represent people who have a history with the God of Abraham and of the Exodus. Jacob/Israel is the name given to the holy nation. But the heads are not speaking the truth. To make matters worse, the heads—rulers and priests and prophets—invoke the Lord's name for support. They constantly speak good news. By saying "the LORD is with us" (3:11) they ignore the problem the nation faces and the evil that is approaching. Micah's indictment therefore concludes in verse 12 with a stirring prediction about the fall of Judah's holy city. He uses three expressions that all emphasize the city that houses the Temple, the symbol of God's presence. "Zion" refers specifically to the hilltop where the Temple was built; "Jerusalem" refers to the city more generally; "mountain of the house" describes in a more picturesque way the location of the Temple. Although Zion was not literally a mountain, in the poetic conception it was the highest place on earth (see Psalm 48:1-2). But Micah's message about this place was clear: It would be destroyed. The people would no longer be able to live under the delusion that God would protect them regardless of how they lived.

INTERPRETING THE SCRIPTURE

What Is a Prophet?

The lesson Scripture provides great insight into what the Old Testament means by the word "prophet" and gives a helpful starting point for people of faith today who wish to be part of ministry that is deemed prophetic. Micah's purpose here is to call the prophets into question. But as he does, we are able to observe the characteristics and typical activities of prophets and we get a clear idea of how prophets in Israel were *not* to conduct themselves in order to fulfill God's calling for them. As such, Micah's words provide direction for our ministry and Christian testimony as well.

Micah reveals the nature of prophets and prophecy in part by the other titles he gives in parallel to the word "prophet." For example, he refers to "seers" (3:7) in the same context. Prophets were essentially people whose role was to let humans in on what God was doing. They gained such information through extraordinary means such as visions and special experiences of divine revelation. These were experiences the average person did not have. The prophet "saw" what God revealed to them, which was not available to everyone. The prophet then had responsibility for communicating the content of what was learned or perceived in the vision and telling people what it meant. Micah also uses the word "diviner" (3:7). These were people who sought answers from God concerning the problems and questions people had. Diviners often sought such answers through rituals thought to prompt a word from God. The story in 1 Samuel 9 illustrates this role of prophets. Saul is looking for this father's donkeys and cannot find them. His servant suggests they go to see the "man of God" (9:6) to locate them. The one they sought out was none other than the prophet Samuel, who would seek an answer to their problem from God.

Because prophets were in charge of divine revelation, they had great responsibility. The nature of the message they proclaimed was somewhat mysterious. They did not hear the direct voice of God. Indeed, Numbers 12:6-8 notes that Moses was different from the prophets in that he did receive direct revelation; God spoke to him, in literal terms, "mouth to mouth." The prophets got their words through visions and dreams (Numbers 12:6). Therefore, there was always a temptation for the prophets to manipulate the message or to cast it in ways that favored those they wanted to please.

Our culture does not widely recognize prophets of the same type as those Micah spoke about. Nevertheless, the problems he sees with the prophets still remain today. The crucial role of hearing, interpreting, and announcing God's word is laid on the church. That word sometimes offers comfort, and sometimes offers critique and a call to repentance. The latter message takes courage and sensitivity to deliver. But when the message of judgment is turned into comfort, the hearer is allowed to continue in an unhealthy condition and the word of God cannot do its healing and correcting work. The disaster Micah 3:9-12 predicts is the direct result of Judah not hearing such a word earlier. The experience awaits anyone today who is not able to hear the word. Often the hearing of it depends on the messenger being faithful to his or her calling to speak the truth. Speaking the truth does not mean preaching *at* people or chastising them. It does mean, however, to let the words of Scripture that convict us and call us into question do their work. The prophets of Micah's day were doing the opposite. Thus, they exchanged the word of God for a lie.

Filled with the Spirit

When Micah contrasts his own role as spokesperson of God's word with that of the prophets, he declares he is filled with power and with the spirit of the Lord. It is important that he states this before giving details for what he says, for what he says is the natural result of his being empowered by God's spirit and given power from God.

Micah's identification of the spirit of God that "filled" him is a key to his word being powerful and true. Other prophets also speak of God's spirit as the animating force that propels them into their work. Ezekiel may be the best example. Several times he speaks of being transported in or by the spirit of God. On one occasion God's spirit took him into Jerusalem to see the abominations taking place in the temple (Ezekiel 8:1-4). Another time God's spirit took him through a valley filled with dry bones in order to reveal that God even had power over death (Ezekiel 37:1-14). In each case it is obvious that Ezekiel did not have control of the experience. The spirit of God was in control. That seems to

be largely what Micah is saying about being filled with the spirit. The spirit gives him the message; it is not his own.

Because Micah is filled with the spirit of God, he also has courage to speak the truth. The spirit is that force that gives life and animation. Indeed, the word for spirit also means "wind" and "breath" and refers to the power of God that gives life (see Genesis 2:7; Ezekiel 37:10). It gives Micah strength. The prophets around Micah are speaking out of their own strength and their own concerns. But Micah is being led by and empowered by the spirit.

The Purpose of Judgment

The last four verses of Micah 3 declare destruction for Jerusalem because of the corruption of its leaders. There are two interesting features of this prophecy of destruction that make it important for us. First, the prediction of destruction did not come true immediately, as Micah probably imagined it would, and yet it was judged to be true nonetheless. Jerusalem was not destroyed by the Assyrians, the dominant force in Micah's time. The Babylonians destroyed the city about 150 years later, but that is hardly what Micah had in mind. His prophecy was judged to be true not because the prediction of destruction was immediately accurate, but because the truth of Micah's critique was accurate. It required the people of Judah to take a hard look at themselves and consider how they might live differently. That is ultimately the most important feature of prophecy, then or now.

Second, Micah's prophecy was remembered precisely for the positive effect it had on the people of Judah. Jeremiah 26:18 recalls the prophecy during the trial of Jeremiah two generations after Micah. Jeremiah was accused of treason because he predicted Jerusalem would be destroyed. Jeremiah's supporters defended him by recalling that Micah was not brought up on charges for his prediction. Instead, the people repented and Jerusalem was spared. Thus, Jeremiah's defenders said that he was not guilty of treason. Instead, he was a true patriot. He was speaking of things that, if the nation listened, would save it in the end. The memory of Micah's sharp critique and prediction of destruction was positive precisely because it had the intended effect of bringing repentance.

SHARING THE SCRIPTURE

PREPARING TO TEACH

Preparing Our Hearts

Meditate on this week's devotional reading from Matthew 7:15-20. As you read Jesus' teachings on trees bearing either good or bad fruit, what kind of tree would he say that you are—and why? What would this Gospel passage say to the prophets that Micah speaks of in 3:5?

Pray that you and the students will strive to be like trees that bear good fruit for the kingdom of God.

Preparing Our Minds

Study the background Scripture from Micah 3 and the lesson Scripture from Micah 3:5-12.

Consider this question as you prepare the lesson: *What can be done to end the dishonesty practiced by corrupt leaders?*

Write on newsprint:

❏ information for next week's lesson, found under "Continue the Journey."

❏ activities for further spiritual growth in "Continue the Journey."

Review the "Introduction," "The Big Picture," "Close-up," and "Faith in Action," which all precede the first lesson of this quarter. Consider how you might use any of this material in today's lesson.

Borrow or buy (perhaps from a thrift store) a scarf, tie, or other small piece of clothing or jewelry that is totally out of character for you. It may be outdated, gaudy, or otherwise not your style. Wear this to class and leave it on at least through the "Gather to Learn" segment.

LEADING THE CLASS

(1) Gather to Learn

❖ Greet the class members and introduce guests.

❖ Pray that those who have come today will recognize God's desire for honest leadership.

❖ Point out your scarf, jewelry, or tie. Comment on how much you love this new piece of clothing or jewelry, perhaps mentioning what a bargain you got. Call on several people and ask what they think of your great find.

❖ Reveal to the class that you wore

your new clothing as an object lesson. Make the point that since most people want to hear complimentary remarks, class members were (mostly) willing to oblige. Likewise, in today's lesson we will learn from Micah about prophets who say pleasant lies when other words are called for.

❖ Read aloud today's focus statement: **Some leaders are corrupt, lie to the people they are charged to protect, and then find associates who will support their evil ways. What can be done to end this dishonesty? God will judge and punish corrupt leaders and prophets.**

(2) Goal 1: Explore How Micah Confronted Corrupt Leaders

❖ Read "What Is a Prophet?" in Interpreting the Scripture to help the students understand this important role.

❖ Select a volunteer to read the words of the Lord according to Micah 3:5-12.

❖ Discuss these questions:
1. **Who do these words describe?** (Verses 5-7, 11 refer to prophets; verse 9 calls out "chiefs of the house of Israel"; verses 9-11 refer to rulers; and verse 11 includes priests.)
2. **How does Micah distinguish himself from other prophets?** (See 3:8 and "Filled with the Spirit" in Interpreting the Scripture.)
3. **Micah points out corruption among the leadership of Israel, which according to verse 11 includes taking "a bribe," "a price," and "money." Why does the leadership think they can get away with selling their services and**

influence? (See verse 11 concerning the Lord's presence and protection.)
4. **What does Micah say will happen to Israel because of these corrupt leaders?** (See 3:12, "Micah 3:9-12 in Understanding the Scripture, and "The Purpose of Judgment" in Interpreting the Scripture.)
5. **What would you say to these corrupt leaders?**

(3) Goal 2: Reflect on Reactions to Leaders Who Mislead and Deceive People

❖ Form small groups and assign each group to answer one of these questions, which you will read aloud?
Group 1: How do you react when you hear that a leader has betrayed trust by stealing from the church?
Group 2: How do you react when you hear that a church leader has been involved in an inappropriate sexual relationship?
Group 3: How do you react when you hear that a leader has engaged in behavior not condoned by the church such as drug or alcohol abuse?
❖ Brings the groups together. Invite each one to state their reactions in a few words. Then ask: **Recognizing that any response needs to be in proportion to the offense, what steps can the church take to restore a leader who has deceived its members?**

(4) Goal 3: Address Corruption in Leadership Within the Church and the Broader Community

❖ Read: **Although we have to be very careful about labeling specific groups of Christians or eras of** church history as corrupt, we can find particular instances of corruption that needed to be addressed with sweeping changes. One such corruption was the sale of indulgences during the Middle Ages. By purchasing an indulgence, one could receive forgiveness for personal sins, and even for the sins of others who were deceased. This became a huge moneymaking business that went far beyond the limits that the church had set. Because it brought much-needed money into the church coffers, even popes looked the other way as these sales soared between 1507 and 1567 when the indulgences were outlawed. As both a professor of theology at Wittenberg University and the priest at the City Church in the same city, Martin Luther spoke forcefully against this exploitative practice. His disdain for the sale of indulgences, which purportedly allowed people to buy salvation rather than rely on God's grace, played an important role in Luther's work in what would later be known as the Protestant Reformation. He was not taking potshots at the church from outside, but rather was intimately involved in the life and teachings of the church. Thus, he addressed corruption from the inside.

❖ Discuss these questions:

1. Where are we seeing corruption within the church?

2. What impact does this corruption have on the church itself?

3. What impact does this corruption have on the church's credibility in the wider community?

4. What steps can we take to address this corruption?

(5) *Continue the Journey*

❖ Pray that as the learners depart, they will vow to stand against corruption in the church and the broader community.

❖ Post information for next week's session on newsprint for the students to copy:

- Title: Justice, Love, and Humility
- Background Scripture: Micah 6
- Lesson Scripture: Micah 6:3-8
- Focus of the Lesson: People sometimes forget what a benefactor has done for them or they make insincere efforts to show gratitude. How will benefactors react to such forgetfulness or ingratitude? God instructs the unjust to be just, to love kindness, and to walk humbly with God.

❖ Challenge the adults to grow spiritually by completing one or more of these activities related to this week's session, which you have posted on newsprint for the students to copy.

(1) Be alert for information in the media about corrupt individuals who have damaged business, government, or the church. What prompted their actions? Who has been hurt? How can you speak out against this corruption? Is there anything you can do to help bring about healing?

(2) Read Jeremiah 26. Notice that verses 7-16 include conflicting responses to Jeremiah's message, including a call for his death (26:11). For what purpose is Micah's

work quoted in Jeremiah 26:18?

(3) Think about how conscientiously you approach whatever tasks God has called you to do. How faithful are you in fulfilling your responsibilities?

❖ Sing or read aloud "Go Forth for God."

❖ Conclude today's session by leading the class in this benediction adapted from Micah 6:8, which is the key verse for July 19: **Let us depart to do justice, and love kindness, and walk humbly with our God.**

UNIT 2: MICAH CALLS FOR JUSTICE AMONG UNJUST PEOPLE

JUSTICE, LOVE, AND HUMILITY

PREVIEWING THE LESSON

Lesson Scripture: Micah 6:3-8
Background Scripture: Micah 6
Key Verse: Micah 6:8

Focus of the Lesson:
People sometimes forget what a benefactor has done for them or they make insincere efforts to show gratitude. How will benefactors react to such forgetfulness or ingratitude? God instructs the unjust to be just, to love kindness, and to walk humbly with God.

Goals for the Learners:
(1) to learn how to honor God gratefully by exhibiting the character traits that God requires.
(2) to express feelings about living up to God's expectations for them to be just, loving, and humble.
(3) to lead the community into making God's requirements a reality.

Pronunciation Guide:

Baal (bay´ uhl) or (bah ahl´)   Moab (moh´ ab)
Balaam (bay´ luhm)   Naboth (nay´ both)
Balak (bay´ lak)   Omri (om ri´)
Beor (bee´ or)   Shittim (shi´ tim)
Gilgal (gil´ gal)   Sidon (si´ duhn)
hesed (hee´ sid)

Supplies:
Bibles, newsprint and marker, paper and pencils, hymnals

READING THE SCRIPTURE

NRSV

Lesson Scripture: Micah 6:3-8

3"O my people, what have I done to you?
 In what have I wearied you?
 Answer me!
4For I brought you up from the land of Egypt,
 and redeemed you from the house of slavery;
and I sent before you Moses, Aaron, and Miriam.
5O my people, remember now what King Balak of Moab devised,
 what Balaam son of Beor answered him,
and what happened from Shittim to Gilgal,
 that you may know the saving acts of the LORD."
6"With what shall I come before the LORD,
 and bow myself before God on high?
Shall I come before him with burnt offerings,
 with calves a year old?
7Will the LORD be pleased with thousands of rams,
 with ten thousands of rivers of oil?
Shall I give my firstborn for my transgression,
 the fruit of my body for the sin of my soul?"
8He has told you, O mortal, what is good;
 and what does the LORD require of you
but to **do justice, and** to **love kindness,**
 and to **walk humbly with your God?**

CEB

Lesson Scripture: Micah 6:3-8

3"My people, what did I ever do to you?
 How have I wearied you? Answer me!
4I brought you up out of the land of Egypt;
 I redeemed you from the house of slavery.
I sent Moses, Aaron, and Miriam before you.
5My people, remember what Moab's King Balak had planned,
 and how Balaam, Beor's son, answered him!
Remember everything from Shittim to Gilgal,
 that you might learn to recognize the righteous acts of the LORD!
 What does the LORD require?
6With what should I approach the LORD
 and bow down before God on high?
Should I come before him with entirely burned offerings,
 with year-old calves?
7Will the LORD be pleased with thousands of rams,
 with many torrents of oil?
Should I give my oldest child for my crime;
 the fruit of my body for the sin of my spirit?
8He has told you, human one, what is good and
 what the LORD requires from you:
  to **do justice, embrace faithful love, and walk humbly with your God.**

UNDERSTANDING THE SCRIPTURE

Introduction. Micah 6 contains a series of indictments and promises of punishment. The opening call for Judah to plead its case, as if in court, sums up the mood of this chapter. The Lord has a case against the people because they have disregarded the covenant. They have not worshiped God purely and, as a result, they have not acted with justice toward one another. This is the situation despite the fact that God has worked faithfully to save and preserve them (6:3-5). When the people have responded, they have responded the wrong way with outward signs of devotion (sacrifices) rather than true devotion that results in right living. Because of this God will bring disaster on Judah. The exact nature of the punishment is not specified, but it is clear that it will feature the basic and foundational features of life—food and harvest—failing to produce what they need.

Micah 6:1-2. Micah opens this section with a summons to court. Indeed, the language the prophet uses is common to legal cases. When the prophet says "the LORD has a controversy with his people" (6:2), he uses a term that literally means "court case." The case is not literally "tried," but the form of speech makes clear that the Lord has a formal indictment against the people. It is a common theme to call the natural elements to hear a case (Deuteronomy 32, especially verse 1). The call in Micah 6:1 to "rise" or literally "stand up" is also common in passages that challenge people to speak in their own defense (Jeremiah 1:17). The call to the mountains and hills is consistent with Israel's tradition of having multiple witnesses for a trial (Deuteronomy 19:15).

Micah 6:3-5. God calls Israel to remember its experience of salvation in order to return to faithful relationship with God. The rehearsal of Israel's history focuses on God rescuing the people from slavery in Egypt and guiding them to the Promised Land. The first note concerns God's gift of leaders: Moses, Aaron, and Miriam. These three siblings are prominent in the story of the Exodus, but the mention of Miriam is somewhat unique in passages like this. Next, Micah mentions Israel's experience with Balaam, the prophet-for-hire whom King Balak summoned to curse the Israelites (Numbers 22–24). Despite Balaam's intention to curse Israel, however, God caused his curse to come out as a blessing instead. Finally Micah mentions the trek to the Promised Land by referring to "from Shittim to Gilgal," the two camps on the east and west of the Jordan River, respectively.

Micah 6:6-7. The description of sacrifices is meant to answer the question of what is needed to humble oneself before God. The list of possible sacrifices progresses from possible to impossible to unthinkable. The expression "burnt offering" (6:6) is the only type of sacrifice the prophet mentions. This refers to an offering that was consumed completely on the altar, as opposed to some offerings that were eaten in whole or part by priests (Leviticus 2:3). Calves were typical animals used for burnt offerings, so it is not surprising that they are named as an example of a sacrifice. Next, Micah gives an incredibly large number in reference to the sacrifice of rams and oil. First Kings 3:4 says Solomon made a thousand sacrifices. Micah's reference, therefore, is meant to portray a number of sacrifices that is only possible for the wealthiest man in Israel! The final sacrifice named is the firstborn child. Although it is not known how widespread the practice of child sacrifice was in the ancient Near East, the Old Testament includes several examples of it (2 Kings 3:27). To make clear that God did not desire such a sacrifice, it was banned in Old Testament law (Leviticus 18:21). Micah mentions it here to raise the level of sacrifice to the ridiculous in order to show that God does not want sacrifices as the primary offering no matter what their price or value.

Micah 6:8. In contrast to Judah's readiness to offer sacrifices, God presents what is truly "good." This term refers to God's will for the world. Similar to Isaiah 1:17, Micah here presents the good in terms of how to treat one another as influenced by God's mercy.

Micah 6:9-12. In verse 9 the Lord here speaks to "the city," that is to Jerusalem, as a personification of the people of Judah. The problem God identifies is the same that Micah has already highlighted: The people cheat people in the marketplace ("wicked scales," 6:11) and oppress their neighbors (6:12). This activity is identified as "violence" (6:12) because it represents action directly opposed to the will and purpose of God.

Micah 6:13-15. God's punishment has already begun because God has spoken it. These verses are essentially a curse that Judah will recognize taking hold in the near future. The curse pertains to the frustration of the basic functions of life. Each step in a process of producing food or seeking nourishment will result only in failure of the goal. Verse 14 begins with the basic problem Judah will have: "You shall eat, but not be satisfied." Verse 15 speaks of the agricultural process that will not be finished: "You shall sow, but not reap."

Micah 6:16. The final indictment compares the people of Micah's time to Omri and Ahab, kings of Israel about one hundred years earlier. Omri was a very successful king by secular standards. But he introduced the worship of foreign gods into his kingdom. This came to a head when he married his son Ahab to Jezebel, the daughter of the king of Sidon. Jezebel was a worshiper of Baal and she made the Baal cult popular in Israel. Along with this worship of foreign gods came ethical practices that departed from Israelite traditions that emphasized justice. A prime example is when Ahab took the field of Naboth and had Naboth killed (1 Kings 21). Thus, Micah accused the wealthy Israelites of coveting fields and taking them (Micah 2:2).

INTERPRETING THE SCRIPTURE

Remember

Prophets like Micah seem supremely concerned about the actions of God's people. Indeed, as we have seen, they call out Israel for oppressing the poor or for abusing the powerless, to mention but two examples. But this concern for right action begins with right thinking, the right awareness of the nature of God. Or, put another way, the prophets call God's people to reflect on God's actions as preparation for doing the right thing. This way of approaching Judah's injustices recognizes that right action grows out of right thinking and right attitudes.

As Micah calls the people of Judah to reflect on God's deeds, his primary command is for them to "remember" (6:5). What they are to remember is the ways God delivered them, particularly how God brought them up from Egypt and escorted them safely to the land of Canaan. The importance of this brief sketch of Israel's salvation story is expressed in the statements that begin and end the historical summary. It begins in verse 5 with God asking, "O my people, what have I done to you? In what have I wearied you?" That is, God asks the rhetorical question, "In what ways have *I* depended or put demands on *you*?" The intended answer, of course, is "In no way." Israel's salvation was due to God's action alone. Israel did nothing to deserve it or to make it happen. At the end of the summary of Israel's experience, God says the purpose of remembering is "that you may know the saving acts of the LORD" (6:5). Micah summarizes what is to be remembered by mentioning specifically the experience Israel had with Balaam (Numbers 22–24). But then Micah gives the general reference "from Shittim to Gilgal," which encompasses the movement from wilderness to Canaan (Joshua 2:1; 4:19). The focus, however, is not on specific events, but on the memory of the past deeds that such memory might produce humility and compassion in God's people, people who had received compassion from God.

On Making Sacrifices

In Micah 6:6-7 the prophet downplays the practice of making sacrifices. The argument, however, is not against the practice of sacrifice per se, but against sacrifices made with the assumption that God wants primarily the sacrificial animal. Micah makes clear that first and foremost God wants the person who gives the sacrifice. A gift on an altar may be a legitimate expression of devotion to God if it is a sign of the human heart turned toward God. But Micah spoke to people who lacked the latter.

Micah's description of sacrifices begins with ordinary offerings. A burnt offering was a sacrifice of an animal that was completely consumed by fire. A calf could be given as a sacrifice after it was eight days old. Year-old calves would be more valuable as sacrifices (Leviticus 22:27). After these references, however, Micah begins to give increasingly extraordinary examples of sacrifices: "thousands of rams" and "ten thousands of rivers of oil." The final one is the most extreme: "my firstborn" (6:7). This reference is meant to be shocking. Child sacrifice is forbidden (Deuteronomy 12:31), and the prophets speak against anyone who practices it (Jeremiah 7:31). Nevertheless, it was known in the ancient world, and many non-Israelites thought of it as the ultimate sign of devotion to a god. Being aware of this practice, the Israelites specify that a sacrificial animal substitute for the firstborn child as a sacrifice (Exodus 13:11-13). By listing the firstborn child as though this were an acceptable sacrifice,

Micah raises to the absurd the value of things that could be sacrificed. The point is that no outward expression like this, no matter how valuable the sacrifice, did God desire.

What Does the Lord Require?

If God does not require sacrifices in the form of burnt offerings and physical gifts on altars, what is expected from those who are in relationship with God? When Micah asks this question, he poses it literally as, "What does the Lord seek from you?" This is a helpful way of putting it because the prophet says God does *not* seek sacrifices from us. Micah then answers this question of what God wants to get from us with three beautiful phrases: "do justice, love kindness, and walk humbly with your God" (6:8). These three expressions present three increasingly broad characterizations of life before God. They describe a way of life that ensures the kind of other-centeredness that would prevent the abuses and injustices Micah railed against.

To "do justice" means to do what is right in terms of God's expectations for the world. For Micah, as with Amos, this includes particularly the right treatment of the poor in the legal system and in settings in which the rich could take advantage of them. There is a tangible quality to this expectation. There is something to do. For Christians in North America, what needs to be done is perhaps more subtle or harder to determine than it was for people in Micah's day. Nevertheless, there are issues of justice related to the poor that are all around us. The treatment of those who are mentally ill, the conditions of our world that keep people in

poverty, and the fact that multitudes of people deal with hunger every day are but a few examples. Micah suggests God intends a world without the conditions that produce inequities and poverty. But God seeks us individually, and the church corporately, to do something to make the world fairer and more just.

While the first statement refers to specific action, the second describes a more general orientation in life: "love kindness." The word "kindness" is a rich term that may require more comment perhaps than justice. It translates a Hebrew word, *hesed*, that often refers to God's faithfulness to God's promises and the prophet's use of the term should be measured against such references. The word is sometimes translated "steadfast love" or "faithful loving kindness" or "covenant love." The term implies steadiness, reliability, and faithfulness to one's obligations. Since God's *hesed* for Israel is characterized by graciousness and unmerited care, it also implies mercy. Human expressions of *hesed* therefore include showing mercy and forgiveness and compassion to those around us. Micah says God requires us to "love" this way of life. That is, God requires a way of life oriented toward God's mercy and kindness. The word "love" in the Old Testament, however, does not refer to sentimental attachment or warm feelings; rather, love is also a covenant word. Thus, "love kindness" means "devote oneself to kindness."

The final statement of verse 8 is broader than the second, but it adds yet another characteristic of the person who stands in right relationship with God. "To walk humbly with your God" refers to action that is modest and careful. The term translated "humble" appears in the Old Testament otherwise only in Proverbs 11:2. It does not refer to downplaying one's ability, but to constant awareness of God's sovereignty. Such awareness produces in turn an awareness and consideration of other people. This broadest requirement to be in relationship with God sums up the first two. If a person really lives in humility before God, he or she will naturally do justice and show mercy and compassion as a result of having experienced justice and mercy from God.

SHARING THE SCRIPTURE

PREPARING TO TEACH

Preparing Our Hearts

Meditate on this week's devotional reading from Deuteronomy 10:12-22. What do you learn about God from this passage? What does the writer say that God requires of us? What comparisons can you draw between these verses and today's lesson Scripture from Micah 6:3-8?

Pray that you and the students will do what God wants so as to bring justice to all people.

Preparing Our Minds

Study the background Scripture from Micah 6 and the lesson Scripture from Micah 6:3-8.

Consider this question as you prepare the lesson: *How might a benefactor react to ingratitude?*

Write on newsprint:

❑ information for next week's lesson, found under "Continue the Journey."

❑ activities for further spiritual growth in "Continue the Journey."

Review the "Introduction," "The Big Picture," "Close-up," and "Faith in Action," which all precede the first lesson of this quarter. Consider how you might use any of this material in today's lesson.

LEADING THE CLASS

(1) Gather to Learn

❖ Greet the class members and introduce guests.

❖ Pray that those who have come today will commit themselves to be just, love kindness, and walk humbly with God.

❖ Read this story: **For many years, the small village of Elora in Ontario, Canada, was the beneficiary of financial gifts from Jack MacDonald, whose unpretentious manner and modest lifestyle in Seattle concealed his considerable wealth. Although Jack had never lived in Elora, his father, Frederick MacDonald, was born there in 1885. Jack honored a promise he had made to his dying father in 1970 to help look after this small town where the family's roots stretched back to the 1830s. He kept that promise by annually mailing a donation that was to be used for projects to benefit the entire community. Jack did so without fanfare, preferring to remain anonymous except to the small group of village leaders who received the money and determined how it was to be spent** for the good of the community. His donations helped build a new town hall, upgrade the park, provide new playground equipment, and construct an ice rink and community center. Jack's most recent gift was used to install an elevator so as to make the town hall accessible to everyone. When Jack died in 2013 at the age of 98, town leaders were surprised to hear from his estate lawyers that the town would continue to receive an annual gift of $25,000. The mayor remarked, "We had no idea how to react. . . . We were grateful for the money, but were still sad. It was like the end of a friendship with someone you never met."

❖ Ask: **Had you been a resident of Elora, what would have been your opinion of your town's benefactor and the gifts he provided?**

❖ Read aloud today's focus statement: **People sometimes forget what a benefactor has done for them or they make insincere efforts to show gratitude. How will benefactors react to such forgetfulness or ingratitude? God instructs the unjust to be just, to love kindness, and to walk humbly with God.**

(2) Goal 1: Learn How to Honor God Gratefully by Exhibiting the Character Traits that God Requires

❖ Solicit one volunteer to read Micah 6:3-5 and a second to read 6:6-7. Encourage the entire class to read verse 8, using whichever translations they have.

❖ Read "Micah 6:1-2" and "Micah 6:3-5" in Understanding the Scripture to help the adults understand that Micah is using the language of a court trial and that God recalls Israel's history.

❖ Ask these questions:
1. **What might God hope to accomplish by asking the people to remember their history with God?** (Micah is affirming the role of memory in encouraging the people to be unwavering in their commitment to follow God. See "Remember" in Interpreting the Scripture.)
2. **Micah 6:6-7 raises the issue of sacrifice as the worshiper inquires as to what kinds of offerings are needed to satisfy God. What offerings are suggested?** (See "On Making Sacrifices" in Interpreting the Scripture.)

(3) Goal 2: Express Feelings about Living Up to God's Expectations for the Learners to Be Just, Loving, and Humble

❖ Invite the adults to read again today's key verse, Micah 6:8, in unison.

❖ Read or retell "What Does the Lord Require?" in Interpreting the Scripture to clarify God's expectations as enumerated in Micah 3:8.

❖ Go around the room and ask each person to express his or her feelings about living up to these expectations in two or three descriptive words. Encourage the adults to be honest by expressing both positive and negative feelings. If they feel God's requirements are overwhelming, for example, they are free to say so. If they feel that acting with justice, loving-kindness, and humility will put them in a difficult position in their business or another setting, they are free to say so.

❖ Try to summarize the positive feelings you heard expressed as well as the negative feelings. Challenge the adults to see God's expectations as positive, even—and especially—if they prompt actions and attitudes that run counter to cultural expectations.

(4) Goal 3: Lead the Community into Making God's Requirements a Reality

❖ **Option:** Use the activity for Group 1 found on the page near the beginning of this quarter titled "Faith in Action: Acting with Justice"

❖ Form two groups and give each group a sheet of newsprint and a marker. Explain what each group is to do by reading the following bold-faced information aloud. Add ideas only if a group has difficulty getting started.

1. **Group 1 is to brainstorm mission and ministry opportunities that exist within our congregation and encourage participants to act with justice, kindness, and humility.** Ideas may include, for example, a church food pantry, a good Samaritan fund to help people pay rent and utilities, or a child care program that charges on a sliding scale based on income.

2. **Group 2 is to brainstorm currently existing projects within the community, perhaps through ecumenical or nonprofit groups, that encourage participants to act with justice, kindness, and humility.** Ideas may include a Christmas in July program that works on homes of people who cannot afford to paint, build a ramp, or make repairs; a literacy program at the local library to help adults learn to read; a friendly caller program where one person calls at a specified time each day to check in on someone who is ill or lonely.

❖ Reunite the groups and ask each one to present their ideas. Poll the class to see who is already involved in each project, and who else might be involved.

❖ Challenge the class members to make a commitment to take steps to act with the justice, love, and humility that God expects. Note that one does not need to be involved in a formal program to meet God's expectations, but programs such as those you have discussed today do provide a framework for active participation.

(5) Continue the Journey

❖ Pray that as the learners depart, they will make a commitment to act as God expects them to with justice, love, and humility.

❖ Post information for next week's session on newsprint for the students to copy:
- **Title: God Shows Clemency**
- **Background Scripture: Micah 7:11-20**
- **Lesson Scripture: Micah 7:14-20**
- **Focus of the Lesson: Sometimes evil and injustice are met not with corrective justice but are trumped by mercy. Who will meet evil and injustice with mercy rather than punishment? God will show compassion and faithfulness to God's people, even to the unjust.**

❖ Challenge the adults to grow spiritually by completing one or more of these activities related to this week's session, which you have posted on newsprint for the students to copy.

(1) Check out Heifer International (http://www.heifer.org) or another organization that works toward peace and justice by providing people with a way to better their own lives and the lives of others. Donate an animal to Heifer International on your own or in cooperation with several class members.

(2) Look for projects in your community that show love and kindness to people by doing something important for them that they cannot do for themselves. Find a hands-on way to participate in one of these projects.

(3) Pray that you and others will "walk humbly with your God" (3:8). In doing so, may you naturally show kindness and justice toward all people.

❖ Sing or read aloud "What Does the Lord Require."

❖ Conclude today's session by leading the class in this benediction adapted from Micah 6:8, which is the key verse for today's lesson: **Let us depart to do justice, and love kindness, and walk humbly with our God.**

UNIT 2: MICAH CALLS FOR JUSTICE AMONG UNJUST PEOPLE

GOD SHOWS CLEMENCY

PREVIEWING THE LESSON

Lesson Scripture: Micah 7:14-20
Background Scripture: Micah 7:11-20
Key Verse: Micah 7:18

Focus of the Lesson:

Sometimes evil and injustice are met not with corrective justice but are trumped by mercy. Who will meet evil and injustice with mercy rather than punishment? God will show compassion and faithfulness to God's people, even to the unjust.

Goals for the Learners:

(1) to learn of God's mercy even when punishment seems in order.
(2) to reflect on experiences when God's mercy and compassion were more than expected.
(3) to carry out acts of mercy and compassion.

Pronunciation Guide:

Bashan (bay´ shuhn)
Gilead (gil´ ee uhd)
hesed (hee´ sid)

Supplies:

Bibles, newsprint and marker, paper and pencils, hymnals

READING THE SCRIPTURE

NRSV
Lesson Scripture: Micah 7:14-20
¹⁴Shepherd your people with your
    staff,
  the flock that belongs to you,
which lives alone in a forest
    in the midst of a garden land;

CEB
Lesson Scripture: Micah 7:14-20
¹⁴Shepherd your people with your
    staff,
  the sheep of your inheritance,
  those dwelling alone in a forest in
    the midst of Carmel.

let them feed in Bashan and Gilead
as in the days of old.
[15]As in the days when you came out
of the land of Egypt,
show us marvelous things.
[16]The nations shall see and be
ashamed
of all their might;
they shall lay their hands on their
mouths;
their ears shall be deaf;
[17]they shall lick dust like a snake,
like the crawling things of the
earth;
they shall come trembling out of
their fortresses;
they shall turn in dread to the
LORD our God,
and they shall stand in fear of you.
**[18]Who is a God like you, pardoning
iniquity
and passing over the
transgression
of the remnant of your
possession?
He does not retain his anger forever,
because he delights in showing
clemency.**
[19]He will again have compassion
upon us;
he will tread our iniquities under
foot.
You will cast all our sins
into the depths of the sea.
[20]You will show faithfulness to Jacob
and unswerving loyalty to
Abraham,
as you have sworn to our ancestors
from the days of old.

Let them graze in Bashan and Gilead,
as a long time ago.
[15]As in the days when you came out
of the land of Egypt,
I will show Israel wonderful
things.
[16]Nations will see and be ashamed of
all their strength;
they will cover their mouths;
their ears will be deaf.
[17]They will lick dust like the snake,
like things that crawl on the
ground.
They will come trembling from their
strongholds to the LORD our
God;
they will dread and fear you!
**[18]Who is a God like you, pardoning
iniquity,
overlooking the sin of the few
remaining for his inheritance?
He doesn't hold on to his anger
forever;
he delights in faithful love.**
[19]He will once again have compassion on us;
he will tread down our iniquities.
You will hurl all our sins into the
depths of the sea.
[20]You will provide faithfulness to
Jacob, faithful love to Abraham,
as you swore to our ancestors a
long time ago.

UNDERSTANDING THE SCRIPTURE

Introduction. Micah 7:11-20 concludes the Book of Micah with hope
of restoration and assurance that God
will forgive the people of Judah for
their sins. This hope includes three
main features: God will lead the people as a shepherd; the nations that
once oppressed and abused God's

people will be ashamed of their actions; and God will forgive the people of Judah whom God punished. By concluding this way, the Book of Micah conforms to the pattern of other prophetic books that begin with and/or are dominated by proclamations of judgment and then move to promises of restoration. This pattern reflects more broadly an understanding of God in the Old Testament. God judges and punishes indeed, but God's judgment is for the purpose of restoration and renewal.

Micah 7:11-13. The first three verses of the background Scripture present a grand vision of a day that is completely new for Judah and the world. "Day" here does not mean a twenty-four-hour period, but an epoch that begins definitively at a point in time. The expression is similar to the "day of the LORD" in Amos 5:18-20 and other prophetic texts. It is a world-changing "day." This day in Micah will be marked first and foremost by the rebuilding of the walls of Jerusalem. This does not refer merely to urban renewal or a city's revitalization. Reference to tearing down the walls had come to signify God's judgment (see Psalm 80:12). Now the rebuilding of the walls signals God's forgiveness and restoration. The second part of verse 11 refers to borders expanding, but the meaning is not clear. This cryptic line may speak, as Isaiah 26:15 does, of expanded borders as another sign of renewed life and vigor brought on by God's forgiveness. The next major event of this "day" will be the movement of nations to Judah that once oppressed Judah. Later in the passage the prophet will speak of the nations being ashamed of their prior abuses of power (see 7:16). The image

here seems to be like Isaiah 2:2-4 and Micah 4:1-5, passages that depict the nations streaming to Jerusalem to receive instruction from Israel's God. Jerusalem will be recognized as the place of universal truth and blessing. But the rest of the earth on that day will become desolate. Zion and the rest of the earth will be separated sharply by fruitfulness and blessing on the one hand and devastation on the other hand.

Micah 7:14-15. Micah draws on one of the most enduring images of God in the Old Testament: God as shepherd. Although best known from Psalm 23 in which an individual speaks of God as "my shepherd," the label is more commonly applied to God's leadership of Israel. For example, Psalm 100 uses the language of sheep and shepherd to describe Israel's relationship to God. Micah alludes to the Exodus event, which was the primary time that God shepherded the people as a whole (see Psalm 80). The reference to the Lord's staff is reminiscent of Psalm 23:4 ("your rod and your staff—they comfort me"). Micah extends the imagery to speak of God taking God's people into good pastures, and he also identifies the places of pasturing: Bashan and Gilead. These are areas just east of the Jordan River in what today is known as the Golan Heights. They are areas well known for having lush pastures and therefore producing healthy livestock (see the reference to cows of Bashan to refer to rich Israelites in Amos 4:1). Hence, the image of God as shepherd does not suggest God provides merely the necessities of life, but rather provides abundantly for the Israelite people.

Micah 7:16-17. When God leads the people into their good pastures, the nations who oppressed them "shall see and be ashamed" (7:16). "Ashamed" may have the connotation of "be shamed," that is, they will have public opinion turn on them. Once they were considered powerful and mighty. Their armies conquered vast territories; they took whatever they wanted. But when God comes as shepherd of Israel their power will be revealed as an illusion. It cannot match the power of the King of the universe. This notion of the nations turning in fear and awe to Israel's God is a common one in the Old Testament. In Micah 4:1-5 the prophet pictures the nations streaming to Jerusalem to be instructed by God's law. This image in turn provides the basis for the Gentile mission in the New Testament. The hope for and openness to people outside the covenant community is grounded in passages like Micah 7:16-17. To be sure, the language here is of shame and fear, but the attitude of the nations that the prophet envisions is repentance. Repentance will be required for anyone who seeks the kingdom of God. It is, in fact, an important dividing line between those who are in right relationship with God and those who are not.

Micah 7:18-20. The Book of Micah ends with a declaration about God's character. God is by nature patient and forgiving. This declaration is almost a paraphrase of a formula that appears numerous times in the Old Testament: The Lord is "merciful and gracious, slow to anger, and abounding in steadfast love" (Exodus 34:6). God's forgiveness is a sign of God's "faithfulness." As noted in the previous lesson, this word translates the Hebrew term *hesed*, which is sometimes rendered "steadfast love." The term refers to covenant love or covenant faithfulness. Thus, God fulfills the promises to Abraham by forgiving Abraham's descendants and allowing them to continue in divine favor. God promised Abraham that he would be the father of a great nation (Genesis 12:1-3), and Micah 7:11-20 promises that pledge will still be realized. The people of Judah will remain, if only as a remnant, in order to realize this promise. But more important, God promised to work through Abraham to bring blessing to all humankind. Abraham would be the conduit of blessing to every tribe. So here God continues to show that work for the human race by showing to the descendants of Abraham mercy and forgiveness.

INTERPRETING THE SCRIPTURE

The Lord, Merciful and Gracious

The Book of Micah ends appropriately with a grand statement about the nature of God as forgiving and forbearing. Until this point the book has been dominated by Micah's critique of Judah and his promise of Jerusalem's destruction. Time and again the prophet cataloged Judah's unfaithfulness to God, which was expressed in the mistreatment of the poor and vulnerable. The cry "the faithful have disappeared from the land" (Micah 7:2) characterized the state of Judean society.

Therefore, Micah declared, "Zion shall be plowed as a field; Jerusalem shall become a heap of ruins, and the mountain of the house a wooded height" (Micah 3:12). But judgment is not the last word. God will forgive and restore Judah.

This conclusion to the Book of Micah is important both to understand the nature of true prophecy in the Old Testament and to understand the true nature of God as the Old Testament presents it. The image some people have of the prophets is that that of angry messengers of a wrathful God. But Micah 7:18-20 would seem to argue that the opposite is true, at least concerning the nature of God.

The prophet begins the presentation of God's character with a question: "Who is a God like you, pardoning iniquity and passing over the transgression of the remnant of your possession?" (7:18, key verse). The question is rhetorical. It expects the answer "No one!" The prophet then makes a declaration about God's character: "He does not retain his anger forever, because he delights in showing clemency" (7:18). This hardly sounds like the vengeful God many imagine they find in the Old Testament. The prophet does not say God does not get angry and does not punish God's people. He does insist, however, that God's anger and judgment are not the final word on God's interaction with the people. There is, in the end, forgiveness and reconciliation. Most important, the accent is on the latter.

What Micah says about God seems to be drawn from a well-known theological statement that recurs throughout the Old Testament. It appears first in Exodus 34:6: "A God merciful and gracious, slow to anger, and abounding in steadfast love and faithfulness." As the statement continues in verse 7, it does include God's wrath but clearly focuses on divine grace. The context of the declaration is God's response to the Israelites worshiping the golden calf. Instead of destroying the people as God considered doing (Exodus 32:10), God forgives. Often when these words about God are repeated, only God's grace is mentioned. One of the most famous examples is Jonah 4:2 in which the prophet sent to Nineveh complains that God is gracious! Indeed, God is much more forgiving than Jonah, who would have destroyed the residents of Nineveh. Hence, the question in Micah 7:18, "Who is a God like you," is meant perhaps to compare God in God's mercy to us with our bent toward anger and retaliation. God is more gracious than we can ever comprehend, and Micah makes that clear about God's nature.

But Micah's statement about God's nature is not just that God forgives, though that is quite significant. The prophet also says God deals with our sins and overcomes them: "he will tread our iniquities under foot" (Micah 7:19). Indeed, God treats our sins as an enemy and conquers them. Micah also says in the next part of the same verse that God "will cast all our sins into the depths of the sea." So Micah ends not just with restoration and the promise of God's grace but also with the declaration that God takes the initiative in overcoming our sin.

The Nations Shall See

One of the most striking themes in Micah 7 is the idea that the nations will perceive the power of Israel's God and cower in fear before this God. In verse 12 Micah refers to two nations, Egypt and Assyria, who were traditional foes. At the time of Micah's ministry Assyria was a major threat from the east, and Egypt was always a dominant power to the south and west of Judah. Hence, Micah promises a grand reversal of fortunes. The language, however, poses at least two problems. First, it seems to suggest a triumphalism in which Judah basks in its superiority over these nations. Second, the description of the nations' response to the Lord may sound cruel. Images of them licking the dust (see 7:17) seem sadistic and the question of how this imagery fits Christian theology is appropriate to ask.

To address the question of triumphalism, we must recognize the setting of Micah's audience. They are at the mercy of the great empires of their day, especially Assyria. Therefore, this passage does not and cannot encourage gloating over victory or excessive pride over Judah's place in the world. In fact, Micah's grand predictions about the nations humbly coming to Judah seem almost delusional given the state of military affairs in that day. But the predictions are neither arrogant and triumphal nor delusional. They are faith-filled visions of the world ruled by God, a world in which powerful nations will come under the rule of the heavenly king.

Concerning the question of cruelty, we should recognize two points about this passage. The language of "licking the dust" is an exaggerated way of saying the nations will come humbly before God. Indeed, the message here is that they "shall see and be ashamed" (of *their* arrogance and cruelty) and "they shall come trembling" (7:17) before God. The other point, to which we have already alluded, is that the picture the prophet paints is of nations brought to justice. The Assyrians were particularly well known for their ruthless assaults on local populations. They even left behind artwork of their exploits that sometimes depicted piles of dead bodies. So the language that the prophet uses is in response to the terror such nations struck in their enemies. The aim of the promise therefore is that these perpetrators of violence would one day be brought to justice.

Shepherd of Israel

The image of God as shepherd is the dominant image in Micah 7. The modern Western reader may get sentimental impressions from this image. For the people of Judah, however, it has profound theological and spiritual effects that were not at all sentimental. The shepherd image was a distinctly royal image in the ancient Near East. So for Judah to call on God to "shepherd your people" (7:14) was to ask God for protection as a king would be expected to give to his people. They expected the Lord to come to their aid, just as people expected their human kings to fend off enemies who would threaten them.

The expectations Judah had when it called on God as shepherd also carried with them a sense of dependence and helplessness. The people looked to God for direction and care. They did not pretend they could protect themselves or secure their own future. In the Old Testament this way of being before God is a model of how to live in relationship with the Lord. It implies humility and faith, trust and dependence. This is the type of relationship assumed whenever God's people collectively or individually called on God as shepherd (Psalm 23; 80; 100).

SHARING THE SCRIPTURE

PREPARING TO TEACH

Preparing Our Hearts

Meditate on this week's devotional reading from Psalm 13 in which the psalmist cries out for deliverance from his enemies. How would you describe the psalmist's relationship with God? What do you learn about the psalmist and his faith? How can this psalm, which includes both a complaint and confident praise to God, be a model prayer for you?

Pray that you and the students will recognize and give thanks for God's mercy.

Preparing Our Minds

Study the background Scripture Micah 7:11-20 from and the lesson Scripture from Micah 7:14-20.

Consider this question as you prepare the lesson: *Who responds to evil and injustice with mercy rather than punishment?*

Write on newsprint:
❏ information for next week's lesson, found under "Continue the Journey."
❏ activities for further spiritual growth in "Continue the Journey."

Review the "Introduction," "The Big Picture," "Close-up," and "Faith in Action," which all precede the first lesson of this quarter. Consider how

you might use any of this material in today's lesson.

LEADING THE CLASS

(1) Gather to Learn

❖ Greet the class members and introduce guests.

❖ Pray that those who have come today will be open to receiving God's mercy for themselves and extending that mercy to others.

❖ Read this story as reported by Rose Arce of CNN in April 2013: **A chance meeting between Anthony Colon, who was visiting an imprisoned friend, and Michael Rowe, who, along with two other men, had gunned down Anthony's unarmed older brother in East Harlem, became a turning point in the lives of both men. Anthony at first had been filled with rage, but in the intervening years had married, became the father of two children, and became a man of faith. When the two men first saw each other, Mr. Rowe's response was to duck, fearing reprisals. Mr. Colon, however, walked over to him and said, "Brother, I've been praying for you. I forgave you. I've been praying I would see you again." Mr. Rowe had taken responsibility for his actions. He was married, had three children, and had earned college degrees, all while serving a sentence of twenty years to life. Mr.**

Colon began to visit and offer regular support. He credits his faith in God with being able to forgive. And his forgiveness and works of mercy have enabled Mr. Rowe to declare, "God has a purpose for me. God has a purpose for us," to which Mr. Colon added, "Yes, *us*."

❖ Provide a few moments of silence for the adults to reflect on these questions: **Had you been Mr. Colon, would you have allowed God's mercy to work through you in such a life-changing way? Why or why not?**

❖ Break the silence by reading aloud today's focus statement: **Sometimes evil and injustice are met not with corrective justice but are trumped by mercy. Who will meet evil and injustice with mercy rather than punishment? God will show compassion and faithfulness to God's people, even to the unjust.**

(2) Goal 1: Learn of God's Mercy Even When Punishment Seems in Order

❖ Observe that we will conclude our study of Micah today. Set the final scene by reading "Micah 7:11-13" in Understanding the Scripture.

❖ Choose a volunteer to read Micah 7:14-20.

❖ Discuss these questions:

1. **Much of Micah's prophecy has been a scathing critique of God's people and a foretelling of the destruction of Jerusalem. How has the tone of his prophecy changed here in chapter 7?**

2. **What do you learn about God from this passage?** (See "The Lord, Merciful and Gracious" in Interpreting the Scripture.)

3. **What associations does the**

image of the shepherd have for the people to whom Micah prophesied? (See "Shepherd of Israel" in Interpreting the Scripture.)

4. **What do you learn about "the nations" in verses 16-17?** (See "The Nations Shall See" in Interpreting the Scripture.)

5. **Where do you see hope in today's passage?**

6. **Micah received prophecies from the Lord in the eighth century before Jesus. We can read them in light of the history of Israel and Judah, and we can also read them as words for God's people in the twenty-first century. What might God be saying to the church today through Micah?**

❖ Summarize this portion of the lesson by reading the "Introduction" in Understanding the Scripture.

(3) Goal 2: Reflect on Experiences When God's Mercy and Compassion Were More Than Expected

❖ Lead the class in reading today's key verse, Micah 7:18.

❖ Encourage the students to discuss these two questions with a partner or small group.

1. **How have you found Micah's description of God to be true in your own life?**

2. **What instances can you recall of God's mercy being far more than you had expected?**

(4) Goal 3: Carry Out Acts of Mercy and Compassion

❖ Read: **John Wesley, the founder of Methodism, not only talked about "works of mercy," which he defined** as "doing good," but he also practiced a wide range of such works. His acts of mercy helped the whole person—body, mind, and soul. According to http://gbgm-umc.org/umw/wesley/mission.stm, he is reported to have:

1. "lived modestly and given all he could to help people who were poor;
2. visited people in prison and provided spiritual guidance, food, and clothing to them;
3. spoken out against slavery and forbade it in Methodism;
4. founded schools at the Foundry in London, Bristol, and Newcastle;
5. published books, pamphlets, and magazines for the education and spiritual edification of people;
6. taught and wrote about good health practices and even dispensed medicine from his chapels."

❖ Discuss these questions:

1. Wesley demonstrated Christian love and mercy by addressing the issues of his day: poverty, prison conditions, slavery, inadequate education, and health care. What issues need to be addressed in your community? (Make a list on newsprint.)
2. Which of these issues might we as a class or congregation try to address?
3. Which groups in the community or church could we work with to show mercy to others?
4. Who will take responsibility for pursing our idea(s) and report back with a plan of action?

(5) Continue the Journey

❖ Pray that as the learners depart, they will seek opportunities to tell the good news of God's mercy and to demonstrate that mercy to others.

❖ Post information for next week's session on newsprint for the students to copy:

■ Title: Our Redeemer Comes
■ Background Scripture: Isaiah 59; Psalm 89:11-18
■ Lesson Scripture: Isaiah 59:15-21
■ Focus of the Lesson: Sometimes everything around us seems violent, cruel, and immoral. Who will bring justice and righteousness to a troubled world? Isaiah and the psalmist promise a time when God will come as a redeemer with a foundation of righteousness and justice and will place God's spirit on those who repent of their sins.

❖ Challenge the adults to grow spiritually by completing one or more of these activities related to this week's session, which you have posted on newsprint for the students to copy.

(1) Recall and give thanks for the mercy and forgiveness God has shown to you. Pass that clemency on to someone who has wronged you.

(2) Examine your attitudes toward persons who have committed serious crimes. Would you be able to forgive them? Could you go offer forgiveness and support to such persons, even as Anthony Colon befriended and supported his brother's killer?

(3) **Write a poem or prayer in which you express your gratitude for God's mercy in your life.**

❖ Sing or read aloud "There's a Wideness in God's Mercy."

❖ Conclude today's session by leading the class in this benediction adapted from Micah 6:8, which is the key verse for July 19: **Let us depart to do justice, and love kindness, and walk humbly with our God.**

UNIT 3: ADVOCATES OF JUSTICE FOR ALL
OUR REDEEMER COMES

PREVIEWING THE LESSON

Lesson Scripture: Isaiah 59:15-21
Background Scripture: Isaiah 59; Psalm 89:11-18
Key Verse: Isaiah 59:20

Focus of the Lesson:
Sometimes everything around us seems violent, cruel, and immoral. Who will bring justice and righteousness to a troubled world? Isaiah and the psalmist promise a time when God will come as a redeemer with a foundation of righteousness and justice and will place God's spirit upon those who repent of their sins.

Goals for the Learners:
(1) to explore how God promises a renewed covenant relationship.
(2) to share feelings about the cruelty and violence of society.
(3) to express gratitude and joy for God's salvation from worldly dangers and work toward a renewed community.

Pronunciation Guide:
shalem (shaw lame´)   shalom (shah lohm´)

Supplies:
Bibles, newsprint and marker, paper and pencils, hymnals, news magazines, scissors, glue, large sheets of construction paper

READING THE SCRIPTURE

NRSV
Lesson Scripture: Isaiah 59:15-21
15bThe LORD saw it, and it displeased him
   that there was no justice.
16He saw that there was no one,
   and was appalled that there was

CEB
Lesson Scripture: Isaiah 59:15-21
The LORD looked and was upset at
   the absence of justice.
16Seeing that there was no one,
   and astonished that no one would
   intervene,

no one to intervene;
so his own arm brought him victory,
　and his righteousness upheld him.
[17]He put on righteousness like a
　　breastplate,
　and a helmet of salvation on his
　　head;
he put on garments of vengeance for
　clothing,
　and wrapped himself in fury as in
　　a mantle.
[18]According to their deeds, so will he
　repay;
　wrath to his adversaries, requital
　　to his enemies;
　to the coastlands he will render
　　requital.
[19]So those in the west shall fear the
　name of the LORD,
　and those in the east, his glory;
for he will come like a pent-up
　stream
　that the wind of the LORD drives
　　on.
**[20]And he will come to Zion as
　　Redeemer,**
**to those in Jacob who turn from
　　transgression, says the LORD.**
[21]And as for me, this is my covenant
with them, says the LORD: my spirit
that is upon you, and my words that
I have put in your mouth, shall not
depart out of your mouth, or out of
the mouths of your children, or out
of the mouths of your children's children, says the LORD, from now on and
forever.

God's arm brought victory,
upheld by righteousness,
　[17]putting on righteousness as
　　armor
and a helmet of salvation on his
　head,
putting on garments of vengeance,
and wrapping himself in a cloak
　of zeal.
[18]God will repay according to their
　actions:
wrath to his foes, retribution to
　enemies,
retribution to the coastlands,
　[19]so those in the west will fear the
　LORD's name,
and those in the east will fear
　God's glory.
It will come like a rushing river
　that the LORD's wind drives on.
**[20]A redeemer will come to Zion
　　and to those in Jacob who stop
　　rebelling,**
says the LORD.
[21]As for me, this is my covenant
with them, says the LORD. My spirit,
which is upon you, and my words,
which I have placed in your mouth
won't depart from your mouth, nor
from the mouths of your descendants,
nor from the mouths of your descendants' children, says the LORD forever and always.

UNDERSTANDING THE SCRIPTURE

Introduction. Both passages that
make up the background Scripture
are liturgical in character and both
focus on the issues of justice and
righteousness. Isaiah 59 seems to be
part of a service of worship in which
the people complain that God has
forsaken them. (The complaint is
assumed in Isaiah 59 but not stated.)
The passage probably dates to the
Babylonian exile, that time when
the people of Judah were defeated

and carried away to live in a foreign land. The prophet declares, however, that their trouble has come because they acted unjustly by deceiving and abusing their fellow Israelites (Isaiah 59:2-8). The people then confess their sinfulness and look to God as their redeemer (Isaiah 59:9-20). The passage concludes with God's assurance that a better day is coming and that day would be identified by God's salvation and Israel's faithfulness (Isaiah 59:21). Psalm 89:11-18 presents the Israelites' confession that God is both powerful and good and therefore should be praised. This psalm thus presents the foundation for Israel's goodness: God is righteous and just by nature and calls God's people to be the same.

Isaiah 59:1-8. The beginning of Isaiah 59 sounds like part of a lament or complaint like those that appear in the Psalms (for example, Psalm 74). That is, verse 1 seems to respond to a complaint that God is unable or unwilling to save God's people. The prophet responds to this charge by saying that God is not withholding salvation. The problem is Israel's sin. It is creating a barrier to the Israelites receiving the mercy God intends for them to have. The statement in verse 2 is quite striking. It declares that Israel's sins have hidden God's face. The psalmist often complains that God hides God's face, a sign of divine displeasure. But here it is the sins of the people that cause God's face to be hidden. How powerful sin is! It can blind people even to the goodness and power of God that is right in front of them. The specific sins listed in verses 3-4 are similar to those noted by Amos and Micah: The people have dealt with others dishonestly and have brought unjust lawsuits. As the prophet expands on these sins, however, he describes them in terms of the characteristics of people, not just things people do. They hatch evil and spin it like a web (59:5); they travel paths of violence and injustice (59:7-9). The people who act this way act against justice and do not understand peace. But their sins are so shockingly bad that they are obvious to anyone who has eyes to see. They cannot be covered up (59:6).

Isaiah 59:9-11. This section continues the prophet's response to the complaint that God's hand is too short to save (see 59:1). It declares that Israel gropes in darkness because of the abundant sins described in verses 2-8. The dominant image is of Israel as a blind person who feels her way along a wall but who stumbles readily. Nevertheless, the people know of God's salvation and hope for it. It is currently absent, however, because of their sinfulness.

Isaiah 59:12-20. Following the prophet's declaration of the people's sins, this section now seems to present the people's confession of that sin. "Our transgressions before you are many" is similar to David's confession when Nathan confronted him about Bathsheba (2 Samuel 12:13). But the confession turns to confidence that God will save since no human can act rightly. This section assumes Israel has suffered defeat and humiliation at the hands of enemies. At other places in Isaiah such defeat is interpreted as a sign of God's wrath (Isaiah 10:5). This may be the understanding here as well. But this section seems also to say that the punishment has been enough. A common theme of the prophets is that God sends enemy armies to punish Israel, but those armies go too far.

They act arrogantly and strike too hard. So God must come and correct the enemy. For example, Zechariah 1:15 declares, "I am extremely angry with the nations that are at ease; for I was only a little angry, they made the disaster worse." This or a similar idea may lie behind Isaiah 59. Now God will come to Jerusalem as "Redeemer" (59:20). The background for the concept of redemption in the Old Testament was the realm of inheritance, commerce, and financial debt (see, for example, Ruth 4:1-12). If a person became indebted, for example, he might have to sell his land that was inherited and passed on through his family in order to pay off what he owed. (I use the masculine pronoun here because males would have been responsible for such economic matters in ancient Israel.) If things got worse he might have to sell his children into slavery or sell himself into slavery in order to satisfy the indebtedness. The only person who might help someone in situations like these would have been a near relative who had financial means to buy back, or "redeem," those sold or lost.

Isaiah 59:21. Now God's voice enters the liturgy, declaring that a new day is coming for the Israelites. The new day will be marked by God's continual presence. God's face will no longer be hidden and God's word will be heard and honored by the people.

Psalm 89:11-18. This portion of Psalm 89 includes a grand declaration that God reigns over the whole cosmos because God created it all (89:11-12). But most important, divine power is directed by God's fairness and goodness. The psalm expresses this by saying that "righteousness and justice are the foundation of your throne" (89:14). After this declaration of God's character the psalmist describes the fortunate state of those who recognize God's reign (89:15-17). Such people find their strength in God, not in themselves. Moreover, they understand all legitimate authority acts in ways that are consistent with God's reign (89:18).

INTERPRETING THE SCRIPTURE

A Redeemer Will Come

One of the most powerful images for God in the Old Testament is the image of redeemer. The word is used often in contemporary religious speech that draws from passages like Isaiah 59:20. A popular hymn by Fanny Crosby proclaims, "redeemed, how I love to proclaim it!" Despite the popularity of this description of God, however, the image is often not appreciated for the radical idea about God it communicates.

It is hard to imagine the shame a person would feel if he lost his ancestral land and, worse, members of his family because he was in such debt. People today who have experienced the trauma of bankruptcy or foreclosure may have some sense of what this would have been like. The deep feelings of failure and loss may also be present in those who go through divorce or similar disruptions. But the extent of loss and the feelings of guilt and shame probably cannot be appreciated completely. Nevertheless, this type of circumstance is the backdrop to the notion of God as redeemer. Furthermore, if we truly consider our own lives and the moral and spiritual debt we have due to our unfaithfulness to God, we will begin to gain some appreciation for the power of the image.

Isaiah 59:20, today's key verse, speaks of God as redeemer specifically in relation to the city of Jerusalem and the central place in the city where the Temple once stood. It declares, "he will come to Zion as Redeemer." When the Babylonians destroyed the city, the Israelites interpreted the event as punishment for their sin. Isaiah 40:2 speaks of the city's circumstances as one of indentured servanthood, as though Zion had been sold for its debts of sinfulness. But the prophet also declares that now Zion's service is over. Isaiah 59:20 makes clear that the end of that service comes because God acts as a redeemer.

The image of God as redeemer is powerful for at least two reasons. First, it speaks of the magnitude of God's love and the intimacy of God's relationship with us. As redeemer, God acts as "next of kin." Second, the redeemer image suggests that we who are redeemed are completely dependent on God's goodness, on God's willingness to "buy us back" from the sinfulness that enslaves us.

The Warrior Dressed in Righteousness

In Isaiah 59 God appears also as a warrior to defeat those who do harm to God's people. The idea that God is a warrior is one of the most disturbing presentations of God in the Bible. What does it mean to suggest God "fights" and that God makes war?

Furthermore, what does it say about God and God's relationship with humankind that God considers some people enemies so as to fight with them?

It is important to recognize first that God comes as a warrior to fight for justice and to fight for those who have no ability to fight for themselves. For anyone who would argue that the divine warrior supports or goes out with a human army, Isaiah 59 will hardly allow it (as does practically every passage that portrays God as warrior). Note that Isaiah 59 says that God comes as a warrior because no human actors have acted justly. God must take the matter of justice on God's own self. Note also that Zion, which God defends, is helpless to act on its own. This passage is not a justification for humans to act violently. In fact, the passage suggests just the opposite. Zion cannot act on its own, and that is why God acts.

The descriptions of God's dress for battle also indicate much about what it means for God to do battle as a warrior. It is perhaps not surprising that the prophet says the Lord is "wrapped in fury" and comes wearing "garments of vengeance" (Isaiah 59:17). This sounds like war language, but it is crucial to recognize that God's armor—the implements of the warrior's uniform—consists of "a helmet of salvation" and "righteousness" as a breastplate (59:17). Christian readers will perhaps recognize these expressions as part of the "whole armor of God" Paul urges Christians to put on in Ephesians 6:10-17. When Paul instructs members of the church to put on these protective coverings, he is really urging them to depend on God. Isaiah 59 indicates that God comes to people in need of help with salvation and righteousness. The two terms help explain what it means for God to be a warrior. God comes to save, not to destroy. God's fury may cause harm to those who are unjust, but that is God's attempt to correct and set the world aright. God comes to uphold righteousness. Righteousness is that force that holds the creation together in right order. So God's work as warrior is intended to restore the harmony and well-being that God intended but has been disrupted by injustice.

One final note about the portrait of God as warrior establishing well-being: When Isaiah 59:18 says God "repays" and brings "requital" it uses a verb from the Hebrew root *shalem*. This is the same root word from which *shalom* comes. Often translated "peace," this word, like the verbs that come from the same root, really refers to wholeness and completeness. It is much like "righteousness" in that sense. So God does not repay enemies as if to get even or seek revenge. Rather, God acts to restore order, to reestablish shalom. That is the work of God as warrior.

God Comes for Zion

It has already been noted that God comes to fight for those who cannot defend themselves. Isaiah 59:20a identifies those God defends as "Zion," as the city of God personified to represent its people. Two features of Zion help us understand why this city is so important. First, Isaiah 59:20b identifies the people of Zion as those "who

turn from transgressions." That is, these are people who repent. Repentance refers to living without pretense or pride, without confidence in one's own ability or goodness. Such people live in humility, and God relies on them to work for peace in the world. So it is logical that God defends them, for the world's future hinges on their well-being. Second, in other passages that speak of Zion as an ideal place that God defends, the people there are those who participate in God's attempt to establish righteousness and justice on earth (see Psalms 15 and 24). They are people with "clean hands and pure hearts" (Psalm 24:4). In other words, Zion is presented as the place where human beings fully acknowledge God's reign over the earth and over the human community. Zion represents the ideal community in which God's vision for the world—mercy, compassion, justice, and truth—actually controls the community.

With this understanding of Zion and its people, it is no wonder Isaiah 59 says God comes to defend and redeem it. We must acknowledge that this understanding of Zion is a vision, a dream of sorts. No gathering of human beings ever lives up to such an ideal. Nevertheless, it is important that we do not lose such gatherings of people who strive to represent God's will. On its best days the church is such a gathering. As we come together to worship we declare, "The Lord reigns!" and strive to allow God's reign to be a reality in our lives.

SHARING THE SCRIPTURE

PREPARING TO TEACH

Preparing Our Hearts

Meditate on this week's devotional reading from Exodus 6:2-8. What good news does God have for the Israelites who are enslaved in Egypt? How did the people receive this news? For what reasons in your own life do you need a deliverer—someone to rescue you from a difficult situation? Whom will you call?

Pray that you and the students will trust God to fulfill covenant promises.

Preparing Our Minds

Study the background Scripture from Isaiah 59 and Psalm 89:11-18. The lesson Scripture is from Isaiah 59:15-21.

Consider this question as you prepare the lesson: *Who will bring justice and righteousness to a troubled world?*

Write on newsprint:

❏ information for next week's lesson, found under "Continue the Journey."
❏ activities for further spiritual growth in "Continue the Journey."

Review the "Introduction," "The Big Picture," "Close-up," and "Faith in Action," which all precede the first lesson of this quarter. Consider how you might use any of this material in today's lesson.

Gather news magazines or other print media that would include pictures of violence for the activity under "Share Feelings about the Cruelty and Violence of Society." Also collect scissors, glue, and large sheets of construction paper or poster board. You will also need tables for this collage-making activity. Contact students during the week if you need them to supply additional magazines.

LEADING THE CLASS

(1) Gather to Learn

❖ Greet the class members and introduce guests.

❖ Pray that those who have come today will express joy for God's salvation in the midst of a troubled world.

❖ Read: **A sixty-five-year-old man boarded an Alabama school bus, abducted a five-year-old boy, and fatally shot the bus driver who tried to protect the children in his care. Held captive in a reinforced bunker for nearly a week, the boy was safely rescued when SWAT agents stormed the hideout. The agents had been able to communicate with the abductor and send food, medication, and toys to the boy through a plastic pipe. They attacked when, by means of a camera, they could see that the abductor was brandishing a gun. Although the boy did not appear to be physically injured, it is unclear what the long-term effects of being held hostage will be on this child. The community and family of the driver were left to mourn the loss of a hero who saved other children aboard the bus.**

❖ Ask: **What questions does this incident raise in your mind, particularly about justice in a seemingly violent world?**

❖ Read aloud today's focus statement: **Sometimes everything around** us seems violent, cruel, and immoral. Who will bring justice and righteousness to a troubled world? Isaiah and the psalmist promise a time when God will come as a redeemer with a foundation of righteousness and justice and will place God's spirit upon those who repent of their sins.

(2) Goal 1: Explore How God Promises a Renewed Covenant Relationship

❖ Set the stage for today's study by reading "Introduction," "Isaiah 59:1-8," and "Isaiah 59:9-11" from Understanding the Scripture.

❖ Choose a volunteer to read Isaiah 59:15-21.

❖ Discuss these questions:
  1. **What does the text reveal about God as Redeemer?** (See "Isaiah 59:12-20" in Understanding the Scripture; "A Redeemer Will Come" and "God Comes for Zion," both found in Interpreting the Scripture.
  2. **What is God's response to the fact that "truth is lacking" (59:15)?** (See "The Warrior Dressed in Righteousness" in Interpreting the Scripture.)
  3. **How does the image of God as a warrior fit with your understanding of the nature of God?** (Be sure that the adults understand that God takes the stance of a warrior to uphold justice.)

❖ Conclude this portion by reading responsively the background Scripture from Psalm 89:11-18. Note that this psalm, like today's reading from Isaiah, emphasizes the righteousness, justice, love, and faithfulness of the Holy One of Israel who is in covenantal relationship with the people.

(3) Goal 2: Share Feelings about the Cruelty and Violence of Society

❖ Form small groups and have each group gather around a table. Set out news magazines (that may be cut), scissors, glue, and construction paper. Tell the groups that they are to find pictures that depict cruelty and violence anywhere in the world. Each group is to make a collage (a display of pictures that are placed randomly and may overlap) that illustrates this violence. Encourage the groups to talk as they work about the impact this violence has on them and their families, even if they have not been directly affected.

❖ Bring the groups together and encourage people to talk about the pictures they have selected and how they feel about the violence these pictures represent.

❖ **Option:** If it is not possible to make a collage, encourage small groups to talk together about violence and its effects on people.

(4) Goal 3: Express Gratitude and Joy for God's Salvation from Worldly Dangers and Work Toward a Renewed Community

❖ Look again at Isaiah 59:16-17, where it is clear that there is no one but God who can intervene to save the people and bring about justice.

❖ Observe that many people in our society do not look to God for salvation or justice. Ask: **By what means do people seek to protect themselves from whatever dangers they believe threaten them?** (List ideas on newsprint. Some ideas may include locks, security systems, weapons, withdrawal from community, joining like-minded groups for protection and survival.)

❖ Discuss how effective (or ineffective) these means of protection seem to be.

❖ Read in unison today's key verse from Isaiah 59:20. Note that as Christians we can rely on God our Redeemer to be present with us, no matter what the circumstances.

❖ Read these words from Isaiah 51:11 (KJV). Then invite the adults to echo the words as you read one line at a time:

Therefore the redeemed of the LORD shall return,

and come with singing unto Zion;

and everlasting joy shall be upon their heads:

they shall obtain gladness and joy;

and sorry and mourning shall flee away.

❖ Encourage the adults to repeat these words throughout the week as an expression of gratitude and joy for God's redemption and salvation.

(5) Continue the Journey

❖ Pray that as the learners depart they will give thanks that their Redeemer, who Christians know as Jesus, has come.

❖ Post information for next week's session on newsprint for the students to copy:

■ **Title: A Choice to Be Just**

■ **Background Scripture: Ezra 7:1, 6, 21-28; Jeremiah 7:1-15**

■ **Lesson Scripture: Jeremiah 7:1-15**

■ **Focus of the Lesson: Many people show partiality, oppress the weak, and break the law as though they are** unaware of the error of their ways. What are the consequences for persons who will not change their ways? Through Ezra and Jeremiah, God sent messages of hope to those who will amend their ways and messages of doom to those who will not.

❖ Challenge the adults to grow spiritually by completing one or more of these activities related to this week's session, which you have posted on newsprint for the students to copy.

(1) **Compare Isaiah 59:3-8 with Paul's language in Romans 3:15-17. Also compare Isaiah 59:17 (which describes the armor of God) to Ephesians 6:11-17 (which describes the armor of the believer).**

(2) **Research "covenant" online or in a Bible dictionary. What covenants has God made with humanity? How have people been obedient—or disobedient—to these covenants? What lessons can you learn from the people of the Bible about what it means to be faithful to God?**

(3) **Take some time each evening to ponder ways you have been faithful or unfaithful to God that day. Offer prayers of repentance and "turn from transgression" (Isaiah 59:20).**

❖ Sing or read aloud "All Praise to Our Redeeming Lord."

❖ Conclude today's session by leading the class in this benediction adapted from Micah 6:8, which is the key verse for July 19: **Let us depart to do justice, and love kindness, and walk humbly with our God.**

UNIT 3: ADVOCATES OF JUSTICE FOR ALL
A Choice to Be Just

PREVIEWING THE LESSON

Lesson Scripture: Jeremiah 7:1-15
Background Scripture: Ezra 7:1, 6, 21-28; Jeremiah 7:1-15
Key Verse: Jeremiah 7:3

Focus of the Lesson:
Many people show partiality, oppress the weak, and break the law as though they are unaware of the error of their ways. What are the consequences for persons who will not change their ways? Through Ezra and Jeremiah, God sent messages of hope to those who will amend their ways and messages of doom to those who will not.

Goals for the Learners:
(1) to review the messages of doom and hope found in Jeremiah.
(2) to regret the error of their ways and resolve to change.
(3) to address their personal unfaithfulness and their community's corruption.

Pronunciation Guide:
Artaxerxes (ahr tuh zuhrk´ seez) *hesed* (hee´ sid)
Baal (bay´ uhl) or (bah ahl´) Shiloh (shi´ loh)
Ephraim (ee´ fray im) Uzziah (uz zi´ uh)

Supplies:
Bibles, newsprint and marker, paper and pencils, hymnals

READING THE SCRIPTURE

NRSV
Lesson Scripture: Jeremiah 7:1-15
   ¹The word that came to Jeremiah from the LORD: ²Stand in the gate of the LORD's house, and proclaim there this word, and say, Hear the word of the LORD, all you people of Judah,

CEB
Lesson Scripture: Jeremiah 7:1-15
   ¹Jeremiah received the LORD's word: ²Stand near the gate of the LORD's temple and proclaim there this message: Listen to the LORD's word, all you of Judah who enter these gates

you that enter these gates to worship the LORD. ³**Thus says the LORD of hosts, the God of Israel: Amend your ways and your doings, and let me dwell with you in this place.** ⁴Do not trust in these deceptive words: "This is the temple of the LORD, the temple of the LORD, the temple of the LORD." ⁵For if you truly amend your ways and your doings, if you truly act justly one with another, ⁶if you do not oppress the alien, the orphan, and the widow, or shed innocent blood in this place, and if you do not go after other gods to your own hurt, ⁷then I will dwell with you in this place, in the land that I gave of old to your ancestors forever and ever.

⁸Here you are, trusting in deceptive words to no avail. ⁹Will you steal, murder, commit adultery, swear falsely, make offerings to Baal, and go after other gods that you have not known, ¹⁰and then come and stand before me in this house, which is called by my name, and say, "We are safe!"—only to go on doing all these abominations? ¹¹Has this house, which is called by my name, become a den of robbers in your sight? You know, I too am watching, says the LORD. ¹²Go now to my place that was in Shiloh, where I made my name dwell at first, and see what I did to it for the wickedness of my people Israel. ¹³And now, because you have done all these things, says the LORD, and when I spoke to you persistently, you did not listen, and when I called you, you did not answer, ¹⁴therefore I will do to the house that is called by my name, in which you trust, and to the place that I gave to you and to your ancestors, just what I did to Shiloh. ¹⁵And I will cast you out of my sight, just as I cast out all your kinsfolk, all the offspring of Ephraim.

to worship the LORD. ³**This is what the LORD of heavenly forces, the God of Israel, says: Improve your conduct and your actions, and I will dwell with you in this place.** ⁴Don't trust in lies: "This is the LORD's temple! The LORD's temple! The LORD's temple!" ⁵No, if you truly reform your ways and your actions; if you treat each other justly; ⁶if you stop taking advantage of the immigrant, orphan, or widow; if you don't shed the blood of the innocent in this place, or go after other gods to your own ruin, ⁷only then will I dwell with you in this place, in the land that I gave long ago to your ancestors for all time.

⁸And yet you trust in lies that will only hurt you. ⁹Will you steal and murder, commit adultery and perjury, sacrifice to Baal and go after other gods that you don't know, ¹⁰and then come and stand before me in this temple that bears my name, and say, "We are safe," only to keep on doing all these detestable things? ¹¹Do you regard this temple, which bears my name, as a hiding place for criminals? I can see what's going on here, declares the LORD. ¹²Just go to my sanctuary in Shiloh, where I let my name dwell at first, and see what I did to it because of the evil of my people Israel. ¹³And now, because you have done all these things, declares the LORD, because you haven't listened when I spoke to you again and again or responded when I called you, ¹⁴I will do to this temple that bears my name and on which you rely, the place that I gave to you and your ancestors, just as I did to Shiloh. ¹⁵I will cast you out of my sight, just as I cast out the rest of your family, all the people of Ephraim.

UNDERSTANDING THE SCRIPTURE

Introduction. The passages in the background Scripture all deal with the delicate question of the significance of the Temple and its worship for the people of God to experience the presence of God. On the one hand, the Temple building itself is quite important. It was ordained by God as a place God would appear and speak to the people in a way that was perhaps not possible anywhere else. The place was sacred. But on the other hand, the Temple was not a source of security in and of itself. God did not guarantee the Temple would never be destroyed just because God chose to "reside" there. More than anything God desired the worship of the Temple to urge the people to do justice and to show compassion. The emphasis on this expectation of right living dominates Jeremiah 7:1-15. Here the prophet gives a sermon in the Temple and about the Temple. He speaks against the deluded notion that the Temple building is inherently secure. Ezra 7 deals with this idea in a more subtle way. The Temple had been rebuilt and was dedicated to the worship of God (Ezra 6). But the restored community was not complete until Ezra brought the law of Moses to Jerusalem to be the standard by which the people would live.

Ezra 7:1, 6. The story of the return from exile in Babylon begins in 539 B.C. when King Cyrus of Persia defeated the Babylonians and sponsored a return from exile of the various peoples the Babylonians had displaced. Some of the exiles returned and the Persians supported the rebuilding of the Temple, which was finally completed in 515 B.C. The story of Ezra bringing the Law to Jerusalem is set at least a generation after exiles began to return to Jerusalem, in 458 B.C. ("in the seventh year of King Artaxerxes"; 7:7). The content of the document Ezra brought to Jerusalem is not completely clear. It is simply called "the law of Moses that the LORD the God of Israel had given" (7:6) or "the law of the God of heaven" (7:21). It seems likely, however, that Ezra's scroll was a form of the books of Genesis, Exodus, Leviticus, Numbers, and Deuteronomy. This section of the Old Testament came to be called "the Law" and was the first major division of the Jewish Bible, to be followed by "the Prophets" and "the Writings" (see Luke 24:44).

Ezra 7:21-24. Artaxerxes' letter gives authority for Ezra and any Israelite priest who so desires to return to Jerusalem. It also endows Ezra with authority to request funds from officials in Jerusalem to establish the law of Moses as the law that organizes these returned exiles. "The Province Beyond the River" was the Persian name of the territory west of the Euphrates.

Ezra 7:25-26. Ezra was appointed head of the province's government. The law of God would stand alongside the law of the Persian king as the law of the land. This was typical of the Persian administration. The Persians allowed local people to use their religious law to guide them, along with certain regulations from the Persian king. This practice created much goodwill between the local people and the Persians. For the Israelites it also allowed the law of Moses to be recognized as the primary authority in the lives of the people.

Ezra 7:27-28. Ezra now speaks. He first praises God for guiding the Persian king to favor Jerusalem and its Temple. Ezra speaks here like the prophet of Isaiah 40–55 who identified the work of Cyrus on Jerusalem's behalf as God's doing (Isaiah 44:28). He then recognizes that his role as scribe is a result of God's steadfast love (*hesed*), or faithfulness to the covenant with Israel. Finally, Ezra speaks like a prophet by declaring that "the hand of the LORD my God was upon me" (7:28). Ezekiel uses similar language to describe God transporting him in a visionary state to receive divine revelation (Ezekiel 37:1). For Ezra, however, the hand of the Lord empowered him to travel, not in a vision but physically back to Jerusalem.

Jeremiah 7:1-4. Jeremiah's sermon begins as a report that "the word . . . came to Jeremiah from the LORD" (7:1). God commands Jeremiah not only to proclaim a particular message, but to proclaim it in a certain place: the gate of the Temple. He delivers the sermon to all those who walk through the gate to worship. The message is simple: "Amend your ways and your doings" (7:3). What needs to be amended is listed in verses 6 and 8, but the list merely illustrates the problem. The real issue is that the people of Judah act contrary to God's intentions and still they believe that God is with them. God pleads "let me dwell with you" (7:3), but this is only possible if the people live in obedience. Instead, however, they falsely believe the Temple will retain the presence of God simply because it is the Temple.

Jeremiah 7:5-7. Jeremiah communicates requirements for God to "dwell" with the people of Judah. The expectations named in verse 6 represent various acts of compassion and justice to the most vulnerable members of society along with fidelity to God in worship. Such faithfulness ensures God's enduring presence and protection.

Jeremiah 7:8-15. Jeremiah offers a lesson from Israel's history. During the time of Samuel, the sanctuary at Shiloh was the place God chose to make the divine name dwell. Jeremiah refers to God's name as a way of speaking about God's presence (Ezekiel speaks of God's "glory" in a similar way). But the sons of Eli, the priest at Shiloh, were not faithful (1 Samuel 4). God rejected Shiloh and chose a new place. The lesson was that God could depart from Jerusalem just as God departed from Shiloh. There was nothing sacred about the stones of the Temple or the hilltop on which the Temple was built. The place was holy because God chose to be there. God's presence, however, demanded faithful living characterized by justice and mercy. Without these marks of faithfulness, God would depart and leave the place a heap of ruins.

INTERPRETING THE SCRIPTURE

False Security

In churches that say a communal prayer of confession, a common way of introducing that prayer is to say, "If we say we have no sin we deceive ourselves, and the truth of God is not in us" (adapted from 1 John 1:8).

Although that well-known saying is accepted as true and is important, the flip side, positive version of the statement perhaps deserves attention as well: "If we say we have sin, we live in the truth and we stand ready to receive God's salvation." Indeed, Jeremiah 7:1-15 suggests the dividing line between those whom God makes secure and those whom God gives over to judgment is a line drawn by confession of sin.

The issue is not simply whether or not we make a verbal confession of our sinfulness. Rather, the point is that those who confess their sins live in ways that are different from those who do not. Their relationship with God is based on trust in God—that God is gracious and merciful—and gratitude for their experience of God's goodness. In other words, people who live with a full awareness of their sins take nothing for granted. Jeremiah spoke to people who trusted in a view of themselves as privileged and automatically protected. He essentially called them to be aware of their sins on the one hand and of God's grace on the other hand.

Those who live with full awareness of their faults also are more likely to be attentive to the needs of others than those who deny their faults. Note that for Jeremiah's audience, the denial of sinfulness went hand in hand with their oppression of the poor. Because they took their relationship with God for granted, they also took for granted their responsibility to other human beings.

It is important to note that self-confidence, self-care, and love of self all have an important place in the life of every believer. The call to confession of sins is not a call to self-hatred. Indeed, if we do not love ourselves we will focus on ourselves as much as the person who is arrogant and overconfident. The proper love of self, however, should grow out of a profound sense that we are loved by God unconditionally. That awareness should, in turn, produce humility and joy and cause us to see every person as an object of God's love as well. If we are able to acquire this kind of love of self we will be more likely to act justly. In so acting, we experience the presence of God. For as God said through Jeremiah, "then I will dwell with you in this place" (7:7).

Does God Dwell in a Place on Earth?

Jeremiah 7:1-15 deals with the assumption that God dwells in a certain place on earth in a way that is not true of every other place. But in what sense did Jeremiah believe God dwelled on earth? Two points are important to understand this fundamental feature of Old Testament faith.

First, Jeremiah 7:1-15 shares with other Old Testament texts the idea that God's dwelling on earth is a place that gives access to God's actual dwelling place in heaven, but it was not a place God was thought to be exclusively. Perhaps the best illustration of this connection between the Temple on earth and the heavenly throne of God is the story of Isaiah's call in Isaiah 6. Isaiah reports, "In the year that King Uzziah died, I saw the Lord sitting on a throne, high and lofty; and the hem of his robe filled the temple" (Isaiah 6:1). In other words, while standing in the Temple in Jerusalem, Isaiah saw a vision of God sitting on the throne in heaven. The Jerusalem Temple was not the place God dwelled in fullness. It was, however, a portal into the actual throne of God. The idea is similar to that expressed in Plato's allegory of the cave, that things on earth are shadows, imperfect expressions of real things in heaven. But as the story of Isaiah's call story suggests, the earthly Temple was considered the link between heaven and earth.

Second, as a link between heaven and earth, a portal to the divine realm, the Jerusalem Temple was necessarily secondary to the real temple in heaven. This meant that the earthly house could be replaced if God so chose to replace it. This was the point at which Jeremiah said the people of Judah were confused about the importance of the Temple. They thought it was *the* house of God and therefore it provided security for them simply by its presence. Jeremiah reminded them, however, that God had chosen the Temple in Jerusalem to be called by God's name. It was God's choice. The Jerusalem Temple was not inherently holy. It was crucial because God chose to make it the place at which the people of Judah could experience God's presence. Jeremiah recalled that the temple at Shiloh had once been the place God designated as the connecting point between heaven and earth. The ark of the covenant was housed there and God spoke to people like Samuel there (1 Samuel 3). But the disobedience of worshipers in that place led to God rejecting it. The Jerusalem Temple could likewise be rejected. The key to God continuing to "dwell" in the Temple was for the people to live in humility with God and to live justly with one another.

The Nature and Origins of Morality

An important part of the church's expression of faith has always been concern for moral issues. The question of how Christians should live and how they should treat one another is paramount. The church today wrestles with certain moral issues that divide the body of Christ. How Christians should respond to these issues is of great interest. It is instructive, however, to observe the particular issues Jeremiah identified as central to Judah's relationship with God and how the prophet said these matters affected that relationship.

Jeremiah gives two lists of moral concerns. The first list is in verse 6. It speaks against oppressing the alien, the orphan, and the widow. The threefold formula is shorthand for the most vulnerable people in Israelite society. The second list in verse 9 sounds like an abbreviation of the second half of the Ten Commandments. Jeremiah refers to stealing, committing murder and adultery, and swearing falsely (see Exodus 20:13-17). These two lists both focus on right treatment of one's neighbor with an emphasis on not abusing or taking advantage of the neighbor. It is also important to note that both lists also include "going after other gods." Jeremiah does not elaborate on the latter point, but the reason he includes this in a list of offenses against the neighbor seems clear. The Ten Commandments begin with extensive commands about how to love God (Exodus 20:1-7). These commandments then give rise naturally to commands on how to treat others. The love of God that comes from gratitude for God's grace is the foundation of our faith. But such love of God is made real to the world when we treat those around us as people God loves and cares for as well.

SHARING THE SCRIPTURE

PREPARING TO TEACH

Preparing Our Hearts

Meditate on this week's devotional reading from Jeremiah 26:8-15, which records responses to Jeremiah's prophecies in the Temple. Scholars interpret this passage as a further development of the sermon at the center of today's lesson in chapter 7. How did various listeners react to the prophet's words from the Lord? What hope does Jeremiah offer to the people, even to those who threaten him? What often happens when people speak truth to power?

Pray that you and the students will choose justice over any attempt to tell people what they want to hear.

Preparing Our Minds

Study the background Scripture from Ezra 7:1, 6, 21-28; Jeremiah 7:1-15. The lesson Scripture is from Jeremiah 7:1-15.

Consider this question as you prepare the lesson: *What are the consequences for persons who show partiality, oppress the weak, break the law, and refuse to change their ways?*

Write on newsprint:

❏ information for next week's lesson, found under "Continue the Journey."
❏ activities for further spiritual growth in "Continue the Journey."

Review the "Introduction," "The Big Picture," "Close-up," and "Faith in Action," which all precede the first lesson of this quarter. Consider how you might use any of this material in today's lesson.

LEADING THE CLASS

(1) Gather to Learn

❖ Greet the class members and introduce guests.

❖ Pray that those who have come today will make the choice to live according to God's justice.

❖ Read: **Although the "Pledge of Allegiance" of the United States affirms "liberty and justice for all," we as a people have not always lived up to our ideals. The oppression by slave owners, the legalized partiality of Jim Crow laws, the segregation of schools and public accommodations, and acceptance by many citizens of the status quo in terms of second-class citizenship for those of African American heritage finally reached a turning point on July 2, 1964, when President Lyndon B. Johnson signed into law the Civil Rights Act. This law prohibited discrimination based on race, color, religion, or national origin, and it gave the federal government power to enforce desegregation. Although great strides have been made, more than fifty years later, the struggle for true equality continues. Laws have changed, but the hearts and minds of some groups remain biased in their words and deeds.**

❖ Read aloud today's focus statement: **Many people show partiality, oppress the weak, and break the law as though they are unaware of the error of their ways. What are the consequences for persons who will not change their ways? Through Ezra and Jeremiah, God sent messages of hope to those who will amend their** ways and messages of doom to those who will not.

(2) Goal 1: Review the Messages of Doom and Hope Found in Jeremiah

❖ Solicit a volunteer to read Jeremiah 7:1-15.

❖ Unpack the meaning of these verses by using the information concerning Jeremiah found in Understanding the Scripture.

❖ Discuss these questions:
1. **What words of judgment do you hear from Jeremiah?**
2. **What words of hope do you hear?**
3. **Jeremiah speaks in verse 10 about people feeling safe in the Temple, despite their unholy actions. How might this message apply to Christians?**
4. **Through Jeremiah the Lord says, "I too am watching" (7:11). What kinds of behaviors do you think people would change if they were constantly aware of God's watchful presence?**

(3) Goal 2: Regret the Error of the Learners' Ways and Resolve to Change

❖ Read "False Security" from Interpreting the Scripture.

❖ Encourage the class members to consider their personal unfaithfulness by reading the following script:
- **Imagine yourself sitting in a favorite chair at home. Visualize your surroundings. Notice how the chair feels to your skin. Inhale pleasant aromas from the kitchen.** (Pause)
- **Suddenly Jesus appears before you. He looks at you lov-**

ingly as he points out ways you have been unfaithful. Listen as he speaks to you. (Pause)
- **Jesus assures you that he has not come to judge you. Instead, he says to you, "Amend your ways and your doings, and let me dwell with you in this place." Speak silently to Jesus any words of repentance.** (Pause)
- **Ponder this encounter for a few moments and then look up when you are ready to move on.** (Pause)

(4) Goal 3: Address the Learners' Personal Unfaithfulness and Their Community's Corruption

❖ Read "The Nature and Origins of Morality" in Interpreting the Scripture. Point out that Jeremiah is dealing not only with issues of personal unfaithfulness but also with unfaithful behavior within the community.

❖ Look together again at the lists in verses 6 and 9. Recall that those named in verse 6 are a shorthand way of saying "the vulnerable groups of people in our society." The actions in verse 9 concern unjust treatment of one's neighbor and the wider community. Ask:
1. **Who are the vulnerable groups of people in our society?**
2. **What are some modern ways that we break the Ten Commandments?** (In our day, stealing, for example, refers not just to a mugging or bank robbery but also to theft that occurs when corporations cheat those who use their

products or services or fail to pay their employees fairly.)

❖ Form small groups and distribute paper and pencil to each. Encourage them to (1) identify a source of corruption in their own community or state and (2) determine ways that they might deal with this corruption. For example, if gang violence is an issue, what steps can the church take to provide a safe haven for gang members who want to change and for youth before they become involved in gangs? If there is political corruption, how can citizens be encouraged to shine a spotlight on the problem and bring in fresh leadership?

❖ Come together and discuss ideas. Decide what the class or individual members can do to address the problems they have identified.

(5) Continue the Journey

❖ Pray that as the learners depart, they will amend their ways and make a choice to act with justice.

❖ Post information for next week's session on newsprint for the students to copy:

- **Title: A Call for Repentance**
- **Background Scripture: Ezekiel 18; Proverbs 21:2-15**
- **Lesson Scripture: Ezekiel 18:1-3, 30-32**
- **Focus of the Lesson: People are aware of behavior that is harmful to the life of a community. What can be done to build and maintain the health of a community? Ezekiel advises confession and, along with Proverbs, exhorts the people to do the right**

thing and thereby build a just community.

❖ Challenge the adults to grow spiritually by completing one or more of these activities related to this week's session, which you have posted on newsprint for the students to copy.

(1) **Write a personal prayer of confession and offer this prayer each day this week. Be mindful of how your actions and attitudes are changing as a result of your repentance.**

(2) **Check yourself whenever you are tempted to engage in biased or unjust behavior. Apologize if you accidentally harm someone by such behavior. Ask God to continue to lead you toward the just behavior that is expected of you as a Christian.**

(3) **Recall that Jeremiah challenged God's people concerning their behaviors and called them to amend their ways. When you witness unjust behaviors, particularly among those who claim the name of Christ, privately call out these people and explain how they have crossed a boundary. Offer to pray with them.**

❖ Sing or read aloud "I Surrender All."

❖ Conclude today's session by leading the class in this benediction adapted from Micah 6:8, which is the key verse for July 19: **Let us depart to do justice, and love kindness, and walk humbly with our God.**

UNIT 3: ADVOCATES OF JUSTICE FOR ALL
A CALL FOR REPENTANCE

PREVIEWING THE LESSON

Lesson Scripture: Ezekiel 18:1-13, 30-32
Background Scripture: Ezekiel 18; Proverbs 21:2-15
Key Verses: Ezekiel 18:30-31

Focus of the Lesson:
People are aware of behavior that is harmful to the life of a community. What can be done to build and maintain the health of a community? Ezekiel advises confession and, along with Proverbs, exhorts the people to do the right thing and thereby build a just community.

Goals for the Learners:
(1) to encounter the message of Ezekiel concerning personal responsibility for one's actions.
(2) to feel accountability for personal acts of omission that damage community.
(3) to pray for discernment in how to build communities of justice.

Supplies:
Bibles, newsprint and marker, paper and pencils, hymnals

READING THE SCRIPTURE

NRSV
Lesson Scripture: Ezekiel 18:1-13, 30-32

¹The word of the LORD came to me: ²What do you mean by repeating this proverb concerning the land of Israel, "The parents have eaten sour grapes, and the children's teeth are set on edge"? ³As I live, says the Lord GOD, this proverb shall no more be used by you in Israel. ⁴Know that all lives are mine; the life of the parent as well as

CEB
Lesson Scripture: Ezekiel 18:1-13, 30-32

¹The LORD's word came to me: ²What do you mean by this proverb of yours about the land of Israel: "When parents eat unripe grapes, the children's teeth suffer"? ³As surely as I live, says the LORD God, no longer will you use this proverb in Israel! ⁴All lives are mine; the life of the parent and the life of the child belong

the life of the child is mine: it is only the person who sins that shall die.

[5]If a man is righteous and does what is lawful and right—[6]if he does not eat upon the mountains or lift up his eyes to the idols of the house of Israel, does not defile his neighbor's wife or approach a woman during her menstrual period, [7]does not oppress anyone, but restores to the debtor his pledge, commits no robbery, gives his bread to the hungry and covers the naked with a garment, [8]does not take advance or accrued interest, withholds his hand from iniquity, executes true justice between contending parties, [9]follows my statutes, and is careful to observe my ordinances, acting faithfully—such a one is righteous; he shall surely live, says the Lord GOD.

[10]If he has a son who is violent, a shedder of blood, [11]who does any of these things (though his father does none of them), who eats upon the mountains, defiles his neighbor's wife, [12]oppresses the poor and needy, commits robbery, does not restore the pledge, lifts up his eyes to the idols, commits abomination, [13]takes advance or accrued interest; shall he then live? He shall not. He has done all these abominable things; he shall surely die; his blood shall be upon himself.

[30]Therefore I will judge you, O house of Israel, all of you according to your ways, says the Lord GOD. **Repent and turn from all your transgressions; otherwise iniquity will be your ruin. [31]Cast away from you all the transgressions that you have committed against me, and get yourselves a new heart and a new spirit!** Why will you die, O house of Israel? [32]For I have no pleasure in the death of anyone, says the Lord GOD. Turn, then, and live.

to me. Only the one who sins will die.

[5]People are declared innocent when they act justly and responsibly. [6]They don't eat on the hills or give their attention to the idols of the house of Israel. They don't defile the wives of their neighbors or approach menstruating women. [7]They don't cheat anyone, but fulfill their obligations. They don't rob others, but give food to the hungry and clothes to the naked. [8]They don't impose interest or take profit. They refrain from evil and settle cases between people fairly. [9]They follow my regulations, keep my case laws, and act faithfully. Such people are innocent, and they will live, proclaims the LORD God.

[10]But suppose one of them has a violent child who sheds blood or does any one of these things, [11]even though his parents didn't do any of them. He eats on the mountains, defiles his neighbor's wife, [12]oppresses the poor and needy, robs others and doesn't fulfill his obligations, pays attention to the idols and does detestable things, [13]and takes interest and profit. Should he live? He should not. He engaged in all these detestable practices. He will surely die, and his blood will be on him.

[30]Therefore I will judge each of you according to your ways, house of Israel. This is what the LORD God says. **Turn, turn away from your sins. Don't let them be sinful obstacles for you. [31]Abandon all of your repeated sins. Make yourselves a new heart and a new spirit.** Why should you die, house of Israel? [32]I most certainly don't want anyone to die! This is what the LORD God says. Change your ways, and live!

UNDERSTANDING THE SCRIPTURE

Introduction. The background Scripture includes a chapter from the Book of Ezekiel and part of a chapter from the Book of Proverbs. The two sections are very distinctive. Ezekiel is a prophet who was also a priest. His prophecy includes many features that focus on priestly issues such as dietary laws, ritual purity, and the proper worship practices in the Temple. Ezekiel prophesied to the people of Israel when they were in exile in Babylon. Thus, the emphasis he places on individual responsibility speaks not just to individuals but to the fate Israel suffers at present. Proverbs is largely a collection of wisdom sayings that give advice about successful living.

The two passages are quite different, but they share two important features in common. First, Ezekiel quotes a popular proverb that *could* have been in the Book of Proverbs. He does so, however, to argue against it. Second, the Proverbs passage speaks, like Ezekiel 18, of what is "right" or "righteous." On this point the wisdom material speaks about righteousness in terms of ensuring justice for the lowly. But the primary characteristic of the righteous is humility before God. The wicked are exactly the opposite. They operate out of pride (Proverbs 21:4) and that pride produces violence (Proverbs 21:7).

Ezekiel 18:1-4. The popularity of the proverb Ezekiel quotes is illustrated by its appearance also in Jeremiah 31:29. Apparently the saying had become a cynical response to suffering that reflected a belief that a person's own sins had no role in his or her well-being. Thus, Ezekiel (like Jeremiah) rejects this idea and argues for individual responsibility. The shift is good news for the people's relationship with God. It assured them that God paid attention to the individual and rewarded them for right actions.

Ezekiel 18:5-9. Ezekiel gives a list of offenses a righteous person avoids. The list includes some concerns that are particularly geared toward the priests of ancient Israel. The other offenses, however, are common to other prophets who call for justice for the poor (Amos 2:6-8 for example). The righteous man, the one who acts faithfully and obeys God's statutes, will "surely live" (18:9).

Ezekiel 18:10-20. Ezekiel makes a case that father and son each bears his own responsibility for sins. The guilt for a father's sins is not passed on to his son. Here Ezekiel makes a strong case for individual responsibility and the punishment and reward that each individual experiences.

Ezekiel 18:21-24. Following the insistence that each person is responsible for his or her own sins, Ezekiel makes the case for repentance as a way out of guilt and punishment. God's wrath is not irrevocable. God does not delight in punishing the wicked. It is not possible to bank righteousness, nor is it inevitable that a person suffers for sins. Repentance is a key to life in relationship with God. If a person truly repents, God does not remember his or her sins.

Ezekiel 18:25-29. The prophet continues the argument by declaring that God's ways are more than fair. God is gracious and stands ready to forgive and restore the one who is unfaithful. Therefore, Israel has no reason to accuse God of being unfaithful to them. God's punishment of Israel is the direct result of Israel's unfaithfulness and lack of repentance.

Ezekiel 18:30-32. The call to repentance is repeated now with additional language about getting a new heart and spirit. Repentance is not just stopping injustice. It is the turning of a person's thoughts (in the Old Testament the heart is the seat of reason) and the person's life energy (the spirit) toward God and God's ways.

Proverbs 21:2-3. God, who judges the heart, is more concerned about justice than sacrifice. This does not mean that God rejects sacrifice. Rather, sacrifice must grow out of a pure heart. If it does, then righteousness and justice will result. If righteousness and justice are not evident, then sacrifice is meaningless.

Proverbs 21:4-8. The next cluster of wisdom sayings continues the theme of righteousness and justice. They focus is on the character of the righteous and the wicked who either do or do not do justice. The wicked are characterized by arrogance, and from their arrogance grows injustice. The wicked are also characterized by hasty actions and shortcuts to prosperity (lying and unjust conduct).

Proverbs 21:9. The material in Proverbs was addressed mainly to young men who were preparing to serve as public officials. So the subject of what type wife a man had (and in other passages the importance of being faithful to that wife) was crucially important. The basic truth of Proverbs 21:9 is that strife in the home makes all of life difficult. If this particular proverb were translated into the circumstances of our society it might read "Marry for love, not for money." That is the core of the issue, namely that married life is better with meager resources and love than with riches and marital strife.

Proverbs 21:10-12. These verses contain more instruction about the wicked and their eventual fate. God, the "Righteous One," will eventually bring an end to the actions of the wicked. This idea reveals the central message behind the comparison of the righteous and the wicked: The wicked are those opposed to God and God's plans for the world. Therefore, God will bring an end to the wicked in order to preserve creation.

Proverbs 21:13-15. The final segment of the background Scripture emphasizes the importance of justice for the poor, which is a central concern of the righteous. Verse 14 distinguishes between a gift and a bribe. They are like the righteous and the wicked, respectively. The one is welcomed and brings joy; the other brings anger and wrath.

INTERPRETING THE SCRIPTURE

Are Your Sins Your Own?

One of the most difficult aspects of human sinfulness to accept is that each person's sins are passed on to others. Our sins are not just our own. The whole community, and all humankind, shares them. This is particularly evident in the way sins of parents are shared by their children. We wish this were not so. The Old Testament sometimes speaks of successive generations experiencing punishment for the sins of another generation. This makes sense theologically in that the Old Testament presents a sense of collective punishment and does not focus primarily on individuals and their good or evil deeds as the sole cause of blessing or punishment. Passages like Psalm 79:8 assume the present generation suffers for the sins of the ancestors and the prayer is that it will not be so: "Do not remember against us the iniquities of our ancestors."

This struggle between corporate and individual responsibility appears in a song by Bruce Springsteen titled "Long Time Coming." Springsteen tells the story of a man struggling to be the husband and father he wants to be. A crucial part of the story was the man's experience with his own father. He recalls that when he was a child, his dad was a stranger who did not live with him. The man realizes that his father's problem with commitment has affected him, indeed scarred him, and he wishes things to be different for his children. Furthermore, the man, who is now a father himself, wants his children to live free of his mistakes. If he could make one wish, "It'd be that your mistakes will be your own/That your sins will be your own." Ezekiel 18 gives the remarkable promise that this man's wish will be a reality for the people of Judah.

On the one hand, this sense of collective guilt and punishment is healthy in that no one is completely responsible for his or her own sins or suffering. There is not a one-to-one correspondence between our disobedience and our hardships. There is certainly truth in the proverb Ezekiel mentions. But on the other hand, the idea that the children's teeth are set on edge because the parents have eaten sour grapes can be a cynical excuse to overlook one's own sinfulness.

Ezekiel speaks in part to this tendency. Jeremiah also gives a similar message when he quotes the same popular saying (Jeremiah 31:29).

Repentance: The Basic Act of Faith

The final verses of our lesson Scripture reveal the ultimate purpose of Ezekiel's pronouncement on individual retribution. Namely, he makes the point that the people of God are in charge of their own futures. They may have success and blessing or tragedy and hardship depending on how they respond to God. They can be sure that God wants to do good for them. God declares, "I have no pleasure in the death of anyone" (18:32). Therefore, the final word God gives through Ezekiel on this matter is a charge to the people of Judah to "Turn, then, and live" (18:32). The imperative "turn" could also be translated "repent." But "turn" is a good rendering in that it communicates the literal meaning of the word and hence the essence of repentance. To repent is to turn from one way and to go another. Ezekiel declares that turning toward God is the key to life and health.

It should be said that Ezekiel's words are true for his audience, but the issue is more complicated for people in different times and circumstances. Suffering is much more complicated and mysterious than is indicated in Ezekiel 18. Nevertheless, Ezekiel's message is what we all need to hear at times. It is possible to become so jaded by an overemphasis on communal sin that we fail to see how essential our own repentance and obedience to God are. Although Ezekiel is speaking about it as a key to life and prosperity, we should be careful in how we think about this connection. The real key to what Ezekiel is saying is not that God will reward those who repent with money or material success. Rather, the main point is Ezekiel's command to the people to "get yourselves a new heart and a new spirit" (18:31). True repentance means to turn from present ways of acting as well as from present ways of thinking about success. The Old Testament testifies that real prosperity is being in the presence of God. Psalm 27:4 perhaps says it most directly, *"One thing* I asked of the LORD, that will I seek after: to live in the house of the LORD all the days of my life, to behold the beauty of the LORD, and to inquire in his temple" (emphasis added). The new heart Ezekiel imagines for the people of God has such an orientation toward God's presence, with a desire to experience and live in ways consistent with God's holiness. The true turning is toward this desire to be near God, toward a life in God's presence.

One clear sign of the importance of repentance is the place it plays in the gospel story. John the Baptist came "proclaiming a baptism of repentance" (Mark 1:4). When Jesus began his ministry, he declared, "The time is fulfilled, and the kingdom of God has come near; repent, and believe in the good news" (1:15).

The Meaning of "Righteous"

In the middle of Ezekiel's treatment of individual reward and punishment he outlines what it means to be "righteous" (Ezekiel 18:5-9). This term in the Old Testament is often understood as a description of a person who is morally pure, who does certain things according to the law or a moral code. Ezekiel *seems* to be saying just that.

He characterizes the righteous person as one who "does what is lawful and right" (18:5). Then the prophet lists certain acts of righteousness. The list is quite similar to the moral concerns of other prophets in this unit. Ezekiel lists not committing adultery, not stealing, and performing acts of compassion among the characteristic acts of the righteous. Ezekiel adds certain characteristics that are distinctively priestly, related particularly to ritual purity. As good as all these actions and character features are, the idea that one can be righteous through human obedience seems at odds with the New Testament's insistence that righteousness comes only through faith (Romans 3:21-26).

A careful reading of Ezekiel 18:5-9 reveals that the prophet does not actually say that right actions *make* a person righteous. Rather, these are things a righteous person *does*. Indeed, Ezekiel gives the list of actions and then says of the one who does them, "such a one is righteous" (18:9). The subtle distinction between a *righteous person* and *righteous acts* appears in both Testaments. For the Old Testament righteousness is a characteristic of God; humans merely share in God's righteousness as a gift. For example, Psalm 72:1 prays for God to give God's righteousness to "a king's son." Likewise, humans are righteous because they enter into right relationship with God who alone is righteous. As Psalm 143:2 declares, "no one living is righteous before you." But Ezekiel makes the important point that those who are righteous will naturally act in ways that are consistent with the righteousness of God.

SHARING THE SCRIPTURE

PREPARING TO TEACH

Preparing Our Hearts

Meditate on this week's devotional reading from Hosea 14. How does the prophet try to persuade the Israelites to change their ways and return to the Lord? What changes does Israel need to make in its relationship with Assyria? Would you feel assured of God's forgiveness after hearing Hosea's words? Why or why not? How does verse 9 address the issue of God's justice and how people respond to it?

Pray that you and the students will recognize the error of your own ways and stand ready to repent.

Preparing Our Minds

Study the background Scripture from Ezekiel 18 and Proverbs 21:2-15. The lesson Scripture is from Ezekiel 18:1-13, 30-32.

Consider this question as you prepare the lesson: *Given that some behaviors are harmful to the community, what can be done to build and maintain the health of a community?*

Write on newsprint:
❏ information for next week's lesson, found under "Continue the Journey."
❏ activities for further spiritual growth in "Continue the Journey."

Review the "Introduction," "The Big Picture," "Close-up," and "Faith in Action," which all precede the first lesson of this quarter. Consider how you might use any of this material in today's lesson.

LEADING THE CLASS

(1) Gather to Learn

❖ Greet the class members and introduce guests.

❖ Pray that those who have come today will be aware of what needs to be done to build and maintain a healthy, just community.

❖ Read: **Domestic violence is a growing problem in the United States. According to an October 14, 2013, article that appeared on UMC. org, the leading cause of injury to women in the United States is domestic violence. A woman is assaulted or beaten every nine seconds. Each day, three women die as a result of violence by their abusers. Victims are found across all spectrums of society, including within religious groups. The church, therefore, needs to be involved. First United Methodist Church, Anchorage, Alaska did step up to the plate and holds an annual "Shed the Light on Domestic Violence" service. Time is provided for sharing and discussion, as well as lighting candles for victims of such violence. When asked why people of faith should care about this family violence, First UMC member Jennifer Miller replied that victims "are in our congregations. They are seeking the love and support of our faith community. The Scripture says that Christians should stand in defense of others being harmed and stand against injustice, especially as it relates to children or helpless members of our society."**

❖ Read aloud today's focus statement: **People are aware of behavior** that is harmful to the life of a community. What can be done to build and maintain the health of a community? Ezekiel advises confession and, along with Proverbs, exhorts the people to do the right thing and thereby build a just community.

(2) Goal 1: Encounter the Message of Ezekiel Concerning Personal Responsibility for One's Actions

❖ Select a volunteer to read Ezekiel 18:1-13, 30-32.
  ❖ Discuss these questions:
  1. **How do you interpret the meaning of the proverb in verse 2?** (See "Are Your Sins Your Own?" in Interpreting the Scripture.)
  2. **Verses 5-18 explore three hypothetical legal cases, two of which are in today's lesson Scripture (18:5-9, 10-13). Verses 5-9 deal with a righteous man. What kinds of behaviors does he avoid? What does he do?** (See "The Meaning of 'Righteous'" in Interpreting the Scripture.)
  3. **Verses 10-13 show a contrast between the way a father, who has set a good example, acts and how his son acts. What does this passage suggest about the ability of the righteousness of one generation to cover the sins of another generation?**
  4. **Read together today's key verses, Ezekiel 18:30-31. What do you learn about God's desire for humanity?** (See "Repentance: The Basic Act of Faith" in Interpreting the Scripture.)

(3) Goal 2: Feel Accountability for Personal Acts of Omission that Damage Community

❖ Read: **Perhaps you have heard of the "bystander effect," a term coined by psychologists John Darley and Bibb Latané following the 1964 stabbing death of Kitty Genovese at her home in New York. According to some reports, many people heard Ms. Genovese's cries for help, but no one was willing to get involved. As shocking as this situation was, there are psychological reasons that explain why people ignore an emergency. When many other people are present during an emergency, a process known as "diffusion of responsibility" kicks in, making each person feel less responsible for taking action. Moreover, people tend to look to others for guidance as to how to handle situations. If no one else seems to be doing anything, others assume that nothing needs to be done.**

❖ Suggest that the adults think about a situation where they could have acted but did nothing. Ask them to silently consider these questions: Why did you refuse to get involved? How might the situation have been different if you had been involved? Did you hold yourself more accountable in subsequent situations so that you were willing to intervene?

❖ Bring everyone together and invite volunteers to comment on any insights they gleaned.

(4) Goal 3: Pray for Discernment in How to Build Communities of Justice

❖ Invite the adults to be in an attitude of prayer as you read these prayers for justice that are adapted from biblical verses:
  1. **Gracious God, we pray for**

communities where all recognize that you give justice
to the weak and the orphan
and maintain the right of the
lowly and the destitute. We
call upon your name to rescue
the weak and the needy, and
deliver them from the hand
of the wicked. And we call
upon people of faith to build
together those communities
that support justice for all
(Psalm 82:3-4).

2. Lord, we know that you will
maintain the cause of the
needy and will execute justice for the poor. Help us as a
community of faith to usher
in this justice for all (Psalm
140:12).

3. Loving God, help us to build
just communities by learning to do good, seek justice,
rescue the oppressed, defend
the orphan, and plead for the
widow (Isaiah 1:17).

❖ Form small groups and distribute paper and pencils. Invite each
group to search the Scriptures for
verses they could adapt, as we have
already done, or to write their own
prayers in which they ask God to be
the kind of community where divine
justice is found.

(5) Continue the Journey

❖ Stand in a circle and invite one
person from each group to read the
prayer the group has written. When
all have finished, add the words,
"And all God's people said, 'Amen.'"
❖ Post information for next week's
session on newsprint for the students
to copy:

■ Title: God Demands Justice
■ Background Scripture: Zechariah 7:8-14; Isaiah 30:18-26

■ Lesson Scripture: Zechariah
7:8-14
■ Focus of the Lesson: Some people show no kindness, mercy,
or justice to others. Who will
protect the weak from their
oppressors? Zechariah says
that God requires kindness
and mercy for the widows,
orphans, aliens, and the poor,
while Isaiah says that God
will heal the wounds of the
afflicted and shower prosperity on the people.

❖ Challenge the adults to grow
spiritually by completing one or more
of these activities related to this week's
session, which you have posted on
newsprint for the students to copy.

(1) Read theologian Dietrich
Bonhoeffer's classic book,
Life Together. What do you
learn about living in Christian community within
the home and within the
church?

(2) Identify situations in which
you can act as a peacemaker
and call people to repentance.
Where can you help build
community among people
who have been estranged?

(3) Recall from the "Gather to
Learn" activity that a church
in Alaska stepped forward
to shed light on domestic
violence and offer help to
local victims. What can you
and your congregation do to
assist those displaced due to
violence?

❖ Sing or read aloud "Just as I Am,
Without One Plea."
❖ Conclude today's session by
leading the class in this benediction
adapted from Micah 6:8, which is the
key verse for July 19: Let us depart to
do justice, and love kindness, and
walk humbly with our God.

UNIT 3: ADVOCATES OF JUSTICE FOR ALL
GOD DEMANDS JUSTICE

PREVIEWING THE LESSON

Lesson Scripture: Zechariah 7:8-14
Background Scripture: Zechariah 7:8-14; Isaiah 30:18-26
Key Verses: Zechariah 7:9-10

Focus of the Lesson:

Some people show no kindness, mercy, or justice to others. Who will protect the weak from their oppressors? Zechariah says that God requires kindness and mercy for the widows, orphans, aliens, and the poor, while Isaiah says that God will heal the wounds of the afflicted and shower prosperity on the people.

Goals for the Learners:

(1) to study the punishment meted out by God for those who reject God's demands.
(2) to make confessions concerning how they abandon the weak.
(3) to show kindness to the oppressed and the weak.

Supplies:

Bibles, newsprint and marker, paper and pencils, hymnals

READING THE SCRIPTURE

NRSV
Lesson Scripture: Zechariah 7:8-14

⁸The word of the LORD came to Zechariah, saying: **⁹Thus says the LORD of hosts: Render true judgments, show kindness and mercy to one another; ¹⁰do not oppress the widow, the orphan, the alien, or the poor; and do not devise evil in your hearts against one another.** ¹¹But they refused to listen, and turned a

CEB
Lesson Scripture: Zechariah 7:8-14

⁸The LORD's word came to Zechariah:

⁹The LORD of heavenly forces proclaims:

Make just and faithful decisions; show kindness and compassion to each other! ¹⁰Don't oppress the widow, the orphan, the stranger, and the poor; don't plan evil against each other!

stubborn shoulder, and stopped their ears in order not to hear. ¹²They made their hearts adamant in order not to hear the law and the words that the LORD of hosts had sent by his spirit through the former prophets. Therefore great wrath came from the LORD of hosts. ¹³Just as, when I called, they would not hear, so, when they called, I would not hear, says the LORD of hosts, ¹⁴and I scattered them with a whirlwind among all the nations that they had not known. Thus the land they left was desolate, so that no one went to and fro, and a pleasant land was made desolate.

¹¹But they refused to pay attention. They turned a cold shoulder and stopped listening.

¹²They steeled their hearts against hearing the Instruction and the words that the LORD of heavenly forces sent by his spirit through the earlier prophets. As a result, the LORD of heavenly forces became enraged.

¹³So just as he called and they didn't listen, when they called, I didn't listen, says the LORD of heavenly forces. ¹⁴I scattered them throughout the nations whom they didn't know. The land was devastated behind them, with no one leaving or returning. They turned a delightful land into a wasteland.

UNDERSTANDING THE SCRIPTURE

Introduction. The two sections of background Scripture feature very different prophecies. Zechariah 1–8 originated during the period just after the people of Judah returned from exile in Babylon. (Much of Zechariah 9–14 seems to come from a later time period.) They were struggling with rebuilding the Temple and rebuilding their society. Thus, Zechariah had much in common with the prophet Haggai and with the concerns expressed in the books of Ezra and Nehemiah.

Isaiah 30:18-26 was composed in very different circumstances. This passage spoke to the people of Judah during the exile as the people awaited deliverance and an opportunity to return to their land. While Zechariah explains why the exile occurred and now urges faithfulness to those who have returned to Jerusalem, Isaiah 30:18-26 gives assurance that they

will return and Zion will be restored. Thus, the Zechariah passage speaks on both sides of the message of Isaiah 30:18-26. The two passages have in common, however, the faith that God alone is the deliverer and God desires faith and obedience.

Zechariah 7:8-10. Zechariah speaks like Amos and Micah about justice for those who are most vulnerable: widow, orphan, resident alien (Amos 2:4-8; Micah 3:1-3). He echoes Micah 6:8 with the call to show kindness and mercy ("to do justice, and to love kindness"). These actions are quite tangible. But Zechariah also instructs the people to cultivate justice in their thoughts: "Do not devise evil in your hearts against one another" (7:10). "Heart" here refers to the seat of reason, not sentimentality or emotion. Hence, what happens in the heart should not be conceived as something out of control or irrational. In fact, it is quite rational. The message is that in all the thoughts and plans of the people justice should be paramount. It should not be an afterthought or something that is neglected. It is too important for that.

Zechariah 7:11-12. The prophet gives exaggerated images of Judah's failure to hear God's word. They turned their shoulders and "stopped their ears" (7:11). Zechariah also says this not hearing has a history. Not only have they not listened to him but they also did not listen to prophets who came before him. The reference to "former prophets" in verse 12 may simply refer to prophets before Zechariah. But the label eventually refers to the story of Israel's experience in the land recorded in Joshua, Judges, Samuel, and Kings. Even if that is not the intention here, the statement is quite strong against the people who would not heed God's warning and be led by God's direction. Whether they have refused to listen to prophets or to the words of the prophets that became Scripture, Zechariah indicts Judah for not taking seriously God's greatest efforts to lead them in the right way. Judah has been like a stubborn child who will not recognize that her parents' warnings are meant to lead her into life that is good and full and not destructive. Judah chose destruction and now suffers the consequences.

Zechariah 7:13-14. The end of the chapter records the natural outcome of God's people not listening: God also does not listen to them. The result is that God allows them to be scattered "among all the nations" (7:14). This is a reference to exile and the situation of the people of Judah living in various parts of the Mediterranean world after the traumatic event.

Isaiah 30:18-22. Isaiah promises God's grace to the people of Jerusalem. The reference in verse 19 to tears and cries for help probably means the passage comes from the period of the Babylonian exile (587–539 B.C.). This is the only time when Jerusalem was destroyed and there is hardly another circumstance that provides the logical backdrop to such language of pain, grief, and desperation. The promise in verse 19 that "he will answer you" probably refers to the return from exile and the rebuilding of Jerusalem and its Temple. The primary sign of God's grace, however, will be divine revelation: God will not withhold the word from the people. Indeed, God will lead them directly. In verse 20 God is uniquely called Judah's "Teacher." God will provide such clear direction that divine instruction will be almost like a light that shows the path (30:21). The result will be that the people will purify their faith by getting rid of the idols that lead them into ways of believing and living that are contrary to God's desires. We should note that the term "teacher" could refer to the prophet or to all the prophets together who speak God's word. If that is what the passage intends, then it has a very concrete message. God's message through the prophetic word will once again direct the people. Regardless of the exact meaning on this matter, the promise is much like Jeremiah's promise of a new covenant that will be given by God and will produce faithfulness in God's people (Jeremiah 31:31-34). Just as Jeremiah says God will put the law within the heart of the people to produce faithfulness, so also Isaiah 30:18-22 points to God's initiative in Judah's obedience.

Isaiah 30:23-26. The second half of

the promise to the people who have experienced trauma portrays the non-human world in complete harmony and cooperation with humans. Verses 23 and 24 describe an abundance of produce from the lush ground and cattle that grow well from eating in good pastures. This may sound like simply a good crop. The next verse, however, indicates that something more is being said. Verse 25 promises that on every hill there will be "brooks running with water." The next verse promises that the light of the moon "will be like the light of the sun," that is, darkness will be overcome by the light. These two verses indicate the prophet is here imagining the renewal of creation. All the challenges humans face now—lack of rain, lack of light—will be no more. Judah's restoration will be like the renewal of the whole earth. Or perhaps the prophet intends to say it will be a precursor to the larger restoration of all creation.

INTERPRETING THE SCRIPTURE

Do Not Even Think About Evil

Zechariah communicates to the people of Judah God's command to act justly and to show mercy as the centerpiece of the human response to God. Like prophets before him, Zechariah brings a message about just treatment of those members of society who are most vulnerable: the widow, orphan, and alien. He also adds the blanket label "poor" (7:10) to those whom the people should treat with care. These concerns are addressed in the legal material of the Old Testament in very concrete ways (see Deuteronomy 15, for example). Zechariah adds, however, that the people should also act with right intentions. He says, "Do not devise evil in your hearts against one another" (7:10). It is not enough simply to follow certain regulations about how to treat the poor. It is also important to have the right attitudes toward other citizens.

Zechariah's words are important to note since many people assume the Old Testament is dominated by law in the narrow sense of that term. In reality, however, the legal provisions of the Old Testament are usually accompanied by instructions on how to be committed in spirit to what God expects, and Zechariah illustrates that point. A better known example of what Zechariah is saying appears in the Ten Commandments (Exodus 20:1-17). Some of the laws concerning treatment of other people may be judged rather objectively. For example, compliance with the commands "you shall not murder" and "you shall not commit adultery" (Exodus 20:13-14) is easy to determine. But the Commandments end with the remarkable demand: "You shall not covet" anything that belongs to your neighbor (20:17). "Covet" refers to having desire for, longing for, and wanting to possess something. It refers to internal rather than external obedience. In a similar way Zechariah instructs God's people not to "devise evil" in their hearts.

Zechariah's words are similar to, though not as explicit as Jesus' instructions in his Sermon on the Mount (Matthew 5–7). Jesus famously cites certain Old Testament laws (and sometimes popular sayings or customs, as in Matthew 5:21-24) and then presents an additional expectation that involves internal commitment. For example, Jesus adds to the commandment against murder, "But I say to you that if you are angry with a brother or sister, you will be liable to judgment" (Matthew 5:22). He also adds to the commandment against adultery, "But I say to you that everyone who looks at a woman with lust has already committed adultery with her in his heart" (Matthew 5:28). What Zechariah's words tell us is that Jesus was not repudiating the Old Testament with his own added commands, as though the Old Testament were inadequate. Rather, he was highlighting the deeper level of commitment that was already present in the Old Testament. For Christians, however, the emphasis Jesus puts on intent changes the way passages like Zechariah 7:8-10 are read. Instead of only focusing on external actions, we are also directed to consider our thoughts: "do not devise evil in your hearts against one another." Indeed, Jesus prompts us now to find those Old Testament calls to right thinking and feeling toward our neighbor as the starting point of the practice of our faith.

For Zechariah there is yet another way that fair treatment of the poor and vulnerable are matters of the heart. Just before the lesson Scripture the prophet speaks about the proper time and purpose of fasting. God asks the people concerning the fasting they did in the past, "Was it for me that you fasted?" (7:5). Fasting was an outward sign of worship, of devotion to God. It should be accompanied by and reveal an inner commitment to God. Hence, the prophet's words here are related to other prophetic calls for

worship that is pure, worship that is linked to justice, that grows from true concern for all God's people. Later, in Zechariah 8:18-19 the prophet answers the question about fasting directly by saying a fast should be a time of joy and gladness because it emerges from the love of "truth and peace" (8:19). Fair treatment of the widow, orphan, and alien are surely expressions of such love.

Scripture Shows the Way

Part of Zechariah's complaint against the people of Judah was not only that they did not listen to him but they also did not heed the law of Moses or the words of the prophets who went before him. As noted already, the reference to "former prophets" in verse 12 may refer simply to previous prophets. But "law" clearly refers to the written instruction that appears in Genesis through Deuteronomy. At some point "prophets" comes to designate the next segment of Scripture.

Scripture is the most readily available source of God's revelation and instruction to us in how to live. Therefore, it is remarkably sad that we so easily ignore this source of direction God gives us, just as those in Zechariah's audience did. It is easy to conclude that people in biblical times who actually heard the prophets, or heard Moses or Jesus, are guiltier of stopping their ears to God's truth than we are since they were so close to the living word of God. But Luke 16:19-31 suggests that is not the case. Jesus there tells the story of a rich man who ignored the poor. When he died he was taken to a place of torment. From there he begged Abraham to send someone back from the dead to warn his brothers to change their lives. But Abraham replied that the brothers had the Law and the Prophets of Scripture, and if they would not listen to them they would also not pay attention to someone from the dead.

The Land Is Desolate

Land in the Old Testament is crucially important. It is at the heart of God's promises to Abraham and a primary sign of God's blessing and God's grace (Genesis 15:18-21). But land is more than something God gives to God's people. It is God's creation, and its health and vitality mirror the spiritual well-being of the people who occupy it. So, for example, when the psalmist in Psalm 72 prays for a king to rule in justice and righteousness, the prayer also includes the fertility of the land, a natural outgrowth of the king's just reign. Zechariah 7 ends with a dire description of the opposite case. The people refused to act justly and to protect the poor (Zechariah 7:8-12). Consequently, God scattered them among the nations. This explanation of what happened to the people of Judah includes two references

to the land being "desolate" (7:14). Although the CEB uses two different words in its translation ("devastated" and "wasteland"), the NRSV reflects the fact that the same Hebrew term appears two times. The repetition of the term "desolate" emphasizes the point that the land suffered from the disobedience of the people.

This way of understanding the natural world—as directly affected by the immoral acts of humans—may seem naive to modern people who are accustomed to putting into distinct categories matters of morality, human society, and nature. But the Old Testament's holistic understanding has potential to inform our faith in a much better way. We should recognize that every action, whether good or evil, has an impact on the world around us, even the nonhuman world. This is immediately obvious, for example, when a military action leaves a landscape scarred along with its human casualties. But it is also true that every other action, however subtle it may be, affects the whole world. Therefore, it is truly our choice, either to do good to the benefit of the whole world, or to do evil and therefore to leave other people and the land "devastated."

SHARING THE SCRIPTURE

PREPARING TO TEACH

Preparing Our Hearts

Meditate on this week's devotional reading from Psalm 147:1-11, which is a hymn of praise to God. What reasons does the psalmist have to praise God? What specific reasons do you

have to praise God for being compassionate to you? Give resounding praise to God as the Creator. What hope do you have in God's "steadfast love" (147:11)?

Pray that you and the students will give thanks for the difference that God makes in your lives.

Preparing Our Minds

Study the background Scripture from Zechariah 7:8-14; Isaiah 30:18-26. The lesson Scripture is from Zechariah 7:8-14.

Consider this question as you prepare the lesson: *Who will protect the weak from their oppressors?*

Write on newsprint:

❏ information for next week's lesson, found under "Continue the Journey."

❏ activities for further spiritual growth in "Continue the Journey."

Review the "Introduction," "The Big Picture," "Close-up," and "Faith in Action," which all precede the first lesson of this quarter. Consider how you might use any of this material in today's lesson.

LEADING THE CLASS

(1) Gather to Learn

❖ Greet the class members and introduce guests.

❖ Pray that those who have come today will stand with God to protect those who are weak from their oppressors.

❖ Read this dialogue between Ebenezer Scrooge and his nephew Fred from the beginning of Charles Dickens's beloved classic, *A Christmas Carol:* **"There are many things from which I might have derived good, by which I have not profited, I dare say,"** returned the nephew. **"Christmas among the rest. But I am sure I have always thought of Christmas time, when it has come round—apart from the veneration due to its sacred name and origin, if anything belonging to it can be** apart from that—as a good time; a kind, forgiving, charitable, pleasant time; the only time I know of, in the long calendar of the year, when men and women seem by one consent to open their shut-up hearts freely, and to think of people below them as if they really were fellow-passengers to the grave, and not another race of creatures bound on other journeys. And therefore, uncle, though it has never put a scrap of gold or silver in my pocket, I believe that it has done me good, and will do me good; and I say, God bless it!"** . . . **"Let me hear another sound from you,"** said Scrooge, **"and you'll keep your Christmas by losing your situation!"**

❖ Ask: **How would you describe the difference in attitude between Scrooge and his nephew concerning the treatment of others?**

❖ Read aloud today's focus statement: **Some people show no kindness, mercy, or justice to others. Who will protect the weak from their oppressors? Zechariah says that God requires kindness and mercy for the widows, orphans, aliens, and the poor, while Isaiah says that God will heal the wounds of the afflicted and shower prosperity on the people.**

(2) Goal 1: Study the Punishment Meted Out by God for Those Who Reject God's Demands

❖ Read "Do Not Even Think About Evil" in Interpreting the Scripture to introduce the class to Zechariah's message.

❖ Choose a volunteer to read Zechariah 7:8-14.

❖ Point out that in verses 9-10 Zechariah makes reference to earlier prophecies. Call on volunteers to read these passages: Isaiah 1:16-17; Amos 5:14-15, 21-24; Micah 6:8; Malachi 3:5. Note that we have discussed these passages from Amos and Micah; we will discuss Malachi next week. Discuss common concerns among these prophets.

❖ Ask these questions:

1. **How does Zechariah say that the people responded to God's messages sent through the prophets?**
2. **How did God respond?**
3. **What happened to the land because of the people's refusal to listen and obey God?** (See "The Land Is Desolate" in Interpreting the Scripture.)

(3) Goal 2: Make Confessions Concerning How the Learners Abandon the Weak

❖ Read: **Reports of devastating fires in factories plagued by unsafe working conditions make headlines. In November 2012, 112 workers were killed in a blaze at the Tazreen factory in Bangladesh. Then in April 2013 the world was again grieved and shocked when 1,131 workers were killed when the Rana Plaza Factory, also in Bangladesh, collapsed. Fifteen different brands of clothing are manufactured at this factory. Major changes need to occur to protect these vulnerable workers from death and serious injury, but consumers neither demand nor are willing to pay for sweatshop-free products. Consequently, the companies that order these clothes are not motivated to renovate buildings, pay fairer wages, or provide better working conditions. And so the tragic cycle continues.**

❖ Choose several volunteers to debate this statement: **While recognizing the need for employees in low-wage countries to support their families *and* the need for lower-income workers in the United States to be able to purchase essential items at discount prices, as Christians we are called to ensure that all workers are treated ethically and with regard for their health and safety.**

❖ Provide quiet time for class members to think about the criteria they use to purchase products. Are they aware of the hidden human cost of the cheap products that they buy? What can they do to insist that people be fairly compensated for their labor and able to work in a safe environment?

❖ Conclude this portion of the lesson by reading: **God of all, we confess that at times we have failed to support those who are vulnerable. Help us to learn the true cost of everything we buy and to recognize those who work to create the products we consume as our brothers and sisters in Christ. Amen.**

(4) Goal 3: Show Kindness to the Oppressed and the Weak

❖ Read today's key verses, Zechariah 7:9-10, in unison.

❖ Explore ways to show kindness to the oppressed and weak by selecting one of these two options.

Option 1: Use the suggested activity for Group 2 in "Faith in Action: Acting with Justice," found near the beginning of this quarter's lessons.

Option 2: Call on persons who have investigated ways for the class to reach out to others, based on previous activities throughout the quarter. Hear their suggestions and decide how the class will become engaged.

(5) Continue the Journey

❖ Pray that as the learners depart, they will go forth knowing that they can make a difference in bringing about justice for all.

❖ Post information for next week's session on newsprint for the students to copy:

- Title: Return to a Just God
- Background Scripture: Malachi 3:1-12; Matthew 7:12
- Lesson Scripture: Malachi 3:1-10
- Focus of the Lesson: Fairness and philanthropy are most apparent during times of great tragedy and loss. How do the faithful demonstrate the same benevolent and just spirit all the time? Malachi and Matthew inform the faithful that God requires justice and faithfulness and will bestow bountiful blessings in proportion to what they are willing to give.

❖ Challenge the adults to grow spiritually by completing one or more of these activities related to this week's session, which you have posted on newsprint for the students to copy.

(1) Compare and contrast the people in Zechariah 7:1-11 with "the least of these" in Matthew 25. What is God's message in both the Old and New Testaments concerning such people? How are you obeying the message?

(2) Select a social issue of concern to you. Check your denomination's stance on that issue. How does that square with your own stance? What further information do you need? What will you do?

(3) Help a young student whose family has limited financial resources get ready for school by purchasing supplies and a backpack. Check with your local school system or department of social services to see what is needed and how you can help.

❖ Sing or read aloud "The Voice of God Is Calling."

❖ Conclude today's session by leading the class in this benediction adapted from Micah 6:8, which is the key verse for July 19: **Let us depart to do justice, and love kindness, and walk humbly with our God.**

UNIT 3: ADVOCATES OF JUSTICE FOR ALL
RETURN TO A JUST GOD

PREVIEWING THE LESSON

Lesson Scripture: Malachi 3:1-10
Background Scripture: Malachi 3:1-12; Matthew 7:12
Key Verse: Matthew 7:12

Focus of the Lesson:

Fairness and philanthropy are most apparent during times of great tragedy and loss. How do the faithful demonstrate the same benevolent and just spirit all the time? Malachi and Matthew inform the faithful that God requires justice and faithfulness and will bestow bountiful blessings in proportion to what they are willing to give.

Goals for the Learners:

(1) to explore Malachi's prophecy about possessions, wealth, and hospitality in light of their faithfulness and justice.
(2) to confess personal unfaithfulness to God and pray for forgiveness.
(3) to institute a personal plan for charitable living.

Supplies:

Bibles, newsprint and marker, paper and pencils, hymnals

READING THE SCRIPTURE

NRSV
Lesson Scripture: Malachi 3:1-10

¹See, I am sending my messenger to prepare the way before me, and the Lord whom you seek will suddenly come to his temple. The messenger of the covenant in whom you delight—indeed, he is coming, says the LORD of hosts. ²But who can endure the day of his coming, and who can stand when he appears?

CEB
Lesson Scripture: Malachi 3:1-10

¹Look, I am sending my messenger who will clear the path before me; suddenly the LORD whom you are seeking will come to his temple. The messenger of the covenant in whom you take delight is coming, says the LORD of heavenly forces. ²Who can endure the day of his coming? Who can withstand his appearance?

For he is like a refiner's fire and like fullers' soap; ³he will sit as a refiner and purifier of silver, and he will purify the descendants of Levi and refine them like gold and silver, until they present offerings to the LORD in righteousness. ⁴Then the offering of Judah and Jerusalem will be pleasing to the LORD as in the days of old and as in former years.

⁵Then I will draw near to you for judgment; I will be swift to bear witness against the sorcerers, against the adulterers, against those who swear falsely, against those who oppress the hired workers in their wages, the widow and the orphan, against those who thrust aside the alien, and do not fear me, says the LORD of hosts.

⁶For I the LORD do not change; therefore you, O children of Jacob, have not perished. ⁷Ever since the days of your ancestors you have turned aside from my statutes and have not kept them. Return to me, and I will return to you, says the LORD of hosts. But you say, "How shall we return?"

⁸Will anyone rob God? Yet you are robbing me! But you say, "How are we robbing you?" In your tithes and offerings! ⁹You are cursed with a curse, for you are robbing me—the whole nation of you! ¹⁰Bring the full tithe into the storehouse, so that there may be food in my house, and thus put me to the test, says the LORD of hosts; see if I will not open the windows of heaven for you and pour down for you an overflowing blessing.

Key Verse: Matthew 7:12

¹²"In everything do to others as you would have them do to you; for this is the law and the prophets.

He is like the refiner's fire or the cleaner's soap. ³He will sit as a refiner and a purifier of silver. He will purify the Levites and refine them like gold and silver. They will belong to the LORD, presenting a righteous offering. ⁴The offering of Judah and Jerusalem will be pleasing to the LORD as in ancient days and in former years.

⁵I will draw near to you for judgment. I will be quick to testify against the sorcerers, the adulterers, those swearing falsely, against those who cheat the day laborers out of their wages as well as oppress the widow and the orphan, and against those who brush aside the foreigner and do not revere me, says the LORD of heavenly forces.

⁶I am the LORD, and I do not change; and you, children of Jacob, have not perished. ⁷Ever since the time of your ancestors, you have deviated from my laws and have not kept them. Return to me and I will return to you, says the LORD of heavenly forces. But you say, "How should we return?"

⁸Should a person deceive God? Yet you deceive me. But you say, "How have we deceived you?" With your tenth-part gifts and offerings. ⁹You are being cursed with a curse, and you, the entire nation, are robbing me. ¹⁰Bring the whole tenth-part to the storage house so there might be food in my house. Please test me in this, says the LORD of heavenly forces. See whether I do not open all the windows of the heavens for you and empty out a blessing until there is enough.

Key Verse: Matthew 7:12

¹²Therefore, you should treat people in the same way that you want people to treat you; this is the Law and the Prophets.

UNDERSTANDING THE SCRIPTURE

Introduction. Although the Jewish Scriptures place the Prophets earlier, just after the books of Moses (Genesis through Deuteronomy), the Prophets come last in the Christian canon. Thus, for Christians Malachi is both the final prophetic book in the Old Testament and also the final book in the Old Testament. As the final word in the Old Testament, the prophetic books point directly to the ministry of Jesus. This role of the Prophets in the Old Testament is particularly evident in the background Scripture for this lesson. Malachi 3 speaks of a messenger who will come to prepare the way for the Lord's coming. The Gospel writers understood this messenger as John the Baptist. They illustrated his role primarily by quoting from Isaiah 40:3, "the voice of one crying out in the wilderness" (Matthew 3:3; Mark 1:3; Luke 3:4; compare John 1:2). Mark 1:2 also clearly refers to Malachi 3:1 when it says, "see, I am sending my messenger." Hence, the language and themes of Malachi 3 resonate with the beginning of the Gospels. Matthew 7:12, another part of the background Scripture and today's key verse, also makes the connection. This passage declares that love of one's neighbor sums up the Law and the Prophets. Such right action is necessary to prepare for God's presence.

Malachi 3:1-4. The name Malachi means "my messenger." Therefore it is not certain whether "my messenger" mentioned in verse 1 is a name, or if the name of the book does not refer to a name but instead makes a general reference to one who delivers the word of the Lord. Malachi 4:5 speaks of God sending Elijah. Perhaps this is the messenger referred to here.

Regardless of the identity, the messenger comes to remind the people of their covenant with the Lord. His coming will be related closely to—and perhaps identical—to the day of the Lord (see 4:5). His coming will prepare for God's coming into the Temple. Thus, the messenger's arrival is for the purpose of purifying the people of their uncleanness. God is holy and so God will not stand for what is unholy.

The messenger's cleansing work will focus on the priests who serve in the Temple. The priests are descendants of Levi (3:3). Throughout the Book of Malachi the priests are criticized for making impure offerings and for not treating the altar with proper respect. They presented impure offerings (1:7), offerings of animals that were blind or had blemishes (1:8). One issue seems to be that the priests have more respect for the Persian governor sent to oversee the territory than for God. After cataloging the problems with the sacrifices being offered, Malachi 1:8 declares, "Try presenting that to your governor; will he be pleased with you or show you favor?" This is not a statement against the governor or a suggestion that the governor does not deserve respect. Rather, it is a recognition that the priests give out respect with the wrong priorities. They should honor God first. Then their honoring of other people will take care of itself. When the messenger finishes his work, however, the priests will be purified and their offerings will be acceptable (3:4).

Malachi 3:5. Although Malachi is chiefly concerned with proper sacrifices and the ritual purity of the Temple, he speaks, as do the other prophets in these lessons, about the central importance of treating justly the most vulnerable people in society. By making this point the prophet here also makes a point similar to Micah 6:6-8: that sacrifices are only meaningful if they are expressions of the heart turned to God. Malachi seems to value sacrifices more than Micah for the value of the sacrifice itself, but he emphasizes that sacrifice is only meaningful if it grows from true devotion. That devotion is seen concretely in treating hired workers fairly, in looking out for those without a protector, and ensuring justice for the resident alien. All of these actions show the fear of God, that is, proper worship.

Malachi 3:6-7. God gives a striking contrast: The people of Israel have always been wishy-washy, regularly turning away from God who showed them compassion and rescued them from slavery in Egypt. But God has been steadfast, always faithful. Israel has only survived, God declares, because God has not changed. Although God has punished God's people, this has always been for the larger purpose of redemption. Israel, on the other hand, has been willing to go completely away from the God who loved them. Therefore, the command is to return. "Return" could also be translated "repent." This awakened sense of the importance of relationship with God is the essence of repentance.

Malachi 3:8-12. God puts the actions of the people in very human terms by declaring they are "robbing" God. They are not giving the full offering and so are not recognizing God fully with that offering. This is similar to Malachi's earlier point (1:8) that they would not try to give such inferior gifts to their human rulers. Surely God is more important, and more powerful, than the governor sent by the Persians. So surely God deserves an offering at least as acceptable as that given to the governor. But the priests are cheating God while giving the full payment to human rulers. Therefore, one of Malachi's primary concerns is the way the priests handle the sacrifices of the Temple. How sacrifices are made indicate something of how the priests relate to God. The prophet encourages the offering of "the full tithe" (3:10), for when that is given God promises to pour out "overflowing blessings" (3:10), which will create "a land of delight" (3:12).

Matthew 7:12. Jesus restates what is known as the Golden Rule. It comes from Leviticus 19:18, which commands each Israelite to "love your neighbor as yourself." Malachi, along with other prophets, often expresses this love of neighbor in terms of treating justly the widow, orphan, and stranger (as in Malachi 3:5). Also, the prophets identify these actions as expressions of the love of God or, as Malachi 3:5 puts it, the fear of God. Because right and just action is directly linked to right relationship with God, Jesus refers to the Golden Rule as the summation of the Law and Prophets.

INTERPRETING THE SCRIPTURE

The Fire that Cleanses and Purifies

"You are about to experience baptism by fire," the seventh-grade football coach said to his team as they prepared for their first game. And, he continued, "that's the best kind of baptism." Such words and images are common in athletics. They dramatize what the participant faces in a contest and may inspire greater effort in order to "survive" the fire. On the other side of the experience the person is more skilled and more confident in his or her capacity to face adversity. The point of the language in circumstances like this is neither a prediction of failure nor a promise of trouble and woe. Rather, it simply recognizes that some experiences bring radical change that is accompanied by profound discomfort. But such change can be good if the person who experiences it embraces it properly.

The language about fire in Malachi 3:1-10 speaks of this type of positive, yet uncomfortable, change. Although the image of fire in the Bible is often taken as a reference to judgment and punishment, this is clearly not the case here. The fire is a "refiner's fire" (3:2). It is meant to purify, as ancient people used fire to purify precious metals like gold and silver. Malachi says specifically that this fire is for the purpose of purifying "the descendants of Levi," those charged with carrying out the service of the Temple in Jerusalem (3:3). This identification of the purpose of God's fire and the object of purification has important implications for us. It suggests we should read most of the Bible's promises of God's fiery presence that judges and purges as promises for us, not for those who are outside the church. Although we may be tempted to focus on biblical passages that speak of God's judgment on people outside God's fold, the most common promise of judgment is a promise for those in relationship with God. The reason for this is that God has expectations of us that God does not have of everyone. God expects more of us in part because we have

responsibility for carrying out God's work and for sharing the good news. We, like the priests of ancient Israel, are the objects of God's refining fire because we "belong to the Lord" and the Lord needs us to be prepared for service. The Lord promises to use the fire to purify the priests so their offering "will be pleasing" (3:4). So also God expects us to have a pleasing offering as well.

But more generally, God's refining fire is aimed at us simply because we are in relationship with God and that relationship demands our attention. Malachi suggests the priests who were supposed to be most attentive to their relationship with God had in fact taken that relationship for granted. They offered God inferior offerings while paying great attention to what they gave to secular officials (1:8). But the Old Testament time and again testifies that God is a "jealous God" (Exodus 20:5; Joshua 24:19). To say God is jealous is to say God cares deeply about the relationship God has with us. Therefore, God will not tolerate half-hearted commitments or insincere service.

It is also important that we read the promise of God's purging fire as a central message in both Old and New Testament. Many people associate the fire of God with Old Testament judgment, particularly as it appears in prophetic books like Malachi. But when John the Baptist described the ministry of Jesus he said, "he will baptize you with the Holy Spirit and with fire" (Matthew 3:11). Moreover, concerning the unproductive and inadequate parts of our lives, John promised, "the chaff he [Jesus] will burn with unquenchable fire" (Matthew 3:12). Malachi anticipates this role Jesus will have in our lives and in the world when he promises "the messenger of the covenant" who will come (Malachi 3:1).

The Human Response to the Unchanging God

Malachi 3:1-10 emphasizes the human response to God. Several times the prophet calls on God's people to return or repent, to come back to God. This raises a question for our understanding of what it means to be in relationship with God. Do we not believe that our salvation depends on God's grace and not our actions? If so, then doesn't Malachi's focus on the human response to God undermine this core theological tenet?

The larger point of Malachi's message is that God does not change. God continues to reach out and seek us in grace. The problem is always our desire or ability to perceive God's grace. Hence, Malachi emphasizes human response precisely because that is the only unknown, potentially changing factor. He urges the people to return to God, whose promise that "I will return to you" (3:7) is not a conditional arrangement that predicates God's grace on human response. Rather, it recognizes that unless the human turns to God he or she will not experience the love and mercy God is extending.

This is a crucial point as we think about what it means for God to take initiative in our salvation and in our relationship with God. Indeed, God does make the way for us and continually seeks us. Malachi makes the point of God's unchanging grace by saying that the people of Jacob have not perished. If God did change, if God were irrational or given to flights of emotion, then surely God would not have allowed the unfaithful people to survive. But unless we turn toward God, unless we are conscious of the precious nature of the relationship we have with God, we will not experience God's remarkable kindness and mercy.

On Giving and Receiving

The kind of response God requires of us may be summed up in the words of the second verse of the old hymn "Give of Your Best to the Master."

> Give of your best to the Master;
> Give Him first place in your heart.
> Give Him first place in your service;
> Consecrate every part.
> Give, and to you will be given;
> God His beloved Son gave.
> Gratefully seeking to serve Him,
> Give Him the best that you have.

The hymn sums up Malachi's call for us to give the best offering we have. Interestingly, when Malachi addresses the question of how we should respond to God with our gifts, he speaks in terms of our giving inadequate gifts as "robbing" God. He speaks in very tangible ways about giving the full tithe, a tenth of the produce of the land as thanksgiving for God's goodness. But just before this call to give a proper offering, the prophet says that God will come to judge oppressive acts like the mistreatment of hired workers and thrusting aside the needs of the widow and orphan. It is appropriate that Malachi has these two types of actions side by side in his proclamation. Other prophets we have discussed cried out against outward signs of piety that lacked any conviction that led to acts of kindness and compassion (for example, Micah 6:6-8). Sacrifice and gifts on the altar are meaningless if they are not accompanied by justice. This seems to be Malachi's message as well. Both justice and tithe are signs of giving the best of one's life to God.

SHARING THE SCRIPTURE

PREPARING TO TEACH

Preparing Our Hearts

Meditate on this week's devotional reading from Psalm 25:4-11. What does the psalmist seek from God? Which of God's character traits does the psalmist name or imply? What do you need to seek from God today? Which of God's character traits compel you to believe that God will provide what you seek?

Pray that you and the students will keep God's covenant.

Preparing Our Minds

Study the background Scripture from Malachi 3:1-12; Matthew 7:12. The lesson Scripture is from Malachi 3:1-10.

Consider this question as you prepare the lesson: *How do the faithful demonstrate on a regular basis the spirit of benevolence that is so apparent during times of tragedy and loss?*

Write on newsprint:
❏ information for next week's lesson, found under "Continue the Journey."
❏ activities for further spiritual growth in "Continue the Journey."

Review the "Introduction," "The Big Picture," "Close-up," and "Faith in Action," which all precede the first lesson of this quarter. Consider how you might use any of this material in today's lesson.

LEADING THE CLASS

(1) Gather to Learn

❖ Greet the class members and introduce guests.

❖ Pray that those who have come today will consider what they can give to others.

❖ Discuss the following and record students' responses on newsprint:

1. **Identify reasons you feel motivated to give a monetary donation for a particular cause.**
2. **Identify types of situations to which you are most likely to contribute.**

❖ Read this summary of a British report, "Predictors of Monetary Donations Following Humanitarian Disasters": **Based on extensive research, Dr. Hanna Zagefka and Dr. Masi Noor have identified several factors that prompted people to give more generously following a humanitarian disaster. For example, if those needing assistance were perceived to be innocent victims, donors were more likely to give than if they thought the victims played a role in bringing disaster upon themselves. Consequently, people tended to contribute more in the aftermath of a natural disaster, such as famine** caused by a drought, than to relief in the wake of a disaster triggered by human actions, such as famine caused by war. Other factors that influence giving were a donor's level of empathy with the victims; a donor's assessment that the recipients of a monetary gift were willing to work to improve their situation; a donor's belief that financial assistance could make a "real difference," particularly in a widespread disaster; and a donor's perception that a positive relationship existed between his or her country and the country where assistance was needed."

❖ Encourage the adults to compare their responses (recorded on newsprint) to the reasons identified by psychologists Dr. Hanna Zagefka and Dr. Masi Noor.

❖ Read aloud today's focus statement: **Fairness and philanthropy are most apparent during times of great tragedy and loss. How do the faithful demonstrate the same benevolent and just spirit all the time? Malachi and Matthew inform the faithful that God requires justice and faithfulness and will bestow bountiful blessings in proportion to what they are willing to give.**

(2) Goal 1: Explore Malachi's Prophecy about Possessions, Wealth, and Hospitality in Light of Our Faithfulness and Justice

❖ Read "The Fire that Cleanses and Purifies" in Interpreting the Scripture.

❖ Choose a volunteer to read Malachi 3:1-12.

❖ Discuss these questions:
1. **Why is God sending a messenger?** (See "Malachi 3:1-4" in Understanding the Scripture. Note that in this context the messenger will come to purify the priests.)
2. **What point is the prophet making in verse 5?** (See "Malachi 3:5" in Understanding the Scripture.)
3. **According to verse 11, an infestation of locusts caused a scarcity of food. How did people respond to this scarcity—and what did God tell them to do instead?** (They have held on to what they had, thereby robbing God rather than trusting in divine generosity. See "Malachi 3:8-12" in Understanding the Scripture.)

❖ Conclude by reading or retelling "The Human Response to the Unchanging God" in Interpreting the Scripture.

(3) Goal 2: Confess Personal Unfaithfulness to God and Pray for Forgiveness

❖ Lead the class in reading Psalm 25 responsively as a personal confession and prayer for forgiveness. If you have access to hymnals that include a Psalter, distribute them. If not, ask half of the class to read the even-numbered verses and the other half to read the odd-numbered ones from their own Bibles.

❖ End this confession with some quiet time for the adults to consider how Psalm 25 speaks to their own lives.

❖ Offer these words of assurance: **The God who is gracious and just, slow to anger and abounding in steadfast love, will cleanse you from all unrighteousness and make you whole. Amen.**

(4) Goal 3: Institute a Personal Plan for Charitable Living

❖ Note that this goal uses the phrase "charitable living," rather than "charitable giving." Point out that whereas one can have a plan for charitable giving that determines how much per year or month one plans to give to a particular cause, charitable living entails a way of relating to God and neighbor that flows from the center of the lives of believers. Money is included in the charitable living plan, but so are ways that believers treat their neighbors and stand up for God's justice.

❖ Read in unison today's key verse, Matthew 7:12, often called "the Golden Rule," which compels the faithful to care for the needs of others.

❖ Distribute paper and pencils. Challenge the adults to list five actions they could take within the next two weeks to help others. These actions may include giving money, but do not limit actions to writing a check. Think outside the box to find ways to lend a helping hand or a listening ear.

❖ Wrap up by urging the adults to follow through on the actions they have listed.

(5) Continue the Journey

❖ Pray that as the learners depart, they will resolve to take the actions they have proposed so as to help to meet the needs of others.

❖ Post information for next week's session on newsprint for the students to copy:

- **Title: Praying for One Another**
- **Background Scripture: Acts 4:1-31**

- **Lesson Scripture: Acts 4:23-31**
- **Focus of the Lesson: At critical times in their lives, people search for strength to weather the storm. Where do they find the necessary strength? The followers of Christ raised their voices together to God in prayer, and the Holy Spirit filled them with strength to speak God's word with boldness.**

❖ Challenge the adults to grow spiritually by completing one or more of these activities related to this week's session, which you have posted on newsprint for the students to copy.

(1) **Be aware of opportunities to give to others. Your goal may be to meet the need of someone local or to assist with relief efforts after a major tragedy.**

(2) **Research the concept of the tithe in the Bible and your denominational resources. What difference does it make if one gives a tithe out of a sense of duty or a sense of gratitude to God?**

(3) **Keep a log this week of the blessings God has bestowed upon you and the gifts that you have given to others. Were you able to give more than you received from God?**

❖ Sing or read aloud "O For a Thousand Tongues to Sing."

❖ Conclude today's session by leading the class in this benediction adapted from Micah 6:8, which is the key verse for July 19: **Let us depart to do justice, and love kindness, and walk humbly with our God.**